W9-BMZ-888

THE COMPLETE IDIOT'S GUIDE® TO

Internet Privacy and Security

by Preston Gralla

ALPHA

A Pearson Education Company

International Standard Book Number: 0-02-864321-6
Library of Congress Catalog Card Number: 2001098465

04   03   02   8   7   6   5   4   3   2

Interpretation of the printing code: The rightmost number of the first series of numbers is the year of the book's printing; the rightmost number of the second series of numbers is the number of the book's printing. For example, a printing code of 02-1 shows that the first printing occurred in 2002.

Printed in the United States of America

Note: This publication contains the opinions and ideas of its author. It is intended to provide helpful and informative material on the subject matter covered. It is sold with the understanding that the author and publisher are not engaged in rendering professional services in the book. If the reader requires personal assistance or advice, a competent professional should be consulted.

The author and publisher specifically disclaim any responsibility for any liability, loss, or risk, personal or otherwise, which is incurred as a consequence, directly or indirectly, of the use and application of any of the contents of this book.

Publisher: *Marie Butler-Knight*
Product Manager: *Phil Kitchel*
Managing Editor: *Jennifer Chisholm*
Acquisitions Editor: *Eric Heagy*
Development Editor: *Nancy D. Warner*
Production Editor: *Billy Fields*
Copy Editor: *Molly Schaller*
Illustrator: *Jody Schaeffer*
Cover/Book Designer: *Trina Wurst*
Indexer: *Angie Bess*

Contents at a Glance

Contents

Introduction

You can't pick up a newspaper or magazine, or turn on the news these days without reading or hearing about yet one more invasion of your Internet privacy and security. Hackers, snoopers, virus-writers, and identity thieves are the modern equivalents of those people who preyed on pioneers and settlers of the Wild West. The Internet and the Wild West have much in common: Both involve forays into uncharted territories where evil-doers are more than happy to take advantage of the unwitting.

Think of this book as the equivalent of an Internet sheriff—except in this instance, it puts the power into *your* hands. It warns you about the dangers you face online, and teaches you to protect yourself against them. As you find out as you go through this book, the dangers are many. But as you also find out, it's easy for you to defeat them.

I don't mean to imply that the only dangers you face online are posed by shady characters that are outside the law. In fact, many of dangers to your privacy are posed by law-abiding, upright citizens and companies. Take this example. Someone pointed out to the head of one of the world's largest computer companies, Scott McNealy of Sun Microsystems, that a new Internet technology his company was developing could lead to a massive invasion of people's privacy. His terse response: "You have zero privacy now. Get over it."

This book is devoted to showing you just how wrong he is. Yes, it's true that your privacy and security can be endangered when you use the Internet. But as I show you, you can do much more than merely try to "get over it." You can fight back, take control of your online life, and make sure that you're safe and secure whenever you use the Internet or online services.

There's been nothing in the history of humankind like the Internet. Nothing else can give you access to such a vast amount of information; nothing else enables you to communicate in so many ways with so many other people whether they be down the street or on the other side of the globe; nothing else gives you such power over the way you shop, the way you live, the way you work, and the way you have fun.

And nothing else can allow your privacy to be invaded or security threatened so easily. Sure, you already know it's the greatest information-gathering resource ever invented— but that also means it's an easy way to gather information about *you*. And in many ways, it's also easy to threaten your security.

This book teaches you all the essentials about staying safe when you go online. Whether you're worried about details of your private life being gathered, scared that your e-mail can be intercepted and read, frightened by mysterious technologies like spyware and Web bugs, or concerned that your Web surfing habits are being watched, I teach you how to fight back. If you're worried about being scammed and spammed, no problem. I show you what you can do. Whether the issue be fear of viruses, worries about the safety of your kids when they log on, concern that your credit card number will be stolen when you buy at a Web store, or anything else related to privacy and security, I teach you how you can be safe and secure whenever you get onto the Internet or an online service such as America Online.

Here's some more good news: Staying safe and protecting your privacy on the Internet need not be a chore. It doesn't have to get in the way of enjoying the Internet or gaining access to its vast resources. I show you simple things you can do to protect yourself and your family, no matter what you do online or how you use the Internet.

I've been using the Internet since before the days when the World Wide Web was invented, so I've been concerned with these kinds of security and privacy issues for quite a while. Over the years, I've gathered scores and scores of ways to keep myself, and my family, safe and secure no matter what we do on the Internet. As a newspaper and Web columnist, executive editor for major Web sites, and magazine and newspaper writer, I constantly get e-mail from people wanting advice on how to fight viruses or keep their e-mail secure. I've offered them advice over the years on what to do, and now I'm passing all that on to you.

So check out this book, follow my advice, and you'll never have to worry again when you head online. And by the way, if you're interested in getting my free e-mail newsletter about the Internet, send e-mail to me at pgralla@tiac.net with the word Subscribe in the subject line. That way, you'll be kept abreast of the latest Internet happenings and how they affect your privacy and security.

How to Use This Book

I've organized this book into six parts. I start off teaching you about the basics of Internet privacy and security, so that you fully understand how the Internet works, why it can be used to gather information about you, and why it can be such an unsecure place. Next, you see how you can put up your first line of cyberdefense with your Internet Service Provider. We move on from there to learn about how to protect yourself and your privacy when using e-mail, when on the Web, or when chatting or participating in public discussion groups. There's a section devoted to keeping your children and family safe, and another shows you how to stay safe when shopping online. You also learn how to protect yourself against viruses. And you get tips and advice on how to protect your PC and how you can use the Internet to track down privacy-related information. And if you're worried about your privacy when you use a cellular telephone or Internet connection, this book provides help for you, as well.

In **Part 1, "The Lowdown on Internet Privacy and Security,"** you learn all the basics of Internet privacy and security. You get an understanding of how the Internet works and why it's such an unsecure place. You learn how to take the first steps to ensure that you're safe when you go online and that no one snoops on you. You see how to remove your name from Web databases so that no one can gather information about you, what you can do to make sure that your Internet Service Provider (ISP) doesn't invade your privacy, and how to create hacker-proof passwords, so they can't be stolen. You also learn how to protect yourself against online scams.

Part 2, "Hack Attack: How to Protect Yourself Against Hackers," shows you how to make sure you're never victimized by hackers and crackers. You discover how to protect yourself against worms, viruses, and other programs that might do damage. You also find out how to use a personal firewall, the ultimate defense against hackers. And if you've set up a network at home, you learn how to protect that, as well.

Part 3, "It's None of Their Business: How to Protect Your Privacy Online," shows you how to protect yourself against one of the most insidious of online threats: identity theft. You find out all the ways in which you can make sure your personal information can't be stolen, and used against you. This section also shows how to protect against spyware and Web bugs, two of the more recent ways that your privacy can be invaded online. And you learn how you can stop cookies from peering into your activities, how you can stop Web sites from snooping on you, and how you can surf the Web in absolute anonymity. This section also covers all of the many the dangers posed by the most popular part of the Internet—the Web. Your surfing habits can be traced, put into databases, and sold to the highest bidder. Registration forms can be used to gather huge amounts of personal information about you. Web sites can look inside your browser and find out a surprising amount of information about you. This section of the book shows how you can fight against all that, so that your privacy need not be invaded.

In **Part 4, "Snoopers Everywhere: Keeping Safe When Using E-mail, Instant Messaging, and Chatting,"** learn about all the dangers of e-mail, chats, and instant messaging—everything from your private messages being read by others to getting viruses from files attached to e-mail to how you can be targeted by scammers and junk e-mailers, called spammers. But you do more than just learn about the dangers—I give you easy-to-follow advice on how you can keep your e-mail private and make sure you aren't targeted by junk mailers. And you see the dangers posed by chatting and joining public discussions—and what you can do to make sure that you're never a victim. Personal profiles can be built about you based on what you say online, and in this section, you learn how to make sure you're never profiled.

Part 5, "Protecting Your Children and Family Online," covers the very serious issue of how to keep your children safe when they surf the Web, chat, send or receive e-mail, or do anything else on the Internet or online services. You can take some simple steps to keep your kids safe and secure. I have two children of my own who are online all the time, and I give advice about what I've learned in my years of teaching them how to use the Internet safely.

Finally, in **Part 6, "Even More Privacy and Safety Issues: Work, Cybershopping, and Beyond,"** you find how to keep yourself safe and protect your privacy when at work, when shopping, and beyond. You find out that at work, your boss can snoop on anything he wants—but you also find out what you can do about it. You learn how to shop safely online, and how to make sure that your credit card information isn't stolen and your privacy isn't invaded. You learn how to check out a site to make sure that it's one you can trust. And you learn how to make sure that when you buy at auction sites, you never get burned. The section also covers how to protect your privacy and security when using cell phones and wireless Internet connections. It covers the basics of protecting your PC from other threats, such as co-workers snooping on you. I show you how to password-protect your computer so that no one else can use it and snoop on you. You find out that even when you delete a file, someone can still read it—but I show you how to make sure that when you delete it, it can *never* be read. You also see how you can use the Internet to get information about privacy and security issues of all kinds, not just those related to your online life. And you find out how you can best use the Internet to get information about privacy and security, and do things such as get your credit report—in some cases, for free.

The book also includes a glossary, called "Speak Like a Geek," that defines computer and technical terms to clear up any confusion you might experience.

Finally, there's an appendix with a listing of the best Internet sites about privacy and security issues.

Extras

To help you understand the online jungle, this book also gives you extra secrets, inside tips, and bits of information that help you get the most out of your money. They are sprinkled throughout the book in these boxes:

Check This Out!

The Check This Out! sidebars throughout the book point out things that are noteworthy, stuff to be leery of, and great tips. Basically, they're full of information that adds to your understanding of security or gives insightful background.

Techno Talk

Techno Talk boxes highlight terms, methods, or brainy stuff that you don't necessarily need to know, but that definitely helps you make more sense out of security and privacy.

Notes
The Notes boxes are used as a catchall to pass along cross-references that point you to other sections of the book, provide interesting facts, and add anything else you should take a look at.

About the Author

Preston Gralla has been hailed as "one of the Web's true editorial pioneers" by USATODAY.com's technology editor, and is the author of over 20 books, including the best-selling *How the Internet Works*, as well as *How Wireless Works, How to Expand and Upgrade PCs*, and *The Complete Idiot's Guide to Protecting Your Child Online*. He has written about the Internet and computer technology for many magazines, newspapers, and Web sites, including *USA Today, PC Magazine*, the *Los Angeles Times*, the *Dallas Morning News, Computerworld, CNet, ZDNet*, and *PC/Computing*, among many others. He has won several writing and editing awards, including one for the best feature article in a computer magazine from the Computer Press Association. As a well-known Internet guru, he appears frequently on TV and radio shows such as the *ABC World News Now*, the *CBS Early Show, CNN, MSNBC*, and he has done commentary for National Public Radio's *All Things Considered*. He was the founding managing editor of *PC Week*, and a founding editor, then editor and editorial director of *PC/Computing*. Gralla lives in Cambridge, Massachusetts with his wife Lydia, children Gabriel and Mia, a rabbit named Polichinelle, and two gerbils named Dr. Evil and Mini-Me.

He also writes the free *Gralla's Internet Insider* e-mail newsletter. To subscribe to it for free, send e-mail to preston@gralla.com with the words SUBSCRIBE NETINSIDER in the subject line.

Acknowledgments

This book, as any, is the work of many people. I'd like to thank Eric Heagy, acquisitions editor, for all his help in making this book happen. And I'd also like to thank all the people involved in the editing and production of this book, including Nancy Warner, Chris McGee, Billy Fields, and Molly Schaller.

And, as always, thanks to my agent, Stuart Krichevsky, my wife, Lydia, and my kids, Gabriel and Mia.

Special Thanks to the Technical Reviewer

The Complete Idiot's Guide to Internet Privacy and Security was reviewed by Christopher McGee, an expert who double-checked the accuracy of what you'll learn here, to help ensure that this book gets all its facts straight.

Christopher McGee is an accomplished computer programmer and graphic designer with more than 5 years of experience in information technology, graphic design, and system security. A native of Mt. Airy, North Carolina, he lives in Indianapolis, Indiana, chained to a dozen or more computers. He can be reached online via e-mail at evisium@yahoo.com.

Trademarks

All terms mentioned in this book that are known to be or are suspected of being trademarks or service marks have been appropriately capitalized. Alpha Books and Pearson Education, Inc., cannot attest to the accuracy of this information. Use of a term in this book should not be regarded as affecting the validity of any trademark or service mark.

Part 1

The Lowdown on Internet Privacy and Security

There are hackers and crackers out there. There are people who want to snoop into your e-mail and flood your e-mail box with junk mail. They want to con you out of your money, invade your privacy, steal your identity, get your credit-card number, find out your Social Security number, and put viruses on your hard disk. They want to find out why your Aunt Mary spent two months away from home just before she was married, they want to tie you up with rope and tickle your feet, they want to …

Oops, sorry, got carried away there. Forget about Aunt Mary and your feet. But the truth is, there are people and businesses that want to get information about you, impinge on your security, and invade your privacy when you're online. Luckily, there's a lot you can do to fight back. But before you learn how to fight back, you have to understand the basics of Internet privacy and security. That's what you'll learn in this part. You'll also learn how to put up your first line of cyberdefense, and how to protect yourself against the most common Internet scams.

So come on along. You'll learn about all that and more … and no one will tickle your feet, I promise.

Chapter 1

Why You Need to Worry About Online Privacy and Security

In This Chapter

- ◆ Understanding the origins of the Internet
- ◆ How the Internet works
- ◆ What is TCP/IP?
- ◆ What dangers hackers pose to you
- ◆ The ways your privacy can be invaded
- ◆ Why cable modems and DSL modems pose security problems

Surprise! If you visit the Internet, someone might be watching you. The very thing that makes the Internet a great, freewheeling place to talk to others, find information, do business, and generally have a great time is the same thing that makes it a place to take precautions with your security and privacy.

In this chapter, you'll learn why the Internet can be such a dangerous place. And you'll get an overview of all the kinds of dangers you face when you go online. Don't worry, though—in the rest of the book you'll find out how to protect your privacy and security.

Why the Internet Can Be Such a Dangerous Place

Why is the Internet an insecure place? To understand that, let's look at how the Internet was born. Step with me for a minute into my Wayback Machine and let's go back in time several decades, which, in the computing world, is practically the beginning of recorded history.

In the late 1960s and early- to mid-1970s, the military and computer scientists had some problems. These were big problems, ones that posed even greater challenges to the future of Western Civilization than did disco, bell bottoms, smiley faces, and *The Brady Bunch*—although those were pretty big problems, as well. The two basic problems that the military and computer scientists faced were these:

- How can computer scientists and military researchers better share information and computing resources with each other?
- What are we going to do if World War III breaks out? How can we build a network that can survive the Bomb?

You're probably thinking that if World War III broke out, the last thing you'd worry about is getting a bunch of computers to talk to each other. Instead, you'd like to know something more basic like, "Will I live past 2 o'clock tomorrow afternoon?" Me too. But you're probably not in the military and probably aren't a computer scientist. They're paid to think differently than us. And if you're going to keep the U.S. mail and income taxes going, you need a computer *network*.

Making things even more complicated was that, in those days, people were using all kinds of different computers. People at one university used one kind of computer, a computer scientist used another, the military used yet others. They had to figure out a way to get them to all talk to one another. Considering that computer scientists sometimes didn't talk to their colleagues down the hall, this was no small feat.

They came up with a pretty smart plan, though. There were two parts to the plan:

- Come up with a common way for different kinds of computers to talk to one another—*communications protocols* that enable computers to exchange information with one another.
- The protocols they came up with even allowed someone with a computer in one part of the country to use the resources of a much larger computer in another part of the country.

◆ Develop a system that enables computers to communicate with each other from any-where in the country, even if wires are cut between them.

Techno Talk

For computers to talk to one another, they have to agree on a common language. A common language that lets computers talk to one another is called a **communications protocol**. There are many different kinds of communications protocols, including several that govern how computers talk to one another over the Internet. Computers that are connected to each other and communicate with each other are called a **network**. Many workplaces have networks of computers hooked up to one another in what's called a local area network—a network of computers just for that company. But there are other networks as well. Wide Area Networks (WANs) are networks that span a large geographic region, and are made up of more than one network connected to one another. The biggest WAN of all is the Internet, which is a massive network of networks—a whole lot of networks connected together across the whole planet.

They did this by developing a technique that was smart enough to reroute messages over a different set of wires from one computer to another if anything went wrong between them. In fact, they created a system that enabled hundreds or thousands of computers across the country to be joined in a giant network.

The computers in the network were smart enough to know the fastest route for a message to be sent, and continually checked for the fastest ways for messages to be sent. If a wire or computer got zapped by a nuclear blast in Ohio, the message could be sent by way of Wisconsin.

Eventually, what the computer scientists and Defense Department came up with became what we call the Internet today.

You're probably thinking, what does this have to do with Internet privacy and security? Plenty, as it turns out. Back in those let-it-all-hang-out days of the '60s and '70s, no one thought that malicious people might use the computer network for nefarious purposes. In fact, the entire network was specifically designed to be as open as possible. What could better enable researchers to share information? How else could a scientist in one part of the country control a computer located two thousand miles away?

Back then, people who used computer networks were a small, relatively close-knit group of people, and they never imagined that the network they were working on would one day span the globe and include many, many millions of people. It was kind of like an old-fashioned neighborhood where no one ever locked their front doors because they all knew each other. Try that today, and you'll lose everything in your house that's not nailed down.

It's More Than Magic: How the Internet Works

Since those early Internet days of the late 1960s and 1970s, the network has evolved into today's Internet. Some things still work like they did back then, and some things are different. If you care about your security and privacy, you need to know about how the Internet works today. (Pitch alert! If you want to learn everything you'll ever need to know about how the Internet works, check out my book *How the Internet Works*. Now back to your regularly scheduled program.)

Most people connect to the Internet via an Internet Service Provider (ISP). An increasingly number of people connect via cable or DSL modems or from their computer at work from their workplace's local area network.

When you dial in to your ISP, usually the first thing that happens is you send a password and username to the ISP, which enables you to log in. So right off the bat, something can go wrong. Someone could find out your username and password and pose as you online. For information about how to stop this kind of thing, turn to Chapter 2, "Putting Up Your First Line of Cyberdefense."

While you're logging in, your computer is also establishing a connection with the ISP using the Internet's basic protocols that have the mouth-crushing name Transmission Control Protocol/Internet Protocol, usually called TCP/IP for short.

After you've logged on and your TCP/IP connection is established, you're given what's called an IP address. It's an address that only a computer could love and understand—there are no words in it. Instead, it's a series of four numbers, separated by periods like this: 147.23.0.124. (Periods are called "dots" in Internet-speak, by the way. Why? I don't have a clue. Makes things sound more important, I think.) This IP address identifies you to the computers and servers that make up the Internet. Without an IP address, you wouldn't be able to do things like browse the Web. Your IP address works with the TCP/IP protocols to do all the kinds of Internet magic that you've grown to know and love.

Usually, you're given a different IP address every time you log in to your ISP, although a few ISPs give you the same IP address each time you log in.

You need this IP address to do things like browse the Web. But it can also be used to invade your privacy and compromise your security. This is possible because, essentially, that IP address identifies yourself to computers on the Internet. So, for example, a Web site can track what you do when you visit, because it can identify your IP address and watch what you do on the site.

What's This Client-Server Stuff?

The Internet is based on *client-server* technology. No, it has nothing to do with waiters and fancy restaurants. In client-server technology, the software that runs on your computer is called a client, and the computer on the Internet that you contact is called a server. Your client and the Internet server work together to do the work of the Internet. So, for example, when you go to a Web site, the client (your Web browser) contacts the server (the computer that runs a Web site). The server (the Web server) then sends your computer a Web page, and your client (your Web browser) displays the page on your computer. Why should you care about this? Because in this kind of technology, the server can get information from the client—which means that there are ways for an Internet site to get information about your computer and the way you use it on the Internet.

Check This Out!

The Internet is full of acronyms, each one more difficult to understand than the next. When setting up your e-mail software, you might come across two of them: POP3 and SMTP. POP3 refers to an Internet mail server (Post Office Protocol) that enables you to receive mail. SMTP stands for Simple Mail Transfer Protocol and refers to an Internet mail server that enables you to send mail. Often, you have to identify these servers when you set up your e-mail program. They have names like smtp.bigisp.net or pop3.bigsip.net.

What's This TCP/IP Stuff?

As you've probably noticed by now, I keep mentioning TCP/IP. No, it's not that it makes me feel geeky and super-cool to use those acronyms. It's that no matter what you do on the Internet, you're using TCP/IP. So let's take a look at what TCP/IP does, and why it's what makes the Internet so great—and also why it's one of the main reasons the Internet can be such an insecure place.

Earlier in this chapter, we took a trip in the Wayback Machine to visit the groovy, far-out, right-on late 1960s and early 1970s to look at the origins of the Internet. One of the big things that the military and computer scientists cared about back then was making sure that if World War III broke out, computers could still communicate with each other, even if there were a lot of broken connections in the network. The solution they came up with was TCP/IP.

TCP and IP go together like love and marriage, like a horse and carriage, like—well, you get the picture. They work really well together. Here's how.

Techno Talk

When TCP breaks something into **packets,** it puts information into each packet, things such as the IP address where the information is headed. It puts this information into what's called a *packet header.* **Routers** (which you read about in a second) examine this packet header to figure out where to send each packet.

When you send information over the Internet, TCP immediately springs into action. It takes that piece of information and breaks it up into a whole lot of tiny pieces called *packets.* Then it sticks a bunch of information into each packet—things like the IP address of where the information is being sent, your current IP address, the order of the packet, and similar things. Then it takes those packets and sends them on their merry way across the Internet.

Now IP takes over. Those packets are sent one after another over the Internet. They go to computers on the Internet called *routers.* Routers do pretty much what they say—they route the packets toward their destination. Using the IP protocol, they examine every single packet that comes their way. They look for the IP address where the information is headed. Then they send that packet to the next closest router to the destination. Each packet usually goes from router to router until it reaches its destination.

Routing things this way makes sure that the packets get to their destination, even if routers along the route crash (or in the case of World War III, if they're blown to smithereens). Routers constantly check which routers are live and which are dead. So if one goes down, it simply sends the packet to another router.

Now the packets all start arriving at their destination. TCP takes over again. The receiving computer uses TCP to look inside each packet. Because each packet can take a different route to get to its final destination, packets often arrive out of order. But TCP is able to use the information put into each packet to reassemble the information into its original form. All this, by the way, happens lightning-fast.

You're probably thinking that all this sounds pretty neat, but so what? What does it all have to do with privacy and security?

Plenty, it turns out. Here's the problem: Routers aren't the only computers that can look at all those packets whizzing every which way on the Internet. Hackers can look at those packets, as well. And they can do more than look at them. They can reassemble them, which means they can look at the information people send to each other. They can get information about your IP address and the receiving IP address. And hackers aren't the only problem. Even Web sites on the up-and-up can get information about you.

This means that you have to assume that unless you or a Web site has taken measures to protect yourselves, whatever information you send over the Internet can be read and used by someone else. In the case of buying online with credit cards, Web sites can use technologies to scramble that information so that hackers can't read it.

All the Evils That Hackers Can Do

Okay, if you've gotten this far in the chapter, you're now a certified know-it-all about how the Internet works. But what does that have to do with privacy and security?

Plenty. Hackers can take advantage of the way the Internet works to do all kinds of evil deeds. Here are just some of the ways that they can harm you when you go online:

◆ **They can take control of your computer.** Hackers can plant programs on your computer that enable them, when they want, to take control of your computer, doing things like reading or deleting your files and personal information.

◆ **They can use your computer to launch hacker attacks against other computers and Web sites.** Hackers can plant agents or robots on your PC and automatically have them go on the attack. These bad guys make it look like the attack is coming from your computer.

As you see throughout this book, there are other very bad things they can do to you, as well.

How Your Privacy Can Be Invaded

Hackers aren't the only danger you face on the Internet. Your privacy can also be invaded, and in many cases it can be invaded legally. Just what kinds of dangers to your privacy are out there? A whole lot of them. Here's a short list. This book shows you how you can protect yourself against all these invasions of your privacy and more:

◆ **Web sites can look at your Internet settings and learn a great deal of information about you.** When you visit a Web site, Web servers can often find out the state in which you're located, the operating system you use, the Web browser you use, what site you just visited, what kind of business employs you, and even more information.

◆ **Web sites can track what you do.** Web sites can do more than just get information about you. They can also track what you do when you visit, often by putting bits of data on your computer called *cookies*. So, for example, a Web site can know what pages you look at when you visit, what kind of news and information you like to read, how

Techno Talk

Cookies are little bits of data that a Web site puts on your computer when you visit. That Web site can then use that cookie as a way to track everything you do when you visit. To learn how to handle cookies, turn to Chapter 11, "They're Not Very Sweet: What You Can Do About Cookies."

many minutes you spend at the site, and more. For more information about this and how to combat it, turn to Chapter 13, "How to Surf Anonymously Without a Trace."

◆ **Someone could "steal" your identity.** So much personal information can be gained about you from the Internet that someone can steal your identity—gather all the information about you and then pose as you, not only online, but in the real world. This is called *identity theft*. (Of course, some days, I must admit, I'd *pay* someone to take over my identity for me.) For more information about identity theft and how to combat it, turn to Chapter 9, "How to Keep Yourself Safe Against Identity Theft."

◆ **Web databases can include private information about you.** Free, publicly accessible databases on the Web can contain a good deal of information about you that you'd prefer not be made public. It's easy to find out your home address, phone number, e-mail addresses, and more at many popular Web sites.

◆ **Your e-mail can be read.** Hackers have ways of reading your e-mail as it's sent across the Internet. For more information about this and how to fight it, turn to Part 4, "Snoopers Everywhere: Keeping Safe when Using E-mail, Instant Messaging, and Chatting."

◆ **Information about your interests and personal life can be gathered from public discussion areas.** Old messages on public discussion *Usenet newsgroup* areas never die on the Internet—they live forever and can be easily looked through to find information about you. Someone can easily go to a public site such as Google Groups at http://groups.google.com, type your name, and find out every posting you've made (see Figure 1.1). That means they can find out your personal interests and read notes that you've sent to others. In essence, they can create a personal profile of you and your interests. For more information about this and how to protect your privacy, turn to Chapter 19, "Protecting Your Privacy on Internet Newsgroups and Discussion Areas."

◆ **Someone can steal your passwords.** Think of all the passwords you use online. There are passwords to log on to the Internet, to get your mail, to get onto certain Web sites—a whole lot of

Techno Talk

Usenet newsgroups are public discussion boards where people talk about every topic imaginable, from Japanese cartoons to computers to sports teams to rock stars. To participate, you need a special piece of software called a *newsgroup reader* (which comes with Netscape and Outlook, and Outlook Express), or you can go to a Web site that lets you read newsgroups, such as Google Groups at groups.google.com. Each message you can read contains a header that tells you, among other things, what the subject of the message is, who sent it, and other details. To make it easier to decide which messages you want to read, you can first view newsgroups headers before deciding which messages you want to read.

them, everywhere you go. Some wily hackers have ways of stealing passwords, which means they can read your e-mail and do other nasty things.

◆ **Marketing groups and companies can compile comprehensive profiles about your buying and Web surfing habits.** Knowing how you spend your money and time is big business. If you're not careful, you can be targeted with ads, junk e-mail, and other nasty things that you might not like to see.

Figure 1.1

It's easy to find out someone's personal interests at a site such as Google Groups DejaNews at groups. google.com.

Viruses, Worms, and Data Theft, Oh My!

As if all that isn't bad enough, there's even more to look out for. The Internet poses some other unique dangers:

◆ **You can get a virus from a file you** *download*. *Viruses* are malicious programs that can do all kinds of damage to your computer, such as deleting all the files on your hard disk or attacking your operating system.

◆ **You can get sent a worm via e-mail.** *Worms* are programs that are frequently sent via e-mail. Like viruses, they can also do damage to your computer. They can also attack Internet servers and have been able to shut down corporate and university networks.

Check This Out!

When you transfer a file from somewhere on the Internet to your computer, you're downloading the file. It's sent from a computer on the Internet straight to your computer.

◆ **Data about you can be stolen.** Your credit card number can be stolen, or personal information can be taken off your computer. There are ways to battle credit card fraud. You can make sure that you buy only at secure sites—sites that use encryption to scramble credit card information so that no hackers or other snoopers can read it as it's sent across the Internet.

Dangers to Cable and DLS Modem Owners

If you own a *cable modem* or *DSL modem*, you probably feel as if you're sitting on top of the world. You get super-high-speed access while everyone else pokes along at a measly 56K.

But there's a price you pay for the luxury of speed. Cable and DSL modem owners are more vulnerable than mere slowpokes. That's because cable and DSL modems are different than regular modems—when you have one and you turn your computer on, it automatically connects to the Internet without you having to do anything, and you stay connected for as long as your computer is on. This means that you can be connected for a dozen or more uninterrupted hours a day. When this happens, your IP address stays the same for the entire day. When you have an IP address on for that many hours in a row, there is the potential for a hacker to find it and do some damage. To play it safe, unplug the wire from the cable modem or DSL modem to your network card when you're not using the Internet. It's easy to do. Just unplug the wire right from the modem itself, or from where it plugs into your computer. You can also call your cable modem or DSL modem service and ask if they have any special security features you can turn on to stop hackers from getting at your computer.

Techno Talk _____

When is a modem not a modem? When it's a **cable modem** or **DSL modem.** When you get onto the Internet via a cable modem or DSL modem, you're not really using modem technology. Instead, you install something called a *network card* into your computer, and a special device is attached to the network card to enable you to browse the Internet using the same cable that comes into your house for cable TV, or using a phone line that enables you to access the Internet at high speed.

Hacker target cable modems and DSL modems more than they do dial-up modems. That's because hackers often use other people's computers to launch attacks on other computers and Web sites. And cable modems and DSL modems are ideal launching pads because they offer high-speed connections and so can do more damage than computers with slower connections.

There's another potential problem. When you use a cable modem, you're really part of a computer network, and the people in your neighborhood or town are part of that computer network. If your cable modem service is configured a certain way, and if your Windows computer has certain settings turned on, then anyone in your town or neighborhood can see every single file on your computer—and can copy them to their own computer.

Luckily, there's a way to combat this problem. People can only look inside your computer if you have something called *file sharing* turned on. You might have file sharing turned on if you have a home network in which you want to share files with other computers on your network. Or, for some reason, Windows may have been configured with file sharing turned on when you bought your computer. (For more information about how to protect home networks, turn to Chapter 8, "How to Protect Your Home Network.")

It's easy to see if you have file sharing turned on—and it's easy to turn it off. To turn off file sharing, open Windows Explorer. Scroll down until you see an icon called Network Neighborhood. Right-click Network Neighborhood and choose Properties. Next, click File and Printer Sharing. The dialog box shown in Figure 1.2 is displayed onscreen. Make sure that both boxes are unchecked. If they're unchecked, no one can look at the files on your computer.

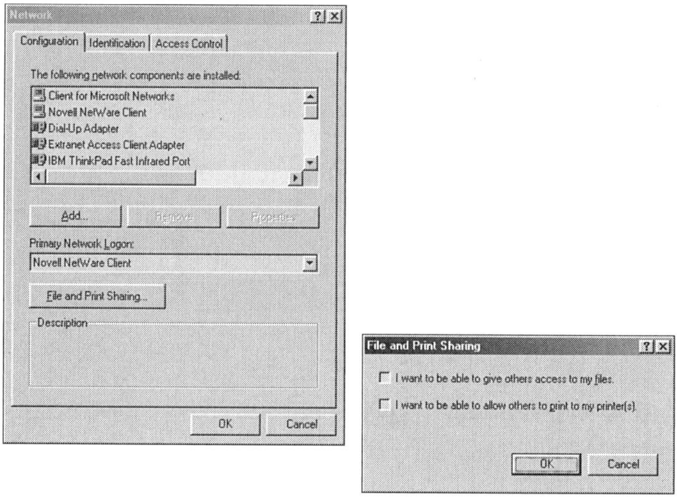

Figure 1.2

If both of these boxes are unchecked, you are safe when using your cable modem.

The Least You Need to Know

◆ The Internet was started in the 1960s and 1970s as a way to help the military and computer researchers share information.

◆ When you go online, people and Web sites can see what information you send across the Internet.

◆ The basic protocol that guides the Internet is TCP/IP.

◆ When you surf to Web sites, those Web sites can gather a great deal of information about you, including what pages you visit and where you're located.

◆ Files that you download from the Internet could contain viruses or other malicious kinds of programs.

◆ Cable modem and DSL modem owners are more at risk than are owners of PCs with dial-up modems.

Chapter 2

Putting Up Your First Line of Cyberdefense

In This Chapter

- What information your ISP has about you—and how to make sure it doesn't invade your privacy
- How to protect your privacy on America Online
- What kind of information is available about you on Web databases
- How to remove your name from Web White Page directories and for-pay databases
- Tips for creating hacker-proof passwords and protecting your passwords
- What you need to know about Microsoft's Windows XP, Passport, and .Net

To be safe and to protect your privacy online, you've got to be strong. Very strong. Stronger than the starting line of the Green Bay Packers. So strong that even the most determined hacker can't bust through your defenses.

But how can you be strong if, when it comes to hacking and cracking Internet technology, you're really just a 98-pound weakling? Easy. Follow the advice in this chapter. You'll learn how anyone—even someone just learning to use the Internet—can put up a powerful cyberdefense. You'll find out how to make sure that your Internet Service Provider doesn't invade your privacy. You'll see how you can create hacker-proof passwords. You'll find out how to get your name out of Web databases. You'll learn what to watch out for in new Microsoft technologies. In fact, after you read this chapter, you won't feel like a 98-pound cyberweakling anymore.

Making Sure Your ISP Doesn't Invade Your Privacy

The greatest threat to your privacy online might not be from the Web sites you visit or from hackers intent on finding out every aspect of your personal life. Instead, the worst threat might come from your Internet Service Provider (ISP). Your ISP can know everything about your Web surfing habits, has access to your e-mail and your credit card number, and can get a lot more information about you. But what can you do about it? In fact, as you see in this section, there's a whole lot you can do.

What Kind of Information Does Your ISP and Online Service Know About You?

Your ISP, more than any Web site, more than any hacker, in fact, maybe even more than your mother, can know just about everything about you. Consider what they can find out if they'd like to know:

- ◆ Your name, address, telephone number, and other identification information
- ◆ Your credit card number
- ◆ Personal information you might have given them when you joined
- ◆ Every Web site you've ever visited
- ◆ The full contents of all e-mail that's ever been sent to you or you've ever sent to anyone else
- ◆ Every chat session you've ever participated in
- ◆ What files you've downloaded
- ◆ What you've bought over the Internet
- ◆ Everything you've ever done online when connecting through them

Check This Out!

If you want to find out all the latest news, information, and links to helpful resources about privacy, check out the Privacy Page at www.privacy.org. It's a great site for learning everything you'll ever want to know about Internet privacy—and if you want to get involved to help protect privacy, it tells you how to do that, as well.

Yikes! That's scary stuff. ISPs know information such as your name, phone number, credit card number, address, and other personal information because you filled out that kind of information when you joined. They can know everything you've ever done when you're on the Internet because of the nature of the Internet—all your Internet communications go through your ISP, who has access to all of it. I mean everything: every letter to your old girlfriend, and every time-wasting Web site you ever visited.

Just because an ISP *can* find out all this information doesn't mean it *will* find out the information. And even if it knows this information, the ISP will *probably not* use it in any way. If the ISP does use it, so what? Read on to see what to worry about, as if you didn't already have suspicions.

Why Should You Care What Your ISP and Online Service Does with Personal Information?

Personal information about you and what you do with your time is worth big bucks to some people—especially to sleazy marketers. So imagine that your ISP sells all your demographic information, including everything you've ever bought online (including that "Full Cleveland" lime-colored polyester leisure suit) to other companies. You might have to spend the rest of your life fighting off telemarketers, junk mailers, junk e-mailers, and others trying to sell you everything under the sun. Including a few more Full Cleveland leisure suits. And you just might bite.

There's more. ISPs could provide that information to various police and law enforcement sources, including the IRS. (No problem, you've never fudged a little on your taxes, have you? You have? Oh, that's a different story.) They could provide personal information to private lawyers in a suit against you, so that whoever is suing could pry into your private life in ways never before possible.

Guaranteeing Your ISP Protects Your Privacy

There are things you can do to make sure your ISP protects your privacy. The primary thing is to find out the privacy policy from its Web site. If, after you've read it, you don't like it, find another ISP. In Figure 2.1, you can see an example of the privacy policy concerning e-mail posted by an ISP called The Internet Access Company (TIAC).

Don't stop with checking out the Web site. Call the ISP and ask for its privacy policies in writing. If it won't give you one, find another ISP. There are many ISPs out there hungry to get your business, so shop around.

When reading ISP privacy policies, you have to read a whole lot of legal mumbo-jumbo and hard-to-follow gobbledygook. After sifting through the lawyerly verbiage, here's what you should look for when checking your ISP's privacy policy:

◆ **Do they share information about you with other companies, especially direct marketers and other businesses?** Selling lists of people and their personal information is big business. Find out if your ISP sells this kind of information. If it does, look elsewhere.

Figure 2.1

Here's an example of a privacy policy concerning e-mail posted by an ISP—Inter.net.

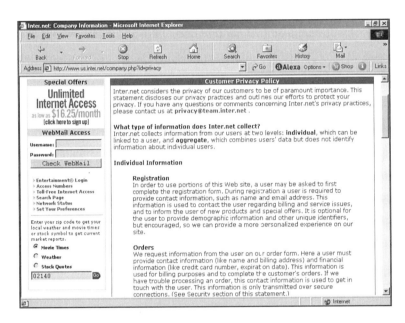

◆ **Do they maintain logs of your activities online?** Just because an ISP can track your online activity doesn't mean it will. Does the ISP maintain logs of your activities? If so, look elsewhere. Even if it doesn't sell that information, someone from inside the ISP could snoop on you by examining the logs.

◆ **Can you see all the information that the company maintains about you—and can you correct it if it's wrong?** It's your information, so you should be able to get access to it.

◆ **Does the service keep copies of your e-mail after you delete it?** Before e-mail makes its way to you, it sits on an e-mail server at the ISP. Does the ISP keep copies of your e-mail or delete the e-mail after you do? You'd like the ISP to delete the e-mail after you've deleted it—or even after you've fetched it from the server. That way, there's less chance that it can be easily stolen.

What Else You Can Do to Protect Your Privacy with Your ISP

There are a few other ways you can protect your privacy with your ISP. The first thing to do is not to give out much private information about yourself. Typically, when you sign up with an ISP, you have to provide information such as name, address, phone number, and credit card number. That's fine. But does the ISP really need to know your annual income? Your favorite hobbies? Your favorite Beatle? (Okay, the world can know it now: Mine was John. Still is, despite his demise.)

Simply refuse to answer any questions beyond the basics. If the ISP won't let you sign up, no problem—tell the ISP to take a hike.

Check This Out! _____

Finger is an Internet service that enables people to find out personal information about you by simply typing in your e-mail address. Usually, finger information is made available only if you specifically ask it to be made available. However, there's a chance that information is available about you without your knowing it. Check with your ISP and ask that the finger information not be available. To check if finger information is available about you, head to www.cs.indiana.edu:800/finger/gateway and search for your e-mail address. It not only shows if finger information is available about you, but you can also see the information that is available.

Also, some ISPs let you maintain public profiles about yourself, things such as your e-mail address, personal interests, and the like. If you don't mind the world—including junk mail marketers—knowing about that kind of thing, fine. (Although, do you really want the world to know that your favorite pets are ferrets, and you spend your free time collecting discarded fingernails?) If you don't want that information made public, tell your ISP to pull your online profile. You might not be aware that those profiles are maintained or kept publicly about you, so check with your ISP.

Protecting Your Privacy on America Online

America Online is a marketer's dream with a vast, captive audience with million of members. America Online recognizes what a goldmine it has, and it's been quite aggressive about mining that gold—namely your personal information. AOL does things such as sell its subscriber list to direct marketers and other businesses. When America Online advertised in a direct marketing magazine, bragging about the value of its vast list, America Online users revolted (and *were* revolted). As a result of the complaints and bad publicity, America Online agreed to allow people to get themselves off these lists.

It is easy to get off the lists. First, use the keyword **CHOICES** or **MARKETING PREFERENCES.** When you do that, you are brought to a screen from which you can choose to be taken off a variety of direct marketing lists, such as receiving e-mail, receiving postal mail, getting telephone calls, and the like. Click the list you want to be taken off of, click **Continue,** and finally, click the button that takes you off the list. You can see the process of getting yourself taken off an e-mail mailing list in Figure 2.2.

Figure 2.2

If you're an America Online member, here's how to make sure that you don't get marketing e-mail from AOL.

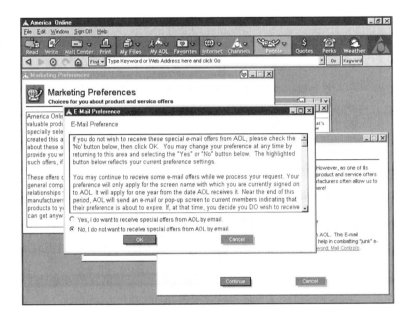

Check This Out!

When you log on to America Online, and at every click of the mouse, it seems like you get a new ad popping up in your face. Don't just sit there—fight back! You can turn those ads off. Use the keyword **CHOICES,** click **Pop-Up,** and turn off the ads.

America Online gives you the option of creating a personal profile—a form, which anyone can see—that includes information such as your name, age, gender, marital status, personal interests, and similar information. If you've been on America Online a while, you might have forgotten you filled one out.

If you're uncomfortable with your profile information being widely available, you can change the information or delete it entirely. It's easy to do. Use the keyword **PROFILE,** and click the **My Profile** button. You can change or delete it. By the way, deleting your profile usually results in one getting less *spam* e-mail, because profiles are used by spammers as a way to gather e-mail lists.

Techno Talk _____

Spam is unwanted e-mail that's sent without asking for it—usually asking you to buy something or sign up for an offer. Don't respond to the offer; the odds are, it's a scam. And don't send an e-mail asking that they not send you the offer again, because that only lets them know your e-mail address is a valid one, and they'll keep sending you mail.

How to Create Hacker-Proof Passwords

One of the biggest threats to your privacy and security is something you have the greatest control over: your passwords. One of the most common ways your privacy can be invaded is by someone getting hold of your password and then wreaking havoc with it.

With a little bit of knowledge, you can create hacker-proof passwords, and you can manage your passwords so that they aren't stolen. Here's what you need to know about managing and creating your passwords so that you don't get burned.

Why You Should Worry About Passwords

On the Internet, you *are* your password. From things as basic as logging on to the Internet through your Internet Service Provider (ISP) to more complicated things (such as checking your e-mail, entering a private area of a Web site, or buying books online), all you are to Web sites and your ISP is a password.

Here are just a few of the things that could be done if your password is stolen:

- ◆ Someone could check all your e-mail and pose as you, sending out threatening phony e-mails and public messages to others.

- ◆ Someone could get access to any private areas of Web sites where you've registered.

- ◆ Someone could "steal" your identity and pose as you, in the real world, as well as online.

- ◆ Someone could use your credit card to buy thousands of dollars of goods online.

Check This Out! _____

Sometimes when you're online you'll find a reference to something called a PIN. PIN stands for Personal Information Number, which is a term often used interchangeably with the term password. If you use an automated teller machine (ATM), your password is probably a PIN.

◆ Someone could use your account to launch hacker attacks all over the world—and people would believe that you are to blame.

How Hackers Steal Passwords—It's Not How You Think

If you know how hackers steal passwords, it can help you know better how to protect yours. So how exactly do they steal them? Surprise: Most hackers don't steal passwords by superhuman feats of programming. They use much more mundane tools.

One of the simplest tools is often called social engineering, which simply means that they ask. A common tactic is a hacker sending you an e-mail or instant message on America Online, claiming that he's working for the service, and asking for your password and username, so that he can fix or check your account. In some cases, hackers call people up, posing as computer security experts, and ask for passwords.

Hackers can look through someone's desk or garbage can at work, for example, and find a username and password written on a sticky note or other slip of paper. In a variation, a hacker could look through your computer while you're away from it and find a list of passwords that you keep on a program.

A very common method is by simply guessing. You'd be surprised at how many people's password is … you guessed it, "password." Or their initials. Or their wife's name. Hackers can use their computers to automate the guessing of passwords. There are programs that keep entering password after password after password—thousands of them—until it finds one that logs on to a system.

The final way hackers can get your password is by sniffing them. It's not that hackers have an especially large proboscis (nose) or sensitive olfactory nerves. Sniffing refers to a way in which hackers examine data moving across the Internet.

How to Handle Passwords So That Hackers Can't Steal Them

It's fairly easy to keep your passwords out of hackers' hands if you just treat your passwords properly. Here's what to do:

◆ *Never* **give out your password when someone asks for it.** If someone asks you for your password—either in an e-mail message, by instant message, or by telephone—don't give it out. Employees of ISPs, America Online, and Web sites never ask you for your password.

◆ **Don't share your password with other people.** Friends and family members might want to use your password to log on to the Internet or America Online. Sure, they're your friends, and yes, they're your family. But are you sure that your 13-year-old son won't inadvertently hand out your password to someone else? Here's one instance where sharing is *not* a good thing to do.

Check This Out!

Increasingly, there are ways that you can check your e-mail when you're away from your own computer. Cybercafes, for example, enable you to log on to your e-mail system to check your e-mail. Or you might be at a meeting and use someone else's computer. Or, there is a growing number of public Internet terminals where people can do things such as check their e-mail, either for free or for a fee. If you check your e-mail from a computer other than your own, change your password after you log in. It's possible that somewhere along the way, a sniffer has been used to find out your password.

- **Change your password weekly or monthly.** There's a small possibility that someone has managed to sniff out your password on the Internet or found out your password in some other way. If you constantly change your password, the thief only has use of your password for a brief amount of time and cannot do a large amount of damage. This is especially important because passwords are easy to "sniff."

- **Never write your password on a slip of paper.** It's too easy to leave it lying around where someone can find it. Unless you have the kind of James Bond technology where paper bursts into flame after you've used it, never write down your password.

- **Use Windows screen saver passwords to protect your PC against password stealers.** One way that people can find out your password is to use your computer when you're away from it, looking for passwords, or using your various Internet accounts. It's easy to thwart this: Use the password protection built into Windows screen savers. To do so, right-click your desktop, choose **Properties,** and click the **Screen Saver** tab. The Screen Saver dialog box appears. Choose a screen saver to use, and check the **Password Protected** box. Click the **Change** button, and type in your password. Now, whenever you're away from your desk for a certain amount of time, a screen saver runs that can only be turned off by using a password. You can also password-protect your entire computer, so that no one can turn it off and restart it to get around your screen saver password. Turn to Chapter 28, "How to Safeguard Your PC," for details.

- **Don't enable the automatic login feature of your ISP and America Online.** When you dial in to your ISP, your connection screen gives you the option of automatically saving your password between logins so that you don't have to retype the password each time you log in. The login screen is pictured in Figure 2.3. Don't check the **Save Password** box; if you do, anyone can log in as you, because your password is automatically sent to your ISP. The same holds true for America Online—don't enable the option that allows your password to be automatically sent to the service.

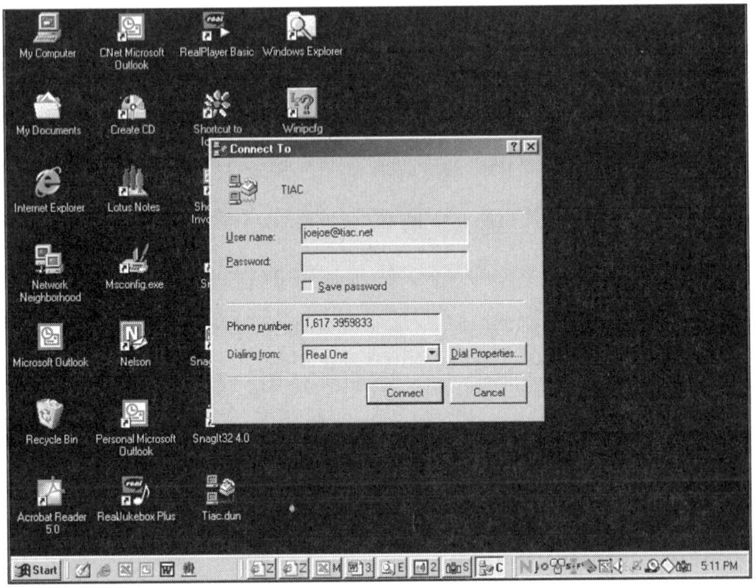

Figure 2.3

To make sure someone can't log in as you to your ISP, make sure you don't tell your PC to remember your password.

◆ **Use different passwords for different Web sites and your ISP.** If you spend any time at all on the Internet, you have many passwords—passwords to log on, to check your mail, to visit certain Web sites, and more. Use different passwords for each site. That way, if someone steals your password, she only has access to a single site, not your entire life.

◆ **If you use Internet Explorer, don't let it save your Web passwords.** Internet Explorer has a time-saving feature that's also a security risk. When you visit a Web site that requires a username and a password, it automatically saves the username and password if you want. Never have it save your passwords. Otherwise, anyone with access to your computer can log in to the Web sites as if they were you.

How to Create Passwords That Even Hackers Can't Crack

Handling your password properly goes a long way toward making sure your password is never stolen. But no matter how you handle them, you're still vulnerable to a hacker who has a program that automatically tries thousands of passwords to see if one is yours. To combat that, you need to create passwords that even hackers can't crack. When choosing a password, there's a lot you can to do make sure it can't be cracked. Follow this advice:

♦ **Never use the name of your spouse, children, pets, or anything else associated with you.** If someone knows anything about your life, these will be the first passwords they try. Also, do not use your address, Social Security number, license plate, initials, or similar information. Remember the principle of "security through obscurity."

♦ **Use at least eight characters in your password.** The longer the password, the harder it is to guess.

Check This Out! _____

Random password generators can create hard-to-crack passwords for you—a combination of random letters, numbers, and characters that is just about impossible to guess. You can download many of them for free from sites such as www. download.com. You can also have a random password generated on the Web at PassGen: A Password Generator Java Applet at www.world.std.com/ ~reinhold/passgen.html.

♦ **Mix letters and numbers.** When you mix these two, it's that much harder to guess a password than if you use only letters or only numbers.

♦ **If you can use upper- and lowercase, use them both.** Sometimes passwords are case-sensitive, which means that the only way to type them correctly is if the proper case is used. If you can create a case-sensitive password, make sure to mix upper- and lowercase letters.

How to Remove Your Name from Web Databases

The whole world is watching! That call from the 1960s should be updated for the new millennium. These days, the call would be about the enormous amount of information about you that's available for the world to see on many databases on the World Wide Web. Web databases are filled to the brim with information about you. Your name, address, phone number, and e-mail address are often only a click or two away from anyone with a mouse and an interest in prying into your life. Your place of employment might be listed, as well.

Things are even worse than that. If someone is willing to fork over some money, they can find out information that you no doubt thought was not available about you publicly anywhere. For a fee, people can visit a variety of for-pay Web sites that are willing to distribute your Social Security number, driving record, credit history, and bankruptcy reports.

Check This Out!

If someone knows a phone number, there is a way for him to find out the name of the person at the number and the person's address—from that, it's a snap to find out an e-mail address. Some Web sites allow reverse phone lookups. Someone could call a phone number repeatedly, and if he continually finds no one home, he could surmise that the people who live there are on vacation. Because he can do a reverse phone lookup, he knows the address, which could be ripe for a burglary.

Here's just a sampling of the information that someone can find out about you for a fee at the A-1 Trace USA Web site—just one of a number of similar sites on the Internet. You can see a portion of the A-1 Web site in Figure 2.4. There's a whole lot more information about you that sites like this are willing to sell:

- ◆ Your driver's license number and driving record. Cost: $24
- ◆ An "Info Probe" that includes your Social Security number, postal address, real estate holdings, bankruptcies, lawsuits involving you, and similar information. Cost: $29
- ◆ Your real estate holdings, including the parcel number of your land, your address, the value of your holding, and the total property value. Cost: $29
- ◆ A history of any civil litigation you've been involved in. Cost: $39
- ◆ Information about your current month's long distance calls, including the dates and frequencies of the calls. Cost: $129

Pretty scary, isn't it? But it's not just investigative sites like these that contain information about you that you might think is private. There are many, many Web sites—including popular search sites—that allow people to search for information about you, such as your address, phone number, and e-mail address.

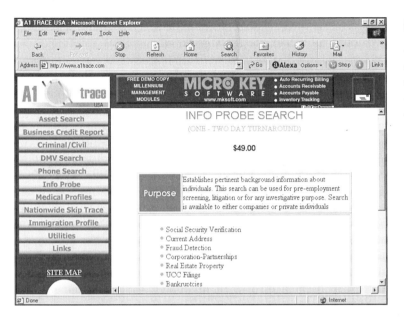

Figure 2.4

Anyone with a credit card and an interest in snooping can find out just about anything about you at sites like A-1 Trace USA.

Why You Should Worry About What's in Web Databases

There's all kinds of information available about you on the Web, either for free or for a few bucks. So what, you might think. After all, you don't have a prison record (although if you did, someone could easily find that out, as well), and you have nothing to hide. Big deal. Let anyone find out anything they want.

Well, in fact, there's a whole lot you *should* worry about. Here are some of the dangers caused by all this information being made public about you in Web databases:

◆ **Identity theft.** If someone finds out your name, address, phone number, Social Security number, bank account information, and similar data, they can in essence steal your identity—and more than that, of course, they can steal your money. With this kind of personal information, someone could take out a credit card in your name, charge thousands of dollars, and have the bills sent to you. He could order new checks from your bank and write out checks from your account. He could get government benefits due to you, such as your Social Security checks. He can pose as you and scam other people, giving your contact information. Turn to Chapter 9, "How to Keep Yourself Safe Against Identity Theft," for more information about this.

- **Stalkers.** It's a scary world out there. Wackos and weirdoes abound. Pick up a newspaper almost every day and you find a story about stalkers, sometimes with tragic results. Women, in particular, need to worry about this possibility. If someone has an abundance of personal information about you, it makes it easier for them to stalk you.

- **Con artists.** If con artists know a great deal of personal information about you, it's much easier for them to gain your personal confidence. They can call up, posing as a bank employee; and, because they have your bank account information, you're likely to believe them. It also makes it easier for them to target you for specific scams.

- **Junk mail.** Direct marketers live on demographic information—targeting junk mail and telemarketing calls at people in specific demographic niches. If they get information about you, you're ripe for unwanted phone calls, junk mail, and junk e-mail.

- **It's just plain creepy.** There's no other way to put it. We all like to think that we're unique individuals, free from privacy intrusions and snooping. The idea that anyone can get extremely personal information about you can be just plain creepy—and you shouldn't have to be subjected to that kind of snooping if you don't want to be.

Check This Out! _____

The Web isn't the only way that people can steal your identity and find out personal information about you. There's another way as well: They can sift through your trash, looking for identifying information about you—for example, bank account slips, ATM slips, anything with your Social Security number, and similar information. People who do this are called dumpster divers. To be safe from them, shred any paper that has any identifying information about you that you'd rather not have the world know about.

What a lineup, huh? Don't worry. There are ways you can fight back. In general, there are two kinds of Web sites that make information about you available. There are the free sites that enable people to look up information such as your name, address, phone number, and e-mail address. These sites tend to have only more public information about you—often called White Page sites. There are also the for-pay sites, such as the A-1 Trace USA Web site. These sites sell the more private information, such as your Social Security number. In general, it's easier to get your name out of the free sites than the for-pay sites.

How to Get Your Name out of Internet White Pages

Internet White Page directories are free, public Web sites that enable people to search for other people, looking for addresses, e-mail addresses, and phone numbers. There are many of them. Unfortunately, there's no central place where you can get your name off all the White Page lists. You have to go to each individual site and request that your name be taken out of that specific White Page directory. They don't always agree to do it—but many do. (By the way, if you want people such as long-lost friends or relatives to be able to find you, you want to keep your name in these databases instead of taking your name out.)

Table 2.1 shows a list of the major White Page directories on the Internet and instructions on how to get yourself out of their listings. You have to contact them individually to remove your name from their lists. In some cases, the exact directions for getting your name off might have changed since this book was published. If you don't find the exact pages listed here for removing your name, don't worry—there is a way to get your name off. Just go to the main page on the site and look for the area that describes how to get your name off the listing. At worst, send a general e-mail to the site, requesting that you be taken off the list.

Table 2.1   Getting Your Name out of White Page Directories

Directory	Web Address	How to Remove Your Name
BigFoot	www.bigfoot.com	Write to help@bigfoot.com and ask to have your listing removed.
Yahoo People Search	www.people.yahoo.com	Go to http://people. yahoo.com/py/ psE-mailSupp.py and fill out the form.
WhoWhere	www.whowhere.com	Go to http://www.whowhere.lycos. com/WriteUs and fill out the form.
Internet @ddress Finder	www.iaf.net	Click **Remove** from the main page and type in your e-mail address.
Switchboard	www.switchboard.com	On the main page, click **My Personal Listing,** then click **Remove your personal listing** and follow the instructions.
Infospace.com	www.infospace.com	Do a White Pages or e-mail search and find your listing. Then click the **update/remove** link and fill out the form for removing your name.
World Pages	www.worldpages.com	Go to http://www.worldpages.com/ docs/forms/res_updates.whtml and fill out the form.

Getting Your Name out of For-Pay Sites

Most of the for-pay sites on the Internet don't compile the information they sell themselves. Instead, they get the information from a wide variety of other places, such as state Departments of Motor Vehicles, registries of deeds, and credit bureaus. So, very few of the for-pay sites provide a way of removing yourself from their databases. In fact, there's an economic incentive for them *not* to remove you—the more information they have, the more information they can sell.

In many cases, there's nothing you can do about getting them to stop providing information about you—especially because many of their sources of information are public records. However, there's still a fair amount you can do.

One of the world's largest—possibly *the* largest—supplier of databases and information about people is Lexis-Nexis. You can find it on the Web at www.lexis-nexis.com.

Lexis-Nexis has a variety of people-finder types of databases. They're designed for attorneys trying to track down people involved in lawsuits and for law-enforcement personnel, as well as for people looking at others' credit histories. They include names and addresses and, at times, other information, such as telephone number and date of birth and credit information. There are several products that provide this kind of information, and you have to do a bit of work to get yourself out of them.

Send an e-mail to remove@prod.lexis-nexis.com, asking that your name be removed, or mail the request to Lexis-Nexis Name Removal, P.O. Box 933, Dayton, OH 45401. You can also fax the request to 1-800-732-7672. Send mail to Consumer Services, Experian, 949 West Bond Street, Lincoln, NE 68521, or call (800) 407-1088.

Check This Out!

The Lexis-Nexis database giant has a variety of people-finder databases. Wouldn't it be nice to know what information, exactly, they have about you in their people-finder databases? In fact, you can find out for a small fee. Send your name and address and an $8 check or money order to Lexis-Nexis Consumer Access Program, P.O. Box 933, Dayton, OH 45401. You get information that they have in their people-finder databases. Keep in mind, though, that this is just a small portion of the databases the Lexis-Nexis sells to people. You aren't able to find out what information Lexis-Nexis's other databases have about you in this way, however.

The Departments of Motor Vehicles have been big violators of people's privacy. In the past, they've disclosed to anyone with a checkbook things such as your driving history and your license number. In many states, your license number is your Social Security number, so in essence, they've given out Social Security numbers. Information from Departments of Motor Vehicles (DMV) have been for sale on Web sites, among other places.

You do have a little bit of consumer protection. There is a way to try and salvage a little of your privacy. The federal Drivers Protection Act gives you some control over how DMV information can be used. DMV information can be given to law-enforcement personnel, insurance companies, and the like. But, if you want to make sure that the information can't be used by anyone else, such as direct marketers, you can ban them from using it. For information how, go to a page put together by the Federal Trade Commission at www.ftc.gov/privacy/protect.htm, as shown in Figure 2.5. The page includes other helpful information, such as how to opt-out of credit card solicitations.

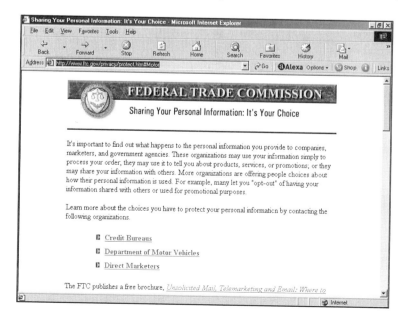

Figure 2.5

For information on how to make sure your state Department of Motor Vehicles doesn't sell information about you, head to this page, run by the Federal Trade Commission.

At the same site, you can also find information on how you can get the major credit bureaus Equifax, Experian, and Transunion Corporation to stop sharing information about you with direct marketers.

Your Public Records Are on the Web

There's another way that anyone can get very personal information about you from the Web. Increasingly, state and local governments are putting public databases online that have information about you.

For example, a site called www.registeredtovote.com allowed its users to find out personal information about anyone in New York City, including address and party affiliation. All one needed to know was a person's name and birthday. And finding out anyone's birthday is easy; the site www.anybirthday.com, divulges birth date information. After an outcry from privacy advocates, the site changed the information it would give out—now it only discloses a name and the borough and zip code where the person lives. It also allows New Yorkers to take their names out of the database.

New York isn't alone in this; governments across the country are starting to put similar databases online that have records the government keeps about people. At this point, unfortunately, there's not a whole lot you can do about it. You can, of course, complain loudly to your local politicians to ask them not to make this information easily accessible on the Web—and you can ask to have your information removed from the database. But as you know from dealing with bureaucrats, the odds of that succeeding are somewhat smaller than the odds of you winning a $300 million PowerBall lottery jackpot.

What About Microsoft's Windows XP, Passport, and .Net?

Ah, Microsoft. The bully everyone loves to hate. There are those who believe that the company is bent on world domination and is willing to do anything it can—legal or not—to get there, including invading your privacy.

Microsoft's Windows XP operating system, along with some other Microsoft technologies, is at the center of a big privacy dispute. Privacy advocates complain that XP steers you toward registering a lot of very private information about yourself with Microsoft Passport, which is a scheme that makes it easier for you to log into and use many Web sites. The idea behind Passport is a compelling one: Just enter your information into Passport, and it automatically logs you in to any Web site, without you having to fill out information.

The problem, these privacy advocates maintain, is that when you use Passport, you're giving Microsoft all kinds of very personal information about yourself. And they don't trust that Microsoft puts it to good use—in short, they believe that Microsoft invades your privacy.

Making matters worse is that there's a whole new technology Microsoft is working on called .Net. I won't bore you with the ultra-techie details, but it's designed to let you more easily use the Internet from cell phones, Palm devices … heck, maybe even from your Dick Tracy–style watch for all I know. At the core of .Net will probably be—you guessed it—Passport, or something very much like it.

What does this all mean? If you trust Microsoft to protect your privacy, go ahead and use Passport. If you don't, though, avoid entering personal information into Passport, if you can. If you can't, put in only the most basic information possible.

The Least You Need to Know

- Before choosing an ISP, get its privacy standards in writing. If you're not happy with the standards, choose another ISP.

- Get yourself off America Online direct marketing and e-mail lists by using the keyword "choices."

- Never give out your password to anyone who asks for it in e-mail or by telephone. They're most likely hackers trying to steal information.

- Make sure your passwords are at least eight characters long and contain a mix of letters and numbers.

- To remove information about yourself from White Page directories, check the list in this chapter or visit the site and send an e-mail asking to be removed from the directory.

- Visit the Federal Trade Commission site at www.ftc.gov/privacy/protect.htm for information on how to make sure your Department of Motor Vehicles doesn't release illegal information about you.

- If you're worried that Microsoft won't protect your privacy, don't use its Passport technology, especially if you use Windows XP.

How to Protect Yourself Against the Most Common Internet Scams

In This Chapter

- ◆ How to recognize Internet scams
- ◆ Ways you can protect yourself against the most common Internet scams and fraud
- ◆ What action you can take if you've been the subject of a scam
- ◆ The best sites on the Internet for getting information about online scams

Con men, scammers, bunco artists, flimflammers, hustlers, smoothies, Ponzi schemers, weisenheimers, and sharpies of all kinds … you'll find them all, and worse, online. They've flocked to the Internet because it's so easy and cheap to do scams there—and because it's so hard to track down the people who've burned you. There's a now-famous *New Yorker* cartoon in which a dog sits in front of a computer and says, "On the Internet, nobody knows you're a dog." In the same way, on the Internet, it can be hard to know that someone is a rip-off artist.

Scams are possible on the Internet because it's so easy for someone to pose as a legitimate businessperson. Spend a few bucks building a nice-looking Web site or sending out mass e-mails, and all of a sudden you're not a chiseler looking to steal someone's life savings; instead, you're a legit businessman trying to help some poor schmoe get rich.

Don't worry. It's easy to make sure you don't get conned. And if you have been the victim of a scam, there's a lot you can do about it. In this chapter, I'll clue you in on how you can avoid Internet scams and what you can do if, for some reason, you've been burned. I'll also show you where to go online to find out the latest information about cons, scams, and other nasty schemes.

Recognizing Online Scams

It's actually pretty easy to spot online scams. Follow this simple, time-honored rule for avoiding any con game: If something sounds too good to be true, then it *is* too good to be true.

Make $100,000 at home in your spare time! Get rid of your credit debt forever—and spend no money! Buy your dream home—with no money down! Sure, and why don't I just give you direct access to my bank account and credit card so you can take out withdrawals whenever you like? And sure, I'll buy that nice bridge you have for sale. What's it called again? The Brooklyn Bridge, you say?

It's not just hype like this that you need to watch out for. If you're sent an e-mail with an impossible-to-believe deal or you happen upon a Web site without an address or phone number on it, be wary. In general, any time a Web site, e-mail, or anything else you come across on the Internet doesn't feel right to you, listen to your instincts—they're almost always right.

Protecting Yourself Against the Most Common Internet Scams

What kinds of things do you need to watch out for on the Internet? There are all kinds of scams. But here are the most common ones to look out for—and how you can make sure that you never get burned:

- **Watch out for rip-off artists at Web auctions.** Web auctions are a great way to buy online. But if you're not careful, you can get burned. You might pay for goods that never get delivered, or you might be told that you're buying a rare collectible only to find out that it's a counterfeit. To protect yourself, don't pay the person from whom you're buying the goods directly; instead, pay what's called an escrow service.

The service holds the money for your goods until the goods are delivered and only releases the money after they have been received by you in good order. Also, never buy collectibles such as rare Beanie Babies or sports collectibles online. Fraud at auction sites has become the most common kind of Internet scam, according to the Internet Fraud Watch at www.fraud.org. For complete information about how to protect yourself when buying at auctions, turn to Chapter 26, "How to Stay Safe When Buying at Auctions."

Check This Out!

There are two types of auction sites: those from which you buy from other individuals, such as at eBay at www.ebay.com, and those from which you buy directly from the site itself. Before buying, know which kind of site you're buying from. If you're buying from individuals, use an escrow service such as Tradenable at www.tradenable.com and Escrow.com at www.escrow.com. If you're buying from the site itself, find out the site's return policies and warranties for the goods that they sell. For more information about protecting yourself when buying at auctions, turn to Chapter 26.

- **Don't download dialer programs that you're told you need in order to access a Web site.** In a recent scam, people were told that to access certain Web sites, they needed to download a special dialer. Surprise! When they did that, their normal Internet connection ended, and the dialer dialed overseas numbers and charged the connection time to the unwitting people who downloaded the dialers. The scammers were eventually caught.

- **Beware of business opportunity schemes.** Sell spotted salamanders and make a fortune! Sounds improbable, doesn't it? Stranger schemes have made con artists money. Here's how these schemes usually work: To make a fortune, you first have to buy marketing materials or merchandise (2,000 spotted salamanders, anyone?). And you keep buying and buying and buying … and the only person making the fortune is the person who sold you a bill of goods—or is that a gross of salamanders? In any event, never respond to a business opportunity scheme on the Internet. The only opportunity they provide are for scamsters looking to turn a quick profit.

- **Don't respond to credit repair offers.** Got yourself into a bit of financial trouble and now have bad credit? You might be targeted by an online shyster promising you he can "repair" your credit rating. Beware—there's no way it can be done. Responding to these offers only results in you getting ripped off.

- **Stay away from pyramid schemes and multilevel marketing (MLM) schemes.** These are some of the oldest scams on the books. They're also called Ponzi schemes after one of the most infamous perpetrators. In them, you're promised a big-time profit if you pay an initial fee and recruit others to join the plan. Oh, and by the way, you also have to buy marketing materials and pay more fees … and you never end up making money, you only keep paying it. This is one of the more common scams on the Internet. The Federal Trade Commission brought a case against a company called the Fortuna Alliance, which allegedly ran such a scheme and then transferred all its loot to a bank in Antigua. Buying this pyramid is like agreeing to buy the Brooklyn Bridge.

◆ **Be wary when signing up for free trials.** Let's face it: You can't get something for nothing. Free trials can end up costing you a bundle. In free trials, you have to first send in your credit card number. You are told that you can back out of the trial before your card is billed. But that free trial might be run by a scammer trying to get his hands on your credit card. Only agree to free trials with large, well-known, reputable Web merchants.

◆ **Don't buy from a site that has no mailing address or phone number.** Anyone can create a slick Web page that looks as if it's on the up-and-up. Behind that page could be a bunco artist looking to get his hands on your credit card. Only buy from a site that has a valid mailing address and phone number—and never buy from a site that lists only a post office box. For more information about shopping on the Web, turn to Part 6, "Even More Privacy and Safety Issues: Work, Cybershopping, and Beyond."

Check This Out!

Not all Web sites include their contact information. But there's often a way to find it out, even if the information isn't listed on the Web site. Point your browser to www.internic.net. Click the button or link to Whois. Type in the name of the site, but leave out the "www." You then get information about the site, often including the site's mailing address, phone number, the names of people who run the site.

◆ **Don't buy stocks based solely on advice you come across on discussion boards, chat areas, or via unsolicited e-mail.** Sure, discussion areas are great places to get inside tips about stocks. They're also the shyster's best friend. People looking to bid up a stock so they can sell it quick and get out for a profit often go into discussion areas, use assumed names, and tell grand lies about the stock to artificially inflate its price. Worthless stocks have been run up this way by con artists, and people have been burned. Scammers send unsolicited e-mail promising that fortunes can be made by buying a stock that proves to be fraudulent. The Security and Exchange Commission has been cracking down on stock scams, but they remain one of the most popular scams on the Internet.

◆ **Look on your credit card bills for suspicious-looking charges from phony Internet Service Providers.** In one of the newest Internet scams, a chiseler starts charging your credit card every month for a fee such as $19.95, so it looks like your normal fee from your Internet Service Provider (ISP). The hope is that you won't notice the fee, because it looks like a normal ISP. Check your credit card account carefully every month.

◆ **Don't respond to spam.** Spam is unsolicited e-mail sent to your inbox, touting too-good-to-be-true offers such as investment schemes. Users of America Online in particular are targeted for spam. Don't be gullible. Never respond to spam—if you do, you could face worse consequences than mere indigestion.

◆ **Stay away from work-at-home offers**. Make $100,000 a year working at home in your spare time? Sounds good. But it's not going to happen in this life. Stay away from Internet work-at-home offers. These guys try to con you into buying a book or series of books or expensive mailing materials and goods. The only person making a number with six zeroes at the end of it is the scammer.

◆ **Don't Call 809 Numbers.** You might get an offer sometime via the Internet, asking you to call a number with an 809 area code. Beware: It's an area code used for numbers outside the U.S. and is a favorite of shysters looking to avoid U.S. fraud laws. Dial the number, and you could be put on hold for a long period of time or talk to an operator who claims he doesn't speak English. The whole time, the meter is running—and you can be charged $25 or more per minute.

◆ **Check out online charities before donating money.** It's sad but true: Con artists have used the Web to set up sites where you can donate money to what you think is a charity. Instead, you're bilked out of money. Before donating money to any online charity, get contact information including name, address (make sure it isn't a post office box), and phone number. Then, check the state where the charity is located to see if the charity is registered and for real.

> **Notes**
>
> There are very few legitimate reasons why you should provide your Social Security number to anyone online. Armed with your Social Security number, a con artist can do a world of damage, including assuming your identity. Never give it out, unless you need to give it to your bank, insurance company or online broker. Other than that, keep it to yourself.

◆ **Always use a credit card when you buy online.** When you pay with a credit card, the most you are liable for, if you've been scammed, is $50. The truth is, most credit card companies waive even that fee, so only pay with your credit card. If a site says it doesn't accept credit cards and instead wants your bank account number, stay away. Armed with that number, they can fleece you for a whole lot of cash. By the way, you should be aware that there is a difference between your credit card and your bank debit card. Generally, if you pay with your bank debit card, you won't get the same protections as when you pay with your credit card. So make sure to use your credit card, not your debit card, when buying online.

What to Do If You've Been Scammed

Okay, so maybe you didn't follow my advice about how to avoid online scams, and you've been scammed. (I bet you never listened when your mother told you to eat your vegetables, either.) There's a lot you can do to fight scammers. You might get your money back, and if not, your credit card company is likely to cover most, if not all, of the costs of your scam. You also have recourse to a wide variety of government and private agencies to help you get your money back—and even to prosecute the scam artist who targeted you.

Dealing with the Company That Burned You

Do you think you've been the victim of a scam? Start off by contacting the company or person you think burned you. Before you do, have all the information about your complaint handy. Here's what you need:

- **Product and sales information**. Have ready the product's name, price, serial number, the date and time you bought it, and any other identifying information. If you were notified by the company via e-mail about your purchase, have a copy of that. If you filled out a Web form to order and printed out that form, have a copy of that, as well. (It's a good idea to print these order forms and e-mail messages and store them in case you need records of your transactions.)
- **A description of your complaint**. Write out exactly why you think you've been wronged.
- **A cancelled check or credit card bill**. If your check has already been cashed or your credit card billed, have that information ready.

Now, call the company, ask to be put through to the person handling consumer complaints, and detail your complaint. Take down the name of the person to whom you talk, and take notes about the call, including the date and time of the call and everything that was discussed. Follow up the call with an e-mail and a letter, preferably via registered or certified mail.

Writing a letter preserves your rights under consumer laws. Include information about the sale, as detailed in the previous bulleted list. Clearly detail your complaint. Include the number of your cancelled check or details about when your credit card was billed.

Include information about who you called at the company and what took place in your discussion. And include information about how you can be contacted.

Give the company 10 to 14 days to act, and tell them you're going to take legal action unless they resolve the complaint to your satisfaction. Make sure they know you're sending copies of your letter to your state consumer agency and your state attorney general. (See the next few sections for information on which groups to contact.)

If you do all this, you'll probably get your complaint resolved. If it does not get resolved, you have a written record of the complaint, which you can then send to the credit card company and government and private consumer agencies.

Getting Help from Your Credit Card Company

When you pay with a credit card, you're covered for all but $50 (at most) if you are the victim of a scam. Credit card companies investigate complaints, and if they find you're in the right, you only have to pay the first $50. Many waive that $50 fee, and you end up paying zero—as in zilch.

As soon as you suspect you've been conned, call your credit card company and give them the dirty details over the phone. Follow up with a letter, detailing your complaint. Include the site that scammed you, its mailing address and phone number, the date and time of the purchase, the product you purchased (or thought you were purchasing), and other pertinent information. Describe how you tried to resolve the complaint and include letters or e-mail that you've sent or received.

Complaining to Private Consumer Agencies

If you've been the victim of a scam, or suspect you have, there are people on your side: private consumer agencies. Here's where to go to complain and get help:

◆ **Better Business Bureaus.** These private agencies are funded by businesses to promote good business practices and are located in each state. They work with businesses to try to get jilted consumers' money back and keep a record of complaints filed against businesses. They keep complaints on permanent file so that other people can be warned about the shysters who've burned others. Complain to the Better Business Bureau in the state in which the company is located. For a list of all Better Business Bureaus in the country, go to the Better Business Bureau Web site at www.bbb.org (see Figure 3.1). You can also file a complaint with the Better Business Bureau's special Web protection site at www.bbbonline.org.

Figure 3.1

Here's where to go to find a Better Business Bureau near you, or to research a company.

- ◆ **The National Fraud Information Center.** This is another good place to make a complaint. It sends your complaint to the proper state, federal, and local law enforcement agencies. Your complaint also goes into the National Fraud Database maintained by the Federal Trade Commission and the National Association of Attorneys General. You can fill out a complaint form online. Head to www.fraud.org and fill out the form. If you prefer the telephone, call 1-800-876-7060.

- ◆ **The Netcheck Commerce Bureau.** This private agency specializes in tracking down online scams and frauds. Head to www.netcheck.com and fill out a complaint form online. The company you're complaining about has 20 days to respond to Netcheck. If they don't resolve it to Netcheck's liking, Netcheck can then forward your complaint to the proper federal organization handling complaints.

- ◆ **Trade associations.** These are good places to make complaints. Just about any kind of business you can imagine belongs to a trade association that, among other things, resolves consumer complaints. (The National Soap and Detergent Association? Yup there is one. The National Turkey Federation? There's that, too—and a lot more where those came from.) For a complete list of trade associations, go to the Federal Trade Commission's Web site at www.ftc.gov and find the Consumer's Resource Handbook. It's a complete guide for consumers that includes a comprehensive listing of trade associations.

Complaining to Government Agencies

A variety of government agencies handle consumer complaints. In some cases, you can file complaints online; in others, you have to do it the old-fashioned way—by writing a letter. Internet fraud has also finally made it onto the radar of the federal government—the Justice Department has begun working with all federal agencies to come up with Internet fraud-busting plans. In any event, here are the agencies to contact when you've been scammed:

◆ **Your state Attorney General's office, or your state's Department of Consumer Affairs.** This is a good place to start. Don't know their addresses? No problem. Head to the Consumer World site at www.consumerworld.org, as shown in Figure 3.2. Here is probably the most comprehensive list in the world of government consumer agencies and Attorneys General offices. When complaining, make sure to contact not just the agencies in your state, but also in the state where the Web site does business.

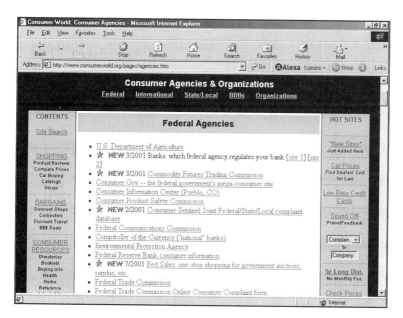

Figure 3.2

The most comprehensive list anywhere of government consumer agencies can be found at the Consumer World site at www.consumerworld.org.

◆ **The Federal Trade Commission.** The FTC is the main federal agency that prosecutes Internet scams. Fill out a complaint at their Web site at www.ftc.org. The complaint goes to the National Association of Attorneys General as well as to the FTC.

◆ **The Security and Exchange Commission.** The SEC at www.sec.gov prosecutes scams involving stocks and securities. They've been extremely aggressive in prosecuting Internet stock scams and fraud and have brought charges against scores of people. You can fill out a complaint on their Web site or e-mail your complaint to enforcement@sec.gov.

Check This Out!

The SEC has put together the most comprehensive page anywhere for information about stock fraud, and it has excellent guidelines to follow when investing over the Internet. Go to the SEC's Investor Assistance and Complaints page at www.sec.gov/invkhome.htm. In addition to lots of articles, tips, and resources, you can make out a complaint online.

Using Small Claims Court

Small claims courts are local courts in which you need no lawyer to represent you. You make your case to the judge and he decides right then and there whether to award you the amount of money you've been scammed. There are only two drawbacks. The first is that you can only go to small claims court in the locality where the Internet business operates. That means you can only take someone to small claims court if they live in your area. The other drawback is that you can't go to small claims court for a huge amount of money—often it's only for cases of under $1,500. It varies according to locality, so check yours.

The Best Sites for Consumer Advice and Scams

Where should you go online if you want to find out about Internet scams and get solid consumer advice? Check out these sites, the best on the Internet:

- **Better Business Bureau (www.bbb.com).** Make a complaint about a site, find a Better Business Bureau near you, check out a business to see if complaints have been lodged against it, get advice about doing business on the Internet ... all that and more is possible here.

- **Better Business Bureau Online (www.bbbonline.com).** Find out if an online site is a reliable and trustworthy one. You can see if sites have complaints lodged against them and lodge your own complaints, as well. It also has a seal that Web sites can display if they're members of the Better Business Bureau Online. When you're on a Web site, Click the Better Business Bureau Online link and you can see whether complaints have been lodged against the company.

- **Consumer World (www.consumerworld.org).** This is probably the most comprehensive site online for finding out information about everything to do with consumers. Especially useful are the links to private and government agencies involved in prosecuting Internet scams or that offer advice on how to avoid scams.

◆ **Web Trust (www.cpawebtrust.org).** A group of wild and crazy accountants has created a sort of Web seal of approval. They check out Web sites, and if that site adheres to security and privacy standards, the site can display the Web Trust seal.

◆ **Federal Trade Commission (www.ftc.gov).** Here's the site of the main agency that investigates Internet fraud. You can find information about scams and fraud, advice on how to avoid them, and more.

◆ **National Fraud Information Center (www.fraud.org).** This site provides information about the latest Internet scams, getting advice on avoiding con artists, and making out complaints if you think you've been burned.

◆ **ScamWatch (www.scamwatch.com).** This is a great place to find out about the latest scams on the Internet. Over the years it's had comprehensive reports on everything from Furby fraud (people claiming they had the much-desired Furby toys to sell when they didn't) to a bizarre scam involving someone who claimed to be the legal adviser to the former president of Zaire, Mobutu Sese Seko, trying to get people to open a bank account in the Ivory Coast. ScamWatch also provides great advice on how to avoid scams and links to other anti-scam sites.

◆ **Security and Exchange Commission (www.sec.gov).** Stock scams have become one of the most common frauds on the Internet. This site clues you in on all the latest scams (one warning is shown in Figure 3.3), offers great advice on how to avoid them, and lets you make complaints if you think you've been the victim of a scam.

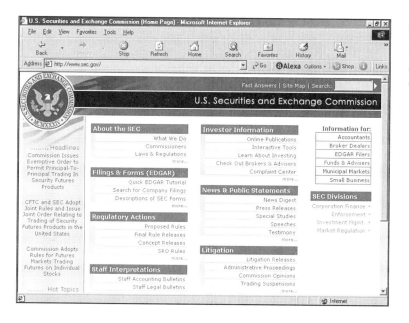

Figure 3.3

Catch up on the latest Internet stock scams at the SEC site at www.sec.gov.

◆ **U.S. Consumer Gateway (www.consumer.gov).** Here's the best place to go to find out all the information federal agencies have about anything to do with consumers—including Internet scams. It links you to great articles, advice, and advisories.

The Least You Need to Know

◆ If you find an offer that sounds too good to be true on the Internet, it might be a scam.

◆ Never respond to spam; many such e-mails are scams.

◆ Be careful when buying at auction sites. It's best to pay an escrow service instead of a person and never buy collectibles there.

◆ Don't buy stocks based solely on advice you come across on message boards or via unsolicited e-mail.

◆ If you believe you've been the victim of a scam, make out complaints with your credit card company and with consumer and government agencies.

◆ Check the Web sites listed in this chapter for the latest information on Internet scams.

Part 2

Hack Attack: How to Protect Yourself Against Hackers

Evil people are out there, wanting to do evil things to your computer. They're creating nasties that want to trash your hard disk. They're building viruses, Trojan horses, time bombs, evil ActiveX controls, and worms. (Worms? Yes, worms.) And there's more nastiness out there, as well.

But fear not, dear reader. You have your trusty anti-hacker fighter here to help. You'll learn in this part that it's exceedingly easy to protect yourself against hackers, as well as viruses and other beasties and nasty creatures you might come across online. You'll see how to make sure you never get a virus or have your computer damaged or privacy invaded by oddball things called Java applets or ActiveX Controls. (Do ActiveX Controls have something to do with the X-Files? Check out this part to find out.) You'll find out how to protect your home network if you have one. And you'll see how you can put up your ultimate cyberdefense—using a personal firewall to keep out any hackers that want to invade your domain.

How the Worm Turns: Protecting Yourself Against Worms, the Most Common Internet Danger

In This Chapter

- ◆ What are worms?
- ◆ Understanding how worms do their damage
- ◆ The difference between server worms and other worms
- ◆ Why worms target Microsoft Outlook
- ◆ How to protect yourself against worms
- ◆ What to do if a worm attacks you

Code Red. Melissa. I Love You. Sircam. The Love Bug.

If you've paid attention at all to Internet security in the last few years, you might have heard one or more of those names. They're all worms—destructive programs intended to harm the Internet itself and anyone who uses it. They've caused billions of dollars in damage to date—and new worms are popping up all the time.

Worms have become the most common threat on the Internet. In this chapter, you'll find out what worms are, how they do their damage, and how you can protect yourself against them. So read on, and you'll learn how to stay away from these slithering, slimy beasts.

What Are Internet Worms?

Many different kinds of destructive programs wreak havoc on computers and on the Internet. In recent years, though, the ones that spread most widely and quickly are called worms.

In general, worms are programs that are designed to spread by themselves from computer to computer, and that attack not just individual computers, but the workings of the Internet itself. So a worm could, for example, attack Internet servers, or be designed to flood the Internet with so much traffic that it makes the Internet more difficult to use.

The line between a virus and a worm is razor thin; in fact, the terms can be used somewhat interchangeably for some pieces of destructive software. Worms, generally, are primarily designed to harm the workings of the Internet; although they often cause destruction to individual computers along the way, their primary purpose is to (in one way or another) cause widespread disruption to the Net itself. Viruses, on the other hand, are designed to hurt individual computers.

The classic definition of a worm is a program that spreads all by itself—it doesn't require any human intervention to do so. Viruses are spread by people sending an infected file to someone else. But that definition really only fit in the early days of the Internet. In those days, sophisticated e-mail programs like Outlook had yet to come into being. Today, many worms use Outlook as a way to spread themselves.

Check This Out!

The most famous worm of all time was released onto the Internet by Cornell graduate student Robert Morris Jr. in 1988. He had written it, hoping to cause mild consternation, but he made a mistake in programming it. It replicated out of control at a breakneck pace; and in short, it closed down the entire Internet. It worked by attacking the UNIX operating system that in those days powered most, if not all, Internet servers. (Of course, the Internet was much smaller in 1988, but still, it was quite a feat.) Morris, who ironically was the son of the world-famous computer security expert Robert Morris, Sr., was convicted of violating the federal Computer Fraud and Abuse Act, and was sentenced to probation, 400 hours of community service, and a $10,000 fine.

For the purposes of this book, a worm is considered to be any program that is primarily spread by e-mail contact and uses the inner workings of e-mail software to spread itself without the software's owner knowing about it. A program that slithers through the Internet, attacking computers as it goes, is also considered a worm.

How Worms Wreak Their Havoc

There are many different worms, and they work in different ways; but in general there are two types—those that directly target Internet servers, and those that target individual computers and use individual computers to spread. This section covers how each works.

Worms That Use Individual Computers to Spread

Question number one: What's the main way that people communicate over the Internet? Answer: Via e-mail.

Question number two: If you wrote a worm and wanted it to spread as fast as possible, how would you get it to spread? Answer: Yes, you got it. Via e-mail.

The most infamous worms of recent time spread via e-mail, and they do so in a very tricky way. Let's take a look at how you could become an unwilling victim, and how you could unknowingly spread a worm.

It starts out when you receive an e-mail message with an attachment. An attachment is a picture, graphic, program, or other file that you receive via e-mail. To use the attachment, you have to detach it from the e-mail, with your e-mail software. The e-mail might be from a friend, a co-worker, or an acquaintance, so you're not suspicious. The e-mail's subject might be something innocuous, like "Check this out," or "Thought you'd want to see this."

 **Check This Out!**

The first worms weren't created to do damage. Instead, they were intended to do good. John Scoch is credited with creating the idea of a worm at the Xerox Palo Alto Research Center in the late 1970s. The worm was supposed to travel through computers on a network, looking for computers that were idle and not at work. The worm would then allow people who needed computer time to "borrow" the idle computer's processing power.

You open the attachment and nothing seems to happen, so you quickly forget about it. Without you knowing it, however, when you opened the attachment, the worm was set loose. It looks through your e-mail address book, and without your knowledge sends a

Check This Out!

Worms are more than mere nuisances—they can cause billions of dollars in damages. They can harm servers, shut down businesses, and require the hiring of extra security staff to exterminate them. The Love Bug worm is thought to have caused the most damage of any worm—an astonishing estimated $8.7 billion.

message to everyone in your address book, with itself attached. The message is the same one you received. Everyone who receives the message then opens the attachment, and the worm sends itself to every person in their address books, and so on. Soon, hundreds of thousands of messages are sent this way, and the e-mail servers on the Internet can't keep up with all the traffic and they crash. Entire corporations can't send and receive e-mail. The Internet gets so clogged with traffic it slows down. The worm has succeeded.

Sometimes these worms also damage your system. One worm, called Sircam, was especially pernicious. It mailed random documents from a person's computer to addresses in the e-mail address book.

Worms That Spread from Server to Server

The other kind of worms are those that don't use e-mail to spread, but rather spread by themselves, slithering from Internet server to Internet server. The most famous recent case of this was the Code Red worm and several variants.

Worms that wiggle from server to server all spread differently. In general, though, they exploit some kind of hole in the operating system or other software that servers use, or in the Internet's TCP/IP protocols. For example, the Code Red worm and its variants exploited a hole in Microsoft Web server software called Internet Information Server (IIS). Not only did the worm attack the server, but it used the server as a launching point for attacks against other servers. So every server infected became a launching site for attacks.

A Cloudy Outlook: Worms and Microsoft's E-mail Software

There's one common thread that ties together worm attacks that spread via e-mail—they use the Microsoft Outlook e-mail program as a way to spread.

Why is that? The reasons depend on who you talk to. If you ask Microsoft they'll say that it's because more people use Outlook than any other e-mail program, and so it makes sense worm writers would write programs that use Outlook to spread themselves—it's the widest possible pool of people.

Others say that Microsoft hasn't done a very good job of building protections into Outlook, and that's why worm writers target it.

They're probably both right. And there's another reason, as well. Outlook is part of the Microsoft Office software suite. That suite enables programmers to write code that can automate different kinds of tasks. But the same tools that automate tasks can also be used to help spread worms.

What this means is that if you use Outlook, you're more vulnerable to worms than if you use other e-mail programs. So Outlook users, be vigilant! Consider yourself always under attack. Pay special attention to the next section of the chapter, which teaches you how to make sure you don't become the victim of a worm.

Check This Out!

Worms are frequently spread via e-mail, but they can also be spread with other communications programs. Recently, worms have started to spread via instant messenger programs. One popular worm targets users of the MSN Messenger instant messenger program: the Choke worm. This worm pretends to be a joke entitled ShootPresidentBUSH.EXE.

How to Protect Yourself Against Worms

Although worms have become a daily part of life on the Internet, they're not that hard to fight. In fact, if you follow these tips, the odds are that you'll never be victimized:

- ◆ **Don't open e-mail attachments from people you don't know.** Worms spread when you open an e-mail attachment. If you get an attachment from someone you don't know, don't open it. Case closed.

- ◆ **If you get an e-mail attachment from someone you know, but weren't expecting it, check with the person before opening it.** As I explained earlier in the chapter, many worms spread by mailing copies of themselves to addresses in Outlook address books. That means even an attachment from someone you know might have been sent by a worm instead of that person. Always check before opening. I once received an innocuous looking e-mail attachment from my then-boss, but hadn't been

Check This Out!

How's this for an irony? The FBI's unit charged with cyber-protection was attacked by the Sircam worm. This worm, in addition to spreading itself, also looks through people's hard disks and mails documents at random to addresses in the infected computer's address book. The Sircam worm sent out at least eight documents from the special unit to people outside the FBI, including one that was marked "official use only."

expecting it. I sent him a note asking if he had sent it, and sure enough, he hadn't; he'd been victimized by a worm.

♦ **Use anti-virus software and keep it updated.** Anti-virus software can check for worms as well as viruses, so always run it and keep it updated. Every month, the anti-virus software companies get a new list of worms and viruses to check for, using a list called virus definitions. Make sure your anti-virus software always has the latest virus definitions. For more information about anti-virus software, turn to Chapter 5, "How to Keep Your Computer Safe from Viruses."

♦ **Use a personal firewall.** Some personal firewalls, such as ZoneAlarm, include anti-worm protection. For more information about how to use personal firewalls, turn to Chapter 6, "The Ultimate Defense: Keeping Safe with Firewalls."

♦ **Consider getting a "security patch" for Outlook.** You can download a "security patch" from Microsoft that stops Outlook from receiving files that might have worms in them. After you download and install this patch, Outlook strips off certain attachments from e-mail. The theory is if you can't open the file, you won't get a worm. For information about the patch, go to www.microsoft.com/office/outlook/. Figure 4.1 shows you the security patch in action.

Be aware that if you install the Outlook security patch, it can be a royal pain in the you-know-what. It doesn't really know which attachments have worms in them and which don't, so it blocks all attachments of certain types—useful ones as well as ones with worms in them. For example, it blocks any attachment ending in .exe from being sent to your PC. So before installing the Outlook security patch, keep in mind that it will keep you from receiving certain kinds of attachments.

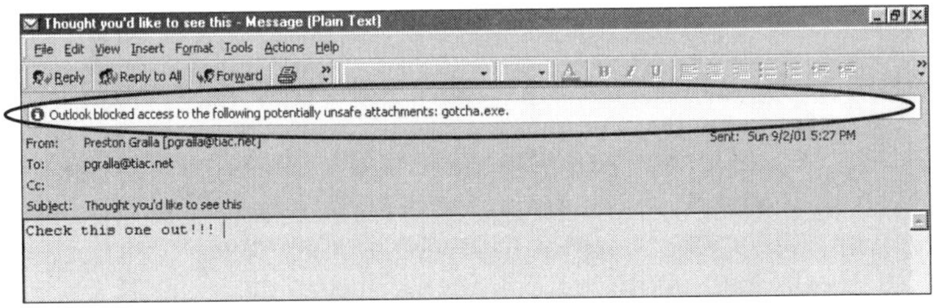

Figure 4.1

Safety first: An Outlook security patch stripped off a file attachment before it could be opened.

♦ **Keep on top of worm alerts.** If you know that there's a new worm on the loose, and you know how to fight against it, you're more likely not to get infected. Keep on top of the latest worm alerts. Head to a news site like www.news.com, the Symantec security alert page at www.symantec.com/avcenter, or the McAfee Regional Virus Info page (go to www.mcafee.com/antivirus and click **Free Regional Virus Info**). That page even tells you which worms and viruses are most popular in different regions of the world.

◆ **Turn off scripting in Outlook**. Another way to protect yourself against worms is to turn off scripting in Outlook. That way, certain worms aren't able to attack you. To find out how to do it, turn to Chapter 7, "Keeping Safe from Java, JavaScript, and ActiveX Applets."

Don't Hide Your File Extensions in Windows

Worm writers are very devious folks, and they use every tool in their arsenals to fool people into running file attachments. One way they do it is by hiding the real name of files attached to your e-mail. Here's how to make sure that they never fool you that way.

In Windows, by default, your file extensions are hidden and you can't see the extensions of common file types, so that if you get an e-mail attachment, you aren't able to see the full name of the file. (An extension is the three letters that follows the dot in a file; so, for example, in the file runme.vbs, "vbs" is the extension.)

Worm writers take advantage of this trick, and mask the fact that a file attached to an e-mail message is in fact a virus. For example, the infamous LoveLetter worm was a file attachment called LOVE-LETTER-FOR-YOU.TXT.vbs. The "vbs" is a giveaway—it's a script that could be dangerous. But to people who had their file extensions hidden, the file looked like an ordinary text file, LOVE-LETTER-FOR-YOU.TXT, and they didn't realize it could be dangerous. So they opened it.

Protect yourself. Show file extensions in Windows by opening Windows Explorer, choosing Folder Options from the View menu, clicking View and unchecking the **Hide file extensions for known file types** box, as shown in Figure 4.2. That way, you always know the true file extension. And if you see .vbs, beware.

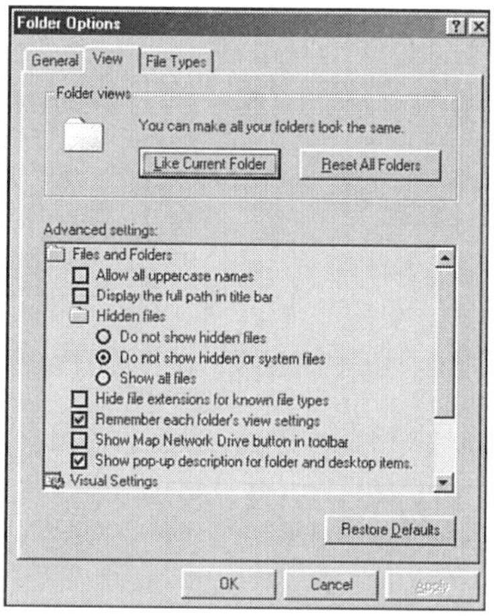

Figure 4.2

Use this dialog box to make sure that you're always able to see true file extensions. This way, you're more likely to know if you've been sent a worm.

What to Do If You've Been the Victim of a Worm

Despite your best efforts, a worm has hit you. Help! What to do now?

That depends on the worm that's attacked you. The first thing you should do is to make sure that your anti-virus definitions are up to date. Many anti-virus programs cannot only detect worms, but can eradicate them, as well. They can only do it, however, if your definitions are the most recent.

After you've gotten the most up-to-date definitions, check the anti-virus program's Web site to see if there are any special instructions on how to kill the worm. Be forewarned, you might have to delete entire programs.

How to Protect Your Web Server

Maybe you run your own Web server (or maybe you run an FTP server that enables other people to download files from you). Or maybe you run a Web server or your own e-mail server.

If you do, you're vulnerable to the kinds of worms that target servers, notably the Code Red worm, one of the most destructive server worms ever released.

Check This Out!

Wonder which worms and viruses were the most prevalent on the Internet last month? You can find out, by going to the www.centralcommand.com Web site. The site, run by an anti-virus company, lists the dozen most prevalent malicious programs every month.

You don't have to be a hard-core techie to protect yourself. Microsoft has made available a free piece of software that can check certain servers for vulnerabilities. It's called HFNetChk. To get it, go to www.microsoft.com/security/ and click **Tools and Checklists.**

To protect your server against the Code Red worm, look for information about it on that page. Here is a patch for you to install that protects your server against the Code Red worm. Also check out the site for instructions on what to do if you've been infected.

The Least You Need to Know

◆ Worms are destructive programs designed to harm the Internet that are often spread by e-mail, or directly from server to server.

◆ Microsoft Outlook users are particularly vulnerable to worms because many worm writers target that e-mail program.

◆ Never open e-mail attachments from people you don't know.

◆ If you get an unexpected e-mail attachment from someone you know, check that the person really sent the attachment before you open it.

◆ Use anti-virus software and make sure the virus definitions are up to date.

◆ If you run a server, get Microsoft's HFNetChk tool at www.microsoft.com/security/ as a way to help protect against worms.

How to Keep Your Computer Safe from Viruses

In This Chapter

- ◆ What damage computer viruses can do
- ◆ How you can get a computer virus
- ◆ Top tips for making sure you don't get hit by a virus
- ◆ How anti-virus software works
- ◆ How to use anti-virus software to protect your computer
- ◆ What you can do if you've been infected
- ◆ Common myths about viruses

Malevolent programs that delete every file on your hard disk. Nasty programs that lie in wait until a certain date, and then spring into action, doing evil on your computer. Files attached to e-mail programs that can steal your America Online password. These are a few examples of the malicious programs called viruses that can harm the data and software on your computer.

There are all kinds of viruses out loose on the Internet and other places, such as your business's network, disks your friends give you, and more. The potential dangers are no doubt overblown. Isn't that why we have newspapers and magazines, after all? But they're very real, as well. And it is small comfort to you to know that there aren't that many viruses online if one is eating your computer and spitting it out right now.

Luckily, it's easy to protect your computer from viruses. You'll find out how in this chapter. So read on—and you won't need to worry about anything chomping on your programs or data.

What Are Viruses?

You're running your computer, and all is normal—except you notice that your files start acting funny. For some odd reason, they keep growing in size. One day you try and run your computer, and whammo!, it doesn't start. Maybe files start vanishing, your hard disk crashes, or you get odd messages on your screen from time to time.

Unfortunately, I've got bad news for you. You've most likely been hit by a computer virus.

Computer viruses can do all kinds of damage to your computer. They can be as harmless as merely displaying a silly message on your screen, or as destructive as wiping out your hard disk or deleting your operating system. And as more and more computers hook up to the Internet, there are greater and greater chances that viruses are spread from computer to computer.

Check This Out!

It's hard to fathom why someone would do something destructive like create a computer virus. Sometimes someone is out for revenge or wants to attack a company or group, and writes a virus to put directly onto someone's computer or network. Other times, virus creators are looking for some kind of odd fame; sometimes it's to see if they can do it. And often, it's just plain maliciousness.

There are many different kinds of computer viruses, as you see later in this chapter. But they all have one thing in common—they do something that you don't expect them to do; and they do it stealthily, hiding their action, possibly until it's too late for you to do anything about it. Usually, they're destructive, but they don't have to be; sometimes they just display a message on your screen. And viruses can be very ... well, eccentric is a nice way to put it. Take the "Smiley" virus, for example. When it's active, "smiley" faces suddenly appear and start bouncing around your screen—kind of like a horrifying flashback to the 1970s. You almost expect polyester-suited John Travoltas to start discoing around the screen beneath a big, glittering mirrored ball. Now *that* would be a virus to stay away from!

How Do Computer Viruses Work?

Literally thousands and thousands of different computer viruses are out there, and more are created every day. But there are some general types of viruses, and all have similarities.

In some ways, a computer virus is very much like a biological virus. When you get a biological virus, it burrows into cells, takes over those cells, and in essence turns them into little virus factories. Each infected cell manufactures copies of the virus; then the cell dies and releases all the new viruses ... and each of these new viruses in turn infects a cell, and turns *it* into a little virus factory, and so on.

Computer viruses work in much the same way. They don't exist by themselves. Rather, they burrow their way into a file on your hard disk—usually a program file that ends in the extension .EXE or .COM, such as WORD.EXE. But they can also infect other kinds of files, such as Word documents and files needed to start up your computer.

After the virus infects a file, you need to run that file for it to do its dirty deeds. It can't run by itself. When you run the infected file, it starts its nefarious work. One kind of virus looks for another program file to infect; and after it infects that one, it looks for another file to infect, and so on. No matter how the virus works, though, after you run an infected program, it does whatever damage the virus programmer instructed it to do. (Oh, no! Not the Polyester Travolta virus, please!)

Check This Out!

Computer viruses get a great deal of news coverage and publicity, but the truth is, they're pretty rare. I've been using computers for 15 years, and have downloaded thousands of files from the Internet, and I've only gotten two viruses in all that time. And the viruses weren't even from downloaded files. One was in a Word document sent over a corporate network to me, attached to a memo (many other people got the virus, as well), and the other was an attachment to a mail message. Killing them was a simple matter—virus killers and virus scanners did the trick and my computer was none the worse for wear.

What Kinds of Viruses Are There?

A whole lot of different kinds of nasty viruses exist. Although there are many different kinds of viruses, here are some common types:

 ◆ **Time bombs.** These viruses are programmed to do their damage at a certain date, or after a certain amount of time has elapsed. For example, the infamous Michelangelo virus was programmed to lie dormant until March 6th, when it was supposed to spring into action. (This might have been the most over-hyped virus of all time, with news stories around the world warning about it just before March 6, 1992. In fact, very few computers ended up being infected.)

◆ **Trojan Horses.** These viruses take their name from the Trojan Horse of Greek legend, which appeared to be a gift, but in fact harbored the Greek army within, which sacked the city of Troy. In the same way, a Trojan horse virus appears to be an innocuous or helpful program, such as a piece of personal finance software, when in fact, when you run the program, it instead damages your computer. Probably the most infamous Trojan Horse of all time is a program called Back Orifice. When you install this piece of software, it enables someone to completely take over your computer—the person has the power to delete files, copy files, and even remotely control your computer by issuing it commands.

◆ **Self-replicating viruses.** This is the kind of virus most like a biological virus—when you run an infected file, it looks for other files to infect, and when those are run, they look for other files to infect, and so on. Sometimes, these kinds of viruses make each file they infect larger—and can end up clogging your hard disk. Other times, they lie dormant until a critical mass is reached, and then they spring into action.

◆ **Boot viruses.** These viruses infect the boot sector of your PC—the files that start up your PC. These can be deadly, because they can make your computer unable to start, and because they're started before other programs, can easily infect other programs, as well.

◆ **Memory resident viruses.** These viruses, when run, stay in your computer's memory. When there, they can infect other programs that you run.

◆ **Document viruses.** At one time, it was thought that viruses could only infect programs, and could not infect data files, such as Word or Excel documents. In fact, viruses *can* infect Word and Excel documents. That's because Word and Excel allow you to run things called macros, which are little programs embedded in the documents. Viruses can run in macros, and in that way can infect document files.

◆ **Dangerous Java applets and ActiveX controls.** Java applets and ActiveX controls are technologies used to make World Wide Web pages more interactive and useful. In essence, they're kinds of programs. Although viruses can't actually infect Java applets and ActiveX controls, the applets and controls can be programmed to do damage to your computer when you visit a page and run them. For more information on what to watch out for, turn to Chapter 7, "Keeping Safe from Java, JavaScript, and ActiveX Applets."

How You Can Get Infected

For your computer to be infected by a virus, a virus has to get onto your system, and then you have to run it. But how might you get a virus? More ways than you can imagine. Here are the most common:

♦ **By downloading an infected file from the Internet.** Some files on the Internet are infected with viruses. If you download one that's infected and then run it, you get the virus.

♦ **From software you buy in the store.** Yes, there have been instances where software you buy from a store has been infected by a virus.

♦ **By using a disk a friend gave to you.** A friend gives you a copy of the latest "MegaKiller SuperDeath Shoot'em'up" game. It has a virus on it. You run the program. You get the virus.

♦ **By loading a document file that someone gives to you.** Someone—maybe someone at work, maybe a friend—gives you a Word file. If it has a virus on it, your computer could get infected.

♦ **By opening and running an e-mail attachment.** If you open and run an e-mail attachment—a file attached to the e-mail message—you could get a virus. In fact, a very common kind of virus is aimed at America Online users. When the AOL user opens and runs the attached file, it finds the user's username and password and sends it to someone else, giving someone else access to the America Online account.

Safety First: How to Protect Yourself Against Viruses

As you see later in this chapter, one of the best ways to make sure you don't get attacked by a virus is to use anti-virus software. But that, on its own, isn't enough. There's a lot more you can do to make sure you don't get attacked by a virus. Here's what to do:

♦ **If someone gives you a floppy disk with files on it, virus-scan the files on it before you copy it to your computer.** You want to know whatever you're being given is safe, so that you don't infect your computer. Keep in mind that even document files such as Word files (that end in a .doc extension) and Excel files (that end in an .xls extension) can carry viruses, so check them, as well.

♦ **If someone sends you a file over your business network, virus-scan it before using it.** A common way of getting a virus is from someone at work giving you a file that contains one.

♦ **Never open a file sent to you via e-mail from someone you don't know.** This is a common way of spreading viruses. The stranger might tell you that it's a screen saver or some other program, but it might be a virus. This is also a way that some hackers steal your password. They send out a file that appears to be a useful program, but behind the scenes it's stealing passwords and sending them off to the hacker. Even when someone you know sends you a file, you should virus-scan it before opening it. To do that, save the file to your hard disk, but don't open it. Then run your virus scanner on it to see if it's infected.

♦ **If possible, copy files you download to a floppy disk, and virus-scan them there.** For absolute safety, virus-scan a program on a floppy disk before running it on your system. This isn't always possible, though, because many files you download are too large to fit onto a floppy disk.

♦ **Notice the size and date of your system files, and check if there's been a change if you suspect a virus.** Some viruses do their dirty deeds by attacking system files. When they do this, they often change the size and date of system files. Write down the size and date of system files, such as command.com. Command.com and other system files are usually found in the C:\ directory. If you notice your system behaving oddly, check those file sizes and dates. If they've changed, you might have a virus.

♦ **Consider disabling macros in Word and Excel documents.** The reason that Word and Excel files can be infected with viruses is that they contain *macros*, which are little programs inside the files that can automate certain tasks and give you extra features. To be safe, disable the macros in any Word or Excel file before you open it. Because viruses can only be spread if the macro is run, a virus inside the file isn't able to spread, because you disabled the macro. When you open a Word or Excel file that has a macro in it, you get a note asking you if you want to disable the macros in the file. Say yes. If for some reason you're not able to use the file because the macro has been disabled, close the file, then check with a virus scanner to see if it contains a virus. If it's clean, open it back up and enable the macros.

♦ **Always run a virus scanner.** The way to make sure you stay safest is to always run a virus scanner, and to keep it in auto-protect mode so that it checks for viruses all the time, not just when you remember to run it. For more details on how to use virus scanners, read the rest of this chapter. Figure 5.1 shows the virus scanner Norton Anti-Virus in action.

It's easy to have Microsoft Word warn you every time it opens a file with macros in it. This feature gives you the option to disable the macros and protect yourself against viruses. How you do this varies from version to version of word. In Word 97, choose **Options** from the **Tools** menu, then click the **General** tab. Click **Macro virus protection** and you're set. In later versions of Word, choose **Options** from the **Tools** menu, then click **Macro and Security** and make sure the Security Level is set to Medium or High. A dialog box explains what each setting means.

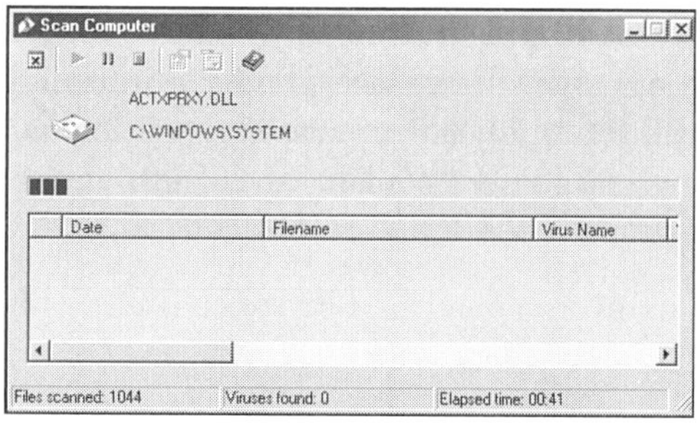

Figure 5.1

Checking that your machine is clean: The Norton Anti-Virus scanner looks for viruses.

How Does Anti-Virus Software Work?

The best way to guarantee that a virus does not harm you is to run anti-virus software. This software looks for viruses on your system, and kills them if you tell it to. It detects viruses in several ways. It looks for tell-tale "signatures"—information embedded in virus files or that viruses leave behind that are sure signs that a virus is present. And it can also check your computer for odd behavior that indicates that a virus is present.

Anti-virus software can help protect your system in these ways:

- ◆ **It checks the files on your system to see if they've been infected.** Just run the software, and it does the rest. It reports if it finds any infected files.

- ◆ **It can check files before you run them to see if they're infected.** You can tell anti-virus software to automatically scan files before they're run.

- ◆ **It can check system files to make sure they haven't been infected.** The software can keep a constant vigil, watching your system files to make sure nothing nasty is happening to them.

- ◆ **It can remove viruses from your system.** When it finds a virus, it can kill it.

- ◆ **It can repair files that viruses have damaged.** When viruses do their dirty work, they typically damage the files that they infect. Anti-virus software can not only kill viruses; it can also repair the damaged files so that you can still use them. Keep in mind, however, that this isn't always the case. Sometimes anti-virus software can't repair the damaged file, and you have to delete the infected file entirely.

How to Use Anti-Virus Software to Keep Your Computer Safe

There's a simple first step you need to take before running anti-virus software—get a copy of one. Any one. Any anti-virus software is better than none. You can buy the software in a retail store or on the Web. And if you want, you can try out a copy for free—you can download and use all major anti-virus software for free for a certain amount of time. Head to any of the major download site such as CNet's Download.com.

I have to be clear about my prejudices here, though. From my point of view, the best anti-virus software is Norton Anti-Virus, from Symantec Corp. It's the most comprehensive, is the easiest to use, has the best features and, I believe, is the most reliable as well. I've tried them all, and it's the one that I use. Another popular piece of anti-virus software is McAfee's VirusScan.

McAfee also offers a unique way to scan your computer for viruses—rather than download software to your computer, you can visit the McAfee Web site and have the site scan your computer for viruses.

Using anti-virus software is fairly simple. Start off by reading the manual. (Well, read it as much as you can stand it—it's usually written in a language that only occasionally resembles English.)

When you're familiar with how your anti-virus software works, follow this advice:

◆ **Set your virus scanner to Autodetect.** Most anti-virus software lets you keep it running permanently on your system, scanning files for viruses before they're run, or while they are copied or moved. Always use the Autodetect option. It's the best way to make sure you don't get infected. You might also be given various options on how to use Autodetect; in other words, whether to use the feature only when you run files, only when you copy them, or only when you download them from the Web. Use Autodetect all the time.

◆ **"Inoculate" your system.** Many anti-virus programs include an inoculation feature. In essence, it takes a "snapshot" of your system files, and then regularly compares that snapshot to the current state of your files. If it notices a difference, this could mean you've been hit with a virus, and it alerts you.

◆ **Set your virus scanner to automatically check files as they're downloaded from the Web.** Virus scanners can check files for viruses before you save them on your system. Make sure to set yours to do this, for maximum safety.

◆ **Even if you've virus-scanned a file downloaded from the Web, virus-scan it again after you install it.** Often, when you download a program from the Web, it comes as a single, compressed file. Your virus scanner will check that file for viruses. But after you install the program, it expands into many files, and the scanner might not have been able to check them all for viruses during the download.

Check This Out!

Some programs require that you disable your virus scanner while you download and install them. The most notable example is Microsoft Internet Explorer. It's fine to disable your virus scanner temporarily when downloading Explorer so that you can install it. But only do this for a file from a well-known source that you know does virus scanning. And as soon as you install the file, turn on your virus scanner.

♦ **Scan regularly for viruses, even if you use Autodetect.** Yes, Autodetect scans all the time for viruses, so in theory, you don't need to tell your virus scanner to look for viruses. On the other hand, it can't hurt. I do it all the time, just for safety's sake.

♦ **Regularly visit the Web site of the company that makes your anti-virus software.** Companies continually release new versions of anti-virus software, and to be safe, you should always have the newest version. To make sure you have the newest version, and to get any other news about viruses, regularly visit the Web site of the company that makes your anti-virus software.

♦ **Download new virus definitions every month.** New viruses are coming out all the time. If your anti-virus software doesn't know about them—and their unique signatures—it might not be able to protect you against them. So make it a habit to download new virus definitions every month. You can get them from the Web site of the company that makes your anti-virus software. Most anti-virus software has a built-in feature that enables you to download and install these virus definitions easily.

Check This Out! _____

Can my anti-virus software report a false virus reading? Yes. It's possible that you'll get a report that you have a virus, when in fact, you don't. There can be a number of causes for this, including an error in the program's virus definition file. Still, it's a good idea to listen to your program's advice when it tells you that you have a virus.

What to Do If You've Been Infected

You've got a virus. What to do. Take two aspirin, get plenty of bed rest and …. Okay, let's get serious here. Computer viruses, after all, are a serious matter.

If you get a virus, I have only one piece of advice for you: Follow the directions that your virus scanner gives to you. If it detects a virus, it usually asks whether it should try to get rid of the virus—and yes, that's certainly a good idea. It will kill the virus and try to repair the file. If it can't repair it, it deletes it. Bite the bullet and go ahead. It's good for you.

Virus Myths, Hoaxes, and Urban Myths

Consider these horrifying stories:

♦ The Federal Communications Commission has uncovered a virus that you can get if you read an e-mail message with the subject of "Good Times" in it. If you read the message, your computer's processor is sent up in smoke because it is set to an "nth complexity infinite binary loop."

◆ If you read an e-mail greeting card sent to you over the Internet from a certain card company, your computer will be infected by a virus.

◆ Companies that sell anti-virus software also create viruses and set them loose, as a way of scaring people into buying more anti-virus software.

◆ If you receive an e-mail message with the subject "It Takes Guts To Say 'Jesus'" and then read that message, every file on your hard disk is deleted.

Yes, you should consider those horrifying stories all you want. Because they're all untrue. Every last one of them. And there are hundreds of more hoaxes and myths like them. Viruses are surrounded by more fear, hype, and hoax than just about any computer technology you can name. To get the lowdown on the latest hoaxes and myths (and old ones, as well) and to get great information on the truth about viruses, visit the Vmyths.com Web site (see Figure 5.2). It's run by security expert and old friend Rob Rosenberger, and is a great place to get the real rundown on the truth about viruses.

Figure 5.2

Read about myths at the Computer Virus Myths home page.

The Least You Need to Know

◆ You can get a virus by downloading an infected file, having one given to you on disk, or even by using commercial software.

◆ Always run anti-virus software on your computer to make sure that you don't get infected.

◆ Virus-scan any file that someone gives to you, whether it be on disk, over your company's network, or via e-mail.

◆ Never open a file attachment sent via e-mail by someone you don't know.

◆ Set your virus scanner to "Autodetect" so it's always checking for viruses—even files as they download from the Web.

◆ Get new virus definitions once a month from the anti-virus maker's Web site.

Chapter 6

The Ultimate Defense: Keeping Safe with Firewalls

In This Chapter

- What firewalls are and how they work
- The difference between corporate and personal firewalls
- Why you need a personal firewall
- All about the best personal firewall
- How to use a firewall to protect yourself on the Internet
- How to get the best firewalls—often for free

The Internet was designed to be as open a network as possible—to allow free communications between computers. That openness is the reason that the Internet has become so popular.

But that openness is also the reason that the Internet has become a potentially dangerous place. Hackers and other unpleasant folks exploit the openness, and attack your computer in various and sundry ways.

That's where firewalls come in. They block hackers and others from doing evil deeds to your computer, while still letting you access the Internet in the ways that you'd like to. In this chapter, you'll learn all about firewalls, and most importantly, you'll learn how to use them to protect yourself against hackers and others.

No Asbestos Needed: What Are Firewalls?

Despite it's name, a firewall doesn't have to be a physical object. It can be a piece of software designed to stop intruders from getting into your system. There are many different kinds of firewalls. Some are used by businesses, others by individuals.

Corporate firewalls are often expensive, sophisticated devices. They're usually a combination of hardware and software. These firewalls don't run on a person's computer. Instead, they're computers that are put on the outside of a company's network to protect it against hackers and snoopers. The firewall computers also use a variety of software to stop hackers.

Notes
Some corporate firewalls use a component called a proxy server. When someone inside a company wants to visit a Web page, he uses his browser to do so. But when he does, the proxy server springs into action. It contacts the Web page, downloads it, and then delivers it to the browser. In other words, the Web page is first looked at by the proxy server and only then delivered, so the proxy server can make sure that the page isn't a destructive one.

And they also often come with sophisticated software for analyzing Internet activity, so that computer professionals can find out whether a hacker has been able to get past the firewall.

Personal firewalls, on the other hand, are much simpler. They're usually just a piece of software that runs on your computer—and many of the best ones are available for free. And although they're certainly not as powerful as corporate firewalls, they don't need to be, because hackers target businesses more than individuals, and businesses have a lot more that requires protection.

Why You Need a Firewall

Everyone who is worried that their PC could be invaded by hackers and snoopers can use a personal firewall. But for cable modem users and DSL modem users, it's especially important—far more important than if you dial into the Internet using a regular modem.

That's because if you're a cable modem or DSL modem user, you're vulnerable. You have an "always-on" connection—from the moment you turn on your computer, you're on the Net. So you're online for far more hours than people who dial in to the Internet—and your computer is also connected to the Net when you're away from it.

You're vulnerable also because cable and DSL modem users are in fact connected to the Internet just like computers on a local area network at work, and these can be more vulnerable to hackers. And because cable and DSL modem users have high-speed connections, hackers target them to try and use those high-speed connections to attack other computers and Internet servers.

 Check This Out! _____

Hackers use all kinds of software and tools to break into other people's computers and do damage. One kind of software is called a script—an automated program that automatically checks for vulnerabilities in thousands of computers at the same time. You don't have to be a particularly sophisticated computer user to use these scripts—anyone can use them. People who don't know much about hacking, but use these scripts are often derisively called "script kiddies." And they're also derisively called "lamers" as well.

Firewalls protect you in two major ways. They stop hackers from breaking into your computer. But they also stop programs on your computer from connecting to the Internet without you knowing about it. Why is that important? Because one way that hackers can get at you is by using what are called back-door programs. These are programs that you unwittingly install on your computer without realizing what they are—and they can connect to the Internet to hackers, who can then use them to take control of your computer and everything on it.

How Personal Firewalls Work

So how do personal firewalls work their magic? After all, they're just pieces of software. How can they keep out hackers?

To understand that, you need to learn a bit about how the Internet works. As I explained in Chapter 1, "Why You Need to Worry About Online Privacy and Security," the Internet is based on communications protocols known as TCP/IP. These protocols are, in essence, a set of rules that tells computers how to communicate with each other. Information is sent back and forth using what are called packets—bits of information.

These packets travel into and out of your computer over what are called ports. These ports aren't real physical objects—instead, they're kind of virtual pathways, and they all have a number. There are thousands of these virtual pathways (to be exact, 65,535, but who's counting?). Certain ports are used for certain kinds of Internet services. For example, when you browse the Internet, you use port 80, and when you send and receive e-mail, you use port 110.

> ### Notes
>
> If you've set up a home network using a hub/router to share an Internet connection, it most likely comes with some kind of firewall built into it. (For more information about home networks and security, turn to Chapter 8, "How to Protect Your Home Network.") But to be absolutely secure, you should use a personal firewall as well. That's because the firewalls on most home networks don't block programs from connecting to the Internet on their own, and so won't protect you against back-door programs such as Back Orifice.

Hackers have figured out ways to use these ports to attack your computer. So if you're using the Internet without a personal firewall, a hacker could use one of the ports to weasel his way into your system.

Personal firewalls hide these ports from the Internet, while still allowing you to use them. That means you're virtually invisible to hackers when you browse the Web—they literally aren't able to see your computer or its ports. Every time someone "probes" your computer to see if a port is open, nothing happens. The packet is turned back, and to the hacker it looks as if a computer isn't even there.

You can check to see how vulnerable your ports are to attack at the home page of the Gibson Research Corporation. Go to www.grc.com and look for the Shields Up area. From there, the site probes your computer's ports and reports on its results. And it shows that personal firewalls really work. In Figure 6.1, you can see the results of a probe of my computer when I was using a personal firewall—with the firewall in operation it operates in "stealth" mode and is invisible to the Internet.

Personal firewalls protect you in one other way, as well. They block any program on your computer from connecting to the Internet. Any time a program tries to connect, or you use a program to try to connect, you get a notice from the firewall software. It asks you if it's okay to connect. If you're using your e-mail software, you say yes. But if the inquiry is about a piece of software you've never heard of, just say no; you've stopped a back-door program from doing its dirty work.

Your computer at IP:

24.128.40.56

Is now being probed. Please stand by. . .

Port	Service	Status	Security Implications
21	FTP	Stealth!	There is NO EVIDENCE WHATSOEVER that a port (or even any computer) exists at this IP address!
23	Telnet	Stealth!	There is NO EVIDENCE WHATSOEVER that a port (or even any computer) exists at this IP address!
25	SMTP	Stealth!	There is NO EVIDENCE WHATSOEVER that a port (or even any computer) exists at this IP address!
79	Finger	Stealth!	There is NO EVIDENCE WHATSOEVER that a port (or even any computer) exists at this IP address!
80	HTTP	Stealth!	There is NO EVIDENCE WHATSOEVER that a port (or even any computer) exists at this IP address!
110	POP3	Stealth!	There is NO EVIDENCE WHATSOEVER that a port (or even any computer) exists at this IP address!

Figure 6.1

Stealthy as she goes: With a personal firewall, you're invisible to hackers on the Internet, and you operate in full stealth mode.

How to Protect Yourself with Personal Firewalls

You can get many different personal firewalls, from major companies with names you might have heard of like Symantec and McAfee to smaller companies that are less well known. They have different capabilities, but generally all work similarly, by hiding your ports from the Internet and stopping programs on your computer from connecting to the Internet without you knowing about it.

Some personal firewalls—like those from Symantec and McAfee—you can buy in a store. Others you download from the Internet, and can often use for free.

The one I use all the time is ZoneAlarm. It's a great firewall, it's easy to set up and use, and it has one more big advantage—it's free.

Check This Out!

There are some advantages to using for-pay firewalls. For example, ZoneAlarm is a great free firewall, but firewalls from Symantec and McAfee do some things that ZoneAlarm doesn't—and that can be helpful to parents. The for-pay firewalls include features that block children from visiting certain sites, for example, and also make sure that personal information isn't sent over the Internet in chat rooms or in instant messages. So if those kinds of things are important to you, consider getting firewalls from Symantec or McAfee.

How to Use ZoneAlarm

To use ZoneAlarm, you first have to download it from the Internet. Go to a download site, such as www.download.com, or download it directly from the ZoneAlarm Web site at www.zonealarm.com. Follow the instructions for downloading it and installing it. Make sure you download the free version, rather than the for-pay version, which is called ZoneAlarm Pro.

When you install ZoneAlarm, a section at the bottom of one of the setup screens entitled Configure Browser appears. It asks whether you want to let ZoneAlarm automatically give your browser and other Internet surfing software access to the Internet. Make sure that box is checked. If it isn't, you have to take several extra steps when setting up the program—leaving it checked helps the program automate its setup.

When you run the program, a screen like the one in Figure 6.2 appears. This enables you to set your security level. There are three settings: low, medium, and high. To change the level, move the slider. As you can see, there are two types of security levels you can set— local and Internet. If you aren't using a network like a home or corporate network, you only need to worry about the Internet setting. It's best to leave that on high. This way you're as safe as possible.

Figure 6.2

This screen sets up all your firewall protection. The great odds are that the original settings are right for you.

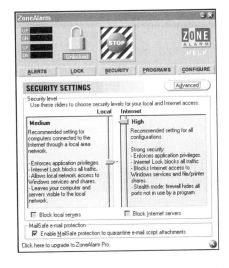

If you're on a network—for example, a home network—you might want to keep the local setting on medium rather than high. When you do that, you're able to share printers and files with other computers on your network. But because your Internet setting is on high, no one outside your network is able to use those printers and files.

That's all there is to basic setup. You're protected: When there's an attempt to get access to your computer from the Internet, ZoneAlarm blocks it. You get an alert when that happens, like the one shown in Figure 6.3. The alert is often in a language that bears only a passing resemblance to the English language, however. To get more information about what's going on, click **More Info** to be sent to a Web site with a bit more of an explanation, as you can see in Figure 6.4. Unfortunately, the information on that page can be hard to decipher unless you're somewhat technically sophisticated.

Figure 6.3

*Gotcha! ZoneAlarm at work, keeping intruders away. But it doesn't give much of an explanation, unless you click on the **More Info** button …*

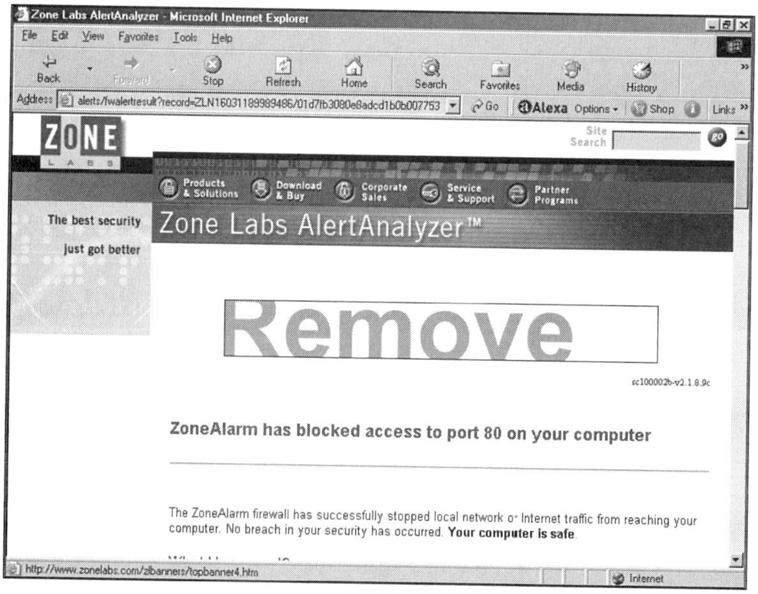

Figure 6.4

… and then you get a fuller explanation. But that explanation might be a bit techie.

Very often, these probes aren't done by hackers. Sometimes your ISP sends out probes like this for a variety of benign reasons. Don't assume that all the hackers in the world are

Check This Out!

After you've gotten a few alerts from ZoneAlarm, you'll probably start to get annoyed; all the program is doing is telling you it's doing its job. You can have ZoneAlarm keep protecting you, but without the alerts popping up all the time. Just check the **Don't show this dialog again** box, and the program continues its protection without all the pop-up alerts.

targeting you if you get a lot of alerts like this. In fact, these kinds of probes are constantly going on all over the Internet, so much so that some people refer to them as the Internet's background noise.

ZoneAlarm Additional Protection

As I mentioned before, ZoneAlarm protects you in another way, as well. It stops programs on your computer from accessing the Internet without you knowing about it. Whenever a program tries to access the Internet— even if you've launched the program—ZoneAlarm pops up a warning (it has a habit of doing that, doesn't it), asking you if you want to let the program go onto the Net. You can see the warning in Figure 6.5.

Figure 6.5

Here ZoneAlarm is asking whether a program can use the Internet.

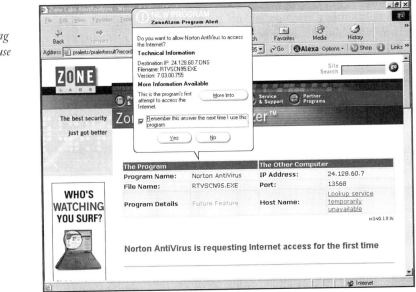

If it's a program you know about, let it go onto the Net by clicking **Yes.** And I'd also suggest that you check the box telling the program to remember the answer the next time the program wants to go online. That way, you don't get bombarded with these kinds of requests constantly.

If it's a program you don't know about, don't let it go online. It could well be a dangerous program.

There's one more primary way that ZoneAlarm protects you. It can completely block all Internet communications between your computer and the Net. And I do mean completely. You won't be able to browse the Web, send or receive e-mail, or communicate in any way. It's like unplugging the wire between your computer and your Internet connection. To do that, click the **Lock** icon. No traffic is able to make its way between the Internet and your PC. I suggest using this lock if you have a cable modem or DSL modem and you're about to be away from your computer. When you click the icon, it's like locking down your PC. Because you don't need Internet access, you might as well do it.

Wait a minute! I spoke too soon. There is, in fact, a way for you to cheat on the lock. If you'd like to use certain programs—for example, your browser or e-mail program—while the rest of the PC is blocked from the Internet, there's a way to do it. Click the **Programs** button in ZoneAlarm, look for the program that you want to allow to get onto the Internet even when your PC is blocked, and then click on the **Pass Lock** box next to it. From now on, even when your PC is locked down, you're able to use that program to get online.

> **Notes**
>
> Firewalls are great for keeping hackers from invading your PC. But they can't do anything about other privacy and security issues, such as cookies being put on your computer or Web sites tracking what you do online.

Where to Get the Best Firewalls

ZoneAlarm is just one of many firewalls that you can get. There are many other good ones, and many of them are also free. Although you can go from site to site, looking for the best ones, my recommendation is to go to a good download site like CNet's Download.com at www.download.com, or ZDNet Downloads at www.zdnet.com/downloads, and get them from there. Download sites have many firewalls to choose from, so it's much simpler to go to one place to get them.

Although ZoneAlarm is my favorite free firewall, here are some other good firewalls to look for at download sites:

◆ **Norton Personal Firewall.** In addition to protecting your ports and stopping back-door programs like Back Orifice, Norton Personal Firewall adds extra protection, such as blocking personal information from being sent over the Internet. You can try it for free, but if you use it for more than 30 days, you have to pay $49.95 to keep using it.

Check This Out!

If you have Windows XP, the latest Microsoft operating system, you have a firewall built into your operating system. Does that mean that you're as safe as possible from hackers? No. The firewall isn't as powerful as ZoneAlarm and most others you can download from the Internet. The XP firewall, for example, doesn't stop programs on your computer from trying to access the Internet—which means it can't protect against dangerous back-door programs such as Back Orifice. If you want solid firewall protection, you should download a free firewall, or get a for-pay one.

♦ **McAfee Firewall.** Like Norton, it provides all the normal firewall protection, and it also adds extra features, such as blocking personal information from being sent over the Internet and stopping children from using instant messenger software.

♦ **Tiny Firewall.** Like the name says, this firewall is a very small download, but it's still effective. Some people have had problems with setting it up, though. Like ZoneAlarm, it's free, although if you use it for business, you're supposed to pay $39.95 for it.

♦ **ConSeal PC Firewall.** If you're a techie who likes to fine-tune firewalls, this is the one for you. You can use it for free for 15 days, but after that you have to fork over $49.95 to keep using it.

♦ **Sygate Personal Firewall.** Like ZoneAlarm, it's free for personal use, although business users are supposed to pay $39.95.

The Least You Need to Know

♦ Personal firewalls are pieces of software that block Internet "ports," making your computer invisible to hackers.

♦ Firewalls can stop hackers from using malicious back-door programs like Back Orifice to attack your computer.

♦ ZoneAlarm is an excellent personal firewall that you can download and use for free.

♦ When using a firewall, place your firewall settings on high and your local network firewall settings on medium for the best protection.

♦ Norton Personal Firewall and McAfee Firewall are both excellent for-pay firewalls that give you some protection that the free ZoneAlarm doesn't.

♦ Good download sites like www.download.com and www.zdnet.com/downloads are good places to find and try personal firewalls.

Chapter 7

Keeping Safe from Java, JavaScript, and ActiveX Applets

In This Chapter

- ◆ Understanding how Java works
- ◆ How you can protect yourself against dangerous Java applets
- ◆ Learning about JavaScript
- ◆ How you can turn off JavaScript
- ◆ Understanding how ActiveX works
- ◆ How to set your security to make sure you don't get harmed by ActiveX controls

The Web has become a dynamic, interactive place in large part because of technologies that enable you to do more than just read pages and look at pictures. Three technologies—Java, JavaScript, and ActiveX—enable you to do some pretty amazing things on the Web. They'll let you play games, they'll track stock quotes for you and issue warnings when a certain price is reached, and they'll help you navigate and a lot more.

But these technologies can present some dangers, as well. In this chapter, we'll take a look at what you need to know about them, and how to make sure that they won't damage your computer or invade your privacy.

Java ... Does That Have Something to Do with Coffee?

Has the coffee culture gone crazy? Isn't it enough that Starbucks (a chain otherwise known to me as McCoffee) has a caffeine stand on every urban, suburban, and rural corner in this country? I mean, there's a limit to things, isn't there? (Don't get me wrong—I'm a big fan of cappuccino. In fact, as I write this I'm sitting in a café in my Cambridge neighborhood with a big double cup of it steaming right in front of me—decaf, of course, otherwise I won't sleep for the next two weeks.)

But does the coffee culture have to invade our *computers*? And how in the world do they get Java coffee into our computers, anyway? Won't it gum up the hard disk?

Rest easy; the Java in this case isn't the common slang term for a caffeine-laced drink. Instead, it's a kind of computer technology—and it can, in fact, jazz up your computer in the same way that a strong cup of Java can set your head buzzing.

Java is a *computer language* that can be used to create programs that can be run by your browser when you're on the Web. So when you visit a Web page, instead of you merely reading text, you can do all kinds of things. You can track your investments as stock tickers and other gizmos run on your screen, for example. You can play interactive games. You can create charts and graphs, and change them as you go. There are all kinds of gee-whiz things you can do. In short, Java can make the Web come alive in a way not possible before.

Techno Talk

Your computer runs programs that have been written by someone. But how are those programs written? A computer programmer uses a **computer language**, which has a set of commands and instructions that tells a computer what to do. Java is one of the many different kinds of computer languages.

Java programs that do this are called applets. (Kind of sounds like cute little baby apples, doesn't it?) Tech-types often call programs applications; and Java programs are called applets because they're generally small, and not as big as Office, for example. (Which is about as big as the state of Montana, give or take a few acres.)

All this sounds good. The Web becomes more interactive, you can play games and track your stocks, and everyone is happy. What could be wrong?

Sorry. There's some bad news. (You knew there had to be some of that, didn't you? Seems to be the way of the world—for every piece of good news, there's one of bad.) Java can also potentially be used to create destructive programs that do nasty things to your computer and invade your privacy.

To understand how that can happen, we're going to have to venture into tech-talk for a minute or two. Don't worry, though. We'll come back into the real world after a short while.

How Does Java Work—and How Can It Harm Your Computer?

It all starts when a programmer creates a Java applet and puts it on a Web page. The applet sits there, doing nothing—until visitors come along. When you visit the Web page, your computer downloads the Java applet to your computer. Your browser then starts something called a byte-code interpreter that runs the applet. The applet then runs in your browser window, and you zap the aliens, or watch your Internet stock hit rock bottom, or do whatever else the applet was designed to do.

The people who created Java recognized that this could cause trouble. They didn't want people writing Java applets that could maraud through your hard disk, deleting everything in sight. So they built security into Java. The security is fairly complicated, but the short version is this: The Java applets were designed to be restricted into what techies call a "sandbox." And from that sandbox, they're not supposed to be able to look at your files or change them, or invade your privacy in any way.

Sounds nice in theory, doesn't it. Ah, but in practice … that's another matter. Security experts have found all kinds of holes in the theory, and point out that "rogue" Java applets can potentially do nasty things. They say that the applets can figure out ways to jump out of the sandbox and delete files on your computer, or invade your privacy. An applet can figure out a way to crash your computer when you visit a Web page. The risks are generally small, because a lot of this stuff is tough to do—and in fact, to date, Java applets haven't wreaked destruction anywhere on the Net. Still, the possibility is there, and you should know about it and know how to keep yourself safe.

Protecting Yourself Against Rogue Java Applets

The possibility is small that you'll be harmed by a rogue Java applet, but the possibility is still there. If you're visiting a Web site you know is safe, or a well-known popular one, you most likely won't have any trouble. But you might be concerned that you could get harmed if you find yourself in one of the many out-of-the-way dark corners of the Internet.

Both Microsoft Internet Explorer and Netscape Navigator include ways that enable you to decide whether to run Java applets on your computer. It's fairly straightforward to do it in each. The next section covers how.

Handling Java Applets in Netscape Navigator

If you're worried about Java applets, you can stop them from running when you use Netscape Navigator. It's easy to do. Here's how to do it in Netscape 4.0 and above.

Check This Out!

Keep in mind that if you completely disable Java applets, you'll be locked out from using some parts of the Web. Decide whether the theoretical possibility of danger is worth not getting access to these parts. Your best option is to ask to be informed before a Java applet is run, so you can gauge the risk on a case-by-case basis.

Choose **Preferences** from the **Edit** menu, and then click **Advanced.** A screen, like the one in Figure 7.1 appears. To make sure that Java applets can't run, uncheck the box next to **Enable Java.** From now on, when you visit a Web page with a Java applet on it, it won't download to your computer.

The problem with this, of course, is that you won't be able to do any of the neat things that Java enables you to do. So how are you going to kill those aliens in that game you want to play? Here's my suggestion: If you're worried about Java applets, disable them, like this. But when you visit a Web site you know you can trust, turn them back on. This way, you can have the best of both worlds.

Figure 7.1

Here's how to stop Java applets from running when you use Netscape Navigator.

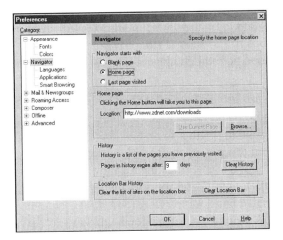

Handling Java Applets in Microsoft Internet Explorer

Microsoft Internet Explorer 5.0 and above give you more ways to handle Java applets than does Netscape Navigator. Internet Explorer enables you to set a variety of security settings for Java, so that you're still able to run it, but the program does some security checks for you. And you have several levels of security to choose from.

Here's how to do it. Choose **Internet Options** from the **Tools** menu, and then click **Security.** Several "Security zones," are listed, and the Internet option is highlighted. That's what you want to customize. Now click **Custom Level.** A new window entitled Security Settings pops up. Scroll down until you come to the section titled Microsoft VM. Here's where you're able to customize how to run Java on your computer. If you want to disable Java completely, click **Disable Java.** If you don't want to disable it, but are a little leery of running just any applet that comes your way, you have three levels of security to choose from, as shown in Figure 7.2: High Safety, Low Safety, and Medium Safety.

I'm not going to go into all the technical details of what each of those levels mean, because it's full of mind-numbing jargon and technical detail that could even cause a geek to run out of the room, tearing his hair and shrieking. But choosing a higher level of safety means you might not be able to run as many Java applets. I've opted to keep mine at High Safety, and haven't yet run into Java applets that don't run, so I suggest you keep yours at High Safety as well.

Check This Out!

If you're a Java jockey, you can customize how Internet Explorer runs Java programs. Click **Custom** in the Microsoft VM section of Security Settings, and then fill out the screens of information you see. You have to know about things like File I/O, Reflections, Threads, and Client Storage. But if you're a true Java jockey, all that stuff is second nature to you.

Figure 7.2

Microsoft Internet Explorer gives you more flexibility than Netscape Navigator in protecting against Java applets.

Hey, What Gives? My Computer Won't Run Java!

Now it's time to get really confusing. It turns out that not every computer can run every Java program. For that, we have Microsoft to thank.

Bear with me on this. It's off to techie-land again for a while. To run Java, a computer needs something in its operating system called a Java Virtual Machine. So far, so good. But it turns out that there are several different versions of this Java Virtual Machine, one released by the computer giant Sun, and one by Microsoft. The Sun version is newer and cooler, but Microsoft decided to ship Windows XP with its own version of the software. So if there's a Java program designed for Sun's version of Java, and you have Microsoft's version, you're out of luck.

To make matters more confusing, some versions of XP might include Sun's version, not Microsoft's.

The upshot? If you can't run a Java program and you think this is the problem, head to www.sun.com. There you can find advice on how to handle the problem.

Now I Have to Worry About JavaScript, Too?

Get ready to be confused. You just learned about the dangers of Java, and now it's time to learn about JavaScript. Guess what? They have nothing in common. That's right, nothing—apart from the letters J-a-v-a, that is. But aside from that, the technologies have nothing to do with one another. Go figure. Because I sure the heck can't.

JavaScript can't do things that a true program does, so in that way it's not like a Java applet, which is a true program. But it can add all kinds of interactivity and animations to Web pages. It's used all over the place on the Web, and has become ubiquitous. For example, when you move your cursor over text and it changes color, or over a graphic and it changes to something else, JavaScript might be working behind the scenes. It's a way for nonprogrammers to better control Web pages.

But JavaScript can do some malicious things as well, such as sending information about your computer back to a Web site.

As with Java, there are ways to control how it's run in both Microsoft Internet Explorer and Netscape Navigator.

Controlling JavaScript in Netscape Navigator

If you're worried about the dangers of JavaScript, you can tell Netscape Navigator not to run it. You do it in the same way as telling Navigator not to run Java. In Netscape 4.0 and above, choose **Preferences** from the **Edit** menu, and then click **Advanced.** To make sure that JavaScript won't run, uncheck the **Enable JavaScript** check box. From now on, when you visit a Web page with a JavaScript on it, Netscape doesn't run it.

The problem is that when you do this, you miss out on a good part of the Web. A workaround is to always enable JavaScript to run, except when you visit an unfamiliar page. When you visit a new page, turn it off so that JavaScript cannot run.

Handling JavaScript in Microsoft Internet Explorer

Microsoft Internet Explorer 5.0 and above give you more ways to customize running JavaScript than does Netscape Navigator. You're able to turn JavaScript on or off, or instead you can be prompted before deciding whether to run it.

Check This Out! _____

Computer guys and gals are always finding security holes in browsers—ways to use Java applets, or JavaScript and similar technologies to invade your privacy or do nasty work to your computer. In response, Microsoft and Netscape have come up with browser patches. These are files you download to your computer and run, and that fix the newly discovered security hole. It's always a good idea to have the latest patches for your browser. Get them from www.microsoft.com and www. netscape.com.

You do it a lot like you customized Java. Choose **Internet Options** from the **Tools** menu, and then click **Security.** Several Security zones are listed, and the Internet zone is highlighted. That's what you want to customize. Now click **Custom Level.** A new window entitled Security Settings pops up. Scroll down until you come to the Scripting section and look for Scripting of Java applets. You have three choices: **Disable, Enable, Prompt.** If you're worried about running JavaScript, either choose **Disable** or **Prompt.** When you choose **Prompt,** you get a message every time JavaScript attempts to run, asking you if you want to run it.

Beware of JavaScript in Your E-mail

Most e-mail programs, including the popular Outlook program from Microsoft, enable you to get e-mail that doesn't just include plain text. In essence, you can get sent entire Web pages.

That's the good news. Here's the bad news: That means that when you read e-mail, you can be attacked by a nasty JavaScript doo-hickey cooked up by a hacker or Internet snooper. In one variation of this theme, someone could use JavaScript to snoop on what you're doing on the Internet, just by embedding some evil commands in an e-mail message you get.

There's something you can do about that, though. You can disable JavaScript from running in Outlook. It's simple to do. To do it, go into Outlook and choose **Options** from the **Tools** menu, then click the **Security** tab. Click **Zone Settings**, and then click **Restricted Sites**. Click the **Custom Level** button and scroll down until you find the Scripting section. Click **Disable** for each of the sections and you're all set. Figure 7.3 shows how to do it.

Figure 7.3

Here's how to stop JavaScript from attacking you when you use Outlook.

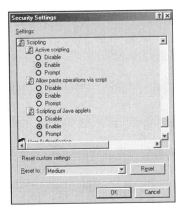

Does ActiveX Have Something to Do with the X-Files?

Sorry, conspiracy fans. ActiveX doesn't have anything to do with the X-Files. Instead, it's a kind of technology developed by Microsoft that enables programs to be downloaded to your computer and run on Web pages. I know that this sounds a lot like Java. But it's very different than Java, in some technical ways that I can assure you, you don't want to know about. In ActiveX, the kinds of things that get downloaded to your computer are called ActiveX controls.

Notes

Outlook, like many e-mail readers, enables you to read HTML, the language of Web pages. That means you could get sent, via e-mail, a dangerous ActiveX control on a Web page. That's exactly what happened with a malicious ActiveX control called Offensive. It was put on a Web page, and the Web page was mailed to people. The Web page displayed a **Start** button that, if clicked upon, started the control doing its dirty work, not allowing any programs to work, not allowing Windows to shut down, and assorted other evil things.

There are a lot of potential security problems with ActiveX. It can potentially delete files from your computer and invade your privacy in a number of ways. Microsoft recognized that, and built some security into ActiveX. The main security precaution has to do with what are called certificates. When someone creates an ActiveX control, they're supposed to go to a company called Verisign and get a certificate that identifies who created the ActiveX control. The idea is that no one would create a dangerous control and then sign their name, address, and other information to it. When they get that certification, the control is referred to as signed.

By default, in Microsoft Internet Explorer, your security settings are set to High for ActiveX controls. That means that when you go to a Web page with a signed ActiveX control on it, you get a warning, like the one pictured in Figure 7.4. The warning tells you who created the ActiveX control, and gives you the option of downloading it or not, depending on whether you trust the control or not. Internet Explorer automatically rejects any control that hasn't been signed with a certificate.

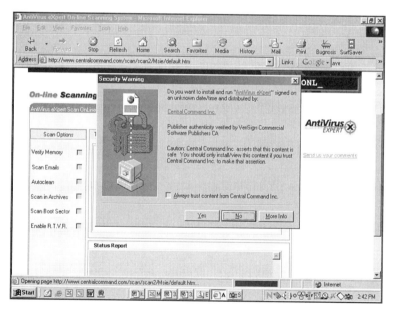

Figure 7.4

Here's the warning you'll get before installing an ActiveX control.

If you'd like, you can change these security settings so that they're less stringent, in the same way that you can change Java and JavaScript settings. But don't do it. You want to be safe, so don't take any chances.

The Least You Need to Know

♦ Java applets are downloaded to your computer and run in your browser—and can cause problems.

♦ You can tell your computer not to download and run Java applets by changing settings in your browser.

♦ You can tell your computer not to run JavaScript by changing settings in your browser.

♦ You receive a warning before an ActiveX control is downloaded to your computer. Only accept it if you trust the person who wrote it. The author's name is listed.

♦ Never download an ActiveX control that doesn't have a signed certificate.

♦ Make sure to keep you ActiveX security settings set to High.

How to Protect Your Home Network

In This Chapter

- ◆ Dangers to your privacy and security when you have a home network
- ◆ What kinds of protection are built into home networks?
- ◆ How to turn off file and printer sharing
- ◆ How to customize file sharing for maximum protection
- ◆ How you can beef up your network's built-in security

So, Mr. or Ms. Smartypants, I bet you're feeling pretty smug and pleased with yourself. You're probably feeling pretty techie: You've set up a home network. If you're like most people, you're probably doing it in large part to share a high-speed Internet connection such as a cable or DSL modem.

You might also be sharing a printer among all your home computers, exchanging files, and maybe even playing a few network games. Congratulations!

There's just one problem. When you use a home network, you open yourself up to all kinds of hacker attacks. But, if you take some simple precautions, you can protect yourself against them. So read on. In this chapter I'll show you how to ward off hackers and snoopers. And then you can feel *really* smug.

What Dangers Are There in Home Networks?

When you set up a home network, you might also expose yourself to all kinds of privacy and security problems—things like hackers getting access to all your personal files and information, or taking control of your computers and using them to launch attacks against Web sites and private businesses. Here are the main dangers in home networks:

♦ **Someone could steal your files.** Your network might expose your computers to hackers who could waltz right in and take any files that they want.

♦ **Someone could delete your files.** It's bad enough that a hacker could steal files on your computer. But they could also go in and delete them as well.

♦ **Someone can steal all your personal information—such as passwords, bank information, and more—and use it for personal gain.** If you store this kind of information on your computer, a hacker could get in through your network, steal this information, then use it to access your bank accounts, Web sites, and more.

♦ **Someone can take complete control of your computers.** Certain back-door programs, such as one called Back Orifice, enable a hacker to take complete control of computers on your network. It's as if the hacker is sitting at your own keyboard, except he's doing it remotely. And you won't even know about it.

♦ **Hackers could crash your computer.** Through various means, a hacker could crash your computer and its network and make it pretty much unusable. Not very nice, is it? Why would they do it? Who knows—but they could, and they have.

♦ **Hackers could track what you do.** Hackers can get onto your network, and then plant goodies that do report back to them every site you visit and the e-mails that you send and receive.

♦ **Hackers could use your computer as a launch pad for other attacks.** A hacker could install an "agent" on your computer that sits idle until the hacker tells it to spring into action. The hacker could then use that agent to attack other computers and Web sites, making it look as if you were the one doing the attacking.

Not very pleasant stuff, is it? As you see in the rest of this chapter, though, there's a lot you can do to foil hackers.

Understanding Your Network's Built-In Protection

When you install a network, it most likely includes some kind of built-in protection. The protection it includes varies depending on the kind of network you've installed and the specific make and model of your network.

One of the most common kinds of networks are called *hub/routers*, which are often used to share high-speed cable or DSL Internet access. Because those are the most common, and the kind that hackers are most likely to target, that's what we concentrate on in this chapter.

Techno Talk _____

Networks that you buy might go under many different names. Although they're commonly called **hub/routers,** sometimes they're called broadband routers, Cable/DSL or other similar names. Usually, these devices all do the same thing, and work the same way—they are designed to let all the computers connected to them get Internet access, and they let all those computers share files and resources like printers. Some people use the terms "hub" and "router" interchangeably; but in fact, they mean different things. A **hub** connects computers to one another and lets them share files, printers, and other resources. A **router** routes information and lets the networked computers connect to the Internet. That's why the devices are called hub/routers—they allow computers to connect to one another, and they allow each of those computers to connect to the Internet.

These kind of networks typically offer built-in protection against hackers, and that protection is often quite good.

The most effective way that your network stops hackers is through a technique called Network Address Translation, commonly called NAT. It's a way of hiding the computers on your network from the Internet. In fact, to the Internet, they're invisible. And if they're invisible, it's just about impossible for anyone to get into them. So you're safe and secure.

Your network uses a nifty bit of magic to do this. Here's how it works. As you learned in Chapter 1, "Why You Need to Worry About Online Privacy and Security," every computer connected to the Internet has its own IP address, such as 146.23.112.34. In order to do anything, from browsing the Web to sending and receiving e-mail, the computer needs to identify itself to the Internet using its IP address.

Here's where NAT does its magic. Your hub/router has an IP address that the Internet can see, for example, 124.78.89.11. But all the computers connected to the hub/router in essence have addresses that the hub/router gives to them. Only computers inside the network can see and use these addresses. Typically, these addresses start with 192.168.1 and then have a number after that, for example, 192.168.1.1, 192.168.1.2, 192.168.3, and so on.

To the outside Internet, though, your entire network has only a single IP address—the IP address of the hub/router. The computers inside your network are invisible. And there's nothing a hacker can do to your hub/router—it has no hard disk on it, no information, nothing at all. So hackers can try to hack to their heart's content, but they won't be able to do a thing.

What to Do About Printer and File Sharing

One of the main reasons to set up a home network is to share files and printers with other computers at home. But there's a problem with that: When your network is connected to the Internet, there's a chance that you allow hackers to get at your files and printers, as well.

If you're the paranoid type, and have no need to share files or printers with other computers on the network, you can turn off file and printer sharing. It's easy to do. Click the **Start** button, and then choose **Control Panel** from **Settings**. Double-click the **Network** icon. Now click **File and Print Sharing.** A screen like the one shown in Figure 8.1 appears.

Figure 8.1

Here's where you can turn on or turn off File and Print Sharing.

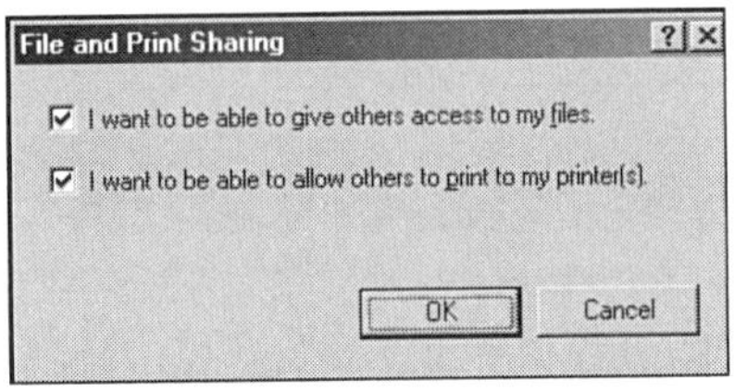

To disable file sharing, uncheck the first box, and to disable print sharing, uncheck the bottom box. If the boxes are already unchecked, you have nothing to worry about—they're already disabled.

There's one problem with turning off file sharing—it defeats one of the main purposes of a network. One of the big benefits of networking is not only sharing a high-speed Internet connection—it's also sharing files among different computers.

There's a way that you can get the best of both worlds. You can be secure and still have a way to share files on your network.

You can do that by enabling file sharing, but customizing how you allow files to be shared; for example, you can allow some to be shared but not others, or you might require a password to be entered if someone wants to gain access to files on certain folders.

Check This Out!

What if you'd like to be as safe as possible and are worried that merely customizing file sharing won't let you be as secure as possible, but you still want to share files on your network? Are you out of luck? No. There's a way out, although it takes a bit of work. When you're connected to the Internet, turn off file sharing, as detailed in this chapter. Then when you want to share files, turn file sharing back on and also unplug the connection between your hub/router and the Internet. That way, you can share files, but because you don't have a connection to the Internet, no hackers can get into your network.

To do that, first enable file sharing on your computer—in other words, make sure the file sharing box in Figure 8.1 is checked. Now you must decide which folders on a computer can be shared and which can't—and you also need to decide what kind of access people on your home network have to the files inside those folders.

You do this by allowing certain folders to be shared, and certain ones not to be shared. And you can also set what kind of access is allowed for the shared folders.

After you've enabled file sharing, start Windows Explorer. Click on a folder, and then choose **Properties** (see Figure 8.2).

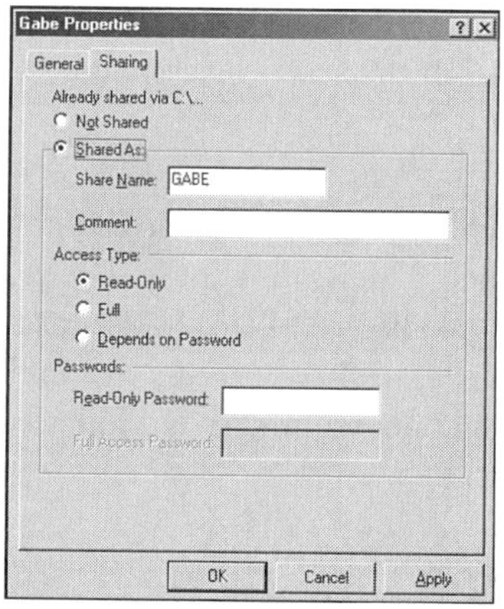

Figure 8.2

Here's how to set which folders you allow to be shared and which are off-limits.

If you don't want anyone to have access to this folder and its files, click the **Not Shared** option. That's it. You've locked out anyone from using the files and this folder.

If you'd like people on your home network to have access to the folder and its files, choose the **Shared As** option. That allows others to use the folder and files in it.

You might notice that when sharing a folder, you get to choose the Share Name. The Share Name is the name that other people on the network see when they look at this folder. By default, the Share Name is the same name as the folder. If you'd like to change it, however, you can. Even when you change the Share Name, the folder name, as seen on your computer, doesn't change.

From this screen, you also have the option to decide how you want the folder and its files to be shared. You have three options:

- **Read-Only.** When you check this, it means that other people can read and copy the files in the folder, but they can't edit them or delete them. So this doesn't protect the files and folder from being looked at—but it does protect them from being changed in any way.

- **Full.** This means other people are allowed to do anything they want with the files in this folder. They can read them, edit them, and delete them to their heart's command.

- **Depends on Password.** This enables you to give people different kinds of access to different files and folders by allowing them access to the folder only if they have a password that you create. So you could give some people full access to files, and some people read-only access. Like all the other options, here you can determine this on a folder-by-folder basis. So a person might have full access to some folders, read-only access to others, and no access to others—it depends how you set the access levels and passwords.

Check This Out!

If you have a wireless network, you can be hacked just as easily (or perhaps more easily) than people with a wired network. For more information about hacking and wireless networks, turn to Chapter 27, "Wireless Insecurity: Protecting Yourself When Using Cellular Devices."

Set these options for every folder on each of the networked computers. Think hard about what kind of access each folder should have. For example, you might want to give no access to a folder that has financial information, read-only access to a folder with information about family outings, and full access to a folder of pictures.

Customizing Your Network's Built-In Protection

As I explained earlier in the chapter, home networks built with hub/routers typically use NAT to protect you from invaders. But they protect you in other ways, and you can customize that protection.

Each network offers slightly different kinds of protection. In the rest of this chapter, I cover how you can customize the popular Linksys hub/router router. Other routers offer similar protections. Read your system's documentation for more details.

As with many other hub/routers, you can change the Linksys router's settings by way of a Web browser. Launch a Web browser, and go to http://192.168.1.1 (see Figure 8.3).

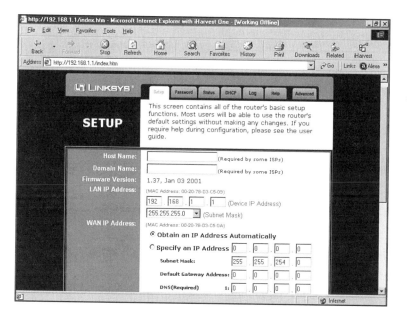

Figure 8.3

Command central: Here's where you customize your hub/router's settings for maximum security.

Setting Password Protection

Start with the most basic protection: Set a password for your router. When you do this, no one can muck around with its settings, making it less secure. The only people who can change the settings are those who have the right password. Setting a password is simple; just click the **Password** tab, then type in the password you want to use twice, once in each box. From now on, only a person who knows the password can change the settings.

Having the Network Automatically Disconnect from the Internet

Another way to protect your network is to have it automatically disconnect itself from the Internet when you don't need an Internet connection. To do that, from the main screen pictured in Figure 8.3, scroll down until you see a box labeled **Connect on Demand: Max Idle Time.** When you check the box, your router automatically disconnects you from the Internet

Check This Out!

Here's the best way to make sure you don't get hacked: Unplug the Ethernet cable that runs from your hub/router to your cable or DSL modem. With it disconnected, no one on the Internet can get into your network.

after you haven't used the Net for a specific amount of time. To set the amount of time, enter it in the entry box.

For example, if you want your network to be automatically disconnected from the Internet after you haven't used any Internet resource for 20 minutes, check the box, and type 20 into the entry box. Then, after 20 without Internet use, the network disconnects itself from the Internet. When you want to use the Internet again, just use it as you normally would—your router automatically connects you.

Blocking WAN Requests

One more way to make sure that your network is safe against intruders is to block what are called WAN (Wide Area Network) requests from going through the router. In essence, blocking these requests help make sure that the PCs on your network are invisible and their ports are hidden from intruders. Turning it off in Linksys is easy. Click the **Advanced** tab, then click the **Filters** tab, scroll down, and click **Enable** next to Block WAN Request.

Check This Out!

One more way to make sure your home network doesn't get hacked is to use a personal firewall on each of the computers on the network. A personal firewall is a piece of software that helps repel hackers. It does one major thing that the NAT protection built into your router doesn't do—it helps make sure that back-door programs like Back Orifice don't make a connection from any of your computers out to the Internet. For more information on how to set up and use personal firewalls, turn to Chapter 6, "The Ultimate Defense: Keeping Safe with Firewalls."

The Least You Need to Know

- ◆ Hackers can steal information from you, take control of your computers, and use your network to launch hacker attacks if your home network is left vulnerable.
- ◆ Your home network probably has built-in protection called Network Address Translation (NAT) to hide your network's computers from the Internet.
- ◆ For absolute safety, turn off file and printer sharing.
- ◆ You can customize the way that you share files and folders on your network, so that you give some people complete access, some people partial access, and some people no access at all.
- ◆ Make sure that you password-protect your hub/router so that no one else can change its settings.
- ◆ Set your router to block WAN requests, and to disconnect from the Internet after a certain amount of idle time, for maximum security.

Part 3

It's None of Their Business: How to Protect Your Privacy Online

To be safe and to protect your privacy online, you've got to be strong. Very strong. Stronger than the starting line of the Green Bay Packers. So strong that even the most determined hacker can't bust through your defenses.

But how can you be strong if, when it comes to hacking and cracking Internet technology, you're really just a 98-pound weakling? Easy. Follow the advice in this section. You'll learn how anyone—even someone just learning to use the Internet—can put up a powerful cyberdefense. You'll find out how to protect yourself against identity theft, cookies, spyware and Web bugs. You'll discover how you can make sure that Internet sites can't invade your privacy.

In fact, after you read this part, you won't feel like a 98-pound cyberweakling anymore. You'll put up a line of defense so powerful that even the Green Bay Packers of hackerdom won't be able to break through.

How to Keep Yourself Safe Against Identity Theft

In This Chapter

- ◆ Understanding what identity theft is
- ◆ How your identity can be stolen
- ◆ What can happen to you if you're a victim of identity theft
- ◆ Steps to take to help ensure you're never a victim
- ◆ What to do if you've been a victim of identity theft
- ◆ How to make complaints to the major credit bureaus

Imagine this: Someone poses as you and cleans out your bank account, runs up tens of thousands of dollars in credit card debt, or uses your Social Security number to take out loans or mortgages in your name, and then takes the money and runs, leaving you holding the bag. Maybe someone falsely files for obtaining federal benefits of some kind—using your identity. Or someone assumes your identity and does all that and more—transfers all the money out of all your bank accounts, commits crimes with your identity, and the police come after you. Sound like a horror story?

It is a horror story, and unfortunately, it's a true one. In this chapter, you'll learn all about identity theft, and particularly how to help make sure you don't become a victim, and what you can do if you're ever victimized.

What Is Identity Theft?

Every day, people across the country are victims of identity theft. Identity theft refers to a whole family of crimes in which someone's personal information is stolen and then used in some illegal way, usually for financial gain. It can be as simple as a telephone calling card being stolen and used, or as sophisticated as a complete identity takeover, in which Social Security numbers and IDs are used to open false bank accounts and credit card accounts. Typically, identity thieves try to spend as much money as quickly as they can, before they can be tracked down and caught.

Identity theft is far more common than you might imagine—and it's getting more common by the day. The Federal Trade Commission (FTC), for example, was getting from 100 to 200 calls a week on its identity theft hotline in November, 1999. A little over a year later, the number of calls had skyrocketed to more than 2,000 calls per week.

Identity theft has become common for a very simple reason—in a world where people's private information has become increasingly public, it's easier than ever to steal personal information about people. The famous bank robber Willie Sutton was asked why he robbed banks, and he replied, "Because that's where the money is." Today, the money is in identity theft.

Identity theft has been around since well before the Internet, but the Internet has made it easier than ever to steal someone's identity. One of the biggest problems is that the Internet makes it easier than ever to find out personal information about someone. Additionally, personal information about people is often shared among commercial Web sites, meaning that personal information about you is available at more places than ever before—and the more places it's available, the more likely your identity is to be stolen. And there are also "identity mills" on the Internet—sleazy Web sites that

Check This Out!

If you think you're immune to identity theft, think again. During a meeting of the World Economic Forum (WEF) in Davos, Switzerland, hackers broke into WEF servers and stole the credit card numbers and personal information of attendees, who included many powerful business and political leaders, including Bill Gates and former President Bill Clinton.

Check This Out!

According to the FTC, the typical victim of identity theft is 42 years old and lives in a large population center in a state such as California, Arizona, Nevada, New York, and Florida. Some 88 percent of victims have no relationship to the thief. And typically, the victim doesn't notice the crime for 14 months.

sell Social Security numbers as well as documents and technology that can be used to create forged drivers' licenses, Social Security cards, and other false means of identification.

How Your Identity Can Be Stolen

Identity thieves have many ways in which they can steal your identity. Here are just a few of the main ones:

♦ **By stealing or finding wallets or purses.** Think of all the personally identifying information you carry around with you in your wallet or purse—credit and bank cards, driver's license, and more pieces of plastic with information about you than you can count. Lose your wallet or purse, and you lose your life. Even if it's returned, the thief can steal the information in it and pose as you.

♦ **By "dumpster diving."** Dumpster diving refers to the practice of looking through someone's trash in search of things such as credit card receipts and bills, banking information, and similar personally identifying data. It's more common than you think. Some people have turned to using shredders at home to shred any piece of paper that contains personally identifying information.

♦ **From Internet identity mills.** These sites illegally sell Social Security numbers as well as blank forms that can be used for creating drivers licenses and other forms of false identification.

♦ **From Internet "private eye" services.** For a fee, these services track down information for you about people, such as their current and past addresses, court records, property they own, long-distance calls they've made, and more.

♦ **From public court information.** If you've ever been involved in any kind of lawsuit, divorce, or similar court proceedings, your life could be an open book. And even if you haven't been involved, if you own property or a house, information about you is public. People can even get hold of your state Department of Motor Vehicles information.

♦ **By "pretexting."** People frequently steal personal information by using a technique known as pretexting. They pose as a person, and then contact banks or other institutions and manage to get information they can use in identity theft.

 Check This Out!

The biggest case of identity theft in history was committed by a New York City restaurant worker, Abraham Abdallah, who used pretexting and other techniques to get into the bank, brokerage, and credit card accounts of celebrities and tycoons such as Stephen Spielberg, Ted Turner, Oprah Winfrey, Disney CEO Michael Eisner, and others, and steal millions of dollars. He was eventually caught.

- **By stealing your mail.** When they do this, they can get your bank and credit card statements, tax information, and more.
- **By buying information from "inside" sources.** They might pay a retail store employee, for example, for credit card or other information about you.
- **By hacking into Web sites or private businesses.** Online shopping sites and private businesses keep credit card records and other personal data about people who buy from them. Hackers can break into those computers and get personal information.

What Evil Can Be Done If Your Identity Is Stolen

There are all kinds of evil things that someone can do if he steals your identity. Here are the most common ones:

- **He can open up a credit card account in your name, or take over your existing account.** The thief then runs up many thousands of dollars in charges and leaves you holding the bag.
- **He can open up a bank account in your name and write fraudulent checks.** Again, guess who's left holding the bag?
- **He can write checks on your account.** And you have to prove that you didn't write the checks.
- **He can open up telephone, cellular, or other communications services in your name.** Yes, you know the drill by now. It's you they come after for payment.
- **He can take out fraudulent loans in your name.** For example, he can take out a car loan.
- **He can call your credit card company, pretend to be you, and have the bills sent to another address**. He runs up credit card charges, but you don't know it because you aren't getting the bills.
- **He can ruin your credit rating.** When he does any or all of the above, your credit rating suffers—and you can spend years trying to get the damage fixed.

How to Protect Yourself Against Identity Theft

Whew! That's a whole lot of bad stuff. Luckily, there are a lot of precautions you can take to help make sure you're never a victim. Here's what to do, both on the Internet and off:

- **Never give your Social Security number to Web sites.** There's no reason that a Web site should ask for your Social Security number. Never give it out. The only exception is if you're opening some kind of brokerage or bank account that requires it. In that case, however, make sure that the site uses encryption so that the number can't be stolen by snoopers.

♦ **Give as little identifying information about yourself to Web sites as possible.** They often ask for your name and address, and sometimes your age, employer, number of children, whether you're married, and similar information. The more of this information you give out, the more susceptible you become to identity theft. Give out the minimum information possible.

♦ **Don't have your Social Security number printed on your checks.** Do that, and you're asking for identity theft. In general, protect your Social Security number at all costs.

♦ **Don't post personal information on Web sites.** You might want to post a great deal of personal information about yourself on your college alumni site or on genealogical sites, for example. But do that and you increase your chances of being victimized by identity theft.

♦ **Use the fewest credit cards possible.** These days, everyone and his brother want to offer you a free credit card. But the more you have, the more can be stolen. And if you have a lot of them, you're less likely to pay attention to the charges on any individual one.

♦ **Carefully check your credit card bills every month.** Account for every single charge. If any seem suspicious, immediately contact your credit card company.

♦ **Safeguard your canceled checks and other financial data.** Keep them in a safe place. And if you want to be super-paranoid, buy a personal shredder and shred any sensitive documents before throwing them away.

♦ **Once a year, get your credit reports from the three major credit bureaus and review them carefully for signs of fraud or errors**. For information how to do it, go to Equifax at www.equifax.com, Experian at www.experian.com, and Trans Union at www.tuc.com.

Check This Out!

In some states, your Social Security number is also used as your driver's license number. That's a very bad idea, because whenever you hand your license to someone for identification—or if you lose your license—someone can easily get your credit card number. Generally, states let you choose something other than your Social Security number for your driver's license number, so make sure to do that.

Check This Out!

One way that your identity can be stolen is by someone stealing or guessing your password to Web sites, ATM machines, and other services that require passwords. To find out how to lessen the chances that your passwords are stolen, turn to Chapter 2, "Putting Up Your First Line of Cyberdefense."

What to Do If You've Become Victimized

If the worst happens, don't despair—there are in fact ways that you can fight back. If you suspect that you've been a victim of identity theft, here's what you should do:

♦ **Contact your bank, credit card company, and any other financial institutions.** Tell them what's happened, and close your existing accounts. Then open new accounts, making sure to use new Personal Information Numbers (PINs).

♦ **Contact the fraud departments of the three big credit bureaus.** Tell them you've been a victim of fraud, have them append a warning to your file that there's a fraud alert, and make sure they alert creditors that they should obtain your permission before any accounts can be opened using your name. For Equifax, call 1-800-525-6385 and write P.O. Box 740241, Atlanta, GA 30374. For Experian, call 1-888-397-3742 and write P.O. Box 949, Allen, TX 75013. For Trans Union, call 1-800-680-7289 and write Fraud Victim Assistance Division, P.O. Box 6790, Fullerton, CA 92634.

♦ **File a report with your local police department, or where the identity theft took place.** By doing this, you not only increase the chances of catching the thief, but it can also help you clear your credit rating later on.

Check This Out!

The FTC has very helpful online resources for anyone concerned about identity theft. Head to www.consumer.gov/idtheft.

♦ **File a report with the Federal Trade Commission.** Call the FTC's Identity Theft Hotline at 1-877-438-4338. You can also write to the Identity Theft Clearinghouse, Federal Trade Commission, 600 Pennsylvania Avenue, NW, Washington, DC 20580.

♦ **If mail theft is involved, report it to your local postal inspector.** Go to your local postal office for information on how to get in touch with him or her. You can also get information on how to do it at www.usps.gov/websites/depart/inspect.

♦ **If your checks have been stolen, stop payment on all your checks.** You can also tell your bank to notify the check verification service it uses not to accept the checks, and you can ask the large check verification services to tell retailers not to accept your checks. The major ones are National Check Fraud Service: (843) 571-2143; SCAN: 1-800-262-7771; TeleCheck: 1-800-710-9898 or 927-0188; CrossCheck: (707) 586-0551; Equifax Check Systems: 1-800-437-5120; and International Check Services: 1-800-526-5380.

♦ **Cancel your phone service, cellular service, and other communications service if they've been compromised.** Make sure to check that someone hasn't assumed your identity with your Internet Service Provider, as well.

Resolve Your Payment and Credit Problems

One of the biggest headaches you'll face if you've been victimized is resolving your credit and payment problems. Two laws govern your credit rights: the Truth in Lending Act, which limits your liability to $50 per credit card; and the Fair Credit Billing Act, which spells out what you can do to resolve billing errors and get your credit restored. You have to take lengthy steps to deal with your credit card company. For information on how to do it, go to www.ftc.gov/bcp/conline/pubs/credit/fcb.htm.

For information on how to resolve all your payment and credit problems, go to the helpful FTC page at www.ftc.gov/bcp/conline/pubs/credit/idtheft.htm.

The Least You Need to Know

◆ Identity theft can be as simple as someone stealing a credit card number or as sophisticated as assuming a person's identity.

◆ Never give your Social Security number to Web sites, unless you're required to in order to open a bank, brokerage, or similar financial service account.

◆ Don't give out unnecessary information to Web sites such as your income, number of children, and other personal information.

◆ If you've been victimized, contact credit card companies, banks, and other financial institutions, and file reports with your local police and the Federal Trade Commission.

◆ Cancel any accounts—such as bank accounts and phone accounts—that have been compromised, and open up new ones.

Chapter 10

I Spy: How to Protect Yourself Against Spyware and Web Bugs

In This Chapter

◆ What is spyware?

◆ All the ways that spyware can invade your privacy

◆ How you can tell if a piece of software contains spyware

◆ What to do if you find spyware on your computer

◆ What are Web bugs?

◆ How to fight back against Web bugs

There seem to be no limits to ways in which your privacy can be invaded when you head onto the Internet. Each year that passes, some new marketer or scamster comes up with yet more innovative ways to try and find out about your Internet habits or private life.

In the last few years, no privacy topic having to do with the Internet has been hotter than so-called spyware and Web bugs. Spyware is software that can track your online activities and report on it; Web bugs are bits of data placed on Web sites that can trace your surfing habits and more.

In this chapter, you'll learn all about how those privacy-invading technologies work—and more important, how you can protect yourself against them.

What Is Spyware?

It seems like the world's greatest deal: download software and use it for free forever. No muss, no fuss. No strings attached.

There are many sites at which you can find free software like this that you can download and use for free, and in particular at popular download sites like www.download.com and www.zdnet.com/downloads.

It seems too good to be true. After all, we know there's no such thing as a free lunch. Well, the offer might or might not be too good to be true. But for many such pieces of free software, there is a potential price to pay, although you don't pay in cash. And there *are* a few strings attached. It's just that those strings might be invisible. The price you might pay is the price of your privacy.

The free software might contain what is called spyware—software modules that track your Internet activities, and then report those activities back to marketers. Those marketers might use the information to target ads at you. And some people worry that the information could be sold to the highest bidder without your knowledge.

The actual software that you download isn't the spyware itself. Instead, the spyware comes along for the ride and works in concert with the main software you download. For example, you might download a free piece of personal finance software. The personal finance software doesn't spy on you. Instead, a separate spyware module does the spying.

As you use the personal finance software, ads would be delivered to you, much like the ads you see on a Web page. The spyware module watches what you do as you surf the Net, and then reports that activity back to a central database. Based on your surfing activities, a profile can be created about you, and then based on that profile, specific ads can be sent to you. For example, if you frequently visit pet sites, you might get ads about pets delivered to you.

Check This Out!

Just because you can download a program and use it for free forever doesn't mean that the software contains spyware. In fact, many programs you can use for free don't contain any spyware modules. So just because a program doesn't cost anything doesn't mean that it spies on you.

The Great Spyware Debate

There's a great debate about what constitutes spyware, and whether, in fact, spyware is a bad thing.

There are those who say the name is misleading, and that the software doesn't do anything that every major Web site does not do. And they note that usually, the information gathered doesn't include any personal information—in other words, you can't be personally identified, and so your privacy isn't being invaded. And they contend that targeting ads at you is in fact a service being provided to you, because you get relevant information about products and services that you otherwise might not have gotten.

Check This Out!

At least one U.S. senator is concerned enough about spyware that he has introduced a law that would control it. U.S. Senator John Edwards of North Carolina has proposed the Spyware Control and Privacy Act that would require any software that includes spyware to warn people of that fact and must explicitly detail what information is being collected, and to whom it's being sent. Under the law, people would be able to try to collect up to $500,000 for every violation. The law has been proposed in several Congressional sessions by Edwards, but has yet to pass.

The anti-spyware people, on the other hand, point out that when you download software with spyware in it, you're typically not informed that there's a spyware module that tracks what you do. You don't know how the information about you is used, and you don't know whether the spyware might accidentally open a back door that can be used by hackers to invade your computer.

Where do I come down on the debate? I don't think that ad modules by themselves are necessarily evil things. But I do believe that you should be told ahead of time that you're installing software that might include tracking modules, that you should be in control of what information can be garnered about you, that no unnecessary information be tracked, and that you can block it being sold to third parties.

Why You Should Worry About Spyware

So what's the big deal about a little bit of snooping? Should you really care about spyware, or is it all much ado about nothing?

Anyone concerned about their Internet privacy needs to be concerned. Here are the reasons why:

◆ **You don't know how marketers will use the information.** Will they use it to identify you and sell information to other third parties? If you care about your privacy, you don't want this to happen.

◆ **You don't know if it will introduce a security hole in your system.** As I mentioned, spyware communicates information about you without you knowing about it. Could hackers figure out a way to hack into this back-door communications channel used by spyware? It hasn't been done yet, but that doesn't mean it can't be done.

◆ **You should have control over what's on your computer.** As a general principle, when installing software, you should be informed about what you're installing. So you should be alerted if any modules are being installed.

◆ **When you uninstall the program you downloaded, the spyware module might not uninstall and can keep spying on you.** Unfortunately, this is a relatively frequent occurrence. You might be surprised at how much spyware is left behind, even after you've uninstalled the program the spyware came with.

Check This Out!

Here's a tricky way to stop spyware, but still keep using the program the spyware came with: Use your personal firewall to block it. Personal firewalls like ZoneAlarm enable you to block software on your computer from contacting the Internet. So when you run a program that includes spyware, you get a notice from ZoneAlarm asking if you want the program to access the Internet. Just say no, and from that point on the spyware isn't able to report on your activities.

How to Spot Spyware Before It Gets You

If you're worried about spyware, the best way not to get victimized by it is simply not to download and install it.

Sounds simple, no?

Unfortunately, it's not so simple. Programs with spyware modules don't tell you that they have them. However, there are a few things you can do if you're interested in spotting spyware:

◆ **Watch out for ad-supported programs.** Not all ad-supported programs include spyware modules. However, it's your first clue that perhaps spyware is included. Download sites generally tell you if a download is ad-related, so read descriptions before you download.

◆ **Check out the Gibson Research "Known Spyware" page**. Steve Gibson, owner of Gibson Research, is the foremost expert on spyware. He maintains an enormous amount of information on his site about the subject, including a Known Spyware page at http://grc.com/oo/spyware.htm (see Figure 10.1).

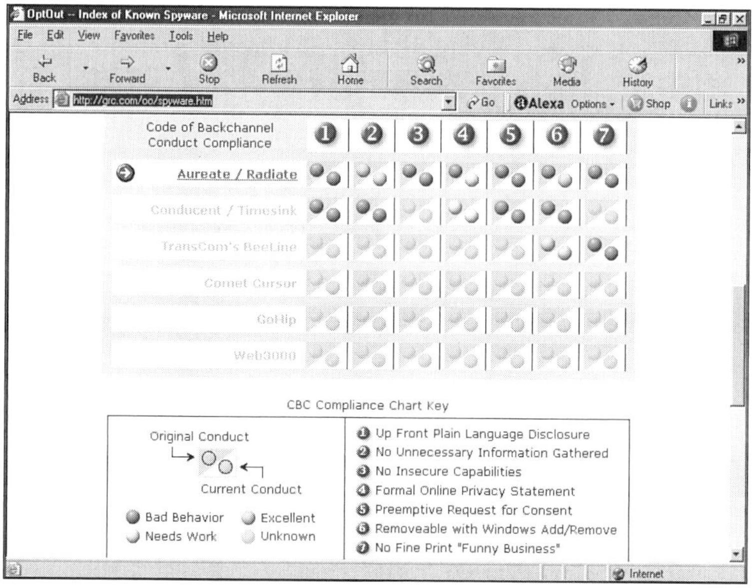

Figure 10.1

Spying on spyware: The Gibson Research Known Spyware page gives you the lowdown on spyware the company has found.

◆ **Use a spyware detector.** Some programs analyze your system and report on spyware they find. An excellent spyware detector is Ad-aware, available from download sites like www.download.com, or directly from the maker of the software at www.lavasoftusa.com.

Notes

The record industry can spy on the MP3s you download. If you've ever used a program like Napster or one of its relatives to download MP3 music files from the Internet, here's an eye-opening piece of news for you: The record industry can keep track of what music you download. Press reports say that using software with names like Copyright Agent and Media Tracker, the industry has tracked what music individuals have downloaded. In some instances, the industry has then sent a warning to the person's Internet Service Provider, demanding that the person be banned from sharing music online. And Roy Orbison's estate forced Napster to ban 60,000 people from the service after a company called Copyright.net discovered the identities of those people who had downloaded Orbison's songs using Napster.

How to Protect Yourself Against Spyware

No matter how vigilant you are, you might have spyware on your system. Many free programs come with spyware piggybacking onto them, and frequently you won't know it's happened.

The best way to find out if you have spyware on your system, and then delete it, is to use anti-spyware software. A number of good ones are available, including Ad-aware, as well as SpyBlocker and Spy Chaser. Get them at popular download sites. My favorite is Ad-aware as seen in Figure 10.2.

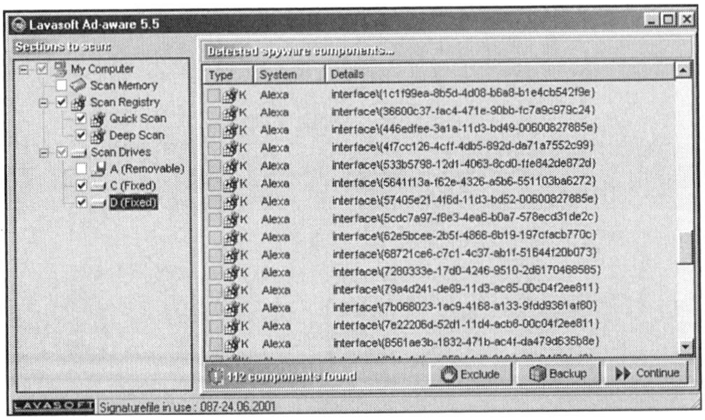

Figure 10.2

Be aware of spyware: Ad-aware in action, scanning a system for software it considers spyware.

Ad-aware does more than tell you that you have what it considers spyware on your system. It also deletes the spyware modules. However, be aware that frequently, if you delete the spyware module, the program it came with will no longer work. My suggestion is to use Ad-aware to first find out what it considers spyware. Then decide if you want to continue using the program or not. If you don't, delete the program as you would any other program. Then run Ad-aware again, to see if the spyware modules were deleted when you deleted the program. If they weren't, use Ad-aware to delete the spyware module.

What Are Web Bugs?

Any time you surf the Net, what you do can be tracked. There are a number of ways you can be tracked, but a popular technique is to use something called a *Web bug*. When used like this, the term "bug" doesn't mean an error in computer coding. Instead, it refers to the kind of bug that can electronically eavesdrop on people. Think of a Web bug as a way of eavesdropping on your activities as you surf the Internet.

Web bugs aren't used by hackers. Instead, they're used by folks of a more respectable sort—people who run Web sites. (Although you can find many people who don't count those who run Web sites as reputable sorts at all, and rate them below used car salesmen, and just above politicians.)

Web bugs are tiny, invisible bits of data put on a Web page that can be used to track what you're doing, and can gather information about you from your computer and send that information to a Web site. You can't see these bits of data, and so there's no way to know that they're there. They work by gathering information on your computer and sending it back to a Web site. At times, the Web site to which they're sending information isn't the one that contains the Web bug; for example, they might send information back to an online advertising network.

Techno Talk

Another name for a **Web bug** is a "transparent GIF." A GIF (Graphics Interchange Format) is a kind of graphic often used on Web pages. Web bugs are very tiny GIF files that can't be seen—hence the name transparent GIFs.

Web bugs are becoming increasingly common. In fact, the security firm Cyveillance did a study in which it found that the use of Web bugs has increased by 448 percent over the last three years.

Although Web bugs might be tiny bits of data, they can do some pretty serious data gathering. Here are some of the main things that they can track and do:

- **They can find out and report on your IP address.** This makes it much easier for Web sites and marketers to track your wanderings through the Internet.
- **They can report on the URL of the page on which the Web bug was located.** Again, this makes it easier to know what sites you've visited.
- **They can report on the time the Web bug was viewed.** So marketers can know the date and time you visited.
- **They can report on what kind of browser you have.** So marketers can know whether you have a PC or a Mac, and your browser.
- **They can read cookies.** This is a particularly dangerous capability. Normally, cookies can only be read by the sites that place them. Web bugs, however, can get around that, and so can help build sophisticated profiles of your surfing habits.

Your E-mail Can Also Be Bugged

It's bad enough that your Web habits can be bugged. But there's another potential problem with Web bugs—they can be attached to e-mail messages sent to you, and your e-mail can be spied upon, as well.

The technique is similar to how regular Web bugs work. For your e-mail to be bugged, you need to use an e-mail reader, like Microsoft Outlook, that can read HTML e-mail. Most e-mail readers, not just Outlook, can do this.

You get bugged when someone sends you a message with a Web bug in it. The bug can then do a variety of things, depending on how it was designed:

- In spam or e-mail advertising, the Web bug can track whether you've viewed the advertising. It can then track how well a particular advertising campaign worked.

- It can tie a cookie to an e-mail address. Normally, when a cookie is put on your computer, the Web site doesn't know your e-mail address. But if you're first sent a Web bug via e-mail, that Web bug can be used to tie your e-mail address to the cookie. That way, the advertiser finds out not just your IP address, but your e-mail address, as well.

- It can tell if an e-mail message has been read, and at what time it was read.

- If you forward or respond to the e-mail, it can allow the sender of the bug to read your response. Through a complicated technique, the Web bug is able not only to track to whom the message was forwarded, but can even send the text of your response or forwarding message.

Check This Out!

Web bugs can be used for many different purposes, often having nothing to do with tracking what you do as you surf the Net. For example, Web counters, which count the number of people who visit a Web page, and then publicly report the results, frequently use Web bugs—and nothing about these Web counters invades your privacy.

What You Can Do About Web Bugs

The first thing you can do about Web bugs is to know when they're on a Web page that you're visiting. You can then decide whether you want to keep frequenting that site, knowing that it uses Web bugs.

But if the bugs are essentially invisible, how do you know if there are Web bugs on a Web page?

Use a free program called Bugnosis that works in concert with Internet Explorer. Go to the Privacy Foundation Web site at www.privacyfoundation.org and click the **Bugnosis Web Bug Detector** icon. Follow the instructions for installing the program. Then, when you visit a Web site, you know whether it contains a Web bug. Figure 10.3 shows Bugnosis in action.

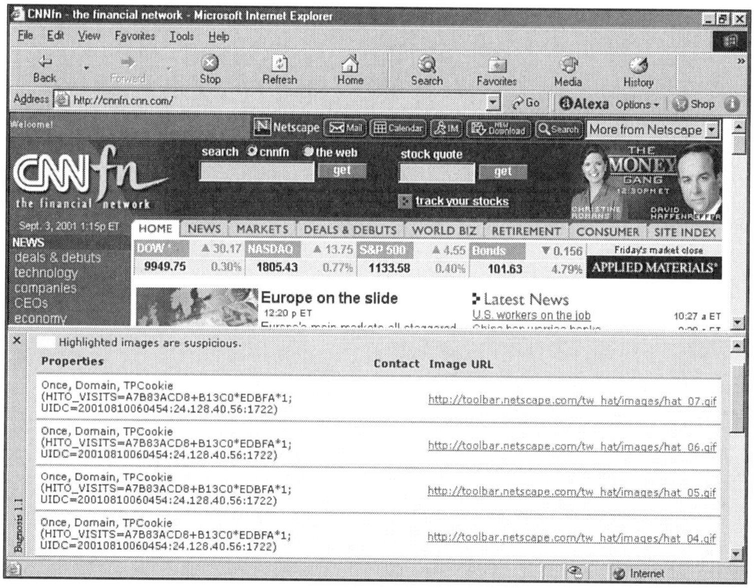

Figure 10.3

There's a whole swarm of them! Bugnosis finds a lot of potential Web bugs on the CNNfn Web site.

Try checking out sites' privacy policies. In general, you won't get much help, because most sites make no mention of Web bugs. However, some do, and increasingly there is pressure for sites to mention whether they use Web bugs. For more information on how to check out a site's privacy policies, turn to Chapter 25, "How to Protect Your Credit Card When Buying Over the Internet."

To be absolutely safe, learn to surf anonymously so that you can't be identified when you visit sites. For detailed information on how to do that, turn to Chapter 13, "How to Surf Anonymously Without a Trace."

To keep yourself safe from e-mail-based Web bugs if you use Outlook, you should turn off scripting in that program. With scripting turned off, you're safe from some of the worst problems with e-mail Web bugs, such as people reading e-mail when you forward it. For information on turning off scripting in Outlook, turn to Chapter 7, "Keeping Safe from Java, JavaScript, and ActiveX Applets."

The Least You Need to Know

◆ Spyware tracks your surfing activities and reports it to a database, and is often used in concert with software to deliver ads to you.

◆ Spyware might come along with a piece of software you can use for free on your computer.

◆ To get rid of spyware, use spyware-killing and detection software like Ad-aware.

◆ Web bugs are invisible pieces of data put on a Web site that can be used to track your surfing activities or report information about your computer to a Web site.

◆ Web bugs can also be used to track whether you read a piece of e-mail.

◆ To be safe against Web bugs, surf anonymously and turn off scripting in your Outlook e-mail program.

Chapter 11

They're Not Very Sweet: What You Can Do About Cookies

In This Chapter

◆ What Web cookies are, and why Web sites use them

◆ The sweet and sour of Web cookies

◆ Where your browser stores its cookies

◆ How to delete cookies from your hard disk

◆ How to stop Web sites from putting cookies on your hard disk

Who doesn't like cookies? They're sweet, they come in all flavors and sizes and every time you buy one from a Girl Scout, you do a good deed.

But when it comes to the Web, cookies leave a bad taste in some people's mouths. Cookies are little bits of information that Web sites put on your computer's hard disk when you visit them. They use those cookies to track what you do on the site, and to offer you extra services, such as customized Web pages. They're also used to deliver ads pitched to your interests.

If you don't like the idea of Web sites putting cookies (or anything at all) on your hard disk, there's something you can do about it. This chapter will show you how. And even if cookies don't bother you, read on, because you'll learn everything there is to know about cookies, except for how to bake mocha chocolate chip ones.

What Are Web Cookies?

It's strange but true: When you visit Web sites, they actually put information on your hard disk that you don't know about. Those bits of information are cookies.

Each cookie a site leaves on your hard disk is a very small text file. If you looked at most of these files, they would make about as much sense to you as would an ancient Sanskrit manuscript. (Although if you were a Sanskrit scholar or an Internet geek, it might make a lot of sense to you.) If you look close enough inside them, you might be able to make a little sense out of them, but not enough to be useful.

Cookies have become ubiquitous on the Web. Just about any Web site you visit uses them, and many Web sites use more than one. If you were to look at your hard disk and see them all, you'd be amazed at just how many there are. Figure 11.1 shows some of the cookies from sites that I've visited. I'm a busy guy on the Web, I know, but this is ridiculous!

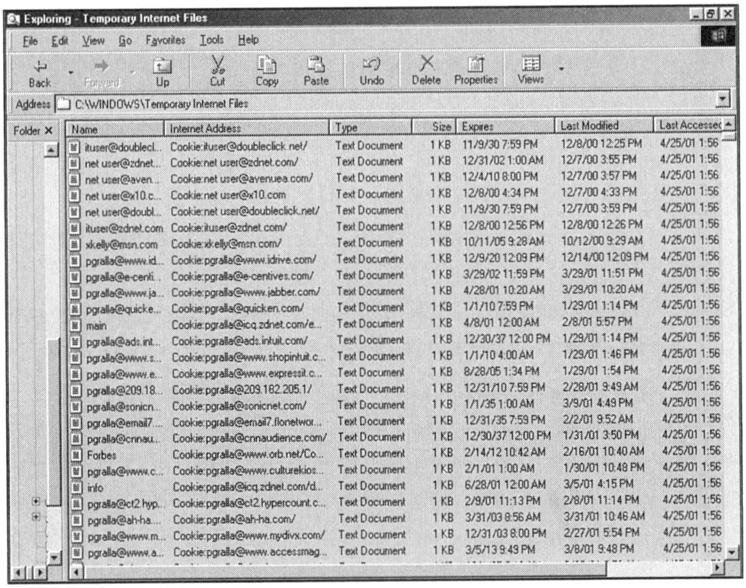

Figure 11.1

More cookies than the Girl Scouts! Here's a list of some of the cookies that sites have put on my hard disk.

Why Are Web Sites Serving Cookies?

Why should a Web site go to the trouble of storing cookies on your computer? A big reason is that it gives them an easy way to track what you do when you visit their site. It uniquely identifies you, so the Web server can find out what you're doing whenever you visit. From visit to visit, the Web server can easily build up a profile about you. That profile is worth a lot of money to Web sites, because after they have that profile, they can sell advertising targeted at people's specific interests. Spend a lot of time on a site reading about childcare for children under the age of one? Diaper companies would love to advertise to you. Do you retrieve stock quotes quite frequently from a site? Online brokerages would pay big money to put an ad in front of your face. And Web sites would love to get that money.

Generally, only the Web site that places the cookie on your hard disk can read that cookie. So when you go to *The New York Times* site on the Web and it puts a cookie on your hard disk, the Web portal Yahoo! isn't able to read that cookie, and vice versa. This exclusivity helps ensure your privacy to a certain degree. If sites could read each other's cookies, the amount of information that could be obtained about you would be absolutely mind-boggling—and it would mean that sites could obtain your username and password at other sites, and other information you don't want made public.

The people who designed the technology of the Web made sure that sites couldn't read each other's cookies, as a way to protect your privacy. But some companies have managed to find their way around the technology. I won't go into all the technical mumbo jumbo and rigmarole of how it's done, but the Internet advertising agency DoubleClick.com has built up a network of Internet sites that in essence can read each other's cookie information. Based on the information gathered from your cookies from all those sites, DoubleClick can put together a profile about your Web surfing habits and interests. It's not the kind of information that's dangerous, and it's based on the Web pages you visit so that advertising can be targeted at you. But it makes some people uncomfortable.

Notes

Cookies are data files placed on your hard disk. Each cookie is made up of two elements—the cookie's name and the cookie's value. The value is the actual data in the cookie itself; each Web site can put all kinds of different data into the value. The value often includes an expiration date (the date the cookie expires—kind of like the sell-by date on real cookies), the domain (the address of the server that delivered the cookie to you), and things such as usernames and passwords. Usually, much of the data is scrambled so that only the Web server can understand it; you're left in the dark.

Cookies Can Also Be Sweet

I don't want to give you the impression that cookies are some wicked plot to destroy civilization as we know it. In fact, some cookies provide the coolest services and content for you on the Web—and you won't even get fat using them. Here's a list of some of the things that cookies can do:

◆ **Log you in automatically to Web sites.** Many sites offer extra services in areas for which you need to log in. It's a pain to type in your username and password each time. Cookies can log you in automatically. Keep in mind, though, that this can be a security risk if anyone else ever uses your computer. When logging in, you're given the option of whether the username and password should be stored on your computer. When you say "yes," the information is stored in your cookie. When you say "no," it isn't.

◆ **Enable you to customize what you see on a Web page.** Maybe you want information about politics and entertainment, but not about business and sports. Or when you visit a Web page, you want to see your local weather and news, as well as a listing of local movies. Some sites recognize that the Web isn't one-size-fits all, and so they enable you to choose the information you want to see whenever you visit. To do that, they need to use cookies. Figure 11.2 shows how you can customize a section of Yahoo! to give you the precise information you want every time you visit. To customize it in this way, you need to use a cookie.

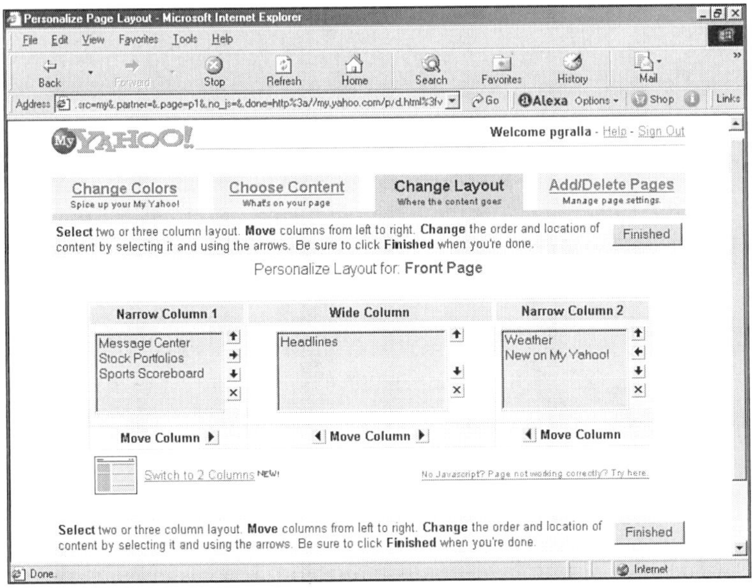

Figure 11.2

Have it your way: Cookies enable you to customize the information you see on a Web site. Here is the customization of a portion of Yahoo!.

◆ **Give you information you want without your having to ask for it.** From your previous Web surfing, a Web site knows that you always check the Celtics box score, the Boston traffic, the Massachusetts lottery number, and the weather in the Bahamas (if your number hits, you'll be able to afford a vacation in some balmy place). The Web site can then use a cookie to show you the information you usually view without you having to ask for it.

◆ **Show you advertising you're interested in.** Don't smirk, now. Some people actually *like* advertising, because it can tell them about good deals on products they're interested in buying. If your cookie tracks that you've been checking out information on a new Palm VII pocket computer, an ad telling you about a cheap deal for one would be welcome.

◆ **They can do much more, as well.** The mind of man and woman is infinite in its capacity for figuring out creative ways to use technology. Have no doubt—new ways of using cookies are being cooked up right now; and I'm assuming they won't be half-baked.

Where Are Cookies Stored?

When a Web server puts a cookie on your computer, it puts it into a specific location on your hard disk. Sounds simple. But, of course, this is the Internet, and nothing is simple. Where that cookie is put depends on whether you use Microsoft Internet Explorer or Netscape Navigator, and even on what version of those browsers you use. Thank you, technology companies, for making all our lives so much easier.

Microsoft Internet Explorer and Netscape Navigator handle cookies a bit differently from each other. Here's what you need to know about each.

Where Microsoft Internet Explorer Stores Its Cookies

If you're using Microsoft Internet Explorer, look in the Windows\Cookies or Windows\ Profiles\UserName\Cookies directory, where UserName is your name. (And it might even be in yet a different directory. Thank you, Microsoft, for making our lives even more confusing.) That's where you'll find all your cookies … and your cookies … and your cookies. If you spend much time on the Web, that folder will be chock full of the little goodies.

Believe it or not, you can tell a good deal about a cookie just by looking in a directory that holds it. In Internet Explorer, each cookie is a separate text file, and ends with the extension .txt. The cookie starts with your abbreviated name, is followed by the "at" sign (@), and then is followed by the name of the Web site that put the cookie on your hard disk.

So, for example, if your abbreviated name was joejoe, and you visited the Web site www.homeruns.com, the cookie put on your hard disk would have the name of joejoe@homeruns.txt.

On the other hand, your computer might use a slightly different scheme for naming the cookies on your hard disk. It might add a [1], [2], or another number to the cookie, so that the www.homeruns.com cookie would be named joejoe@homeruns[1].txt.

Whichever scheme your computer uses, however, you can find out which Web sites have put cookies on your hard disk just by looking in the Cookies folder, or at whatever folder stores your cookies.

You can also see the date and time each cookie was put there or modified. Just look at the date and time for the file in the directory—that's the latest time that the Web site touched the cookie.

Sometimes you can find out more about the cookie. For example, you might be able to see whether it's used to put in your name and password, and other information. Of course, usually, you find garble and incomprehensible characters, but it can't hurt to take a look.

To look inside a cookie, double-click it. You should see something that looks like Figure 11.3.

Figure 11.3

What's inside this cookie? As usual, it's a bunch of garbled text and letters.

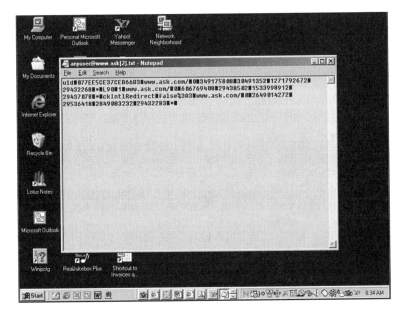

Sometimes you might see English words in there that give you a clue as to what the cookie is doing, and you might even see your username and password.

Where Netscape Navigator Stores Its Cookies

Netscape handles cookies differently from Internet Explorer. Instead of creating separate text files for each, it stores all your cookies in a single text file called … yes, what else, cookies.txt. (How surprisingly logical. They'll never let *that* happen again.) Look for the file in the folder C:\Program Files\Netscape\Users\Username, where Username is, of course, your username.

Check This Out!

Some cookies can reveal your Web passwords to snoopers. If you look through your cookie files, you might be surprised to notice that some cookies list your usernames and passwords for Web sites. Usually cookies encrypt those usernames and passwords on your cookies, but not all do. If it's not encrypted on your cookie, that means that anyone with access to your computer can open your cookie files and steal your passwords. So if you're worried that someone other than you has access to your computer, delete those cookies that show your username and password. See the section later in this chapter "Fight Back: How to Make Cookies Crumble," for information on how to kill cookies.

Figure 11.4 shows a typical cookies.txt file. You're able to see the name of the Web site that put the cookie on your hard disk, and the usual incomprehensible information, along with the occasional English word. You won't see the date and time the cookie was put there, though.

```
cookies.txt - Notepad
File  Edit  Search  Help
# Netscape HTTP Cookie File
# http://www.netscape.com/newsref/std/cookie_spec.html
# This is a generated file!  Do not edit.

secure.webconnect.net   FALSE   /cgi-bin        FALSE   1234117633      A300
0009210953477817100210 01
.netscape.com   TRUE    /       FALSE   1293839763      UIDC    155.40.99.115:0936292922:587344
.zdnet.com      TRUE    /       FALSE   1041310954      cgversion       4
.zdnet.com      TRUE    /       FALSE   1041310954      browser 9B286373383AB856
.doubleclick.net        TRUE    /       FALSE   1920499140      id      ade18804
.imgis.com      TRUE    /       FALSE   1093830404      JEB2    BE9D1CA0DF3ACAB29B2863733004A9D6
.avenuea.com    TRUE    /       FALSE   1261957903      AA002   936300180-101612538/947878412
.focalink.com   TRUE    /       FALSE   1293796546      SB_ID   0937838463000044166320803965550
.amazon.com     TRUE    /       FALSE   2082786702      x-main  eKQIFwnxuF7qtmM40x6UWAXh0Ih6Uo5H
www.myfamily.com        FALSE   /       FALSE   2145945625      IsMember
LASTLOGINDATE=3%2F14%2F00
www.myfamily.com        FALSE   /       FALSE   2145945625      Security
MEMBER=5F616F8B97D53C5
.preferences.com        TRUE    /       FALSE   1268662462      PreferencesID
019W2reo9VAXaQUmU4Lj2V
ads.admaximize.com      FALSE   /       FALSE   1260366384      i33004900010EUMA01
http://www.Furniture.com|002640b
.cdnow.com      TRUE    /       FALSE   2145913273      cookTrack       1811774958-953088507
.altavista.com  TRUE    /       FALSE   1388491225      AV_USERKEY
AVSdde883b82F000024001 0ac00081a8
.emusic.com     TRUE    /       FALSE   981224885       SID     6058F3a05a851a952dd
.emusic.com     TRUE    /       FALSE   1604168885      FIRST_SID       6058F3a05a851a952dd
.mediaplex.com  TRUE    /       FALSE   1245628800      svid    9734493002226510110411052180
.mediaplex.com  TRUE    /       FALSE   1245628800      mojo1   10sb191236
.zdnet.com      TRUE    /       FALSE   979435716       chkpt   regextra_imp
.peapod.com     TRUE    /       FALSE   1010948342      podToken
810L8FmHn3HPV10nRUcbzAyQXi0zYMWrdTt
.peapod.com     TRUE    /       FALSE   980643688       firstorder      true
```

Figure 11.4

Here's how to look at cookies in the cookies.txt file of Netscape Navigator.

Fight Back: How to Make Cookies Crumble

You don't have to allow Web sites to put cookies on your hard disk—after all, whose computer is it, anyway? And you can also clean cookies off your hard disk. In fact, there's a good deal you can do to ensure your privacy and make cookies crumble. Without a whole lot of work you're able to …

- ◆ Check out a Web site's cookie policy.
- ◆ Delete cookies from your hard disk.
- ◆ Stop new cookies from being put on your hard disk.
- ◆ Allow some cookies to be put on your hard disk and stop others from being put on.

In the next section, I show you how to do all that and more.

Check Out a Web Site's Cookie Policy

If you're worried about cookies and how they're used by Web sites, there's something easy you can do—check out a site's policy. Unfortunately, not many sites post those policies, but some do. Look for the area of the site entitled "Privacy Policies," "FAQ," "Help," or something similar. Some sites spell out in great detail exactly what they use cookies for. In fact, if you find a site willing to publish this information so freely, it often means they're not using cookies to invade your privacy, because that's not something they're likely to want to share with the world. You can see Yahoo!'s cookie policy, available in their Privacy Center area, in Figure 11.5.

Figure 11.5

It's open to the world: Yahoo!'s cookie policy.

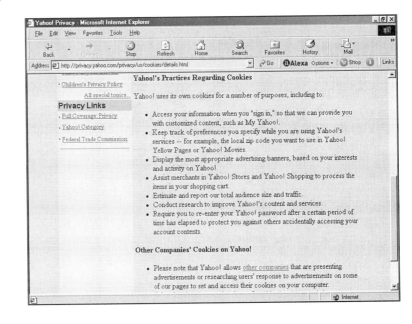

If you don't find a cookie policy at a site, go to the Contact area and send an e-mail requesting it. Often you won't get a note back, but sometimes you will.

How to Delete Cookies from Your Hard Disk

It's quite easy to delete cookies from your hard disk. You can do it yourself, but a much better way is to use a "cookie-killer" program, a program that enables you to delete and manage cookies. If you're worried at all about cookies, I strongly recommend that you get one of these programs. Many are available. My favorite is CookiePal—it's the most comprehensive solution I've found to killing and managing cookies. You can get it at many download sites on the Internet, such as the ZDNet Software Library at www.zdnet.com/downloads. You can also find it www.kburra.com. You're able to try the program for free before deciding whether to buy it, so it's a can't-lose deal.

If you're not using a cookie-killer program, you can still delete cookies from your hard disk. In Microsoft Internet Explorer, go to the Windows\Cookies or Windows\Profiles\UserName\Cookies directory, or other directory where your cookies are stored. Then, to delete a cookie, simply delete it as you would any other file. That's it. It's over. The cookie is history. Delete as many or as few as you'd like.

In Netscape Navigator, you aren't able to delete cookies one by one. Instead, you have either delete every Netscape cookie or none at all. To delete all the cookies, go to \Program Files\Netscape\Users\Username, and delete the cookies.txt file. There. All gone. To leave them, don't do a thing.

By the way, a word of warning here: Don't try to edit your cookies.txt file. Bad things could happen. Netscape didn't design the file to allow it to be edited.

Programs such as CookiePal enable you to delete individual cookies, whether you use Netscape Navigator, or Microsoft Internet Explorer.

Check This Out!

If you've deleted Internet Explorer cookies, you might be surprised to see them in the directory that temporarily stores Internet files. Well, believe it or not, you see the cookies in that directory, but they don't really exist! Because of the peculiar way that Internet Explorer handles cookies, the names of those cookies show up, even though they've been deleted.

How to Stop Cookies from Being Put on Your Hard Disk

If you don't like the taste of cookies, you can do something even better than deleting them—you can stop them from being put on your computer in the first place. To do so, you can use a program like CookiePal, or you can customize Microsoft Internet Explorer and Netscape Navigator to block the cookies.

To do this in Internet Explorer, choose **Internet Options** from the **View** or **Tools** menu. (It varies according to what version of Internet Explorer you have.) Then click the **Advanced** tab and scroll down until you see the Cookies section, as seen in Figure 11.6. In some versions of Internet Explorer, you instead click the **Security** tab, highlight the **Internet** icon, and click **Custom Level.** In both cases, you get the screen pictured in Figure 11.6.

Figure 11.6

Here's how to turn off cookies in Microsoft's Internet Explorer.

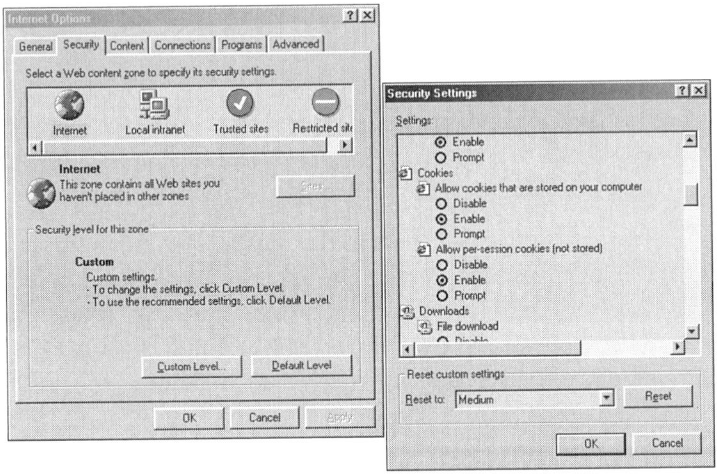

What you do now varies according to your version of Internet Explorer. In some versions, to stop all cookies from being put onto your hard disk, choose **Disable all cookie use.** When you do this, every cookie is automatically rejected. I don't suggest going this far— after all, many cookies have their uses. Instead, I recommend choosing the **Prompt Before Accepting Cookies** option. That way, before a cookie is put on your hard disk, you're asked if it's okay; you have the option to accept it or not.

In other versions of Internet Explorer, you disable cookies by choosing **Disable** from the section that says Allow cookies that are stored on your computer. And you can also choose to allow cookies to be used, but only for your current Internet session. To do that, choose **Disable** from the Allow per-session cookies section.

To do this in Netscape Navigator, choose the **Edit** menu and then choose **Preferences.** Then click **Advanced.** As in Internet Explorer, you're able to reject all cookies or instead be asked whether to reject individual cookies.

> **Notes**
>
> A word of warning—if you disable all cookies, you also give up special Web services, such as customization. And you aren't able to use some Web sites at all.

Handling Cookies in Microsoft XP and Internet Explorer 6

If you use Windows XP or Internet Explorer 6 or later, you're in luck. Microsoft has given you a better set of tools for handling cookies than you've ever had before.

With that operating system or browser, you can have your browser automatically accept or reject cookies based on: whether the site has an privacy policy that you can easily read from inside your browser; whether it uses cookies that gather information that can identify you, without asking you first; and other information. And you can customize it site by site, allowing only some sites to put cookies on your hard disk.

To customize how or whether to accept cookies with XP or Internet Explorer 6, choose **Internet Options** from the **Tools** menu of Internet Explorer, and click the **Privacy** tab. A screen like the one in Figure 11.7 appears. Privacy settings enable you to determine how to handle cookies. You can accept all cookies, reject all of them, or you can accept some and reject others, depending on whether they violate your privacy. Settings range from accepting all cookies to rejecting all cookies, with Low, Medium, Medium High, and High settings in between. Change the settings by moving the slider.

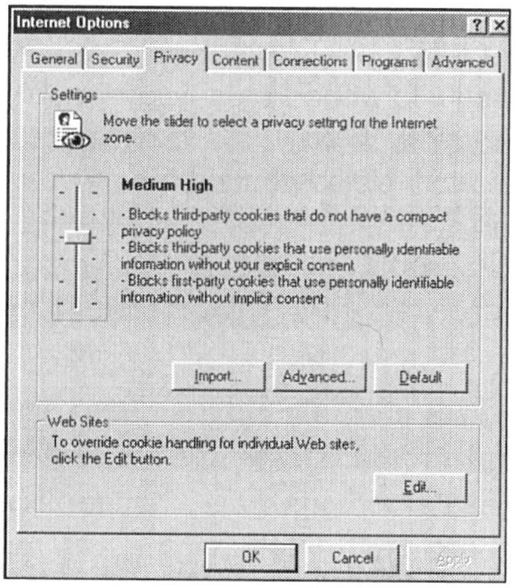

Figure 11.7

Here's how to customize the way you accept cookies in Windows XP and Internet Explorer 6.

In general, I leave my settings on High. That blocks all cookies that use personally identifiable information, unless you give your explicit approval. And it blocks cookies from Web sites that don't have a privacy policy that your browser can read. That might be too high for some people, because it blocks a lot of cookies, so you might want to leave yours on Medium or Medium High.

When you block cookies in this way, your browser automatically blocks the cookies without your having to do anything. The first time a cookie is blocked, you get a notice telling you that a cookie is blocked. After that, it doesn't appear automatically unless you tell it to. And whenever a cookie is blocked, you see a small icon of an eye appear near the bottom of your browser. Figure 11.8 shows you the notice and the icon.

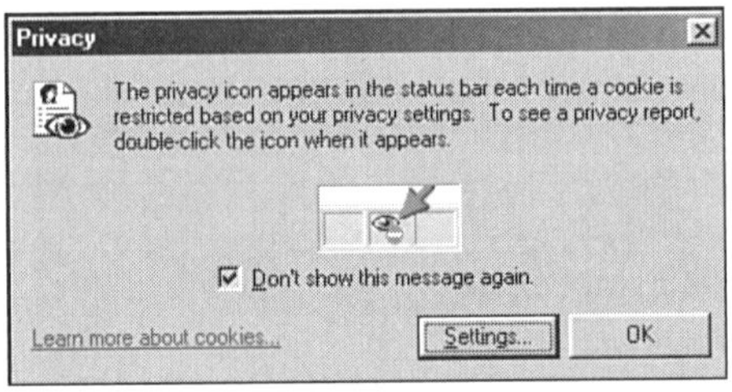

Figure 11.8

Block that cookie! Here's Internet Explorer in action, killing a cookie.

You can customize the way cookies are handled by Windows XP and Internet Explorer 6 even further. You're able to block or allow cookies on a site-by-site basis. To do it, from the **Privacy** tab, click **Edit.** Then type in the address of the Web site and click **Block** to block all cookies from the site or **Allow** to allow all cookies from the site.

You Should Really Get a Cookie Killer

The best option when dealing with cookies is to get a cookie killer such as CookiePal. Rejecting all cookies means you give up a lot of great Web content and services. Accepting all cookies leaves your privacy vulnerable to invasion. And being asked every time a cookie is about to be put on your computer can be very annoying, indeed.

That's where a program like CookiePal comes to the rescue. It enables you to automatically allow some sites put cookies on your computer, but it automatically rejects others. You tell it which sites to accept and which to reject. It's very easy to use, and also enables you to easily delete cookies.

It's the solution I use. For sites at which I get great extra services by allowing cookies, I tell CookiePal to accept cookies. All others I tell CookiePal to reject.

How to Selectively Stop Advertising Cookies

Earlier in this chapter I explained that cookies put on your computer by one Web site usually can't be read by anyone else. Note the word "usually." As I noted, that isn't always the case.

Cookies can be put on your computer not only by Web sites, but also by advertisers—you know, those annoying banner or pop-up ads you see everywhere on the Internet. Many of those advertisers are part of giant advertising networks, such as the DoubleClick network.

Many of these networks have cooked up a way to read and add the same cookie to your hard disk, no matter where you are on the Internet. That way, the networks can build up a substantial profile about you—they can track the sites you visit and the pages you visit on those sites. In short, they can create a personal profile about you, and then sell that profile to advertisers, who personally target obnoxious ads your way.

Not a pretty picture.

There's something you can do about it, though. There has been such an outcry against Double-Click and its advertising cousins that you can opt out of having their cookies track you. All you have to do is go to a Web site, click a button, and their cookies will leave you alone. To opt out of DoubleClick cookies, go to www.doubleclick. net/us/corporate/privacy/privacy/ad-cookie/ and click **Opt Out Click here**. That's all it takes.

Check This Out!

Just about every site I go to uses annoying pop-up ads that appear in a separate browser window. You can kill these pop-ups. Go to a download site, such as ZDNet Downloads at www.zdnet.com/downloads or http://software. xfx.net/, and get a copy of Popup Killer. It's a free program that kills pop-up ads so they stop annoying you.

DoubleClick isn't the only advertising network out there. There's a simple way you can opt out of many others as well. From www.networkadvertising.org/optout_nonppii.asp you're able to opt out of many ad networks from one spot, including DoubleClick's. Figure 11.9 displays the message you get after opting out.

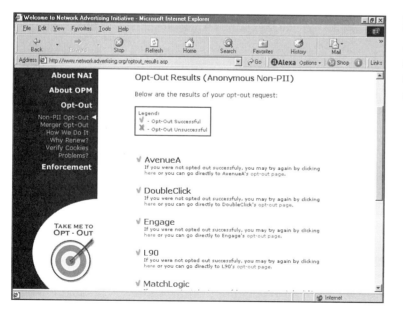

Figure 11.9

Success! The big ad networks are now unable to track your computer use with their cookies.

The Least You Need to Know

◆ Web cookies can invade your privacy, but they also enable you to get special Web services and content.

◆ Microsoft Internet Explorer stores cookies in the Windows\Cookies or Windows\Profiles\UserName\Cookies directory. You can delete individual cookies there.

◆ Netscape Navigator stores cookies in the \Program Files\Netscape\Users\Username directory. You can delete the cookies.txt file there, but you can't edit it.

◆ Both Explorer and Navigator enable you to automatically reject cookies, or can also ask whether to accept cookies every time a Web site wants to serve one.

◆ Windows XP and Internet Explorer 6 enable you to customize the way that your computer handles cookies.

◆ The best way to handle cookies is to use a cookie-killer utility, such as CookiePal.

How to Make Sure Internet Sites Don't Abuse Your Privacy

In This Chapter

◆ How to check out a site's privacy policies

◆ Learning to decipher a privacy policy's fine print

◆ How to use Internet Explorer 6 or Windows XP to get information about a site's privacy policies

◆ Privacy dangers posed by financial sites and job-hunting sites

◆ How TRUSTe protects your privacy

◆ How to fill out Web registration forms and be sure your privacy isn't invaded

It's sad but true: Web sites, including very good Web sites, and often your favorite ones, might invade your privacy. They can watch what you do, gather information about you, and sell that information to the highest bidder.

But if you're worried about that, there's a lot you can do, as you'll see in this chapter. I'll show you how to check out a Web site's privacy policies, how to protect your privacy when filling out registration forms, and more.

Checking Out a Site's Privacy Policies

Your first line of defense against sites invading your privacy is a simple kind of diligence—check out a site's privacy policies before you give it any information.

Sounds easy, right? Unfortunately, it's not. The first problem is that Web sites frequently hide their privacy policies so deep within their pages, you have to be a miner to find them. And even when you do find them, the language they're in often only vaguely resembles English—it's in classic legalese.

Still, if you work a bit at it, you should be able to check out a site's policies. Some sites include a link to the policies at the top or bottom of the page. When it's at the bottom of the page, the link is frequently in very small type. If you don't find it at either of those places, look for a Help section or an FAQ (Frequently Asked Questions) section. Most sites have search boxes in which you can type the word privacy and do a search. One way or another, you should find it. If you don't, don't give the site your personal information.

Figure 12.1 shows the publicly posted privacy policy (say *that* three times fast!) of the CNet technology site.

Check This Out!

If you can't find the site's privacy policy anywhere, there's one more solution—send an e-mail to the site and ask for it. You can usually find the e-mail address on the Contact Us page.

Figure 12.1

The lowdown: Here's the privacy policy of the CNet technology site.

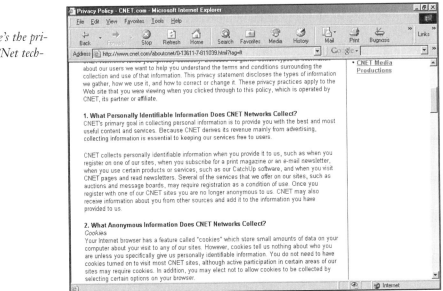

I hate to tell you this, but finding the policy is the easy part. Now you have to actually understand it. Be prepared to plow through some pretty dense language.

If you stick at it, you'll be able to decipher it. So read on; the next section tells you what you need to know.

What Does All That Fine Print Mean?

Most privacy policies are written in a language that only lawyers could love. But when you throw away much of the verbiage, what you're looking for is really quite simple. Here's what to watch out for:

- ◆ **Does the site collect personally identifiable information about you without your knowledge?** Many Web sites track your activities when you're on them. You want to know whether that information is used to personally identify you or not. And if it is, you'd like to be warned about it. In general, you'd prefer a site not to gather personally identifiable information, but if it does, you should know about it.

- ◆ **What kind of personally identifiable information is gathered—and how is it gathered?** If the site does get personal information about you, what kind of information is it? Your e-mail address? More? And how does it gather that information?

Check This Out!

Don't be surprised if you don't find anything on a Web site's privacy page about Web bugs and cookies—many don't bother to tell you about them. As a practical matter, though, almost every Web site you visit uses cookies, and many of them use Web bugs. If you don't find mention of them in a privacy policy, assume that the site uses them.

- ◆ **Does the site use cookies and Web bugs?** Cookies are bits of data put on your computer to track what you do on a site, and to help you customize your experience on the site. Web bugs are tiny graphics put on Web pages that can track what you do on the site. Find out whether the site uses either of these technologies.

- ◆ **What kind of anonymous information does the Web site gather?** Web sites frequently gather information about the surfing habits of their users and aggregate that information as a way of telling advertisers who their audience is. You need to know if anonymous information is gathered, and if so, what kind of information it is.

- ◆ **How does the site use the information?** Does it use it to target advertising? Will it send you unsolicited e-mail based on your surfing activities? See if you can find out how information about you is used.

◆ **Does the site share the information with other businesses?** Many sites share information that they gather with other businesses, often as a way to get money. You want to make sure that no personal information about you is shared unless you give your consent. And you want to make sure that if non-identifiable information is shared about you, that it can't be used by a third party to identify you.

◆ **Can you opt out of certain services?** You're on more e-mail lists than you know. Some sites allow you to opt out of receiving "special offers" and other kinds of spam.

◆ **Is your credit card information or buying habits shared with other sites?** This is a big no-no. You don't want this done—period.

◆ **Can you opt out of mailings?** Web sites ask for your e-mail address not because they're curious (although, I must admit, most Webmasters I've know are very curious people, indeed), but because they want to send you e-mail asking you to buy things or to visit the site. You want to be able to opt out of getting those mailings— in other words, you don't want to get them. You should be allowed to opt out, and you should be shown how to do it.

◆ **Is there contact information?** To whom can you complain if you think your privacy has been violated? There should be a person or e-mail address to whom you can send your complaints.

◆ **Can you update your personal information?** If the site does gather personal information about you, you should be able to view it and change it if it's inaccurate.

Check This Out!

A while back, Web sites began dropping like flies and going out of business or being sold—and many of those sites contained enormous amounts of private information about people, including their buying habits and credit card numbers. In some instances, when Web sites have gone out of business, they've tried to sell personal information about people to businesses, even though they promised that they would never do it. In fact, the Federal Trade Commission successfully sued Toysmart.com for violating its privacy statement by agreeing to sell information about users of its Web site. Toysmart ended up not selling the data. Similar actions by the courts have taken place against other sites as well.

Using Internet Explorer 6 or Windows XP to Check Out Web Sites

Internet Explorer 6 or later and Windows XP give you a great tool to check out Web sites. Built into them is a technology that can give you immediate access to a site's privacy policies.

When you're using Internet Explorer 6 or better, and you're visiting a Web site whose privacy policy you want to read, choose **Privacy Report** from the **View** menu. A screen that lists cookies that have attempted to be placed on your computer appears (see Figure 12.2).

To check out the privacy policy of the site, highlight the cookie and click on **Summary.** The privacy policy of the site is shown, as seen in Figure 12.3.

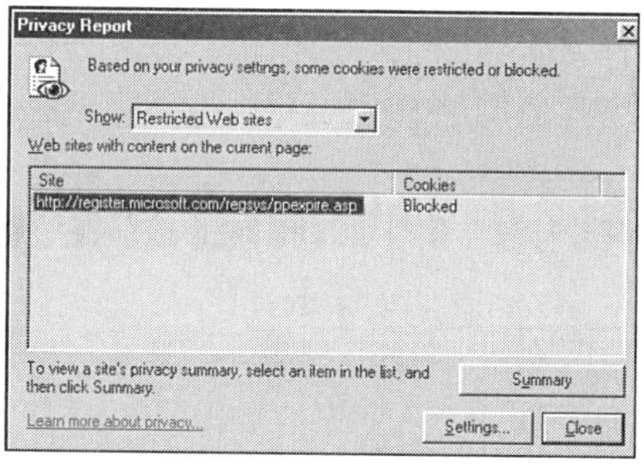

Figure 12.2

Internet Explorer 6 enables you to view cookies that have been attempted to be put on your computer ...

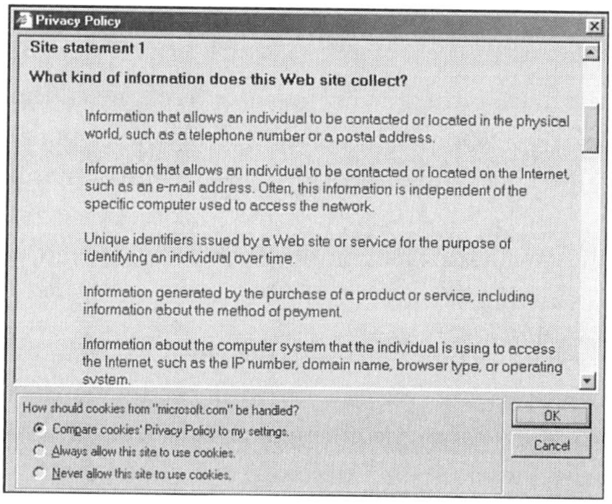

Figure 12.3

... and then enables you to check out the privacy policy of the site.

Well, in theory at least, you see the privacy policy of the site. In practice, you aren't able to read that many privacy policies. That's because you're only able to read the privacy policy if the site puts it into a special format called the Platform for Privacy Preferences (*P3P*). And very few Web sites, as of this writing, put their policy into that form.

Techno Talk

P3P was developed so that there could be a standard way for people to get privacy information about Web sites. The standard requires that the information be put into a format that can be read by Web browsers such as Internet Explorer 6. And it requires that certain basic information be included in that policy. However, nothing in P3P makes sure that those policies are actually followed; that's left up to consumers and watchdog groups.

What You Need to Know About Financial and Job Search Web Sites

The Web sites that contain the most sensitive information about you are financial sites—online banks, brokerages, and similar destinations. They have your account numbers, your holdings, often your credit card number, your bank information, and much more. And so they have quite sophisticated profiles about your financial life, and private life as well.

That's pretty dangerous stuff. The federal government, for once, recognized the potential privacy dangers inherent in that; as a result, provisions about privacy were built into the Gramm-Leacy-Fliley Act, a law about financial services. The law requires that financial companies—both online as well as the bricks-and-mortar type—protect your private information. It also requires that the businesses let you opt out of having your personal information being sent or sold to other businesses.

There's only one problem: Financial sites regularly violate the law, according to the Center for Democracy and Technology. According to a study of 100 financial Web sites by the group, only 22 percent of the sites gave customers an easy way online to opt out of having information about them shared with others. And even worse, some online mortgage companies don't give their customers any notice at all about their privacy practices, which is a violation of the law.

Check This Out!

If you're interested at all in privacy issues, the Privacy Foundation site at www. privacyfoundation.org is a great resource. It has reports, advice, and columns chock-full of help for all kinds of privacy issues.

Another kind of site that has a great deal of personal information about you is a job-hunting site—after all, not only does it have your resumé, but it often asks personal questions, as well—often questions that employers might not be allowed to ask by law.

A report by the privacy advocacy group the Privacy Foundation, criticizes several job-hunting sites, particularly the well-known Monster.com site. According to the group, the site has discussed selling resumé information to marketers, and it posts resumés from private sites without the job seekers even knowing about it. And a collegiate job service called MonsterTRAK asks for information from people that the law bans employers from asking—things such as age, race, and gender.

You Can Trust TRUSTe

When it comes to checking out the privacy policies of Web sites, the TRUSTe site at www.truste.com is one of your best friends. It's an independent service with the sole purpose of making sure that people's privacy is protected online. It has a logo that Web sites that follow its privacy policies can display on their sites (see Figure 12.4).

Privacy Policy [x]
 	
Privacy Summary for:
 	
    Microsoft Corporation
    To read this Web site's complete privacy policy, click here.
 	
Privacy Certificate:
 	
    TRUSTe
 	
    Register a dispute
 	
Site statement 1
What kind of information does this Web site collect?
 	
How should cookies from "microsoft.com" be handled?
○ Compare cookies' Privacy Policy to my settings.
○ Always allow this site to use cookies.
○ Never allow this site to use cookies.   [OK] [Cancel]
	Figure 12.4
	
	You can trust the TRUSTe logo to protect your privacy.

TRUSTe creates standards about how personal information can be used that's gathered by Web sites. If a Web site wants to use the TRUSTe logo on its site, it has to adhere to those standards—and TRUSTe checks to make sure that the standards are adhered to. TRUSTe also resolves privacy complaints filed against Web sites that display the TRUSTe logo. TRUSTe sets rules so that you control your own private information and keeps Web sites from misusing information you give to them.

A Web site with the TRUSTe seal is a site that adheres to TRUSTe standards. In general, the standards include the following:

Check This Out!

You can complain to TRUSTe if a site displaying its logo invades your privacy. Have you gone to a site with a TRUSTe logo and suspected the site has invaded your privacy? Don't just sit there and stew—take action! Go to www.etrust.com/users/users_watchdog.html and fill out a form complaining about the site. TRUSTe will investigate.

♦ The site has implemented a privacy policy and made it readily available on the Web site.

♦ The site discloses precisely how it collects and uses information about visitors to the site.

♦ Consumers are given the opportunity to control their private information.

♦ The site protects the security of the information it gathers so that it can't be stolen.

Protect Your Privacy When Filling Out Registration Forms

To get any kind of special service on the Web, you have to fill out a registration form. It doesn't matter whether you want to get special information from a Web site, get a free e-mail newsletter, or buy something from a site.

These registration forms can gather very personal information about you. But there's a whole lot you can do to protect your privacy when filling out these forms. Because, after all, you're the one filling in the information on the forms—the power is in your hands. Follow this advice for filling out forms to protect your name—and your demographic information.

♦ **Look for the opt-out policy.** Most Web forms tell you, in very innocuous terms, that they're going to send you mass or targeted e-mail, or they're going to let advertisers send you e-mail. In essence, that means you've been put onto someone's list. Usually, the site lets you opt out—that is, ask that you not be put on the list so that no mail is sent to you. It's usually a small check box, somewhere at the bottom of the form. Read the form carefully to see whether you need to check or uncheck the box if you don't want to receive mail. It's often hard to tell.

♦ **Only fill out the fields that are required.** Most registration forms have fields that you're required to fill out in order to register, and they also include many fields you don't need to fill out. Often, people miss the distinction. Those fields you need to fill out often have asterisks or other small marks next to them, or note that they're required. Fill those out, and leave the others blank.

♦ **Is there a way to correct errors in the registration information you give?** Your personal information, in the long run, should belong to you. So if you want to correct it, there should be a way for you to do so.

♦ **Read the fine print.** You might be surprised at what you agree to when you fill out a registration form. Even though most of the fine print is dull and written in legalese, read all of it before signing up. You don't want to find out that you've given away your first-born child (then again, maybe you do ....).

◆ **Get a second, free e-mail address that you use whenever you enter your e-mail address.** Web sites ask for e-mail addresses so that they (and their advertisers) can send you e-mail. If you don't want your main e-mail box littered with junk, get a second (or third or fourth), free e-mail address, and use that when filling in your information. That way, the junk mail is sent to the other addresses, not your main one. You can get free e-mail addresses at many sites, including www.yahoo.com, www.hotmail.com, www.bigfoot.com, www.zdnet.com, and many others.

◆ **When all else fails, lie.** Let's not beat around the bush here—feel free to lie on Web registration forms. It's a war, after all—they want to invade your privacy and you want to protect it—and all's fair in love and war. If they ask questions that are too personal, they should expect to be lied to. They want to know your profession? Fine; no problem. Tell them you're the Emperor of Ice Cream. Want to know your annual income? Sure, let them go ahead and ask—it's $2.5 billion. How many children do you have? Thirty-seven sounds like a good round number. Look at it this way: They can't invade your privacy if nothing you tell them is true.

Check This Out!

There are many other ways you can protect your privacy when visiting Web sites, such as blocking cookies, watching out for Web bugs, and surfing anonymously. For more information, see Chapter 10, "I Spy: How to Protect Yourself Against Spyware and Web Bugs," Chapter 11, "They're Not Very Sweet: What You Can Do About Cookies," and Chapter 13, "How to Surf Anonymously Without a Trace."

The Least You Need to Know

◆ Before giving information to a site, check out its privacy policies. If you can't find them at the top or bottom of the site's front page, look for the Help or FAQ section of the site.

◆ When you read a privacy policy, look in particular at whether the site gathers personally identifiable information about you, and at how that information is used.

◆ Look for the TRUSTe trustmark logo on a Web site—it means the site adheres to TRUSTe's privacy standards.

◆ Use the opt out options on registration forms if you don't want to receive a lot of e-mail.

◆ Only fill out the required fields in a registration form—these are often marked with an asterisk.

◆ Feel free to lie about your profession, income, and other questions that seem too personal.

Chapter 13

How to Surf Anonymously Without a Trace

In This Chapter

- ◆ What information Web sites can find out about you from your browser
- ◆ How to delete information out of your browser's cache
- ◆ Making sure that no one can see which Web sites you've recently visited
- ◆ Keeping your e-mail address and Usenet Newsgroup information private
- ◆ How you can surf the Web anonymously

When you head onto the Web with your browser, you announce all kinds of personal information about yourself: your e-mail address, what newsgroups you're interested in, recent Web sites you've visited ... and a whole lot more.

In this chapter, you'll see all the kinds of information that your browser can reveal about you—and you'll see how with just a little bit of work, you can protect your privacy so that it need not tell the world about you, no matter how much of a blabbermouth it is.

All the Information Your Browser Reveals About You

By merely pointing your browser to a site, you can reveal an enormous amount of information about yourself. Just what kind of information? You probably won't believe it. Read this list and weep.

- **Detailed information about your browsing habits.** What pages do you click to on a site? Do you prefer reading about sports or financial information? All that and more can be revealed by the use of cookies that Web sites place on your hard disk, as well as by other techniques. For information about how to handle cookies to protect your privacy, turn to Chapter 11, "They're Not Very Sweet: What You Can Do About Cookies."

- **Your IP number.** An IP number, such as 24.234.23.23, identifies your computer on the Internet. If a hacker knows your IP number, it's easier for you to be attacked.

- **Your e-mail address.** Yes, your browser reveals that about you, as well. Isn't anything secret any more?

- **Detailed information about the newsgroups you've visited.** It can reveal the newsgroups you've visited, the headers you've downloaded, and any graphics files you've viewed. (Of course, you haven't visited any adult-oriented newsgroups. But some spammers post naughty pictures to all the newsgroups they can think of, so you might still have some explaining to do to.) And Internet Explorer can even reveal the full text of everything you've read in those newsgroups.

- **Your user ID.** When you install Internet Explorer and Netscape Navigator, you're asked to provide a user ID. Web sites can look inside your browser and find out what it is.

- **What browser and operating system you use.** No great surprise here: Your browser can tell a Web site whether it's Internet Explorer or Netscape Navigator, what version of Explorer or Navigator it is, and what operating system you use.

- **Whether you're using a PC or a Macintosh.** It might also be able to know if you're using a different operating system, such as Linux.

- **Recent Internet sites that you've visited.** It's easy for a Web site to find out which sites you've visited. Your browser keeps this kind of information in several places. It keeps it in the URL window itself at the top of the browser; click the drop-down arrow to the right to see the history of sites you've visited. And it keeps even more detailed information in a special area of your computer called a *browser cache*. That cache contains not merely a record of where you've visited, but graphics, text, and other pieces of the actual Web pages.

It's pretty amazing what your browser can reveal about you, isn't it? But don't worry—you don't need to give away all this information every time you visit a Web page. Because, as I show you in the rest of this chapter, there's a lot you can do to protect your privacy when your browser hits the Web.

Techno Talk

When you visit a Web page, the information on that page is downloaded to your computer, including all the graphics, the HTML pages, and anything else on that page, so that you can view the page. All the elements of the page are put into a directory on your hard disk called a cache directory or **browser cache**. That's why, when you hit your browser's **Back** button, you're able to see the page or pages you visited so quickly—it's viewing them from a cache on your computer, and doesn't have to go out to the Internet and grab them.

What Your Browser Cache Tells About You

As I explained before, when you visit Web sites, entire Web pages and all their elements are kept in a special browser cache on your computer in a special directory. Exactly where these files are kept depends on the browser you use and its version number. However, Internet Explorer usually puts them in the C:\Windows\Temporary Internet Files folder, and Netscape Navigator puts them in C:\Program Files\Netscape\Users\username\ Cache, where username is your Netscape username. Figure 13.1 shows the Netscape cache on my computer.

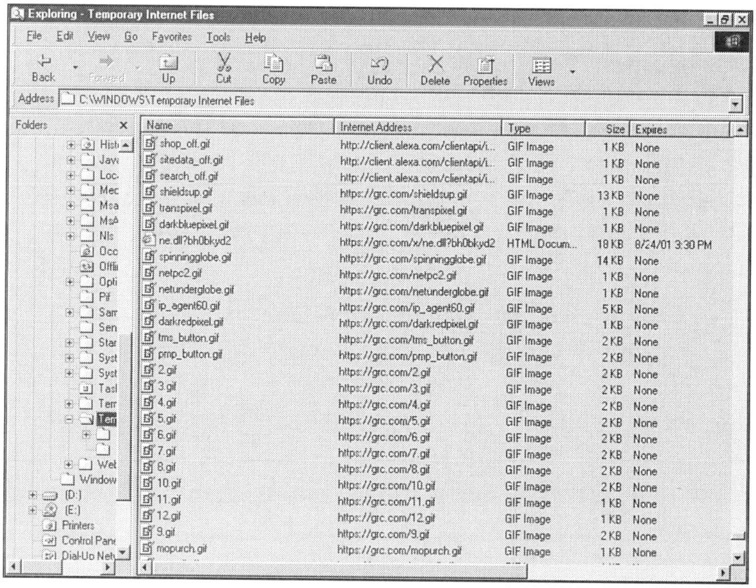

[Screenshot: Exploring - Temporary Internet Files window showing cache contents]

Figure 13.1

Here are just some of the contents of my Internet Explorer cache directory.

As you can see in this picture, it's pretty tough for normal human beings like you (assuming, of course, that you're a normal human being—a big assumption, I know) to see what's going on in your cache, because it looks like a bunch of weird-looking names. But in fact, there are ways to reconstruct the Web pages you've visited from this browser cache. You can even download programs from the Internet that can do that for you.

It's pretty easy to clean out your browser caches. Both Internet Explorer and Netscape Navigator have ways to let you do that. In Internet Explorer, choose **Internet Options** from the **Tools** menu. Then, in the section under Temporary Internet Files, click **Delete Files.** That cleans out all the files in your Internet Explorer browser cache (see Figure 13.2).

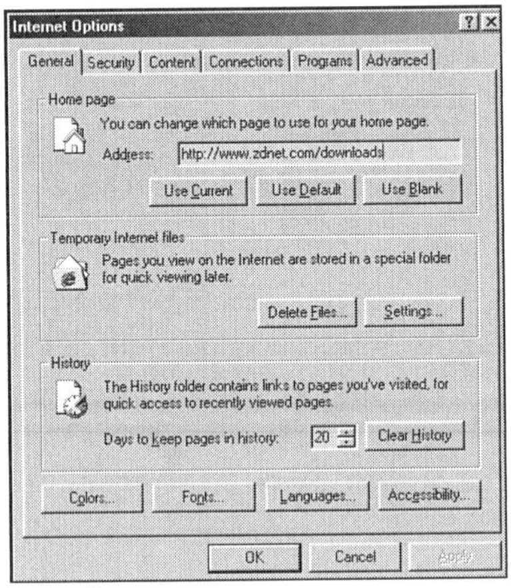

Figure 13.2

Here's how to clean out your Internet Explorer cache.

Internet Explorer also has a neat feature that cleans out your browser's cache for you every time you shut down the program. That means you don't have to do it yourself—your browser does your housecleaning for you. To set up this feature, choose **Internet Options** from the **Tools** menu. Then click the **Advanced** tab. Scroll down until you see the Security section. Then check the box next to **Empty Temporary Internet Files when browser is closed.** Now, every time you close down your browser, your cache is cleaned, with no muss and no fuss.

To clean out your Netscape Navigator 4.0 cache, choose **Preferences** from the **Edit** menu. Then click the **+** sign next to Advanced, and choose **Cache.** Click **Clear Disk Cache.** That action deletes all the files from your browser cache. You can also click **Clear Memory Cache.** Doing so deletes all the files currently in your computer's memory. If you use a version other than Navigator 4, the procedure might be slightly different.

Check This Out!

It can be kind of a pain to have to remember to constantly clean out your browser cache. Many programs, though, automatically clean your cache for you, at intervals you specify. For example, Cache and Cookie Washer (there are separate versions for Internet Explorer and for Netscape Navigator) and Cache Killer Pro do that for you. To get them, and other similar programs, go to any of many popular Internet download sites, such as the ZDNet Software Library at www.zdnet.com/downloads. You're able to download them and try them out, but if you want to keep using one, you're expected to pay a fee to the author of the program.

Hiding Your Browsing History

Your browser has a much better memory than you do. (At least, it has a better memory than *I* do. But then, I can't even remember simple things like where I put my car keys whenever I need to leave the house.) It remembers where you've been on the Web. And it's a blabbermouth—it'll hand over that information to any Web site that wants it. How indiscriminating!

If you'd like your browser to keep its mouth shut and not reveal where you've been, you can clean out your history list. It's easy to do. In Internet Explorer, it's on the same screen from which you can delete files from your cache. To get there, first choose **Internet Options** from the **Tools** menu. Then in the section under History, click on **Clear History.** That deletes all your history files.

In Netscape Navigator, choose **Preferences** from the **Preferences** menu. Then click **Clear History.** You can also clear the listing of recent files in your location bar by clicking **Clear Location Bar.** If you don't like continually having to kill your history list, you can kill it altogether. In Internet Explorer, in the History portion of the Internet Options screen, set the days to keep pages in history to zero. In Netscape Navigator, set the pages in history to expire after zero days. In both instances, you're able to browse without a history list.

Hiding Your E-mail Address

When you surf the Web, your browser can reveal your e-mail address to the world. It's not that hard for sites to find it out.

However, if you do a little bit of work, you can hide your e-mail address—or even put in a false e-mail address if you like. You only need to change your browser settings or the settings in your e-mail program.

In Netscape Navigator, hiding your e-mail address is a straightforward process. If you use Netscape 4.0 or above, choose **Preferences** from the **Edit** menu. Then click **Identity.** Three fields show up onscreen: one for your name, one for your e-mail address, and one that displays your organization. Delete the text from any of those that you wish to keep secret. (Write down the information somewhere, though, so that you can put it back in if you wish.) Your e-mail address and name are now hidden when you visit a Web page.

In Microsoft Internet Explorer, click the **Mail** button and choose **Read Mail.** Doing so launches your e-mail program. You now have to delete your name and e-mail address from your e-mail program. Every program handles this differently, so check your manual on how to do it.

In Outlook, you do this in slightly different ways, depending on the version of the program you have; but the general idea in all of them is the same. In Outlook 2000, choose **Services** from the **Tools** menu. Then click your e-mail account (or accounts). Click **Properties.** Fields for your name, e-mail address, and organization are displayed (see Figure 13.3). Delete the text from any of those that you want to keep secret. (Write down the information somewhere, though, so that you can put it back in if you wish.) Your e-mail address and name are now hidden when you visit a Web page. Be aware that this makes it more difficult for you when you want to send e-mail—you need to put all that information back in so that people know who's sending them the mail. Security and privacy have their price at times.

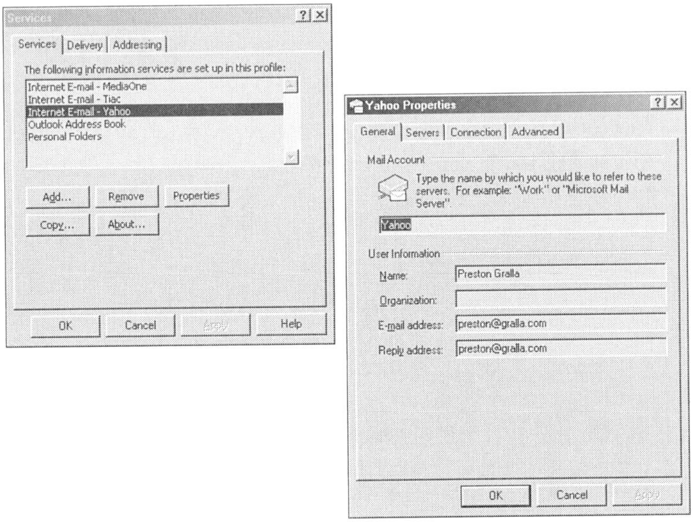

Figure 13.3

Use this screen to hide your e-mail address in Outlook.

Keep Newsgroup Information from Prying Eyes

When you're browsing the Web, sites can look into your browser and see information about how you use Usenet newsgroups. Sites are able to see your address information, and might also be able to see which newsgroups you read and subscribe to.

In Internet Explorer 4 and above, you have to first launch the Outlook Express newsgroup reader. To do that, click the **Mail** button and then choose **Read News.** Outlook Express's newsgroup reader loads. Right-click your newsgroup server. Fields there display your name, your e-mail address, and your organization. Delete the text from any of those that you want to keep secret. (Write down the information somewhere, though, so that you can put it back in if you wish.) Your e-mail address and name are now hidden when you visit a Web page.

Check This Out!

The simplest way to make sure that no site can check what newsgroups and messages you're reading is to not bother with newsgroup software. Instead, you can use the Web itself to read and post to newsgroups. Go to Google Groups at http://groups.google.com/ to participate in newsgroups right from the Web. If you're worried about anonymity, simply don't use your real name or e-mail address. And there are other ways to post anonymously to newsgroups. To see how, turn to Chapter 17, "Staying Anonymous with Anonymous Remailers," and Chapter 19, "Protecting Your Privacy on Internet Newsgroups and Discussion Areas."

You might also like to make sure that Web sites can't tell which messages and headers you've been reading in newsgroups. To do that, click the newsgroup server. A listing of all the groups to which you're subscribed is displayed. Right-click each one, choose **Properties,** and then click the **Local Files** tab. To get rid of all the information about what you've read in each of the newsgroups, click the **Delete** button. Everything you've read in those newsgroups is deleted.

Of course, still listed are the newsgroups that you subscribe. To hide that, you have to unsubscribe to the newsgroups. To do that, right-click the newsgroup and choose **Unsubscribe from this newsgroup.**

In Netscape Navigator 4.0 and above, follow the directions as outlined in the previous section to hide your e-mail address. That should do the trick for you. To hide other details about newsgroups, also choose **Preferences** from the **Edit** menu and click **Identity.** Delete the information in the other fields listed there, then click the **Mail Server** category, and delete information listed there. If your server information doesn't show up, you can get to it by clicking **Mail & Groups** instead of Identity.

In Navigator 3.0, select **Mail and News Preferences** from the **Options** menu. Then click the **Servers** tab and delete information from there. After that, click the **Identity** tab, and delete that information as well.

Surfing Anonymously Without a Trace

As you can see from the rest of this chapter, surfing the Web while protecting your privacy takes a whole lot of work. In fact, you can spend all your time deleting your cache, killing cookies, hiding your e-mail address ... which leaves you no time at all to surf the Web. (Good solution, in a weird way, I guess; if you don't surf the Web, you don't need to worry about protecting your privacy there.)

In fact, there's a much easier way. You can use a Web site designed to let you surf anonymously. It's simple to do. You go to a Web site designed to hide your identity when you browse the Web. Then you type in the name of the Web site you want to visit. When you do that, you go to the site you want to visit, but all traces of your identity are wiped clean. No cookies. No e-mail address. No newsgroup information. No nothing. Nada.

In a variation on the theme, you can go to a site and download a small button that appears in Internet Explorer. When you want to surf anonymously, you click that little button, and that's it—you're anonymous.

There are several of these kinds of services around. Many are free, but increasingly, you have to pay for them. The best-known site is the Anonymizer at www.anonymizer.com. It has a free service as well as a paid service that offers more protection and features. I haven't yet found it worth my while to pay for the extra features, but check it out—it might be worth it to you.

Check This Out!

Here's yet another way that a Web browser can invade your privacy: In Internet Explorer 5.0, when you bookmark a page, the site that you bookmark might be able to know that you've bookmarked it—and it knows the exact time that you bookmarked it, and the precise page that you bookmarked. So if you're at a large site with a lot of pages, the site is able to track all the pages on the site that you've bookmarked.

An excellent free site for anonymous surfing is SafeWeb at www.safeweb.com. In fact, this site is so good that many people in China, whose government blocks access to many sites, use SafeWeb as a way to get around the government limiting their access to sites such as the *Washington Post* news site. In fact, the U.S. government has even been funding SafeWeb so that people in China can use the Internet free of censorship.

I could explain how this anonymous surfing works, but it would get pretty technical pretty fast (and pretty dull, too). It has to do with things like proxy servers ... and I can see your eyes glazing over already. So I'll spare you the details. Believe me, though, it works. If you want a few details about proxy servers, though, check out the nearby sidebar.

Notes
Proxy servers can keep you safe because they hide your identity from Web sites. Here's how they work. When you want to visit a Web site, you don't go directly to the site. Instead, your request goes to a proxy server. The server goes to the site, and grabs the page, and you then get the page from the server. So you never actually visit the site yourself, and your identity is kept safe.

Protect Your Identity Online– Become Schizophrenic

How can you be in two places at once if you're not anywhere at all? Easy. Use one of the new identity-hiding and identity-switching programs that make it easy to hide your identity online. These programs do more than merely hide your identity—they actually enable you to create different identities for yourself when you surf online, complete with different e-mail addresses, different newsgroups information, and more for each. Kind of like that old movie *The Three Faces of Eve*, except you're in control, not your different personae. And there isn't an evil one ... unless, of course, you want to create one.

You download these programs to your computer, and they then enable you to create different personalities with your browser. As of this writing, these identity-switching programs haven't been released, but by the time you read this, they might be. The networking company Novell has one called DigitalMe at www.digitalme.com. And a company called Zero Knowledge Systems at www.zks.net, has software called Freedom that not only enables you to create several different identities, but also protects your privacy in many other ways.

The Least You Need to Know

- Browsers can reveal a surprising amount of private information about you.
- Delete information out of your browser's cache directory and kill your history list to keep your browsing habits private.
- To participate in newsgroups without people knowing your identity, go to http://groups.google.com/.
- You can easily delete information about your e-mail address and newsgroups you visit from your browser, so Web sites can't find it.
- For the most privacy when browsing the Web, go to a site that lets you surf anonymously, such as www.anonymizer.com.

Part 4

Snoopers Everywhere: Keeping Safe When Using E-mail, Instant Messaging, and Chatting

Remember that e-mail you sent last month about your company's private plans for expansion into Bali? A snooper could have read it. Or that e-mail your sweetheart sent you last week, pledging undying love? Someone might have intercepted it en route and be cackling about it right now. All those times you've chatted and sent instant messages with people—the world might be laughing at them right now.

And think of all the junk mail you get in your e-mail inbox—what people refer to as *spam*. Get-rich-quick offers, scams, solicitations to visit pornographic Web sites—all that and more litter your e-mail box.

Well, Chucky, there's good news on the way. You can protect your privacy and you can fight back against spammers. This part of the book will show you how. You'll learn how e-mail works and how hackers can snoop into it. You'll find out about dangers in e-mail, such as e-mail viruses. And you'll see how you can vanquish them all. You'll even learn how you can send "anonymous e-mail" so that you can send e-mail and participate in Internet newsgroups without people knowing your true identity.

Chapter **14**

Dangerous Delivery: What Dangers Are There in E-mail?

In This Chapter

- ◆ How others can snoop through your e-mail
- ◆ Why your e-mail can legally be read by your place of employment
- ◆ What is spam?
- ◆ What you need to know about e-mail spoofing and mail bombs
- ◆ How viruses can spread via e-mail

E-mail … can't live with it, can't live without it. It's one of the most revolutionary ways ever created that enables people to communicate. It has changed the way we do business, the way we communicate with family and friends, and the way we live our lives. It's been a great boon to us all.

But there are some dangers in e-mail. Because the Internet is not a very secure place, your e-mail can be intercepted and read by others. You can be swamped by unsolicited e-mail, called *spam*, and your computer can get a virus from opening an attachment to an e-mail message. In this chapter, we'll look at all the dangers e-mail poses—and in future chapters, you'll see how you can keep yourself safe.

How E-mail Works

To better understand the dangers of e-mail, you need to know how e-mail works. When you send a message, it doesn't immediately go directly to the recipient. Instead, it's sent to a special computer called a *mail server*.

Techno Talk _____

There are two different kinds of **mail servers**—you connect to one to send mail and connect to another to retrieve it. The server that sends mail uses a protocol called POP3 (for Post Office Protocol 3). The one that receives mail uses a protocol called SMTP (for Simple Main Transfer Protocol).

The mail server takes your mail, and sends it over the Internet to the mail server of the recipient. The recipient then connects to his or her mail server and retrieves the message.

The mail server, and the Internet, needs information in order to deliver your message, in the same way that the post office needs addressing information to deliver your mail (that's assuming that they *do* deliver the mail, of course, which is sometimes a risky proposition). In the same way, when you send an e-mail message, extra information needs to be added—and because this is the Internet we're talking about, your mail program adds more than just addressing information.

To handle this extra kind of information, an e-mail message is divided into two parts: the *header* and the *body*.

- The body is the message that you compose.
- The header contains the information that's needed to deliver the e-mail message to the proper address.

There's not a whole lot you need to know about the body of the message—after all, you composed it! But the header … ah, now, that's where things get tricky. Understanding the header is key to knowing things such as how your e-mail can be snooped on and how you can combat spam. So let's take a closer look at the e-mail header.

The most basic information in an e-mail header is stuff you put there yourself. You type in the e-mail address of the person to whom you're sending the mail. You put in the subject of the message. If you're sending copies to others, you put in their e-mail addresses. You see all this information as you compose the message.

The program puts other information into the header, as well, though. Usually, you don't see this information. When you compose an e-mail message, your e-mail program automatically adds information to the header. It adds the date and time that the message was composed and two other pieces of information: It creates a message ID, which is a super-long number, followed by your e-mail address; and most e-mail programs put in a piece of information identifying the program that created the e-mail.

Check This Out!

Usually, you only view a small portion of the header information in a piece of e-mail—important information such as addresses, the subject line, and the date and time. But e-mail programs also let you see the full header of an e-mail message. Seeing the whole header can help you stop spam. To view the full message header in your e-mail program, read carefully through the documentation—very carefully, because that information is often buried deep. In Microsoft Outlook, when you're viewing a message, choose **Options** from the **View** menu; you see the header in the scrollable window in the screen that appears.

You can see header information as shown by Microsoft Outlook in Figure 14.1.

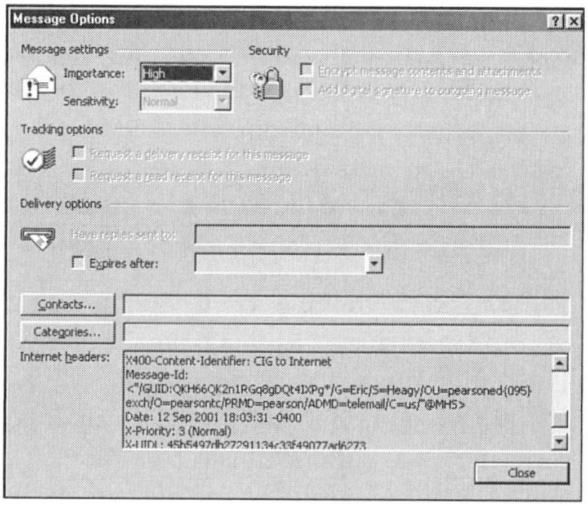

Figure 14.1

Header information in an e-mail, as shown in Microsoft Outlook.

So, for example, if your e-mail address were joe@joejoe.net, and the e-mail program you used to create an e-mail was the Windows version of Eudora Pro, version 3.0, your e-mail program would add that information to the header. Generally, you don't see that information and neither does the person receiving the mail. If you want to, you can see it, but you have to configure your e-mail program in a special way to peek in.

Now, you probably wonder, why spend all this time talking about headers? Because they're key to your e-mail privacy and to stopping Internet spam. Hackers and snoopers can read that header information as your mail message travels across the Internet. And in examining the header information of e-mails you receive, you can help stop spam.

How Your E-mail Can Be Read by Others

Every time you send out a piece of e-mail, you should assume that it can be read by some-one other than the person you sent it to. That memo you wrote about launching a new business on the Internet, selling spotted salamanders and painted turtles online (www.buyamphibians.com, anyone)? Assume your competitor can read it. A nasty note about your boss? Yup, it can be snooped on. A too-friendly note to an old high-school flame of yours? Yes, it can be perused.

That's due to the nature of how e-mail is sent and received. After e-mail leaves your mail server, it's sent over the public Internet.

Hackers and snoopers can examine your mail as it travels. They can read the message. And they can read the headers, which have identifying information about you and who you're sending the e-mail to, so not only can they read your mail, they can also know who you are. Then, armed with your e-mail address, it's a snap to find out where you live, your phone number, and other personal information. And of course, they can read your message itself. So if you're sending any information that you'd like to be kept secret—like your amphibian business plan—you could be in big trouble.

> **Notes**
>
> To keep your e-mail private, you can encrypt it so that only the intended recipient can read it. Encryption scrambles your e-mail so that anyone looking at it (except the recipient) sees a bunch of random letters, num-bers, and other incomprehensible gobbledygook. That way, no one can snoop on your mail as you send it across the Internet.

What to do? If you're worried about e-mail privacy, turn to Chapter 15, "Keeping Your E-mail Private with Encryption," to see what you can do to keep your e-mail private. It tells you what you can do to make sure your www.buyamphibians.com business plan—or any other e-mail—can't be snooped on by anyone as it makes its way across the Internet.

Your Boss Owns Your E-mail

Before you hit the Send button at work, consider this: Your boss owns your e-mail. Any e-mail you send and receive at work can legally be snooped on, saved, and used in any way your employer wants. That means anything—e-mail complaining about your superi-ors, love letters to your spouse (and love letters *not* to your spouse), jokes that you send and receive, that note to your friend in accounting in which you called your boss Big Butt. Every bit of every note is the legal property of your company.

There's not much you can do about your company snooping on your e-mail, because it's perfectly legal. The best advice is this: Never send an e-mail that you don't want your bosses to see. And never, ever call your boss Big Butt.

Check This Out! _____

You're at work. You send an e-mail. Afterward, you think that perhaps you shouldn't have sent it, so you delete it. Think it's gone from your work's e-mail system? Well, it isn't. When you send e-mail at work, it's stored in various places in your company, such as on an e-mail server and possibly on backup disks. Even if you delete it, that e-mail lives on in company archives. Companies have different rules about how long they keep the e-mail. You should assume that it's kept forever.

Why Spam Can Leave a Bad Taste in Your Mouth

If your e-mail inbox is like mine, it's filled—absolutely to the brim—with unsolicited e-mail, the equivalent of junk postal mail; although from my point of view (and many others') it's worse. E-mail you never asked for from people you don't know is called "spam."

It's not uncommon to receive dozens of pieces of spam in a day, and sometimes even more. America Online users are particularly targeted by spammers and tend to receive more spam than do people with other Internet Service Providers. There's all kinds of spam, but most are commercial offers, often offering shady products and services: work-at-home offers, pyramid schemes, products that don't do what they promise, health and diet scams (Herbal Viagra seems to be a big one these days), phony investment opportunities and stock offers … the list goes on and on. All that and more is offered thanks to spam. Much spam is also pornographic in nature, trying to get you to visit for-pay pornographic sites on the Web.

Spam is offensive and litters your mailbox with so much unwanted mail that sometimes it's hard to get to the real mail that needs reading, because there's so much junk. And as spammers get more sophisticated, it's becoming increasingly difficult to figure out what's spam and what isn't. It used to be that you'd see something like "Great business opportunity!!" in the subject line of an e-mail, and you'd know to ignore the message. No longer. Now spammers write in things like "Hi," "About our talk," or "Good news"—anything that makes it sound like the message is from a friend instead of a spammer.

Don't think all you need to do to stop getting spammed is to write back to the spammer, asking that they stop bugging you. This doesn't help. In many cases, they've forged their return address, so

Check This Out! _____

One reason spam is so popular with spammers is because it's so cheap to send out. But because you're paying for your connection time one way or the other, you're actually paying to receive it. You're only paying a few cents at a time, but that does add up. Think of it this way, would you accept a collect call from a telemarketer?

that if you answer them, it goes to a phony address. In other cases, if you write back, the spammer knows that your e-mail address is a valid one—and he sends even *more* spam.

Often, spammers don't want you to know it's them sending you spam. They hide their addresses by faking information such as who is sending you the message. When a spammer does this, it's called "spamoflauge."

There are many ways to fight spam, including getting spam-fighting software that automatically detects spam and deletes it before you ever see it. Most e-mail software, including Microsoft Outlook, includes spam-fighting features. Figure 14.2 shows how you can use Outlook to fight spam.

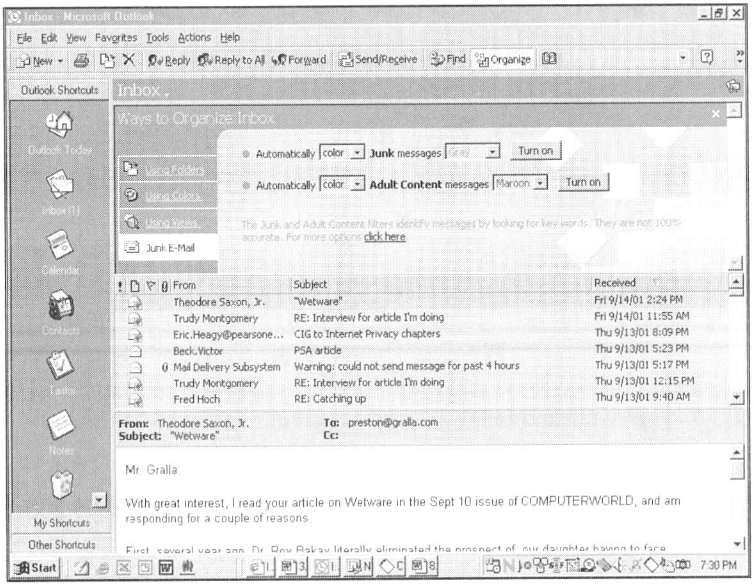

Figure 14.2

Using Outlook's Junk E-mail feature to fight against spam.

There are many other ways to fight spam. For the complete rundown, head to Chapter 16, "Beyond Luncheon Meat: How to Protect Yourself Against Spam."

Why E-mail Spoofing Is No Joke

Imagine this: Your boss gets a message, apparently from you, calling him Big Butt, telling him he's the worst boss you've ever had, and then resigning. Or your spouse gets an e-mail, also apparently from you, saying it's all over between the two of you; you want a divorce. Or a piece of offensive spam is sent to thousands of people with your return address, so it looks as though you've sent it. You, of course, have to put up with the hundreds of angry messages sent in response.

Those are all examples of *e-mail spoofing*. In e-mail spoofing, someone sends an e-mail and forges an address so that it looks as if someone else sent the e-mail. E-mail spoofing is tough to track down. The best way to combat it is to forward any spoofed mail to your Internet Service Provider and ask it to track down the source of the mail. The ISP might or might not be able to do it, but it doesn't hurt to try.

Is There Such a Thing As a Mail Bomb?

Mail bombs. Pretty frightening-sounding words. It conjures up visions of e-mails arriving in your in-box and then blowing your computer to smithereens—or at least crashing your hard disk. The mail simply arrives, and the damage is done; there's nothing you can do about it.

Well, breathe a sigh of relief. It's not going to happen. No one can send you an e-mail message that on its own destroys your computer.

A mail bomb is when someone sends you (or someone else) massive amounts of mail, so that you get dozens or even hundreds of messages or more, all at once. In the worst case, this can overwhelm your ISP's e-mail server, causing it to crash. In the best case, you are forced to delete hundreds of pieces of e-mail—a very annoying, time-consuming chore.

There are a few things you can do if you get a mail bomb. First, alert your ISP and send it the e-mail. The ISP can then try to track down the perpetrator.

Check This Out! _____

I can write about mail bombs from experience. Several years ago my daughter, who was 11 years old, was subjected to a harassing mail bomb. She received dozens of e-mail messages from a single sender in a short period of time, with a not-very-friendly, although not specifically threatening, message. It was quite frightening to her—so much so that she didn't want to use e-mail any more.

The first thing I did was check the address of the sender of the message. It didn't appear to be forged. From the content and wording of the message, including its poor spelling and grammar, I guessed that the message was coming from a pre-teen or young teen, which made it more likely that the address wasn't forged. First, I sent a note to the ISP, telling about the mail bomb. Next, I used America Online's e-mail filters to tell the service to reject any e-mail to my daughter coming from the offending address. It worked like a charm—after I took action, she never received another message from the bomber.

Next, you can take some action on your own. Send a message to the ISP of the sender of the message, telling it about the mail bomb. Depending on the sophistication of the sender of the mail bomb, that might or might not work. If the mail bomb sender doesn't bother to hide his or her identity, then the ISP can take action. If the identity is hidden well, you might not be able to track down the sender of the message.

Many e-mail programs also enable you to reject messages from certain senders, or at least flag them or put them into a common folder where you can easily delete them. Turn to Chapter 16 for details on how to do that. America Online enables you to block messages coming from specific e-mail addresses. Chapter 21, "The Best Rules for Keeping Kids Safe on the Internet" shows you the steps for that.

Can You Get a Virus from an E-mail Message?

Probably more myths surround e-mail and viruses than any other single thing about the Internet. All kinds of crazy messages fly around claiming, among other things, that you can get viruses if someone sends you a simple text message, for example.

Let me put your mind at ease. You can't get a virus by simply reading a text e-mail message.

Now let me disturb you. E-mail *can* spread viruses. But to get a virus from an e-mail, you have to open a document attached to the e-mail or run a program attached to the e-mail. And there is a possibility that damage can be done to your computer by reading HTML e-mail. But there's a very simple way to make sure you don't get a virus from e-mail: *Never* open a file or run a program sent to you via e-mail from someone you don't know. And to be perfectly safe, you shouldn't even run a program sent to you via e-mail from someone you *do* know. If you do open a program from someone you know, though, you should run a virus-checking program, such as Norton Anti-Virus. For information about viruses and preventing them, turn to Chapter 5, "How to Keep Your Computer Safe from Viruses."

Check This Out!

You can't get a virus from merely reading e-mail, but if you're reading HTML-based e-mail, you can get into trouble. Various nasty things can be done to you when you get an HTML message with technologies such as Java, JavaScript, and ActiveX. Some e-mail readers that read HTML enable you to turn those technologies off to keep yourself safe. For example, if you use Outlook, you can turn them off by choosing **Options** from the **Tools** menu, then clicking the Security tab. Now click **Zone settings.** From here, you're able to turn those technologies off. For more information on the technologies' dangers, and more details of turning them off in the Zone settings, turn to Chapter 7, "Keeping Safe from Java, JavaScript, and ActiveX Applets."

You can even get a virus from a document, such as a Word document, sent to you via e-mail. For example, the most widespread virus in recent years, named Melissa after a certain "exotic dancer," was spread by a Word document sent via e-mail. The Word document had a virus in a macro inside it.

Beware of E-mail Web Bugs

The minds of hackers are devious beyond description. How else can we account for e-mail Web bugs?

The bugs we're talking about here aren't the kind that cause a problem with a program. We're talking about bugs as in bugging someone's room. Hackers and Web marketers can use a technique to plant a kind of bug in an e-mail, and in that way track what you do when you read the e-mail.

Web bugs can only work in HTML e-mail—they can't be planted in text e-mail. A Web bug is a tiny, invisible graphic in a format called GIF. That little graphic communicates with a server or a hacker. It can do things such as tell the sender whether you read the e-mail message and what links you clicked, which is why Web marketers use them. And it can also be used along with cookies—little bits of data that Web sites put on your computer—to personally identify you to Web sites. Normally, when a cookie is put on your computer by a Web site, the site isn't able to find out your e-mail address. But when used with a Web bug, the site can learn your e-mail address, can know whether you read e-mail it sends to you, and can put together a very sophisticated profile about who you are and what you do online.

Hackers can also use Web bugs to read your e-mail, although in a limited and roundabout way. If you get an e-mail with a Web bug on it, and forward it to someone, and make a comment on it, a hacker can read the e-mail, along with your comments. That's the only e-mail the hacker is able to read—he or she isn't able to read other e-mail on your computer.

It's not that hard to fight Web bugs. Turn to Chapter 10, "I Spy: How to Protect Yourself Against Spyware and Web Bugs," to learn how to do it.

The Least You Need to Know

◆ Your e-mail can be read by snoopers as it makes its way across the Internet.

◆ Your employer can legally read your e-mail—and many employers do. Don't send e-mail that you don't want read by your boss and others at work.

◆ One way to avoid spam is to use spam-blocking software.

◆ Never open a file or document that you're sent via e-mail from someone you don't know.

Chapter 15

Keeping Your E-mail Private with Encryption

In This Chapter

- ◆ Understanding how encryption can keep your e-mail safe from prying eyes
- ◆ What steps you take when you encrypt and sign your e-mail
- ◆ How to use Pretty Good Privacy to encrypt and sign your e-mail
- ◆ How to use a digital certificate to encrypt and sign your e-mail

As you've seen in other chapters, any time you send e-mail over the Internet, it can be snooped on. One way to make sure that your e-mail stays private is by using *encryption*—a way of scrambling information so that only the intended recipient can read it.

Encryption solves another problem, as well. It's fairly easy for someone to do e-mail spoofing—that is, to forge a message so that it looks as if it comes from someone else. How can people be sure that the message they get from you really *is* from you? And how can you be sure that the message you get from someone really is from the person who it appears to be from? (All this spy stuff is starting to give me a headache!) The answer, again, is encryption, because encryption can create a digital signature that can't be forged. Get an e-mail with a digital signature, and you can be sure it's from who it says it's from. If you send out an e-mail with your digital signature, the recipient can rest assured that it's from you.

In this chapter, I'll take a look at how you can use encryption to keep your e-mail secure and private.

What Is Encryption, Anyway?

What is encryption? You actually know more about encryption than you realize. It's just a fancy way of saying you're applying some kind of secret code to something as a way to try to hide it from someone. Spies use this kind of thing all the time. Here's your chance to play at being James Bond—or at least Maxwell Smart.

Let's take a simple example of encryption. See if you can decipher this sentence: "on'tday ouyay ovelay ogsfray?"

If you ever spoke Pig Latin as a kid, you'd know that the original sentence was, "Don't you love frogs?" When speaking Pig Latin, you take the first letter of a word, move it to the back of the word, and add the letters "ay" to the end of it. That, in essence, is a way of encrypting information—scrambling it so that it doesn't look like the original sentence.

Think of all the times you created secret codes as a kid. (Well, at least *I* was creating them all the time. Then again, maybe I was a weird kid.) Maybe you came up with a code where you substituted the letter z for a, y for b, and so on. You shared the code with a friend, and the two of you could exchange secret messages with each other. It wasn't as though you really *knew* anything so important that it needed to be kept from prying eyes, but still, the whole *idea* of the secret code was what was important.

Now, you don't want to send messages out over the Internet in Pig Latin—at least, not if you want to keep your message private—because there are ways to crack encryption codes, especially when someone has a computer to help. And yes, I'm fairly sure that a hacker with a little bit of time will be able to translate "Assordwaypay orfay ouyay: uitfray oopslay" into "Password for you: Fruit Loops."

> **Notes**
>
> When data is encrypted, a code or set of formulas is used—one so complex that it is extremely difficult for anyone to crack. The code used to encrypt information is called a cipher.

But you *do* want to send out your e-mail using encryption if you want to keep it private. Encryption can be used in another way, as well. It can be used to create a unique digital signature that you attach to your messages so that whoever gets the message knows that the message came from you and not from someone posing as you.

Here's How Encryption Works—And How to Use It

Before you learn how to encrypt your e-mail, it's a good idea to get an understanding of how encryption works. We're not spies or spooks here, so I'm going to keep it pretty basic. You should still learn everything you need.

Encryption is based on the idea of keys. A key on your computer, which is basically a file or program of some sort, is used to encrypt information so that it can't be read. You encrypt your e-mail with a key. Then, another key is used to decrypt the information—put it back into its original form. When sending e-mail on the Internet, you encrypt your e-mail with a key before sending it. That way, no one on the Internet can read your mail, because it's encrypted and looks like a whole bunch of random letters, numbers, and characters. But the person you're sending the message to has a key that can decrypt the e-mail, and when the message gets to his computer, he uses the key and reads the mail.

Encryption programs create these keys. The encryption programs can be completely separate from your e-mail program, or they can be integrated into the program. It's easier to use encryption programs integrated into your e-mail program, because they enable you to do everything from one program: your e-mail software. If you use an encryption program that's separate from your e-mail program, you have to do a bit more juggling to get everything done. Pretty much any good encryption program works with any e-mail software, so you're in luck.

In general, there are two encryption technologies that use keys. One is called *private key encryption* and the other, not surprisingly, is called *public key encryption*. Here's what you need to know about each.

What Is Private Key Encryption?

In private key encryption, you use a key to encrypt your e-mail, and the person receiving the e-mail uses the same key to decrypt it. Sounds simple and secure, doesn't it? Well, there's a problem with it. How do you get that key to the person receiving the e-mail? If you send the key via e-mail, you defeat the whole purpose of encryption, because the key could be intercepted en route, and the e-mail could be read. In that case, for sending and receiving e-mail, private key encryption isn't really workable. (I guess you could mail the key on a floppy disk, but that's getting a bit complicated for our purposes.)

What Is Public Key Encryption—And How Do You Use It?

The other kind of encryption—public key encryption—is much more workable on the Internet. Just about every encryption program uses public key encryption—and I suggest that public key encryption be the only kind of encryption you use.

In public key encryption, the encryption program creates two keys for you. They're a matched pair that work together to encrypt and decrypt e-mail. One key is called your private key, and the other is your public key. Figure 15.1 shows the Pretty Good Privacy (usually called PGP) program creating a pair of keys. The public and private keys work together to encrypt your e-mail when you send it, and they decrypt your e-mail when it's received.

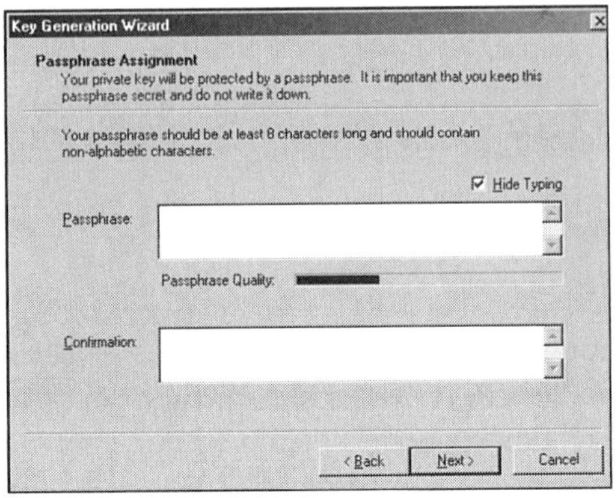

Figure 15.1

Here's the PGP program as it starts to create a set of keys for you—one private and one public.

You're the only person in the world who has your private key, so it stays on your computer. But you send your public key out to the world—you want as many people as possible to have a copy of it. To do that, you can put your public key on a public site on the Internet so that other people can download it. Also, you can attach your public key to your e-mail messages, so that anyone who receives your message can have a copy of your public key. You should also get copies of other people's public keys.

Here's how public and private keys work together. To send someone secure, encrypted e-mail, you need to have his public key on your computer. You use that public key to encrypt mail. After you encrypt it, you send it over the Internet.

After you encrypt the mail with the person's public key, no one can read it except the person you're sending it to. That's because all the public key can do is encrypt e-mail. It can't decrypt it. When it's sent out over the Internet, it looks like a bunch of gobbledygook to anyone trying to snoop on it.

The encrypted e-mail gets sent to your friend. Here's the cool thing: Your friend can read the e-mail, because his private key decrypts it. In fact, the only way that mail can be read is with his private key, because he's the only person in the world with his private key.

It works the other way, as well. When someone wants to send you secure e-mail, he uses your public key to create the encrypted message, sends it over the Internet, and when you get it, you can read it with your private key—no one else can read your mail.

Got that? Good. Let's get away from theory and back to reality now (always a good idea unless you're stuck in a university somewhere, where theory *is* reality). Here are some step-by-step instructions on how you actually use an encryption program:

1. Get an encryption program, such as Pretty Good Privacy. (Very important first step, that. I'll show you where and how later on in the chapter.)

2. Next, use it to generate two keys—one private and one public.

3. Then, make your public key available to as many people as possible by posting it on servers on the Internet and by sending it to friends using e-mail.

4. Get other people's public keys.

5. When you want to send someone secure e-mail, encrypt the message with the recipient's public key and send it. The recipient of the e-mail is the only person who can read the e-mail, using his or her private key.

6. When you get e-mail from someone who has encrypted it with your public key, you are the only person able to read it, using your private key.

Check This Out!

The only way you can exchange secure e-mail with people is if you have copies of their public keys, and they have copies of your public key. Otherwise, encryption doesn't work. So make sure that you get your public key into the hands of as many people as possible—and always ask to be sent copies of their public keys.

Using Pretty Good Privacy to Encrypt E-mail

There's a fair number of encryption programs available. The best one is Pretty Good Privacy (PGP). Don't be fooled by its name: Pretty Good Privacy is more than pretty good. In fact, it's great. It features super-strength encryption and is probably the most common encryption program used on the Internet, so it has become a standard of sorts. That means that, by using PGP, you have the widest number of people with whom to exchange secure, encrypted e-mail. Sometimes, encryption programs don't work with one another. But because so many people who use encryption use PGP, it's a good place to start. Even if people use an encryption technology other than PGP, you can still send and receive secure e-mail to and from them.

Here's even more good news: There's a version of PGP you can use for free, if you plan to use it for your personal use and not for business. The program is called PGPFreeware. It's owned by the Network Associates security company, which sells for-pay versions of the software, as well. The truth is, the free version is every bit as good as the for-pay version that you can buy on the Web site or in a retail store. True, there are a few bells and whistles missing, but for most purposes, you do just as well with the free version of the program.

Although Network Associates makes the free version available for download, they don't make it very easy to find. So you don't have to go nosing around the Web site, here's where to find it to download it: www.pgp.com/products/freeware. If for some reason that page has vanished, then do a search on the www.pgp.com or www.nai.com site for PGP Freeware. You should be able to find out the location that way.

PGP comes with a manual, so I'm not going to spend time here telling you all the ins and outs of using the program. It works just like encryption programs described earlier in the chapter. Here's a brief rundown, along with tips, on how to use PGP to exchange secure e-mail with people:

- When you first run the program, you are asked to generate a set of keys—one private and one public. One of the options you have is to determine how many bits you want to use when creating the key. In general, the larger the number of bits you use to create the key, the more secure your e-mail is. But when you choose a larger number, it also means it takes longer to encrypt the message. My general rule is the larger the better. I suggest using a number no smaller than 2048.

- The program is designed to work well with e-mail programs such as Eudora, Microsoft Outlook, and Microsoft Outlook Express. When you install the program, make sure to install the plug-ins that work with your program. That way, it is easier to encrypt and decrypt e-mail.

- After you install the program, new icons show up in your e-mail program. When you create mail, an icon for signing the message and one for encrypting the message appear. If you only want the person receiving the mail to be sure it's coming from you, click the icon for signing the message. That way, the recipient knows it's from you when he or she receives it. If you only click that icon, though, the mail isn't encrypted—it merely carries your digital signature, and the recipient knows the message is from you. If you want to encrypt the message, click the icon for encrypting the message.

◆ When you send a message that carries your digital signature, you have to type your PGP password before sending the message. You are prompted to supply your password.

◆ To send the person encrypted e-mail, you need his or her public key. If you have the public key on your computer, the message is sent automatically. If you don't, you are shown a list of all the public keys you have on your computer, as shown in Figure 15.2. Choose a public key from the list, and the person's key is added to the e-mail message. Then, send the message. It is sent, encrypted, and signed, if you chose to digitally sign the message. If you don't have the intended recipient's key on your computer, ask him or her to send you a copy. Some people include their keys on their Web pages or in their e-mail messages.

◆ You can search for people's public keys on the Internet. Some people upload their public keys to servers on the PGP site or other sites so that anyone who wants to can easily get their public keys. To find keys like this, click the **Open Key Search** icon from the PGPKeys portion of the PGP program and fill out a form for finding someone's key. Then right-click the keys you want to put on your computer, and select **Import to Local Keyring.** A search for public keys is shown in Figure 15.2.

Check This Out!

The latest version of PGP includes a firewall to help protect your computer against hackers and other ne'er-do-wells. For more information about firewalls, how they can help you, and how to use them, turn to Chapter 6, "The Ultimate Defense: Keeping Safe with Firewalls."

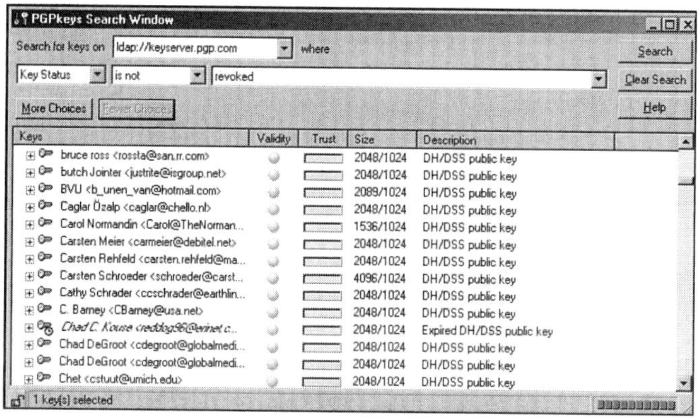

Figure 15.2

Here's how to find public keys over the Internet.

◆ When you receive an encrypted e-mail message, it looks like a whole bunch of random numbers, letters, and characters. An icon in your e-mail program automatically decrypts the message and verifies that the name in the From field is the actual sender. Click it, and those random numbers, letters, and characters turn into a readable e-mail message. Figure 15.3 shows the message as it's received—encrypted and unreadable. Figure 15.4 shows the same message after it's been decrypted.

Check This Out! _____

If PGP doesn't have a plug-in for your e-mail program, don't despair. You can still use PGP. PGP comes with two programs: PGP Tray and PGP Tools. Each enables you to encrypt and decrypt messages, although it takes a little bit longer and a bit of juggling. If there's no PGP plug-in for your program, use one of these tools.

There are many more ins and outs to PGP. If you want to get down and geeky, there are some truly nifty things you can do with it. But if you're just looking to encrypt and decrypt e-mail, it's pretty straightforward to use. Just remember: You need to have the intended recipient's public key if you want to send him or her encrypted e-mail, and the recipient needs to have your public key to send you encrypted e-mail.

Figure 15.3

What in the world is this message saying? It's been encrypted with PGP.

```
The project - Message [Plain Text]                                    _ 6 X
File  Edit  View  Insert  Format  PGP  Tools  Actions  Help
Send     x           !  +   ▼  Options...  A  ? 
To...   | Joanna Claus                                              |
Cc...   |                                                           |
Subject: | The project                                              |

-----BEGIN PGP MESSAGE-----
Version: PGPfreeware 7.0.3 for non-commercial use <http://www.pgp.com>

qANQR1DBwU4DZnVX3SxZE+4QB/91DsZ/cmgxpdfUuf/gVsIx4MZr2DonBQxiO7kj
5XbaLY11j8umX4NbFVJvnZPYfRxe7DtmO6iL9B4KVPo/OqqW46uRrIo//N5zsIRx
JUHyMg8DWOZBzldeHiHnmBtB5+PZ6h8eyJTeCipgQ8thACiiCVJDhsIt5fTKbmXO
+r7VoiFKTEJLTt2WdUH7ba/NqYPbJvt+QrdhAmCuLyNeUO7sJ7NemSONdLMfOi4W
UOQaNjO+f7/GpbfW3tOfmSigYA9CuwrSoNvCLpAlhi6aQGQ8M1TzXlZR1ZaDzqtF
fs9CBtZowT/9QJgRa8vjBNKy/FQ+L1gSyQIQFb1zwCfKUo7LCADRIpYwu3V+8hjs
EzEFjXEzbmKHjlsepB1rcRxyKDCAbsMp4VnliM9YLCokepVc2EXFCmDSb4Dh1DbW
pfQyoFHZLoGvR9L7+Q//AWbEe4LSziF1WbYZbxf9OHW/CZ/aqxJ9IXUtCArRbUZ2
nLn7aRATbP9sccsLWy+KQcst7uX6Lx+C9iaNZtMD6Jroc1+bWGXIMhPtBuuDUKgX
+KDUQzakmdQ7IQgOCtXLsRZ2rpibY/npc/tPbf1b7vbuK+JI1QQcY1nDP9ISqoeU
iMzT9ZytAWtOLoPviHtqOhciN9Ou6Sz/cmO1fdmn+ega9bLMKoz1XtSE9hUckOsq
EsDKq/jHycAQxyFDq12LqEKzzp7fOZeAb7oVbjfiXimvKWc+1AC8R6blt54m+i3R
cs67YThbvJMEwoY+IOIFq1J6TD5WwfXiSz1R+Ov8OTOaunhjfhxH7BYfsxwsIT1t
em2vFyPDavdTTnVIhKm5YV86JPfGMOsH5j/IUx6BNCZ/9cvOfRGQWbdEaFa51ne1
NcYDhXVcJcRqQW434ou2+Gy+MugnjYkXCayBpSvMXNgimMLgpbaXPNXvuNps5cle
5BGmT+yagmQG8Hqtslmwk24VBOF3Zn5LpA==
=Qrgm
-----END PGP MESSAGE-----
```

Figure 15.4

Ah, now I see. PGP comes to the rescue and decrypts the message.

```
The project - Message (Plain Text)                                    _ 6 X
File  Edit  View  Insert  Format  PGP  Tools  Actions  Help
Send     x           !  +   ▼  Options...  A  ? 
To...   | Joanna Claus                                              |
Cc...   |                                                           |
Subject: | The project                                              |

Joanna:

I just got word --- the project is a go! So let's go ahead and start talking. Before we meet,
check out the following Web site. www.ivegotasecretnow.com I've password-protected it. Password
is swordfish. User name is MarxBros.
```

How to Use a Digital Certificate to Encrypt E-mail

A *digital certificate* does pretty much the same thing that PGP does. It uses private and public keys, and it can digitally sign and encrypt your e-mail. Digital certificates are often called *digital IDs*.

You can get a digital certificate or digital ID from a Certificate Authority. (Sounds impressive and formal, doesn't it?) The most popular one on the Internet is VeriSign at www.verisign.com. Unlike PGP, it isn't free—it costs $14.95 per year for the certificate. After the year is up, you have to pony up the money again, because your certificate won't work any longer.

If you want someone to be able to send secure e-mail to you, you have to send him a copy of your digital certificate—although, in essence, you're really just sending him the public key part of it. And to send secure e-mail to him, you have to get a copy of his digital certificate—although he's really just sending you his public key.

You use your digital certificate to sign and encrypt outgoing e-mail. You also use it to decrypt incoming e-mail. A digital certificate works right within your e-mail program—there's no other way to use it. How you use it depends on your e-mail software, so if you decide to use a digital certificate, check on the authority's Web site for information on how to use it with your e-mail program.

 Techno Talk _____

You don't need to have an encryption program to use encryption with your e-mail. You can also use what's called a **digital certificate**. A digital certificate is, in essence, a key used to encrypt and decrypt your e-mail. But the key isn't created by an encryption program on your computer. Instead, a private company called a Certificate Authority, such as a company called VeriSign at www.verisign.com, creates it. You download the key to your computer and can use that key to encrypt e-mail. Often, these Certificate Authorities charge you for the use of the digital certificate, but the price is fairly low.

The Least You Need to Know

◆ Encryption programs require that you have two keys—a private key and a public key. You share your public key with the world, but keep your private key to yourself.

◆ Send your public key to as many people as possible and post it on public Web sites. That way, people can send you encrypted e-mail.

- Before sending an encrypted message to someone using Pretty Good Privacy or another encryption program, you need his public key. Ask him to send you a public key if you don't already have it.

- When you install Pretty Good Privacy, make sure to install the plug-ins specifically designed for your e-mail program.

- Digital certificates work much like encryption programs, such as Pretty Good Privacy, but you have to pay an annual fee to use them.

Chapter

16

Beyond Luncheon Meat: How to Protect Yourself Against Spam

In This Chapter

   ◆ What is spam, and how is it created?
   ◆ Techniques to hide your name and e-mail address from spammers
   ◆ How to use e-mail software and spam-fighting tools to stop spam from ever reaching you
   ◆ What you can do if you've been spammed

We've all been deluged by the e-mail offers: "Make a million dollars in your spare time!" "New, Guaranteed: Herbal Viagra!" "New Stock—Can't Miss!"

There's more as well … a lot more. E-mail boxes all over the world are filled daily with junk mail like these offers, called *spam*. Spam is the electronic equivalent of junk mail and telemarketers calling you during dinner to get you to get a new credit card or switch your long-distance phone carrier. Any time you're sent an e-mail message from someone you don't know, making you an offer of some kind, or trying to get you to take an action, you're a victim of spam. Multiply the spam you get in a day by millions and millions of people—and that figure by the cost of transmitting, receiving, and deleting this e-mail—and you have an idea of the scope of the problem.

Spam is one of the most annoying problems you'll face on the Internet. But you're in luck, because there's a lot you can do to stamp out spam and even help lock a spammer in the slammer, as you'll see in this chapter.

What Is Spam, and How Is It Created?

So what is spam, exactly? It's e-mail that you never asked to get, sent to you by someone you don't know. Usually, the identity of the sender of the e-mail has been forged, so it's difficult to know who is sending it. Spam is a popular way to do scams on the Internet, through various get-rich-quick schemes—and it might also offer pornography for sale, or ask you to visit for-pay pornographic Web sites.

Check This Out!

E-mail isn't the only thing that's bedeviled by spam. So are Usenet newsgroups—worldwide public bulletin boards in which people carry on discussions. Spam is frequently posted on these newsgroups, often to such an extent that it completely overwhelms any legitimate discussion.

Many spam offers are scams, although not all are. (For information on how to recognize an Internet scam, see Chapter 3, "How to Protect Yourself Against the Most Common Internet Scams.") Spam has become popular because it's cheap and easy to create, it's often difficult to track down its creator, and there are gullible people out there who respond to the offers. In other words, there's money to be made, and it doesn't cost spammers a lot to try to make it.

Money Matters: The True Cost of Spam

Sure, spam is an annoyance. But in fact, it's worse than a mere annoyance—it costs time and money for nearly everyone but the sender. It clogs up Internet e-mail boxes and mail servers so that mail gets delivered more slowly or not at all. It forces Internet Service Providers to buy extra bandwidth to be able to deliver all the extra mail. There are other costs and problems, as well. Here are the main ones:

◆ **Because of the massive volume of spam, you have to pay more for your Internet connection than if there were no spam.** Estimates of how much e-mail on the Internet is actually spam range from 10 percent to 30 percent or even more. To deliver all that spam, Internet Service Providers (ISPs) need to buy extra computers and faster connections to the Internet. They have to hire extra staff. The Netcom ISP has estimated that about 10 percent of its customer's bills is devoted to handling spam issues. Guess who pays the cost? That's right, you. ISPs pass the cost directly on to their customers.

♦ **Spam often disrupts normal Internet traffic.** It can clog up the pipes that deliver e-mail and Web sites to you. Things are delivered more slowly to you, or not at all. Spam has also crashed ISPs and corporate networks.

♦ **Children are subject to sexually related and pornographic messages.** When spammers send out e-mail in bulk, all they have are e-mail addresses—there's no way for them to differentiate adults from children. So, sexually oriented spam— estimated by AT&T to make up some 11 percent of all spam—is sent to children.

♦ **You have to take time out of your day to delete spam.** It takes a few seconds (and often longer) to delete a piece of spam, especially because it's not always easy to know from the subject line what's spam and what isn't. Multiply all the time you spend deleting spam—that's time that you could spend doing other things instead.

♦ **Spam leads to scams.** Much spam is devoted to scamming people. There's more fraud and abuse because spam has not been outlawed.

Check This Out! _____

Spam costs money. It takes up Internet bandwidth and forces Internet Service Providers to buy more bandwidth than they need. It costs money because every time someone at work has to delete a piece of spam, the person's company has, in essence, paid him to delete that piece of e-mail. And it costs money because businesses have to buy larger hard disks and extra servers to deal with the excess mail that spam creates—and they have to pay for staff time to install those disks and servers. Perhaps for a single user, the money doesn't amount to much, but taken over the entire Internet, it adds up to big bucks. A spam-fighting company called Bright Lights calculated that spam costs a staggering $213 million per year.

Nasty Business: How Spam Is Created

Before you learn how to fight spam, you need to know how it's created—don't worry, I'm not talking about odd body parts that might go into luncheon meats.

Let's take an example. Joe Spammer (a.k.a. Joe the Slimeball) decides he's going to try to make a million dollars by sending out spam hyping his extremely illegal business scheme: He wants people to call an 809 number he's set up offshore, so he can charge them each $5 a minute without them knowing about it. As a come-on to get people to call, he's going to claim in the subject line of the mail, "Free money—call now!!!" And for the body of the e-mail, he'll make up some scam about if people call the number listed, they'll get secret details about how to get free cash from the U.S. Treasury.

So what does Joe do? First, he gets a list of e-mail addresses to which to send the spam. There are several ways he can do this. He can take the easy (and more expensive) way and buy the list of addresses from any of the companies that sell bulk e-mail lists. But no, Joe is too cheap to do that—and he has a less-expensive way of doing it, anyway. He's going to harvest the names from the Internet using special address-gathering software. Many spammers and many companies that sell bulk e-mail build their spamming lists this way. Later on in this chapter, in "Hiding Your Name from Spammers," I show you how you can try to make sure that spammers don't grab your name when compiling their spam lists. So how do spammers harvest their names? Let me count the ways:

- **They get names from postings to Usenet newsgroups.** Newsgroups are world-wide, public Internet bulletin boards. When you post a message to Usenet, your e-mail address is also posted. Software can go into newsgroups and automatically grab the e-mail address from every posting. Later on in this chapter, in "Hiding Your Name from Spammers," I show how you can hide your e-mail address so it can't be harvested. And for more information about Usenet newsgroups, turn to Chapter 19, "Protecting Your Privacy on Internet Newsgroups and Discussion Areas."

- **They get names from public Web white page directories.** There are many white page directories on the Internet that have people's e-mail addresses on them. Spammers can automatically grab all those addresses. To get your name out of these directories, turn to Chapter 2," Putting Up Your First Line of Cyberdefense."

Check This Out! _____

The material written to Usenet newsgroups is often kept in public archives that people can look at, including at the popular Web site www.google.com. These archives are then used by spammers as an easy central resource for getting e-mail addresses. To keep your postings out of these archives, add the following line to your posting's header or to the beginning of your message: x-no-archive:yes.

- **They get names from chat rooms, especially on America Online.** Software can automatically watch chat rooms and grab the e-mail addresses of people who come in. Later in this chapter, in "Protecting Your Address in Internet Chats," I clue you in on how to protect your e-mail address when in a chat room.

- **They get names from Internet mailing lists.** Internet mailing lists are discussions carried on via e-mail. You can subscribe to a mailing list by sending a message to a specific e-mail address. Internet mailing lists are also called listservs, and they're managed by special listserv software. But there is a command that a spammer can issue to the software that in some cases gives to the spammer the e-mail address of everyone on the list. Later in the chapter, in "Protecting Your Address in Internet Chats," I give you information on how to fight this.

◆ **They can get names from your ISP's public directory.** Some ISPs, including America Online, post a public directory with information about people on the ISP, including their e-mail addresses. You can get your name off of these public directories. I tell you how later in the chapter, in "Getting Your Name out of Web White Page Directories." For more detailed information, turn to Chapter 2.

◆ **They can get your e-mail address from your Web page, if you've created one.** Many people, when they create a Web page, include their e-mail address on it somewhere. Software can automatically check Web pages and gather e-mail addresses listed on them. There are some tricks you can use to keep your address safe from spammers and yet still let people know your e-mail address. I show you how later on in this chapter, in "Protecting Your Address on Your Web Page."

Hiding Your Name from Spammers

The best way to cut down or eliminate the spam you get is to stop it at the source—don't let spammers get your e-mail address in the first place. Of course, that's a whole lot easier said than done. As you can see from the previous section, your e-mail address might be spread out all over kingdom come on the Internet.

Still, there's a lot you can do to hide your e-mail address from spammers. Here's how to do it.

Hiding Your Real Address When Posting to Usenet Newsgroups

Spammers grab lots of e-mail addresses from Usenet newsgroups. It's a fairly simple matter to make sure they don't get yours. There are a number of ways that you can hide your real address when you post to Usenet newsgroups:

◆ **Post anonymously.** Several Web sites and Internet services let you send out e-mail anonymously or post messages anonymously on newsgroups. This means that your name isn't listed along with the posting—and spammers can't grab it. For example, take a look at the W-3 Anonymous Remailer at www.gilc.org/speech/anonymous/ remailer.html (see Figure 16.1), which enables to you post anonymously. There are many others that do it, as well. There's only one drawback to this technique—in some newsgroups, people ignore anonymous posters, because sometimes spammers post anonymously as a way to send spam to an entire newsgroup without having their identity revealed. For more information on how to post to newsgroups anonymously, turn to Chapter 17, "Staying Anonymous with Anonymous Re-mailers," and Chapter 19, "Protecting Your Privacy on Internet Newsgroups and Discussion Areas."

Figure 16.1

Posting to a newsgroup using an anonymous remailer like the one at www.gilc.org/ speech/anonymous/ remailer.html keeps your e-mail address private.

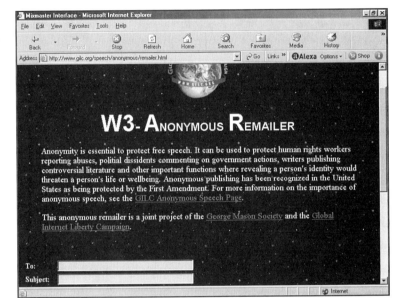

◆ **Use a second e-mail address when posting to newsgroups.** Many sites on the Internet, such as www.hotmail.com, www.bigfoot.com, and www.zdnet.com, give you free e-mail accounts. Get one or more of these free e-mail accounts. Then, when posting to newsgroups, use one of those accounts as your return address— but use it for no other purpose. That way, spam is sent there, but you never have to read it.

◆ **Munge your e-mail address.** *Munging* refers to a technique you can use so that when you post a newsgroup message using your normal Usenet newsgroup software, your real address doesn't show up—instead, no address or a different address shows up. (Munge? What a word! Leave it to Internet geeks to come up with new uses for language on a daily basis.) You can munge your e-mail address using your news-group and e-mail software. Check the documentation for how. If you use the Out-look Express newsreader (it comes with both Microsoft Outlook and Microsoft Outlook Express), here's what to do: Click the **Tools** menu and choose **Accounts.** Look for your Usenet server in the list that appears and click it. Click **Properties.** The screen shown in Figure 16.2 appears. In the E-mail Address field, delete your name. Next, put in a phony e-mail address—but make absolutely sure it's phony, something like adam@do-not-send-me-spam-or-else.net. Now, whenever you post to a Usenet newsgroup, your real e-mail address doesn't appear. The only drawback is that people who want to send you e-mail to follow up on your posting aren't able to because your address isn't listed.

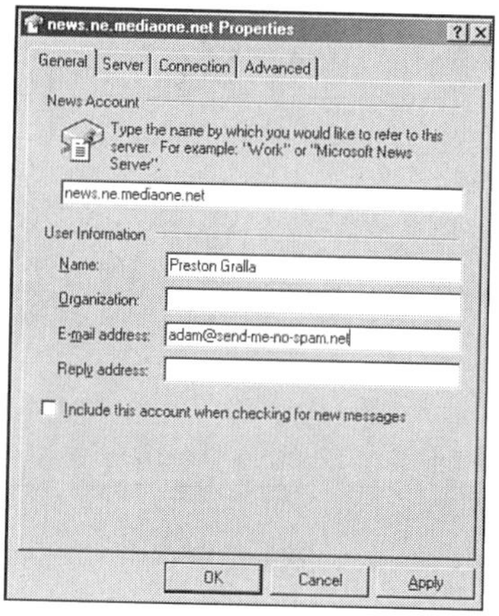

Figure 16.2

Here's how to use the Outlook news reader to change the address that is listed when you post to newsgroups.

Check This Out!

When you munge your e-mail address, there's a generally accepted etiquette about what you should and shouldn't do. An absolute no-no is putting someone else's e-mail address in your postings—whether on purpose or by accident. So check to make sure that any e-mail address you post isn't a real one. And generally, it's considered good form to use a phony address that address-harvesting can't read, but humans can. For example, if your e-mail address is goodguy@pure.net, you could create a phony e-mail address of goodguy@l-want.nospam.pure.net.

◆ **Go to Google Groups at http://groups.google.com to read and post in newsgroups.** When you post to newsgroups at this site, you can use any e-mail address you want—it's easy to munge your address without having to go through setup screens in your newsreader program.

Usenet is a way that spammers get highly targeted spam lists. Let's say a spammer is trying to get people to buy antique cars. Sending a spam out to hundreds of thousands of people might not find the spammer many customers, because not many people are interested in antique cars. But Usenet newsgroups enable spammers to gather a highly targeted list of people interested in a specific topic, such as antique cars, Japanese animation, or

PalmPilots. That's because the newsgroups are organized by specific interests, and spammers can gather names from specific lists. If you have a special interest, that's all the more reason to protect your e-mail address when posting to Usenet.

Getting Your Name out of Web White Page Directories

Spammers also harvest names from Web White Page directories, Web sites where you can search for people's e-mail addresses. There are many of these Web sites on the Internet, such as www.bigfoot.com, www.whowhere.com, and www.people.yahoo.com. If you get your name out of those directories, you can cut down on the spam you receive.

Most of these sites give you the option to delete your name from them, although they don't exactly trumpet that fact. For a list of the major White Page directories on the Web and detailed instructions on how to get your name out of them, turn to Chapter 2. And since many of these directories get their information from local phone companies, you can also call your local phone company and ask to have your phone number unlisted, which should help. Keep in mind, though, that if you do that, people won't be able to find your phone number by calling directory assistance, and it won't be listed in the phone book, so think hard before taking this drastic step.

Removing Your Name from Your ISP's Directory

Another source of e-mail addresses for spammers is your Internet Service Provider's (including America Online's) public directory. You might not even know that your ISP *has* a public directory, but yes, many of them do. Or maybe you joined America Online several years ago and created a profile, but now you've forgotten about it. (Age does that to you. I know from experience.)

Check with your ISP—including America Online—and tell it to remove your name from the public directory. Also, ask if it keeps finger information about you. Finger is a feature of some Internet servers that enables people to type in an e-mail address and get back information about the person at that address. Tell your ISP you don't want your information available via finger. For more information, turn to Chapter 2.

Protecting Your Address in Internet Chats

Yet another way for spammers to get e-mail addresses (boy, they're persistent buggers, aren't they?) is to use software that automatically grabs addresses of people in chat rooms and Internet Relay Chat (IRC) channels. This is a particularly bad problem on America Online.

The best way to outsmart spammers who harvest your name in chat rooms is to use a separate e-mail address or ID from your real one whenever you chat. That way, spam is routed to that address or ID, and you simply never check that account—that way, you're never spammed. To do this, get a free e-mail address as outlined earlier in the chapter and use that when participating in Internet chats. America Online users should create a separate screen name to use whenever they're chatting. The spam is all routed to that screen name, and the spam that piles up there can be ignored.

Check This Out!

Not all spam is made up of commercial offers, but much of the spam sent is commercial offers of some kind—get-rich-quick schemes, come-hither offers to visit for-pay Web sites, goods being sold. There are other kinds of spam, such as e-mail chain letters and political calls to action.

Protecting Your Name in Internet Mailing Lists

Internet mailing lists, often called *listservs*, are great ways to participate in discussions and get information via e-mail. But they can also be a boon for spammers. Several different kinds of software are used to create these discussion lists. Some of them allow anyone to send a "who" message to the software, and the software then dutifully sends back a comprehensive list of e-mail addresses of people who are on the list. This is not a good thing if you want to stop spam. Luckily, there are ways to block the "who" command. The person running the listserv can simply block all "who" requests. If the person doesn't do that, you can take matters into your own hands. Two popular programs for handling listservs are listproc and listserv. You can tell which software manages yours by the address you had to use when subscribing—it should either have the word listproc or listserv in it. If you aren't sure, send a note to the person managing the list, asking which software the list uses. You can give the software a command to block your e-mail address from being given out when someone issues a who command. Here's how:

◆ If you're on a listproc list, compose an e-mail message to the listproc address where you subscribed, with the line SET *listname* CONCEAL YES in the body of the message. For *listname*, substitute the name of the list to which you've subscribed.

◆ If you're on a listserv list, compose an e-mail message to the listserv address where you subscribed, with the line SET *listname* CONCEAL in the body of the message. For *listname*, substitute the name of the list to which you've subscribed.

Protecting Your Address on Your Web Page

When you create a Web page, most likely you include your e-mail address in some way. Spammers use programs to automatically harvest names from Web pages, meaning you could end up being spammed. When you put your e-mail address on a Web page, you most likely did it by including a mailto tag in your HTML code. When others click that link, it automatically launches their e-mail program, with your e-mail address already filled in. The problem is that harvesting programs can get your e-mail by looking for these links.

According to the Multimedia Marketing Group, there's a way around it. Simply put a %20 in front of your e-mail address when you create the link, and you'll foil spammers. Here's an example of the HTML code you would use if your e-mail address was goodgirl@nice.net:

```
<A HREF="mailto%20goodgirl@nice.net">Click here to send me e-mail</A>
```

The mailto link still works with a browser, but the address-harvesting program doesn't recognize there's an e-mail address there and ignores it.

Using Your E-mail Program to Stop Spam in Its Tracks

Maybe you don't want to keep your identity private in Usenet newsgroups. Maybe you want your name published in directories so that old friends and family members can always find you. Maybe you've taken all the steps I outlined previously, but somehow, some way, the spammers are still finding you. What can you do now?

Notes
How in the world, you might wonder, can an e-mail program or spam-killing software automatically know which mail is spam and which isn't? They do it in a variety of ways. They have a list of known spammers, and whenever an e-mail comes from one of them, it considers it spam. They also search for keywords in the header and sometimes the body of the message—words that are commonly used by spammers. And some of them examine the headers of the messages, looking for certain tell-tale signs that show the sender is a spammer.

Pretty much any e-mail program you use these days has a way of filtering out at least some spam so that you don't have to see it. The program either refuses to accept spam, automatically deletes it, or puts it in a folder so that you can delete the spam yourself. I suggest having your e-mail program put all the spam in a folder, so that you can delete it yourself. These programs aren't perfect, after all, and the last thing you want is to delete a message from your mother (eat your vegetables!) because your e-mail software thought it was spam.

If you use Outlook, it's very easy to turn the spam filter on (see Figure 16.3). Click the **Organize** button at the top of Outlook and, from the screen that drops down, click **Junk E-mail.** Then, just turn the spam filters on, and Outlook starts filtering your e-mail. You can tell it to shade the suspect spam a certain color, such as gray or maroon, so that you can tell at a glance that you've been sent spam. Or, you can have it send all suspected spam to a folder, and you can then look at all the spam there. That's how I handle spam. Figure 16.3 shows how to turn on the spam filter in Outlook. Note that there are two kinds of spam filters. One covers garden-variety spam. The other filters out adult content spam.

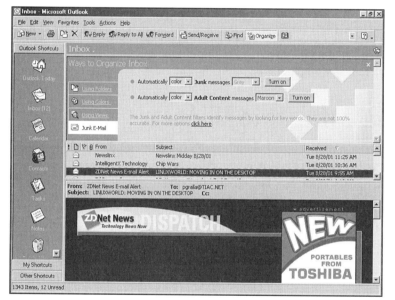

Figure 16.3

Here's how to filter spam using Outlook.

Spam filters don't always know what e-mail is spam and what isn't. Sometimes they miss spam. But you can help your e-mail software detect spam better. When a piece of spam makes it through, you can tell your software that it's spam, and from that point on, all e-mail from that source is marked for what it is—time-wasting, yellow-bellied, nasty spam. The more spam you mark, the smarter your e-mail program becomes. In Outlook, right-click the offending (and offensive) spam, choose **Junk E-mail** from the menu that drops down, and click to add it either to the junk mail sender's list or the adult content sender's list. From then on, the software doesn't let the spam through.

Check This Out!

Sometimes, Outlook (and other e-mail software) mistakenly thinks something is spam when it isn't. You want to let mail from that sender through in the future, without turning off your spam filter. Most e-mail software, including Outlook, has an exception list—e-mail addresses that should never be considered as spam. Here's how to add an address to the exception list in Outlook to always let mail from that address through. From the **Tools** menu, click **Rules Wizard** and then choose **Exception List**. Then, from the **Rule Description** at the bottom of the screen, click **Exception List**. Now, add the e-mail address you want to let through. It is no longer considered spam. Note that this doesn't work with every version of Outlook—in some versions, to do this, follow the directions for creating a new rule with the Rules Wizard, and you're asked what exceptions you want to add—you can add the e-mail addresses that way.

Use Spam-Fighting Software to Kill Spam

There's another way to make sure that spam doesn't reach you—use spam-fighting software. This software works one of two ways: It can work right inside your e-mail software and detect and kill spam; or, you can run it before running your e-mail software to detect and kill spam.

There's a lot of spam-fighting software out there. The software generally offers more capabilities than the filters that come with your e-mail software. Good ones are Spam Exterminator, Spam Buster, and SpamKiller, among others. You can try them all out for free by downloading them from many download sites on the Internet, including CNet's Download.com at www.download.com.

Check This Out!

Users of America Online will tell you they receive tons of junk mail. But you can create filters to try and stem the tide of spam. Use the keywords Mail Controls. Then, click **Set Up Mail Controls**. Follow the directions for putting in the addresses that send you spam. From now on, that mail is blocked from reaching you.

Fight Back! What to Do If You've Been Spammed

One way or another, you're going to be spammed. You might be able to cut down on spam, but you can never kill it entirely. Still, if you've been spammed, there are steps you can take to either make sure it doesn't happen again or to track down the spam senders and curtail their actions (or even put them out of business).

First Find Out Who the Spammer Is

In Chapter 14, "Dangerous Delivery: What Dangers Are There in E-mail?" I gave details of how e-mail works and spent a bit of time looking at headers of e-mail messages. If you want to find out who a spammer is, you have to look in the e-mail header. So turn back to that chapter for a rundown on the ins and outs and the ups and downs of e-mail and its headers.

By the way, before we go on, a warning here: A smart spammer can trick you. The really good ones forge a message so completely, you'll probably never be able to track down who created it.

Check This Out!

When you register at Web sites or fill out forms online, you're often asked to provide your e-mail address. When you do that, you might well be putting yourself on a spam list. But filling in a phony e-mail address might not work—some sites check to make sure the e-mail address you put in is a valid one. Many Web sites, such as www.bigfoot.com, www.hotmail.com, and www.zdnet.com, offer free e-mail boxes. Get a second (or a third) e-mail box at one of these sites and always put in that address when filling out forms. That way, your spam is always sent to that one address.

Spammers can usually forge almost every part of a header, so it's hard to trust any part of a header. But often the most reliable part of the header is the Received header. This part of the header details when various Internet servers received the piece of mail and then forwarded it on to the next server. Often, there are several Received headers, and several of them might be forged. Still, they're worth looking at. Look for the originator of the mail—in other words, the Received header with the earliest date and time. That might be the location of the true sender. Then again, it might not, but at least you have a place to begin. Also look for the Message ID header. Often, that has the name of the ISP where the spam started, so at least you know the origination point of the mail. You can then complain to that ISP.

Take These Steps When You've Been Spammed

So you've looked at the header, and you might or might not know the true spammer. In any event, there are actions you can take, even if you don't know the true identity of the spammer. Here's what to do:

◆ **Complain to your ISP.** Your ISP hates spam as much as you do—it forces ISPs to spend more money on mail servers and other costly Internet stuff. Many ISPs have an e-mail address where you can send spam. Forward all your spam to that address—and include the true address of the spammer if you've been able to find it out from the message header. On America Online, forward the spam to the screen name TOSSpam. In all cases, forward the original e-mail, don't copy and paste the spam into a new message. When you forward the spam, all the headers are left intact, so your ISP can do some detective work.

◆ **Complain to the advertiser.** Sometimes spam mentions the name and phone number of an advertiser sponsoring the spam. Call up the number, complain, and tell them you're going to tell everyone you know never to do business with them unless they stop spamming. A legitimate business might listen to you. Scammers won't.

Notes

When you get spam, you might be tempted to respond to it by sending off an angry note. Or there might be a return e-mail address in the note, saying if you want to get taken off the spam list, send an e-mail message to that return address. Never respond to spam. Spammers rarely take you off their lists. By responding, you're only letting them know that your e-mail address is a valid one—and they'll send you even more spam.

◆ **Complain to the ISP from which you think the mail came.** You might be able to find out where the mail originated by examining its header. If you think you know where it came from, forward the mail to that ISP. The ISP doesn't want spammers on the system and might kick them off.

◆ **Complain to your state attorney general.** In some states, such as California, Virginia, and Washington, spam is more than a nuisance—it's illegal. Although the laws vary from state to state, increasingly, states are passing anti-spam laws. The state attorney general is responsible for enforcing them. These laws can have some pretty stiff penalties. In Washington, for example, spammers can be fined $2,000 for every individual piece of spam they send. Considering that most spammers send out millions of pieces of spam, we're talking some big-time money.

◆ **Get more information at these Web sites.** Web sites can help you complain about spam and learn more about how to track down the true senders of spam. Head to the Fight Spam on the Internet site at //spam.abuse.net/. The How To Complain About Spam, or Put a Spammer in the Slammer site at //dlis.gseis.ucla.edu/people/pagre/spam.html is especially worthwhile for figuring out where to complain.

The Least You Need to Know

- When posting messages to Usenet newsgroups, alter your e-mail address or use an anonymous remailer to post so that spammers can't get your address from the newsgroup.

- Take your name out of Web White Page directories to cut down on the amount of spam you receive.

- Remove your address from your ISP's public directory so that spammers can't get your e-mail address from there.

- Get a second, free e-mail address at a site such as www.hotmail.com, and when filling out Web forms, use that address. That way, spam is sent to that address, not your main one.

- Complain to your state attorney general if you've received spam—several states now have anti-spam laws.

- Never respond to spam—it only proves to the spammer that your e-mail address is a valid one, and might result in you getting even *more* spam.

Chapter 17

Staying Anonymous with Anonymous Remailers

In This Chapter

- ◆ Why you might want to use an anonymous remailer
- ◆ How anonymous remailers work
- ◆ How to use Web-based anonymous remailers
- ◆ How to use your e-mail program along with anonymous remailers
- ◆ The best anonymous remailer sites and services on the Internet

To turn the old *Cheers* theme song on its head: Sometimes you just want to go where nobody knows your name. There might be times when you want to send e-mail to someone or to post a message to a Usenet newsgroup in which you don't want your name known. Maybe you want to blow the whistle on wrongdoing at your company and are worried about the consequences to you if it was known you were the whistleblower. Maybe you're worried that if you divulge certain information about yourself, you could be ostracized in your community. Maybe you don't want your name ending up in spam lists. For whatever reason, there are times when you would like to send information, but don't want your name known.

Anonymous remailers enable you to do just that. You can send e-mail or participate in newsgroups, and your name and address aren't attached to your postings. This chapter shows you how to do it.

What Is an Anonymous Remailer, Anyway?

An anonymous remailer enables you send an e-mail message or post a message on a Usenet newsgroup without anyone knowing your e-mail address. When someone gets the message or sees the posting, he can't tell that it's you who sent it. Most anonymous remailer services are free, although some for-pay services have sprung up.

As you see in this chapter, there are different kinds of anonymous remailers. Some are Web sites where you fill out a form to send anonymous mail. Others are Internet servers to which you send e-mail; with these, you use your own e-mail program to send the anonymous mail, but the server does a bit of magic to make sure that your identity isn't known when the message is delivered.

Generally, here's how most types of anonymous remailers work. When you send your message, the anonymous remailer strips off your e-mail address and other header information that can be used to identify you. After stripping off this header information and putting in new header information, it sends your message on its merry way. Anyone reading the message can't see who originally sent it.

For extra security, some anonymous remailers use what's called chaining. That means the remailer sends your message to yet another anonymous e-mailer, who in turn strips off the header that your initial anonymous e-mailer puts on, and puts a new header on. This chain can go on and on. The chaining technique provides greater assurance that your identity can't be found out.

You can also use anonymous remailers to post messages to Usenet newsgroups. Some let you post directly. Others require that you jump through a hoop or two and have your e-mail sent to a gateway that takes the anonymous mail and posts it to the newsgroup. (The Internet can be pretty complicated sometimes, can't it?) But either way, you can use anonymous remailers to post messages on newsgroups.

Why Would Someone Use an Anonymous Remailer?

You're an honest person. You don't beat your dog, spout obscenities in public, or wear white socks with black shoes (at least not in full public view—what you do behind closed doors is your own business). And you're an upright citizen—you always speak your mind and stand behind your words. So why use an anonymous remailer? What have you got to hide? Isn't there something cowardly about sending messages to people or posting notes on discussion boards in which your identity is hidden?

No, there's nothing cowardly about it. There are times when you might want to be able to make your views publicly known or get a message to someone, but you don't want your e-mail address and identity known.

Almost everyone could use an anonymous remailer at sometime. Here are some of the main reasons you might want to use one:

◆ **You want to keep your name off spam lists.** As you saw in Chapter 16, "Beyond Luncheon Meat: How to Protect Yourself Against Spam," spammers often go to Usenet newsgroups to gather people's e-mail addresses so they can spam them. If you use an anonymous remailer to post messages, your name isn't on your message and you can't be spammed.

◆ **You're a whistle-blower and don't want your name known.** Perhaps you've uncovered illegal activity or some other kind of nefarious business at your company or somewhere else, and you want to alert the right people, but you don't want your name known. Sending information using an anonymous remailer gets the whistle blown on the bad guys without you getting harmed.

◆ **You don't want your beliefs or lifestyle to be known by your employer or the community in which you live.** Maybe your political beliefs or sexual orientation are such that you'd be ostracized in your local community if they were known—but you want to be able to express yourself on the Internet. And perhaps you don't want those beliefs or your orientation known by your employer, either. You can use anonymous remailers to enter discussions while retaining your anonymity.

◆ **You have a medical or mental condition that you would like to discuss with others and get advice about, but don't want your employers, co-workers, or people in your community to know about it.** There are many conditions, such as mental illness, alcoholism, and AIDS, that people like to keep to themselves. Perhaps you have a problem that you'd like to speak with others about for support, but you don't want your employer, co-workers, or people in your community to know about it. Remailers can solve the problem for you.

◆ **You just plain like your privacy.** The truth is, you don't need a reason to want to post messages anonymously. Perhaps you just feel more comfortable expressing yourself when your identity isn't known. It's your right to do so.

> **Check This Out!**
>
> Be aware that when you use many kinds of anonymous remailers, there are ways your identity can be tracked down by law enforcement personnel or others. If you post defamatory anonymous mail, you could suffer the consequences. For example, the Wade Cook Financial Corp. sued 10 people who posted anonymously for allegedly making defamatory comments about the company on Yahoo! message boards.

Using Anonymous Remailers

This being the Internet, there are different kinds of remailers and—surprise!—they work in different ways. Some are Web-based, some require you to simply send an e-mail message, and some require you to practically jump through hoops to use them—you have to do things like encrypt your message and other fancy things before sending the message. In general, the more complicated the remailer, the more secure it is and the harder it is for anyone to trace your address. If you're super-paranoid, you have to do a bit more work because you probably want to use super-secret remailers. The following sections cover the different kinds of remailers on the Internet and how to use them.

Pseudonymous E-mailer

The pseudonymous e-mailer enables you to receive messages, as well as send them, without your identity being known. (Ah, the Internet. Always coming up with new ways to abuse the language.) In a pseudonymous e-mailer, when you send an e-mail, a false e-mail address—in other words, your pseudonym—is put in place of your own. That way, people can send you responses, but they don't really know to whom they're responding.

If you send pseudonymous e-mail and someone responds to you, the response e-mail first goes back to the pseudonymous remailer. The remailer uses Internet magic to figure out that the message should be sent to you. It then sends the message to you. You send and receive e-mail without anyone knowing your true e-mail address. Be aware, though, that in this kind of remailer, your identity can be discovered. The pseudonymous remailer has to keep your true e-mail address, as well as your pseudo address. Theoretically, the remailer could turn that information over to someone else. In fact, that's already happened at the most popular pseudonymous e-mailer of all time, a site called `anon.penet.fi`, hosted in Finland.

In 1995, the Church of Scientology wanted to find out who had posted secret church documents on the Internet. They had been posted using the `anon.penet.fi` remailer. The church asked the Finnish government to get the site to turn over the true name of the person who had posted the documents. The government, in turn, asked that the true address be handed over. The address was revealed, and the church discovered who had posted the documents. The owner of the site eventually shut it down, because he started to get more threats to turn over the names of people who had used the service.

Web-Based Anonymous Remailers

Web-based remailers are the simplest to use. Just go to a Web site, fill in a form, and you're done. No muss, no fuss. Figure 17.1 shows the Web-based anonymous remailer,

Cheech's Anonymous Remailer at www.geocities.com/Area51/2868/remail.html. Many anonymous remailers are small, homegrown sites, often run by a single person, like the one showed in Figure 17.1.

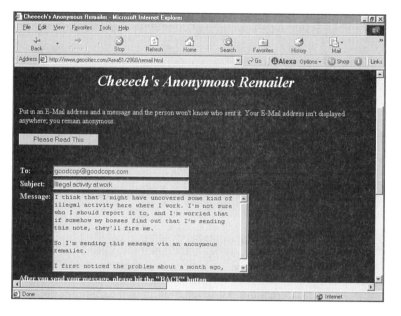

Figure 17.1

It's easy and safe to send anonymous e-mail using Cheech's Anonymous Remailer.

Sometimes, Web-based anonymous remailers don't provide the level of security other types of anonymous remailers do. That's not always true, though. The truth is, unless you're pretty paranoid, even the simplest level of anonymity is good enough for you. Some Web anonymous remailers use very high levels of security. Some of the Web-based remailers enable you to chain remailers, so you can send it from one to the other for greater security. You can even choose which ones to send to from a list. I know, it sounds pretty geeky. But to people who live for the Internet, that's a very cool thing.

The main drawbacks to Web-based remailers is that some are starting to charge a fee for their services; and they tend to come and go because they're often run by volunteers. But there are still enough free ones available that you should never have to pay. A list of free Web-based remailers is provided at the end of this chapter.

Sending Anonymous E-mail Using Your E-mail Program

The other way to use an anonymous remailer is to use your e-mail program. You compose a message, add a few extra bits of information that the remailer needs, and then send the message. The remailer does the work for you.

Notes

Not all remailers are created equal. Some offer higher degrees of safety than others. The Cypherpunk and Mixmaster remailers both offer a whole lot of security. In a Cypherpunk remailer, also called a Type-1 anonymous remailer, you can encrypt your e-mail message and send that through a chain of other remailers. (In fact, some remailers require that you encrypt your mail before sending it.) As you might guess, it's very secure and it is pretty tough to figure out who sent the message. However, for the truly raving paranoids among us (oops, not very politically correct, that; let's just call them very security-conscious folks), there is the Mixmaster remailer, also called a Type-2 anonymous remailer. In this type of anonymous remailer, the message is encrypted and then cut up into a whole lot of tiny little pieces that don't look like they're related to one another. These little encrypted pieces are then sent separately from anonymous remailer to anonymous remailer to anonymous remailer. When the very last remailer gets all these little completely garbled bits of data, it puts them all back together and sends it out as a message. The last remailer hasn't a clue where the original message came from.

The only real problem with these kinds of remailers is that they're kind of tough to use. Here's how to do it using the popular anonymous remailer you can find and use for free by sending your message to `remailer@replay.com`.

First, find out the address of an anonymous remailer you want to use. There's a list at the end of the chapter. In our example, let's say that we're using an anonymous remailer with the address `remailer@sendstuff.com`. And let's say that we want to send an e-mail to `joe@joejoe.com`. (By the way, sometimes an anonymous remailer might have slightly different instructions than are provided here. You should check with the anonymous remailers you want to use to see how to post with them.)

Now that you have the address of the anonymous remailer, start composing your message in your e-mail program. In the To field, put the address `remailer@sendstuff.com`. Leave the Subject line blank.

That's it for the easy part. Now the work begins. There has to be some way for the remailer to know where to send the message. There are two ways to do this: the hard way and the easy way.

If you're feeling particularly techie or know your way around your e-mail program, you probably want to do it the hard way. Here's what to do. With your e-mail program, create a new header that reads like this:

```
Anon-To: <address>
```

In this case, it would read:

```
Anon-To: joe@joejoe.com
```

Your e-mail program might or might not allow you to create headers. And you might or might not know how to do it, even if your e-mail program lets you do it. Check the e-mail's documentation for details.

Okay. Now let's take a look at the easy way. Instead of trying to muck around and edit headers, after you've filled in the address and subject lines, put two colons on the first line of the body of your message, then go to the next line of your message and put in the Anon-To address line. Follow that with a blank line, then ## marks and then a Subject line. Finally compose your message. Now it should look like this:

```
::

Anon-To: joe@joejoe.com


##

Subject: Sending anonymous e-mail
```

You can see here in Figure 17.2 how it would look in the Microsoft Outlook e-mail program.

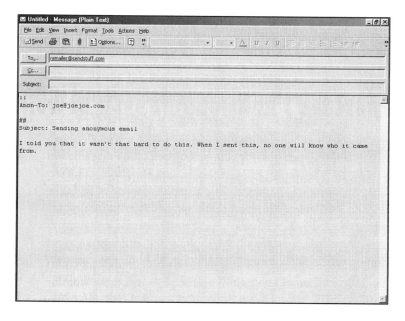

Figure 17.2

Here's how to send anonymous e-mail using an anonymous remailer.

By the way, the anonymous remailers also enable you to post messages to Usenet newsgroups. It's simple to do. In the Anon-To: line, simply put the name of the newsgroup, like this:

```
Anon-To: alt.rabbitlovers.forever
```

Check This Out!

An increasing number of anonymous remailers require that you encrypt your message before sending it. For information about how to encrypt e-mail messages, turn to Chapter 15, "Keeping Your E-mail Private with Encryption." For details about how to send the encrypted message, check the help information of the anonymous remailer.

Check This Out!

Anonymous remailers enable you to speak out anonymously on newsgroups and via e-mail. That's a right you have. But there are some rules you should follow when posting anonymously so you don't abuse that right. You shouldn't use anonymous remailers to spam, stalk, or harass people. You shouldn't use it to commit illegal acts or to espouse hate speech of any kind.

Most anonymous remailers have help information that tells you how to use them. To get information on how to use a specific anonymous remailer, send an e-mail message to the remailer with the Subject line `remailer-help`.

Where to Find Anonymous Remailers on the Internet

There are a fair number of anonymous remailers on the Internet. Here are some good places to go for information and to post mail anonymously:

- **Electronic Frontiers Georgia's Reliable Remailer Lists at http://anon.efga.org/ Remailers/.** This site boasts a big list of anonymous remailers, along with links to related sites and information.

- **www.sendfakemail.com/~raph/remailerlist. html.** This site provides an excellent list of anonymous remailers, along with helpful information about how to use remailers and other anonymity tools.

- **W-3 Anonymous Remailer at www.gilc.org/ speech/anonymous/remailer.html.** This is a very easy-to-use Web-based remailer.

The Least You Need to Know

- Anonymous remailers strip off e-mail header information to keep your identity private.

- Use anonymous remailers to keep your name off spamming lists and when you want to send e-mail or post information that you worry could have consequences for you if your name were known.

- To find out how to use an anonymous remailer along with your e-mail program, send an e-mail to the remailer with the subject line of `remailer-help`.

- Never use an anonymous remailer to harass or threaten others, commit illegal acts, or espouse hate speech.

Chapter 18

Keep Yourself Safe and Protect Your Privacy When Chatting and Instant Messaging

In This Chapter

- What are chat and instant messaging?
- What kinds of dangers are there when you chat and use instant messengers?
- Safety and privacy when using chat programs
- Safety and privacy when using instant messengers
- Ensure that you're protected when using ICQ and Internet IRC chat

For many people, the neatest thing about the Internet is the way it enables them to communicate with people all over the world. And the way they like to communicate is to chat and send and receive instant messages—to talk to others via keyboard.

Chat and instant messaging are both great. But they also carry dangers. In this chapter, you'll find out what those dangers are, and how to keep yourself safe when chatting.

What Kinds of Ways Are There to Chat and Instant Message on the Internet?

What different types of chat and instant messaging are there on the Internet? Let me count the ways … no, that might take too long.

The words "chat" and "instant messaging" when used on the Internet are very confusing, and they're applied to a lot of different things. So first, let's do the rundown on what those terms mean—and what they don't.

When you chat or use instant messaging on the Internet, you don't actually speak to someone else, or hear what they're saying. (Thank you, Internet, for taking even simple-sounding words and making them difficult to understand.) Instead, when you chat online, you type messages on your keyboard, and other people can see what you type; they type messages on their keyboards, and you see what they type. It's all done live.

The primary difference between chat and instant messaging programs is that when you chat, it's like a giant free-for-all—you talk to the entire group of chatters (or is that chatterers?) at the same time (although you can also carry on a side conversation, one on one).

Most chats are focused on a topic, such as pets, car care, romance, or just about any other kind of topic you can name.

To chat, you enter a special area, often called a chat room or a channel. When you're not in that room or channel, you can't chat.

Instant messaging, on the other hand, involves one-on-one talks with "buddies." You run special instant messaging software, such as America Online Instant Messenger or ICQ (pronounced "I seek you"), and can then send and receive instant messages with other people who use that software. You generally create a "buddy list" of friends, family, and co-workers, and are alerted when anyone on your buddy list is online. Then you can start an instant message session with them. They're alerted when you're online, as well. Figure 18.1 shows the Yahoo! Messenger program in action.

Check This Out!

Increasingly, instant messaging programs include the ability not just to type words on a keyboard, but to talk live as well over the Internet. You need a microphone and a set of speakers to participate, and the voice quality leaves much desired, to say the least. But still, you're now able to talk to others live online, not just type and read words. And the service is free, no matter where the chatters are located in the world.

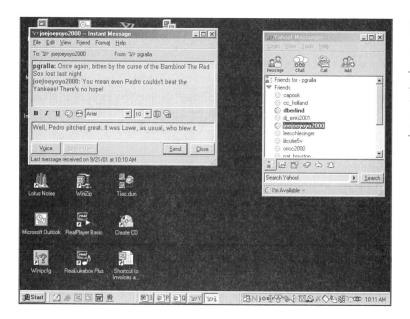

Figure 18.1

Keeping in touch with friends: Instant messaging programs like Yahoo! Messenger enable you to keep in instant touch with friends, family, and co-workers.

All kinds of different technologies are available for chatting and sending instant messages, and there are many different ways you can chat. Here's the rundown of the most popular ones:

♦ **Internet Relay Chat (IRC).** Here's the granddaddy of all chats. This was the first kind of chatting ever available on the Internet, and it's still one of the most popular. You need special IRC software to participate in IRC chats. My favorite is mIRC. You can download it from download sites such as www.download.com or www.mirc.com. You can chat using many other kinds of chat software, as well. There are some potential security holes in using IRC that could cause you trouble. I outline the problems—and how you can easily plug them—in "Don't Let IRC Irk You: The Special Dangers of IRC Chat" later in this chapter.

♦ **Chats on America Online.** To a great extent, America Online was built on chat. It's a yakker's paradise. Pick a subject, and you'll find others who want to chat about it. For those who like to chat, the joint is jumping. Of course, for some, AOL is also synonymous with security holes.

♦ **ICQ (pronounced "I Seek You").** This software started out as an underground phenomenon and took the Internet by storm. Millions of people use it to chat with one

Check This Out!

The lines between an instant messaging program and a chat are becoming more and more blurred. Many instant messaging programs, such as Yahoo! Messenger and ICQ, also include chat capabilities.

another. You can only use it to communicate with others who use ICQ. Get it at download sites such as www.download.com, or at www.icq.com.

♦ **Instant pagers and instant messengers.** There are many of these, as I've mentioned before. Instant messaging is also built into America Online, but a lot of other software enables you to instant message on the Internet, such as the America Online Instant Messenger, Microsoft Messenger, and Yahoo! Messenger. On America Online, it's known as an instant message—"IM" for short. Some people also call it a private message, or "PM" for short.

♦ **Web-based chats.** Some Web sites let you chat right on the site itself. No software is needed—just head to a site and yak away.

♦ **Private chat rooms.** In some kinds of chats, such as on America Online, you can create private chat rooms where you and only those you invite can enter. You might be invited into a private chat room. Kids should never go into a private chat room unless they know the person who created it.

What Dangers There Are in Chatting

You and your family face a number of different dangers while chatting—everything from simply having to deal with a rude or unpleasant person, to having your e-mail address taken and put on spam lists, to having your children targeted by adults, and even more. In this section, I look at advice on how you can avoid dangers when you chat. The use of IRC has a different set of dangers associated with it. I cover all that, as well as the dangers of instant messengers later in the chapter in the section "Don't Let IRC Irk You: The Special Dangers of IRC Chat."

> **Notes**
>
> You might sometimes hear the phrase *real-time chat*. It just means that you're chatting live—you see what people type at that moment, and they see what you type at that moment. And because all chat is live, the phrase doesn't really add any meaning to the term *chat*.

People Might Not Be Who They Say They Are

There's a famous cartoon in the *New Yorker* magazine in which a dog, poised near a keyboard, says something like "On the Internet, no one knows you're a dog."

Well, take that a little bit further. On the Internet, you don't know whether the 12-year-old girl your daughter is chatting with is really a 45-year-old male pedophile. You don't know whether the pleasant, mild-mannered man you're chatting with who says his hobbies are raising orchids and studying chess, is really a raving lunatic. The whole point of chatting is to make friends, and it's hard for you to believe that people can be hiding identities like that. But they can. So be careful what information you give out about yourself to anyone you meet in chats.

Moderated Chats Are Safer Than Unmoderated Ones

Most chats are freewheeling: Anybody can say anything they want, and they usually do. But some chats are moderated, which means that someone watches what goes on and can kick people out of the chat area if they're getting out of hand. (Hanging from the chandeliers is usually considered okay, though, so you're safe on that account.) It's best if children participate only in moderated chats. And if you're offended by sexually oriented talks or abusive behavior, consider looking for moderated chats.

Report Abusive Behavior to Moderators or the Online Service

There's something about chats that pushes some people over the edge. The partial anonymity—and the fact that nobody's liable to punch them out for being rude—gives them a license to act abusively, to harass people, and to act as all-around jerks.

If you're in a chat area and someone is exhibiting abusive behavior, in particular if they're harassing you, report them to a moderator (if there is one). And if it's a chat on America Online, report their behavior to the service. On a service like America Online, people can be kicked off the service for abusive behavior. If the behavior bothers you, leave the chat area. To report abusive behavior of any kind on America Online, use the keywords NOTIFY AOL and follow the instructions.

> **Notes**
>
> People who moderate chat areas go by a number of different names. A common one is SYSOP—short for System Operator.

Using the Bozo Filter to Block Messages from Bozos

If someone is being abusive on a chat, but you don't want to leave the chat room, don't let the jerk force you off—there's a way you can stay in the chat room without having to put up with abusive behavior or harassment. Many chats enable you to block messages from certain people so that you never see any of their messages. Think of it as a Bozo filter. If only we could do this in real life! Of course, if we could, no one would ever have to hear another word any politician ever spoke … not a bad thing, when you think about it.

Check the specific kind of chat software you're using to see how you can block the Bozos. (Don't look under Bozo in the documentation, though, because you won't find it listed there.) Figure 18.2 shows how you do it when using Yahoo! Messenger to participate in a chat.

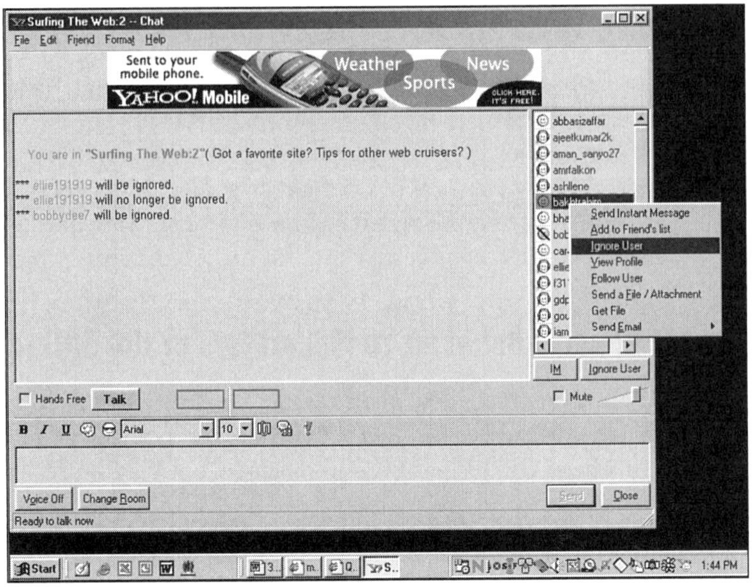

Figure 18.2

The fastest way to get rid of the Bozos is to block messages from people when you use Yahoo! Messenger.

Check This Out!

America Online's Internet Instant Messenger enables you to block people from sending you messages—but it goes well beyond that. You can also issue a "warning" to someone. When you issue a warning to someone, that person can send and receive fewer messages than they could before the warning. And if they receive enough warnings from people, they aren't allowed to send and receive messages at all. It's the best way of all to block the Bozos.

Never Give Out Your Real Identifying Information

People can often seem so friendly, so good-natured, and just so plain nice in a chat room or via an instant message that you'll be tempted to give out identifying information about yourself. Well, I have three words for you if you face that temptation: *Don't do it!* Stalkers and harassers can seem charming at first—that's how they can insinuate their way into people's lives. But remember, if you give out identifying information about yourself, you can be stalked. The identifying information can be used in scams, as well. Remember, on the Internet, no one knows you're a dog—or a stalker or a scam artist.

Meet in a Public Place

Sometimes relationships born online can blossom into real-life friendships. I can speak from personal experience here: Someone who I met in a writer's discussion area later became a good friend of mine after we found out we lived in the same area and met for lunch. But you need to be careful when meeting someone in real life—you don't really know what that person is like. So if you agree to meet someone in person, only agree to do it in a public place, such as a coffee shop or a restaurant. *Never* agree to meet at or very near your home.

Don't Give Up Your Life for an Online Stranger

The story has become such a commonplace that it's become a cliché. Two people meet online. One or both might already be married. They develop such a close relationship that one decides he's head over heels in love with the other, and gives up his entire life—friends, family, job, and all. And in brief order the relationship turns sour, because real life can never stand up to fantasy. And so a person's life is destroyed … and in some cases, there's physical violence, as well.

So never give up your life for an online stranger. It won't work out. Keep fantasy a fantasy and real-life, real-life.

Check This Out!

Kids love to chat. But they're also more vulnerable than adults to stalkers and harassers. There's a lot you can do to protect your kids when they chat. Turn to Chapter 21, "The Best Rules for Keeping Kids Safe on the Internet," and Chapter 22, "Playing It Safe on America Online," for advice on how to do that.

Keep Your E-mail Address from Spammers

People who send out spam often gather e-mail addresses from chat rooms as a way to build up their junk e-mail lists. This is a particular problem on America Online. There are ways to make sure that you won't be subject to spam after entering chat areas. America Online users should create a separate screen name to use whenever they're chatting. That way, the spam is all routed to that screen name, and the spam that piles up there can be ignored. America Online users can also create a new screen name every time they chat, and then abandon that screen name. That way, the screen name no longer exists by the time it's spammed. Of course, it's harder for friends to keep track of you if you use disposable screen names.

For other kinds of chats, outsmart spammers by using a separate e-mail address or ID from your real one when you chat. That way, spam is routed to that address or ID—and you simply never check that account, so you're never spammed. To do this, get a free e-mail address and use that when participating in Internet chats. To find out how to get free e-mail addresses, turn to Chapter 16, "Beyond Luncheon Meat: How to Protect Yourself Against Spam."

Don't Let IRC Irk You: The Special Dangers of IRC Chat

When you chat using IRC, you should heed all the advice about chats in general to keep yourself safe. But IRC poses its own special dangers. Because of a security hole in IRC, it's easy for people to send you viruses and Trojan horses, and damage your computer, or even steal your passwords and take control of your computer.

The cause of the potential trouble are two IRC features. One is the ability to run what are called "scripts." The other is a way to communicate known as "DCC." Here's what you need to know to keep yourself safe if using each.

Beware When Running IRC Scripts

Chatting on IRC is pretty simple. But the truth is, underneath it all, IRC is extremely complex and has all kinds of hidden capabilities and powers. One of those capabilities is the ability to run *scripts*. When you run an IRC script, your computer performs a series of commands that the script tells it to. Commonly, you get scripts when people send them to you over IRC.

The problem is that unless you know what you're doing—and I mean *really* know what you're doing—you won't know before a script runs what it will really do. Sure, a person might *tell* you it'll do all kinds of neat stuff, but for all you know, the script might in fact search through your computer for all your passwords and then silently send those passwords back to a hacker.

Even if a friend tells you a script is safe, don't believe him. Unless your friend is a true wizard, there's no way for him to know what the script really does. And some legitimate, useful scripts have been hacked to do damage.

So unless you're a wizard yourself, don't run scripts. They're too dangerous to mess around with.

Beware When Using DCC

When you issue a *DCC* command in IRC, you open up a direct connection between you and another person. This can be helpful because it enables the two of you to chat directly, and with no lag time as sometimes happens in normal IRC. When using DCC, you can send and receive files with the person with whom you've opened up the connection.

And therein lies the rub. When you open up a DCC connection with someone, you're opening yourself up to all kinds of attacks. Someone can send you files of all kinds— including Trojan horses. And when they do that, they can literally take control of your PC, without you knowing about it.

A DCC connection was used by hackers to get an infamous Trojan horse called Back Orifice onto thousands of computers. Back Orifice enables a hacker to take complete control of a computer across the Internet. A hacker can look at every single file on the computer, steal passwords, delete and move files, run programs—in fact, can control a computer just as if he were sitting at a keyboard.

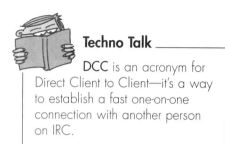

Techno Talk

DCC is an acronym for Direct Client to Client—it's a way to establish a fast one-on-one connection with another person on IRC.

Normally, if someone wants to open a DCC connection with you, you get a request. And then, if they want to send you a file, you get another request. That means that there's an easy way to make sure you don't run into trouble—when someone wants to open a DCC connection with you, turn it down. And if you've opened a DCC connection with someone and they want to send you a file, just say no.

Simple, yes? Ah, but this is the Internet we're talking about, so nothing is truly simple. When you're using IRC software, you get to set the DCC options. Check those settings. There's a setting in DCC that leaves you open to any passing hacker or cracker out there. If your DCC settings are set to Auto-Get, then you never get a warning when someone tries to send you a file—it's sent to you automatically. And after you get that file, you could be in big, big trouble.

So read your chat software documentation, and check your DCC settings. Make sure it is *not* set to Auto-Get. For maximum safety, set it to Ignore All. When you do that, no one can ever send you files. You don't even get a warning—the file is automatically turned away.

Protecting Yourself When Using Instant Messengers

When you use instant messengers, the same rules of safety apply as when you're chatting. So when using these programs, follow that same advice.

However, there are some special issues concerning instant messengers. The foremost is to beware of accepting files from anyone. Instant messaging programs enable you to exchange files with others. It's a great way for sharing information and files, but it's also a great way to get a virus or Trojan horse.

The first rule is simple: Don't accept files from people you don't know. Ever. Case closed.

Be very leery of accepting files from people you do know, as well, in the same way as you would be leery of accepting files via e-mail. If a friend offers to send you a file, ask what it is and whether it's been checked for viruses.

Also check the settings of your instant messenger program to make sure that it's not set to automatically accept files. That way you're more secure. Figure 18.3 shows the screen you use in ICQ to make sure you don't automatically accept files.

Figure 18.3

Here's how to make sure that you can't automatically accept files when using ICQ.

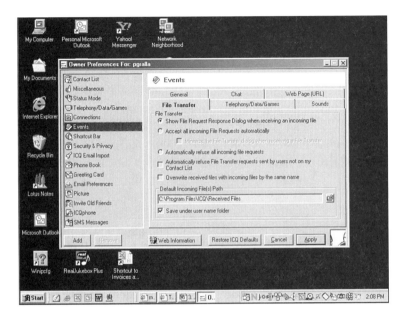

When you install an instant messenger program, you're asked to register and provide information about yourself. The information can be as basic as your gender. But you can also provide a great deal more information about yourself, including your real name, address, phone number, occupation, and other personally identifying information.

For safety's sake, leave these profiles about yourself as generic as possible. If you give too much information about yourself, it can potentially lead to identity theft. I leave my profiles as blank as possible.

Special Issues When Using ICQ

ICQ is an exceedingly popular instant messenger program. It's also a bit confusing to use, and contains all kinds of hidden features.

But some of those features are important if you want to ensure your privacy and safety.

The first is one I've already mentioned. Turn off the feature that automatically accepts files sent to you by others. To get to that screen, when you get to the program's **Preferences** screen, click **Events,** then the **File Transfer** tab, and make sure it's not set to automatically accept files.

To handle most of the other privacy and security features, click **Security & Privacy** from the **Preferences** screen, and then click the various tabs that appear. Particularly important is to click the **Direct Connection** tab, and make sure that you don't allow a direct connection with any user. When you allow that, you're allowing others to see your IP address, and if a hacker has your IP address, it's easier for him to break into your PC.

ICQ users soon find out that they can easily be inundated by spam. These are often links to pornographic Web sites. To stop spam, from the **Security & Privacy** tab click **Ignore** and check the box that says **Do not accept Multi-Recipient Messages from Users not on my Contact List** (see Figure 18.4). Spam is then blocked.

> ### Notes
>
> Pitch alert! Want to learn more about ICQ, the world's most popular instant messenger? Then check out *Teach Yourself ICQ in 24 Hours* written by (blush, blush) me.

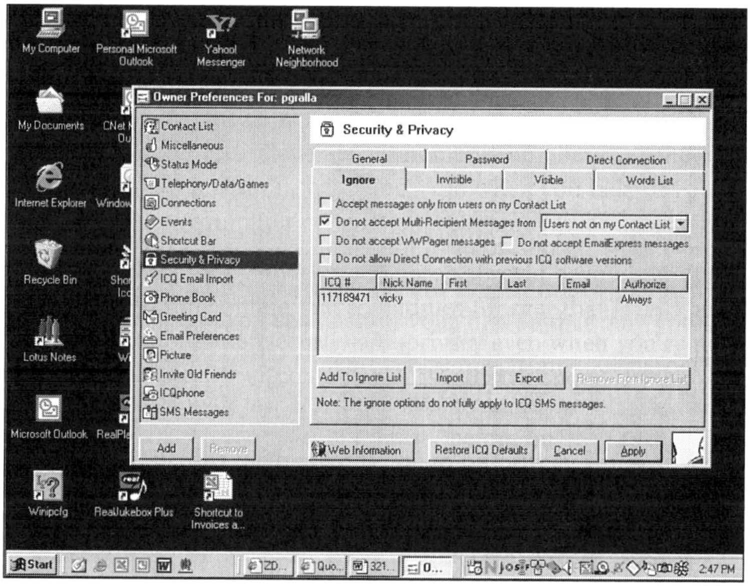

Figure 18.4

Here's how to block spam in ICQ.

The Least You Need to Know

◆ Realize that people often disguise their identities and personalities when they chat and use instant messengers.

◆ Moderated chats are safer to participate in than ones that aren't moderated.

◆ Never give out your real name, address, telephone number, or other identifying information in chat rooms or in instant message program profiles.

◆ Use Bozo filters to block messages from people who are abusive or harassers.

◆ In instant messenger programs, never accept files from people you don't know, and make sure the program does not automatically accept files from everyone who wants to send them to you.

Protecting Your Privacy on Internet Newsgroups and Discussion Areas

In This Chapter

- ◆ What are Usenet newsgroups and other online public discussion areas?
- ◆ Privacy invasion when joining public discussions online
- ◆ Protect your privacy when participating in online public discussions
- ◆ Abusive or harassing behavior on newsgroups and in discussion areas
- ◆ Getting your postings out of sites that archive newsgroup postings

Cyberspace is a vast, freewheeling place where you can talk to others in public discussions about anything under the sun and over the stars … and all places in between.

That's the good news. The bad news is that these freewheeling discussions can be used to invade your privacy. When you participate in discussions, people can put together a profile about your likes and dislikes, put you onto spam mailing lists, and abuse your privacy in other ways. In this chapter, you'll see how you can protect yourself when participating in public discussions on the Internet and online services.

What Are Usenet Newsgroups?

Quick, without thinking, tell me what you think newsgroups are. Are they (a) Roving packs of journalists; (b) The usual gang of gasbags and blowhards who talk about current events on cable news channels; or (c) None of the above?

If you answered (c) None of the above, you're right on target. You'd think that something called newsgroups would have something to do with the news, but nooooo. This is the Internet we're talking about, and nothing is what it says it is. As for why they're called Usenet newsgroups …. Suffice to say the name was derived from the term "User Network."

Newsgroups are discussion areas on the Internet in which you can talk about anything you want. Like talking with others about pranks? Head to alt.shenanigans. Are you a fan of the TV show *Buffy the Vampire Slayer*? You're not alone, as you'll find out at alt.tv.buffy-v-slayer. A space cadet, are you? Meet like-minded others at sci.astro.

To participate in newsgroups, you need a piece of software called a *newsreader*. Both Netscape Navigator and Microsoft Internet Explorer have newsreaders built into them, and there are many others you can find at download sites such as www.download.com. Figure 19.1 shows Internet Explorer's newsreader that is built into Outlook Express and Outlook.

You can also participate in newsgroups by going to the Google Groups at //groups.google.com/. You don't need any special software—you're able to do everything right from that page via your Web browser.

> **Notes**
>
> A "flame" is when someone in a newsgroup or other discussion area verbally and vociferously attacks someone else—often for no clear reason. It can also be used as a verb, as in "to flame, or to be flamed" (that is the question …). There are people who love nothing more than to go online and flame people, just for their little bit of fame. (A fame flame?)

> **Notes**
>
> In most newsgroups, people post directly to the newsgroup and it immediately goes. That's one reason why so many newsgroups are filled with spam these days. However, in moderated newsgroups, you post a message, but it doesn't immediately go live. Instead, it goes to a moderator who checks each message, making sure it's not spam and it fits the newsgroup topic.

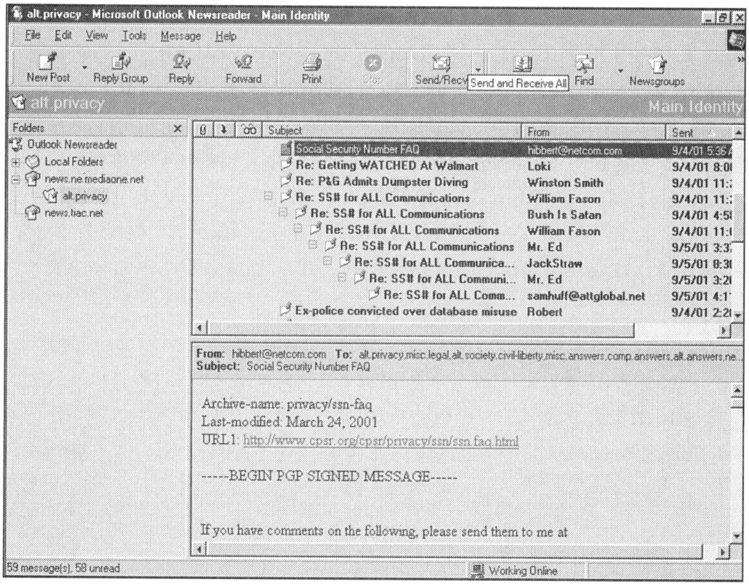

Figure 19.1

My newsreader of choice is Microsoft's Outlook Express.

What Other Kinds of Discussion Areas Are There?

Newsgroups aren't the only kinds of discussion areas on the Internet and online services. America Online has very active message boards and many Web sites have Web-based discussion areas as well.

Although these discussion areas use different technology than newsgroups, many of the privacy issues they pose are the same, as you see in the following section.

What Dangers Are There in Newsgroups and Discussion Areas?

What could be wrong with talking to people about *Buffy the Vampire Slayer*, whether Pluto is truly a planet (at last look it still is), or good April Fool's jokes? By itself, maybe nothing. But there are a lot of problems you might come across when participating in public discussions—everything from getting your name on spam lists to being harassed, to people being able to put together a profile of your interests with only a few mouse-clicks. Here are issues you should be concerned about:

◆ **You might reveal information about yourself that you don't want an employer or people in your local community to know about.** Maybe you've talked in discussion areas about your personal life, medical condition, or your political beliefs—and they're things that you don't want employers, would-be employers, or people in your local community to know about. It's easy for employers or would-be employers to check out your postings.

◆ **Anyone can put together a detailed profile of your interests and personality by doing a search at Google Groups at //groups.google.com/.** Google Groups is a Web site that enables you to post and read newsgroup messages. But it also enables people to search for every posting you ever made to Usenet newsgroups, making it very easy for someone to put together a personality profile about you.

◆ **You might be put on spam lists.** Spam is unsolicited e-mail sent to you from people you don't know about things you don't want. It's very annoying and can clog up your e-mail box. Spammers often go to Usenet newsgroups and "harvest" names to put into their spam lists.

◆ **You might be harassed by people online—and they could also find out your e-mail address and harass you via e-mail.** Most people on the Internet are normal (well, at least *near*-normal), but there are also a lot of weirdos out there who might harass you because they object to something you said about Buffy or for no discernable reason.

Protecting Your Privacy on Newsgroups and Discussion Areas

You can see there are many reasons why you want to protect your privacy in newsgroups and discussion areas. Don't let that scare you away, though. There's a lot you can do to protect your privacy online. Here's everything you need to know.

Hide Your E-mail Address in Your Newsreader

When you post a message to newsgroups, your e-mail address is right there, for the entire world to see. That's because you put information into your Web browser or newsreader that included your e-mail address.

But what you put in, you can also take out. And you can also make a phony address. Taking out your e-mail address or replacing it with a phony one helps to hide your identity from spammers and others.

Check your specific newsreader to see how to hide your e-mail address. If you use Outlook's or Outlook Express's built-in newsreader, it's easy to hide your address. First launch the newsreader. (This varies according to what version of Outlook you have. Commonly, though, you choose **Go To** from the **View** menu, and then choose **News.**) Then right-click your newsgroup server—for example, news.ne.mediaone.net. Now, click **Properties.** In the General tab is an input box where your e-mail address goes. Simply delete your e-mail address to make it unavailable to anyone when you use newsgroups (see Figure 19.2).

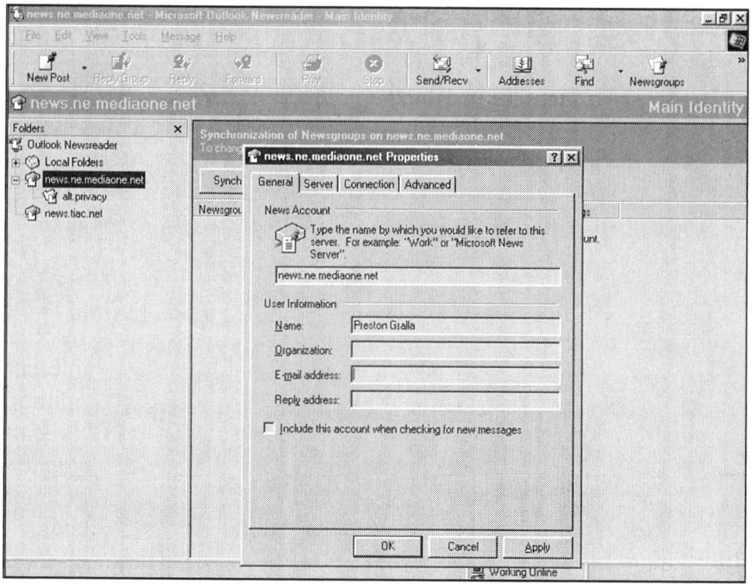

Figure 19.2

Here's how you can make sure that your e-mail address doesn't show up when you post to newsgroups using Outlook's newsgroup reader.

Make Sure Your Posts Aren't Put into Databases

Sites such as Google Groups take every post made in Usenet newsgroups and, in essence, put them into an easy-to-search database so anyone, anywhere, anytime can search through them. That means your words live forever. And someone can put together a profile of you based on all your postings.

There's a way for you to keep your name out of these kinds of databases. You can add a special header to your posting that alerts sites that you don't want your posting put in their databases.

Put this line into the header of your message: X-no-archive:yes.

When you do that, sites like Google Groups won't put your post into their database. Check your newsgroup reader's manual to see how to edit the header. And see the section later in this chapter in "Your Permanent Profile and What You Can Do About It," for more information about Google Groups and privacy.

Use an Alias on Google Groups

If you'd like to post messages, but don't want your real identity known, register with Google Groups under a different name. This way, all your postings appear with that name. You have to supply a valid e-mail address, but you can easily get one specifically for this purpose from a free e-mail site like www.hotmail.com.

Use a Separate Screen Name When Posting Messages on America Online

America Online enables you to create several screen names. When you post a message on America Online, it automatically identifies you by your screen name. So create a separate screen name to use whenever you're posting a message. (Perhaps you want to create a new name in addition to the separate screen name you use to chat, as I suggest in the previous chapter.) That way, you're identified by that screen name, and if anyone sends you spam or harasses you, it's on a separate screen name. You can also create a new screen name every time you want to post a message, and then abandon that screen name. That way, the screen name no longer exists after you get rid of it.

Report Any Harassing Behavior to Your Online Service or Internet Service Provider

If you're being harassed in postings, report the harasser to your online service, such as America Online. If the harassment occurs on a newsgroup, report it to your Internet Service Provider (ISP).

> **Check This Out!**
>
> Being able to hide your identity when posting messages can be liberating—but you don't want to abuse the privilege of privacy. When posting anonymously, you shouldn't use hate speech, harass people, try to manipulate stocks by planting false rumors, or send out spam.

Use an Anonymous Remailer to Post Your Messages

An anonymous remailer enables you to post a message on a Usenet newsgroup without anyone knowing your e-mail address. (As you might guess from the name—smart you!—you can send e-mail with them anonymously, as well.)

Many different kinds of anonymous remailers enable you to do this. For more information about how to use anonymous remailers, and how to post Usenet messages with them, turn to Chapter 17, "Staying Anonymous with Anonymous Remailers."

Your Permanent Profile and What You Can Do About It

As I've mentioned several times in this chapter, Google Groups keeps a permanent record of every posting made to newsgroups. This makes it easy for someone to put together a profile of your likes, dislikes, hobbies, and personality. (Likes rabbits, hates sea monkeys, hobby is collecting toenail clippings, personality is multiple.)

But Google Groups also gives you ways to protect your privacy. You can delete any posting you want out of the site, so that when people search through it, they'll find only the postings you want them to find. (It's okay to let them find postings on your affection for rabbits; it's not okay to find postings on your toenail collection.)

In Google parlance, when you want to delete a posting, you "nuke" it. So how to nuke a posting? It's easy to do. Send an e-mail to groups-support@google.com with the following information:

- ◆ Your name and contact information, including an e-mail address at which you can be reached.

- ◆ The entire Google Groups URL (or message ID) for each message you want deleted.

- ◆ The statement "I swear under penalty of civil or criminal laws that I am the person who posted each of the foregoing messages or am authorized to request removal by the person who posted those messages."

If someone is using Google Groups to post messages that you feel are abusive or harassing, you can report them to the site, which may take action against the person. To do that, send information about the posting(s) to groups-abuse@google.com.

The Least You Need to Know

- ◆ To protect your privacy when you post messages, hide your e-mail address in your newsreader.

- ◆ To keep your posts out of sites that archive newsgroup messages, put this line into the header of your message: X-no-archive:yes.

- ◆ To hide your true identity when posting to a newsgroup, you can use an anonymous remailer.

- ◆ Report any abusive posting behavior to your online service or your Internet Service Provider.

Part  Protecting Your Children and Family Online

Many parents are justifiably worried about their children using the Internet. They've heard stories of stalkers, they worry that their children might come across inappropriate material online, and they worry that their kids' privacy might be invaded when they surf the Web.

But the truth is, there are ways to keep your kids safe online. It's not hard at all—and it won't interfere with their enjoyment of the Internet, either. In this part, you'll find out the best tips for teaching your kids so they'll stay safe online, you'll get parenting and technical advice on keeping them safe, and you'll see how to use site-blocking software so that they don't come across inappropriate material online. And because so many children use America Online, I'll also teach you how you can customize that service to keep your children safe and secure.

So when it comes to your kids getting online, don't worry, be happy. They'll be able to get all the amazing resources of the Internet, and they'll be safe and secure, as well.

Chapter 20

Online Dangers That Kids Face

In This Chapter

♦ What you should know about online stalkers

♦ How children can come across inappropriate material online

♦ What is site-blocking software?

♦ The e-mail dangers kids face

♦ The ways in which your children's privacy can be violated online

The Internet is a great place for kids—it's a combination of the world's biggest library, playground, amusement park, school, and den for hanging out with their friends.

But it can pose dangers, as well. Your children can be stalked online, can come across inappropriate material, or can have their privacy violated. That doesn't mean they shouldn't spend time online, because they should. But you should know the dangers they can face online—and know what to do about them. In this chapter, we look at the kinds of dangers your children face online, and I give brief advice on how to handle them. Then in the next chapters, I give in-depth advice on how you can keep your kids safe and protect their privacy online.

The Dangers Children Face Online

Just about every week, it seems, you hear yet another story about the dangers posed by the Internet to children. Of how easy it is for them to come across pornographic or other kinds of inappropriate material. Of how they can be targeted by stalkers. Of how their privacy can be invaded by marketers of every kind and stripe. Of how they've been lured by strangers into real-life meetings, with disastrous results.

Yes, the stories are true. But considering how many children use the Internet, they're also relatively rare. You shouldn't be frightened away from letting your children use the Internet any more than you should be frightened away from letting them walk in your neighborhood or go to the public library.

Because the truth is, the Internet is a great place for kids to go. They can visit amazing locations, they can learn from the earth's largest virtual library, they can get homework help, they can make friends on many continents, and they can learn a great deal about the world and their place in it. And let's not forget that they're kids—so they can have loads of fun, as well.

I know all this from experience—I have two children of my own, Gabriel and Mia. (Hi, kids! Nice seeing your name in print again, isn't it?) They've learned and grown from using the Internet, they've done better in school because of it, and they've certainly had fun on it. (Right now, I'll bet Gabe is continuing his quest for world domination online in Diablo II. And Mia, no doubt, is chatting with her online buddies on America Online—about 17 at the same time.)

Just as you need to make sure that your children are safe in the real world, you also need to make sure that they're safe when they're online. In general, there are three types of dangers that you need to be concerned about when your kids go online:

◆ **They can be targeted by stalkers or those who might take advantage of them.** Your adolescent daughter might think she's becoming best online friends with a 14-year-old girl, when in fact, it's a 45-year-old man—and he wants to set up a meeting with her.

◆ **They can come across inappropriate material such as pornographic pictures or violence and hate sites.** The Internet is a vast, free-wheeling place, and there are nasty nooks and crannies they might come across.

◆ **Their privacy can be invaded.** Kids love contests. They love games. They love getting things for free. Big companies and advertisers know this, and they often induce children into giving away information about themselves and their family online, so that your and your kids' privacy might be invaded.

Check This Out! _____

The Internet is a vast place, and often the best way to find information on it is to go to a search site or Web portal such as Yahoo! or Excite. But when kids do searches on those sites, they might find inappropriate material in the searches—and the searches generally are targeted at adults, not kids. The solution to the problem: Have your kids visit a kid-centric search site such as Yahooligans! at www.yahooligans.com. It's safe, the information your kids find across the Internet from there is designed for kids, and there's a lot of cool kid stuff for them to check out, as well.

Are There Really Stalkers Online?

Perhaps the thing that kids love to do the most online is communicate with others. They love making friends, learning about other people and places, and hanging out with their friends. To a great extent, that's how kids learn who they are—by talking with others. Chat, e-mail, and instant messengers all make it easy for kids to find friends. And the Internet's international reach enables kids to have pen pals from all over the world.

That's great and should be encouraged. But there are dangers to that, as well. Your child can be harassed and stalked or victimized by adults looking to take advantage of children's trust and innocence. There is a set of rules your kids should follow to make sure that they aren't victimized. Two of the most important are:

◆ They should realize that the people they are communicating with might not be who they say they are.

◆ They should never agree to meet any of their online acquaintances unless you're present with them and it's in a public place.

For more rules your children should follow, turn to Chapter 21, "The Best Rules for Keeping Kids Safe on the Internet," and Chapter 22, "Playing It Safe on America Online."

Check This Out! _____

As a parent, you like to know who your kids' friends are. The same should hold true in the online world—try to get to know their online buddies. You often can tell more clearly than your child if those buddies really are your children's age or are pretending to be their age. Drop in on your kids when they chat online, ask them to tell you about who's in the chat room with them, and look at the screen to see what the chat is about.

How Can Kids View Inappropriate Material Online?

Free speech is messy, especially on the Internet. The same basic right that has protected us from tyranny for over 200 years is also used to post material online that is truly objectionable—sexually oriented material, violent material, and sites devoted to hate.

If children want to find that material, they will no doubt be able to find it. All they need to do is spend a few minutes at a search site or Web portal, and they can find what they want.

Even if a child doesn't go searching for that material, he or she might find it anyway. Surfing the Web, visiting chat rooms, participating in Usenet newsgroups, even just getting e-mail can all inadvertently expose your children to material that you find objectionable.

There are many things you can do about your kids finding objectionable material online. Here are some of the most important:

◆ **Use common-sense parenting.** Your children are bombarded daily with objectionable material on television and the radio, in newspapers and in magazines—just remember the often-salacious reporting on President Clinton and Monica Lewinsky several years back, or the nightly news. Just as you discuss objectionable material available on the airwaves and in print, also discuss with them anything they find on the Internet that's objectionable. Encourage them to come to you with questions they have.

◆ **Use site-blocking software.** You can get software that blocks objectionable sites on the Internet, such as those that are sexual or violent in nature. This is called *site-blocking software*. You can also block the kinds of sites your children visit on America Online. For more information about site-blocking software, turn to Chapter 21 and Chapter 22.

◆ **Know where your children spend time online.** When your children leave the house, you want to know where they're going. If they go somewhere after school, you want to know where they are, as well. The same should hold true for the online world; knowing where your children spend their time helps make sure they aren't visiting inappropriate sites. Drop in on your children when they're using the Internet, see where they visit, and talk with them about it.

◆ **Find out your library and school's Internet access policies.** Many libraries and schools offer

Check This Out!

Site-blocking software is far from a perfect solution to the problem of your children seeing objectionable material online, and many parents might not want to use it. The software might also block important, useful sites that you would like your children to see, such as sites about breast-cancer prevention or the dangers posed by AIDS.

access to the Internet, and your children might be getting onto the Internet there. Find out what those policies are. Do they use site-blocking software? What can you do if you want your children to have full access to the Internet, without site-blocking software? What are the policies for chatting? Do more than just find out—get involved in setting those policies, if they're still being set, by attending and speaking at public meetings.

There are many more tips about what you can do about your children coming across inappropriate sites online. Turn to Chapter 21 for more details.

How Kids' Privacy Can Be Violated

To many companies, your child is a potential gold mine. Children spend billions of dollars a year and they influence the spending of many billions of other dollars. (Don't believe they influence billions in spending? Just try taking your child to the supermarket and passing the candy aisle. Or count the number of times you've bought Beanie Babies or Furbies, and countless other dolls, toys, and games in the past year.)

Not only that, kids are impressionable and, at an early age, begin to notice brands. If a company can get your kids to become loyal customers, that company might have customers for life. Have you noticed how often your kids sing jingles from commercials—or worse yet, extol the virtues of MCI over AT&T? They're a marketer's best dream.

Many kid-oriented sites on the Web gather personal information about children and then use that information themselves or sell it to other marketers. And we're not talking just names and e-mail addresses. Web sites have gathered highly personal information from children, such as whether the child has gotten gifts in the form of savings bonds, stocks, mutual funds, cash, or other financial services—and whether the children's parents own mutual funds. That same site publicly posted the full names, ages, and full addresses—including city, state, and ZIP code—of kids who won a contest.

There is a piece of good news, though. The law is on your side. The federal Children's Online Privacy Protection Act has a set of guidelines that cover the information Web sites can gather about

> **Check This Out!**
>
> The Federal Trade Commission, looking into the issue of how kids' privacy can be invaded online, did a survey and found that nearly ninety percent of child-oriented sites it visited collected personal information from children. They did this by using contests, games, guest books, and other means. Less than 10 percent of those sites tried to obtain the parents' consent about collecting that information.

children, and what those sites can do with that information. It even *prohibits* Web sites from gathering information about your kids without your express approval.

Still, creating a law is one thing, and enforcing it is another. So you shouldn't rely on the government to protect your kids' privacy. The best way to do it is to make sure that they never give out any information about themselves or your family that you don't think should be revealed. For more information on how to protect your children's privacy online, turn to Chapter 21.

The Dangers for Kids in E-mail

Kids love to send and receive e-mail. They make new friends this way, keep in touch with old ones, and, in general, have a grand old time.

> **Notes**
>
> According to lawyers we've talked to, sending spam that has links to pornographic sites to kids is apparently legal. That's because the sender doesn't knowingly send the spam to kids—the spam is sent to many thousands of e-mail addresses, and the spammer doesn't know who's at each address. However, if the spammer actually sends pictures, that might not be legal.

> **Techno Talk**
>
> To you or me, an e-mail chain letter is an annoyance. Ah, but to kids it's the very stuff of life. Kids love to send and receive chain letters. So if you notice your kid's mailbox is stuffed with chain letters, don't worry. It's not a mail bomb. Your kids just wanna have fun.

All that should be encouraged. But e-mail also poses dangers for kids. Here's the rundown of some potential problems with e-mail.

- **Your kids can be sent unwanted e-mail (called spam) that contains inappropriate material, such as links to pornographic sites.** Millions of pieces of unwanted e-mail—commonly known as spam—are sent over the Internet every day. A surprisingly high percentage of such mail includes links to pornographic sites. To visit the sites, your kids need only click the links.

- **A stalker can target your kids via e-mail, posing as a child.** A stranger can send e-mail to your children, and there's no way for your kids to know that the sender of the mail is really a 35-year-old man, not a 10-year-old boy, as he claims.

- **Your child can be sent harassing e-mail.** Someone can target your child and send him or her harassing e-mail—the e-mail might be as dangerous as a threat, or as innocuous as teasing. But even innocuous teasing can seem dangerous and harassing when it's received via e-mail.

- **Your child can be sent an attachment that contains a virus or is pornographic in nature.** Files can be attached to e-mail messages. Kids love to send attachments to each other—things such as pictures or funny little programs. But there's a chance that your child can be sent an attachment with pornographic material or a virus in it.

◆ **Your child can be sent a mail bomb.** A mail bomb isn't a file that blows up a computer. Instead, it's a constant series of e-mails—possibly hundreds or more—that makes it difficult, if not impossible, for your child to use e-mail or the computer.

It sounds scary, I know. But you don't really need to be concerned. As I show you in the next chapter, there's a lot you can do to protect your kids from any e-mail dangers.

The Least You Need to Know

◆ To help your kids avoid stalkers, teach your children that people can disguise themselves online and might not be who they say they are.

◆ Tell your children never to agree to meet anyone they've made friends with online unless you're present and it's in a public place.

◆ Site-blocking software can block your children from seeing inappropriate material—but it can also block them from seeing informational sites you'd like them to be able to visit.

◆ Ninety percent of kid-oriented sites collect personal information from children.

◆ Your children shouldn't give out any personal information about themselves to a Web site without your approval.

Chapter 21

The Best Rules for Keeping Kids Safe on the Internet

In This Chapter

- ◆ How good basic parenting helps keep your children safe online
- ◆ The best rules for making sure your kids stay safe online
- ◆ Protect your children's privacy on the Internet and the Web
- ◆ Protect your kids in chat, using instant messaging, and sending and receiving e-mail
- ◆ Should you use filtering software?

There's a lot that technology can do to help you keep your kids safe and secure when they're online, as you'll see in the next few chapters. But even more important than technology is to teach your kids how to stay safe and protect their privacy when they're connected. There's a lot of rules you should know for making sure that your kids' online experience is a happy one.

In this chapter, you'll take a look at those rules. And you'll spend time learning how to protect your kids' privacy when they hop onto the Net, not just how to keep them safe.

In addition to those rules, you'll also get detailed advice on how to protect kids when they surf the Web, chat, use instant messaging and e-mail. And you'll get the rundown on using filtering software, sometimes called parental control software, to protect your kids.

The Best Line of Defense: Good Parenting

There are all kinds of advice, tips, software, and Web sites that can help you keep your kids safe and protect their privacy when they go online. They're all necessary and they're all useful. But the truth is, there's something a whole lot more important than all of that put together—and that's being a good parent. It sounds trite, I know. After all, aren't we all good parents?

Yes, we're undoubtedly all good parents. But I've noticed that when it comes to the Internet, parents can get strange. They act as if somehow the Internet is separate from the rest of their and their children's lives. They can start to trust their children less, or be less secure that the things they've taught their children about the real world will carry over into the online world.

So overriding everything else in this chapter is to apply the same common-sense rules of parenting to the Internet that you do in the real world. Go back to the basics: Teach your kids right from wrong; let them know what's appropriate for them to do and view online and what isn't. Recognize that the online world is like the real world; you want to know who their friends are and where they're visiting, but you don't want to be overbearing or intrusive about it. Most of all, you want your children to trust you enough that they'll come to you if they need advice, want to know whether visiting certain Web sites is suitable, or are made uncomfortable by things that have been said to them in chat rooms or via e-mail.

And, as many of us have learned the hard way, often the best way to get your kids to trust you is to show that *you* trust *them*. That means that although you want to know what your kids are doing online, you should be careful about not being intrusive, and you shouldn't try to find out what your kids are doing online without them knowing about it.

Check This Out! _____

You can get a helpful, free pamphlet on how to protect your children. An excellent resource for any parent concerned about how to keep their children safe online is "Child Safety on the Information Highway," by the National Center for Missing and Exploited Children and the Interactive Services Association (8403 Colesville Road, Suite 865, Silver Springs, MD 20910). Much of the information in this section of the book is inspired by that pamphlet. You can also read the entire pamphlet and get more information at the National Center for Missing and Exploited Children Web site at www.missingkids.org.

I can tell you from personal experience that this works: I've given my kids pretty free rein in what they do online, and it's paid off. They regularly ask me before they download files from the Internet whether they can register at certain sites, and they come to me when they come across something online that makes them uncomfortable. So just make sure that, however you handle your kids' online use, it brings you together instead of pushes you apart.

Rules for Keeping Kids Safe Online

Good parenting is the basis of how to keep kids safe—but still, there are things you need to do specifically about the Internet and online services to protect your kids. It's best to teach them rules about how to stay safe—in essence, teach them to be what's known in the real world as "street smart," but what we'll call "CyberSmart."

The children most at risk online tend to be teenagers. One reason is that you're more likely to leave them unsupervised than you would younger children. And teenagers go online largely to meet other kids, send and receive e-mail, participate in bulletin boards, and chat, and chat, and chat. You can see a chat in Figure 21.1. Now not only do teens tie up your phone line by talking on the telephone, they also tie it up by dialing in to the Internet to chat and send and receive instant messages. In fact, my teenage daughter Mia can often be found talking into the phone, while chatting online and *instant messaging* at the same time—often to the same people! Talk about wanting to stay in touch!

This tendency to talk and chat has always been normal for teens—but online it has the potential for danger, because a person might pose as someone your child's age, but really be an older person targeting your child.

Check This Out!

One of the best places to get advice about online kid safety is at the www.safekids.com Web site. Run by well-known journalist and columnist Larry Magid, it offers excellent advice and links to other safety sites.

Your kids face three kinds of risks online. He or she might be exposed to inappropriate material of a sexual or violent nature. Your kid also might give out information to a stranger online, or arrange a face-to-face encounter that could risk his or her safety—witness cases in which pedophiles gained a child's confidence, and then arranged a personal meeting and molested the child. And your kid might be exposed to messages via e-mail, bulletin boards, chats, or instant messages that are harassing, demeaning, or hostile.

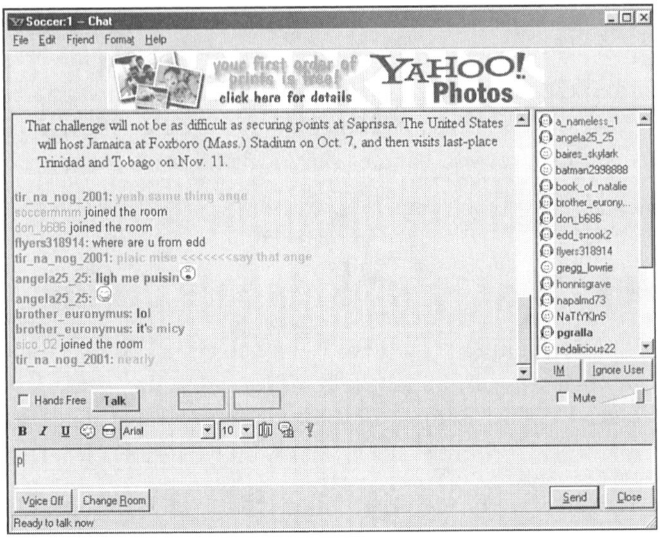

Figure 21.1

Kids love to chat, as you can see here in a Yahoo chat about soccer. But make sure they know safety rules before going online.

Notes

What does "IM me" mean? Watch your kids online in a chat session, and you might frequently see the phrase "IM me." What in the world does that mean? IM stands for Instant Message which is a way for two people to have a private, one-on-one chat, especially on America Online or using America Online's Instant Messenger on the Internet. So when one kid asks another to IM him or her, it's an invitation to a personal chat. Kids often participate in a public chat room as well as several Instant Message sessions simultaneously.

There are ways to protect them against all these dangers. Here's how to do it:

◆ **Block their access to certain portions of the Internet.** There are ways that you can block kids' access to certain Web sites and other areas of the Internet and online services that might be unsuitable for them. You can do this using what's called site-blocking software, or by using the parental control areas of online services. To learn about site-blocking software, turn to the section later in this chapter titled "Using Site-Blocking Software." For how to use America Online parental controls, turn to Chapter 22, "Playing It Safe on America Online."

◆ **Spend time with your children online.** Site-blocking software is no substitute for spending time with your kids when they're online. Ask them where they go, watch what they're doing, and suggest places that you think they might want to visit. That doesn't mean you need to always be there when they go online, but regularly dropping in to ask what they're doing goes a long way to ensure that they aren't visiting inappropriate places or doing inappropriate things.

♦ **Make sure they don't give out personal information.** Data such as home address, school name, or telephone number should never be revealed in public or private message areas such as bulletin boards, chat rooms, or via Instant Messages or e-mail. The person who your 11-year-old daughter believes is another 11-year-old girl might well be a 40-year old man. Also consider unlisting your child's name in public directories on America Online. For how to do it, turn to Chapter 22.

Check This Out!

You can block e-mail from specific individuals to your kids. If your children complain that a specific person is sending e-mail that makes them uncomfortable, or for some other reason they don't want to get messages from someone, there's a simple action you can take. You can configure their e-mail software to block messages from a certain sender, or have the offending messages put automatically into a special "Junk" folder, to be easily deleted. And on America Online, you can block e-mail from specific individuals. For details on how to do it in e-mail, turn to Chapter 16, "Beyond Luncheon Meat: How to Protect Yourself Against Spam." For how to do it on America Online, turn to Chapter 22.

♦ **Don't allow your child to meet someone person-to-person that they've met online without getting your approval.** If you agree to such a meeting, you should go along, and the meeting should be held in a public spot.

♦ **Tell them not to respond to messages that are suggestive, obscene, threatening, or that make them feel uncomfortable.** If your children come across any messages like that, they should tell you about it. Then contact your online service or service provider, send them the message, and ask for their help. If the message is truly threatening, contact the police.

♦ **Child pornography is illegal.** Laws regarding adult content on the Internet are currently being tested in the courts, but child pornography is illegal on or off the Internet. If you become aware of any use or transmission of child pornography online, contact the National Center for Missing and Exploited Children at 1-800-843-5678 and notify your online service.

♦ **Make sure your children know that people might not be who they say they are.** They should always keep in mind that it's easy for someone online to pose as someone else. It's easy for a 45-year-old man to pose as a 10-year-old boy. Even having a scanned picture should not be taken as proof.

Have Your Kids Agree to These Rules Before They Go Online

The National Center for Missing and Exploited Children and the Interactive Services Association have come up with a set of rules that kids should agree to before going online, to protect their safety. Here are their rules—have your kids agree to them before going online:

◆ I will not give out personal information such as my address, telephone number, parents' work address or telephone number, or the name and location of my school without my parents' permission.

◆ I will tell my parents right away if I come across any information that makes me feel uncomfortable.

Check This Out!

Teach your kids not to pose as someone else or harass others. It's not enough to teach your kids how to be safe online—you should also teach them to respect the rights of others. Some kids bully, harass, and demean other kids in chat rooms— so teach your children never to do that. Most of this kind of behavior online probably comes from children, not adults. And tell your kids they shouldn't pose as someone else. Too often, posing as someone else makes kids more likely to exhibit the kind of harassing or unfriendly behavior they'd never show if they were using their real name.

◆ I will never agree to get together with someone I "meet" online without first checking with my parents. If my parents agree to the meeting, I will make sure that it is in a public place and bring my mother or father along.

◆ I will never send a person my picture or anything else without first checking with my parents.

◆ I will not respond to any messages that are mean or in any way make me feel uncomfortable. It is not my fault if I get a message like that. If I do, I will tell my parents right away so that they can contact the online service.

◆ I will talk with my parents so that we can set up rules for going online. We will decide upon the time of day that I can be online, the length of time I can be online, and appropriate areas for me to visit. I will not access other areas or break these rules without their permission.

Protecting Your Children's Privacy Online

When you look at your children, you see sweetness and innocence and light (well, sometimes). But when direct marketers, advertisers, and sellers see them, they see big fat dollar signs. They see those dollar signs because kids spend billions of dollars a year—they're a huge consumer market. And they influence the spending of many billions of dollars more—and if you don't believe that, look in your cupboard and count the boxes of cereals with names like "Super-Cocoa Marshmallow Sugar Flakes," or look at the toys littering your living room.

There are other reasons marketers target your children. Your kids are very susceptible to advertising, and have a hard time distinguishing advertising from non-advertising, which makes them prime targets. And if marketers can get your kids as customers now, when their buying habits are still being formed, they'll have them as customers for life.

But there are bigger dangers than being targeted by marketers. Some Web sites have posted public information about children, including their names, addresses, and e-mail information—and so the site could provide a stalker with information about your child.

Check This Out!

Why would an oil company create a site for kids? The idea, on the face of it, makes absolutely no sense. The oil giant Chevron has created a site for kids at www.chevroncars.com that offers games, coloring books, cartoon-like cars, and free stuff for kids. Why would they do that? When was the last time your 7-year-old filled up her car at the gas pump? (Don't answer that question—it could be held against you in court.) They, and other marketers do it because they're trying to buy customer loyalty at the earliest possible age; if they can hook your kids on their brand when they're young, the company's got a lifetime customer.

The Law Is on Your Side

Reading all this bad news isn't much fun, I know. Well, it's time to cheer up, because there's some very good news: When it comes to protecting your kids' privacy on the Internet, the law is on your side.

And the law even has a name. It's called the Children's Online Privacy Protection Act (COPPA), and it puts forward a set of guidelines about what Web sites can and can't do with information they gather from your kids. In fact, it even *prohibits* Web sites from gathering information about your kids without your express approval.

It's hard to believe, I know; it seems that Congress never did anything intelligent when it comes to the Internet. But in this instance, the members of Congress were right on target.

The Federal Trade Commission enforces the law, which is pretty strict. Here's what the law says about what Web sites can and can't do with regard to children's privacy:

◆ **Web sites directed at children, or that collect information from kids under 13, have to post their privacy policies.** They have to spell out, online, what kind of information they gather, how the site will use the information, and whether the information is sent to third parties, such as advertisers or marketing firms. And the sites must post a person to contact about the policies at the site.

◆ **Web sites must get parental consent before collecting, using, or disclosing personal information about a child.** So that means that you must be contacted before any of this happens—and you also must give explicit consent that it's okay to do all this. There's a three-part process for getting parental consent via e-mail, by phone, and by other means. And if the site shares information about kids with others, there's an even more complicated consent process it has to follow. If a site doesn't do this, it's breaking the law.

Check This Out! _____

One unintended consequence of COPPA is that some sites no longer give kids free e-mail accounts. That's because they ask for personal information from people who sign up for the accounts, and the sites don't want to have to go through the bother of asking for parental consent. For example, the Web site www.snap.com stopped giving kids free e-mail accounts because of the passage of COPPA. Oh, well. You have to take the bad with the good.

◆ **Web sites must get parental consent again if their information-gathering policies change.** That means if a site has a set of policies for gathering information, and you say it's okay, the site has to get your consent again if their policies change.

◆ **Parents are allowed to review the personal information gathered about their children.** So you have the right to see exactly what information a Web site has about your kids.

◆ **Parents have the right to revoke their consent, and to delete information collected about their kids.** So if you change your mind and don't want information collected, you can stop that. And you can delete any information that you want.

You can get more information about all this at the Federal Trade Commission Web site. Head to www.ftc.gov/bcp/conline/pubs/online/kidsprivacy.htm for information about COPPA. The FTC also posts information to help kids learn how to protect their privacy, as you can see in Figure 21.2.

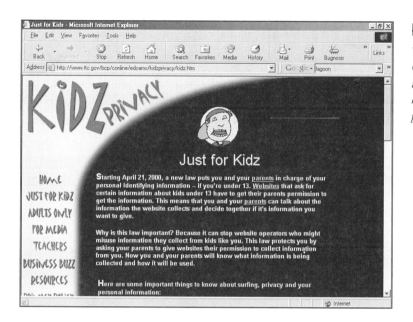

Figure 21.2

The Federal Trade Commission Web site has information for kids about how they can protect their privacy.

Making Sure the Law Is Followed

As we all know, passing a law is one thing, and getting people to follow it is another. A law is only as good as whoever is enforcing it.

The good news is that the FTC takes its job seriously. Even before COPPA was passed, it was using its power to help protect kids' privacy. For example, under rules in effect before COPPA, it took action against a site called Young Investor. The site asked kids to give information about their allowance and savings habits, and collected personal information such as names and addresses. In return, the site said it would keep the identities of the kids anonymous. The site, however, tracked the identities of the kids. It didn't sell that information or give it away, but it did keep the identities. In reply, the FTC took action against it.

If you believe that a site is breaking the law, it's easy to ask the FTC to investigate. You can call a toll-free number to complain, at 1-877-382-4357, or send in a complaint by mail to Consumer Response Center, Federal Trade Commission, 600 Pennsylvania Avenue, NW, Washington, DC 20580. You can fill out a complaint form online at www.ftc.gov/ftc/complaint.htm. A site found breaking the law must pay a $10,000 fine. And more importantly, the fine is announced publicly, which would mean that parents would steer their kids away from the offending site.

What to Watch for on the Web

The Web's a big place, with all kinds of great sites for kids and adults to visit. But it's also a place where kids can come across inappropriate material of many kinds, such as pornography, hate-filled sites, and commercial sites that pitch products such as alcohol to your kids. Just as you want to make sure that your kids are safe in the real world, you want to make sure that they're safe when they head out to the Web.

The first thing you can do to keep your kids safe when surfing the Web is to talk to them. And make sure not to do all the talking—listen to what they have to say, as well. These are the kinds of things you should do when having a talk with them:

♦ **Warn them about the kinds of sites they should stay away from.** Make clear that you don't want them visiting pornographic sites, hate sites, or any other kinds of sites you find inappropriate. Don't merely issue a command—explain why you don't want them visiting those sites, and listen to what they say in response.

♦ **Explain to them that sites might not be what they seem.** The many hate groups that create Web sites have gotten increasingly sophisticated about disguising their ulterior motives and who they really are. Often, a hate site won't at first blush appear to be one—in fact, one racist site even has photos that apparently extol Martin Luther King, until you read more closely. Teach your kids how to recognize the real thing from a phony.

♦ **Let them know that if they're in doubt about whether they should visit a specific site, they should come to you.** Make sure your kids trust you, and tell them that if they have any doubt, they should come to you to see whether a site is suitable for them to visit.

Spend Time Surfing with Your Kids

If you spend time browsing the Web with your kids, they'll soon learn what's an appropriate site and what isn't. So guide them—but make sure to look for sites that they're interested in, or it won't be of much use. (So, no, your favorite license-plate collecting site or the site listing the top mutual funds might not be the best place to show them.)

And check in regularly on your kids when they're on the Web, so you can see where they're visiting and so they know you're close at hand. If you're especially worried about where your kids have been online, you can also look in the History list of their Web browser.

Check This Out! _____

Beware of sellers of alcohol and other inappropriate products targeting your kids online. Remember Joe Camel? That cigarette cartoon character is widely attributed to have led to an increase in smoking among children—and many people believe that the character was created primarily to hook kids on cigarettes. Well, Joe is not alone in appealing to children. Another kids' favorite are the Budweiser Beer cartoon-like lizards—and kids can head straight to the Budweiser site and download a Budweiser lizards screen saver. They can also sign up for a free NASCAR racing fantasy league game, and more. To get into the site, they only have to fill in a form saying that they're over 21—but of course, there's no checking, so kids of any age can enter.

Lead Them to Kid-Friendly Search Sites

Kids spend a lot of time looking for stuff on the Web—for hints about playing the Pokemon video game, for information about Furbies, for pictures of animals … for just about anything you can name. The best way to find things on the Web is to go to a search site like Yahoo!. The only problem with those kinds of sites is that they're for adults as well as kids—this means that kids might come across inappropriate material when searching on them.

There are, however, a number of kid-friendly search sites you can introduce to your kids. They're able to find what they want fast on these sites; and they won't come across any inappropriate material—unless you consider information about Barbies and toy action figures inappropriate. (Where I live, in Cambridge, Massachusetts, you can find a load of parents who think that.)

Check This Out! _____

How's this for an idea: A browser that's kid-friendly, easy-to-use, guides kids to safe Web sites, and includes safe e-mail? That's the idea behind the free Web browser, SurfMonkey. Get it for your kids at www.surfmonkey.com.

The best one (and the favorite of my kids) is Yahooligans! at www.yahooligans.com. My kids have been using it for years and always keep returning to it. There are others as well, though, so check them out. You might want to consider making that page your kids' "start" page, so that whenever they run their browser, that's the first page that shows onscreen. Your browser's help menu has information on how to do that. Take some time to check out the listing of kid-friendly sites at the end of this chapter for more ideas on where to send your kids.

What to Watch for in Chat and Instant Messaging

For many kids, chat is the whole reason to go online. Teens, in particular, are hooked on chat. As the parent of a teen, some days I think they all live in a parallel universe, hooked together by chat rooms, instant messaging software, and telephones.

Check This Out!

You can block your kids from chatting at all by using site-blocking software. I don't recommend using site-blocking software that blocks your kids from chatting at all, because chat seems to be such a vital part of kids' lives. If you want to block it, technology allows it. For more information on site-blocking software, see the "Using Site-Blocking Software" section later in this chapter.

There are some general rules you can give your children to follow to make sure your kids stay safe when they chat or use instant messengers.

- Recognize that people might not be who they say they are.

- Never give out personal information in chat rooms.

- Never agree to meet someone in real life that you've met online unless you've okayed it with a parent—and then only meet in public.

- If you're in a chat area and the talk makes you feel uncomfortable, leave and tell your parents about it.

- If anyone exhibits abusive behavior, tell your parents about it.

Protecting Your Kids from the Evils of E-mail

Oh, yeah, kids like to communicate in other ways than online chat. They also like to send and receive e-mail. Lots of it. Lots and lots and lots of it.

E-mail is great for kids, but kids should also be careful how they use it. They could get inappropriate messages, pictures, and files sent via e-mail; they could be harassed or stalked via e-mail; and they could pick up viruses from e-mail. Here's how to make sure that they stay safe:

- **Your kids should never open file attachments from people they don't know.** File attachments can be anything—a nice picture of a pet cat, pornography, or a file containing a computer virus. So they should never open file attachments from strangers—they should delete them instead.

- **If your kids are made uncomfortable by a message, they should tell you about it and show you the message.** You should then contact your Internet Service Provider and ask them to track down the sender and take action.

◆ **You should set up e-mail filters to filter out junk e-mail, adult e-mail, and e-mail that might be harassing in nature.** Pretty much all e-mail software enables you to set these filters. America Online also lets you set filters. Figure 21.3 shows how to set filters using Microsoft Outlook. For more information on how to set e-mail filters, turn to Chapter 16 and Chapter 22.

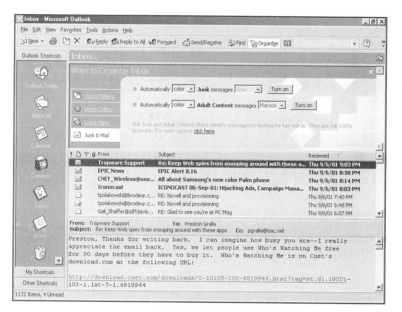

Figure 21.3

Here's how you can set filters to keep your kids from seeing junk mail and mail with adult content in Microsoft Outlook.

Should Your Kids View Newsgroups?

Newsgroups are Internet discussion areas in which anyone can participate. They're wide-ranging discussions about anything under the sun, moon, and stars—and judging from the oddballs you sometimes come across in them, from beyond space, as well.

There are a number of dangers for kids on newsgroups. A major issue is that many newsgroups, even those not connected with adult topics, can contain pornographic pictures and videos that can be downloaded and viewed. Another issue is that many newsgroups use language that I'd rate well beyond PG-13.

So what to do? If your kids are on America Online, there are a number of useful filters you can use to limit your kids' use of newsgroups. For example, you can opt to not allow them to visit newsgroups that have pictures in them. And you can also buy site-blocking software (explained later in this chapter) that doesn't allow them to visit certain newsgroups. Finally, you can simply not allow them to visit newsgroups at all. I recommend limiting kids' use of newsgroups in some way, though. Perhaps only let them view the sites that trade video game secrets.

Using Site-Blocking Software

If you're looking for an all-in-one solution to keeping your kids safe on the Internet, you should look into site-blocking software such as NetNanny, CyberPatrol, Norton Internet Security, and Network Associates Guard Dog. This software all works in a similar way. It limits your kids' use of the Internet. You're able to block them from using certain parts of the Internet entirely, such as newsgroups. And you're able to limit their use of certain parts of the Internet, such as only allowing them to visit certain Web sites. Often, you get to mix and match the controls, so that you can customize your kids' use of the Internet.

But before using this kind of software, there are a few things to keep in mind. Not all parents want to use this kind of software, for a number of reasons that I outline below. I've never used it for my kids, for example. But I know a lot of parents who have used it and feel it's useful. Before using site-blocking software, here are two things to think about:

- **Site-blocking software might block useful sites as well as inappropriate sites.** One thing to realize about site-blocking software is that it might block useful sites as well as inappropriate ones. For example, it might block sites concerned with breast cancer, because the word "breast" is found on the site. And it might block out sites that provide information as AIDS and other important topics.

- **Will it affect the sense of trust you have with your kids?** Putting site-blocking software on your kids' computer might say to them that you don't trust them. And the ultimate way to keep kids safe online is by making sure they trust you enough to ask for help and advice. So consider whether putting site-blocking software on your computer will affect that sense of trust.

The Least You Need to Know

- Apply the same common-sense rules of parenting and safety that you use in the real world to the Internet.

- Make sure your kids never agree to meet anyone in person that they've met online before they've checked with you. Be present at the meeting and make sure it's in a public place.

- Tell your kids never to give out personal information about themselves, such as their address, school, and telephone number.

◆ More important than technology is to make sure that your kids trust you and seek your guidance when they go online. So, have a heart-to-heart talk with them about their use of the Net.

◆ It's best if your kids participate in moderated chats rather than freewheeling ones.

◆ Site-blocking software can keep your kids from visiting unsafe sites, but it can block them from useful sites as well. Think hard before deciding whether to use it.

Chapter 22

Playing It Safe on America Online

In This Chapter

◆ The dangers your kids might face on America Online

◆ How Parental Controls can help you keep your kids safe

◆ Using the basic Parental Controls

◆ How to customize Parental Controls

◆ What to do if your children have been harassed on America Online

◆ Tips for kids and parents on how to stay safe on America Online

Any parent who subscribes to America Online (known as AOL, for short) knows that the service is heaven on earth to kids far and wide. After all, what's not to like? Every hour of the day and night there are thousands of kids chatting and ready to talk. There are tons of cool areas for kids to visit. There's easy e-mail. There's instant access to the Internet. There are ways for kids to easily create their own home pages. What else could a kid want? (Aside from free Britney Spears tickets, a Nintendo GameCube, and a lifetime supply of M&Ms, that is.)

I can attest from long personal experience that both of my kids, Gabe and Mia, spend tons of time on the service. Trying to take away AOL from them would be like trying to take away MTV, the *Harry Potter* books, or their CD players. It's just not going to happen.

But although America Online has just about everything that kids want, it also has some things that parents *don't* want: potential dangers. There is a host of dangers that America Online poses for kids. Because it allows kids easy access to the Internet, it enables them to easily get into trouble. And because it's so easy for people to disguise their identities on the service, it's easy for adults to target kids while posing as youngsters.

In this chapter, I'll show you the kinds of dangers your kids face on America Online. More important, I show you how you can make sure that your kids stay safe when using the world's most popular online service.

What Dangers Are There on America Online?

America Online has gotten so big in large part because of how family-friendly it is, and because kids spend so much time on the service. But its very size means that there are potential dangers lurking. After all, with over 10 million subscribers, it's the size of a world-class city—and any city of that size has some bad neighborhoods and bad characters. It's your job as a parent to keep your kids away from the bad neighborhoods and make sure they know how to handle any bad characters they might come across.

Here's the rundown of the dangers on America Online you need to be worried about:

◆ **Your kids could be targeted in chat areas.** As you already know, your kids love to chat … and chat … and chat … and chat. They might not talk to you, but they'll gab for hours online with their friends and strangers. Unfortunately, adults can hang out in chat areas, posing as kids, looking for vulnerable, gullible kids to target. In fact, this is one of the biggest concerns that parents have about kids' use of the Internet. According to a study by National Public Radio, 85 percent of people surveyed worried that dangerous strangers might make contact with children.

◆ **Your kids could be targeted via instant messaging.** High up on the kids' popularity list on America Online is instant messaging, the ability to hold private one-on-one conversations with others. There's a special danger in instant messaging—these conversations can't be monitored by anyone else, and so they're a perfect way for strangers to target your kids. Making them

Check This Out!

Some chat areas on America Online are monitored by adults to make sure that no kids are targeted, and that no inappropriate language is being used. Mostly these chat areas are found in the Kids Only area of the service. To get there, use the keywords Kids Only.

even more dangerous is AOL Instant Messenger. This is a free program on the Internet that anyone on the Internet can use to send instant messages to anyone on America Online. So it's not just America Online users you have to worry about—it's literally anyone with access to the Internet. Figure 22.1 shows an instant message session.

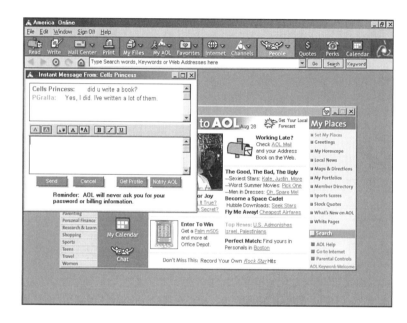

Figure 22.1

Instant messaging is one of the most popular activities for kids on America Online.

◆ **Your kids can be targeted or harassed via e-mail**. Just as adults can disguise themselves while chatting, they can disguise themselves via e-mail. Your kids can also be sent harassing messages from other kids, as well as from adults.

◆ **Your kids can receive inappropriate material via e-mail.** Sending and receiving pictures on America Online is a breeze. It's great for sharing family photos. But it also means that your kids can be sent pornographic or other inappropriate pictures. Making things worse is that there's no way for your kids to know before looking at a picture whether it's pornographic. And making things even *worse* is that you can count on your kids being sent junk e-mail asking them to visit pornographic or other inappropriate sites.

◆ **Your kids' passwords can be stolen**. Possibly the most common scam on America Online is people posing as America Online employees, asking users for their passwords via e-mail or instant messaging. The requests are *always* false. America Online employees will never ask for a password.

◆ **Your kids can get viruses.** It's easy to download things on America Online. That means it's easy for kids to download virus-ridden files.

◆ **Your kids can visit Internet sites and areas that are inappropriate.** America Online makes it very easy for kids to use the Internet. That means they might come across areas that you consider inappropriate, such as pornographic or hate sites.

◆ **Your kids can have their privacy invaded.** It's amazingly easy to gather information about people on the Internet. That means that whenever your kids are online, their privacy can be easily invaded.

Notes

Kids don't have to download software to catch viruses on America Online. They can also get computer viruses via e-mail. If your kid opens up a file attachment and that attachment has a virus in it, then your kid gets that computer virus. So make sure your kids know never to open file attachments from strangers. And even if they know the person who's sent them the file, they should always virus-check it. For information on virus-checking software, turn to Chapter 5, "How to Keep Your Computer Safe from Viruses."

Pretty scary-sounding, I know. But I didn't tell you all this just to scare you. It's to make you aware of what you're up against. And there's good news here: America Online gives you tons of tools you can use to make sure that your kids stay safe whenever they log on. So read on to see what those tools are and to learn how to use them.

Taking Control with Parental Controls

There are a number of ways you can protect your kids on America Online, but the best and most comprehensive way to do it is with a service called Parental Controls. From this single area on America Online, you can control just about every aspect of the way your kids use the Internet and America Online. For example, you can block them from viewing pornographic or inappropriate Web sites, and you can limit the way they can use chat and e-mail. There's a lot more you can do, as well, and I show you how to do it all in this section. What's great about this area is that you set all the rules for how your kids use the service, and you can change the rules whenever you want. For example, you can have more stringent rules for a young child, but when the child gets older and you're more confident the child can explore areas on his own, you can set less restrictive rules.

Getting Started with Parental Controls

First things first. To get started, you have to go to the Parental Control area of America Online. To get there—surprise!—use the keywords Parental Controls. Figure 22.2 shows the screen that is displayed.

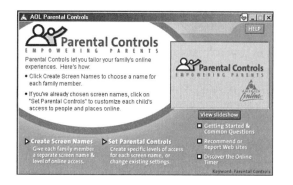

Figure 22.2

Here's the area where you set Parental Controls on America Online.

Before you set the controls, you need to create a separate screen name for each of your children. A *screen name* is the identity that each kid uses to get onto America Online. It gives them each a separate account, including a separate e-mail address, and enables you to set different levels of control for each. If you've already done this, you don't need to do it again; so if your kids already have screen names, you're ahead of the game.

It's simple to create a screen name from the Parental Control area. Click **Create Screen Names.** Then, just follow the directions. Believe me, it really is that easy. If only raising kids was this simple!

Check This Out!

Perhaps you don't want to go through the trouble of creating a separate screen name for each of your children. Take our advice—create a separate screen name for each. If you don't, you aren't able to control what your kids can and can't see and do on America Online. Just as important, if you don't create separate screen names for them, they'll have access to your e-mail, and can even send out e-mail under your name. (Just try explaining to your boss why you included him on a chain e-mail letter warning that he'll die within the next three days unless he sends the letter on to 15 friends.) And if you don't create separate screen names, you'll get your kids' e-mail, which generally means many of the aforementioned chain letters, silly jokes, incomprehensible missives from the world of Kid Culture, and general all-around goofiness.

What's great about Parental Controls is that you can set different rules for each of your kids. So if you have a brood of kids, you can have one set of rules for your 5-year-old son, another for your 8-year-old daughter, another for your 12-year-old son, and yet a different set for your 14-year-old daughter. (Four kids under the age of 15! Are you ready for a rest home yet?)

When you set Parental Controls, you block kids from going to certain parts of the Internet and America Online, and you restrict their access to certain services such as chat and downloading software that could lead to problems. Internet sites are blocked by special site-blocking software built into America Online that's much like the site-blocking software people buy to block kids from visiting certain Internet sites. On America Online, because the software is built into the service, this service is free.

How to Set Basic Parental Controls

When you use Parental Controls, you have two main choices: You can use a set of pre-fabricated built-in controls, or you can mix and match to create customized controls based on what you want each of your kids to be able to do online. It's much simpler to use the built-in ones, but they're less flexible than the custom controls.

To use the basic, built-in controls, click **Set Parental Controls** when you get to the Parental Controls area. A screen like the one in Figure 22.3 should appear. It lists all of the screen names in your account and enables you to set the Parental Controls for each one individually.

Figure 22.3

Here's how to set Parental Controls on America Online.

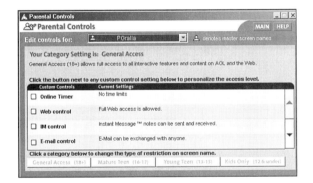

For each screen name, click the controls you want to set. The choices are Kids Only, Young Teen, and Mature Teen. (If you don't want any controls set for a screen name, leave it at General Access, which is the default.) America Online recommends that Kids Only be set for kids 12 and under, Young Teen be set for kids 13 through 15, and Mature Teen be set for kids 16 to 17.

When you do this, you might notice that it's not all that clear what these controls actually do. You only get a very brief description, as you can see in the Figure 22.3. That brief description helps a little bit, but not a whole lot. So here's the rundown on exactly what each of the settings mean:

- **Kids Only.** This lets kids visit only one area of America Online: the Kids Only channel. And it only allows kids to visit Web sites that are selected for age-appropriate content for kids up to 12 years old. Everything else is blocked. So kids can't send or receive Instant Messages. They can't join member-created or private chat rooms—although they can visit public chat rooms in the Kids Only area. They can't send or receive file attachments or pictures in their e-mail. They're also blocked from Internet newsgroups that allow file attachments. (That's because objectionable pictures and other material can sometimes be found in newsgroups that allow file attachments, regardless of the newsgroup's subject.)

- **Young Teen.** This lets teens visit some chat rooms—but they can't visit member-created chat rooms or private chat rooms. They can only visit Web sites that have been judged appropriate for kids under 15. They're also blocked from Internet newsgroups that allow file attachments.

- **Mature Teen.** This restricts teens access to certain Web sites—they can only visit sites that have been judged appropriate for kids under 17. They're also blocked from Internet newsgroups that allow file attachments.

 Check This Out!

Parts of America Online charge fees in addition to your normal monthly fee. For example, some online gaming areas charge a per-hour fee. Kids can run up big bills playing online games or visiting other premium areas. Parental Controls blocks access to these premium services, which is a good idea for anyone worried about financial health.

Have It Your Way: Customizing Parental Controls

Basic Parental Controls are great. They're easy to set up, and they do the job. But they treat all kids the same, and you might want to allow your kids freedoms in certain areas but restrict them in others. For example, maybe you trust your kids to visit only appropriate Web sites, but you're worried about their use of chat or e-mail. Or maybe you're not worried about chat, but don't want them to visit certain newsgroups. In that case, you're in luck, because America Online offers a way to mix and match controls in any way that you'd like.

To customize controls, after you've gone to the area where you can set controls, select the screen name for which you want to set controls. Now you can customize how your kids can use chat, Instant Messages, e-mail, the Web, and newsgroups, as well as how they can download files. For example, you can allow them full access to Instant Messages, but restrict their use of newsgroups.

For each screen name, click the kind of access you want to customize. For example, if you want to customize the chat setting, click the button next to **Chat control.** (For once—logic on America Online!) When you do that, a screen like the one in Figure 22.4 shows onscreen. You can set controls for each screen name just by clicking the controls you want to set.

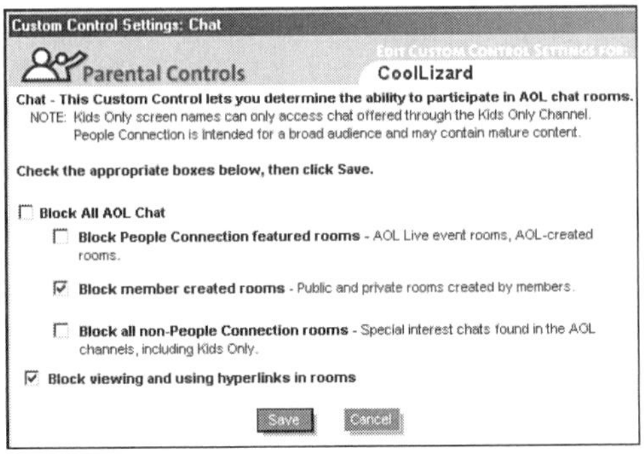

Figure 22.4

Customizing Parental Controls on America Online.

As you can see, there's a whole lot of choices, and not a lot of explanation of what they all mean. So here's the rundown on each:

- **Chat control.** You can block different parts of chat in several ways. You can block chat hyperlinks—that way, if someone sends your kid a link to a Web site, inappropriate or not, he cannot click the link and go there. You can also block kids' access to chats in the People Connection, which is aimed at an older audience than kids and includes a number of adult topics. You also can block access to member-created chat rooms in the People Connection and to access to conference rooms—large chat rooms on America Online. You get to choose which of these to block and which to enable.

- **Instant Message control.** As I explained before, Instant Messages are private, live, one-on-one conversations. You can choose to block your kids from using Instant Messages. Whether someone is trying to send your kid a message from directly within America Online, or from the Internet using AOL Instant Messenger, the messages are blocked.

- **Downloading control.** Worried that your kids might download inappropriate pictures, programs, or a file with a computer virus in it? Then block their ability to download files. You can block them from downloading files directly on America Online or via an Internet service called FTP, a popular way to download files.

> **Notes**
>
> After you set controls for your kids, sign off and exit AOL. Only then let your kids onto the service. If you set the controls, don't log off, and let them use your screen name, they could go into the Parental Control area and undo the controls you've set for them.

- ◆ **Web control.** If you're worried that your kids are viewing inappropriate sites on the Web, use this control. You can limit them to sites appropriate for kids 12 and under, ages up to 16, or ages up to 17.

- ◆ **E-mail control.** This one offers a mind-boggling number of choices. You have an incredible amount of control over how your kids can send and receive e-mail. You can block your kids from exchanging e-mail with anyone. You can also allow them to get e-mail only from America Online members or only from specific Internet e-mail addresses. And you can block them from getting e-mail from specific America Online members and addresses. You can also block them from getting pictures or attachments in any e-mail messages.

- ◆ **Newsgroup.** As with e-mail, you have a whole lot of control over how your kids access newsgroups. You can block all access to newsgroups. You can instead block their access to specific newsgroups. Alternately, you can only allow them to go to certain newsgroups. You can even block your kids' access to newsgroups that contain specific words in their description. And you can block them from getting any of the graphics, sounds, animations, and photographs found on newsgroups by not allowing them to download files from newsgroups.

Check This Out!

The software that America Online uses isn't perfect—there's no way it can know about every site on the Internet that might not be good for your kids to visit. If you come across a site that you think should be blocked, go to the Parental Controls area and click **Recommend or Report Web Sites.** Then fill out a form giving the site's location as well as a description of the site and why it should be blocked. You can also ask that a certain site not be blocked—for example, a site about breast cancer that the software might have inadvertently blocked. In both cases, your request goes to the company that does the site-blocking, and they make the final determination about what should be blocked and what shouldn't.

What to Do If Your Child Has Been Harassed on America Online

No matter how good a job you do as a parent protecting your kids on America Online, your child could possibly be harassed. They could get harassing e-mail or Instant Messages, or they could be harassed in a chat room. If that happens, immediately report the harassment to America Online at keyword TOS.

Keep detailed information about the harassment. Make sure that your child has the screen name of the person doing the harassing. Note the time and date that the harassing occurred. Most important, print out a copy of the harassment and send that along, as well. If you don't, America Online might not take any action at all. One of my daughter's friends received a death threat on America Online via an Instant Message. Her parents contacted America Online, and had the screen name of the person who sent the threat. But because they had no actual record of the threat, America Online refused to take action.

What can you do if your child receives harassing or annoying e-mail from an individual? You don't want to block your kids' use of e-mail altogether, but on the other hand, you want to solve the problem. It's simple—you can block your kids from getting e-mail from individual addresses. To do that, customize Parental Controls and choose **E-mail control.** Then follow the directions for blocking an individual address. I can vouch from personal experience that this works. Someone harassed my daughter via e-mail, so I blocked the address, and my daughter was never bothered again.

Kids' Safety Tips on America Online

Technology can help keep your kids safe on America Online—but technology can go only so far. Teaching your kids how to stay safe works even better than depending on technology to do it for you.

America Online has put together a good set of simple safety tips. Give it to your kids and have them read it and follow it:

1. Don't give your AOL password to anyone, even your best friend.
2. Never tell someone your home address, telephone number, or school name without your parent's permission first.

 Check This Out!

How much do you and your kids really know about online safety? You can find out in a special America Online area. Head to the Safe Surfin' Challenge area (at keyword Safe Surfin') to find a site full of safety information, tips, and quizzes to make learning about online safety fun.

3. If someone says something that makes you feel unsafe or funny, don't respond. Take charge— keyword Kid Help.
4. Never say you'll meet someone in person without asking your parent's permission first. Your parent should accompany you to the first meeting, which should be in public.
5. Always tell a parent about any threatening or bad language you see online.
6. Don't accept things from strangers (for example, e-mail, files, or Web page addresses).

A Final Word to Parents

Remember, the best way to keep your kids safe anywhere online, including America Online, is to be a good parent and follow safety tips. For more information on general Internet safety tips, turn to Chapter 21, "The Best Rules for Keeping Kids Safe on the Internet."

To protect your kids' privacy, make sure that they don't create an America Online member profile or, if they do, that they don't give out any personal information in it. To do that, have them use the keyword Profile and click **Create or Modify My Profile.** Check the profile they create so you can be sure that they're not giving out personal information.

And for an excellent central place to go for advice of all kinds on safety on America Online, go to the Neighborhood Watch area by using the keyword Neighborhood Watch.

The Least You Need to Know

- Adults can disguise their identities in America Online chat areas, bulletin boards, and e-mail when communicating with your kids.

- Basic Parental Controls enable you to make sure that your kids don't do things or access areas that could be harmful. To get there, use the keyword Parental Controls.

- If you want more control over how your kids use America Online, customize the Parental Controls.

- If your child has been harassed, keep a record of all the relevant information about the harasser and report him or her to America Online.

- Have your kids read and agree to follow America Online's safety tips for kids.

- Go to the Neighborhood Watch with the keyword Safety to get advice and help on how to keep your kids safe on America Online.

Part 6

Even More Privacy and Safety Issues: Work, Cybershopping, and Beyond

The next time you send an e-mail to a co-worker calling your boss Big Butt, consider this: Your boss can read every e-mail you send and receive. He can see what sites you surf to. He can read every file on your computer. And he can do it legally.

Oh, you're looking for more things to worry about? Okay, before you take out your credit card and start sending its number over the wires, there are precautions you ought to be taking. And when you talk on your cell phone, or use a wireless computer connection, someone might be listening in.

And it's strange but true: There's a world beyond the Internet. I spend so much time online that sometimes I forget that fact. There are dangers to your computer security and privacy even when you're not online. Someone could steal your computer's password or snoop through your computer, for example—and they can even read files that you thought you had deleted.

This part of the book fills you in on privacy issues at work, when you shop online, and when you use wireless technologies. It shows you how to protect your PC, as well. And it also shows you how you can use the Internet to fight back and get information about privacy and security online, as well as in the real world, so that you can follow the cardinal rule of Massachusetts politics: Don't get mad, get even.

Chapter 23

Your Life Is Not Your Own: What You Need to Know About Privacy at Work

In This Chapter

- ◆ What kind of Internet and computer monitoring employers engage in
- ◆ Is it legal for employers to snoop on their employees?
- ◆ Consequences to violating your employer's Internet and e-mail policies
- ◆ Laws governing what employers can and can't do when it comes to monitoring employees
- ◆ What you can do to try to protect your privacy at work

It's something most of us don't like to think about: When you're at work, your boss might be watching everything you do on your computer. From sending and receiving e-mail to surfing the Web, to the very files on your computer, your boss can see it all.

But what do you need to know about workplace surveillance? does your boss have free rein in examining everything you do? And do you have any recourse? Read on, because you'll learn all about that and more in this chapter.

Do Employers Really Monitor What Employees Do At Work?

Next time you pass along a slightly risqué joke via e-mail to your friends at work, or spend a few minutes buying a pair of jeans online on your lunch hour, or create a party list and invitations after-hours at work, think twice. Your employer might be watching what you do. And the company is perfectly within its rights.

That's because when it comes to personal use of a company computer, the law is clear: Everything that people do on a work computer belongs to their place of business. That means every e-mail, every file, every document, every bit of Web surfing—in fact, every single keystroke a person makes is not their own.

When it comes to the workplace and computers, there is no privacy.

Think that *your* boss isn't legally snooping on you? Think again. Monitoring of employees is on the rise and shows no signs of slowing down. Consider these facts from the American Management Association's 2001 survey of workplace monitoring and surveillance:

◆ Sixty-three percent of companies monitor their employees' use of the Web and Internet.

◆ Forty-six percent of companies store and review their employees' e-mail—a more than three-fold increase since 1997, when only 15 percent of companies did it.

◆ Thirty-six percent of companies store and review files on employees' computers.

◆ Nineteen percent count the number of keystrokes that people make, or count the time logged on.

Check This Out!

If you have a company laptop that you also use at your home at times, everything you do on that laptop can be legally monitored by your employer—even personal activities such as newsletters you create for your PTA, private e-mail to friends and family, and the Web surfing you do at home. That's because the laptop belongs to your company, making everything on it theirs. If you're worried about privacy, your best bet is to have a separate computer for home use, even if you're allowed to bring a laptop home from work.

Sheesh! Are we all working for private employers or for Big Brother? (Being a freelance writer, I don't need to worry about Big Brother, because I work for myself. Hey, does that mean I have to monitor what I do?)

What Actions Do Employers Take Against Employees?

Employers do more than just monitor what their employees do—they act on what they find, as well. And just as monitoring is becoming more common, so are actions taken by employers. Again, consider these facts from the American Management Association survey on workplace monitoring and surveillance:

- Forty-six percent of companies have taken disciplinary action against employees for sending sexually suggestive or explicit material via office e-mail.

- Thirty-six percent of companies have taken disciplinary action against employees for downloading, uploading, or viewing pornographic material over the Internet.

- Thirty-four percent of companies have taken disciplinary action against employees for connecting to unauthorized, restricted, or non-business-related Web sites.

- Twenty-eight percent of companies have disciplined employees for sending a discriminatory, harassing, or another kind of objectionable e-mail.

What all this means is that you should assume that at work, every keystroke you make, every e-mail you send and receive, and every Web site you visit can be seen by your boss.

Check This Out!

Some companies allow employees to connect to corporate networks from home using what's called a Virtual Private Network (VPN). And some companies provide dial-in accounts that enable people to connect to the Internet from home. If you use a VPN or a company-provided dial-in account at home, your employer is able to monitor your Internet connection just as if you were at work. In fact, I know of one instance in which an employee dialed in to the Internet using a company dial-in account, and visited risqué Web sites—and when the company's tech support department found out, instead of telling their bosses, they told fellow employees, and the offending employee's questionable surfing habits became publicly known at work.

Why Your Boss Might Be Snooping on You

Is your boss just nosey? Does he get his kicks by looking at what other people are doing when he thinks no one is looking?

For all I know, the answer to those questions might be "Yes." But that's not the primary reason that employers are increasingly snooping on their employees. They do it for a number of reasons: to make sure employees aren't spending their time surfing the Net instead of working; to protect sensitive company information from being released; and to protect themselves from a variety of lawsuits. (You just *knew* that lawyers were going to be at the bottom of this, didn't you?)

It might seem odd that employers snoop on their employees to protect themselves against lawsuits, but in our litigious society, it's all too true. Here are the legal reasons employers snoop on employees:

- **To protect themselves in harassment suits.** If employees visit pornographic Web sites, and those Web sites can be seen by other employees, the company could potentially be sued for sexual harassment, because it wasn't diligent enough in making sure the company atmosphere was free of harassment. The same holds true for e-mail—if employees send out suggestive e-mail that could be considered harassment, the company can be held legally liable.

- **As part of "due diligence" procedures.** Companies are required to keep adequate files and records—if they don't, they can be legally liable, and can run into serious problems, particularly if they're part of a lawsuit. So many companies keep employee e-mails and backups of employee files as part of their due diligence procedures.

Check This Out!

Finger is an Internet service that enables people to find out information about others by typing in a simple command over the Internet. The only way it works is if information about you is provided by someone—either by yourself or someone else. Some places of work automatically provide finger information, possibly without telling their employees about it. If they do that, anyone with an Internet connection can find out that information. Find out if your company provides finger information about you, and if they do, you could ask them to delete that information if you don't want it made public.

What the Laws Say About Work and Online Privacy

There's a good chance that you've read all this and said to yourself, "There oughta be a law!"

In fact, there is one. And it gives employers the right to monitor their employees' computer use. The law is the federal Electronic Communications Privacy Act (ECPA) and it pretty much lets your employer monitor all your e-mail traffic and Internet activity.

However, that doesn't mean that employees have no rights at all. And in fact, there's a bit of murkiness in the law, and the possibility that laws might give employees some recourse.

Where the law becomes murky is in whether employees have a right to know that they are being monitored, or that they might be monitored. A law considered by Congress, the Notice of Electronic Monitoring Act, would require that companies notify employees if they are being watched electronically. The law actually has some teeth: It requires that detailed notice be given to employees before monitoring takes place. And if that notice isn't given, employees can sue and recover damages from employers. The proposal doesn't limit in any way what information can be monitored—it lets employers check up on whatever they want. And employees have no right to look at the personnel file created by the surveillance. Still, however, it's a big step forward.

The law has been shot down at least once in Congress, but it keeps getting re-filed. And considering that online privacy is a big hot button with a lot of people, there's a chance that it could become law someday.

In absence of federal regulation, at least one state has gotten into the act. Connecticut now requires that employers notify employees when they are being monitored. The law is pretty toothless, though. Employers only have to post a notice saying that they might monitor e-mail and Internet use. They don't have to provide any kind of details or information about that monitoring. Employees have no right to review information gathered about them. And even if an employer violates the law, it leads only to a slap on the wrist—$500 for a first offense, and a maximum of $3,000 for the third offense and beyond.

A similar law was passed in California twice, but it was vetoed each time by Governor Gray Davis. In any event, it's even weaker than the Connecticut law, and it doesn't even establish penalties for violations.

Here Comes Da Judge!

There is a small, bright ray of hope for those people who believe they should have some kind of privacy zone when it comes to computer use at work. A proposal in 2001 would have allowed the computer use of employees of federal courts—all 30,000 of them—to be monitored. In fact, what was being proposed was no different than what can legally be done in corporations across the country. Their e-mail and Web and Internet use was going to be monitored.

But for some federal judges, this hit home. After all, this was going to affect *them* and the people who work for them.

So the judges fought back, and when the men and women in black robes get riled, you don't want to be in their way. First, the 9th Circuit Judicial Council ordered that intrusion detection software be shut down, as protection against monitoring efforts. Then a number of other federal judges spoke out against the proposal, and got Congressmen on their side.

Check This Out!

Computer surveillance is only one kind of workplace monitoring you need to worry about. The American Management Association survey found out that 43 percent of employers monitor telephone use (things such as the numbers that people call and the amount of time spent on the phone), 38 percent use video surveillance for security purposes, 15 percent use video surveillance to check on employee job performance, and 12 percent record and review telephone conversations.

Finally, Federal Judge Alex Kozinski of the 9th Circuit Court went on a one-man crusade to kill the monitoring. He publicly spoke out against it, offering interviews to TV, radio, newspapers, and magazines. He flooded the proponents with memos. (And if countless memos from a judge aren't mind-numbingly powerful, I don't know what is.) And he wrote an op-ed piece in *The Wall Street Journal* speaking out against it. The upshot is that he won, and personally shut down the software that did the monitoring.

Big deal, you might be thinking. How does that affect me? I'm not an employee of the federal courts. It could affect you big-time. Because it means that the federal courts have been sensitized to the issue, and if suits concerning monitoring Internet activities come before the courts, the rulings could go against employers. And it also gives impetus to federal and state laws that might limit the practice, or at least require that employees be told about the monitoring.

What You Can Do About Workplace Monitoring

You're not completely powerless when it comes to workplace monitoring. Although the law isn't on your side, there are still some things that you can do if you're concerned about your privacy at work:

- ◆ **Find out your company's monitoring policies.** Does your company monitor your e-mail and your Web and Internet use? If so, what kind of monitoring do they do?

- ◆ **Find out what is off-limits and what is allowed.** Are you allowed to send and receive personal e-mail at work? Can you surf for your own pleasure during lunchtime and breaks? Find out the answers to these and other questions.

- ◆ **Ask that the policies be posted.** Even though the law might not require it, most people would probably feel that people have a right to know if they're being monitored. It's in a company's best interest to do this, because if a policy is publicly posted, people know what they can and can't do.

♦ **Follow the policy.** Be clear about this: If you don't follow the policy, you could face serious consequences. So even if you don't agree with it, toe the line.

♦ **Remember that you're covered if you use a company computer at home.** If you use a company laptop or desktop at home, the same rules apply as if you're in the workplace, so follow the law at home as well. If you use a company computer for personal use at home, strongly consider buying a separate one for your personal use.

♦ **Check the state and federal laws.** By the time you read this, the federal law about monitoring might have changed. Check with your state and federal representatives to see if there have been any changes in the law.

Check This Out!

According to the privacy watchdog group the Privacy Foundation, the two most popular pieces of software for monitoring employees are WebSense and MIMEsweeper. WebSense is used to monitor employees' Web surfing habits, and as of mid-2001 was used to monitor 8.25 million employees, says the watchdog group. The group says that MIMEsweeper, used to monitor e-mail, was monitoring 10 million employees in mid-2001.

The Least You Need to Know

♦ Assume that you're being monitored at work—63 percent of companies monitor their employees' use of the Web and 46 percent store and review their employees' e-mail.

♦ Employers often take disciplinary action against employees for their computer use: 46 percent of companies have taken disciplinary action against employees sending sexually suggestive or explicit material via office e-mail, and 36 percent have taken disciplinary action against employees for downloading, uploading, or viewing pornographic material over the Internet.

♦ The law allows employers to monitor employee use of the Internet and e-mail, as well as the examination files on employees' computers.

♦ Find out what your company's policies are, and ask that they be publicly posted—and make sure that you follow them.

♦ Check to see whether federal or state laws about workplace monitoring have changed recently—there's a movement afoot to give employees some kind of privacy rights.

Chapter 24

What Dangers Are There for Online Shoppers?

In This Chapter

◆ What you need to know about shopping before buying online

◆ All about shopping carts and one-click shopping

◆ What dangers are there in shopping online?

◆ How to protect yourself against shopping fraud and other problems

◆ What you can do if the site you buy from goes out of business

◆ How to make sure you don't get burned when buying stocks on the Internet

I hate malls. I hate stores. I hate everything to do with having to trudge to some godforsaken place in the middle of a huge parking lot, plunk down my filthy lucre and trudge back home with what I've bought. I've got better things to do with my life.

But I love to buy things online. It's simple, it's easy, I can do it in my pajamas at home, and I can get great deals on things. I've bought everything from computers to scanners to software, CDs, and more.

And I'm not alone. Millions of people spend billions of dollars a year shopping online. They're shopping online for its convenience, because you can get great deals, and yes, because it's even fun. (I never thought I would ever include the words "shopping" and "fun" in the same sentence. Live long enough, I guess, and *anything* can happen.)

But you don't want to head willy-nilly into shopping online without taking note of the dangers, and without making sure that someone doesn't abscond with your credit card information, or scam you out of your life savings. So read on to see how to stay safe when you shop online.

What to Watch for When Buying Online

Shopping online is about as easy as things get. Just point your browser at a shopping site, click around until you find what you want, and pay. You usually have to pay shipping charges, and whatever you've bought is delivered to you via mail or a delivery service within a few days of the purchase.

Notes
Expect that some day you might shop with an "ewallet"—an electronic "wallet" on your computer that has information about you such as your credit card. Then, when you visit a shopping site, you don't need to input any information, the site can get it from your ewallet when you tell it to. But if others have easy access to your computer, be careful about using an ewallet; anyone using your computer might be able to charge things to your account.

A lot of different kinds of buying sites are available online. Here's the rundown on the major kinds:

◆ You can buy directly from the manufacturer of a product, such as from computer maker Dell at www.dell.com.

◆ You can buy from the online version of a retail store or mail-order outlet, such as the Gap at www.gap.com.

◆ You can buy from a store that exists only in cyberspace, such as Amazon at www.amazon.com.

◆ You can buy from an online mall that sells products from many different online stores, much like a real-life mall, such as at the Internet Mall at www.internetmall.com. (The good news here is that you don't have to visit the food court. Virtual food is never very tasty, anyway.)

◆ You can buy from online auction sites, such as ebay at www.ebay.com. These work much like real-life auctions, except that you bid online. Turn to Chapter 26, "How to Stay Safe When Buying at Auctions," for more information on how to buy at auction sites.

◆ You can buy stocks and financial services from investment sites, such as eTrade at www.etrade.com. Be careful when buying stocks online—there's a lot of fraud out there. Turn to the section later in this chapter titled "Taking Stock: How to Make Sure You Don't Get Burned When Buying Stock Online," to see how to stay safe.

> **Check This Out!**
>
> The biggest scams on the Internet, according to the anti-fraud group the National Fraud Information Center at www.fraud.org, are found at auctions—such as not delivering the goods after they've been paid for. So you have to take extra care when buying or selling at auctions. That's why there's a whole chapter in this book, Chapter 26, which gives you the scoop on online auction safety.

How Do I Buy Online?

After you've visited a site and found what you want to buy, you go to a special, secure area of a site, and pay using your credit card. You fill out a form that asks for your name, address, and credit card information, and sometimes more information, as well. Click again (yes, there's a lot of clicking when you buy online, but it's better than waiting in lines) and you get some kind of verification about what you've bought. Some sites send you e-mail verifying your order.

That's it. Now sit back and wait for the goodies to arrive.

To make shopping easier for you, most sites enable you to establish a standing account. (After all, the easier it is for you to shop, the more money they take in.) This way, when you visit, you don't have to type in your name, credit card information, and other things when you want to shop—all of that is already on record. In fact, some sites require that you establish an account before shopping there. Often, for you to access your account, you need to type in a username and password, or possibly just a password. Sometimes, the site creates the username and password for you, but more often than not, you get to create both.

Many sites utilize virtual shopping carts—places where you put things you're thinking of buying. You can stack your shopping cart as high with items as you want, and then proceed to a virtual "checkout" when it's time to fork over the moolah. It works like a real-life shopping cart, except that the wheels aren't bent. As you go through a site, you click items to put them into the cart. When you're finished shopping and have found whatever you want to buy, you fill out a form with your credit card information (or else the site already has your account information), and you buy. Figure 24.1 shows a shopping cart at Amazon.com.

Figure 24.1

Get ready to buy! You can fill a virtual shopping cart at Amazon.com.

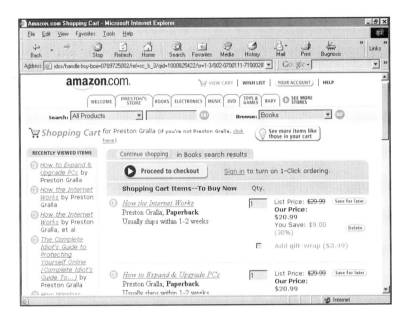

Many sites also offer "Express Shopping" or "one-click shopping" in which you don't need to fill out a form or put anything in a shopping cart. Just click that you want to buy, and bingo!—it's charged to your credit card, and it's winging its way to you.

Dangers of Online Shopping: How to Protect Yourself

There are all kinds of dangers you might face when you shop online. Your credit card information might be stolen, or someone might take your money and run. You could be the victim of a scam, or your privacy might be invaded. But yes, you guessed it, help is on the way. Follow my advice and you should never go wrong.

◆ **Always pay with your credit card.** When you pay with a credit card, you're given a great deal of consumer protection—your credit card company stands behind you. At most, you'll be out $50 if you've been subject to a scam, and the truth is, with most credit card companies these days, you won't even be liable for that much. For more information about shopping with credit cards, turn to Chapter 25, "How to Protect Your Credit Card When Buying Over the Internet."

◆ **Know the site you're buying from.** You want to make sure you buy from creditable sites that won't take your money and head to Bermuda with it. Does the site look as if it'll be around for a while? During the great "dot-bomb" bust, many shopping sites went belly-up. You don't want to buy from a site that's likely to go bankrupt. For more information on what to do if that happens to you, check later in this chapter in the section titled "What to Do If a Shopping Sites Takes Your Money and Goes out of Business." And turn to Chapter 25 for information on how to check out a site.

- **Only shop at secure sites.** You want to make sure that when you send your credit card information, it's scrambled so that hackers can't steal it. For information on how to know you're shopping at a secure site, turn to Chapter 25.

- **Always print out your order form and keep a copy of it.** If you don't have evidence of what you've bought, what you've agreed to pay, and when you did the buying, it's tough to prove that you've been ripped off. So print out all order forms and keep them in a safe place.

- **If other people can gain easy access to your computer, be leery of signing up for one-click shopping.** When you sign up for one-click shopping, it takes only one click to buy something; you don't go to a checkout area or a virtual shopping cart. Instead, your credit card is charged, and the goods are shipped to you. So if other people can gain easy access to your computer—such as at work, or if your kids use your computer—be leery of setting up any one-click shopping accounts. One-click shopping just makes it too easy to charge things to your credit card by surfing to a site and clicking.

- **Check out hidden costs before buying.** Remember, there are shipping and handling costs when you buy, so make sure that you know the true cost of a product before turning over your plastic. And depending on where you live, you might have to pay sales taxes at some sites. Look around a site to see where these costs are spelled out—often in the Help or FAQ areas. If you can't find information about the costs, buy at another site.

- **Know what the return policies and warranties are.** How long do you have to return something you buy? If the goods arrive damaged, and you have to return them, who pays shipping costs? Who covers the warranty—the manufacturer of the goods, or the site from which you bought the product? Know all this before buying.

- **Watch out for Internet scams.** You run into all kinds of buying scams on the Internet—get-rich-quick schemes (although only the scammer ends up getting rich), stock fraud, and more. For information on how to protect yourself against them, turn to Chapter 3, "How to Protect Yourself Against the Most Common Internet Scams."

 Check This Out!

If someone has your Social Security number, they can do almost anything-steal your identity, get into your bank account, and more. So never give out your Social Security number when filling out a shopping form. There's no reason any site should ever ask you for it.

◆ **If you've been scammed, you can fight back.** In Massachusetts where I live, where politics is a contact sport, there's a saying: *Don't get mad, get even*. If you've been scammed, you can still fight back. Turn to Chapter 3 to see how.

Check This Out! _____

When you buy computer products at some sites, you might notice in small type something called a "restocking fee." That means that if you return something you buy there, you're charged a fee. This restocking fee can be shockingly high, sometimes as high as 25 percent of the cost of the product. That means if you return a $2,000 computer, you might have to pay $500 to return it. Never pay restocking fees, and look closely at any site that sells hardware to make sure they don't charge one.

What to Do If a Shopping Site Takes Your Money and Goes out of Business

How the mighty have fallen! The list of shopping sites that have gone belly-up is long indeed, including the infamous www.pets.com, and others too numerous to mention.

But what happens if you buy from a site that goes out of business? How do you handle getting the goods, or getting issues resolved like returns or warranties? Do you need to stand in line with creditors and hope the site makes good?

In fact, there are many things you can do to make sure that you're not burned if your e-shopping site goes into bankruptcy or is bought out. Here's advice on what to do:

◆ **Gather the information about what you've bought and your problem.** Get all e-mail correspondence, information about phone calls, your credit card bill, regular mail sent to you, and a print out of your payment confirmation. You need much of that to resolve your problems.

Check This Out! _____

Many states have consumer protection offices that are usually run by the state Attorney General. If the site at which you're shopping goes out of business and you can't reach a resolution with it, contact your consumer protection office and ask that they take action. Also contact the consumer office in the state where the shopping site is located. These offices might be able to resolve the issue if no one else can.

- **If the site was bought by another one, contact the purchasing site, explain the problem, and send along any correspondence.** The odds are great that this will resolve the issue.

- **If that doesn't resolve the problem, or if the site has declared bankruptcy and is unreachable, contact your credit card company.** Explain the problem, and tell the company you want a credit for the cost of the sale. The most you'll be out is $50, but most credit card companies will waive even that fee.

- **Make a complaint to the Federal Trade Commission (FTC) at www.ftc.gov/ftc/complaint.htm or by calling 1-877-382-4357.** The FTC doesn't act in behalf of individual consumers, but if it finds a pattern of abuse, it can act against a company. So encourage any others in a similar situation to contact the FTC, as well.

- **If it's a warranty issue, contact the manufacturer.** Manufacturers make good on warranties on their products, no matter where those products were bought. In fact, if you need to return goods, and you can't return them to the site, try returning them to the manufacturer. Although the manufacturer has no legal obligation to accept the return, they might do so, to maintain good consumer relations.

Making Sure You Don't Get Burned When Buying Stock Online

When it comes to the stock market, everyone wants to make a fast killing.

Unfortunately, a lot of the people making quick killings on stocks these days are scamsters of all kinds, who prey on our desire to get an inside deal. Online stock scams and schemes have become so frequent that they're now one of the top scams on the Internet. The Security and Exchange Commission (SEC) has targeted the problem, recently rounding up and charging nearly four-dozen people in a national anti-stock-scam sweep. But there are many others waiting in the wings to take the scamsters' places.

However, forearmed is forewarned. With the right information, you can make sure that you won't get scammed when buying stocks online. Here's what to know:

- **Watch out for "pump and dump" schemes.** It's one of the oldest stock scams in the book—a group of people claim they're disinterested parties giving out advice about a previously unknown stock that's about to go through the roof. You buy the stock at a high price, and it instead heads for the cellar, and you're out a lot of money. And the "disinterested parties" were in fact the stockowners, trying to get the price on their stock bid up so they could sell at a high price and get out. On the Internet, people sometimes send out free newsletters touting great stock deals, not telling you that they're the owners of the stock. And unsolicited e-mail and messages in bulletin boards might tout stock, as well. The general rule: Don't believe anything anyone says online about stocks unless you know for an absolute fact that you can trust them.

♦ **Check out the SEC Web site for advice on how to avoid scams and be a savvier online investor.** The SEC Web site at www.sec.gov, and pictured in Figure 24.2, is a great source of information on how to avoid scams. Check it out regularly to make sure you don't get burned.

♦ **Watch out for people who don't use their real names online.** People online often use "handles" or aliases instead of their real names. Only deal with people who give you their real name, address, phone number, and other contact information.

Check This Out! ___

No one really knows how much money is wasted on online stock fraud. But consider this: Marc Beauchamp of the North American Securities Administrators Association (www.nasaa. org) believes that "investors are losing about $1 million an hour from stock fraud," a fairly astounding number.

♦ **If anyone offers a "guarantee" on a high rate of return, run the other way.** All investment entails risk, and the higher the rate of return, the greater the potential risk. The SEC warns that language such as "guarantee," "high return," "limited offer," or "as safe as a C.D." might be a sign of a scamster.

♦ **Be leery of offshore investments.** When you send your money overseas, it's hard to track what happens to it, and you don't have the same protections as when you invest in the United States. Be very careful about directly investing overseas.

Figure 24.2

Great advice from the feds: Check out the SEC Web site at www.sec.gov for advice on avoiding online stock scams.

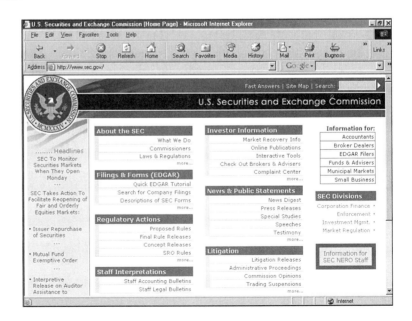

♦ **Watch out for those who offer "inside" information, or try to pressure you to invest before you can check out the offer.** That's often a sign that a scamster is at work.

♦ **Check out online investment news-letters carefully.** There are tons of online investment newsletters that promise big returns on your money. Be careful, though: Unscrupulous ones spread false information or promote worthless stocks and make a profit by doing so. You can check with the SEC or your state regulatory agency to see if the newsletter has ever been investigated. And read the fine print in the newsletter carefully—it might say that it receives payment from companies it writes about. If that's the case, don't trust it.

Check This Out!

You can find out your bro-ker's employment history, whether there's been disci-plinary action taken against him, and much more at the National Association of Security Dealers (NASD) Web site at www.nasdr.com.

The Least You Need to Know

♦ Always pay with your credit card when you shop online, because it offers complete consumer protection.

♦ Check out a site before buying; make sure it's reputable, and that it's a "secure" site that scrambles credit card information so that hackers can't steal your information.

♦ Look for hidden costs, and understand warranties and return policies before buying.

♦ Always print out your order form and keep it in a safe place.

♦ If you buy from an online site that goes out of business and you run into a problem, gather all the pertinent information and contact your credit card company, the Federal Trade Commission, and your state Attorney General.

♦ Beware of "pump and dump" online stock scams—people who claim to be giving objective advice, but are trying to get a stock bid up so they can sell at a profit.

25

How to Protect Your Credit Card When Buying Over the Internet

In This Chapter

- ◆ How to make sure that your credit card information can't be stolen
- ◆ Figuring out whether a site uses a secure connection for protecting your credit card
- ◆ Special free protections you can get to protect your credit card
- ◆ How to check out a site before buying to make sure it's a reputable one
- ◆ Where to get the lowdown on shopping sites online

Before you put your plastic on the line and shop till you drop in cyberspace, you want to know that your credit card information won't be stolen. And you'd like to make sure that the site from which you're buying is a legitimate one that won't take your money and run.

Luckily, it's easy to make sure that your credit card will never be stolen—and it's simple to check out a site before you buy to make sure it's a legitimate one.

How do you do that? I thought you'd never ask. Check out this chapter and you'll never go wrong.

How to Know You're Buying Through a Secure Site

The biggest fear that many people have about buying online is whether their credit card information will be stolen. What's to stop a hacker from intercepting your credit card information as it makes its way across the Internet? Will some 16-year-old cracker capture your credit card information, and then use it to buy Megadeath CDs, life-sized posters of Pamela Anderson, a five-year supply of pepperoni pizza (and so a five-year-supply of pimple cream), and round-trip tickets to Tahiti for him and his adolescent friends?

Not if you buy at a secure site. When you buy at a secure site, your credit card information is scrambled as it's sent across the Internet so that no one can read it except the site to which you're sending it. This means your credit card information is safe from hackers, crackers, and other assorted ne'er-do-wells.

"That's all well and good," you're no doubt thinking, "But how do I know when I'm shopping at a secure site?"

It's actually exceedingly easy to know. When you've put everything you want into your shopping cart (don't forget the tea caddy with the knitted figurine of George Bush and the Pope on top, please) and it's time to pay with plastic, you're sent to a page where you're supposed to enter your credit card information. If you're on a secure site, before you get to that page, a window pops up (see Figure 25.1), alerting you that you're about to enter a secure site. (Figure 25.1 shows the message you get in Microsoft Internet Explorer. The one for Netscape Navigator is slightly different.) Click **OK,** and you're sent to the secure site where you can go ahead and buy.

Figure 25.1

Here's how to know you're entering a secure site. If you don't see this screen, it's not a safe place.

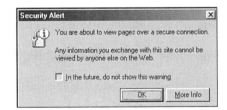

Now, here's something peculiar. See the little check box in the window? If you'd like, you can use that check box to tell your browser *not* to alert you each time you visit a secure site. Why would you *not* want to be alerted? I haven't a clue. But this is the Internet, after all, and it sometimes seems to be a looking-glass world. My strong advice is to make sure that you tell the browser to alert you every time you're about to visit a secure site. And never, even in your wildest imagination, enter credit card information in a site that isn't secure.

By the way, if things aren't confusing enough for you, think about this one: If you want to always be alerted when you visit a secure site, make sure the box is checked in Netscape Navigator, but in Microsoft Internet Explorer, make sure the box is *unchecked*. It must be just Netscape and Microsoft's way of making sure you're paying attention. Ain't the Internet grand?

Check for the Locked Lock

That pop-up window is one clue that you're entering a secure site. But there's another way to check. Look for the little icon of a lock on the bottom bar of your browser. In Netscape Navigator, if the little lock is unlocked, it means that the site is not a secure one. If the lock is locked, it means the site is secure.

In Microsoft Internet Explorer, if there is no lock at the bottom of the browser, it means the site is not secure. If there is a lock there, it means the site is secure. Figure 25.2 shows the secure icon in Microsoft Internet Explorer.

Check This Out!

SET stands for Secured Electronic Transaction, and it's the electronic encryption and payment standard that a group of big companies, including Microsoft, Netscape, Visa, MasterCard, and others are pushing to become the standard for doing electronic commerce on the Internet. Some sites are already using it; soon every site might be using SET.

Done	🔒 💿 Internet

Figure 25.2

To make sure you're at a secure site, look for the locked padlock icon in Microsoft Internet Explorer.

Failsafe Credit Card Protection—It's Free!

Credit card companies know that one of the main reasons people are worried about shopping online is fear of their credit card information being stolen. So they've done a lot to allay people's fears. And more than just allaying people's fears, they also have taken some solid steps to offer you credit card protections.

The first thing to keep in mind is this: The most you'll ever have to pay if your credit card is stolen—online or in the real world—is $50. Not a penny more. And the truth is,

Check This Out!

When you shop online, always pay with your credit card rather than by check or some other method. If you pay by check, you don't get the same kinds of consumer protections—such as capping your losses at $50—that you do when paying with a credit card.

credit card companies are hungry for business, and most of them waive even that fee. For example, Visa has put into effect its Zero Liability plan, which says that if you buy anything over the Internet using your Visa card and it's stolen, you're not liable for a single penny.

But when you lose your credit card, there's a bigger issue than money—it's the time you have to spend dealing with credit card companies and repairing your credit if the person who's stolen it has run up big bills. Because of that, credit card companies have built protections into their credit cards you should be aware of. Here's the rundown on each.

American Express and Discover Card Protections

American Express and Discover Card have both come up with similar programs for protecting your credit card. Each time you shop with either of those credit cards online, you can have a unique credit card number generated. That number is valid only for that single transaction. So if someone steals the credit card number, it won't do them any good—that number can only be used for a single transaction. The American Express program is called Private Payments, and the Discover Card program is called Deskshop.

There are some slight differences between the programs. At deskshop, for example, you generate a unique number for each store or service, and can keep using that number each time you shop at the online store. So, for example, you can continually use the same number each time you shop at Amazon.com, or you can have the same number used every month to pay your Internet Service Provider (ISP).

Check This Out!

Be warned not to use one-time numbers to buy airline tickets and tickets to entertainment and sporting events. Often, you have to present your real-life credit card to pick up tickets. When you go to pick them up, your real-life credit card number won't match the unique credit card number generated online, and so you might not be allowed to pick up the tickets.

With Private Payments, on the other hand, that number is good only for that single payment. The next time you want to pay at Amazon.com, for example, you have to generate a new number. And you aren't able to use Private Payments for paying a recurring payment such as to your ISP.

What this means is that the Discover plan is a bit more convenient than the American Express plan, but it's also less safe. So decide whether convenience or safety is more important to you, and then use the plan that suits you best.

Visa Protections

Visa offers a different way to protect your credit card online, through its Visa Authenticated Payments plan. In essence, it password-protects your Visa card. If you choose to use the plan, whenever you use your Visa card online, you enter a password. That way, even if someone steals your credit card, they aren't able to use it online because they also need your password.

How to Check Out a Site Before Buying

Making sure a site is secure ensures that no hackers can steal your credit card when you send it to that site, as does using the special credit card protections. But what about the site itself? What if the Web site you're buying on is a scam? The truth is, it doesn't take a whole lot of skill or money to put together a professional-looking Web site (although considering all the crud you come across when surfing the Web, that might come as a surprise to you). In a real-life store, by checking out how well a store is maintained, seeing what the merchandise is like, talking to the staff, and other means, you can often tell if the store is an honest one. But just because a Web site has a pretty face doesn't mean much—lurking behind that pretty face could be a scam artist, just itching to get his hands on your money.

But fear not, dear reader; there are ways you can check out a site before buying, so that you're able to tell whether the site's on the up-and-up or is a lowdown crook. Here's what to know:

- ◆ **Does the site make available contact information?** You want to know things such as the address (or at least the city) of the site's main headquarters. Better yet, does it list the names of the company's officers (not many sites do this, by the way)? Is it a publicly traded company (if it is, it'll tell you so)? How about a contact telephone number? Is one listed? The more of this kind of information a site is willing to post, the more likely it is that it's an honest one. If you can't find any of this kind of information about the site, be leery.

- ◆ **Does it prominently post important information, such as its shipping and return policies and warranties?** Make sure this kind of information is posted. If it's not, it could be a sign that there's a shady character in there somewhere. If it's not posted, send an inquiry e-mail to the site. Do they respond quickly and with the specific information you've asked for? If you can't find out this kind of information, then take a hike, because the site might take a hike with your money if you buy through them. Figure 25.3 displays a page detailing shipping charges at Amazon. com.

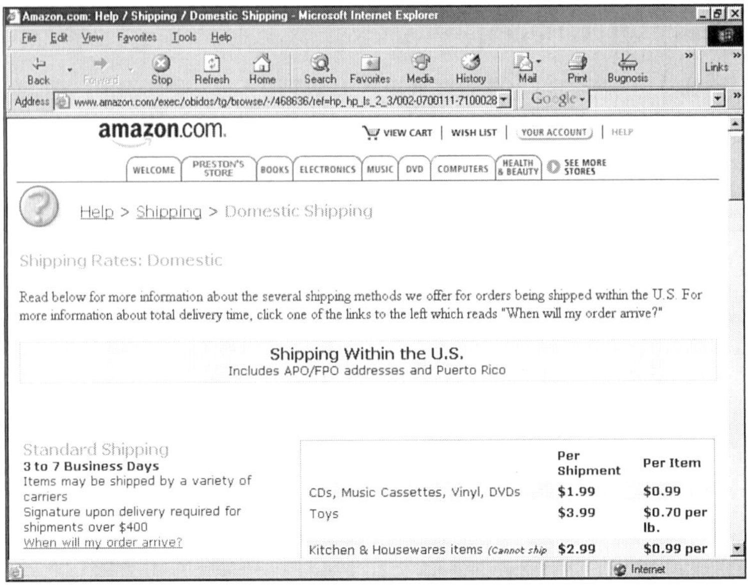

Figure 25.3

Before buying at a Web site, look for clear information about policies like shipping charges, as pictured here at Amazon.com.

◆ **If the site has message boards, check them out.** Busy message boards often mean a lot of active users, and it might be a sign that the site has return visitors. If people keep returning, the site can usually be trusted. But check out what kinds of messages are being posted—if it's loads of complaints, that's a bad sign. Be careful not to rely too heavily on message boards, though. The site can forge messages and weed out complaints.

◆ **Have you heard of the site before?** A site associated with a well-known bricks-and-mortar store can usually be trusted. And if the site has shelled out big bucks for a national advertising campaign, it often means it's well-funded and should be around for a while.

Check This Out!

Know your rights about shipping times. You have the force of the law behind you when it comes to knowing when the goods you've ordered will be delivered to you. Internet shopping is covered by the Federal Trade Commission's Mail Order Rule. That rule says that companies must ship orders to you within the time they've promised—and if they haven't promised a time, then they must ship them within 30 days of when you've ordered them. If there's a delay, they have to notify you, and ask whether you agree to the delay, or else let you cancel the order—and you then get a full refund within seven days, or one billing cycle of your credit card account. If they don't notify you of a delay, and the goods still aren't shipped, you have the right to cancel the order and get a refund.

Where You Can Get the Lowdown on Shopping Sites

There are a variety of ways to get the inside scoop on online shopping sites to see whether they're honest. Here's where to go.

Check Out the Better Business Bureau

Better Business Bureaus are local, non-profit corporations that can give you the inside skinny on businesses that have less-than-savory reputations. They can tell you if businesses have any outstanding complaints lodged against them.

You can get a free report from the Better Business Bureau about any company that they have a record of. This report tells you how long the company has been in business, whether complaints have been filed with the Better Business Bureau about the company, and how the complaints were resolved—if they were resolved at all. And if a government agency such as the Federal Trade Commission or a state Attorney General has taken actions against the company, the Better Business Bureau also tells you that. The reports usually cover the past three years, and show if the company is a member of the Better Business Bureau.

Keep in mind that the bureau doesn't have reports on every business. If it doesn't have a report, it generally means that either the company is a new one, or that there have been no complaints against it.

Check This Out! _____

Some things you should never buy online because the possibilities for fraud are simply too great. Don't buy collectible Beanie Babies. As any 10-year-old child or toy collector can tell you, collectible Beanie Babies are big business, and commonly sell for hundreds or even thousands of dollars. Although buying garden-variety Beanie Babies online for $5 and $10 is fine, buying expensive collectibles is a very bad idea—it's too easy for scamsters to sell counterfeit goods. And I wouldn't buy sports memorabilia, either. As with Beanie Babies, you aren't able to examine the goods before you buy. In a recent case, baseballs were being offered that were supposedly signed by baseball great Roberto Clemente. The only problem was that the baseballs were manufactured five years after Clemente had died.

Better Business Bureaus are all local. So a Better Business Bureau in Peoria, Iowa, for example, can't tell you about a business based in Hackensack, New Jersey. So before checking in with a Better Business Bureau, you need to find out where the Web site's main offices are. If you can't find out where the main offices are, you've answered the question already—stay away.

To find contact information for a Better Business Bureau near you, check the Yellow Pages or call directory assistance. If you're like me and would rather do things on the Web, go to the bureau's Web site at www.bbb.com to find contact information. And you can also search for reports on the Web site.

Check This Out! _____

The federal Fair Credit Billing Act covers credit card transactions over the Internet. It gives you legal rights if there's an error on your credit card bill because of a transaction you made over the Internet, or if you're disputing a credit card bill because of a transaction over the Internet. If you find that you've been billed incorrectly for some reason (such as for goods and services you haven't received, an error in the amount charged, or unauthorized charges), the law covers you. Under it, you must write a letter to the company that made the incorrect charge, describing the error, and including your name, address, and charge card number. When you send the notice, the company must, by law, send you a written acknowledgment of your claim within 30 days, and must resolve the problem within 90 days.

Head to the BBB*Online* Site

So much business is being conducted on the Internet that the Better Business Bureau has hung out its shingle online—it's put together a program for checking out online sites in the same way that it checks out bricks-and-mortar businesses. The program is called BBB*Online* and you can get information about it at the BBB*Online* site at www.bbbonline. com.

Here's how it works: A Web site agrees to participate in the program, and so has to abide by BBB*Online* standards. This means that the company agrees to resolve complaints quickly and fairly, that it has a satisfactory record with the Better Business Bureau, that it be in business at least a year, that it agrees to correct or withdraw misleading Internet advertising, and that it provides contact information such as addresses, phone numbers, and the names of company officials. The company must also agree to binding arbitration with a consumer if there's been a complaint. All in all, it's a pretty good deal for consumers.

Companies who participate can also place a BBB*Online* seal on their site. When you see that seal, you know the site is willing to abide by strict standards. And even better, you can click the seal to get a full rundown about the company. This rundown includes the company's address, phone number, contact information, and the like, as well as information on how long the company has been in business. And if there have been any complaints against the company, you're shown that as well.

Take a Close Look at the ePublicEye

Here's a great idea for a site: Have the people who actually shop at sites rate the sites for reliability, customer satisfaction, and sensitivity to privacy issues. That's what the ePublicEye at www.epubliceye.com does (see Figure 25.4). The ePublicEye gathers information from consumers about their experiences at sites, and uses the information to rate sites. It does more than merely rate sites—it also publishes comprehensive information about the sites, including ratings for reliability, safety, privacy practices, customer support, and more. And you can even see individual comments that people have made about a site. It's a great way to get a true picture of a shopping site.

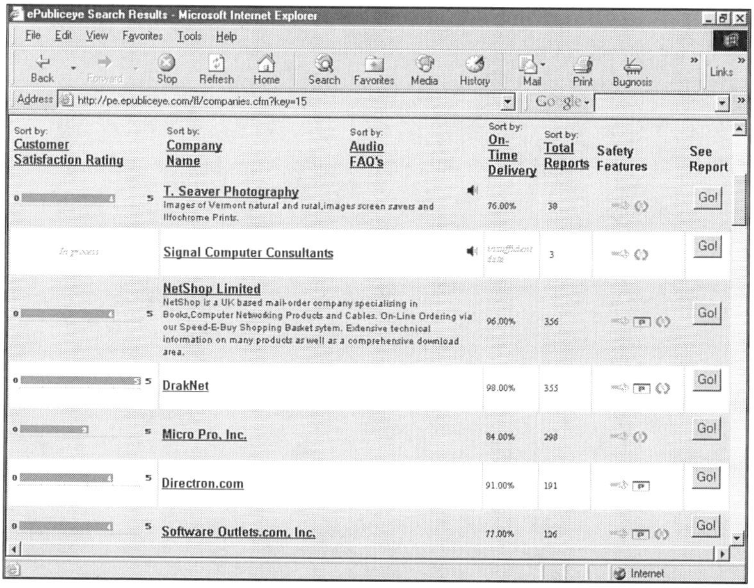

Figure 25.4

Take a close, close look at a site at www.epubliceye.com. You get comprehensive consumer ratings of buying sites.

Head to Usenet Newsgroups

One of the best places to find out the goods on an online merchant is in newsgroups and online discussion boards. There are many newsgroups you can head to, but I've found that for information about which online sites to stay away from, misc.consumer is the best by far. In a single day, for example, there were three messages posted warning people to stay away from buying at certain Web sites. Head there, read the messages, and post questions of your own. You can be sure you get answers—honest ones.

Check This Out!

To read newsgroups, you need a special piece of software called a newsgroup reader. Netscape Navigator and Microsoft Outlook include them. You can also read newsgroups at the Google Groups at www.groups.google.com.

The Least You Need to Know

◆ Only buy through sites that feature secure transactions. You can tell they're secure by looking for the locked padlock at the bottom of your browser.

◆ Use the special, free protections for online shopping that credit card companies offer their customers.

◆ Check out the sites you patronize with the Better Business Bureau and other consumer sites.

◆ Make sure that the sites you patronize list contact information, including address and phone numbers.

◆ Check out return policies and warranties online before buying—and don't buy from a site that doesn't tell you its policies.

Chapter 26

How to Stay Safe When Buying at Auctions

In This Chapter

- ◆ What kinds of online auctions are there?
- ◆ How do you bid at online auctions?
- ◆ How to check out an auction site to make sure it's a reputable one
- ◆ How to check out sellers to make sure they won't burn you
- ◆ Top tips for making sure you won't be scammed at auctions

Where can you get the best deals on the Web? At online auctions. Where are the most common scams committed on the Web? At online auctions, according to the Internet Fraud Watch site.

It's no accident that auctions offer you the best deals, and are also places where the most scams are committed. They're incredibly popular sites, drawing many thousands of people bidding on millions and millions of items a day. The vast majority of them are safe—but before bidding, you want to make sure you know what's up so you don't get scammed.

Read this chapter, and you can be a bidder, too—one who can bid without getting burned. I'll let you know everything there is about how to stay safe and steer clear of scams while you pursue great deals.

Sold American! What Are Online Auctions?

An auction done online? How is that possible? How can a smooth, fast-talking auctioneer rattle off bids and bargains rat-a-tat style over the wires and modems that make up the Internet?

Not only are online auctions possible, they're about the hottest things going these days. The basic idea of an online auction is the same as a traditional auction: You bid against others, trying to buy something at the lowest price possible. But in online auctions, there's no live auctioneer, there's less pressure, and you don't need to show up at a certain time and place to participate—auctions take place twenty-four hours a day, seven days a week, at sites all over the Internet. Many hundreds of thousands—and possibly millions—of items are being auctioned off online right now as you read these words.

 **Check This Out!**

It's easy to get carried away at an auction, assuming that you're getting the best deal possible … but are you? Before bidding on an item, make sure to find out its true retail price; otherwise, you might end up paying more than you would in a store.

Keep in mind that auctions aren't just for buyers. You can make a pretty penny by cleaning out your attic and putting things up for sale as well. Don't look down your nose at those odd items you have lying around your house. (And if your house is like mine, those items can be very odd, indeed. As I write this, I'm looking at a goat skull hanging on my wall, a telescope on the floor, and an old ant farm near the window. Wonder how much they'd sell for?) Realtors say that every house, no matter how eccentric, has its buyers. And when you're selling at auctions online, all old junk might have a buyer as well.

Biding Your Time: How Do Online Auctions Work?

The basics of buying at an auction are pretty simple. You bid by going to an auction site, browsing for things you're interested in buying, and then making bids. To make a bid, you first register, for free, at the site. In some instances, such as if you're buying the item directly from the site itself, you have to enter your credit card number and information. In other instances, you won't have to enter your credit card number because you won't be buying the item from the site, but rather from a private person who put the item up for bid.

Every auction lasts for a certain amount of time. Most auctions lasts for several days, and often up to a week or more. If you're making a bid, it makes sense to check in regularly, to see how the bidding is going, because you're probably not the only person who absolutely has to have those wind chimes that play the theme to *Love Story* every time a breeze blows by. When you check in, you're able to see the history of the bidding, which includes information on how many other people are bidding, and what they've bid. Figure 26.1 shows a typical auction on the popular eBay auction site at www.ebay.com.

Figure 26.1

Get ready to bid! A DVD player up for bidding at the eBay auction site.

At the end of the auction, if you're not the highest bidder, you've only spent your time, not your money—although you might never forgive yourself for not spending an extra $5 for those *Love Story* wind chimes.

However, let's say that your dream came true, and you snagged the wind chimes for a mere $27.50 (and a bargain at half the price …). You're told by e-mail that you're the winning bidder. If the auction site is the one selling the item, you pay the auction site using your credit card. If instead you're buying it from a private seller at the auction site, you make arrangements with that private seller.

What Kinds of Auction Sites Are There?

Auctions might look the same, but very often, they're quite different from one another. The first step to making sure that you don't get burned at an auction is to know what kind of auction you are buying at. You face different dangers depending on the kind of auction where you buy.

In general, there are two types of auctions. The following sections tell you what you need to know about each.

Check This Out!

Whether auction scams are common or not is, to a great extent, in the eye of the beholder. The Internet Fraud Watch site at www.fraud.org reports that auction scams are by far the most common scam on the Internet, accounting for 78 percent of all reported scams in 2000. However, the eBay auction site counters that fraud is exceedingly rare, occurring in only about 27 of every one million transactions. Of course, if you're one of those 27, it doesn't seem rare at all. It feels more like well-done.

Auctions in Which You Buy Primarily Directly from the Site

At some auction sites, such as www.ubid.com, you buy some or all of the goods directly from the site. You have to be careful when buying at these sites to make sure that the site is on the up-and-up. They need to actually deliver the goods at the agreed-upon price—goods that aren't damaged in any way. And you also want to make sure that the site protects your privacy. These sites can gather an incredible amount of information about you. It includes not just your credit card information, but also information about the products you buy and bid on; and that information is quite valuable to marketers and sellers. Later on in the chapter, in "Check Out the Auction Site Before Bidding," I show you how to safeguard your privacy at sites like these.

Auctions Where You Buy Primarily Directly from Individuals

At many sites, such as the popular eBay auction site, you primarily buy from other individuals.

A big draw at these kinds of auctions is the incredible variety of stuff you can buy there. On the monstrous eBay site, for example, on any given day there are two million or more different items for sale. Groovy drinking birds, powerful computers, potato peelers, Martin 0042 guitars, glass pigs … pretty much anything you can imagine, and a whole lot of things you've never imagined (and might never want to), are for sale here.

But because you buy at these sites directly from individuals, there's more danger in getting burned when using them. After all, you're buying from someone, sight unseen—how can you ensure the goods will be delivered? Often, you don't pay with your credit card, so you might lack basic consumer protections, as well. As you see in this chapter, though, there's a lot you can do to make sure that you don't get burned when you buy at auctions.

What Are the Most Common Auction Scams?

So, what are the most common dangers when you visit auction sites? According to the Federal Trade Commission, based on complaints it's received, these are the most common scams:

- People who don't deliver the goods they've promised.
- People who deliver goods that are much less valuable than the ones they claimed to be selling.
- People who don't deliver goods in a timely fashion.
- People who don't fully explain all the information about the goods they're selling, or improperly describe the terms of the sale.

Check Out the Auction Site Before Bidding

The best way to make sure you don't get burned at an auction is to check out the site first. It's important to check out an auction site even if you're not buying from the site itself, because there's a lot an auction site can do to cut down on scams. For added safety, some sites even offer free or low-cost insurance to reimburse you if you get burned. The following is a list of what you can do to learn about a site before bidding:

- **Check out its privacy policies.** Auction sites of any kind can track what you buy—and if you're buying directly from the site, you're giving them your credit card information as well. Make sure that what they do with the information doesn't invade your privacy. Look for privacy seals, such as the TRUSTe seal, which indicates that they adhere to strict privacy guidelines. For more information about checking privacy on the Web, turn to Chapter 12, "How to Make Sure Internet Sites Don't Abuse Your Privacy."

- **Look for insurance and guarantees.** Auction sites have recognized that if they don't stamp out scams, they'll put themselves out of business. So some of them, such as www.amazon.com and www.ebay.com, have put insurance and guarantees into effect. These anti-scam features guarantee that the site will reimburse your money if you've been scammed. Typically, sites cover items that cost up to a certain amount of money, often $200 or $250. In some instances, for example at eBay, you have to pay the first $25. Sometimes you have to pay some kind of annual fee for the insurance guarantees. But guarantees are helpful—they help protect you against scams, and they're a sign that the site is a reliable one that takes scams seriously.

◆ **Find out if the site is policed for scam artists.** Some sites take a laissez-faire attitude towards scamsters, claiming that the site acts only as a middleman, not a policeman, and has no responsibility for policing the site. Other sites, though, have started to crack down by actively looking for scamsters and then ejecting them. eBay, for example, looks for and ejects "shillers" who artificially bid up the costs of items. They eject sellers for other reasons as well. Click around the auction site to see if it provides information on how it polices itself.

Check This Out!

Insurance and guarantees often don't cover everything for sale on an auction site. Read the fine print about insurance and guarantees, because they don't always cover all the items up for sale, even if those items cost less than $200 or $250. Some sites put a label of some kind next to items that are covered.

◆ **If you buy from the site, do they post warranty, shipping, and return policies?** You want to make sure that you can return things, that what you buy is covered by a warranty, and you know what the shipping costs are. If you can't find that information, head to an auction elsewhere.

◆ **Is there a comprehensive help section detailing safety, privacy, and consumer issues?** Auction sites can be confusing places, and if you have a problem, it's often hard to know where to go to solve it. You want a site that spells out all its policies in explicit detail and is easy to find. Figure 26.2 displays the Safe Harbor section of eBay.

Figure 26.2

Staying safe at eBay: Here's the Safe Harbor section detailing all its consumer, safety, privacy, and related issues.

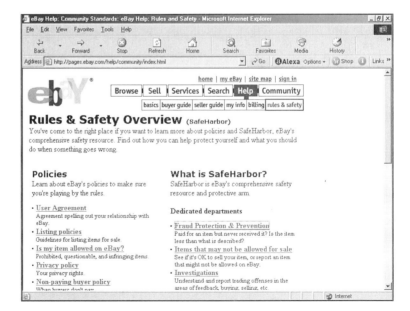

◆ **Can you view information about how reputable the sellers and buyers are?** A good way to make sure you don't get burned is to make sure you buy from someone reputable. But if you're buying from someone sight unseen, how can you check on them? Some auction sites enable buyers and sellers to rate others for reputability. That way you're able to see others' records. Look for sites that allow these kinds of ratings, because at them, you have better ways to make sure you don't get burned.

◆ **Does the site have rules about not allowing illegal or other inappropriate items to be sold?** Some auction sites have been used to sell a variety of items that are either illegal or inappropriate to sell online, such as handguns and firearms. Sites have started to crack down on this, and some have formulated specific policies against the sale of inappropriate or illegal items. A site that has policies against selling this kind of thing is a site that's more likely to be reputable.

Check This Out!

eBay has banned a variety of illegal or inappropriate items from being sold on the site. The list is long, but here's a small selection of what can't be sold: firearms; bazookas; explosives; beta or pre-release software; pirated movies and music; illegal animal parts; Federal, New York, and Seattle police badges; live animals; Cuban cigars; skulls; and human remains. Talk about a mixed bag!

How to Make Sure You Don't Get Scammed at Auctions

Checking out an auction site before bidding can help make sure you don't get burned—but it only takes you so far. There are many thousands of people who bid on auctions, so how can you make sure that when you buy that matched set of salt and pepper shakers in the shape of Minnesota, you'll really be delivered the goods?

If you've bought an item at an auction where you buy directly from the site, you're okay, because you're paying by credit card, and you've checked out the site. But what do you do if you've bought an item at a site in which you buy from a private seller? How can you make sure the seller won't just take the money and run? It's actually not that hard to do. Follow these tips and you should be just fine.

Research the Seller

How trustworthy is the person who's doing the selling? Some sites such as eBay enable you to get detailed information about how the seller has treated other buyers. At eBay, for example, you can see a profile detailing how other sellers have rated the buyer—you can see a tally of the total number of positive, neutral, and negative comments, and you can read the individual comments, as well. If someone has several negative comments, stay away. (In fact, if someone too many negative comments, and eBay confirms they're accurate, that person is kicked off the service.)

The auction site provides you with the e-mail address of the seller. Send an e-mail to the seller asking a question, and see how fast you get a response. If you don't get a response, or you get a slow one, that's a bad signal. And certainly if you can't get an address and phone number, stay away.

If the site has a message board or chat area, head there and ask if any other people have had dealings with the seller. If they have, they'll be happy to share them with you—both good and bad.

Understand How the Site Works Before Buying

Auctions can be confusing, and you want to know how they work before you buy—you don't want to face the equivalent of a situation in a real-life auction when you swat at a mosquito buzzing around your face, only to find out that you've just made the winning bid on the $25 million Picasso up for sale. You want to know details such as whether you pay for an item before the seller ships it, or whether you're shipped the item, and then you pay for it.

Check This Out! _____

"Flash" or "express" auctions are auctions that are done very quickly—often, they take an hour or less. In that way, they're similar to real-life auctions. These kinds of auctions get your adrenaline flowing, because you're in pitched battle against other bidders. When your adrenaline is flowing at one of these auctions, it's easy to get carried away—especially because some of them allow you to chat online with other bidders, which means a bit of taunting can take place. In a hothouse atmosphere like this, macho posturing sometimes takes over, and you might find yourself bidding very high prices on an item, just to prove you can win. But when the bidding is over, you might find yourself paying well over top-dollar for an item that isn't worth a plug nickel. So make sure before you bid at one of these to set a top price over which you won't go.

Get Contact Information from the Seller

You want to get the seller's real-life mailing address and phone number, as well as e-mail address. If the seller isn't willing to provide that information, don't trust him or her. Most sites only provide e-mail addresses, so you have to contact the seller via e-mail.

Find Out About Warranties, Returns, and Deliveries

How long until the goods are shipped to you? Who pays for shipping? What kind of warranty do you get? How do you get service if there is a warranty? Sometimes this information is covered in the auction listing itself, but it isn't always. Get all the details—in writing—before closing the deal.

Don't Buy Expensive Collectibles

One of the biggest scams going is the sale of collectibles online. Don't trust buying "retired" Beanie Babies, sports memorabilia, and other expensive collectibles—they're all very common scams. In one particularly noteworthy scam, someone offered for sale a baseball signed by baseball great Roberto Clemente. The only problem is that the ball was manufactured five years after the ballplayer's death!

Check This Out! _____

The eBay auction site, recognizing the possibility for fraud in buying products such as rare coins and trading cards, has created a page with links to many different companies that authenticate that the items being sold are real. There are authentication services for everything from coins to Beanie Babies, stamps, trading cards, autographs, and more. Get to them at http://pages.lebay.com/help/community/auth-overview.html.

Never Pay by Cash or Money Order

When you send cash or a money order, you have absolutely no recourse when someone takes the money and runs. If someone demands cash, it's a possible sign that you're about to be scammed.

Ask That Shipping Be Done Cash on Delivery (C.O.D)

Here's a simple way to ensure that someone can't cash your check without sending you the goods: Ask that they ship it cash on delivery. When something is shipped C.O.D., it means that you pay for the item only when you receive it. It costs a few dollars extra compared to regular shipping, but if it's the first time you're dealing with a seller, it might be worth the cost. And you can always try to get the seller to pay for the extra C.O.D. charge, or to at least split the charge with you.

Check This Out! _____

When you buy something sight unseen, such as a CD, it's hard to know whether what you're buying is illegal—that it hasn't been pirated, for example. Some warning signs include: the documentation is photocopied, a CD is sent only in a jewel case, you're asked to send money to a Post Office box instead of a street address, and you're asked to send cash.

Use an Internet "Escrow" Service

If it's the first time you're buying, or you're spending serious money (more than $100 or so), you might want to use an Internet escrow service. These services act as a good-faith go-between between the buyer and the seller. Generally, here's how it works. You make your payment to the escrow service, but the service doesn't immediately turn the money over to the seller. Instead, it keeps the money in escrow. The seller then sends you the goods. You inspect them, then tell the escrow service you've gotten what you paid for. The escrow service then releases the money to the seller.

The biggest escrow site is Tradenable at www.tradenable.com. The fee varies according to the purchase price of the item. For items up to $25,000 (which I'm certain should cover whatever you're bidding on), the fee is four percent of the amount of the purchase price, with a minimum $7.95 fee if you pay by credit card. If you pay by case, the fee is two percent, with the same $7.95 minimum.

The Least You Need to Know

- ◆ Before bidding at an auction, know whether you're buying from the site or a private individual.
- ◆ Shop at auction sites that offer insurance and guarantees against fraud and scams.
- ◆ It's best to shop at auction sites that actively police themselves against shillers and scamsters.
- ◆ Before sending money to anyone, check his or her background. For big-ticket items, use an Internet escrow company.
- ◆ Never pay by cash or money order.
- ◆ Don't buy expensive collectibles online—they're too easy to counterfeit, and you can't examine the goods before buying.

Chapter 27

Wireless Insecurity: Protecting Yourself When Using Cellular Devices

In This Chapter

◆ Privacy and security dangers when using wireless technology

◆ Understanding how different wireless technologies work

◆ How to be safe when using a wireless network in the office

◆ How to protect a home wireless network

◆ Protecting yourself against wireless viruses

◆ How to protect yourself against cell phone snoopers and cloners

Cellular phones, wireless personal digital assistants (PDAs) like iPaqs and Palms, and wireless networks. All these have made our lives more convenient and have created a world in which we have instant, always-on connections. More and more, we're communicating wirelessly, particularly over the Internet.

But we pay a price for these ubiquitous connections. Hackers, snoopers, and evil-doers are able to gain access to your data, private information, and computers literally out of thin air. Viruses might invade not just PDAs, but cell phones as well. Your cell phone calls can be snooped upon.

In this chapter, you'll find out all about the kinds of wireless dangers you face, and how to fight against them.

What Kinds of Cellular Dangers Are There?

It might be hard for some people to take wireless dangers seriously. After all, the whole point of wireless technology is that you don't see anything: Look Ma, no wires! And human nature, being what it is, makes us believe that if we don't see something, it doesn't exist.

But wireless dangers are all too real. There are all kinds of privacy and security problems with wireless communications. Here are some of the main kinds:

◆ **Viruses.** These nuisances can be spread wirelessly, and so pose potential dangers not just to computers, but also to cell phones, PDAs, and wireless networks. The viruses can be as innocuous as a joking text message on a cell phone, or as damaging as deleting all the data from a PDA or crashing a wireless network.

◆ **Cell phone snoopers.** These guys can listen in on cell phone calls and invade your and your company's privacy.

◆ **Cell phone cloners.** The "identity" of your cell phone can be stolen. Cell phone cloners can then use that false identity to make phone calls, leaving you holding the bill.

◆ **Wireless hackers and network snoopers.** These bad guys can see every bit of data traveling through wireless corporate networks, and use that information to gain an advantage on their competitors. Wireless hackers can also steal information, delete files, and destroy software. Wireless hackers and network snoopers can also see all the information traveling on your home wireless network, and they can steal your private information and files, using a technique called *drive-by hacking*.

◆ **Wireless vandals.** These ne'er-do-wells can crash wireless networks by flooding them with phony information and messages so that the networks can't keep up with all the traffic.

◆ **Wireless hackers.** Wireless hackers can snoop on your e-mail while you're using a wireless network in a public area such as an airport or convention center.

Techno Talk

As more businesses and even homes set up wireless networks, a new kind of hacking has appeared: **drive-by hacking.** In drive-by hacking, a hacker takes a laptop and a wireless network card into a car with him, and then drives to a parking lot outside a business or home with a wireless network inside. Then, using the hardware and software, he's able to hack into the wireless network from outside the building. In this way, a drive-by hacker could hack into dozens of wireless networks in a single day. Some people refer to the practice of driving around in search of wireless networks to hack into as "war driving."

How Do Wireless Communications Work?

Before you get the inside scoop on how to protect yourself against wireless dangers, you need some sense of the different kinds of wireless communications out there. Here's the short list:

- **Cell phones.** You know all about these. In fact, you probably walk around all day with one attached to your ear. Hey, unplug for a change and join the real world!

- **Wireless personal digital assistants (PDAs) and e-mail devices.** Gadgets like the Palm, the iPaq, and the BlackBerry all enable you to get information from the Internet and to send and receive e-mail wirelessly.

- **Corporate wireless networks.** These are like normal business local area networks, except they allow computers to get onto the network wirelessly. This requires that a computer have a wireless network card, and that the network have a wireless access point. These networks use a wireless networking standard known as 802.11.

Check This Out!

You can always count on technology to make whatever is simple more complicated, and to make whatever is complicated even more complicated. That's the case with 802.11 networks. There are two kinds: 802.11a and 802.11b. The 802.11a networks offer faster speeds. If you have an 802.11b network card, it won't work with an 802.11a network. But if you have an 802.11a card, it might work with an 802.11b network. Thank you once again, technology, for making life more confusing than it needs to be.

◆ **Home wireless networks.** Increasingly, people who want to share an Internet connection at home network their computers. And if those computers are located in different parts of the house, the easiest way to connect them is with home wireless networks. These are usually 802.11 networks. That standard is also sometimes referred to as Wi-Fi.

◆ **Public wireless networks.** Airports, hotels, and soon even restaurants like Starbucks, will have public 802.11 networks that anyone can use. In some instances, you might have to pay for the service, but in others it'll be free. Either way, accessing the Internet wirelessly from public places is coming in the future—and in some cases you can already do it.

◆ **Bluetooth.** This is a technology that has yet to catch on. It's designed to allow computers, cell phones, entertainment devices, and more to communicate wirelessly with each other.

How to Protect Your Wireless Network

More and more, when people connect to the Internet, they do it via a wireless network, most likely an 802.11 (802.11b Wi-Fi) network of some sort. It might be over a home network, a network at work, or a public network (for example, one in an airport).

No matter how you connect, though, as I've explained before, there are dangers in using wireless networks. But you can fight back against hackers and snoopers. Just follow these tips:

◆ **Encrypt your e-mail.** Drinking cappuccino in a café while sending e-mail? How convenient. How dangerous. A nearby hacker could be reading your e-mail. To be safe, encrypt your e-mail before sending it. For information on how to do it, turn to Chapter 15, "Keeping Your E-mail Private with Encryption."

◆ **Find out if your company has a Virtual Private Network (VPN).** Many businesses allow employees to connect to the corporate network using what's called a Virtual Private Network (VPN). By running a special piece of software that scrambles all communications, you can keep everyone from seeing your activities on the Internet. There are special issues when connecting via a VPN wirelessly, so if you're planning to use a wireless connection, check with your company first.

◆ **Turn on the encryption system for your home network.** Often, a home wireless network

Check This Out!

If you want the real inside scoop on everything you've ever wanted to know about wireless technologies, get a copy of the book *How Wireless Works*, written by none other than yours truly. In addition, check out *The Complete Idiot's Guide to Wireless Computing and Networking* by Paul Heltzel.

includes a built-in encryption system—but that system isn't necessarily turned on when you install the network. Check the documentation, and see how to turn on encryption.

♦ **Ask if encryption is turned on in your corporate network.** You'd like to keep your information private at work. If your company uses a wireless network, ask if encryption is turned on, and if not, recommend that it be used.

♦ **Use a firewall.** When you buy a wireless network, it usually includes a firewall that keeps intruders out. And you can also buy personal firewalls. Just as you use a firewall in a wired network, you should also use a firewall in a wireless network. For more information about firewalls, turn to Chapter 6, "The Ultimate Defense: Keeping Safe with Firewalls."

♦ **Buy a 128-bit wireless network card.** Wireless network cards come with 64-bit or 128-bit security. You're much safer if you use a card with 128-bit security. It costs a little more, but your privacy and peace of mind is well worth the expense.

♦ **Be smart about using your passwords.** You can have powerful encryption and all the safety procedures in the world, but if you choose an easily crackable password, a hacker can get in. For information about the best way to handle passwords, turn to Chapter 2, "Putting Up Your First Line of Cyberdefense."

Watch Out for Wireless Viruses

If you have a PDA like a Palm or an iPaq, you might think you're safe from viruses. You hear all the time about viruses attacking personal computers, but PDAs? You never hear a word.

Well, I hate to break the news to you, but PDAs can get viruses, too. It's true that there aren't that many PDA viruses, but as PDAs get more popular, it's expected that PDA viruses will become more common.

Notes

Nothing, it seems, is immune to viruses. As cell phones get more sophisticated and become more like computers, they also become vulnerable to viruses. In fact, a virus of sorts has already hit them. The Timofonica virus attacked the Telefonica Spanish cell phone network. It started as a PC virus, attacked the Outlook e-mail program on people's PCs, and used Outlook to flood Telefonica cell phones with prank messages. By the way, a good safety precaution for your cell phone is to set the permissions in your network security settings from automatic to manual. That way, you'll never get a download to your phone without your permission.

These kinds of viruses spread wirelessly and could spread even more quickly than computer viruses, because of the "always-on" nature that some devices use to connect to the Internet.

One of the first wireless viruses to spread attacked the Palm PDA. It was called Phage, and was sent from Palm to Palm when the Palms exchanged data wireless via their infrared ports. When activated, the virus blanked the screen and halted the current program being run.

Luckily, there's a fairly simple way to combat wireless viruses: Get software designed to protect PDAs against viruses. A number of software programs are available, including Symantec Antivirus for the Palm and McAfee's VirusScan for Palm OS. In fact, McAfee has an entire line of security products for PDAs. Head to the McAfee Wireless Security Center at www.mcafee.com/wireless/ for more information. And for an excellent all-around piece of safety software for your PDA, head to www.pdadefense.com.

Beware of Cell Phone Snoopers and Cell Phone Cloners

It's not only wireless computer communications you need to worry about. There are also dangers in using wireless phone technologies.

The dangers are twofold: Someone can listen in to your cell phone call or cordless phone call; or someone can "clone" your cell phone and make calls, charging them to your account. The following sections teach what to do about each.

Fighting Snoopers

People can listen in on cell phone calls and calls on cordless telephones using special scanners. These devices scan the surrounding area for calls, then enable people to listen in on them.

Check This Out!

Soon every cell phone manufactured will have the ability to show you exactly where you are, using Global Positioning Satellite technology. This way, if you're in an emergency, police or other emergency personnel will be able to know exactly where you are, even if you can't talk or aren't sure where you are. But privacy advocates worry that the feature might be used by private businesses to violate your privacy.

The Federal Trade Commission ruled back in 1994 that scanners that could listen in on frequencies used by cell phones could no longer be manufactured. That, of course, hasn't stopped the practice. People with scanners who can listen in to cell phone and cordless phone calls are still out there.

The best way to make sure that your cell phone calls aren't listened to is to use only cell phones that use digital technology. (Your cellular provider or cell phone manufacturer will tell you if it is before you buy.) Cell phones that use digital technology have built-in encryption to help foil snoopers. Most new phones and services use digital technology, but it's a good idea to check, just in case. While digital signals can be hacked, digital phones are still more secure than analog ones.

When buying a cordless phone, look for those that have as many channels as possible, and that constantly switch among them. This makes it more difficult for someone to listen in on your cordless calls.

Fighting Cloners

Cell phones identify themselves to cell phone networks using something called an Electronic Serial Number (ESN). It's a unique number that the cell phone manufacturer programs into the phone. Whenever you make a call, the ESN is sent, the network checks it, enables you to make the call, and the call is charged to your account.

Unfortunately, thieves have figured out a way to "clone" that ESN. Using a special scanner and decoder, a thief can find out a cell phone's ESN and then program that ESN into a different phone—in essence, cloning your phone. The thief can then make calls with that cloned phone, and the charges all go to you.

There are ways to fight against cloners. Generally, only analog cellular phones can be cloned, because digital phones have security and encryption technology built into them that makes it more difficult to allow the ESN to be stolen. So your best bet is to buy a digital, rather than an analog, cellular phone.

To be safe, use the lock feature of your phone when you're not using it. Check your cellular bill carefully every month to make sure no unauthorized calls have been made. Report a stolen cellular phone immediately. And keep documents about your ESN hidden and in a safe place so they can't be stolen.

The Least You Need to Know

- When sending e-mail over a wireless network, encrypt it so that snoopers or hackers can't read it.
- Turn on the encryption feature in your home wireless network—and make sure that encryption is turned on at your place of work as well.
- Buy a 128-bit rather than a 64-bit wireless network card for maximum security.

♦ Personal digital assistants can get viruses, so make sure to use an anti-virus program from companies such as McAfee or Symantec.

♦ Digital cellular phones are much more secure than analog cellular phones—They use encryption, which makes them harder to eavesdrop upon and harder to clone than analog cellular phones.

Chapter 28

How to Safeguard Your PC

In This Chapter

- ◆ How to make sure your laptop won't be stolen
- ◆ How to use a screen saver to password-protect your PC
- ◆ Ways you can encrypt your files so that only you can read them
- ◆ How to permanently erase files from your hard disk
- ◆ How to back up your data in case of a crash or other accident

The Internet isn't the only place where your privacy can be invaded. It can also be invaded at the office where you work, or even at your home. Maybe you don't want your children to be able to get at certain sensitive files on your computer, and there are probably many files that you don't want co-workers to see. And if you own a laptop, it's all too easy for a thief to steal it.

In this chapter, I'll show you how you can keep your PC safe from prying eyes, protect your laptop so it doesn't get stolen, and ensure you're the only person who can get access to your computer and all your data. And for extra security, I'll tell you how to back up your data so it's all safe in case of a computer crash.

Protecting Your Laptop Against Theft

Think your laptop is safe? Think again. Even the country's most powerful law-enforcement agency, the FBI, can't keep thieves from snatching their laptops. In July, 2001, the agency revealed that it was missing 184 laptop computers, including 13 that were most likely stolen.

The FBI isn't alone in this: Laptop theft has become an epidemic. According to the Safeware Insurance Company, approximately 387,000 laptops were stolen in 2000—that's more than a billion dollars in stolen equipment. And beyond that are the incalculable costs associated with the potential misuse of proprietary business and personal information.

But fear not. I can teach you how to be smarter than the FBI when it comes to protecting your laptop. And you won't even have to take a civil service examination.

Get Anti-Theft Hardware

One of the simplest ways to make sure your laptop isn't stolen is to buy inexpensive hardware to lock down your computer and sound an alarm if someone tries to steal it. There are several kinds of these locks. The simplest, which typically cost less than $40, are hardened security cables, similar to bicycle locks, that can be locked using a key or a number combination. You attach the cable to your laptop using a small slot on the laptop called the Universal Security Slot. Just about every laptop manufactured in the last several years has such a slot, but if yours doesn't, cable makers can include an adhesive pad with a slot you can attach to your laptop. In both cases, when you attach the cable, you wrap it around something secure, such as a desk, and then lock it.

For a little extra money, usually totaling about $50 or $60 (more for more sophisticated equipment), you can get a lock combined with a sensor alarm. The sensor alarm can be used in concert with the lock or on its own. Motion sensors can sound a loud alarm when your laptop is moved too much—they're either silent or emit small chirps if they're jostled or bumped.

Check This Out! _____

The FBI isn't the world's only law enforcement or intelligence agency that has trouble stopping thieves from stealing its laptops. In 1996, a thief snatched a laptop from an agent of Britain's top-secret intelligence agency, MI5, in the Paddington Railway Station in London. The agency won't reveal what was on the laptop, but many believed that it contained sensitive intelligence information about security in Northern Ireland. James Bond, where are you when we need you?

There are many manufacturers of these kinds of locks and motion sensors, including Kensington at www.Kensington.com, Kryptonite at www.kryptonitelock.com, and Targus at www.targus.com. You can buy them at most computer and electronics stores.

Some locks are also combined with special software. For example, PC Guardian at www.pcguardian.com sells a package that includes a lock plus encryption software. With encryption software, you're the only person who can read what's on your computer; everyone else is locked out. So even if your laptop is stolen, no one is able to read the data.

Use Thief-Tracking Services

Another option is to buy LoJack-style tracking services that can track down your laptop if it's stolen. Typically, a service like this costs from $50 to $80 per year. You install a small piece of software on your computer that, whenever you connect to the Internet, gives the tracking service vital information that can be used to pinpoint its location. When you report your laptop as being stolen, the next time it connects to the Internet the tracking service is able find out where it is, and reports the information to law enforcement authorities. Companies that provide this type of service include CompuTrace (www.computrace.com), Lucira Technologies (www.lucira.com), and Computer Sentry Software (www.sentryinc.com).

Check This Out!

If you want to make sure that your personal or business information can't be stolen, even if your laptop is taken by a thief, consider getting encryption software that can make everything on your computer unintelligible to anyone but you. There's a lot of good encryption software including PGP, Magic Folders, and Encryption Plus Folders. You can try out free versions of any of them by first downloading them from a download site like www.download.com. Later in this chapter, in the section "How to Encrypt Your Files So That Snoopers Can't Get at Them," I show you how to encrypt your data with PGP.

Follow These Anti-Theft Tips

Hardware and monitoring service can only go so far to protect your laptop. The best way to insure that your computer doesn't get stolen is to follow these tips:

- **Carry it in a bag that doesn't look like a laptop case.** Carrying your laptop in an obvious laptop case is like putting on a label that says "Steal me!" There are many kinds of cases, including backpacks, that can carry laptops but don't look like the ubiquitous black laptop carrying case.

◆ **In airports, only put it through the X-ray machine when you're next in line, and then watch it like a hawk.** A common scam is for two thieves to work in concert. One waits at the end of the conveyor belt, and the second steps in front of you when you put your case on it. The second person then takes a long time getting through the security checkpoint and creates some kind of diversion while the first person walks away with your laptop. Also, never check a laptop as luggage if at all possible.

◆ **Engrave your company name and ID on your laptop.** This discourages thieves from taking it, and makes your laptop easier to trace. Also, make sure you have a copy of the laptop's identification number, which you can use if reporting it stolen.

◆ **If you have to leave your laptop in a car, lock it in the trunk, not the passenger compartment.** When driving, store it out of sight and keep your doors locked so no one can do a quick grab-and-run maneuver.

Check This Out!

Worried that if your laptop is stolen you won't be able to afford to buy a new one? Then buy laptop insurance, which insures you against its theft. Several companies offer such insurance, including the Safeware insurance agency at www.safeware.com. A policy for a $2,000 laptop typically costs $120. You can go to the site to get a quote and even buy insurance online.

How About Password Protecting Your PC?

If you work in an office, or any place where other people might have access to your PC, the greatest danger to your privacy might not come from hackers, crackers, spammers, scammers, or other assorted slimeballs. Instead, it might come from your co-workers and other people who have access to your computer.

Yes, it's not something pleasant to think about, but it's true. A co-worker might want to snoop on you by looking at what's on your PC. (Office rivals, take note: There's nothing on my PC worth looking at—unless you think the complete lineup of the 1989 Red Sox is an industrial secret.)

It's not only co-workers who might invade your privacy at work. In most offices, many people pass through (visitors, maintenance people, and others), and it would be easy for them to sit down at your PC and begin snooping around.

If you're a member of the great army of cubicle dwellers in corporations all across the country, you know how many people pass by your little piece of the universe on a given day. Every one of them can look into your PC and invade your privacy.

And you, you with the smug look on your face; yes, that's right—you over there! You have an office, so you think you're immune from this kind of invasion of privacy? Well think again. Do you lock it every time you leave it? And even if you do, cleaning people and maintenance people walk in every night, and they can discover all your secrets just by flipping a switch.

Here are just a few of the things people can do by turning on your computer when you're not there:

♦ They can make copies of all the files on your computer, including sensitive data, personal financial information, and more.

♦ They can copy down all your passwords and any other information you have on your computer that can give them access to your bank account, Web accounts, and other sensitive information.

♦ They can pose as you and send e-mail messages.

♦ They can delete any files on your computer that they want.

There's a lot of other bad stuff they can do, as well—just use your imagination, and you'll get some idea.

There's a simple way to secure your system against prying eyes, though. Read on to see how you can do it in about three minutes.

Password-Protect Your PC with a Screen Saver

It's easy to protect your PC so that when it's turned on and you're not using it, no one else is able to use it either. You do it by telling your PC to run a screen saver, and then password-protecting the screen saver.

Check This Out!

For more sophisticated protection for your computer than password protection can provide, you might want to look at the many programs you can download from the Internet and use. The Lock and WinBlocked are just two of the programs you can use. Many of them are shareware, which means that you can download and try them for free, and pay for them only if you continue using them. You can find them at popular download sites, such as www.download.com.

To do it, right-click your desktop. Then choose **Properties.** Now click the **Screen Saver** tab. The screen pictured in Figure 28.1 appears.

Figure 28.1

Here's the screen that enables you to password-protect your PC.

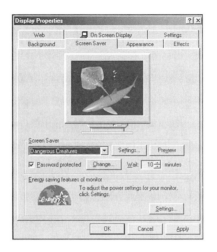

Click the arrow underneath the box that says **Screen Saver,** and choose the screen saver you want to use. (Myself, I'm partial to the Dangerous Creates screen saver. It reminds me that there might be sharks on my screen—but they're nothing compared to the sharks out there in the business world.) A small picture of what the screen saver looks like is displayed, but to get the full effect, click **Preview.** The full-screen version is launched, giving you the whole, full screen saver effect. Warning to refugees from the 1960s: Do not choose The '60s USA screen saver! You'll get serious flashbacks, and you'll find yourself looking for old love beads, flag-bedecked bell-bottom jeans—and you'll wonder what happened to all that lovely long hair you used to have!

Now, to password-protect the screen saver, click the **Password Protected** box. The screen pictured in Figure 28.2 is displayed. Type in the password you want to use. You have to type it in twice to confirm it. That's it! Your PC is now password protected. When your screen saver is running, the only way to get at your PC is to type in your password. For information about creating the best passwords that can't be guessed, turn to Chapter 2, "Putting Up Your First Line of Cyberdefense."

Notes
When you use a screen saver, it automatically starts after a certain amount of time passes in which you don't use your PC—usually about 14 minutes or so. But you can change the time value so that it starts as little as one minute after you stop using your computer. To do that, change the number in the Wait box in the Screen Saver tab, which can be changed to as little as one minute.

Luckily, it's easy to turn that feature off. Here's how. Click on the **Start** button, then choose **Settings,** and then **Control Panel.** Double-click the **Network** icon. Then click

File and **Print Sharing.** If nothing is checked on the screen, you're safe—no one can get at the files on your computer. If anything is checked there, uncheck it. Now you're safe.

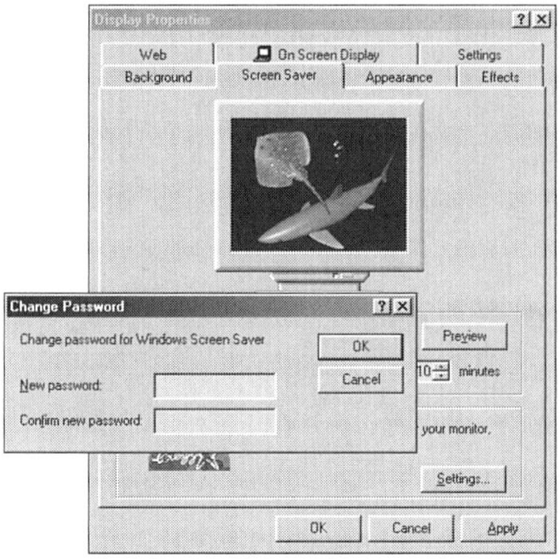

Figure 28.2

Enter the secret word here so no one else will be able to use your computer.

How to Encrypt Your Files So That Snoopers Can't Get at Them

Passwords are good at protecting garden-variety snoopers like your co-workers and the maintenance people from looking into your computer. But a professional hacker might be able to circumvent password protection. Maybe you don't feel the need to password-protect your entire PC, but there are certain files that you want to keep from prying eyes.

In those cases, you can encrypt certain files so that no one—not even the most determined hacker—is able to read them. To encrypt a file means to scramble it using secret codes so that no one except you can read them.

You can try out and use many encryption programs to do this. My favorite is Pretty Good Privacy, more commonly called PGP. It has super-strength encryption that's so powerful the government won't allow it to be exported.

There's even more good news: You can use a version of PGP for free if you plan to use it for your personal use, and not in a business. It's called PGPFreeware, and it's available from the PGP Web site at www.pgp.com/products/freeware. If for some reason that page has vanished, then do a search on the www.pgp.com or www.nai.com site for PGP Freeware. You should be able to find the location that way.

For information on installing it, turn to Chapter 15, "Keeping Your E-mail Private with Encryption." PGP is great for encrypting e-mail, as well.

After it's installed, in Windows Explorer, just right-click the file you want to encrypt, and then choose **Encrypt** from the PGP menu. A screen like the one in Figure 28.3 is displayed. It has a group of "keys" on it. I won't go into the whole key thing here, but it's covered in Chapter 15; go there for the full rundown on keys. From here, drag your name to the bottom part of the screen. Check the box next to **Conventional Encryption** to encrypt the file. When you do that, you create an encrypted file that only you can read, but your original file is still on your hard disk. Check the box next to **Wipe Original** if you want to also delete the original file, so that only the encrypted file is on your hard disk.

Figure 28.3

Here's how to use PGP to encrypt any file so that only you're the only person able to read it.

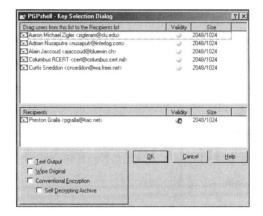

After you do all this, you're prompted for a password. Now you hold the key to the file—only someone who has that password can get at the file.

Check This Out!

PGP isn't the only encryption program out there. There are many dozens of others, and some of them are easier to use. Cryptext, Puffer, and WinXFiles Blowfish are all good encryption programs. They're either free or shareware and are available at many download sites on the Internet, including www.download.com.

How to Permanently Erase Data from Your PC

When you delete a file from your computer, you can feel pretty safe that it's deleted, can't you? You delete it, it gets sent to the Recycle Bin, and then you clean out your Recycle Bin. After it's out of there it's history, right? Gone forever? Sayonara?

I have some bad news for you. The answer is no. When you delete a file from your hard disk, and then empty it from the Recycle Bin, you don't actually delete it. It lives on. Yes, you heard me; delete doesn't really mean delete.

Ah, technology. Ain't it grand?

When you delete a file from your computer, you're not really erasing the data. All you're really doing is erasing the first character of the filename, so that your computer loses track of it, and it *looks* as if the file is deleted. Over time, other files might overwrite your original file, and eventually the deleted files are erased. But you don't know how, and you don't know when.

If you're one of the super-paranoid types, or you need to make sure that you completely erase files from your hard disk, there are ways you can do that. But, you need some extra software to do it.

You can use PGP to kill the data from files. After you've installed PGP, right-click a file in Windows Explorer that you'd like to permanently delete, and choose **Wipe** from the file menu. That wipes the file off your hard disk, and you can bid it good-bye. Mutilate File Wiper is another good program for deleting files. Download it, and other similar programs, from www.download.com.

Three Rules to Keep Your Data Safe: Back Up, Back Up, and Back Up!

In this chapter, I've talked a great deal about how to keep your computer and its data safe from other people. But there's something else you have to worry about when it comes to your data: What happens if your computer crashes? Are all your files lost forever?

They're not lost if you've been a good little boy or girl and backed up your computer. Backing it up means making copies of all its data and putting that backup somewhere safe.

There are several different ways in which you can back up your data. You can back it up to what's called a tape drive, which is a device in your computer that stores data on magnetic tape. These used to be very popular for backups, but there are newer, more convenient, less-expensive options available, so they're not used as much as they used to be. You can back up to a removable drive, such as a Jaz drive. This is an easy, convenient way to back up your data. And because Jaz disks are small, it's easy to put them somewhere safe, or even carry them around in your pocket.

Another option—and my favorite one—is to back up your data to a CD. For this you need a CD drive that you can write to, called a CD-RW drive. They're increasingly becoming standard equipment on many PCs. Finally, you can pay an Internet backup service—like the one pictured in Figure 28.4, @Backup at www.backup.com—to store and perform the backup for you. Be aware that these services charge annual fees based on how much data you want to back up. For example, @Backup charges an annual fee of $49.95 for up to 50 megabytes of back-up space, $199 for 300 megabytes of storage space, and $995 for 3 gigabytes of storage space.

Figure 28.4

One of the many ways you can back up your data is by using a for-pay Web site like @Backup.

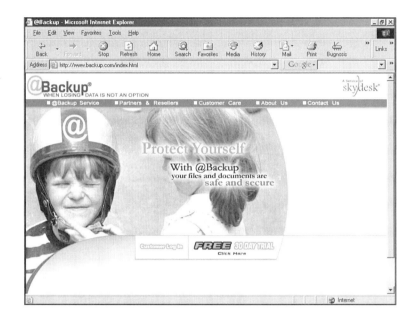

How often should you back up? That depends on how important your data is to you. I back up at least once a day and sometimes more. I'd recommend once a day, but if you can't do that, do it at least once a week.

You back up your data using—surprise!—backup software. (For once, a technology concept that makes sense!) For most purposes, just use the backup software built right into Windows. It's free, easy to get to, and easy to use.

To use it, choose **Programs** from the **Start** menu; choose **Accessories,** then **System Tools,** and then **Backup.** Microsoft Backup software runs. Choose **Create a new backup job** and a wizard appears that walks you through a simple step-by-step process to back up your data. Figure 28.5 shows the program in operation.

> **Notes**
>
> When you back up the data on your PC, you're most likely backing up tens of megabytes of data, and possibly hundreds of megabytes. That means that unless you have a high-speed connection like a cable modem or DSL modem, you shouldn't consider using one of these services. On a dial-up connection, it can take you countless hours to back up your data.

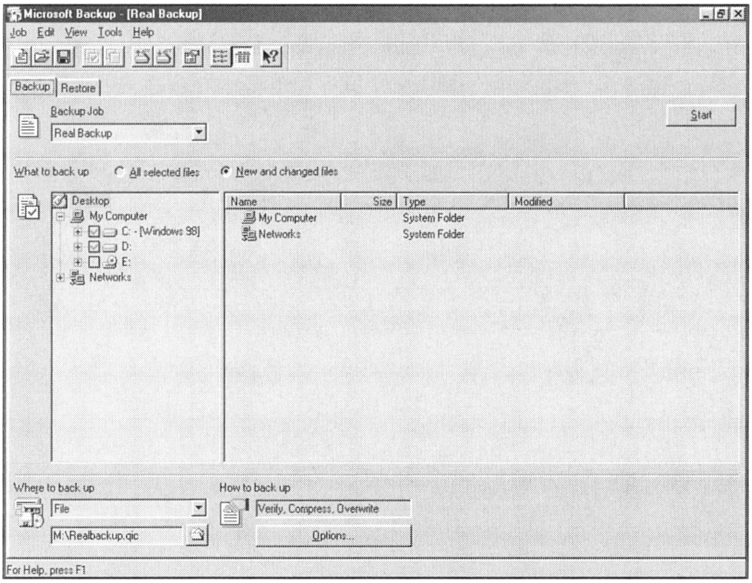

Figure 28.5

Here's Windows built-in backup program, Microsoft Backup, in operation.

That's all there is to it. Use it daily to compute in peace.

The Least You Need to Know

♦ Get an anti-theft lock and motion alarm to keep your laptop safe. When traveling, don't let it out of your sight, and carry it in a nondescript bag that doesn't look like a laptop case.

♦ A good way to protect your PC from others is to password-protect it with Windows' built-in screen savers.

♦ Use Pretty Good Privacy or a similar encryption program to encrypt individual files on your computer so that only you can read them.

♦ When you empty your Recycle Bin, the files aren't permanently deleted—there are ways they can still be read by someone.

♦ Use Pretty Good Privacy or a similar file-wiping program to permanently delete files from your hard disk.

♦ Make sure to back up your data files using Windows' free, built-in backup program.

Chapter 29

Fight Back: Use the Internet to Get Information About Privacy and Security

In This Chapter

- ◆ Using the Internet to protect your privacy and security
- ◆ Private sites that accept complaints about privacy invasions and fraud
- ◆ Government agencies that accept complaints about privacy invasions and fraud
- ◆ How to get your credit report online—and correct it
- ◆ How to use the Web to get your name off telemarketing and junk-mail lists

If you've read much of this book, you know that there are many ways your privacy can be invaded online. (And if you haven't read much of this book, and you're reading this now, you're clearly one of those people who jumps to the end of a mystery novel to find out who 'dun it before you even discover what they 'dun. Shame on you!)

You've also learned that there's a whole lot you can do to protect your privacy and security online. And here's even better news—you can use the Internet to fight back and uncover what kinds of private information is being gathered about you by credit bureaus, databases, and other companies. And in many cases, you're able to use the Web to delete that information, or at least make sure that the information is correct. This chapter will show you how—and give you the rundown on where to complain about invasions of privacy and Internet fraud.

Using the Internet to Protect Your Privacy and Security

The Internet can be used to invade your privacy and endanger your security. But the vast resources of the Web can be used to protect them, as well. Here are some of the things you're able to uncover on the Web:

◆ You can get copies of your credit ratings and history from the top credit bureaus—and you can correct any information that's not right.

Check This Out!

Want to find out how vulnerable your browser is to giving out information about you? Go to www. privacy.net/analyze. It shows what kind of information can be gathered about you—things like the page you visited right before you came there, the browser you use, your operating system, your screen display, and more.

◆ You can find out some of the information that the database giant Lexis-Nexis gathers about you—and you can ask that certain information not be provided about you.

◆ You can learn how to stop the major credit bureaus Equifax, Experian, and TransUnion Corporation from sharing information about you with direct marketers and others.

◆ You can find out how to get your name off of tele-marketing and junk-mail lists.

◆ You can discover an enormous amount of information about protecting your privacy and security by visiting any of the many sites devoted to privacy and security.

So come along. It's time to protect yourself and seek revenge!

Where to Go to Complain About Privacy and Security Issues

Think you've been ripped off or had your privacy invaded? You don't have to take it lying down. You can head to the Internet and complain to sites that will take action. If you have a problem, head to any of these private sites. The section later in this chapter, "Government Sites That Investigate Your Complaints," covers government sites where you can make out complaints.

TRUSTe

www.truste.org

This is the foremost group for helping protect your privacy at commercial sites on the Internet. It has a set of privacy rules to which sites must adhere if they want to display the TRUSTe privacy seal. If you believe that your privacy has been invaded, head to this site and file a complaint by clicking **File a Complaint** on the main page (see Figure 29.1).

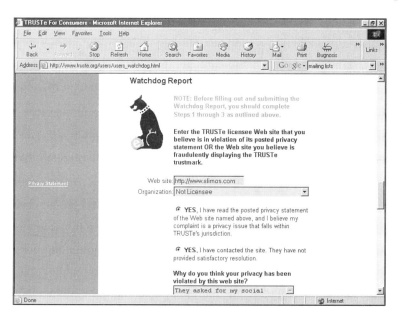

Figure 29.1

If you think a site has violated your privacy, set the dogs on it by filing a complaint at the TRUSTe site.

National Fraud Information Center

www.fraud.org

This excellent site, run by the National Consumer League, is a great place to go to get information and advice about Internet fraud; it's also the place to go if you've been victimized by fraud. Head to the site, click **How To Report Fraud and Ask Questions** and then click the **Online Incident Report Form.** If you're feeling low-tech, you can also call 1-800-876-7060.

BBBOnline

www.bbbonline.org

BBBOnline is the online version of the Better Business Bureaus and so it's a great place to get advice on privacy and fraud issues. It's also the place to go to file a complaint. To do that, click the **File a Complaint** link on the front page. You're able to file complaints about sites that have violated your privacy or defrauded you, but you can also file other kinds of complaints, such as if you suspect a charitable organization of fraud, false advertising claims, and frauds involving new cars.

Check This Out!

Privacy and protection sites like TRUSTe and BBBOnline.org have seals that sites can display on them to show that they follow good practices. But it's easy for a site to fraudulently slap a seal on its site. So check out the seals yourself—check the TRUSTe and BBBOnline.org sites for a listing of sites that are authorized to display their seals.

Identity Theft Resource Center

www.idtheftcenter.org

If you're worried about identity theft, or suspect you've been a victim, here's a great place to go. It has all the information and resources you'll ever need. It also includes an excellent form that you can print out and mail in to various places to help get identity theft problems cleared up. Click **Fraud Form** and follow the instructions.

Government Sites That Investigate Your Complaints

If you'd like the law to come down on people who have invaded your privacy, committed Internet fraud, or done some other kind of nasty deed, you want the government on their tails. Here's where to go to get the government to investigate.

Federal Trade Commission

www.ftc.gov

This is the mother of all government privacy and security sites. This agency, charged with regulating interstate commerce, has an incredible amount of helpful information about protecting your privacy and safety online. Click around to the many parts of the site for help. A great page is www.ftc.gov/privacy/protect.htm, which gives great information about your privacy rights concerning credit bureaus, direct marketers, and whether your state Department of Motor Vehicles may release information about you to direct marketers. To file a complaint online, go to www.ftc.gov/ftc/consumer.htm and click **File a Complaint Online.** If you're filing a complaint about identity theft, look for the link to Identity Theft Complaint Form (see Figure 29.2).

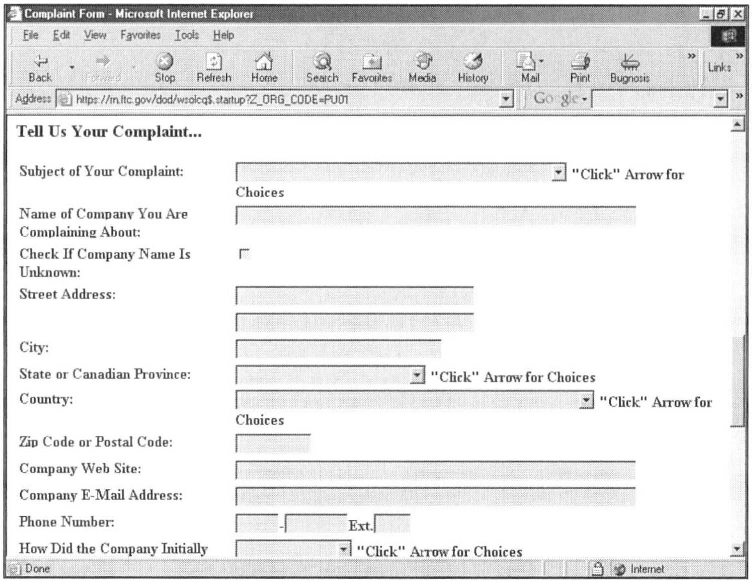

Figure 29.2

The FTC complaint form: If you have a complaint to make, it's the place to go.

Securities and Exchange Commission

www.sec.gov

If you have a complaint about an online stock scam, here's the place to go. In fact, if you want to know anything about stocks, head here. To file a complaint, go to www.sec.gov/complaint/selectconduct.shtml. You're able to file a complaint of any kind about securities here, not just about online scams.

Internet Fraud Complaint Center

www.ifccfbi.gov/

This site, a partnership between the FBI and the National White Collar Crime Center, is a central repository for fraud complaints about the Internet. When you make a complaint here, it might be referred to a variety of law enforcement agencies.

Check This Out!

If you want a great place to find government agencies—including state agencies—who investigate invasions of privacy and fraud, then head to this site, Consumerworld.org. It has the best list of such agencies I've ever found. Find the list at www.consumerworld.org/pages/agencies.htm. There's also a lot of other great information on the site about Internet privacy and security.

U.S. Postal Inspection Service

www.framed.usps.com/postalinspectors/fraud/MailFraudComplaint.htm

The U.S. Postal Inspection Service investigates mail fraud, so if you suspect that you've been a victim, here's where to go. Mail fraud, by the way, takes in a lot of ground and includes identity theft and other kinds of fraud. If any part of a fraud you've been victimized by took place through the mail, it's the place to go.

State Agencies

Many state agencies investigate invasions of privacy, identity theft, and fraud. There's not enough room in this book to list every one from every state. In your state, though, look for the State Attorney General's Office and Consumer Protection Agency. If your county has a District Attorney and Consumer Protection Agency, check with them as well.

Credit Where It's Due: How to Get Your Credit Ratings Online—and Correct Them

These days, without a good credit rating, you practically can't be part of the national economy. Have a good rating, and you're on top of the world—you're able to get a mortgage, a car loan, a college loan, and do any of the myriad other things that good credit can bring your way. But if you have a bad rating … bad news. Don't expect to buy that dream house any time soon.

Who compiles these mysterious credit ratings? Three big companies: Experian, Equifax, and TransUnion Corp. (Interesting how you can't possibly tell from their names that any of those companies are in the credit business. Do you think that maybe they don't want people to know that?)

Check This Out!

One of the most common scams on the Internet is the credit repair scheme—someone promises that if you have bad credit they can "repair" it. If you hear a promise like that, run the other way—it's almost certainly a scam. Often, you end up paying a good deal of money for nothing, or something you could easily do yourself. People have given out personal information, such as credit card numbers, and have been the subject of fraud.

These companies compile a good deal of personal information about you and your credit history—and then they sell that information to companies. So a bank, for example, checks your credit ratings with one of them before extending you a loan. But they also provide that information to other entities, such as your landlord.

Here's some of the information in your credit report:

- Identifying information, such as your name, address and previous address, date of birth, telephone number, and Social Security number.

- Your current and previous employer.

- Your credit history of paying bills with stores, banks, finance companies, and mortgage companies.

- Public records about you, such as tax liens, bankruptcies, and similar information.

Clearly, you want to know what's in your credit report—and you'd like to be able to correct the report if it's wrong. Here's how to get your credit report from each of the big credit bureaus. After you get your credit report, follow the instructions on each credit bureau's Web site to find out what to do if you find errors.

Getting Your Credit Information from TransUnion Corporation

Getting your credit report from TransUnion is about as simple as it comes. Head to the company's site at www.transunion.com, click **order your credit report and score,** and follow the directions. The cost of the service depends on the state you live in. In most states you're charged $8.50, although in some states you pay less. State law governs how much you are charged for your credit reports, so whether you get yours from TransUnion, Equifax, or Experian, the cost is the same.

You're able to order your reports over the Web, using a secure connection, so your credit card information can't be stolen. (If that happened, who knows *what* would happen to your credit?)

TransUnion also has a good deal of helpful information about your rights concerning credit; click **frequently asked questions about credit** and start reading.

Check This Out! _____

If you live in Colorado, Georgia, Maryland, Massachusetts, New Jersey, or Vermont, you don't have to pay to get your credit report—it's free. You can't get them for free over the Web, however. Instead, you have to mail a letter asking for your reports. Include your name, address, date of birth, Social Security number, current employer, and place of residence. You're able to get free credit reports from all three credit bureaus. Check their Web sites to find their mailing addresses.

Getting Your Credit Information from Equifax

At Equifax, as at TransUnion, it's easy to get your credit report. Head to www.equifax. com, click **Equifax Credit Profile,** and then follow the links for ordering your credit report. You have to scroll down to the bottom of the page that appears, because the top part of the page displays all kinds of other services that Equifax tries to sell to you.

Check This Out!

Is your mailbox (your postal one, that is) inundated with offers for credit cards? It could be that credit card companies have checked your credit rating with credit bureaus, figured that you are a good bet, and hope you're an easy mark for their cards. If you want, you can stop getting junk mail based on information garnered from your credit reports at Equifax, TransUnion, and Experian. You can visit their Web sites and look for an opt-out policy. Or you can instead call 1-888-5OPTOUT (1-888-567-8688) and ask to be removed from the lists of all three.

There's a great deal of helpful information about credit at the site, and you can even see a sample credit report, as shown in Figure 29.3.

Figure 29.3

Equifax makes an example of a credit report available for viewing.

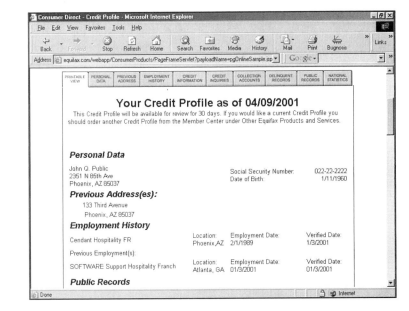

Getting Your Credit Report at Experian

You have to do a bit more clicking around at Experian (www.experian.com) to find out how to get your credit report, but still, it's there to be found. When you get in, click **Personal Credit,** which takes you to a page listing the different reports you can order. You want the **online credit report,** so click that option. Then follow the instructions; as with the other services, you can order online. If you've ordered your credit report and believe that there's an error, you can click **Request and Investigation,** then follow the instructions for putting your report straight.

How to Get Your Name off Telemarketing and Junk-Mail Lists

It's 7 P.M., and you're at home after a long, hard day at work. For the first time all day, you, your spouse, and your kids are all together, having a quiet family dinner. The phone rings. It could be your mother, calling about vacation plans, so you pick it up.

"Hello, Mr. Gralla, I'm calling from the Slimeball Bank of Outer Mongolia, and we have a new credit card with your name on it! Just ask for it now and …."

You slam down the phone. Another dinner ruined. You could have used your favorite technique for getting rid of telemarketers. ("I'm so glad you called," you say. "Because I'm talking to you in my underwear." And for once *they* slam down the phone.) Instead, you just wanted to get off the phone fast. Isn't there anything you can do?

Check This Out!

Lexis-Nexis is a huge database company with an enormous amount of personal information compiled about people. Businesses and others can get that information on the company's Web site at www.lexis.com—by paying a fee. If you'd like to get your name out of Lexis-Nexis's P-Track database—which is designed for attorneys trying to track down people involved in lawsuits, and for law-enforcement personnel—send an e-mail to remove@prod.lexis-nexis.com, asking that your name be removed, or mail the request to Lexis-Nexis Name Removal, P.O. Box 933, Dayton, OH 45401. You can also fax the request to 1-800-732-7672.

Yes, in fact, there is. You can visit the Direct Marketing Association Web site at www.the-dma.org and ask that you be taken off telemarketing and junk-mail (the postal kind) lists. Just head to the site, click **Consumer Information** and then **Consumer Assistance** and follow the directions. It doesn't eliminate every call or piece of junk mail, but it gets rid of many. To get yourself off these lists straight from the Web, it costs five bucks. Otherwise, you can print out a page from the Web and then mail it in. After all, they don't want to make it *too* easy for you to get off the lists—because then they'd be out of business.

The Least You Need to Know

- ◆ You can complain about privacy violations, identity theft, and fraud to www.truste. com, www.fraud.org, www.bbbonline.org, and www.idtheftcenter.org.

- ◆ The Federal Trade Commission at www.ftc.org and the Internet Fraud Complaint Center at www.1ifccfbi.gov are good government agencies to which to make out complaints.

- ◆ You can get a copy of your credit reports at a low cost or for free from www.equifax. com, www.experian.com, and www.transunion.com.

- ◆ You can tell the major credit bureaus Equifax, Experian, and TransUnion Corporation to stop sharing information about you with direct marketers.

- ◆ If you live in Colorado, Georgia, Maryland, Massachusetts, New Jersey, or Vermont, you can get your credit report for free by calling 1-800-888-4213 for your TransUnion credit report, and 1-800-997-2493 for your Equifax report.

- ◆ To get your name off junk-mail lists, head to the Direct Marketing Association Web site at www.the-dma.org and follow the instructions provided.

Speak Like a Geek: The Complete Archive

802.11   A standard that allows networks and devices to communicate wire-lessly. The 802.11b standard is also called Wi-Fi.

ActiveX   A technology for Microsoft Internet Explorer that allows programs to be downloaded and run on your browser.

anonymous e-mail   A way of sending e-mail so that no one can tell the true identity of the sender.

anonymous posting   A way to send messages on Usenet newsgroups so that no one can tell the true identity of the sender.

anonymous remailer   A program or Web site that lets you send out anony-mous e-mail and lets you post anonymously to a newsgroup.

anonymous surfing   A way to browse the World Wide Web so that no in-formation can be gathered about you from your Web browser.

applet   A Java program. *See* Java.

BlueTooth   A wireless technology that allows computers and other devices to communicate with each other.

Bozo filter   A feature of some chat programs that enables you to block mes-sages from individuals who annoy you.

browser cache   A directory on your hard disk that temporarily keeps files such as Web pages and graphics that have been downloaded to your computer when you visit a Web site.

cable modem   A device that hooks you up to the Internet through your cable system at high speed.

chat   A way in which people can communicate in real-time, by typing messages on their keyboard.

chat channel   A place where you chat, particularly when using IRC. *See* IRC.

chat room   A place where you chat, particularly on America Online.

cipher   A code used to encrypt information.

communications protocol   A kind of language that allows computers to talk to one another over a network such as the Internet.

cookies   Bits of data put on your computer by a Web server that can be used to track what you do when you're on the Web.

data mining   A technique in which a statistical analysis of people's Web surfing habits is used to target advertising at them.

digital certificate   A key used to encrypt and decrypt information, which can be used to guarantee that you're the sender of a message, or to verify the authenticity of a person sending you a message.

digital signature   An encrypted electronic "signature" that can't be forged that identifies you as the sender of a message.

download   To transfer information or files from the Internet to your computer.

DSL modem   A device that connects you at high speed to the Internet over telephone lines.

dumpster diver   Someone who sifts through garbage and trash cans, looking for papers with identifying information about people, or their passwords.

e-mail filter   A technology that sorts incoming e-mail so that some are automatically routed to certain folders or deleted, based on the sender and the content of the message. E-mail filters can be used to cut down on spam sent to you.

e-mail spoofing   A way of forging the From address in an e-mail message so that it appears that the message came from someone other than the real sender.

encryption   A method of scrambling information as it's sent across the Internet so that no one can read it.

Ewallet   An electronic wallet that contains your credit card information or electronic money so that you can use it to easily shop at many online shopping sites.

file attachment   A file attached to an e-mail message or a newsgroup posting. Any kind of file can be attached to e-mail or newsgroup postings.

file extension   The three letters on the end of a filename that are used to identify the kind of file it is. For example, files with .doc extensions are Microsoft Word files.

Finger   An Internet service that enables people to find out information about you by typing in your e-mail address.

firewall   A piece of hardware, software, or hardware/software combination that protects a computer or network from being invaded by hackers.

flame   To vociferously attack someone in a newsgroup or other discussion area, often for no clear reason.

FTP (File Transfer Protocol)   A way of downloading files on the Internet. *See* download.

Google Groups   A Web site that enables you to post and read newsgroup messages.

History list   A list, kept by your Web browser, of all the recent Web sites that you've visited.

home network   A network used at home to connect computers, typically to share a high-speed Internet connection such as a cable modem or DSL modem.

ICQ   Software used to chat and communicate with others over the Internet.

identity theft   Using identifying information about someone to commit financial or other kinds of fraud, (or even assume their identity).

infomediary   A site or a piece of software that protects your privacy and that enables you to determine what information should be made public about you on the Internet.

instant message   A message sent privately to an individual when both are online at the same time.

Internet mailing list   *See* listserv.

Internet Service Provider (ISP)   A company that provides you with access to the Internet for a monthly fee.

IP address   The numerical address of something on the Internet—the address that computers understand. It's a series of four numbers, separated by periods, like this: 147.23.0.124.

IRC (Internet Relay Chat)   A way of chatting on the Internet. To chat this way, you need special IRC software.

Java   A kind of language that can be used to run programs in your browser that you get from the Web.

JavaScript   A technology that enables Web designers to use a variety of interactive features on Web pages.

key   A piece of data used to encrypt or decrypt information.

listserv   A public discussion carried on via e-mail.

macro   An automated set of commands in a file such as a word processing file or a spreadsheet. Macros can be infected with viruses.

mail bomb   The automatic sending of dozens, or even hundreds or thousands, of e-mail messages to a single e-mail box or mail server so that it crashes the server or computer.

mail header   The part of an e-mail message that contains the subject line, the sender, the receiver, and similar information.

message board   A public area online where people can read and send messages.

Microsoft Outlook   A popular e-mail program that is often targeted by virus-writers and worm-writers.

moderated chat   A chat in which a monitor can kick people out of the chat room if their behavior is inappropriate. *See* chat.

munge   A way of posting a message to a newsgroup so that the identity of the sender appears different from the true sender. Unlike true anonymous posting, there are ways to discover the true identity of the sender.

.Net   Microsoft's technology for delivering services and software over the Internet.

newsgroup   A discussion area on the Internet.

newsgroup reader   A piece of software used to read newsgroups.

online auction   Just like a real-life auction, except that it's done online.

opt out   A policy that enables you to say that you don't want to receive junk mail or similar information.

parental controls   A feature of America Online that enables parents to decide where kids can go on America Online and the Internet, and how they can use America Online and the Internet.

Passport   A Microsoft technology that enables you to put all your personal information in a single place, and then have that information be sent to do things such as log you into your favorite sites.

password   A set of private letters and numbers or words you type in to give you access to a service or site.

personal firewall   A firewall used at home to protect a computer. *See* firewall.

PIN (Personal Information Number)   A set of private letters and numbers or words you type in to give you access to a service or site. Often used interchangeably with the term *password*.

Platform for Privacy Preferences (P3P)   A standard that allows Web browsers and other software to easily access and display a site's privacy policies.

POP 3 server   A kind of Internet computer that enables you to receive e-mail. You usually have to put in name of your POP 3 server into your e-mail program to receive mail.

port   A virtual connection that enables you to access Internet resources.

pretexting   A technique in which someone poses as someone else in order to get personal information and commit identity theft.

Pretty Good Privacy (PGP)   A program used to encrypt and decrypt information. It's especially useful for sending out private e-mail that only the sender and recipient can understand.

private key   Someone's key in an encryption scheme that only one person can use. It's used in concert with that individual's public key to encrypt and decrypt information. *See* key *and* public key.

pseudonymous e-mailer   A kind of anonymous remailer in which the sender is given a false e-mail address—if someone responds to that e-mail address, the true sender receives that response. *See* Anonymous remailer.

public key   Someone's key in an encryption scheme that anyone can use. It's used in concert with that individual's private key to encrypt and decrypt information. *See* key *and* private key.

registration form   A form on the Web you fill out to enter a special area of the Web site or get special services.

router   A device that sends data over the Internet toward the data's final destination.

screen name   A person's name as it appears on America Online in chat areas and discussion areas. It's also that person's e-mail address on America Online.

script kiddies   People who don't know much about hacking, but run simple programs or scripts to try to attack people's computers. They are often young kids, hence the name script kiddies.

secure site   A site that encrypts your credit card information as it's sent across the Internet so that the credit card number can't be stolen.

SET (Secure Electronic Transactions)   The electronic encryption and payment standard that a group of companies—including Microsoft, Netscape, VISA, and MasterCard—are pushing to become the standard for doing electronic commerce on the Internet.

shareware   Software you can download from the Internet, try out for free, and pay for only if you decide to keep it.

site-blocking software   Software that blocks children from accessing certain sites or resources on the Internet.

SMTP (Simple Mail Transfer Protocol)   A kind of communications protocol that enables you to send e-mail. You usually have to put in name of your SMTP server into your e-mail program to receive mail.

spam   Unsolicited e-mail that is sent to you without you asking for it that usually involves a scam or contains commercial offers or pornography.

spamoflauge   A method by which senders of spam hide their addresses by faking information, such as who is sending the message.

spyware   Software that tracks your Internet activities, and reports on them to Web servers and marketers. Spyware is sometimes built into free software that you download from the Internet.

SSL (Secure Sockets Layer)   A technology that scrambles information as it's sent across the Internet so that hackers can't read it.

SYSOP (System Operator)   Someone who moderates a chat room or is in charge of a message board.

TCP/IP (Transmission Control Protocol/Internet Protocol)   The two basic communications protocols that enable you to connect to and use the Internet.

Trojan horse   A malicious program that appears to be benign, but in fact is doing damage to your computer.

TRUSTe   A company that sets voluntary standards for privacy on the Internet that gives out "seals" companies can post on their Web sites if they adhere to those privacy rules.

Usenet newsgroup   *See* newsgroup.

unmoderated chat   A chat in which there is no monitor or moderator present.

Virtual Private Network (VPN)   Software that enables you to connect to a corporate network over the Internet securely, by encrypting the connection.

virus   A malicious program that can do damage to your computer.

Web browser   A piece of software, such as Netscape Navigator or Microsoft Internet Explorer, which you use to visit Web sites.

Web bug   A tiny, invisible graphic put on a Web site or sent in an HTML e-mail message that can track your activities as you surf the Web or read the e-mail.

Web database   A Web site that contains information that can be searched through, such as e-mail addresses.

Web white pages   Web sites that contain information that can be searched through, for identifying information such as e-mail addresses, phone numbers, and addresses.

Wi-Fi   Also known as 802.11b. *See* 802.11.

wipe   To permanently erase a file from your hard disk so that it can't be recreated.

worm   A malicious program that travels from computer to computer over the Internet or a network without human intervention.

The Best Internet Sites for Privacy and Security Issues

Where do you need to go to get the lowdown in privacy and security issues? What if you want to get a free personal firewall, find out about identity theft, complain to a government agency about a privacy invasion, get the lowdown on shopping fraud, and more? You'll find all you need in this appendix.

General Privacy Protection Sites

Do you want to get advice on keeping yourself safe online, read the latest news about privacy issues, or get involved in the public debate about Internet privacy? Then head to one of these privacy protection sites.

American Civil Liberties Union

www.aclu.org   The privacy area of this well-known civil liberties group is a very good resource for finding out information about privacy online. Especially useful is the Privacy Rights Pocket Card, which gives you a capsule rundown on ways to protect your privacy. There are also updates on privacy- and security-related laws and lawsuits.

The Center for Democracy and Technology

www.cdt.org   This excellent site focuses on providing information about government legislation having to do with online privacy issues. It goes beyond that, though. Especially useful is the privacy area, which gives privacy tips, help on using privacy technologies, and more.

Computer Professionals for Social Responsibility

www.cpsr.com   This group focuses on the impact of technology on society as whole—and as you might expect, they devote a good deal of their time and energy to privacy issues. Their home on the Web is a great place to great privacy-related information, and you can join the group if you want.

Electronic Frontier Foundation

www.eff.org   This is probably the best site in all of cyberspace for getting information on online privacy issues. You get news, government information, the latest doings inside the industry, and much more. You can also subscribe to a free e-mail privacy alert.

Online Privacy Alliance

www.privacyalliance.org   This group is composed of private businesses that push business-oriented privacy proposals. You might not agree with everything on the site, but there's good, useful information to be found here.

Privacy Foundation

www.privacyfoundation.org   This might well be my favorite place to head to about privacy-related issues online. It takes an exceedingly tough line on privacy issues, and is always up-to-date with the latest about privacy-related technologies. The site has a free Web bug detector called Bugnosis. And Richard Smith's Tipsheet, a column about privacy-related issues, is not to be missed. You can see it in Figure B.1.

The Privacy Page

www.privacy.org   This comprehensive site is great for keeping up with the latest news about how to protect your privacy online and in the real world. In addition to news, lobbying efforts and advice on how to protect your privacy are covered.

Figure B.1

My favorite site for privacy information on the Internet: The Privacy Foundation.

Privacy Rights Clearinghouse

www.privacyrights.org   This site provides useful information and articles about privacy, including some good ones for what to do in the event of identity theft. There's a good set of links to other privacy-related sites as well.

Sites for Downloading Firewalls, Cookie Killers, Anti-Virus Software, and Other Programs

As I've told you throughout this book, there's a lot of software available that can keep you safe from hackers, snoopers, and virus writers. Head to these sites to download software to help.

Download.com

www.download.com   Name a piece of software, any piece of software. You'll find it here. From personal firewalls to cookie killers, encryption software and more, you'll find a huge collection. And there are thousands of non-privacy related downloads as well.

McAfee.com

www.mcafee.com   McAfee makes anti-virus software, personal firewalls, and other privacy- and security-related software. Head here to find it. You're able to download and try the software for free, but if you continue to use it for more than 30 days, you have to pay for it.

Simtel.net

www.simtel.net   Here's another excellent download site. It includes tons of files of all kinds, many of which are privacy- and security-related downloads.

Symantec

www.symantec.com   Here's the place to go to get trial versions of anti-virus software, personal firewalls, and other privacy- and security-related programs made by Symantec. You can download and try the software for free, but if you use it for more than 30 days you have to pay for it.

ZDNet Downloads

www.zdnet.com/downloads   Here's one more superb download site for you to check. Tons of files are available, and many of them are privacy-related. And there's one more reason you might want to check out this site—my monthly Preston's Picks column, pictured in Figure B.2. I pick all kinds of software for you to download, often including security- and privacy-related ones.

ZoneLabs

www.zonelabs.com   Here's the place to download the excellent ZoneAlarm personal firewall. You can download and use a free version of the program, or spend $39.95 for a "pro" version that includes extra features.

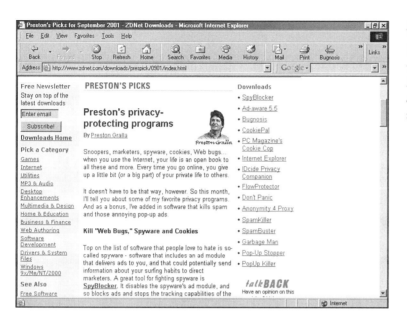

Figure B.2

Who's the guy with the weird 'do? I Is that Elvis? No, it's me on a bad hair day, in my Preston's Picks monthly software column.

The Best Sites to Get the Inside Skinny on Consumer Advice, Privacy Issues, and Scams

Do you want to know where to go online if you want to find out about Internet scams and get solid consumer advice? Check out these sites, the best you'll find on the Internet.

Better Business Bureau

www.bbb.org   Make a complaint about a site, find a Better Business Bureau near you, check out a business to see if complaints have been lodged against it, get advice about doing business on the Internet—all that and more is possible here.

Better Business Bureau Online

www.bbbonline.org   Help find out if an online site is a reliable and trustworthy one. You can see if sites have complaints lodged against them and lodge your own complaints, as well. It also has a seal that Web sites can display if they're members of the Better Business Bureau Online. When you see that seal on a Web site, click the seal's link and you can see whether complaints have been lodged against the company.

Consumer World

www.consumerworld.org   This is probably the most comprehensive site online for finding out information about everything to do with consumers. Especially useful are the links to private and government agencies involved in prosecuting Internet scams or that offer advice on how to avoid scams. You can see the site in Figure B.3.

Figure B.3

Get the inside scoop on scams and information about Internet consumer issues at Consumer World.

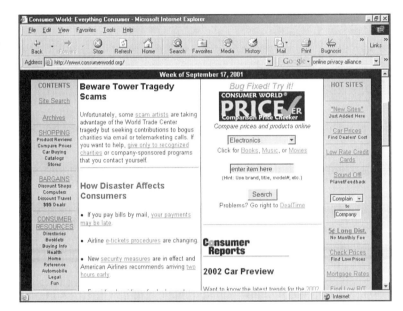

Identity Theft Resource Center

www.idtheftcenter.org   If you're worried about identity theft, or you suspect you've been a victim, here's a great place to go. It has all the information and resources you'll ever need. It also includes an excellent form that you can print out and mail in to various places to help get identity theft problems cleared up. Click **Fraud Form** and follow the instructions.

National Fraud Information Center

www.fraud.org   Learn about the latest Internet scams, get advice on avoiding con artists, and make out complaints if you think you've been burned.

ScamWatch

www.scamwatch.com   This is a great place to find out about the latest scams on the Internet. Over the years, its had comprehensive reports on everything from Furby fraud (people claiming they had the much-desired toys Furbies to sell when they didn't) to a bizarre scam involving someone who claimed to be the legal adviser to the former president of Zaire, Mobutu Sese Seko, trying to get people to open a bank account in the Ivory Coast. There's also great advice on how to avoid scams and links to other anti-scam sites.

TRUSTe

www.truste.org   This is the foremost group for helping protect your privacy at commercial sites on the Internet. It has a set of privacy rules to which sites must adhere if they want to display the TRUSTe privacy seal. If you believe that your privacy has been invaded, head to this site and file a complaint by clicking **File a Complaint** on the main page.

Government Sites That Investigate Complaints

If you'd like the law to come down on people who have invaded your privacy, committed Internet fraud, or done some other kind of nasty deed, here's where to go.

Federal Trade Commission

www.ftc.gov   This is the mother of all government privacy and security sites. This agency, charged with regulating interstate commerce, has an incredible amount of helpful information about protecting your privacy and safety online. Click around to the many parts of the site for help. A particularly helpful page is www.ftc.gov/privacy/protect.htm, which gives great information about your privacy rights concerning credit bureaus, direct marketers, and whether or not your state Department of Motor Vehicles may release information about you to direct marketers. To file a complaint online, go to www.ftc.gov/ftc/consumer.htm and click **File a Complaint Online.** If you're filing a complaint about identity theft, look for the link to **Identity Theft Complaint Form**.

Securities and Exchange Commission

www.sec.gov   If you have a complaint about an online stock scam, here's the place to go. In fact, if you want to know anything about stocks, head here. To file a complaint, go to www.sec.gov/complaint/selectconduct.shtml. You're able to file a complaint of any kind about securities here, not just about online scams.

Internet Fraud Complaint Center

www.ifccfbi.gov   This site, a partnership between the FBI and the National White Collar Crime Center, is a central repository for fraud complaints about the Internet. When you make a complaint here, it might be referred to a variety of law-enforcement agencies.

U.S. Postal Inspection Service

www.framed.usps.com/postalinspectors/fraud/MailFraudComplaint.htm   The U.S. Postal Inspection Service investigates mail fraud, so if you suspect that you've been a victim, here's where to go. Mail fraud, by the way, takes in a lot of ground and includes identity theft and other kinds of fraud. If any part of a fraud you've been victimized by took place through the mail, it's the place to go.

U.S. Consumer Gateway

www.consumer.gov   Here's the best place to go to find out all the information federal agencies have about anything to do with consumers—including Internet scams and where to make a complaint. It links you to great articles, advice, and advisories, as you can see in Figure B.4.

Figure B.4

If you're looking for government information about Internet scams or other consumer issues, head to Consumer.gov.

Where to Get Your Credit Information

If you want to get your credit report to find out whether you're a victim of identity theft or some other kind of scam, here's where to go. From all three, you're able to get your credit profile for a maximum price of $8.50 or possibly for free, depending on the state you live in.

Equifax

www.equifax.com   In addition to getting your credit profile, you can sign up for other services, such as one claiming to protect you against identity theft.

Experian

www.experian.com   As with Equifax, you can get your credit profile as well as a variety of other privacy-related services.

TransUnion

www.transunion.com   As with the other credit bureaus, you can get your credit report here. There's also some very useful information about identity theft and privacy.

Anonymous E-mail and Anonymous Surfing Sites

If you're worried about privacy, you can send e-mail anonymously, or hide your identity when you surf. Here are the places to go to.

Anonymizer

www.anonymizer.com   Here's a long-popular place to go if you want to surf anony-mously. The basic service is free, but if you want extra features—including filtering ads and other extras—you can pay $49.96 per year.

Cheech's Anonymous Remailer

www.geocities.com/Area51/2868/remail.html   This is a very easy-to-use Web-based remailer. Type up your message, send it, and it's done.

Electronic Frontiers Georgia's Reliable Remailer Lists

http://anon.efga.org/Remailers   This is a very good place to go for information about how to find and use remailers.

SafeWeb

www.safeweb.com   This great, free, anonymous surfing site has become increasingly popular—so much so that many people in China use it to surf to Web sites their government doesn't want them to see.

SendFakeMail.com Remailer List

www.sendfakemail.com/~raph/remailer-list.html   Here you can find a huge list of anonymous remailers, along with instructions. The site is kind of techie, so be prepared to be a bit intimidated. It's worth wading through, though.

W-3 Anonymous Remailer

www.gilc.org/speech/anonymous/remailer.html   Anonymous remailers can be difficult and confusing to use. Not this one. It's Web-based, so if you can use a keyboard, you can send anonymous e-mail.

Index

X-Y-Z

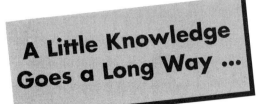
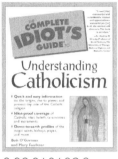

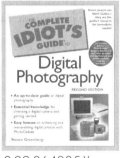
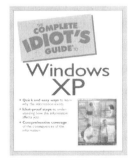

Language Arts

PATTERNS OF PRACTICE

SEVENTH EDITION

Gail E. Tompkins
California State University, Fresno, Emerita

Merrill
is an imprint of

PEARSON

Upper Saddle River, New Jersey
Columbus, Ohio

Library of Congress Cataloging-in-Publication Data

Tompkins, Gail E.
   Language arts : patterns of practice / Gail E. Tompkins. — 7th ed.
      p. cm.
   Includes bibliographical references and index.
   ISBN 0-13-159789-2 (alk. paper)
  1. Language arts (Elementary)   I. Title.
   LB1576.T655 2009
   372.6—dc22

Vice President and Executive Publis
Senior Editor: Linda Ashe Bishop
Senior Development Editor: Hope I
Senior Project Manager: Mary M. Ii
Senior Editorial Assistant: Laura We
Design Coordinator: Diane C. Lorenzo
Cover Designer: Candace Rowley
Cover Images: Cher Cartwright and Linda Bronson
Operations Specialist: Laura Messerly
Director of Marketing: Quinn Perkson
Marketing Manager: Darcy Betts Prybella
Marketing Coordinator: Brian Mounts

This book was set in Optima by S4Carlisle Publishing Services. It was printed and bound by Edwards Brothers. The cover was printed by Phoenix Color Corp.

Photo Credits: "Meeting the Needs" feature photos by Ingram/Jupiter Images, David Mager/Pearson Learning Photo Studio, and Anne Vega. All photos in the color insert by Gail E. Tompkins

Pearson Education Ltd.
Pearson Education Singapore Pte. Ltd.
Pearson Education Canada, Ltd.
Pearson Education—Japan

Pearson Education Australia Pty. Limited
Pearson Education North Asia Ltd.
Pearson Educación de Mexico, S.A. de C.V.
Pearson Education Malaysia Pte. Ltd.

Merrill
is an imprint of

10 9 8 7 6 5 4 3 2
ISBN 13: 978-0-13-159789-1
ISBN 10:   0-13-159789-2

For Judy,
my Cape Cod "sister,"
and the Chase family
with love and gratitude
for adopting me

PREFACE

*H*elping children and adolescents learn to communicate using all six language competencies—reading, writing, listening, speaking, viewing, and visually representing–can seem like an overwhelming task for a new or even an experienced teacher. Making this goal possible for *all* children in our culturally diverse, technologically changing society can be even more daunting. However, this thoroughly revised and streamlined seventh edition of *Language Arts: Patterns of Practice* models for you the integration of the six language arts into the literacy curriculum and presents the most effective and practical methods for working with the diverse abilities and literacy experiences of children in today's K–8 classrooms.

The text begins with the background information you need to understand your students, their classroom environment, and the research and theories behind solid language arts teaching. It goes on to clarify the specific instructional approaches best suited to an integrated study of language arts, modeling instruction and pinpointing the topics, strategies, and skills you will need to cover. Within this presentation, the text describes four patterns of practice—*literature circles, literature focus units, reading and writing workshop,* and *thematic units*—each developed to illustrate how to integrate the teaching of language competencies depending on instructional goals. The use of each of these patterns of practice is clarified within every chapter topic. Seamlessly, the text illustrates the way the language arts and instructional methodologies fit together, like the carefully constructed pieces of a quilt, crafted and organized to form one complete picture.

Language Arts: Patterns of Practice has long been a highly valued resource to preservice teachers. Built on a solid research base, this exceptionally applied and teacher-friendly text brings teaching methods to life through the use of authentic student artifacts, classroom vignettes, and video footage of master teachers in their language arts classrooms. The seventh edition of the text, streamlined to provide a succinct model of language arts instruction, retains the rich classroom orientation, accessible writing style, and numerous features that have been the text's hallmark, adding a sharpened focus on English learners, deepened classroom application of the four patterns of practice, and integrated treatment of the almost limitless resources of MyEducationLab. These new ideas and revisions have been crafted to help you prepare for, plan for, and implement successful language arts instruction.

Preparing for the Language Arts Classroom

▶ **New!** *Patterns of Practice* features pinpoint the ways to use the four patterns of practice—literature focus units, literature circles, reading and writing workshop, and thematic units—with each chapter's topic.

▶ Colorful inserts in Chapter 2 identify the patterns of practice—the four instructional approaches most appropriate for integrating the six language arts. These pages provide detailed classroom examples of teachers in action, identifying procedures and processes for using each instructional approach. These colorful classroom glimpses illustrate how motivating and engaging each approach can be for students learning language arts.

▶ Chapter-opening vignettes describe how individual teachers use the different instructional approaches to develop language arts competencies. These features set the tone for each chapter, clearly illustrating chapter concepts as they are played out in successful language arts classrooms.

▶ Authentic samples of student work pepper every chapter, modeling the kind of interaction and response you can expect in your own classroom.

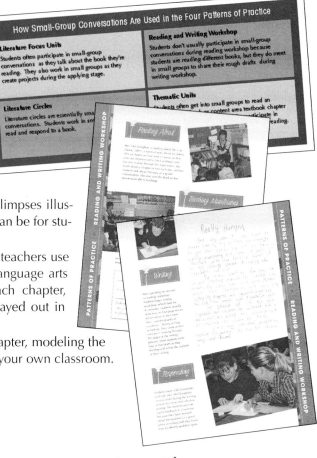

Planning for the Language Arts Classroom

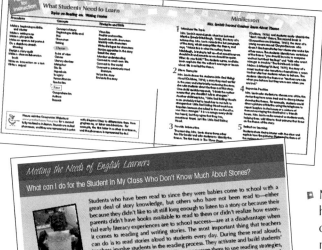

◆ **New!** *Planning for Instruction* features throughout the text help you prepare for teaching with three elements. First, a list of concepts, strategies, and topics help you plan meaningful minilessons. Second, a detailed minilesson example models effective instructional practice. Finally, connection to MyEducationLab deepens the text's authentic classroom exploration by leading you to video clips that illustrate other minilessons from the list of topics in live language arts classrooms.

▶ **New!** *Meeting the Needs of English Learners* features help prepare you for the needs of today's students with concrete advice for planning instruction to address the needs of culturally and linguistically diverse learners.

Tools for the Language Arts Classroom

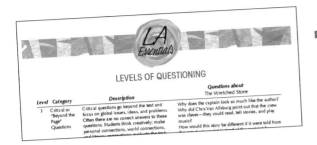

LA Essentials provide guidelines, lists, tools, and resources ready to take right into the classroom. These practical, informative teaching tips are foundational tools all teachers can refer to again and again as they teach.

Step by Step features provide detailed instructions for preparing and carrying out specific instructional strategies. These tools become a clear and precise map for teachers to use in their classrooms.

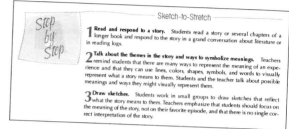

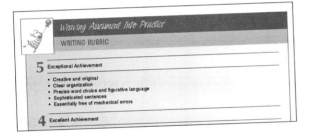

Weaving Assessment Into Practice features present authentic artifacts and guidelines for assessing the development of language arts strategies and skills.

Booklists provide thematically organized lists of trade books that you can incorporate into your teaching.

MyEducationLab This online website, available with this text, contains classroom clips, strategies, artifacts, lesson-planning guidance and software, standards information, and research articles—countless resources for a prospective teacher. Deepen your understanding of language arts teaching by visiting this valuable website.

Language Arts: Patterns of Practice provides consistent models of language arts instruction and is infused with a rich array of strategies and ideas, adaptable to suit your personal instructional style and your students' individual needs.

MyEducationLab

Your Class. Your Career. Everyone's Future.

"Teacher educators who are developing pedagogies for the analysis of teaching and learning contend that analyzing teaching artifacts has three advantages: it enables new teachers time for reflection while still using the real materials of practice; it provides new teachers with experience thinking about and approaching the complexity of the classroom; and in some cases, it can help new teachers and teacher educators develop a shared understanding and common language about teaching. . . ."[1]

As Linda Darling-Hammond and her colleagues point out, grounding teacher education in real classrooms—among real teachers and students and among actual examples of students' and teachers' work—is an important, and perhaps even an essential, part of training teachers for the complexities of teaching today's students in today's classrooms. For a number of years, we have heard the same message from many of you as we sat in your offices learning about the goals of your courses and the challenges you face in teaching the next generation of educators. Working with a number of our authors and with many of you, we have created a website that provides you and your students with the context of real classrooms and artifacts that research on teacher education tells us is so important. Through authentic in-class video footage, interactive simulations, rich case studies, examples of authentic teacher and student work, and more, **MyEducationLab** offers you and your students a uniquely valuable teacher education tool.

MyEducationLab is easy to use! Wherever the MyEducationLab logo appears in the margins or elsewhere in the text, you and your students can follow the simple link instructions to access the MyEducationLab resource that corresponds with the chapter content. These include:

Video: Authentic classroom videos show how real teachers handle actual classroom situations.

Homework & Exercises: These assignable activities give students opportunities to understand content more deeply and to practice applying content.

1. Darling-Hammond, l., & Bransford, J., Eds. (2005). *Preparing Teachers for a Changing World.* San Francisco: John Wiley & Sons.

Case Studies: A diverse set of robust cases drawn from some of our best-selling books further expose students to the realities of teaching and offer valuable perspectives on common issues and challenges in education.

Simulations: Created by the IRIS Center at Vanderbilt University, these interactive simulations give hands-on practice at adapting instruction for a full spectrum of learners.

Student & Teacher Artifacts: Authentic student and teacher classroom artifacts are tied to course topics and offer practice in working with the actual types of materials encountered every day by teachers.

Readings: Specially selected, topically relevant articles from ASCD's renowned *Educational Leadership* journal expand and enrich students' perspectives on key issues and topics.

Other Resources:

Lesson & Portfolio Builders: With this effective and easy-to-use tool, you can create, update, and share standards-based lesson plans and portfolios.

News Articles: Looking for current issues in education? Our collection offers quick access to hundreds of relevant articles from the New York Times Educational News Feed.

MyEducationLab is easy to assign, which is essential to providing the greatest benefit to your student. Visit www.myeducationlab.com for a demonstration of this exciting new online teaching resource.

ACKNOWLEDGMENTS

I'm privileged to work with very talented teachers. I want to express my heartfelt thanks to the teachers highlighted in the Patterns of Practice features: Judith Kenney, Laurie Goodman, Laura McCleneghan, and Susan McCloskey—and the teachers profiled in the chapter opener vignettes—Manuel Hernandez, Kathleen Kakutani, Arnold Keogh, Patty LaRue, Mike Martinez, Kristi McNeal, Ro Meinke, and Jennifer Miller-McColm. I also want to acknowledge the teachers who have influenced my teaching over the years: Eileen Boland, Kimberly Clark, Stephanie Collom, Florence Crimi, Pat Daniel, Roberta Dillon, Whitney Donnelly, Sandy Harris, Terry Kasner, Carol Ochs, Judy Reeves, Jenny Reno, and Susan Zumwalt. Thanks for welcoming me into your classrooms. I learned as I watched you and worked side by side with you and your students. The students whose writing samples and photographs appear in the book deserve special recognition. You've breathed life into the pages of this book.

I am grateful to everyone on Jeff Johnston's remarkable team at Merrill who enthusiastically embrace each new edition of *Language Arts*. I want to thank Linda Bishop, my acquisitions editor, for nurturing our vision for the seventh edition and ensuring that it became a reality. My development editor, Hope Madden, is my taskmaster, nudging me toward impossible deadlines. All taskmasters should have your spirit! My project manger, Mary Irvin, is a marvel! You've moved this book through production with your usual thoroughness and efficiency. Melissa Gruzs, my copyeditor and proofreader, has become an indispensable member of the production team. I appreciate your dogged attention to detail, and since we've been working together, you've taught me to be a more careful writer. Thanks, too, to quiltmaker Cher Cartwright and illustrator Linda Bronson, whose dynamic work is featured on the cover and inside this edition of *Language Arts*. Your talent enriches my words.

Finally, I want to acknowledge my colleagues who served as reviewers for this edition: Diane Bottomley, Ball State University; Helen Hoffner, Holy Family University; Cindy J. Hopper, University of North Carolina – Charlotte; Lonnie R. McDonald, Henderson State University; Debra Price, Sam Houston State University; and Janet Young, Brigham Young University. I also want to thank Patricia DeMay, University of West Alabama; Deanna Gilmore, Washington State University—Tri-Cities; and Rebecca Kaminski, Clemson University, who painstakingly reviewed the ancillaries for instructors to verify their accuracy and usefulness. I remain grateful to reviewers of previous editions, as well: Helen Abadiano, Central Connecticut State University; Doreen Bardsley, Arizona State University; Bobbie W. Berry, Clarion University of Pennsylvania; Scott Busley, Grand Canyon University; Irene Cota, California State University, Northridge; Betty Goerss, Indiana University East; Gail Gerlach, Indiana University of Pennsylvania; Catherine Kurkjian, Central Connecticut State University; Lonnie R. McDonald, Henderson State University; Marjorie S. Wynn, University of South Florida, Lakeland; and Janet R. Young, Brigham Young University. I appreciate your thoughtful analyses and insights. This text is more effective because of your efforts. ▰

ABOUT THE AUTHOR AND ILLUSTRATORS

Gail Tompkins I'm a teacher, first and foremost. I began my career as a first-grade teacher in Virginia in the 1970s. I remember one first grader who cried as the first day of school was ending. When I tried to comfort him, he sobbed accusingly, "I came to first grade to learn to read and write and you forgot to teach me." I've never forgotten that child's comment and what it taught me: Teachers must understand their students and meet their expectations.

My first few years of teaching left me with more questions than answers, and I wanted to become a more effective teacher, so I started taking graduate courses. In time I earned a master's degree and then a doctorate in reading/language arts, both from Virginia Tech. Through my graduate studies, I learned a lot of answers, but more important, I learned to keep asking questions.

Then I began teaching at the university level. First I taught at Miami University in Ohio, then at the University of Oklahoma, and finally at California State University, Fresno. I've taught preservice teachers and practicing teachers working on master's degrees, and I've directed doctoral dissertations. I've received awards for my teaching, including the Provost's Award for Excellence in Teaching at California State University, Fresno, and I was inducted into the California Reading Association's Reading Hall of Fame. Throughout the years, my students have taught me as much as I taught them. I'm grateful to all of them for what I've learned.

I've been writing college textbooks for more than 20 years, and I think of the books I write as teaching, too. I'll be teaching you as you read this text.

When I'm not teaching, I like to make quilts, and piecing together a quilt is a lot like planning effective language arts instruction. Instead of cloth, teachers use the patterns of practice and other instructional procedures to design instruction for the diverse students in today's classrooms. That's why I like to use quilts on the cover of *Language Arts*. ◆

Cher Cartwright After a lifetime of relying on words to communicate—first as a teacher and then as a lawyer—I discovered the language of visual art, which allows more articulate and subtle expression than can be achieved with mere words. Originally drawn to quilting by my appreciation of traditional quilts, I use the quilt form as a springboard for creative expression. I am proud to be an award-winning textile artist, and I rely exclusively on my own hand-dyed fabric, creating purely imaginative visuals that are abstract, bold, and dramatic. My quilts are primarily explorations of form and color and the emotions evoked by these elements, but I also hope to elicit a physical response in the viewer. My work has been exhibited internationally, with pieces juried into the prestigious Quilt National exhibitions in 2003 and 2007. I live with my husband and two dogs in White Rock, British Columbia. You can see more of my work at my website: **www.chercartwright.com** ◆

Linda Bronson I grew up on the hustling bustling Jersey Shore, spending summers at the beach covering my brother up to his neck in sand and decorating him to look like a starfish. At home I played dress up and ran around the backyard pretending to be Wonder Woman, and my mom taught me how to draw.

It wasn't until attending art college at the Rhode Island School of Design that I truly blossomed. Suddenly, I was expected to spend all of my time making art! What a treat! I took so many interesting classes—everything from photography and graphic design to stained glass and ceramics. I learned that artists could make careers out of doing what they love!

Nowadays, you can find my painting in picture books, magazines, advertisements, posters, and greeting cards. I think I have the world's best job! You can see more of my work at **www.lindabronson.com/** ◀

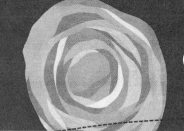

CONTENTS

SPECIAL FEATURES

chapter one

Learning and the Language Arts

The first graders in Mrs. McNeal's classroom are rereading their collaborative retelling of Maurice Sendak's *Where the Wild Things Are* (2003). It's written on three large charts, one for the beginning, one for the middle, and one for the end. Here is their retelling:

Beginning	*Max wore his wolf suit and made mischief. His mother called him, "Wild Thing!" He was sent to bed without any supper!*
Middle	*Max went to his room and a forest grew. Max got into his private boat and sailed to where the wild things are.*
End	*Max wanted to go home to where somebody loved him best of all. When he got home his supper was waiting for him and it was still hot!*

Mrs. McNeal used interactive writing to write the retelling so that all of the words would be spelled correctly, and the children could easily reread it. The "middle" chart is shown on page 4. The boxes around some letters and words represent the correction tape that Mrs. McNeal used to correct spelling errors and poorly formed letters.

How do teachers incorporate the six language arts in their teaching?

Listening, talking, reading, writing, viewing, and visually representing are the six language arts; two of the language arts are oral, two are written, and two are visual. Effective teachers integrate instruction and incorporate opportunities for children to use all six every day in their language arts programs. As you read this vignette about first graders participating in writing workshop, notice that Mrs. McNeal provides opportunities for her students to use all six language arts.

Japmeet holds the pointer and leads the class in rereading the "beginning" chart, moving the pointer from word to word as the children read aloud. Next, Henry leads the rereading of the "middle" chart, and Noelle does the "end" chart. As they finish reading, the children clap their hands because they're proud of their retelling of a favorite story.

Mrs. McNeal's students are learning about stories; they know that stories have beginnings, middles, and ends. They can pick out the three parts in stories that Mrs. McNeal reads aloud, and they try to include all three parts in the stories they write.

The first graders participate in an hourlong writing workshop each day. It begins with a 15-minute word work lesson that focuses on reading and writing high-frequency words. The first graders sit on the floor in front of the word wall, a bulletin-board display with 20 sheets of construction paper on which the letters are printed in alphabetical order and word cards with high-frequency words are posted according to beginning letter. Currently, 52 words are posted on the word wall, and several new words are added each week. The word wall is shown on page 4.

The lesson begins with a review of the words. First, Hanna holds the pointer and leads the children in reading the words. Next, Mrs. McNeal passes out small dry-erase boards, pens, and erasers, and they play a word game: The teacher gives phonological, semantic, and syntactic clues about a word on the word wall, and the first graders identify the word. Mrs. McNeal says, "I'm thinking of a word with three letters. It begins with /y/ and it fits in this sentence: _____ are my friend. What is the word?" The children identify *you* and write it on their dry-erase boards. They hold up their boards so Mrs. McNeal can check their work. Then the children erase their boards and the game continues.

Next, Mrs. McNeal teaches a 15-minute minilesson on a writing concept, such as adding details, writing titles, or using punctuation marks correctly. Today, she reviews beginning, middle, and end. She asks Sachit to read his draft aloud. He reads:

I love school. I have lots of friends. One is Yaman.

Children's Retelling of the "Middle" of the Story

Max w|ent| to |his| room and a forest gr|ew|. Max |got| into his pri|vate| bo|at| and |sailed| to where the wi|ld| things are.

Mrs. McNeal's Word Wall				
Aa at any and are all	**Bb** by	**Cc** can can't	**Dd** do don't	**Ee** eat
Ff fun friend	**Gg** got get going	**Hh** house had her have him how	**Ii/Jj/Kk** I jump	**Ll** like look
Mm/Nn me make new	**Oo** other one of or	**Pp/Qq** quiet play people	**Rr** run	**Ss** sister some said
Tt they there time then	**Uu** used us	**Vv** very	**Ww** went with want was	**Xx/Yy/Zz** You

He is a good friend to me. We play with Alex. We play basketball. We are good friends. I can't get a ball in the hoop.

The children pick out the beginning and middle sections of the story but notice that Sachit's story needs an ending. After several children suggest possible endings, Sachit decides to use Yaman's suggestion and finishes his story this way: *But I still play basketball anyway.*

A 25-minute writing period follows. On most days, children write stories independently, but sometimes they work together to write collaborative compositions, as they did to retell *Where the Wild Things Are.* Today, some children are beginning new stories. They sit knee-to-knee with a classmate and plan their stories by telling them aloud. Some children work on stories they began the previous day, and others meet with Mrs. McNeal to share their writings. They read their stories to Mrs. McNeal and talk about them, checking that they make sense and have a beginning, a middle, and an end. If the story is ready to be published, Mrs. McNeal types it on the computer, leaving space at the top for an illustration and correcting spelling and other mechanical errors so that the children can read it.

Noelle's Story

The Birthday Party

Once it was my grandpa's birthday. We had a party. We played lots of games. My dad played and my sister played and my cousin played. All of us had fun.

For the last 5 minutes of the workshop, children share their newly published compositions. Noelle reads aloud her story, "The Birthday Party," which is shown here. The children tell her that they like her story because it reminds them of the times they spend with their grandparents. Mrs. McNeal ceremoniously hangs Noelle's story in a special section of the bulletin board for everyone to reread.

*T*oday, **teachers face new challenges** and opportunities. The students who come to your classroom may speak a different language at school than they speak at home, and they're growing up in varied family structures: Many live in two-parent families, but others live with single parents or grandparents, in blended families, or with two moms or dads. Far too many children are growing up in poverty, some with parents in prison and siblings in gangs. Still others are homeless. Sadly, some have lost sight

of the American dream, believing that a college education is out of reach. Clearly, the way you teach language arts must address not only your beliefs about how children learn but also the language and culture of the students you teach.

In this chapter, you'll read about theories of language and learning and how they apply to language arts instruction. As you continue reading this chapter, think about these questions:

- How do children learn?
- How do language and culture influence learning?
- What are the language arts?
- How do children learn language arts?

HOW CHILDREN LEARN

Swiss psychologist Jean Piaget (1886–1980) radically changed our understanding of how children learn with his constructivist framework (Piaget & Inhelder, 2000). He described learning as the modification of children's cognitive structures as they interact with and adapt to their environment. He believed that children construct their own knowledge from their experiences. Related to Piaget's theory is information-processing theory (Flavell, Miller, & Miller, 2001), which focuses on how learners use cognitive processes and think about what and how they're learning.

The Process of Learning

Children's knowledge is not just a collection of isolated bits of information; it is organized in the brain, and this organization becomes increasingly integrated as their knowledge grows (Tracey & Morrow, 2006). The organization of knowledge is the cognitive structure, and knowledge is arranged in category systems called *schemata.* (A single category is a *schema.*) Within the schemata are three components: categories of knowledge, features or rules for determining what constitutes a category and what's included in each category, and a network of interrelationships among the categories.

These schemata can be likened to a conceptual filing system in which children and adults organize and store the information derived from their past experiences. Taking this analogy further, information is filed in the brain in "file folders." As children learn, they add file folders to their filing system, and as they study a topic, its file folder becomes thicker.

As children learn, they enlarge existing schemata or construct new ones. Two cognitive processes—*assimilation* and *accommodation*—are responsible (Piaget & Inhelder, 2000). Assimilation takes place when information is integrated into existing schemata, and accommodation occurs when schemata are modified or new schemata are created. Through assimilation, children add new information to their picture of the world; through accommodation, they change that picture to reflect new information.

Learning occurs through the process of equilibration. When children encounter something they don't understand, disequilibrium, or cognitive conflict, results. This disequilibrium typically produces confusion and agitation, feelings that impel children to seek equilibrium, a comfortable balance with the environment. In other words, when confronted with new or discrepant information, children are intrinsically motivated to try to make sense of it. If their schemata can assimilate or accommodate the new information, then the disequilibrium caused by the new experience will motivate them to learn. Equilibrium is then regained at a higher developmental level. These are the steps in the process:

1. Equilibrium is disrupted by the introduction of new or discrepant information.
2. Disequilibrium occurs, and the dual processes of assimilation and accommodation function.
3. Equilibrium is attained at a higher developmental level.

The process of equilibration happens again and again during the course of a day. In fact, it is occurring right now as you are reading this chapter. Learning doesn't always occur when we are presented with new information, however: If the new information is too difficult and we cannot relate it to what we already know, we don't learn. The new information must be puzzling, challenging, or, in Piaget's words, "moderately novel."

Learning Strategies

We all have skills that we use automatically as well as self-regulated strategies for things that we do well—driving defensively, playing volleyball, training a new pet, or maintaining classroom discipline. We unconsciously apply skills we have learned and choose among strategies. The strategies we use in these activities are problem-solving mechanisms that involve complex thinking processes. When we are learning how to drive a car, for example, we learn both skills and strategies. Some of the first skills we learn are how to make left turns and parallel park. With practice, these skills become automatic. One of the first strategies we learn is how to pass another car. At first, we have only a small repertoire of strategies, and we don't always use them effectively; that's one reason why we get a learner's permit that requires a more experienced driver to ride along with us. With practice and guidance, we become more successful drivers, able to anticipate driving problems and take defensive actions.

Children develop a number of learning strategies or methods for learning. Rehearsal—repeating information over and over—is a learning strategy children use to remember something. Here are other learning strategies:

Predicting: Anticipating what will happen
Organizing: Grouping information into categories
Elaborating: Expanding on the information presented
Monitoring: Regulating or keeping track of progress

Information-processing theory suggests that as children grow older, their use of learning strategies improves (Flavell, Miller, & Miller, 2001). As they acquire more effective methods for learning and remembering information, children also become more aware of their own cognitive processes and better able to regulate them. They can reflect on their literacy processes and talk about themselves as readers and writers. For example, third grader Mario reports that "it's mostly after I read a book that I write" (Muhammad, 1993, p. 99), and fifth grader Hobbes reports that "the pictures in my head help me when I write stuff down 'cause then I can get ideas from my pictures" (Cleary, 1993, p. 142).

Children become more realistic about the limitations of their memories and more knowledgeable about which learning strategies are most effective in particular situations. They also become increasingly aware of what they know and don't know. The term *metacognition* refers to this knowledge that children acquire about their own cognitive processes and to children's regulation of their cognitive processes to maximize learning (Tracey & Morrow, 2006).

Teachers play an important role in developing children's metacognitive abilities. During large-group activities, teachers introduce and model learning strategies. In small-group lessons, they provide guided practice, talk with children about learning strategies, and ask them to reflect on their own use of these cognitive processes. Teachers also guide children about when to use particular strategies and which strategies are more effective with various activities.

Social Contexts of Learning

Children's cognitive development is enhanced through social interaction. Russian psychologist Lev Vygotsky (1896–1934) asserted that children learn through socially meaningful interactions and that language is both social and an important facilitator of learning (Vygotsky, 1986, 2006). Children's experiences are organized and shaped by society, but rather than merely absorbing these experiences, children negotiate and transform them as a dynamic part of culture. They learn to talk through social interactions and to read and write through interactions with literate children and adults (Dyson, 1997, 2003). Community is important for both readers and writers: Children talk about books they are reading with classmates, and they turn to classmates for feedback about their writing (Zebroski, 1994).

Through interactions with adults and collaboration with classmates, children learn things they could not learn on their own (Tracey & Morrow, 2006). Adults guide and support children as they move from their current level of knowledge toward a more advanced level. Vygotsky (2006) described these two levels as the actual developmental level, the level at which children can perform a task independently, and the level of proximal development, the level at which children can perform a task with assistance. Children can typically do more difficult things in collaboration than they can on their own, which is why teachers are important models for their students and why children often work with partners and in small groups.

A child's "zone of proximal development" is the range of tasks that the child can perform with guidance from others but cannot yet perform independently. Vygotsky believed that children learn best when what they are attempting to learn is within this zone. He felt that children learn little by performing tasks they can already do independently—tasks at their actual developmental level—or by attempting tasks that are too difficult, or beyond their zone of proximal development.

Vygotsky and Jerome Bruner (2004) used the term *scaffold* as a metaphor to describe adults' contributions to children's learning. Scaffolds are support mechanisms that teachers, parents, and others provide to help children successfully perform a task within their zone of proximal development. Teachers serve as scaffolds when they model or demonstrate a procedure, guide children through a task, ask questions, break complex tasks into smaller steps, and supply pieces of information. As children gain knowledge and experience about how to perform a task, teachers gradually withdraw their support so that children make the transition from social interaction to internalized, independent functioning.

Implications for Learning Language Arts

How children learn has important implications for how they learn language arts. Contributions from the constructivist and sociolinguistic theories include these ideas:

- Children are active participants in learning.
- Children learn by relating the new information to prior knowledge.
- Children organize their knowledge in schemata.
- Children use skills automatically and strategies consciously as they learn.
- Children learn through social interactions with classmates and the teacher.
- Teachers provide scaffolds for children.

Think about these implications and how they will affect your teaching.

LANGUAGE LEARNING AND CULTURE

Language is a complex system for creating meaning through socially shared conventions (Halliday, 1978). Before children enter kindergarten, they learn the language of their community. They understand what community members say to them, and they share their ideas with others through that language. In an amazingly short period of 3 or 4 years, children master the exceedingly complex system of their native language, which allows them to understand sentences they have never heard before and to create sentences they have never said before. Young children are not taught how to talk; this knowledge about language develops tacitly, or unconsciously.

The Four Language Systems

Language is organized using four systems, sometimes called *cueing systems*, which together make oral and written communication possible. Here are the language systems:

The phonological, or sound, system of language

The syntactic, or structural, system of language

The semantic, or meaning, system of language

The pragmatic, or social and cultural use, system of language

The four language systems and their terminology are summarized in Figure 1–1.

Children have an implicit understanding of these systems, and they integrate information simultaneously from them in order to communicate. No one system is more important than any other one, even though the phonological system (sometimes called the *visual system*) plays a prominent role in early literacy.

The Phonological System. There are approximately 44 speech sounds in English. Children learn to pronounce these sounds as they learn to talk, and they associate the sounds with letters as they learn to read and write. Sounds are called *phonemes*, and they are represented in print with diagonal lines to differentiate them from *graphemes*, or letter combinations. For example, the first letter in *mother* is written *m*, and the phoneme is represented by /m/; the /ō/ phoneme in *soap* represented by the grapheme *oa*.

FIGURE 1–1

Overview of the Four Language Systems

System	Terms	Applications
Phonological System The sound system of English with approximately 44 sounds	• Phoneme (the smallest unit of sound) • Grapheme (the written representation of a phoneme using one or more letters) • Phonological awareness (knowledge about the sound structure of words, at the phoneme, onset-rime, and syllable levels) • Phonemic awareness (the ability to manipulate the sounds in words orally) • Phonics (instruction about phoneme-grapheme correspondences and spelling rules)	• Pronouncing words • Detecting regional and other dialects • Decoding words when reading • Using invented spelling • Reading and writing alliterations and onomatopoeia
Syntactic System The structural system of English that governs how words are combined into sentences	• Syntax (the structure or grammar of a sentence) • Morpheme (the smallest meaningful unit of language) • Free morpheme (a morpheme that can stand alone as a word) • Bound morpheme (a morpheme that must be attached to a free morpheme)	• Adding inflectional endings to words • Combining words to form compound words • Adding prefixes and suffixes to root words • Using capitalization and punctuation to indicate beginnings and ends of sentences • Identifying the parts of speech • Writing simple, compound, and complex sentences • Combining sentences
Semantic System The meaning system of English that focuses on vocabulary	• Semantics (meaning) • Synonyms (words with similar meanings) • Antonyms (opposites) • Homonyms (words that sound alike)	• Learning the meanings of words • Discovering that some words have multiple meanings • Studying synonyms, antonyms, and homonyms • Using a dictionary and a thesaurus • Reading and writing comparisons (metaphors and similes) and idioms
Pragmatic System The system of English that varies language according to social and cultural uses	• Function (the purpose for which a person uses language) • Standard English (the form of English used in textbooks and by television newscasters) • Nonstandard English (other forms of English)	• Varying language to fit specific purposes • Reading and writing dialogue in dialects • Comparing standard and nonstandard forms of English

The phonological system is important in both oral and written language. Regional and cultural differences exist in the way people pronounce phonemes. For example, Jimmy Carter's speech is characteristic of the southeastern United States, and John F. Kennedy's was typical of New England. Similarly, the English spoken in Australia is different from American English. English learners must learn to pronounce English sounds, and sounds that are different from those in their native language are particularly difficult for children to learn. For example, Spanish does not have /th/, and children who have immigrated to the United States from Mexico and other Spanish-speaking countries have difficulty pronouncing this sound; they often substitute /d/ for /th/ because the sounds are articulated in similar ways (Nathenson-Mejia, 1989). Younger children usually learn to pronounce the difficult sounds more easily than do older children and adults.

Children use their knowledge of the phonological system as they learn to read and write. In a purely phonetic language, there would be a one-to-one correspondence between letters and sounds, and teaching students to sound out words would be a simple process. But English is not a purely phonetic language, because there are 26 letters and 44 sounds and many ways to combine the letters—especially the vowels—to spell some of the sounds. Consider the different ways of spelling long *e* in these words: *sea, green, Pete, me,* and *people.* And sometimes the patterns used to spell long *e* don't work, as in *head* and *great.* Phonics, which describes the phoneme-grapheme correspondences and related spelling rules, is an important part of beginning reading instruction, because students use phonics information to decode words. However, because readers do much more than decode words when they read, phonics instruction cannot be the entire reading program.

Young children also use their understanding of the phonological system to create invented spellings. First graders, for example, might spell *home* as *hm* or *hom,* and second graders might spell *school* as *skule,* based on their knowledge of phoneme-grapheme relationships and the spelling patterns. As children become better readers and writers, their spellings become increasingly sophisticated and finally conventional. Also, English learners' spellings typically reflect their pronunciations of words.

The Syntactic System. The syntactic system is the structural organization of English. This system is the grammar that regulates how words are combined into sentences. The word *grammar* here means the rules governing how words are combined in sentences, not the grammar of English textbooks or the conventional etiquette of language. Children use the syntactic system as they combine words to form sentences. Word order is important in English, and English speakers must arrange words into a sequence that makes sense. Young Spanish-speaking English learners, for example, learn to say, "This is my red sweater," not "This is my sweater red," which is the literal translation from Spanish.

Children use their knowledge of the syntactic system as they read. They anticipate that the words they are reading have been strung together into sentences. When they come to an unfamiliar word, they recognize its role in the sentence even if they don't know the terms for parts of speech. For example, in the sentence "The horses galloped through the gate and out into the field," children may not be able to decode the word *through,* but they can easily substitute a reasonable word or phrase, such as *out of* or *past.* Many of the capitalization and punctuation rules that children learn reflect the syntactic system. Similarly, when they learn about simple, compound, and complex sentences, they are learning about the syntactic system.

Another component of syntax is word forms. Words such as *dog* and *play* are morphemes, the smallest meaningful units in language. Word parts that change the meaning of a word are also morphemes. When the plural marker *-s* is added to *dog* to make *dogs,* for instance, or the past-tense marker *-ed* is added to *play* to make *played,* these words now contain two morphemes because the inflectional endings change the meaning of the words. The words *dog* and *play* are free morphemes because they convey meaning while standing alone. The endings *s* and *ed* are bound morphemes because they must be attached to a free morpheme to convey meaning. As they learn to talk, children quickly learn to combine words and word parts, such as adding *-s* to *cookie* to create a plural and adding *-er* to *high* to indicate a comparison. They also learn to combine two or more free morphemes to form compound words; *birthday,* for example, is a compound word created by combining two free morphemes.

Children also learn to add affixes to words. Affixes added at the beginning of a word are prefixes, and affixes added at the end are suffixes. Both kinds of affixes are bound morphemes. For example, the prefix *un-* in *unhappy* is a bound morpheme, whereas *happy* is a free morpheme because it can stand alone as a word.

The Semantic System. The third language system is the semantic, or meaning, system. Vocabulary is the key component of this system. Researchers estimate that children have a vocabulary of 5,000 words by the time they enter school, and they continue to acquire 3,000 words each year (Stahl & Nagy, 2005). Considering how many words children learn each year, it is unreasonable to assume that they learn words only through formal instruction. Children probably learn 7 to 10 words a day, many of which are learned informally through reading and through social studies, science, and other curricular areas.

At the same time children are learning new words, they are also learning that many words have more than one meaning. Meaning is usually based on the context, or the surrounding words. The common word *run,* for instance, has more than 30 meanings. Read these sentences to see how the meaning of *run* is tied to the context in which it is used:

Will the mayor run for reelection?
The bus runs between Dallas and Houston.
The advertisement will run for three days.
Did you run in the 50-yard dash?
The plane made a bombing run.
Will you run to the store and get a loaf of bread for me?
The dogs are out in the run.

Children often don't have the full range of meanings of many words; rather, they learn meanings through a process of refinement.

Children learn other sophisticated concepts about words as well. They learn about shades of meaning—for example, the differences among these *sad* words: *unhappy, crushed, desolate, miserable, disappointed, cheerless, down,* and *grief stricken.* They also learn about synonyms and antonyms, wordplay, and figurative language, including idioms.

The Pragmatic System. The fourth language system is pragmatics, which deals with the social and cultural aspects of language use. People use language for many purposes, and how they talk or write varies according to purpose and audience. Language use varies among social classes, cultural and ethnic groups, and geographic regions; these varieties are known as *dialects*. School is one cultural community, and the language of school is Standard English. This register, or style, is formal—the one used in textbooks, newspapers, and magazines and by television newscasters. Other forms, including those spoken in inner cities, in Appalachia, and by Mexican Americans in the Southwest, are generally classified as nonstandard English. These nonstandard forms of English are alternatives in which the phonology, syntax, and semantics differ from those of Standard English, but they are neither inferior nor substandard. They reflect the communities of the speakers, and the speakers communicate as effectively as those who use Standard English in their communities. The goal is for students to add Standard English to their repertoire of language registers, not to replace their home dialect with Standard English.

Academic Language

The type of English used for instruction is called *academic language*. It's different than the social or conversational language we speak at home and with friends in two ways. First, academic language is more cognitively demanding and decontextualized than social language in which speakers carry on face-to-face conversations about everyday topics (Wong-Fillmore & Snow, 2002). Teachers use academic language when they teach language arts, math, and other content areas and when they give directions for completing assignments. It's also the language used in content-area textbooks and standardized achievement tests.

Second, academic language has semantic, syntactic, and pragmatic features that distinguish it from social language. The ideas expressed are more complex; the meaning is less obvious and takes more effort to understand. The vocabulary is more technical and precise; many words are unfamiliar or are used in new ways. The sentence structure is different: Academic language uses longer, more complex sentences that may be difficult to understand. Academic language has a different style, too: Speakers and writers present detailed, well-organized information about complex and abstract topics, usually without becoming personally involved in the topic. The contrasts between social and academic language are summarized in Figure 1–2.

Even when students are proficient users of social language, they are likely to have difficulty understanding and using academic language in the classroom without instruction (Wong-Fillmore & Snow, 2002). Through instruction and frequent opportunities to use talk and other language arts in meaningful ways, children learn the knowledge, vocabulary, and language patterns associated with academic English. Although learning academic language is essential for all children, the challenge is greater for English learners.

Culturally and Linguistically Diverse Students

The United States is a culturally pluralistic society, and our ethnic, racial, and socioeconomic diversity is reflected in classrooms. Today nearly a third of us classify ourselves as non-European Americans (Wright, 2004). The percentage of culturally

FIGURE 1–2

Contrasts Between Social and Academic Language

	Social Language	Academic Language
Topics	Topics are familiar, everyday, and concrete; they are often examined superficially with few details being presented.	Topics are unfamiliar, complex, and abstract. More details are provided, and they are examined in more depth.
Vocabulary	Everyday, familiar words are used.	Technical terms, jargon, and many multisyllabic words are used.
Sentence Structure	Sentences are shorter and dependent on the context.	Sentence structure is longer and more complicated.
Viewpoints	One opinion or viewpoint is shared, and it is often subjective or biased.	Multiple viewpoints are considered and analyzed, usually objectively.

diverse students is even higher: In California, more than 50% of school-age children belong to ethnic minority groups, and in New York state, 40% do. It has been estimated that given current birthrates and immigration patterns, within a few years, Hispanic American and Asian American populations will have grown by more than 20%, and the African American population will have grown by 12%. These changing demographic realities are having a significant impact on schools, as more and more students come from linguistically and culturally diverse backgrounds.

Because the United States is a nation of immigrants, dealing with cultural diversity is not a new responsibility for public schools; however, the magnitude of diversity is much greater now. In the past, the United States was viewed as a melting pot in which language and cultural differences would be assimilated or combined to form a new, truly American culture. What actually happened, though, was that the European American culture remained dominant. The concept of cultural pluralism has replaced the idea of assimilation. Cultural pluralism respects people's right to retain their cultural identity within American society, recognizing that each culture contributes to and enriches the total society.

Children of diverse cultures come to school with a broad range of language and literacy experiences, although their experiences may be different than those of mainstream or European American children (Samway & McKeon, 1999). They have learned to communicate in at least one language, and, if they don't speak English, they want to learn English in order to make friends, learn, and communicate just like their classmates. Brock and Raphael (2005) emphasize that teachers should take children's diverse backgrounds into account as they plan instruction, making sure to provide a variety of opportunities for children to participate in classroom activities.

English Learners. Learning a second language is a constructive process, and children learn English in a predictable way through interactions with other children and with adults. Jim Cummins (1996) theorized that English learners must develop two types of English proficiency. First, children learn social or everyday language, which Cummins called Basic Interpersonal Conversational Skills (BICS). Social language is characterized as context-embedded because context cues that make the language easier to understand are available to speakers and listeners. This type of language is easy to learn, according to Cummins, because it is cognitively undemanding and can usually be acquired in only 2 to 3 years.

Cummins's second type of language is called Cognitive Academic Language Proficiency (CALP). CALP is academic language, the type of language that students need to understand and use for school success, and it's much harder for learners to understand because it's context reduced and more cognitively demanding. Context-reduced language is more abstract and less familiar, and it's cognitively demanding because technical terms, complex sentence structures, and less familiar topics are involved. English learners require 5 to 7 years or more to become proficient in this type of English, and too many English learners never reach proficiency.

How quickly English learners learn academic English depends on many factors, including their native language proficiency, school experiences, motivation, and personality. The family's literacy level, their socioeconomic status, and their cultural isolation are other considerations. In addition, when families flee from social unrest or war in their native countries, children often take longer to learn English because of the trauma they experienced.

Michael Newman/PhotoEdit Inc.

The Four Language Systems
These Spanish-speaking first graders use the four language systems as they learn to speak, read, and write in English. They have already developed the language systems in their native language, and now they add linguistic information about English. Their teacher helps them understand how English is similar to their native language and how it is different. The errors that these English learners make, such as pronouncing *j* like *h* and placing modifiers after the noun instead of before it (e.g., the *baby little* instead of the *little baby*), often reflect the language systems of their native language.

Meeting the Needs of English Learners

How Can Teachers Support English Learners' Language Development?

- Create a stress-free environment in the classroom.
- Show genuine interest in children, their language, and their culture.
- Build students' background knowledge using artifacts, videos, photos, maps, and picture books.
- Use language that is neither too hard nor too easy for students.
- Embed language in context-rich activities.
- Highlight important words on word walls and encourage students to use these words orally and in writing.
- Have students dramatize vocabulary words they are learning, stories they have read, historical events they are studying, and other topics to enhance their learning.
- Demonstrate how to do projects, and show samples so students understand what they are expected to do.
- Read aloud to students every day.
- Avoid forcing students to speak.
- Expand the two- and three-word sentences that students produce.
- Have students work together with partners and in cooperative groups.
- Have students share ideas with a partner as a rehearsal before sharing with the whole class.
- Provide many opportunities for students to listen to and speak English and to read and write English in low-risk situations.
- Don't lower your expectations for any group of students.

So that children can grow in their knowledge of and use of academic language, Courtney Cazden (2001) challenges teachers to make changes in classroom language use to incorporate more academic language. Finding ways to help all children develop academic language has become more urgent because of the enactment of the No Child Left Behind Act of 2001.

Critical Literacy

It's easy for teachers to focus on teaching children how to read and write without considering how language works in our society, but language is more than just a means of communication; it shapes our perceptions of society, justice, and acceptance. Standard English is the language of school, but today, many children speak a different language or a nonstandard form of English at home. These language differences and the way that teachers and classmates respond to them affect how children think about themselves and their expectations for success at school. Some children are more eager to share their ideas than others, and research suggests that teachers call on boys more often than girls. Also, classmates encourage some children to participate more than others. These language behaviors silence some children and marginalize others.

Language is not neutral. The reasons why people use language are another consideration. Both children and adults use language for a variety of purposes—to entertain, inform, control, and persuade, for example. Language used for these purposes can affect our beliefs, opinions, and behavior. Martin Luther King Jr.'s "I Have a Dream" speech, for example, had a great impact on American society, calling people to action in the Civil Rights movement. Essays, novels, and other written materials also affect us in powerful ways. Think about the impact of *Anne Frank: The Diary of a Young Girl* (Frank, 1995): The madness of the Holocaust appalled us.

Critical literacy focuses on the empowering role of both oral and written language. This theory emphasizes the use of all six language arts to communicate, solve problems, and persuade others to a course of action. It emphasizes the interactions of students in the classroom and in their neighborhoods, and the relationship between language and students in the context of the classroom, the neighborhood, and society.

Critical literacy grew out of the critical pedagogy theory that suggests that teachers and students ask fundamental questions about knowledge, justice, and equity (Wink, 2005). Language becomes a means for social action. Teachers do more than just teach students to use the six language arts; both teachers and students become agents of social change. The increasing social and cultural diversity in our society adds urgency to resolving inequities and injustices.

Language arts instruction doesn't take place in a vacuum; the content that teachers teach and the ways they teach it occur in a social, cultural, political, and historical context (Freire & Macedo, 1987). Consider the issue of grammar instruction, for example. Some people argue that grammar shouldn't be taught because it is too abstract and won't help children become better readers or writers; however, others believe that not teaching grammar is one way the majority culture denies access to nonstandard English speakers. Both proponents and detractors of grammar instruction want what is best for students, but their views are diametrically opposed. Think about these issues related to teaching and learning:

Does school perpetuate the dominant culture and exclude others?
Do all students have equal access to learning opportunities?
How are students who speak nonstandard English treated?
Is school more like family life in some cultures than in others?
Do teachers interact differently with boys and girls?
Are some students silenced in classrooms?
Do teachers have different expectations for minority students?
Are English learners marginalized?
Does the literature that students read reflect diverse voices?

Language arts is not simply a body of knowledge, but rather is a way of organizing knowledge within a cultural and political context. Giroux (1997) challenges teachers not to accept the status quo, but to be professionals and to take control of their own teaching and consider the impact of what they do in the classroom.

Luke and Freebody's (1997) model of reading includes critical literacy as the highest level. I have adapted their model to incorporate both reading and writing:

Level 1. Code Breakers: Students learn phonics, word-identification strategies, and high-frequency words to read and write fluently.

Level 2. Text Participants: Students comprehend what they are reading, learn about text structures and genres, and develop coherent ideas in the texts they write.

Level 3. Text Users: Students read and write multigenre texts and compare the effect of genre and purpose on texts.

Level 4. Text Critics: Students examine the issues raised in books they read and write.

Teachers take students to the fourth level, text critics, when they read and discuss books such as *Rosa* (Giovanni, 2005), the story of the Rosa Parks's refusal to give up her seat on a city bus; *The Breadwinner* (Ellis, 2000), the story of a girl in Taliban-controlled Afghanistan who must pretend to be a boy to support her family; *The Watsons Go to Birmingham—1963* (Curtis, 2000), the story of an African American family caught in the Birmingham church bombing; and *Homeless Bird* (Whelan, 2000), the story of an Indian girl who has no future when she is widowed. These stories describe injustices that primary-, middle-, and upper-grade students can understand and discuss (Foss, 2002; Lewison, Flint, & Van Sluys, 2002). In fact, teachers report that their students are often more engaged in reading stories about social issues than other books and that students' interaction patterns change after reading them (Wolk, 2004).

Implications for Learning Language Arts

What you've read about language and culture has important implications for how students learn language arts in school:

- Students use the four language systems simultaneously as they communicate.
- Students need to understand and use academic language.
- Students from each cultural group bring their unique backgrounds of experience to the process of learning.
- Students' cultural and linguistic diversity provides an opportunity to enhance and enrich the learning of all students.
- Students use language arts to reflect on cultural, social, and political injustices and work to change the world.

Think about these implications and how they will affect how you teach language arts.

HOW STUDENTS LEARN LANGUAGE ARTS

Language arts instruction is changing to reflect our greater oral, written, and visual communication needs. The Steering Committee of the Elementary Section of the National Council of Teachers of English (NCTE, 1996) identified seven characteristics of competent language users, which are presented in Figure 1–3. Students exemplify these characteristics of competent language users as they do the following activities:

- Compare the video and book versions for the same story
- Interview community resource people who have special knowledge, interests, or talents in connection with literature focus units and social studies and science thematic units
- Examine propaganda techniques used in print advertisements and television commercials
- Use the Internet to gather information as part of social studies and science thematic units
- Assume the role of a character while reading a story, and write simulated journal entries as that character
- Use the writing process to write stories, and share the stories with classmates
- Analyze an author's writing style during an author unit

These activities exhibit the three characteristics—meaningful, functional, and genuine—of all worthwhile experiences with language. First, they use language in meaningful rather than contrived situations. Second, they are functional, or real-life,

---

FIGURE 1–3

Characteristics of Competent Language Users

Personal Expression

Students use language to express themselves, to make connections between their own experiences and their social world, to choose books they want to read and topics they want to write about, and to create a personal voice.

Aesthetic Appreciation

Students use language aesthetically to read literature, talk with others, and enrich their lives.

Collaborative Exploration

Students use language as a learning tool as they learn in collaboration with class-mates.

Strategic Language Use

Students use strategies as they create and share meaning through language.

Creative Communication

Students use text forms and genres creatively as they share ideas through oral and written language.

Reflective Interpretation

Students use language to organize and evaluate learning experiences, question personal and social values, and think critically.

Thoughtful Application

Students use language to solve problems, persuade others, and take action.

activities. And third, they are genuine rather than artificial activities, because they communicate ideas.

Creating a Community of Learners

Language arts classrooms are social settings. Together, students and their teacher create the classroom community, and the type of community they create strongly influences students' learning. Effective teachers establish a community of learners in which students are motivated to learn and are actively involved in language arts activities. Teachers and students work collaboratively and purposefully. Perhaps the most striking quality of classroom communities is the partnership that the teacher and students create. Students are a "family" in which all the members respect one another and support each other's learning. They value culturally and linguistically diverse classmates and recognize that everyone makes important contributions to the classroom (Wells & Chang-Wells, 1992).

Students and the teacher work together for the good of the community. Consider the differences between renting and owning a home. In a classroom community, students and the teacher are joint owners of the classroom. Students assume responsibility for their own learning and behavior, work collaboratively with classmates, complete assignments, and care for the classroom. In contrast, in traditional classrooms, the classroom belongs to the teacher, and students are simply renters for the school year. This doesn't mean that in a classroom community, teachers abdicate their responsibility to students. On the contrary, teachers retain their roles as organizer, facilitator, participant, instructor, model, manager, diagnostician, evaluator, coordinator, and communicator. These roles are often shared with students, but the ultimate responsibility remains with the teacher.

Researchers have identified many characteristics of effective classroom communities. Ten of these characteristics, which are described in Figure 1–4, show how the learning theories presented earlier in this chapter are translated into practice.

Teachers begin the process of establishing a community of learners when they make deliberate decisions about the kind of classroom culture they want to create (Whatley & Canalis, 2002). School is "real" life for students, and they learn best when they see a purpose for learning to read and write. The social contexts that teachers create are key. Teachers must think about their roles and what they believe about how children learn. They must decide to have a democratic classroom where students' abilities in reading and writing develop through meaningful literacy activities.

Teachers are more successful when they take the first 2 weeks of the school year to establish the classroom environment (Sumara & Walker, 1991). Teachers can't assume that students will be familiar with the procedures and routines used in language arts or that they will instinctively be cooperative, responsible, and respectful of classmates. Teachers explicitly explain classroom routines, such as how to get supplies out and put them away and how to work with classmates in a cooperative group, and they set the expectation that students will adhere to the routines. Next, they demonstrate literacy procedures, including how to choose a book from the classroom library, how to provide feedback in a writing group, and how to participate in a grand conversation or discussion about a book. Third, teachers model ways of interacting with students, responding to literature, respecting classmates, and assisting classmates with reading and writing projects.

FIGURE 1–4

Characteristics of Effective Classroom Communities

Responsibility

Students are responsible for their learning, their behavior, and the contributions they make in the classroom. They see themselves as valued and contributing members of the classroom community. Students become more self-reliant when they make choices about the language arts activities in which they are involved.

Opportunities

Students have opportunities to participate in language arts activities that are meaningful, functional, and genuine. They read real books and write books for real audiences—their classmates, their parents and grandparents, and other members of their community.

Engagement

Students are motivated to learn and to be actively involved in language arts activities. In a student-centered classroom, the activities are interesting, and students sometimes choose which books to read, how they will respond to a book, topics for writing, and the writing form they will use.

Demonstration

Students learn procedures, concepts, skills, and strategies through demonstrations—with modeling and scaffolding—that teachers provide.

Risk Taking

Students are encouraged to explore topics, make guesses, and take risks. Rather than viewing learning as the process of getting the answer right, teachers promote students' experimentation with new skills and strategies.

Instruction

Teachers are expert language users, and they provide instruction through minilessons on procedures, skills, strategies, and other concepts related to language arts. These minilessons are planned and taught to small groups, the whole class, or individual students so that students can apply what they are learning in meaningful literacy projects.

Response

Students have opportunities to respond after reading and viewing and to share their interpretations of stories. Through writing in reading logs and participating in discussions called *grand conversations,* students share personal connections to the story, make predictions, ask questions, and deepen their comprehension. When they write, students share their rough drafts in writing groups to get feedback on how well they are communicating, and they celebrate their published books by sharing them with classmates and other "real" audiences.

Choice

Students often make choices about the language arts activities in which they are involved. They choose what books they will read and what projects they will create after reading. Students make choices within the parameters set by the teacher.

Continues

FIGURE 1–4

Continued

When they are given the opportunity to make choices, students are often more highly motivated to do the activity, and they value their learning experience more because it's more meaningful to them.

Time

Students need large chunks of time to pursue language arts activities. It doesn't work well for teachers to break the classroom schedule into many small time blocks for phonics, reading, spelling, handwriting, grammar, and writing. Students need 2 or 3 hours of uninterrupted time each day for language arts instruction. It is important to minimize disruptions during the time set aside, and administrators should schedule computer, music, art, and other pull-out programs so that they don't interfere. This is especially important in the primary grades.

Assessment

Teachers and students work together to establish guidelines for assessment, and students monitor their own work and participate in the evaluation. Rather than imposing assessment on students, teachers share with their students the responsibility for monitoring and evaluating their progress.

Adapted from Cambourne & Turbill, 1987.

Teachers are the classroom managers or administrators. They set expectations and clearly explain to students what is expected of them and what is valued in the classroom. The classroom rules are specific and consistent, and teachers also set limits. For example, students might be allowed to talk quietly with classmates when they are working, but they are not allowed to shout across the classroom or talk when the teacher is talking or when classmates are making a presentation to the class. Teachers also model classroom rules themselves as they interact with students. According to Sumara and Walker, the process of socialization at the beginning of the school year is planned, deliberate, and crucial for establishing an environment that's conducive to learning.

Not everything can be accomplished quickly, however, so teachers continue to reinforce classroom routines and language arts procedures. One way is to have student leaders model the desired routines and behaviors and encourage classmates to follow the lead. Teachers also continue to teach additional literacy procedures as children are involved in new activities. The classroom community evolves during the school year, but the foundation is laid during the first 2 weeks.

Teachers develop a predictable classroom environment with familiar routines and a consistent schedule. Students feel comfortable, safe, and more willing to take risks in a predictable environment. This is especially true for students from varied cultures, English learners, and less capable readers and writers.

Motivation for Learning

Motivation is intrinsic and internal—a driving force within us. Children in the primary grades are usually eager to learn. They are enthusiastic participants in classroom activities and confident that they will be successful in school. Their teachers play a crucial role in engaging them, monitoring their progress, and providing encouragement. They plan instructional activities that are interesting, incorporate authentic materials, and often involve children in cooperative groups. Pressley, Dolezal, Raphael, Mohan, Roehrig, and Bogner (2003) studied nine second-grade teachers, examined the most engaging teachers' instructional practices, and identified these motivating teacher behaviors:

- Teachers create a community of learners.
- Teachers create a positive classroom environment with books, charts, and posters used as teaching tools, colorful bulletin board displays, and a display of student work.
- Teachers set clear expectations for behavior and learning, and children know what is expected of them.
- Teachers encourage cooperation rather than competition.
- Teachers provide positive feedback and compliment children for good behavior and learning.
- Teachers encourage children to take risks and to be persistent.
- Teachers plan instruction thoroughly with little "down time" between activities.
- Teachers provide authentic, hands-on activities.
- Teachers model and scaffold learning.
- Teachers teach strategies and skills through direct instruction and modeling.
- Teachers monitor children's behavior and learning.
- Teachers stimulate children's creativity, curiosity, and critical thinking.
- Teachers emphasize depth over breadth as they teach.
- Teachers make home–school connections.
- Teachers model interest and enthusiasm for learning.
- Teachers emphasize the value of education.
- Teachers genuinely enjoy being with children and communicate that they care for them.

Edmunds and Bauserman (2006) found similar results when they interviewed students in prekindergarten through fifth grade.

Often students' motivation for language arts diminishes as they reach the upper grades. Penny Oldfather (1995) conducted a 4-year study to examine the factors influencing students' motivation and found that when students had opportunities for authentic self-expression as part of language arts activities, they were more highly motivated. The students she interviewed reported that they were more highly motivated when they had ownership of the learning activities. Specific activities that they mentioned included opportunities to choose their own topics for writing and books for reading, to express their own ideas and opinions and talk about books they're reading, to share their writings with classmates, and to pursue "authentic" activities—not worksheets—using the language arts.

Some students are not strongly motivated for language arts, and they adopt strategies for avoiding failure rather than strategies for success. These strategies are defensive tactics (Paris, Wasik, & Turner, 1991). Unmotivated students often give up or remain passive, uninvolved in reading and other language arts activities. Some students feign interest or pretend to be involved even though they are not. Others don't think language arts is important, and they choose to focus on other curricular areas—math or physical education, for instance. Some students complain about feeling ill or that classmates are bothering them. They place the blame on anything other than themselves.

Other students avoid language arts entirely. They just don't do it. Another group of students read books that are too easy for them or write short pieces so that they don't have to exert much effort. Students use these strategies because they lead to short-term success. The long-term result, however, is devastating because these students fail to learn to read and write.

The Six Language Arts

Traditionally, language arts educators have defined the language arts as the study of the four modes of language: listening, talking, reading, and writing, but more recently, the National Council of Teachers of English and the International Reading Association (*Standards,* 1996) proposed two additional language arts—viewing and visually representing. These new language arts reflect the growing importance of visual literacy (Whitin, 1996).

Listening. Beginning at birth, a child's contact with language is through listening. Listening instruction is often neglected at school because teachers believe that children already know how to listen and that instructional time should be devoted to reading and writing. This book presents an alternative view of listening and listening instruction and focuses on these key concepts:

creatively

- Listening is a process of which hearing is only one part.
- Students listen differently according to their purpose.
- Students listen aesthetically to stories, efferently to learn information as part of thematic units, and critically to persuasive appeals.
- Students use listening strategies and monitor their comprehension in order to listen more effectively.

Talking. As with listening, teachers often neglect instruction in talk because they believe students already know how to talk. Research has emphasized the importance of talk in the learning process (Dwyer, 1991). For example, students use talk to respond to literature, provide feedback about classmates' writing in writing groups, and present oral reports as part of social studies and science units. You'll learn more about these key concepts about talk as you continue reading:

- Talk is an essential part of learning.
- Students use talk for both aesthetic and efferent purposes.
- Students participate in grand conversations as they respond to literature.
- Students give presentations, including oral reports and debates.
- Drama provides a valuable method of learning and a powerful way of communicating.

Reading. Reading is a process, and students use strategies and skills to decode words and comprehend what they are reading. Students vary the way they read according to their purpose: They read for pleasure differently than they do to locate and remember information (Rosenblatt, 2005). Here are the key concepts about reading:

- Reading is a strategic process.
- The goal of reading is comprehension, or meaning making.
- Students read differently for different purposes.
- Students participate in five types of reading: independent reading, shared reading, guided reading, buddy reading, and reading aloud to children.

Writing. Like reading, writing is a strategic process (Dean, 2006). Students use the writing process to write stories, reports, poems, and other genres (Graves, 1994). They also do informal writing, such as writing in reading logs and making graphic organizers. As you continue reading, you'll learn about these key concepts about writing:

- Writing is a process in which students cycle recursively through the stages of prewriting, drafting, revising, editing, and publishing.
- Students experiment with many written language genres.
- Informal writing is used to develop writing fluency and as a learning tool.
- Spelling and handwriting are tools for writers.

Viewing. Visual media include film and videos, print advertisements and commercials, photographs and book illustrations, the Internet, and DVDs. Because visual media, including the Internet, are commonplace in American life today, students need to learn how to comprehend them and to integrate visual knowledge with other literacy knowledge (Williams, 2007). Heide and Stilborne (1999) explain that the Internet has "a wide range of resources available for electronic field trips involving pictures, text, sound, and sometimes interactivity" (p. 19). Here are the key concepts about viewing:

- Viewing is an important component of literacy.
- Students view visual media for a variety of purposes.
- Viewing is much like reading, and students use comprehension strategies in both reading and viewing.
- Students use the Internet as a learning tool.
- Students learn about propaganda techniques in order to critically analyze commercials and advertisements.

Visually Representing. Students create meaning through multiple sign systems such as video productions, Inspiration® and other computer programs, dramatizations, story quilts, and illustrations on charts, posters, and books they are writing (Moline, 1995). According to Harste, "seeing something familiar in a new way is often a process of gaining new insights" (1993, p. 4). Projects involving visual texts are often completed as part of literature focus units, literature circles, and thematic units. This book presents these key concepts about visually representing:

- Students consider audience, purpose, and form as they create visual texts.
- Visual texts, like writing, can be created to share information learned during literature focus units and thematic units.

Relationships Among the Language Arts. Discussing the language arts one by one suggests a division among them, as though they could be used separately. In reality, they are used simultaneously and reciprocally, just as Mrs. McNeal's students in the vignette at the beginning of the chapter used all six language arts during writing workshop. Almost any language arts activity involves more than one of the language arts. In a seminal study, researcher Walter Loban (1976) documented the language growth and development of a group of 338 students from kindergarten through 12th grade (ages 5–18). Two purposes of his longitudinal study were to examine differences between students who used language effectively and those who did not, and to identify predictable stages of language development. Three of Loban's conclusions are especially noteworthy. First, he reported positive correlations among listening, talking, reading, and writing. Second, he found that students with less effective oral language abilities tended to have less effective written language abilities. And third, he found a strong relationship between students' oral language ability and their overall academic ability. Loban's study demonstrates clear relationships among the language arts and emphasizes the need to teach listening and talking as well as reading and writing.

Language Arts Strategies and Skills

Students learn both strategies and skills through language arts instruction. Strategies are problem-solving methods or behaviors, and students develop and use both general learning strategies and specific strategies related to language arts. Although there isn't a definitive list of language arts strategies, researchers have identified a number of strategies that capable readers and writers use (Fletcher & Portalupi, 1998). I focus on these strategies in this text:

Activating background knowledge	Organizing
Blending	Playing with language
Brainstorming	Predicting
Connecting	Proofreading
Evaluating	Questioning
Identifying big ideas	Revising
Identifying root words	Segmenting
Inferencing	Setting purposes
Monitoring	Summarizing
Noticing nonverbal cues	Visualizing

These strategies are described in Figure 1–5. Some strategies, such as blending, are used specifically in phonemic awareness, phonics, and spelling, and many others are applied in all six language arts. Consider revising, for example. Probably the best-known application is in writing: Students revise as they add, substitute, delete, and move information in their rough drafts. Revising visual representations works the same way. But students also revise meaning while they talk on the basis of feedback from the audience, and as they listen to a speaker, view a DVD, or read a book.

Skills, in contrast, are information-processing techniques that students use automatically and unconsciously as they construct meaning. Many skills focus at the word level, but some require students to attend to larger chunks of text. For example, readers use skills such as decoding unfamiliar words, noting details, and sequencing events, and writers employ skills such as forming contractions, using punctuation marks, and capitalizing people's names. Skills and strategies are not the same thing. The important difference between skills and strategies is how they are used: Skills are used unconsciously, and strategies are used deliberately (Paris et al., 1991).

FIGURE 1–5

Strategies That Capable Readers and Writers Use

Strategy	Description
Activating background knowledge	Students think about what they already know about a topic.
Blending	Students combine sounds to pronounce a word.
Brainstorming	Students think of many ideas related to a topic.
Connecting	Students relate a topic to themselves, the world around them, and literature.
Evaluating	Students reflect on, make judgments about, and value an experience.
Identifying big ideas	Students determine the most important ideas.
Identifying root words	Students pick out the root in a longer word.
Inferencing	Students draw conclusions from clues presented in the text.
Monitoring	Students keep track of their understanding or success with an activity.
Noticing nonverbal cues	Students interpret gestures, symbols, and nonalphabetic features.
Organizing	Students put ideas in a coherent and logical arrangement.
Playing with language	Students notice figurative and novel uses of language and use language creatively themselves.
Predicting	Students anticipate events.
Proofreading	Students identify mechanical errors in their writing.
Questioning	Students ask questions to clarify or expand meaning.
Revising	Students make changes or a new version.
Segmenting	Students break a word into sounds.
Setting purposes	Students identify a goal for themselves.
Summarizing	Students pick out the big ideas to remember.
Visualizing	Students draw pictures in their minds.

Students learn to use five types of skills. Although many of the skills are oriented to reading and writing, some are used for listening, talking, viewing, and visually representing. Here are the five types of skills:

◆ *Comprehension Skills.* These include separating facts and opinions, comparing and contrasting, and recognizing literary genres and structures. Students apply comprehension skills as they create meaning using all six language arts.

◆ *Print Skills.* These include sounding out words, noticing word families, using root words and affixes to decode and spell words, and using abbreviations. Students use print skills as they decode words when reading and as they spell words when writing.

◆ *Study Skills.* These include skimming and scanning, taking notes, making clusters, and previewing a book before reading. Students use study skills during thematic units, while reading informational books, and while collecting information to use in writing reports.

◆ *Language Skills.* These include identifying and inferring meanings of words, noticing idioms, dividing words into syllables, and choosing synonyms. Students are continuously interacting with words as they use the language arts, and they use language skills to analyze words when they are listening and reading and to choose more precise language when they are talking and writing.

◆ *Reference Skills.* These include alphabetizing a list of words, using a dictionary, and reading and making graphs and other diagrams. Students learn to use reference skills to read newspaper articles, locate information in encyclopedias and other informational books, and consult library resources.

Examples of each of the five types of skills are presented in Figure 1–6. Students use these skills for various language arts activities. For example, they use some of the skills when giving an oral report and others when writing in learning logs or making a graphic organizer to compare several versions of a folktale.

Teachers often wonder which skills they should teach and when to teach them. School districts often prepare frameworks and curriculum guides that include the skills to be taught at each grade level, and skills are usually listed in basal reading programs. These resources provide guidelines, but teachers should decide which skills to teach and when to teach them based on students' level of development.

Teachers use a combination of direct and indirect instruction to provide information that students need to know about skills and strategies. Direct instruction is planned. Teachers often teach minilessons, brief 15- to 30-minute lessons, in which they explicitly explain a particular strategy or skill, model its use, and provide examples and opportunities for practice. Indirect instruction involves taking advantage of teachable moments to reexplain a strategy or skill to a student or clarify a misconception. Both types of instruction are necessary in order to meet students' needs.

Teachers plan strategy and skill instruction that grows out of language arts activities using a whole-part-whole sequence: The language arts activity is the first *whole*, the minilesson is the *part*, and having students apply what they are learning in other language arts activities is the second *whole*. This instructional sequence is recommended to ensure that the instruction is meaningful and that students learn to use the strategies and skills independently (Mazzoni & Gambrell, 2003).

The goal of instruction is for students to be able to use the strategies and skills that they've learned independently. Dorn and Soffos (2001) have identified four

FIGURE 1–6

Language Arts Skills

Category	Skills	
Print	Sound out words using phonics Notice word families Decode by analogy Use classroom resources Apply spelling rules	Recognize high-frequency words Divide words into syllables Capitalize proper nouns and adjectives Use abbreviations
Comprehension	Chunk words into phrases Sequence Categorize Classify Separate facts and opinions Note details Identify cause and effect Compare and contrast	Use context clues Notice organizational patterns of poetry, plays, business and friendly letters, stories, essays, and reports Recognize literary genres (traditional stories, fantasies, science fiction, realistic fiction, historical fiction, biography, autobiography, and poetry)
Language	Notice compound words Use contractions Use possessives Notice propaganda Use similes and metaphors Notice idioms and slang Choose synonyms Recognize antonyms Differentiate among homonyms Use root words and affixes Appreciate rhyme and other poetic devices	Use punctuation marks (period, question mark, exclamation point, quotation marks, comma, colon, semicolon, and hyphen) Use simple, compound, and complex sentences Combine sentences Recognize parts of sentences Avoid sentence fragments Recognize parts of speech (nouns, pronouns, verbs, adjectives, adverbs, conjunctions, prepositions, and interjections)
Reference	Sort in alphabetical order Use a glossary or dictionary Locate etymologies in the dictionary Use the pronunciation guide in the dictionary Locate synonyms in a thesaurus Locate information in an encyclopedia, atlas, or almanac	Use a table of contents Use an index Use a card catalog Read and make graphs, tables, and diagrams Read and make time lines Read newspapers and magazines Use bibliographic forms
Study	Skim Scan Preview Follow directions	Make outlines and clusters Take notes Paraphrase

behaviors that teachers use as part of both direct and indirect instruction to develop self-regulated learners:

Modeling: Teachers demonstrate how to use strategies and skills.

Coaching: Teachers direct students' attention and encourage their active engagement in activities.

Scaffolding: Teachers adjust the support they provide according to students' needs.

Fading: Teachers relinquish control as students become more capable of using a strategy or performing an activity.

It's not enough to simply explain strategies and skills or remind students to use them. If teachers want their students to be able to use strategies and skills independently, they must actively engage students, encourage and scaffold them while they are learning, and then gradually withdraw their support.

The Goal of Language Arts Instruction

The goal of language arts instruction is for students to develop communicative competence, the ability to use language appropriately in both social and academic contexts (Hymes, 1972). Communicative competence is context specific: This means that students may participate effectively in classroom conversations but not know how to give a more formal oral presentation. Similarly, students may know how to read informational books but not how to write a report to share information. At each grade level, teachers expand students' abilities to use the six language arts in new contexts. Through language arts instruction, students acquire the characteristics of competent language users. They become more strategic and more creative in their use of language, better able to use language as a tool for learning, and more reflective in their interpretations.

In recent years, state and federal mandates have increasingly dictated which instructional approaches and materials teachers use in teaching language arts and developing students' communicative competence. Those that are grounded in scientific evidence are endorsed (Lyon & Chhabra, 2004). The most far-reaching initiative is George W. Bush's No Child Left Behind (NCLB) Act of 2001, which was designed to close the achievement gap between white, affluent students and other students. This initiative, based on the report of the National Reading Panel (2000), has mandated an increased emphasis on teaching basic skills and holds schools accountable for students' performance. Schools are now required to administer standardized tests each year to students in grades 3–8 to monitor their progress. Guidelines for preparing students for "high-stakes" testing are presented in Figure 1–7.

The NCLB Act affects every school in the United States. All schools set annual achievement goals, and those that meet their goals are labeled "schools of choice." If schools don't make adequate yearly progress for 2 consecutive years, they are required to implement special programs to improve test scores, and parents may transfer their children to higher-achieving schools.

The NCLB initiative's emphasis on basic skills has narrowed the goal of language arts instruction in many schools to having students meet grade-level standards on standardized achievement tests; to achieve that goal, teachers are increasingly being required to use scripted basal reading programs under the mistaken assumption that they were recommended by the National Reading Panel (Shanahan, 2003).

Because of the NCLB Act, state-designated lists of grade-level standards, and other mandated programs, teachers feel a loss of professional autonomy in determining what and how to teach. There is increased pressure from parents, administrators, and politicians for teachers to "teach to the test" rather than to develop students' communicative competence by engaging their students in meaningful, functional, and genuine language arts activities. Some teachers have embraced the new instructional programs, and others have quietly resisted them and continued to use student-centered approaches as often as they could. Still others are actively resisting the imposition of these programs because they reject the conformity and loss of teacher control inherent in new state and federal mandates (Garan, 2004; Novinger & Compton-Lilly, 2005).

FIGURE 1–7

How to Prepare Students for High-Stakes Testing

Test-Taking Strategies

Teach test-taking strategies by modeling how to read, think about, and answer test items.

Practice Tests

Design practice tests with the same types of items used on the tests that students will take.

Easy-to-Read Materials

Use easy-to-read reading materials for practice tests so students can focus on practicing test-taking strategies.

Variety of Passages

Include a combination of unrelated narrative and expository passages on practice tests.

Regular Schedule

Have students take practice tests on a regular schedule.

Untimed and Timed Tests

Begin with untimed tests and move to timed tests as students gain experience with test-taking strategies.

Testing Conditions

Simulate testing conditions in the classroom, or take students to where the test will be administered for the practice sessions.

Graphs of Test Results

Graph students' results on practice tests so they can see their progress.

Teachers, administrators, and parents can point to both positive and negative outcomes of these state and federal mandates (Valencia & Villarreal, 2003). Some teachers feel more confident about their teaching ability now because they are being told how to teach language arts, and in many schools, students' test scores are rising. At the same time, however, other teachers are discouraged and frustrated because they are not allowed to use the instructional approaches that have been effective for them in the past. Some of their students continue to fail because they cannot do work at their grade level, and they also are concerned about the amount of time diverted from instruction for testing. In some schools, testing takes more than one month of the school year. In addition, some parents have expressed concern that their children have developed test anxiety and are preoccupied with the "high-stakes" tests they must pass each spring.

Review

Language arts instruction should be based on theories and research about how children learn. Language and culture also have an impact on how students learn language arts. The goal of language arts instruction is for students to develop communicative competence in the six language arts—listening, talking, reading, writing, viewing, and visually representing. Here are the key concepts presented in this chapter:

- Constructivist, information-processing, and sociolinguistic theories of learning inform our understanding of how students learn language arts.
- Students learn through active involvement in listening, talking, reading, writing, viewing, and visually representing activities.

- Teachers should provide instruction within students' zone of proximal development.
- Teachers scaffold or support students' learning.
- Students use all four language systems—phonological, syntactic, semantic, and pragmatic—in listening, talking, reading and writing.
- Students learn cognitively demanding and decontextualized academic language at school.
- Teachers create a community of learners in their classrooms.
- Students learn and use language arts strategies, including predicting, visualizing, revising meaning, summarizing, and monitoring.
- Students learn and use language arts skills, including choosing synonyms, skimming, capitalizing words, and using a dictionary.
- Students need opportunities to participate in language arts activities that are meaningful, functional, and genuine.

Professional References

Brock, C. H., & Raphael, T. E. (2005). *Windows to language, literacy, and culture*. Newark, DE: International Reading Association.

Bruner, J. S. (2004). *Toward a theory of instruction*. Cambridge, MA: Harvard University Press.

Cambourne, B., & Turbill, J. (1987). *Coping with chaos*. Rozelle, NSW, Australia: Primary English Teaching Association.

Cazden, C. B. (2001). *Classroom discourse: The language of teaching and learning* (2nd ed.). Portsmouth, NH: Heinemann.

Cleary, L. M. (1993). Hobbes: "I press rewind through the pictures in my head." In S. Hudson-Ross, L. M. Cleary, & M. Casey (Eds.), *Children's voices: Children talk about literacy* (pp. 136–143). Portsmouth, NH: Heinemann.

Cummins, J. (1989). *Empowering minority students*. Sacramento: California Association for Bilingual Education.

Dean, D. (2006). *Strategic writing*. Urbana, IL: National Council of Teachers of English.

Dorn, L. J., & Soffos, C. (2001). *Shaping literate minds: Developing self-regulated learners*. York, ME: Stenhouse.

Dwyer, J. (Ed.). (1991). *A sea of talk*. Portsmouth, NH: Heinemann.

Dyson, A. H. (1997). *Writing superheroes*. New York: Teachers College Press.

Dyson, A. H. (2003). *The brothers and sisters learn to write*. New York: Teachers College Press.

Edmunds, K. M., & Bauserman, K. L. (2006). What teachers can learn about reading motivation through conversations with children. *The Reading Teacher, 59,* 414–424.

Faltis, C. J. (2006). *Teaching English language learners in elementary school communities* (4th ed.) Upper Saddle River, NJ: Merrill/Prentice Hall.

Flavell, J. H., Miller, P. H., & Miller, S. A. (2001). *Cognitive development* (4th ed.). Upper Saddle River, NJ: Prentice Hall.

Fletcher, R., & Portalupi, J. (1998). *Craft lessons: Teaching writing K–8*. Portland, ME: Stenhouse.

Foss, A. (2002). Peeling the onion: Teaching critical literacy with students of privilege. *Language Arts, 79,* 393–403.

Freire, P., & Macedo, D. (1987). *Literacy: Reading the word and the world*. South Hadley, MA: Bergin & Garvey.

Garan, E. (2004). *In defense of our children: When politics, profit, and education collide*. Portsmouth, NH: Heinemann.

Giroux, H. (1997). *Pedagogy and the politics of hope, theory, culture, and schooling*. Boulder, CO: Westview Press.

Graves. D. H. (1994). *A fresh look at writing*. Portsmouth, NH: Heinemann.

Halliday, M. A. K. (1978). *Language as social semiotic: The social interpretation of language and meaning*. Baltimore: University Park Press.

Harste, J. (1993, April). Inquiry-based instruction. *Primary Voices K–6, 1,* 2–5.

Heide, A., & Stilborne, L. (1999). *The teacher's complete and easy guide to the Internet*. New York: Teachers College Press.

Hymes, D. (1972). On communicative competence. In J. B. Pride & J. Holmes (Eds.), *Sociolinguistics* (pp. 269–285). Harmondsworth, Middlesex, UK: Penguin.

Lewison, M., Flint, A. S., & Van Sluys, K. (2002). Taking on critical literacy: The journey of newcomers and novices. *Language Arts, 79,* 382–392.

Loban, W. (1976). *Language development: Kindergarten through grade twelve* (Research Report No. 18). Urbana, IL: National Council of Teachers of English.

Luke, A., & Freebody, P. (1997). Shaping the social practices of reading. In S. Muspratt, A. Luke, & P. Freebody (Eds.),

Constructing critical literacies (pp. 185–225). Cresskill, NJ: Hampton.

Lyon, G. R., & Chhabra, V. (2004). The science of reading research. *Educational Leadership, 61*(6), 12–17.

Mazzoni, S. A., & Gambrell, L. B. (2003). Principles of best practice. In L. M. Morrow, L. B. Gambrell, & M. Pressley (Eds.), *Best practices in literacy instruction* (2nd ed., pp. 9–22). New York: Guilford Press.

Moline, S. (1995). *I see what you mean: Children at work with visual information.* York, ME: Stenhouse.

Muhammad, R. J. (1993). Mario: "It's mostly after I read a book that I write." In S. Hudson-Ross, L. M. Cleary, & M. Casey (Eds.), *Children's voices: Children talk about literacy* (pp. 92–99). Portsmouth, NH: Heinemann.

Nathenson-Mejia, S. (1989). Writing in a second language: Negotiating meaning through invented spelling. *Language Arts, 66,* 516–526.

National Reading Panel. (2000). *Teaching children to read: An evidence-based assessment of the scientific research literature on reading and its implications for reading instruction, reports of the subgroups.* Washington, DC: National Institute of Child Health and Human Development.

NCTE Elementary Section Steering Committee. (1996). Exploring language arts standards within a cycle of learning. *Language Arts, 73,* 10–13.

Novinger, S., & Compton-Lilly, C. (2005). Telling our stories: Speaking truth to power. *Language Arts, 82,* 195–203.

Oldfather, P. (1995). Commentary: What's needed to maintain and extend motivation for literacy in the middle grades? *Journal of Reading, 38,* 420–422.

Paris, S. G., Wasik, B. A., & Turner, J. C. (1991). The development of strategic readers. In R. Barr, M. L. Kamil, P. B. Mosenthal, & P. D. Pearson (Eds.), *Handbook of reading research* (Vol. 2, pp. 609–640). New York: Longman.

Piaget, J., & Inhelder, B. (2000). *The psychology of the child.* New York: Basic Books.

Pressley, M., Dolezal, S. E., Raphael, L. M., Mohan, L., Roehrig, A. D., & Bogner, K. (2003). *Motivating primary-grade students.* New York: Guilford Press.

Rosenblatt, L. M. (2005). *Making meaning with texts: Selected essays.* Portsmouth, NH: Heinemann.

Samway, K. D., & McKeon, D. (1999). *Myths and realities: Best practices for language minority students.* Portsmouth, NH: Heinemann.

Shanahan, T. (2003). Research-based reading instruction: Myths about the National Reading Panel report. *The Reading Teacher, 56,* 646–655.

Stahl, S. A., & Nagy, W. E. (2005). *Teaching word meanings.* Mahwah; NJ: Erlbaum.

Standards for the English Language Arts. (1996). Urbana, IL: National Council of Teachers of English and the International Reading Association.

Sumara, D., & Walker, L. (1991). The teacher's role in whole language. *Language Arts, 68,* 276–285.

Tracey, D. H., & Morrow, L. M. (2006). *Lenses on reading.* New York: Guilford Press.

Valencia, R. R., & Villarreal, B. J. (2003). Improving students' reading performance via standards-based school reform: A critique. *The Reading Teacher, 56,* 612–621.

Vygotsky, L. S. (1986). *Thought and language.* Cambridge, MA: MIT Press.

Vygotsky, L. S. (2006). *Mind in society.* Cambridge, MA: Harvard University Press.

Wells, G., & Chang-Wells, G. L. (1992). *Constructing knowledge together: Classrooms as centers of inquiry and literacy.* Portsmouth, NH: Heinemann.

Whatley, A., & Canalis, J. (2002). Creating learning communities through literacy. *Language Arts, 79,* 478–487.

Whitin, P. E. (1996). *Sketching stories, stretching minds.* Portsmouth, NH: Heinemann.

Williams, T. L. (2007). "Reading" the painting: Exploring visual literacy in the primary grades. *The Reading Teacher, 60,* 636–642.

Wink, J. (2005). *Critical pedagogy: Notes from the real world* (3rd ed.). New York: Longman.

Wolk, S. (2004). Using picture books to teach for democracy. *Language Arts, 82,* 26–35.

Wong-Fillmore, L., & Snow, C. E. (2002). What teachers need to know about language. In C. T. Adger, C. E. Snow, & D. Christian (Eds.), *What teachers need to know about language* (pp. 7–54). Washington, DC: Center for Applied Linguistics.

Wright, J. W. (Ed.). (2004). *The New York Times 2005 almanac.* New York: Penguin.

Zebroski, J. T. (1994). *Thinking through theory: Vygotskian perspectives on the teaching of writing.* Portsmouth, NH: Boynton/Cook.

Children's Book References

Curtis, C. P. (2000). *The Watsons go to Birmingham—1963.* New York: Delacorte.

Ellis, D. (2000). *The breadwinner.* Toronto: Groundwood Books.

Frank, A. (1995). *Anne Frank: The diary of a young girl* (new ed.). New York: Doubleday.

Giovanni, N. (2005). *Rosa.* New York: Henry Holt.

Sendak, M. (2003). *Where the wild things are.* New York: HarperCollins.

Whelan, G. (2000). *Homeless bird.* New York: Scholastic.

chapter two

Teaching and Assessing Language Arts

Mrs. Miller-McColm sits down on her teacher's stool and picks up Natalie Babbitt's *Tuck Everlasting* (2002), the highly acclaimed story of a family who drinks from a magical spring and becomes immortal. "Yesterday, we stopped halfway through Chapter 6," she says to her sixth graders. "Who remembers what was happening?" A sea of hands go up, and Mrs. Miller-McColm calls on Junior. "Winnie wanted to run away from home, but she got kidnapped by the Tucks. I don't know why though," he says. Next, Isabel says, "I think she goes with the Tucks because she wants to. I think she wants an adventure so she'll stay with them forever."

The students continue talking about the story for several minutes, and then Mrs. Miller-McColm begins reading aloud. After she reads the middle of page 34, she stops and asks, "Why does Mae Tuck say, 'We're not bad people, truly we're not. We had to bring you away—you'll see why in a minute—and we'll take you back just as soon as we can. Tomorrow. I promise'?" The students break into small groups to talk for several minutes about whether the Tucks are "bad" people for kidnapping Winnie and to speculate about why they abducted her. Their desks are arranged in five groups, and the classmates in each group talk eagerly. After several minutes, Mrs. Miller-McColm brings the class back together to continue the discussion. "We don't think the Tucks are bad people," Noemi offers, "because bad people aren't nice, and

How do teachers organize for instruction?

Teachers organize for instruction using four patterns of practice—literature focus units, literature circles, reading and writing workshop, and thematic units. Teachers vary the patterns they choose and sometimes add other programs, including basal readers. No matter which patterns teachers use, they combine direct instruction, small-group activities, and independent activities into their plans. As you read this vignette, notice how Mrs. Miller-McColm incorporates all four patterns of practice in her language arts program.

Mae Tuck is. They must have a good reason for what they did." Donavon says, "They may be nice people but we don't think Winnie will get free 'tomorrow.'" Iliana agrees, "Winnie won't get free until the book ends, and there are a lot of pages still to read." After the students share their ideas, the teacher reads to the end of this chapter and continues reading the next one, where the Tucks explain to Winnie about their "changelessness" and why they abducted her. She finishes reading the last page of Chapter 7, puts the book down, and looks at the students. They look back at her, dazed; no one says a word.

To help the sixth graders sort out their ideas and feelings, Mrs. Miller-McColm asks them to quickwrite in their reading logs. The students take about 5 minutes to write, and then they're ready to talk. Some read their reading log entries aloud, and others share their ideas. Mrs. Miller-McColm asks, "Do you believe the Tucks? Are they telling the truth?" About half of the students agree that the Tucks are telling the truth; others aren't so sure. Next, she asks them to write in their reading logs again, this time about whether they believe the Tucks' story.

Mrs. Miller-McColm uses the novels she reads aloud to teach about story structure. Her focus is on plot development as she reads *Tuck Everlasting*. She has talked about how authors develop stories, and the students understand that in the beginning, authors introduce the problem; in the middle, the problem gets worse; and in the end, it is resolved. Yesterday, they learned the problem in this story—Winnie Foster is abducted by the Tucks. The teacher has also taught them about conflict situations, and at this point in the story, they think the conflict is between characters—between Winnie and the Tucks. Later, they'll see that the conflict is within Winnie herself as she decides whether to drink from the spring and live with the Tucks forever.

Mrs. Miller-McColm spends the first hour of the language arts period teaching a literature focus unit using a book from her district's list of "core" literature selections. She reads the book aloud because about half of her sixth graders couldn't read it on their own. She has already read *Holes* (Sachar, 1998) and

A Wrinkle in Time (L'Engle, 2007); by the end of the school year, she will have read 11 or 12 novels.

Mrs. Miller-McColm's daily schedule is shown in the box below. Her students participate in a variety of language arts activities using the four patterns of practice during the morning and connect language arts to social studies and science through thematic units in the afternoon.

Mrs. Miller-McColm's Daily Schedule

8:30–8:45 *Opening*

8:45–9:45 *Literature Focus Unit*
Mrs. Miller-McColm reads aloud a featured book, involves students in response activities, and teaches story structure, vocabulary, and other strategies and skills.

9:45–10:30 *Book Groups*
Students divide into groups according to reading level and participate in literature circles. They choose books to read, read them independently, and meet with Mrs. Miller-McColm to discuss them. They also apply what they are learning about story structure during the literature focus unit to the books they are reading now and create graphic displays that they post on a special bulletin board.

10:30–10:45 *Recess*

10:45–11:15 *Word Work*
Mrs. Miller-McColm teaches minilessons on word-identification and spelling strategies and skills, including idioms, synonyms, syllabication, root words, and affixes. Students also study spelling words and take weekly spelling tests.

11:15–12:15 *Writing Workshop*
Students use the writing process to write stories and other genres. They meet in writing groups to revise their writing and editing conferences to correct spelling, capitalization, punctuation, and sentence structure errors. They share their published writing from the author's chair. Mrs. Miller-McColm also teaches minilessons on writing procedures, concepts, strategies, and skills.

12:15–1:00 *Lunch and Recess*

1:00–2:00 *Math*

2:00–3:15 *Social Studies/Science*
Mrs. Miller-McColm alternates teaching monthlong social studies and science thematic units. Students apply what they are learning in language arts as they participate in content-area study and develop projects to share their learning.

3:15–3:25 *Clean-up and Dismissal*

Next, Mrs. Miller-McColm's students participate in book groups, another name for literature circles. They read at fourth- through eighth-grade levels, and she divides them into seven book groups according to reading level. The students choose novels to read after their teacher introduces several choices for each group. Currently, they are reading these books:

Stone Fox (Gardiner, 2003) (level 4)

Sarah, Plain and Tall (MacLachlan, 2004) (level 4)

Shiloh (Naylor, 2000) (level 5)

Ralph the Mouse (Cleary, 1993) (level 5)

Maniac Magee (Spinelli, 2002) (level 6)

The BFG (Dahl, 1998) (level 6)

Harry Potter and the Goblet of Fire (Rowling, 2002) (level 8)

The students meet with their groups to set reading schedules. They read during this period and at home and meet with Mrs. Miller-McColm two or three times each week to talk about their books. Groups create displays about the books they're reading on a bulletin board on one side of the classroom. For this round of book groups, the focus is on plot development: Each group makes a sign with the title and author of the book and then creates a graphic display emphasizing the conflict situations in their novel.

Mrs. Miller-McColm meets with the group reading *Sarah, Plain and Tall,* a story about a mail-order bride in the early 1900s. She begins by asking the students to summarize the story so far, and Gabrielle says, "A woman named Sarah is coming to stay at a farm. She might marry the dad and be a mom for the children, Anna and Caleb." "Has she arrived yet?" Mrs. Miller-McColm asks, and April responds, "She just arrived. She came on a train and everyone is very nervous." Then students make connections between the story and their own lives, the world around them, and other literature, and Mrs. Miller-McColm helps them analyze the plot and identify the conflict situation; it's between Sarah and the other characters. The students decide to draw open-mind portraits of the characters to post in their section of the bulletin board. For their portraits, they will draw pictures of the characters and attach three sheets of paper behind the pictures where they will draw and write about the conflict each character feels at the beginning of the story, in the middle, and at the end.

Next, she meets with the group reading *Shiloh*. These students have just finished reading this novel about a boy who sticks out his neck to save an abused dog. They're eager to talk about the book and make connections to personal experiences and to other dog stories they've read. Mrs. Miller-McColm asks them to think more deeply about the story and rereads the last paragraph of the story aloud:

> I look at the dark closing in, sky getting more and more purple, and I'm thinking how nothing is as simple as you guess—not right or wrong, not Judd Travers, not even me or this dog I got here. But the good part is I saved Shiloh and opened my eyes some. Now that ain't bad for eleven. (p. 144)

She asks what Marty, the main character in the story, means when he says, "nothing is as simple as you guess . . . " Omar begins, "At first Marty thought he was all good and Judd Travers was all bad, but then Marty did something dishonest to get Shiloh. He didn't like doing bad things but he did them for a good reason so I think that's ok." The students continue talking about being responsible for your own actions, both good and bad. After the discussion ends, the teacher checks the group's section of the bulletin board, and the students make plans to finish it before the end of the week.

The teacher also takes them over to the classroom library and introduces them to *Shiloh Season* (Naylor, 1996) and *Saving Shiloh* (Naylor, 2006), the other books in the Shiloh trilogy, and the students eagerly decide to read these two books next.

After the recess break, Mrs. Miller-McColm teaches a word work lesson on suffixes, beginning with the word *changelessness* from *Tuck Everlasting*. She points out the two suffixes, *-less*, meaning "without," and *-ness*, meaning "state of being." The students talk about the word's meaning and how the suffixes affect the root word. Then she shares a list of other words ending in *-less*, including *weightless*, *effortless*, and *careless*. They talk about the meaning of each word and how it changes when it takes on the suffix *-ness*, such as *weightlessness*. Then students use the last 10 minutes of the period to practice their spelling words.

Next, Mrs. Miller-McColm begins writing workshop with a minilesson on writing narrative leads. She displays a chart of four techniques that writers use to hook their audience and explains each one:

Action: The main character does something interesting.

Dialogue: The main character says something interesting.

A thought or a question: The main character shares something that he or she is thinking or asks a question.

A sound: The author begins with an interesting sound related to the story.

She reads aloud the first sentences from *The Sign of the Beaver* (Speare, 2005), *The Breadwinner* (Ellis, 2000), and other novels, and the students identify the hook used in each one. Tomorrow, they will work together as a class to write sample leads using each technique, and the next day, they'll write leads with partners.

After the minilesson, students write independently for 40 minutes. For the past month, they've been writing on self-selected topics; many are writing stories, but some are writing poetry and informational books. Mrs. Miller-McColm has already announced that students should finish the pieces they are working on by Friday because beginning next week, they'll be using writing workshop time to write reports as part of their unit on ancient Egypt.

Some students are working independently, and others are meeting in small groups to revise their writing, conferencing with the teacher, or working with partners to proofread their writing. The four computers are all occupied, too, as students word process their compositions and print out final copies. They place their final copies in a box on Mrs. Miller-McColm's desk and she binds their compositions—handwritten or word processed—into books for them.

During the last 5 minutes of writing workshop, students take turns sitting in the author's chair to read their completed writings aloud. Students sit on the floor and listen attentively as their classmate reads. Ricky, who wants to be a race car driver, reads a book he has researched and written about the Winston Cup Series. He has also included this year's schedule of races and a map of the United States showing where the tracks are. After he finishes reading, students clap and ask questions. Junior asks, "What does NASCAR stand for?" and Ricky explains that it is an acronym for the National Association for Stock Car Automobile Racing. Omar asks for more clarification about how the races are run, and Briana asks how winners of each race gain points. The students get so interested that they don't want to end the discussion, even though it is lunchtime!

In the afternoon, Mrs. Miller-McColm teaches thematic units on social studies and science topics. Currently the topic is ancient Egypt. The students are reading from a text set of books and Internet articles, making notes of important information about ancient Egypt in their learning logs. Mrs. Miller-McColm taught a series of mini-lessons on notetaking at the beginning of the unit, and students are applying what they learned as they read and take notes. For 30 minutes, students finish reading text set materials and taking notes.

Next, Mrs. Miller-McColm brings the class together to talk about the reports they will write. She begins by asking them to highlight the achievements of the ancient Egyptian civilization and they brainstorm a list, including:

the remarkable pyramids
gods and goddesses
how the Egyptians farmed near the Nile River
the mummification process
the hieroglyphic system of writing
Egyptian women's make-up and jewelry

Then she explains that students will choose one achievement that particularly interests them, research it, and share what they learn in a report. They'll also make an artifact to go with the report. If their topic is hieroglyphics, for example, they might make a scroll. The students are excited; they quickly choose topics and suggest artifacts they can make. Mrs. Miller-McColm distributes the rubric that students will use to self-assess their projects and that she'll use to grade them and they read it together. Then she passes around several reports from last year, which the students examine and compare to the rubric to better understand what their teacher wants them to do.

---

*T*eachers use four patterns of practice to involve students in meaningful, functional, and genuine language-learning activities: literature focus units, literature circles, reading and writing workshop, and thematic units. Teachers incorporate a combination of these approaches in their instructional programs, just as Mrs. Miller-McColm did in the vignette. It's not enough to teach language arts using a basal reader or other textbook.

Assessment goes hand in hand with teaching. It should be authentic—based on students using the language arts in genuine and worthwhile ways. Teachers begin by determining students' background knowledge before instruction, and they continue as they monitor students' progress during instruction. Teachers and students collaborate to document students' learning; there are innovative ways to involve students in assessing their own learning and determining grades.

As you read this chapter, you'll learn how to organize for instruction and to assess students' learning. Think about these questions as you continue reading:

- What are literature focus units?
- What are literature circles?
- What is reading and writing workshop?
- What are thematic units?
- How do teachers assess students' learning?

PATTERNS OF PRACTICE

Just as there are many quilt patterns, there are many ways to organize language arts instruction. This text focuses on these four patterns or instructional approaches for teaching language arts: literature focus units, literature circles, reading and writing workshop, and thematic units. All four patterns embody the characteristics of learning described in Chapter 1 and provide opportunities for students to use oral and written language in meaningful, functional, and genuine ways. Teachers organize their instructional programs in different ways, but students need to have opportunities to participate in all four approaches during each school year. Figure 2–1 provides an overview of the four patterns of practice.

FIGURE 2–1

Overview of the Four Patterns of Practice

Features	Literature Focus Units	Literature Circles
Description	Teachers and students read and respond to one text together as a class or in small groups. Teachers choose texts that are high-quality literature selections. After reading, students explore the text and apply their learning by creating projects.	Teachers choose five or six books and collect multiple copies of each one. Students choose the book they want to read and form groups or "book clubs" to read and respond to the book. They develop a reading and discussion schedule, and the teacher participates in some of the discussions.
Strengths	• Teachers develop units using the reading process. • Teachers select picture books or chapter books for units. • Teachers scaffold reading instruction as they read with the whole class. • Teachers teach minilessons on reading strategies and skills. • Students explore vocabulary and literary language. • Students develop projects to apply their reading.	• Books are available at a variety of reading levels. • Students are more strongly motivated because they choose the books they read. • Students have opportunities to work with their classmates. • Students participate in authentic literacy experiences. • Activities are student directed, and students work at their own pace. • Teachers may participate in discussions to help students clarify misunderstandings and think more deeply about the book.
Limitations	• Students all read the same book whether or not they like it and whether or not it's their reading level. • Many of the activities are teacher directed.	• Teachers often feel a loss of control because students are reading different books. • Students must learn to be task oriented and to use time wisely in order to be successful. • Sometimes students choose books that are too difficult or too easy for them.

Teachers usually organize their daily schedule to include two or more of the instructional approaches, as Mrs. Miller-McColm did in the vignette at the beginning of the chapter. When teachers don't have that much time available, they alternate teacher-led literature focus units with student-selected literature circles or reading and writing workshop. Both teacher-led and student-selected instructional patterns provide valuable language-learning opportunities, and no one approach provides all the opportunities that students need. The logical solution is to use a combination of patterns.

Literature Focus Units

Teachers organize literature focus units around a featured selection. Books chosen for literature focus units represent the finest in children's literature; they're books that

---

FIGURE 2–1

Continued

Features	Reading and Writing Workshop	Thematic Units
Description	Students choose books and read and respond to them independently during reading workshop and write books on self-selected topics during writing workshop. Teachers monitor students' work through conferences. Students share the books they read and the books they write with classmates during a sharing period.	Students study social studies or science topics. They use the six language arts as they participate in activities and demonstrate learning. Although content-area textbooks may be used, they are only one resource. Students also identify topics they want to study, so thematic units are authentic learning opportunities.
Strengths	• Students read books appropriate for their reading levels. • Students are more strongly motivated because they choose the books they read. • Students work through the steps of the writing process during writing workshop. • Teachers teach minilessons on reading strategies and skills. • Activities are student directed, and students work at their own pace. • Teachers have opportunities to work individually with students during conferences.	• Students read text sets of stories, informational books, and poetry related to the unit. • Students write in learning logs. • Teachers and students make clusters and other charts to organize information. • Teachers scaffold instruction as students work independently, in small groups, and together as a class. • Students use talk to clarify meanings and give presentations. • Students use computers and technology tools to enhance learning. • Students create projects.
Limitations	• Teachers often feel a loss of control because students are reading different books and working at different stages of the writing process. • Students must learn to be task oriented and to use time wisely in order to be successful.	• Teachers must design thematic units and locate needed resources and other materials. • Thematic units are more time-consuming than textbook-driven social studies and science units.

Booklist

BOOKS FOR LITERATURE FOCUS UNITS

Kindergarten --
Brett, J. (1989). *The mitten*. New York: Putnam.
Henkes, K. (1991). *Chrysanthemum*. New York: Greenwillow.

Simont, M. (2001). *The stray dog*. New York: HarperCollins.

Grade 1 --
Choi, Y. (2001). *The name jar*. New York: Knopf.
Dorros, A. (1991). *Abuela*. New York: Dutton.

Rathmann, P. (1995). *Officer Buckle and Gloria*. New York: Putnam.

Grade 2 --
Bunting, E. (1999). *Smoky night*. San Diego: Harcourt Brace.
Look, L. (2004). *Ruby Lu, brave and true*. New York: Atheneum.

Meddaugh, S. (1995). *Hog-eye*. Boston: Houghton Mifflin.

Grade 3 --
Cohen, B. (1998). *Molly's pilgrim*. New York: Lothrop, Lee & Shepard.
MacLachlan, P. (2004). *Sarah, plain and tall*. New York: HarperCollins.

White, E. B. (2006). *Charlotte's web*. New York: HarperCollins.

Grade 4 --
Naylor, P. R. (2000). *Shiloh*. New York: Aladdin Books.
Ryan, P. M. (2000). *Esperanza rising*. New York: Scholastic.

Gardiner, J. R. (2003). *Stone Fox*. New York: HarperTrophy.

Grade 5 --
Curtis, C. P. (2000). *The Watsons go to Birmingham—1963*. New York: Delacorte.
DiCamillo, K. (2003). *The tale of Despereaux*. New York: Candlewick Press.

Lowry, L. (2005). *Number the stars*. New York: Yearling.

Grade 6 --
Babbitt, N. (2002). *Tuck everlasting*. New York: Farrar, Straus & Giroux.
Hale, S. (2005). *Princess Academy*. New York: Bloomsbury.

Paulsen, G. (2006). *Hatchet*. New York: Aladdin Books.

Grade 7 --
Avi. (2003). *Nothing but the truth: A documentary novel*. New York: Orchard Books.
Sachar, L. (1998). *Holes*. New York: Farrar, Straus, & Giroux.

Whelan, G. (2000). *Homeless bird*. New York: Scholastic.

Grade 8 --
Cushman, K. (1994). *Catherine, called Birdy*. New York: HarperCollins.
Hesse, K. (2001). *Witness*. New York: Scholastic.

Lowry, L. (2006). *The giver*. New York: Delacorte.

every student should read. Several books for each grade level are suggested in the Booklist on page 42. The books must be appropriate for students' interest level, but sometimes they aren't written at their reading level. When they're too difficult for students to read themselves, teachers read them aloud.

Students read the featured selection as a class, and they develop their understanding of the story with the teacher's guidance. In the vignette, for example, Mrs. Miller-McColm was teaching a literature focus unit on *Tuck Everlasting* (Babbitt, 2002). Here are the four components of literature focus units:

🔹 *Reading.* Students read books together as a class or in small groups. They may read independently or together with a partner, or they may read along as the teacher reads the book aloud or guides their reading.

🔹 *Responding.* Students respond to the selection to record their initial impressions of it and to develop their comprehension. They write in reading logs and participate in discussions called *grand conversations*.

🔹 *Teaching Minilessons.* Teachers teach minilessons on language arts procedures, concepts, strategies, and skills and connect the minilessons to books students are reading or compositions they are writing (Atwell, 1998). The steps in teaching a minilesson are shown in the Step by Step box below.

🔹 *Creating Projects.* Students create projects to apply their learning (Luongo-Orlando, 2001). Projects may involve any of the language arts, but children usually choose the projects they create based on their interests and the opportunities the selection presents to them.

Literature Circles

Students meet in small-group literature circles to read and respond to self-selected books (Daniels, 2002; Day, Spiegel, McLellan, & Brown, 2002). What matters most is that students are reading and discussing something that interests them and is manageable in a supportive community of learners. As students participate in literature

---

Minilessons

1 **Introduce the topic.** Teachers introduce the strategy or skill by naming it and making a connection between the topic and the activities going on in the classroom.

2 **Share examples.** Teachers show how to use the topic with examples from students' writing or from children's books.

3 **Provide information.** Teachers provide information, explaining and demonstrating the strategy or skill.

4 **Supervise practice.** Students practice using the strategy or skill with teacher supervision.

5 **Assess learning.** Teachers monitor students' progress and evaluate their use of newly learned strategies or skills.

circles, they learn to view themselves as readers. They have opportunities to read high-quality books that they might not have chosen on their own and read widely (Evans, 2001). They also learn responsibility for completing assignments and to self-assess their learning and work habits (Hill, Johnson, & Noe, 1995; Samway & Whang, 1996). Here are the components of literature circles:

◆ **Reading.** Teachers collect five or six copies of each of six books and give a book talk to introduce each book. Students sign up for the book they want to read and form literature circles to read the book. After working together as a group to create a reading and responding schedule, students read the first part of the book to be ready to participate in the discussion.

◆ **Responding.** Students meet to discuss the book and to reflect on their reading. To facilitate their responding, they often assume roles ranging from discussion director to illustrator and word wizard, and they prepare for their roles before they meet to discuss the book. A list of roles is presented in the LA Essentials box on page 45.

◆ **Creating Projects.** After finishing a book, students prepare projects to present when they share the book with classmates. Students choose the type of project they create. Projects range from murals and dramatizations to poems and choral readings of excerpts.

◆ **Sharing.** Students meet as a class, and each group shares its book. Sometimes students prepare a book talk to share the book; at other times, they create projects to tell about the book. They provide enough information to create interest in the book, but they never tell the ending because they want to encourage classmates to read the book through the sharing activity.

Mrs. Miller-McColm's students in the vignette at the beginning of the chapter participated in literature circles that they called book clubs. These sixth graders participated in activities representing all four components of literature circles.

Reading and Writing Workshop

Two types of workshops are reading workshop and writing workshop. Reading workshop fosters real reading of self-selected stories, poems, and informational books, and writing workshop fosters real writing for genuine purposes and authentic audiences (Atwell, 1998; Cohle & Towle, 2001). Teachers often use the two workshops concurrently, but if their schedule doesn't allow them to do so, they may alternate them. Schedules for reading and writing workshop at the second-, fifth-, and eighth-grade levels are presented in Figure 2–2.

Some teachers fear that their students' standardized achievement test scores will decline if they implement a workshop approach in their classrooms, even though many have reported either an increase in test scores or no change at all. Kathleen Swift (1993) presented the results of a yearlong study comparing two groups of her students, one group reading basal reader stories, and the other participating in reading workshop. The workshop group showed significantly greater improvement, and Swift also reported that students participating in reading workshop showed more positive attitudes toward reading.

Reading Workshop. Students read self-selected books independently during reading workshop and respond to books by writing in reading logs (Atwell, 1998). There are many benefits to reading workshop: Students become more fluent readers and deepen their appreciation of books and reading, they develop lifelong reading habits,

ROLES STUDENTS PLAY IN LITERATURE CIRCLES

Discussion Director

The discussion director guides the group's discussion and keeps the group on task. To get the discussion started or to redirect the discussion, the discussion director may ask:

- What did the reading make you think of?
- What questions do you have about the reading?
- What do you predict will happen next?

Passage Master

The passage master focuses on the literary merits of the book. This student chooses several memorable passages to share with the group and tells why he or she chose each one.

Word Wizard

The word wizard is responsible for vocabulary. This student identifies four to six important, unfamiliar words from the reading and looks them up in the dictionary. The word wizard selects the most appropriate meaning and other interesting information about the word to share.

Connector

The connector makes meaningful personal, world, or literary connections. These connections might include events at school or in the community, current events or historical events, or something from the connector's own life. Or the connector can make comparisons with other books.

Summarizer

The summarizer prepares a brief summary of the reading to convey the main ideas to share with the group. This student often begins the discussion by reading the summary aloud to the group.

Illustrator

The illustrator draws a picture or diagram related to the reading. It might involve a character, an event, or a prediction. The student shares the illustration with the group, and the group talks about it before the illustrator explains it.

Investigator

The investigator locates some information about the book, the author, or a related topic to share with the group. This student may search the Internet, check an encyclopedia, or interview a person with special expertise.

FIGURE 2–2

Schedules for Reading and Writing Workshop

Second-Grade Schedule

15 minutes	Reading aloud to students
15 minutes	Teaching a minilesson (on a reading or writing topic)
30 minutes	Reading and responding
15 minutes	Sharing
	—Later—
30 minutes	Writing
15 minutes	Sharing

This 2-hour schedule is broken into two parts. The first 75 minutes, scheduled in the morning, focuses on reading, and the last 45 minutes, scheduled after lunch, is devoted to writing.

Fifth-Grade Schedule

40 minutes	Reading and responding
20 minutes	Teaching a minilesson (on a reading or writing topic)
40 minutes	Writing
20 minutes	Sharing

This schedule is also planned for 2 hours. The minilesson separates the two independent work sessions, and during the sharing session, students share books they have read, response projects they have created, and compositions they have published.

Eighth-Grade Schedule

40 minutes	Reading and responding or writing
15 minutes	Teaching a minilesson (on Mondays–Thursdays)
	Sharing (on Fridays)

The eighth-grade schedule is for 55 minutes. Because of time limitations, students alternate reading and writing workshop, minilessons are scheduled for 4 days each week, and sharing is held on Fridays.

they're introduced to different genres, and they choose favorite authors. Most important, students come to think of themselves as readers (Daniels, 2002). Here are the components of reading workshop:

◆ *Reading and Responding.* Students spend 30 to 60 minutes independently reading books and other reading materials. They also keep reading logs for writing responses to their reading and participate in conferences with the teacher to enrich their understanding of favorite books.

◆ *Sharing.* For the last 15 minutes of reading workshop, the class gathers together to share books they've read and enjoyed.

◆ *Teaching Minilessons.* The teacher spends approximately 15 minutes teaching minilessons on reading workshop procedures, literary concepts, and reading strategies and skills.

Writing Workshop. Writing workshop is a way of implementing the writing process (Atwell, 1998; Calkins, 1994; Fletcher & Portalupi, 2001). Students usually write on topics they choose themselves, and they assume ownership of their learning. The classroom becomes a community of writers who write and share their writing, and students come to see themselves as writers (Samway, 2006). They practice writing skills and strategies and learn to choose words carefully to articulate their ideas. Perhaps most important, they see firsthand the power of writing to entertain, inform, and persuade.

Students' writing grows out of their personal experiences, books they have read or listened to read aloud, and content-area study (Gillet & Beverly, 2001; Graves, 1994; Heffernan, 2004). They write personal narratives about experiences and events in their lives, create sequels to favorite books, and retell stories from different viewpoints. Young children often use the pattern or refrain from a familiar book, such as *Brown Bear, Brown Bear, What Do You See?* (Martin, 2007) and *The Important Book* (Brown, 1990), to structure their stories. Students experiment with other genres, such as poetry and scripts, after reading examples of the genre and learning about them. They also use writing workshop to write letters, book reviews, reports, and other projects as part of thematic units. In the vignette at the beginning of the chapter, Mrs. Miller-McColm's sixth graders were writing reports on ancient Egypt during writing workshop.

Writing workshop is a 60- to 90-minute period scheduled each day. During this time, the teacher and the students are involved in these activities:

◆ **Writing.** Students spend 30 to 45 minutes working independently on writing projects. They move at their own pace through all five stages of the writing process—prewriting, drafting, revising, editing, and publishing. Many times, students compile their final copies to make books during writing workshop, but sometimes they attach their writing to artwork, make posters, write letters that are mailed, or perform scripts as skits or puppet shows.

◆ **Sharing.** Students gather together to share their new publications with the class and to make related announcements. For example, a student who has just finished writing a puppet-show script and making puppets may ask for volunteers to help perform the puppet show, which could be presented several days later during sharing time. Younger children often sit in a circle or gather together on a rug for sharing time. The student who is sharing sits in a special chair, labeled the "author's chair," to read his or her composition. After the reading, classmates clap and offer compliments. They may also make other comments and suggestions, but the focus is on celebrating completed writing projects, not on revising the composition to make it better.

◆ **Teaching Minilessons.** During this 15- to 30-minute period, teachers present minilessons on writing workshop procedures, literary concepts, and writing skills and strategies (Fletcher & Portalupi, 1998; Portalupi & Fletcher, 2001). They also talk about authors of children's trade books and the writing strategies and skills these authors use.

Teachers often add a fourth component to writing workshop in which they read stories aloud to share examples of good writing with students. This activity helps students to feel a part of the community of writers.

Thematic Units

Thematic units integrate language arts with social studies, science, and other curricular areas (Lindquist & Selwyn, 2000). Students use all the language arts as they investigate, solve problems, and learn during a unit (Rief, 1999). They also use language arts to demonstrate their new learning at the end of the unit. These language arts activities occur during thematic units:

◆ *Reading.* Students read informational books and magazines, stories, and poems related to the unit as well as content-area textbooks. They also research topics on the Internet.

◆ *Keeping Learning Logs.* Students keep learning logs in which they write entries about new concepts they are learning, record new and interesting words, make charts and diagrams, and reflect on their learning.

◆ *Making Visual Representations.* Students create clusters, maps, time lines, Venn diagrams, data charts, and other diagrams and displays. They use these visual representations as tools to organize information and represent relationships about the topic they are studying (Moline, 1995).

◆ *Creating Projects.* Students create projects to apply their learning and demonstrate their new knowledge. These projects range from alphabet books and oral reports to posters and dramatizations.

In the vignette, Mrs. Miller-McColm's students were involved in a thematic unit on ancient Egypt, and they participated in all four language arts activities during the unit.

THE TEACHER'S ROLE

The teacher's role is complex and multidimensional. No longer are teachers simply providers of knowledge, nor do they assign an endless series of worksheets and busywork. Instead, teachers understand that students' literacy develops most effectively through meaningful social contexts. These teachers plan for instruction

Bob Daemmrich / The Image Works

A Teacher at Work

This third-grade teacher organizes instruction into literature focus units, literature circles, reading/writing workshop, and thematic units. Now the students are involved in writing workshop. One group meets with the teacher while others write independently or confer with classmates. This teacher is an instructor and a participant; she teaches the students and learns along with them. She manages the classroom effectively; the classroom is arranged to facilitate learning. The third graders understand the routines and their teacher's expectations.

using the four patterns of practice to meet the needs of their students. Their goal is to help children develop communicative competence and to excite them about literacy.

Teachers direct the life of the classroom. They are instructors, coaches, facilitators, and managers. Figure 2–3 lists some of the roles teachers assume.

What About Teaching?

You could say that everything a teacher does during the four patterns of practice is teaching, and in a sense it is. Although teaching is defined as providing information, teachers do two kinds of teaching. One kind is direct instruction, where teachers teach minilessons in which they explicitly present information, provide opportunities for supervised practice, and then have students apply what they have learned through reading and writing activities. Direct instruction has been associated with skill-and-drill activities, but it doesn't have to be. This kind of teaching is necessary to provide information and opportunities for students to apply what they are learning with guidance from the teacher.

The second kind is indirect instruction. Teachers use indirect instruction for brief, on-the-spot lessons as they respond to students' questions or when students demonstrate the need to know something. These interactions take place during whole-class activities, during conferences with students, and while working with small groups.

Differentiating Instruction

Teachers know that students vary—their interests and motivation, their background knowledge and prior experiences, and their culture and language proficiency as well as their language arts capabilities—so it's important to allow for these differences as they plan for instruction. According to Carol Ann Tomlinson (2001), differentiated instruction "means 'shaking up' what goes on in the classroom so that students have multiple options for taking information, making sense of ideas, and expressing what they learn" (p. 1). Differentiating instruction is especially important for students who haven't been successful and who can't handle grade-level reading and writing assignments and for very capable students who aren't challenged by grade-level assignments.

Teachers differentiate instruction as they implement the patterns of practice in their classrooms. Here are five ways to differentiate instruction:

◆ *Offer Choices.* Teachers offer choices when students select books to read in literature circles and in reading workshop, and students often choose their writing topics and genres during writing workshop. Students also make choices about the projects they create during literature focus units and thematic units.

◆ *Use Small Groups.* Teachers group students flexibly for literature circles, guided reading, writing groups, and other instructional activities. Students also work in small groups to develop projects and to write reports and other compositions.

◆ *Set Up Centers.* Teachers set up centers with instructional materials for students to practice concepts they're studying and to extend their learning.

◆ *Integrate All Six Language Arts.* Teachers provide opportunities for students to develop expertise in all six language arts, not just reading and writing. Because many students are better able to understand and express themselves through the oral

FIGURE 2–3

Teacher Roles During Language Arts Instruction

Role	Description
Organizer	Creates a language-rich environment. Sets time schedules. Uses the four patterns of practice. Uses the language arts as tools for learning across the curriculum.
Facilitator	Develops a community of learners. Stimulates students' interest in language and literacy. Allows students to choose books to read and topics for projects. Provides opportunities for students to use language in meaningful, functional, and genuine ways. Involves parents in classroom and out-of-classroom literacy activities.
Participant	Reads and writes with students. Learns along with students. Asks questions and seeks answers to questions.
Instructor	Provides information about books, authors, and illustrators. Explains language arts procedures. Teaches minilessons on concepts, skills, and strategies. Activates and builds background knowledge before reading, writing, and viewing. Groups students flexibly for instruction.
Model	Demonstrates procedures, strategies, and skills. Reads aloud to students every day.
Manager	Sets expectations and responsibilities. Monitors students' progress. Keeps records. Arranges the classroom to facilitate learning. Provides technology hardware and software to support language arts activities.
Diagnostician	Conferences with students. Observes students participating in language arts activities. Assesses students' strengths and weaknesses. Plans instruction based on students' needs.
Evaluator	Assesses students' progress in language arts. Helps students self-assess their learning. Assigns grades. Examines the effectiveness of the language arts program.
Coordinator	Works with librarians, aides, and parent volunteers. Works with other teachers on grade-level projects, pen pal programs, and cross-age reading programs.
Communicator	Expects students to do their best. Encourages students to become lifelong readers and writers. Communicates the language arts program to parents and administrators. Shares language arts goals and activities with parents and the community.

and visual language arts than through the written language arts, using all six language arts scaffolds their learning. Other students who are capable readers and writers may have less expertise in the other language arts and need to develop those abilities, too.

◆ *Incorporate Projects.* Teachers have students create projects as the final step in literature focus units and thematic units so that they have opportunities to explore topics that interest them and demonstrate their learning in authentic ways.

When teachers consider the needs of their students and incorporate these five ways to differentiate instruction into their plans, students are more likely to be successful.

Meeting the Needs of English Learners

How Do Teachers Adapt Instruction for English Learners?

Classroom Environment

Create a community of learners so that students feel valued and are comfortable taking risks and admitting when they are confused or need assistance.

Grouping Patterns

Vary grouping patterns so that English learners have regular opportunities to work in small groups, individually, and with the whole class. When students work in small groups, they collaborate and learn from their classmates.

Minilessons

Teach minilessons regularly, and reteach the minilessons to small groups of English learners who need additional practice.

Visuals

Integrate visuals, including realia, photographs, charts, maps, and diagrams, into the language arts program.

Background Knowledge

Take time to build students' background knowledge, and introduce important vocabulary words before teaching difficult concepts.

Oral Language

Provide opportunities for students to talk with classmates, and use talk to support their written language development.

Centers

Incorporate centers so English learners have an opportunity to work collaboratively on activities and projects and learn from their classmates.

Monitor Students

Monitor students' progress closely and provide assistance when needed so they can be successful.

ASSESSING STUDENTS' LEARNING

Assessing students' learning in language arts is a difficult task. Although it may seem fairly easy to develop and administer a criterion-referenced test, tests measure language skills rather than students' ability to use language in authentic ways. Nor do tests measure listening, talking, and viewing very well. A test on punctuation marks, for example, doesn't demonstrate students' ability to use punctuation marks correctly in their own writing. Instead, such a test typically evaluates whether students can add punctuation marks to a set of sentences created by someone else or proofread to spot punctuation errors in someone else's writing. A far better alternative approach is to examine how students use punctuation marks in their own writing.

Traditional assessment reflects outdated views of how students learn to read and write and offers an incomplete picture of students' language abilities. Tests focus on only a few aspects of what readers do as they read, what listeners do as they listen, and what writers do as they write. Traditional assessment fails to use authentic language tasks or to assist teachers in finding ways to help students succeed.

Assessment should resemble real language use (Valencia, Hiebert, & Afflerbach, 1994). A better approach is authentic assessment, in which teachers examine both the processes that students use as they listen, talk, read, write, view, and visually represent and the artifacts or products they create, such as projects and reading logs. Students, too, participate in reflecting on and assessing their own learning. Authentic assessment has five purposes:

- To document milestones in students' language and literacy development
- To identify students' strengths in order to plan for instruction
- To document students' language arts activities and projects
- To determine grades
- To help teachers learn more about how students become strategic readers and writers

Assessment is more than testing; it is an integral part of teaching and learning (Tierney, 2005). The purpose of classroom assessment is to inform and influence instruction. Through authentic assessment, teachers learn about their students, about themselves as teachers, and about the impact of the instructional program. Similarly, when students reflect on their learning and use self-assessment, they learn about themselves as learners and also about their learning. The LA Essentials box on page 53 presents guidelines for authentic assessment and describes how teachers use authentic assessment tools in their classrooms.

Monitoring Students' Progress

Teachers monitor students' progress as they are involved in language arts activities during literature focus units, literature circles, reading and writing workshop, and thematic units, and they use the results of their monitoring to inform their teaching. Four ways to monitor students' progress are classroom observations, anecdotal notes, conferences, and checklists.

Classroom Observations. Language arts teachers engage in "kid watching," a term that Yetta Goodman coined and defined as "direct and informal observation

LITERATURE FOCUS UNIT

Reading

The fifth graders in Mrs. Kenney's class are reading Roald Dahl's delicious fantasy, *Charlie and the Chocolate Factory* (2004). It's the story of Charlie Bucket, an honest and kind boy, who finds the fifth winning Golden Ticket, entitling him to a visit inside Willy Wonka's famous chocolate factory. Charlie and the four other children who also found winning tickets have a wild time visiting the factory, and, in the end, Mr. Wonka gives Charlie the best present of all—his factory!

Mrs. Kenney varies the ways students read each chapter. She reads the first chapter aloud, using whole-class shared reading, and students follow along in their copies of the book. For the other chapters, students alternate reading independently, reading with a buddy, reading in small groups, and reading together as a class.

Create your own Wonka goodie.

Responding

Mrs. Kenney's students respond to the story in two ways. They participate in small-group and whole-class discussions called grand conversations.

In these lively discussions, they share their ideas about the story, ask questions to clarify misunderstandings, and make connections to their own lives. Mrs. Kenney participates in the whole-class grand conversations and often asks students to think about Charlie and compare him to the other four children who visit Willy Wonka's chocolate factory.

The fifth graders also write in double-entry reading logs. At the beginning of the literature focus unit, students staple together booklets of paper for their journals and divide each page into two columns. After reading each chapter, they choose a quote and write it in the left column and then write a response in the right column.

Quote	Response
Ch. 19 Pg. 94 "The place was like a witch's kitchen!"	I chose this quote because did you know — it's a simile!

QUOTE	MY THOUGHTS
Ch 11 Pg 50 "You've got a Golden Ticket! You found the last Golden Ticket! Hey, what do you know?"	I feel excited and happy because Charlie never had anything much in his life. Maybe now his life will take a turn for the better.

Teaching Minilessons

Mrs. Kenney and her students choose important words from each chapter as they read *Charlie and the Chocolate Factory*. The words are organized by parts of speech on the word wall because Mrs. Kenney is teaching a series of minilessons about the parts of speech. The noun list includes *hooligan*, *precipice*, and *verdict*; the verb list includes *beckoned*, *revolt*, *stammer*, and *criticize*. The adjective list includes *despicable*, *scraggy*, and *repulsive*; *ravenously*, *violently*, and *frantically* are on the adverb list.

Mrs. Kenney also uses the words from the word wall as she teaches minilessons on root words and affixes to small groups of students. Students take turns choosing a word from the word wall and breaking apart the word's prefix, root, and suffix as Mrs. Kenney writes the information on the dry-erase board. Then students record the information on small, individual dry-erase boards.

In this literature focus unit, Mrs. Kenney is focusing on character. During a series of minilessons, students investigate how Roald Dahl developed Charlie's character and compare him with Willy Wonka and the other four children with winning Golden Tickets.

After studying about the characters, students create open-mind portraits of one of the characters. One student's open-mind portrait of Willy Wonka is shown here. The portrait goes on top and the page showing his thoughts goes underneath.

Creating Projects

Students create a variety of projects to extend the book and apply their learning. These two boys created a model of Willy Wonka's chocolate factory. Other students researched how chocolate is made and created a poster to display what they learned, wrote poems about each of the characters in *Charlie and the Chocolate Factory*, or read another of Roald Dahl's stories.

As the concluding activity, Mrs. Kenney and her students view *Willy Wonka and the Chocolate Factory*, the film version of the story starring Gene Wilder. Afterwards, students work in small groups to create Venn diagrams comparing the book and the film versions. One student's Venn diagram is shown here. After discussing the differences, most students agree that they preferred the book.

LITERATURE CIRCLES

Reading

Mrs. Goodman's eighth graders participate in literature circles. Mrs. Goodman introduces eight books written at varying levels of difficulty, and students sign up for the book they want to read. The students are currently reading these books:

- *The Outsiders,* by S. E. Hinton (2006)
- *The Face on the Milk Carton,* by Caroline Cooney (1990)
- *Holes,* by Louis Sachar (1998)
- *I Am the Cheese,* by Robert Cormier (1977)
- *To Kill a Mockingbird,* by Harper Lee (2002)
- *What Jamie Saw,* by Carolyn Coman (1997)

Students have set a reading schedule and they spend time reading during class and at home.

Students in each literature circle assume roles to deepen their understanding of the story and ensure the smooth functioning of their group. They rotate these roles each day so that everyone has the opportunity to experience all roles.

ROLES IN A LITERATURE CIRCLE		
1	Discussion Leader	This student keeps classmates focused on the big ideas in the story.
2	Harmonizer	This student helps everyone stay on task and show respect to classmates.
3	Wordsmith	This student identifies important words in the story and checks the meaning of words in a dictionary.
4	Connector	This student connects events in the story with real-life experiences.
5	Illustrator	This student draws pictures to help classmates visualize events in the story.

Responding

Students frequently meet in their literature circles to discuss the story they are reading, and students fulfill their roles. They talk about what's happening in the story, ask questions to clarify confusion, make connections to their own lives, and predict what will happen next. As students talk, Mrs. Goodman circulates around the classroom, joining each group for a few minutes.

Students also write in reading logs. Sometimes they write summaries and make predictions, and at other times they write reflections and ask questions. After writing, students often divide into groups of two or three to read their entries to classmates.

Reading Log

I am liking To Kill a Mockingbird a lot. But it's very different from other books I've read. Instead of describing the scenery and how the people look, it tells the history of everything. The book tells you what has happened. That makes it harder to picture what is happening but easier to make up what you want. I don't think I've ever read a description of Scout anywhere in the book. I didn't quite understand the beginning of the book because it was introducing everything really fast. But now, I'm beginning to understand what is going on.

Reading Log

My questions are:

- *Why don't Scout and Jim call their father Dad but use his real name (Atticus)?*

- *Why doesn't Scout play with other girls?*

- *What does everyone look like?*

- *Why doesn't anyone search for the truth about the Radleys?*

Creating Projects

Students create projects after they finish reading and discussing a story. They write poems and sequels, research a topic on the Internet, develop PowerPoint presentations, create artifacts related to the story, and design story quilts.

After students identify a project they want to develop, they meet with Mrs. Goodman and she approves their choice and helps them get started.

"When Jamie saw Van Throw Nin"

This picture is a square from a story quilt about *What Jamie Saw*, a story about child abuse. Students in the literature circle draw pictures to represent events from the book and put them together to make the quilt, which presents a strong message about the effects of child abuse.

Sharing

Sharing is the concluding activity. Students in each literature circle share the book they have read and their project with Mrs. Goodman and the class. Sometimes students work together to give a group presentation to the class, and sometimes students develop individual presentations. The students demonstrate their understanding of the story through their presentation, and they hope to interest their classmates in choosing the book and reading the story.

Mrs. Goodman explains how students will be graded before the literature circle begins and posts the criteria in the classroom. For this literature circle, students are graded on four items; each item is worth 25 points. At the end of the literature circle, Mrs. Goodman prepares a grading sheet with the criteria, grades students' work, and assigns the grades.

GRADING SHEET

Name _Justin_

Book _The Face on the Milk Carton_

1. Reading Log _____ 20

2. Roles in the Literature Circle _____ 25

3. Working Together in a Group _____ 25

4. Project at the End _____ 22

_(92)_

READING AND WRITING WORKSHOP

Reading & Responding

Mrs. McClenaghan's fifth and sixth graders participate in reading workshop for an hour each morning. The students read books they have selected from the classroom library, including *A Wrinkle in Time* (L'Engle, 2007), *The Sign of the Beaver* (Speare, 2005), *Harry Potter and the Sorcerer's Stone* (Rowling, 1997), *Missing May* (Rylant, 1992), and *Tuck Everlasting* (Babbitt, 2002).

Students also respond to the books they're reading, and their response activities vary according to what Mrs. McClenaghan is teaching. This week's focus is on a reading strategy—forming interpretations. The students identify a big idea in the chapter they are reading and provide evidence from the text to support the idea on T-charts they have made.

Conferencing

As her students read and respond, Mrs. McClenaghan moves around the classroom, stopping to conference with students. She asks students to read a short excerpt and tell about their reading experience and the reading strategies they are using. They talk about the story so Mrs. McClenaghan can monitor their comprehension and clarify any misunderstandings. She carries a clipboard with her and writes notes about each student, including what book the student is reading and the progress he or she is making.

Reading Aloud

Mrs. McClenaghan is reading aloud *The Cay* (Taylor, 2003), a survival story about an elderly African American man and a Caucasian boy who are shipwrecked in the Caribbean and become friends through the experience. She reads aloud a chapter or two each day, and the students talk about the story in a grand conversation. She also uses the book in the minilessons she is teaching.

Teaching Minilessons

These fifth and sixth graders have been examining the strategies that good readers use, such as asking questions, making connections, and visualizing, in a series of minilessons. Today, Mrs. McClenaghan focuses on making inferences. She explains that good readers read between the lines to figure out the author's message. She rereads a passage from *The Cay* and asks the students to identify the big idea in the passage. Then she makes a T-chart on a dry-erase board and records their answers. In the first column, she writes the big idea, and in the second, a quote from the text to support the big idea. Then she reads another passage several pages later in the text, and they rephrase the big idea to clarify it and finish the chart.

BIG Idea	Text Evidence
It's about friendship.	p. 76 I said to Timothy, "I want to be your friend." He said softly, "Young bahss, you 'ave always been my friend."
It doesn't matter what color you are, you can still be friends.	p. 79 "I don't like some white people my own self, but 'twould be outrageous if I didn't like any o' dem."

Writing

After spending 60 minutes in reading workshop, students begin writing workshop, which lasts for 45 minutes. Students usually write two- to four-page stories about events in their own lives—autobiographical incidents— during writing workshop. They work at their own pace, moving through the stages of the writing process. Most students write four or five drafts as they develop and refine the content of their writing.

Responding

Students meet with classmates and with Mrs. McClenaghan several times during the writing process to revise and edit their writing. The students provide useful feedback to classmates because they have learned about the qualities of a good piece of writing and they know how to identify problem spots.

Really Hungry

One day, when it was close to dinner time, my big brother was so hungry he got there before any of us. He was waiting impatiently and when we were at the table with our food in front of us he already started devouring the vegetables and rice.

My mother looked at him, and he stopped stuffing himself. He waited very impatiently while she said grace. Mother's grace isn't short but it isn't very long either. He fidgeted and squirmed untill she finished. "You should make it shorter," he said.

He gobbled all of his rice, vegetables and chicken. We watched him in amazement. He asked for seconds and he started to swallow his food.

"Don't eat like that," snapped my mother. "Disgusting!" She bit her chicken wing and chewed.

Teaching Minilessons

In this writing minilesson, Mrs. McClenaghan shares an essay written by a student from another class. She asks the students to rate it using their district's 6-point writing rubric. They raise their hands and show with their fingers the score they would give the paper. Most students rate it a 4, and Mrs. McClenaghan agrees. They talk about the strong points in the paper and the areas where improvement is needed.

Then Mrs. McClenaghan reviews the asking-questions and magnifying-a-sentence revision strategies and the symbols students use to represent the two strategies. Next, students reread the essay and attach small self-stick notes to the paper with the symbols written on them to indicate revision points. Students also underline the specific sentence to which each note refers.

Sharing

During the last 5 minutes of writing workshop, one student sits in the author's chair and shares a newly published composition. The classmates clap and offer compliments after the student finishes reading. They are an appreciative audience because Mrs. McClenaghan and her students have developed a supportive classroom community.

THEMATIC UNITS

Reading

Ms. McCloskey works with 40 kindergarten through third-grade students in their multiage classroom. The children are engaged in a thematic unit on insects, integrating all areas of the curriculum. They participate in a variety of reading activities. They listen to Ms. McCloskey read books aloud and read along with her as she shares big books. During centers time, they reread familiar books with buddies and read independently. They also read other books at their own reading levels during guided reading.

Learning Logs

Each day, children write entries for their learning logs at the writing center. They meet with Ms. Russell, a student teacher working in the classroom, to write about insects. Many of the students are English learners, so Ms. Russell helps them to expand their sentences and include science words in their entries. She also reviews spelling, capitalization, punctuation, and grammar skills with individual children. Then children file their papers in their learning log folders, which are kept at the writing center. At the end of the thematic unit, children compile their learning logs and decorate the covers.

This entry, titled "Wings," was written by a kindergartner who is still learning about capital letters and punctuation marks. He added the second part, "because it has wings," in response to Ms. Russell's question, "How can a ladybug fly?"

WFs

A LadeBug can fly,
BeKCse it hs wfs.

Visual Representations

A Bee

Head

Abdomen   Thorax

SPIDERS   INSECTS

2 body parts   3 body parts
1. head   1. head
2. abdomen   2. thorax
                           3. abdomen

8 Legs   6 legs

No wings   Wings

Spin webs   No webs

The children make diagrams, charts, and drawings to record information they are learning about insects. They learn to draw insects accurately with three body parts and six legs. They use diagrams to organize information they are learning as Ms. McCloskey reads a book or presents a demonstration. They also use attribute charts to record descriptive words as they observe insects in the "Look and Learn" science center.

Creating Projects

The children are creating a multigenre display on insects. Each child writes a story, poem, or report for the display, which will cover an entire wall of the classroom. The children use the writing process to develop their compositions, and all children, even the kindergartners, type their final copies on the computer with Ms. McCloskey's assistance.

What body Parts?
thorax
head
abdomen
wings
stinger
antennae
legs
eyes

Where do they live?
colony
hive

Bees

What type of bees?
queen bee
drone bee
worker bees

What do they eat?
Pollen
nectar

The Bees

Bees have three body parts: a thorax, an abdomen, and a head. On their body they have some little and big wings, a stinger, two antennae, six legs, and two large black eyes.

The bees live in a hive. Sometimes bees live in a group of bees, and it is called a colony. A lot of bees live in a colony and a lot of bees live in a hive.

There are three kinds of bees. There is a queen bee, a drone bee, and worker bees. The queen lays eggs on the hive and the worker bees take car of the baby bees. One of the worker bees gets pollen from the flowers. Whe the worker bees get pollen, they danc because they can't talk.

Bees eat pollen and nectar to ma honey. When bees make honey they have to go get pollen and nectar. W need bees because bees could mal honey for us. If bees is not in this stat there will be no honey for us.

Dragonfly

Dragonfly fly, fly, fly.
Dragonfly fly around the pond.
Dragonfly fly by the flower.
Dragonfly fly by me.
Dragonfly fly, fly, fly.

GUIDELINES FOR AUTHENTIC ASSESSMENT

- **Choose Appropriate Assessment Tools**

  Teachers identify their purpose for assessment and choose an appropriate assessment tool. To judge spelling development, for example, teachers examine students' spelling in books they write and their use of proofreading, as well as their performance on spelling tests.

- **Use a Variety of Assessment Tools**

  Teachers regularly use a variety of authentic assessment tools, including anecdotal notes, that reflect current theories about how children learn.

- **Integrate Instruction and Assessment**

  Teachers use the results of assessment to inform their teaching. They observe and conference with students as they teach and supervise students during language arts activities.

- **Keep a Positive Focus**

  Teachers focus on what students can do, not what they can't do. They focus on how to facilitate students' development as readers, writers, and users of language.

- **Examine Both Processes and Products**

  Teachers examine both the language processes students use and the products they create. They notice the strategies students use for language activities as well as assess the quality of students' work.

- **Consider Multiple Contexts**

  Teachers assess students' language arts development in a variety of contexts, including literature focus units, thematic units, and reading and writing workshop. Multiple contexts are important because students often do better in one context than in another.

- **Focus on Individual Students**

  In addition to whole-class assessments, teachers make time to observe, conference with, and do other assessment procedures with individual students in order to develop clear understandings of each student's development.

- **Teach Students to Self-Assess Their Learning**

  Self-assessment is an integral part of assessment. Students reflect on their progress in reading, writing, and the other language arts.

Weaving Assessment Into Practice

NOTES ABOUT MATTHEW

March 5	Matthew selected Ben Franklin as historical figure for American Revolution project.
March 11	Matthew fascinated with information he has found about B. F. Brought several sources from home. Is completing B. F.'s lifeline with many details.
March 18	Simulated journal. Four entries in four days! Interesting how he picked up language style of the period in his journal. Volunteers to share daily. I think he enjoys the oral sharing more than the writing.
March 24	Nine simulated journal entries, all illustrated. High level of enthusiasm.
March 28	Conferenced about cluster for B. F. biography. Well-developed with five rays, many details. Matthew will work on "contributions" ray. He recognized it as the least developed one.
April 2	Three chapters of biography drafted. Talked about "working titles" for chapters and choosing more interesting titles after writing that reflect the content of the chapters.
April 7	Drafting conference. Matthew has completed all five chapters. He and Dustin are competitive, both writing on B. F. They are reading each other's chapters and checking the accuracy of information.
April 11	Writing group. Matthew confused Declaration of Independence with the Constitution. Chapters longer and more complete since drafting conference. Compared with autobiography project, writing is more sophisticated. Longer, too. Reading is influencing writing style—e.g., "Luckily for Ben." He is still somewhat defensive about accepting suggestions except from me. He will make 3 revisions—agreed in writing group.
April 14	Revisions: (1) eliminated "he" (substitute), (2) resequenced Chapter 3 (move), and (3) added sentences in Chapter 5 (add)
April 23	Editing conference—no major problems. Discussed use of commas within sentences, capitalizing proper nouns. Matthew and Dustin more task-oriented on this project; I see more motivation and commitment.
April 29	Final copy of biography completed and shared with class.

of students" (1978, p. 37). To be effective kid watchers, teachers must understand how children develop language and must understand the role of errors in language learning. Teachers use kid watching spontaneously when they interact with students and are attentive to their behavior and comments. Other observation times should be planned when the teacher focuses on particular students and makes anecdotal notes about their involvement in literacy events and other language arts activities. The focus is on what students do as they use oral and written language, not on whether they are behaving properly or working quietly. Of course, little learning can occur in disruptive situations, but during these observations, the focus is on language, not behavior.

Anecdotal Notes. Teachers write brief notes as they observe students; the most useful notes describe specific events, report rather than evaluate, and relate the events to other information about the students (Rhodes & Nathenson-Mejia, 1992). Teachers make notes about students' performance in listening, talking, reading, writing, viewing, and visually representing activities; about the questions students ask; and about the strategies and skills they use fluently or indicate confusion about. These records document students' growth and pinpoint instructional needs (Boyd-Batstone, 2004). A yearlong collection of records provides a comprehensive picture of a student's learning in language arts. An excerpt from a fifth-grade teacher's anecdotal notes about one student's progress during a unit on the American Revolution appears in the Weaving Assessment Into Practice feature on page 54.

Several organizational schemes for anecdotal notes are possible, and teachers should use the format that is most comfortable for them. Some teachers make a card file with dividers for each child and write anecdotes on notecards. They feel comfortable jotting notes on these small cards or even carrying around a set of cards in a pocket. Other teachers divide a spiral-bound notebook into sections for each student and write anecdotes in the notebook, which they keep on their desk. A third technique is to write anecdotes on small sheets of paper and clip the sheets in students' assessment folders.

Conferences. Teachers talk with students to monitor their progress in language arts activities as well as to set goals and help students solve problems (Gill, 2000). Seven types of conferences are described in Figure 2–4. Often these conferences are brief and impromptu, held at students' desks as the teacher moves around the classroom; at other times, the conferences are planned, and students meet with the teacher at a designated conference table.

The teacher's role is to be listener and guide. Teachers can learn a great deal about students and their learning if they listen as students talk about their reading, writing, or other activities. When students explain a problem they are having, the teacher is often able to decide on a way to work through it. Graves (1994) suggests that teachers balance the amount of their talk with the student's talk during the conference and, at the end, reflect on what the student has taught them, what responsibilities the student can take, and whether the student understands what to do next.

Checklists. Teachers use checklists as they observe students; as they track students' progress during literature focus units, literature circles, reading and writing workshop, and thematic units; and as they document students' use of language arts skills, strategies, procedures, and concepts. For example, when students participate in writing conferences in which they read their compositions to small groups of classmates and ask for suggestions for improving their writing, teachers can note whether students participate fully in the group, share their writing with classmates, gracefully accept suggestions about improving their writing, and make substantive changes in their writing based on some of their classmates' suggestions. Students can even help develop the checklists so that they understand what types of behavior are expected of them.

A "Weekly Reading-Writing Workshop Activity Sheet" appears in the Weaving Assessment Into Practice feature on page 57. Third graders complete this checklist each week to monitor their work during reading and writing workshop. Notice that

FIGURE 2–4

Types of Conferences

On-the-Spot Conferences

The teacher visits with students at their desks to monitor some aspect of the students' work or to check on progress. These conferences are brief; the teacher may spend less than a minute at each student's desk.

Prereading or Prewriting Conferences

The teacher and the student make plans for reading or writing at the conference. At a prereading conference, they may talk about information related to the book, difficult concepts or vocabulary words related to the reading, or the reading log the student will keep. At a prewriting conference, they may discuss possible writing topics or how to narrow a broad topic.

Revising Conferences

A small group of students meet with the teacher to get specific suggestions about revising their compositions. These conferences offer student writers an audience to provide feedback on how well they have communicated.

Book Discussion Conferences

Students and the teacher meet to discuss the book they have read. They may share reading log entries, discuss plot or characters, compare the story to others they have read, or make plans to extend their reading.

Editing Conferences

The teacher reviews students' proofread compositions and helps them correct spelling, punctuation, capitalization, and other mechanical errors.

Minilesson Conferences

The teacher meets with students to explain a procedure, strategy, or skill (e.g., writing a table of contents, using the visualization strategy when reading, or capitalizing proper nouns).

Assessment Conferences

The teacher meets with students after they have completed an assignment or project to talk about their growth as readers or writers. Students reflect on their competences and set goals.

---

students are directed to write a letter to the teacher on the back of the sheet, reflecting on their work during that week.

Implementing Portfolios in the Classroom

Portfolios are systematic and meaningful collections of artifacts documenting students' language arts learning and development over a period of time (Porter & Cleland, 1995). These collections are dynamic, and they reflect students' day-to-day learning activities in language arts and across the curriculum. Students' work samples provide windows on the strategies they employ as language users—readers, writers, listeners, viewers, and talkers.

Portfolio programs complement language arts instruction in many ways. The most important benefit is that students become more involved in the assessment of their work and more reflective about the quality of their reading, writing, and other language use. There are other benefits as well:

- Students feel ownership of their work.
- Students become more responsible about their work.
- Students set goals and are motivated to work toward accomplishing them.
- Students reflect on their accomplishments.
- Students make connections between learning and assessing.
- Students' self-esteem is enhanced.
- Students recognize the connection between process and product.

In addition, portfolios eliminate the need to grade all student work. Portfolios are useful for student and parent conferences, and they complement the information provided in report cards.

Weaving Assessment Into Practice

WEEKLY READING-WRITING WORKSHOP ACTIVITY SHEET

Name _____   Week _____

Read independently	M T W Th F	Made a cluster	M T W Th F
Wrote in a reading log	M T W Th F	Wrote a rough draft	M T W Th F
Listened to the teacher read aloud	M T W Th F	Went to a writing group	M T W Th F
Read with a classmate	M T W Th F	Made revisions	M T W Th F
Read at the listening center	M T W Th F	Proofread my own writing	M T W Th F
Had a reading conference	M T W Th F	Had a writing conference	M T W Th F
Shared a book with classmates	M T W Th F	Shared my writing with classmates	M T W Th F
Other		Other	
Interesting words read this week		Spelling words needed this week	

Titles of books read   Titles of writings

Write a letter on the back, thinking about the week and your reading and writing.

Collecting Work in Portfolios. Portfolios are folders, large envelopes, or boxes that hold students' work. Teachers often have students label and decorate folders and then store them in plastic crates or cardboard boxes. Students date and label items as they place them in their portfolios, and they attach notes to the items to explain the context for the activity and why they selected a particular item for inclusion in the portfolio. Students' portfolios should be stored in a place where they are readily accessible to students. Students review their portfolios periodically and add new pieces to them.

Students usually choose the items to place in their portfolios within the guidelines the teacher provides. Some students submit the original piece of work; others want to keep the original, so they place a copy in the portfolio instead. In addition to the writing and art samples that can go directly into portfolios, students also record oral language and drama samples on audio- and videotapes to place in their portfolios. Large-size art and writing projects can be photographed, and the photographs placed in the portfolio. The following types of student work might be placed in a portfolio:

autobiographies	oral readings (on videotape)
biographies	oral reports (on videotape)
books	poems
choral readings (on videotape)	projects
clusters	readers theatre performances
copies of letters, along with replies	(on videotape)
received	reading log entries
drawings, diagrams, and charts	reports
learning log entries	simulated-journal entries
lists of books read	stories
multigenre projects	

This variety of work samples takes into account all six language arts. Also, samples from workshops, literature focus units, literature circles, and thematic units should be included.

Not all work that is placed in a student's portfolio needs to be graded for quality. Teachers, of course, will be familiar with most pieces, but it is not necessary to correct them with a red pen. Many times, students' work is simply graded as "done" or "not done." When a piece of work is to be graded, students should choose it from the items being placed in their portfolios.

Many teachers collect students' work in folders, and they assume that portfolios are basically the same as work folders; however, the two types of collections differ in several important ways. Perhaps the most important difference is that portfolios are student oriented, whereas work folders are usually teachers' collections. Students choose which samples will be placed in portfolios, and teachers often place all completed assignments in work folders (Clemmons, Lasse, Cooper, Areglado, & Dill, 1993). Next, portfolios focus on students' strengths, not their weaknesses. Because students choose items for portfolios, they choose samples that they believe best represent their language development. Another difference is that portfolios involve reflection (D'Aoust, 1992). Through reflection, students become aware of their strengths as readers, writers, and language users. They also use their work samples to identify the language arts skills, strategies, procedures, and concepts they already know and the ones they need to focus on.

Involving Students in Self-Assessment. Portfolios are a useful vehicle for engaging students in self-reflection and goal setting (Courtney & Abodeeb, 2005). Students can learn to reflect on and assess their own reading and writing activities and their development as readers and writers. Teachers begin by asking students to think about their language arts abilities in terms of contrast. For example, in reading, students identify the books they have read that they liked most and least and ask themselves what these choices suggest about themselves as readers. They also identify what they do well in reading and what they need to improve about their reading. By making these comparisons, students begin to reflect on their language arts development.

Teachers use minilessons and conferences to talk with students about the characteristics of good listeners, good writers, good storytellers, and good viewers. In particular, they discuss these characteristics:

- What good listeners do as they listen
- How to view a film or videotape
- What fluent reading is
- How to prepare to give an oral report
- Which language arts strategies and skills students use
- How students choose books for reading workshop
- How students demonstrate comprehension
- What makes a good project to extend reading
- How students decide what to write in journals
- How students adapt their writing to their audience
- How students visually represent important concepts
- How to use writing rubrics
- How to participate in a grand conversation

As students learn about what it means to be effective language users, they acquire both the tools they need to reflect on and evaluate their own language development and vocabulary to use in their reflections, such as *goal, strategy,* and *rubric.*

Students write notes on the items they choose to put into their portfolios. In these self-assessments, students explain the reasons for their selections and identify strengths and accomplishments in their work. In some classrooms, students write their reflections and comments on index cards; in other classrooms, students design special comment sheets that they attach to the items in their portfolios. A first grader wrote this reflection to explain why she chose to make a poster about author Eric Carle and his books and to include it in her portfolio: "I have a favorite author. Mr. Eric Carle. I read five of his books!" A fifth grader chose to put the reading log he wrote while reading *Shiloh* (Naylor, 2000) in his portfolio. He wrote this reflection: "I put my journal on the computer. It looks good! I used the SPELCHEK. I put in lots of details like I was him. I should of put some illustrations in the book."

Showcasing Students' Portfolios. At the end of the school year, many teachers organize "Portfolio Share Days" to celebrate students' accomplishments and to provide an opportunity for students to share their portfolios with classmates and the wider community (Porter & Cleland, 1995). Often family members, local businesspeople and politicians, school administrators, college students, and others are invited to attend. Students and community members form small groups, and the students share their portfolios, pointing out their accomplishments and strengths. This activity is especially useful in involving community members in the school and showing them the types of language arts activities students are doing as well as how students are becoming effective readers, writers, and language users.

These sharing days also help students accept responsibility for their own learning—especially those students who have not been as motivated as their classmates. When less motivated students listen to their classmates talk about their work and how they have grown as readers, writers, and language users, they often decide to work harder the next year.

Assigning Grades

Assigning grades is one of the most difficult responsibilities placed on teachers. "Grading is a fact of life," according to Donald Graves (1983, p. 93), but he adds that teachers should use grades to encourage students, not to hinder their achievement. The authentic assessment procedures described in this chapter encourage students because they document how students are using all the language arts in authentic ways. The difficult part is reviewing and translating this documentation into grades.

Assignment Checklists. One way for students to keep track of assignments during literature focus units and thematic units is to use assignment checklists. Teachers create the assignment checklist as they plan the unit. Students receive a copy of the checklist at the beginning of the unit and keep it in their unit folder. As students complete the assignments, they check them off, so it is easy for the teacher to review students' progress periodically. At the end of the unit, the teacher collects the unit folders and grades the work.

A checklist for a second-grade thematic unit on hermit crabs is presented in the Weaving Assessment Into Practice feature at the top of page 61. Eight assignments on the checklist include both science and language arts activities. Students put a check in the boxes in the "Student's Check" column when they complete each assignment, and the teacher adds the grade in the right-hand column.

Teachers of middle- and upper-grade students often assign points to each activity in the unit checklist so that the total point value for the unit is 100 points; activities that involve more time and effort earn more points. The checklist shown in the Weaving Assessment Into Practice feature at the bottom of page 61 is for a fifth-grade literature focus unit on *Number the Stars* (Lowry, 2005); the point value for each activity is listed in parentheses. Students make checkmarks on the lines on the left side of the grading sheet, and the teacher marks the numerical grades on the right side.

Rubrics. Teachers and students develop rubrics, or scoring guides, to assess students' growth as writers or to evaluate other language arts activities (Skillings & Ferrell,

Weaving Assessment Into Practice

CHECKLIST FOR THEMATIC UNIT ON HERMIT CRABS

Name _____

Begin _____
End _____

	Student's Check	Teacher's Grades

1. Keep an observation log on the hermit crab on your table for 10 days.   ☐ _____
2. Make a chart of a hermit crab and label the parts.   ☐ _____
3. Make a map of the hermit crab's habitat.   ☐ _____
4. Read three books about hermit crabs and do quickwrites about them.   ☐ _____

   _____ Hermit Crabs

   _____ A House for Hermit Crab

   _____ Is This a House for Hermit Crab?

5. Do two science experiments and write lab reports.   ☐ _____

   _____ Wet-Dry Experiment

   _____ Light-Dark Experiment

6. Write about hermit crabs. Do one.   ☐ _____

   _____ All About Hermit Crabs book

   _____ A poem about hermit crabs

   _____ A story about hermit crabs

7. Do a project about hermit crabs. Share it.   ☐ _____
8. Keep everything neatly in your hermit crab folder.   ☐ _____

Weaving Assessment Into Practice

NUMBER THE STARS GRADING SHEET

Name _____   Date _____

_____ 1. Read Number the Stars.   _____

_____ 2. Write 5 entries in a reading log or simulated journal.   (25) _____

_____ 3. Talk about your reading in 5 grand conversations.   (25) _____

_____ 4. Make a Venn diagram to compare characters. Summarize what you learned from the diagram in an essay.   (10) _____

_____ 5. Make a cluster about one word on the word wall.   (5) _____

_____ 6. Make a square with a favorite quote for the story quilt.   (10) _____

_____ 7. Do a project.   (25) _____

Total   (100) _____

Weaving Assessment Into Practice

WRITING RUBRIC

5 Exceptional Achievement

- Creative and original
- Clear organization
- Precise word choice and figurative language
- Sophisticated sentences
- Essentially free of mechanical errors

4 Excellent Achievement

- Some creativity, but more predictable than an exceptional paper
- Definite organization
- Good word choice, but little figurative language
- Varied sentences
- Only a few mechanical errors

3 Adequate Achievement

- Predictable paper
- Some organization
- Adequate word choice
- Little variety of sentences and some run-on sentences
- Some mechanical errors

2 Limited Achievement

- Brief and superficial
- Little organization
- Imprecise language
- Incomplete and run-on sentences
- Many mechanical errors

1 Minimal Achievement

- No ideas communicated
- Lacks organization
- Inadequate word choice
- Sentence fragments
- Overwhelming mechanical errors

Weaving Assessment Into Practice

RUBRIC FOR ASSESSING REPORTS ON ANCIENT EGYPT

4 Excellent Report

_____ Three or more chapters with titles
_____ Main idea clearly developed in each chapter
_____ Three or more illustrations
_____ Effective use of Egypt-related words in text and illustrations
_____ Very interesting to read
_____ Very few mechanical errors
_____ Table of contents

3 Good Report

_____ Three chapters with titles
_____ Main idea somewhat developed in each chapter
_____ Three illustrations
_____ Some Egypt-related words used
_____ Interesting to read
_____ A few mechanical errors
_____ Table of contents

2 Average Report

_____ Three chapters
_____ Main idea identified in each chapter
_____ One or two illustrations
_____ A few Egypt-related words used
_____ Some mechanical errors
_____ Sort of interesting to read
_____ Table of contents

1 Poor Report

_____ One or two chapters
_____ Information in each chapter rambles
_____ No illustrations
_____ Very few Egypt-related words used
_____ Many mechanical errors
_____ Hard to read and understand
_____ No table of contents

2000). Rubrics make the analysis of writing simpler and the assessment process more reliable and consistent. Rubrics may have 3, 4, 5, or 6 levels, with descriptors at each level related to ideas, organization, language, and mechanics. Some rubrics are general and appropriate for almost any writing project, whereas others are designed for a specific writing assignment.

The Weaving Assessment Into Practice feature on page 62 shows a general, 5-level writing rubric that teachers and students can use to assess almost any type of formal writing assignment. In contrast, the rubric shown in the Weaving Assessment Into Practice feature on page 63 is designed to assess a particular writing assignment—a class of sixth graders designed this 4-level rubric to assess their reports on ancient Egypt. In contrast to the general rubric, the report rubric lists specific components that students were to include in their reports.

Both teachers and students can assess writing with rubrics. They read the composition and highlight words or check statements in the rubric that best describe the composition. It is important to note that rarely are all the highlighted words or checked statements at the same level; the score is determined by examining the highlighted words or checked statements and determining which level best represents the overall quality of the composition.

To assess students' learning systematically, teachers should use at least three evaluation approaches. Approaching an evaluation from at least three viewpoints is called *triangulation*. In addition to tests, teachers can use kid watching, anecdotal records, conferences, portfolios, assignment checklists, and rubrics. Using a variety of techniques enables teachers to be much more accurate in charting and assessing students' language growth.

What About Tests? With the current emphasis on accountability, it's important to understand the differences between authentic assessment and tests. Consider the often-confused terms *assessment* and *evaluation*. Assessment is diagnostic and ongoing. Teachers use assessment tools to plan instruction and monitor student progress. In contrast, evaluation is used to judge students' learning (Cobb, 2003). It often involves testing, using teacher-made tests, unit tests that accompany textbooks, or end-of-year standardized achievement tests. Teachers use evaluation after instruction to assign grades and at the end of the year to determine if students have met grade-level standards and should progress to the next grade level.

Authentic assessment tools and tests provide different kinds of information. Authentic assessment gives a more complete picture of what students know about language arts and the strategies and skills they can use, whereas tests judge student performance against a grade-level standard (Wilson, Martens, & Arya, 2005). A student who scores 95% on a unit test is judged to have learned more than one who scores 70%, but it usually isn't clear exactly what the student knows or which strategies and skills he or she has learned to use.

Most teachers are required to administer end-of-year standardized achievement tests to show students' growth and demonstrate accountability. Even with this emphasis on tests, it's important that teachers continue to use authentic assessment to inform their instruction and monitor student learning.

Review

This chapter focused on how teachers teach language arts. Teachers plan language arts instruction using four patterns of practice: literature focus units, literature circles, reading and writing workshop, and thematic units. Key points presented in this chapter include the following:

- Classrooms should be authentic learning environments that encourage students to use all six language arts.
- Literature focus units include four components: reading books, responding, teaching minilessons, and creating projects.
- In literature circles, students read and discuss self-selected books in small groups.
- Reading workshop components are reading and responding, sharing, and teaching minilessons.
- Writing workshop components are writing, sharing, and teaching minilessons.
- Thematic units are interdisciplinary units that integrate language arts with social studies, science, and other curriculuar areas.
- Teachers play many roles during language arts instruction: organizer, facilitator, participant, instructor, model, manager, diagnostician, evaluator, coordinator, and communicator.
- Teachers differentiate instruction to meet the needs of all students.
- Assessment is an integral part of instruction.
- Teachers use authentic assessment procedures, including observations, anecdotal notes, conferences, checklists, portfolios, and rubrics, to monitor and assess students' learning.

Professional References

Atwell, N. (1998). *In the middle: New understandings about writing, reading, and learning* (2nd ed.). Portsmouth, NH: Heinemann.

Boyd-Batstone, P. (2004). Focused anecdotal records assessment: A tool for standards-based, authentic assessment. *The Reading Teacher, 58,* 230–239.

Calkins, L. M. (1994). *The art of teaching writing* (2nd ed.). Portsmouth, NH: Heinemann.

Cambourne, B. (2001). What do I do with the rest of the class? The nature of teaching-learning activities. *Language Arts, 79,* 124–135.

Clemmons, J., Lasse, L., Cooper, D., Areglado, N., & Dill, M. (1993). *Portfolios in the classroom: A teacher's sourcebook.* New York: Scholastic.

Cobb, C. (2003). Effective instruction begins with purposeful assessments. *The Reading Teacher, 57,* 386–388.

Cohle, D. M., & Towle, W. (2001). *Connecting reading and writing in the intermediate grades: A workshop approach.* Newark, DE: International Reading Association.

Courtney, A. M., & Abodeeb, T. L. (2005). Diagnostic-reflective portfolios. In S. J. Barrentine & S. M. Stokes (Eds.), *Reading assessment: Principles and practices for elementary teachers* (2nd ed., pp. 215–222). Newark, DE: International Reading Association.

Daniels, H. (2002). *Literature circles: Voice and choice in book clubs and reading groups* (2nd ed.). Portland, ME: Stenhouse.

D'Aoust, C. (1992). Portfolios: Process for students and teachers. In K. B. Yancy (Ed.), *Portfolios in the writing classroom* (pp. 39–48). Urbana, IL: National Council of Teachers of English.

Day, J., Spiegel, D. L., McLellan, J., & Brown, V. (2002). *Moving forward with literature circles.* New York: Scholastic.

Evans, K. S. (2001). *Literature discussion groups in the intermediate grades.* Newark, DE: International Reading Association.

Fletcher, R., & Portalupi, J. (1998). *Craft lessons: Teaching writing K–8.* Portland, ME: Stenhouse.

Fletcher, R., & Portalupi, J. (2001). *Writing workshop: The essential guide.* Portsmouth, NH: Heinemann.

Gill, R. S. (2000). Reading with Amy: Teaching and learning through reading conferences. *The Reading Teacher, 53,* 500–509.

Gillet, J. W., & Beverly, L. (2001). *Directing the writing workshop: An elementary teacher's handbook.* New York: Guilford Press.

Goodman, Y. M. (1978). Kid watching: An alternative to testing. *National Elementary Principals Journal, 57,* 41–45.

Graves, D. H. (1983). *Writing: Teachers and children at work.* Portsmouth, NH: Heinemann.

Graves, D. H. (1994). *A fresh look at writing.* Portsmouth, NH: Heinemann.

Heffernan, L. (2004). *Critical literacy and writer's workshop: Bringing purpose and passion to student writing.* Newark, DE: International Reading Association.

Hill, B. C., Johnson, N. J., & Noe, K. L. S. (Eds.). (1995). *Literature circles and response.* Norwood, MA: Christopher-Gordon.

Lindquist, T., & Selwyn, D. (2000). *Social studies at the center: Integrating kids, content, and literacy.* Portsmouth, NH: Heinemann.

Luongo-Orlando, K. (2001). *A project approach to language learning: Linking literary genres and themes in elementary classrooms.* Markham, ON: Pembroke.

Moline, S. (1995). *I see what you mean: Children at work with visual information.* York, ME: Stenhouse.

Portalupi, J., & Fletcher, R. (2001). *Nonfiction craft lessons: Teaching information writing K–8.* Portland, ME: Stenhouse.

Porter, C., & Cleland, J. (1995). *The portfolio as a learning strategy.* Portsmouth, NH: Heinemann.

Rhodes, L. K., & Nathenson-Mejia, S. (1992). Anecdotal records: A powerful tool for ongoing literacy assessment. *The Reading Teacher, 45,* 502–511.

Rief, L. (1999). *Vision and voice: Extending the literacy spectrum.* Portsmouth, NH: Heinemann.

Samway, K. D. (2006). *When English learners write: Connecting research to practice, K–8.* Portmouth, NH: Heinemann.

Samway, K. D., & Whang, G. (1996). *Literacy study circles in a multicultural classroom.* York, ME: Stenhouse.

Skillings, M. J., & Ferrell, R. (2000). Student-generated rubrics: Bringing students into the assessment process. *The Reading Teacher, 53,* 452–455.

Swift, K. (1993). Try reading workshop in your classroom. *The Reading Teacher, 46,* 366–371.

Tierney, R. J. (2005). Literacy assessment reform: Shifting beliefs, principled possibilities, and emerging practices. In S. J. Barrentine & S. M. Stokes (Eds.), *Reading assessment: Principles and practices for elementary teachers* (2nd ed., pp. 23–40). Newark, DE: International Reading Association.

Tomlinson, C. A. (2001). *How to differentiate instruction in mixed-ability classrooms* (2nd ed.). Alexandria, VA: Association for Supervision and Curriculum Development.

Valencia, S. W., Hiebert, E. H., & Afflerbach, P. P. (1994). *Authentic reading assessment: Practices and possibilities.* Newark, DE: International Reading Association.

Wilson, P., Martens, P., & Arya, P. (2005). Accountability for reading and readers: What the numbers don't tell. *The Reading Teacher, 58,* 622–631.

Children's Book References

Babbitt, N. (2002). *Tuck everlasting.* New York: Farrar, Straus & Giroux.

Brown, M. W. (1990). *The important book.* New York: HarperCollins.

Cleary, B. (1993). *Ralph the mouse.* New York: Morrow.

Coman, C. (1997). *What Jamie saw.* New York: Puffin Books.

Cooney, C. (1990). *The face on the milk carton.* New York: Bantam.

Cormier, R. (1977). *I am the cheese.* New York: Knopf.

Dahl, R. (1998). *The BFG.* New York: Puffin Books.

Dahl, R. (2004). *Charlie and the chocolate factory.* New York: Knopf.

Ellis, D. (2000). *The breadwinner.* Toronto: Groundwood Books.

Gardiner, J. R. (2003). *Stone Fox.* New York: HarperTrophy.

Hinton, S. E. (2006). *The outsiders.* New York: Penguin.

Lee, H. (2002). *To kill a mockingbird.* New York: HarperCollins.

L'Engle, M. (2007). *A wrinkle in time.* New York: Square Fish.

Lowry, L. (2005). *Number the stars.* New York: Yearling.

MacLachlan, P. (2004). *Sarah, plain and tall.* New York: HarperCollins.

Martin, B., Jr. (2007). *Brown bear, brown bear, what do you see?* New York: Holt.

McMillan, B. (1995). *Summer ice: Life along the Antarctic peninsula.* Boston: Houghton Mifflin.

Naylor, P. R. (1996). *Shiloh season.* New York: Atheneum.

Naylor, P. R. (2000). *Shiloh.* New York: Aladdin Books.

Naylor, P. R. (2006). *Saving Shiloh.* New York: Atheneum.

Rowling, J. K. (1998). *Harry Potter and the sorcerer's stone.* New York: Levine.

Rowling, J. K. (2002). *Harry Potter and the goblet of fire.* New York: Scholastic.

Rylant, C. (1992). *Missing May.* New York: Orchard Books.

Sachar, L. (1998). *Holes.* New York: Farrar, Straus & Giroux.

Speare, E. G. (2005). *The sign of the beaver.* New York: Yearling.

Spinelli, J. (2002). *Maniac Magee.* New York: Scholastic.

Taylor, T. (2003). *The cay.* New York: Laurel Leaf.

The Reading and Writing Processes

During the first week of school, Ms. Kakutani reads aloud *Granny Torrelli Makes Soup* (Creech, 2003) to her fourth graders. It's a story about friendship, which is her theme for the first month of school. In the story, Granny Torrelli helps her granddaughter Rosie smooth out her relationship with best friend Bailey. Ms. Kakutani makes connections between what Rosie learns about being a friend and how she wants the students to behave toward their classmates. It's the teacher's first step in creating a community of learners in the classroom.

After they finish the book, Ms. Kakutani and her students prepare spaghetti and meatballs and invite parents, grandparents, and siblings to join them for a lunch. The students write invitations, and parents volunteer to supply many of the ingredients and help prepare the food in the classroom. Others bring salad, bread, fruit, and dessert to complete the meal. It's a festive occasion where children introduce their families to Ms. Kakutani and show them around their classroom.

For the next 2 weeks, Ms. Kakutani and her students read *Amber Brown Goes Fourth* (Danziger, 1995), the third in a series of chapter-book stories about a spunky girl with a two-color name. This book, also with a friendship theme, is written at the third-grade reading level; it's appropriate for this class because most students read a year below grade level. The teacher has a class set of this Amber Brown book that she

---

*H*ow do teachers use the reading process
to organize literature focus units?

Good teaching isn't accidental! Teachers organize literature focus units to ensure that students comprehend what they're reading. Some
activities introduce the book and activate background knowledge, some guide students as
they interpret the story, and others provide
opportunities to teach students about literature
and for students to apply what they're learning. As you read this vignette, notice how
Ms. Kakutani incorporates the prereading, reading, responding, exploring, and applying stages
of the reading process in the unit.

---

distributes to students and a text set with multiple copies of
the other books in the series that she places in the classroom
library for students to read independently.

Ms. Kakutani reads this story with her students using
shared reading because she wants to ensure that everyone
can read the story, and she wants to introduce the comprehension strategies that she will emphasize this year. The students follow along in their copies as she reads the book
aloud, chapter by chapter. The class spends 9 days reading
the 14 chapters in the book; on some days, they read one
chapter, and on other days, they read two. As they read,
Ms. Kakutani pauses off and on to think aloud about the comprehension strategies she is using—monitoring, visualizing,
connecting, summarizing, and evaluating.

After they finish reading, the students participate in a grand conversation with Ms. Kakutani.
Participating in a free-flowing discussion about the
story is new to many students. The teacher explains the activity, models it,
and teaches them how to ask questions, offer opinions, and make connections to their own lives and to *Granny Torrelli Makes Soup*. They talk about
the events in the story, the importance of having friends, and their own
nervousness about beginning fourth grade.

When the grand conversation slows down, Ms. Kakutani often
returns to the book and rereads a sentence to redirect the conversation.
After reading Chapters 6 and 7, for example, she rereads the
bottom part of page 47 and asks, "What does Brandi
mean when she says, 'I am NOT Justin'?" At first
the students are unsure, but as they talk about how
Brandi might feel, they recognize that one child
cannot replace another one. Then the teacher asks,
"Do you think Brandi and Amber will become best
friends?" The students make predictions that guide their
reading for the second half of the story.

After reading and discussing Chapter 14,
Ms. Kakutani rereads Amber's comment, "I guess there
will always be changes in my life" (p. 100), and
asks students what they think it means.
They reflect on the changes in Amber's
life—her friend Justin moving
away, her parents getting di-
vorced, her father moving
to Paris, her mother
dating Max, and

Amber starting fourth grade. Then Ms. Kakutani asks students if they expect to have changes in their lives, and the conversation continues as they talk about the changes in their lives—parents who are soldiers in Iraq, new babies born into their families, mothers going to work, families moving to a new community, grandparents dying, older siblings being sent to prison, and, of course, starting fourth grade.

After they talk about the story, the students write entries in their reading logs. Ms. Kakutani provides questions to guide their responses. She makes her questions open-ended to encourage students to continue to think more deeply about the story and make connections to their own lives. Here are Ms. Kakutani's questions:

Chapters 1 and 2	*What have you learned about Amber?*
	How do you think her life is going to change?
Chapter 3	*What's hard about starting fourth grade?*
Chapters 4 and 5	*How is Amber's fourth grade different from third grade?*
	How is fourth grade different for you?
Chapters 6 and 7	*Do you think Amber and Brandi will become best friends?*
	Do you agree with Amber that everyone should have a best friend?
Chapter 8	*What funny things have you done with your mom or dad?*
Chapter 9	*Do you think it was fair for the girls to get detention for laughing?*
Chapters 10 and 11	*Why do you think Brandi and Amber are getting to be better friends?*
	Would you want to be the Burp Queen or Burp King of fourth grade?
Chapters 12 and 13	*What should Amber do to be a good friend?*
	Do you think Amber is ever going to like Max?
Chapter 14	*Do you think Max was trying to bribe Amber with the mermaid?*
	What changes have you had in your life?

The students make small journals by stapling together sheets of lined paper and adding construction paper covers. They illustrate the covers to reflect the book they are reading. They begin each entry on a new page and add the chapter number, a title, and the date at the top of the page. Bella writes this entry after reading Chapters 6 and 7, in response to the question, "Do you think Amber and Brandi will become best friends?":

> *I feel sorry for Amber Brown. She has too many changes in her life. She needs a new best friend. Her old best friend moved away and she is lonely. I am thinking Brandi will be her best friend because she needs one, too. I hope there are no more changes for her!*

Jordan writes this entry after reading Chapter 14 and adds this title—"The Change in My Life":

I'm having a change right now and it scares me. My Dad is in Iraq. He is a sergeant. I pray to God to watch over him. He says he's safe but I think he could get killed. I'm proud of him because he is brave. I pray he comes back safe.

Ms. Kakutani also emphasizes the important vocabulary in the story. She posts a word wall—a large chart divided into alphabetized sections—and after reading each chapter or two, students choose the most important words to add to the word wall. They take turns writing the words on the chart, and they refer to the word wall whenever they need help spelling or thinking of a word. The class word wall is shown in the box below. She also points out the wordplay in the story. The students get interested in reading jokes after reading the ones in Chapter 1 and Chapter 6, and Ms. Kakutani locates several joke books in the classroom library to share with them.

Amber Brown Goes Fourth Word Wall			
AB Amber Brown best friend Brandi Colwin Burp Queen bossy	**CD** divorce colorful change do-over detention	**EF** empty feeling feet-feat fourth-forth fiend	**GH** Hannah Burton Her Dweebness humongous
IJ Justin Daniels immature	**KL** London knapsack laughing	**M** Max Mrs. Holt musical mermaid	**NOP** Paris name dropper nervous
QRS sole-soul scared snap fingers spaghetti-slurping contest	**TU** trophy	**VW** vacancies	**XYZ**

Ms. Kakutani also shares information about author Paula Danziger and does a book talk to introduce the other Amber Brown books. Then students spend the last week in the unit reading other Amber Brown stories individually, with partners, and in small groups. Even after the unit ends, many students will trade books and continue reading about Amber Brown's adventures during independent reading time.

Reading and writing involve similar processes. The reading process is a series of stages during which readers read, explore, and reflect on the text they're reading. The writing process is similar, involving a variety of activities as students gather and organize their ideas, write rough drafts, revise and edit the drafts, and, finally, publish their writings. The goal of both processes is making meaning. Readers create meaning through negotiation with the texts they're reading, and, similarly, writers create meaning through negotiation with the texts they're writing. Readers use their life and literature experiences and their knowledge of written language as they read, and writers bring similar knowledge and experiences to writing. It's quite common for two people to read a text and come away with different interpretations and for two writers to write different accounts of the same event. Meaning doesn't exist on the pages of the book that a reader is reading or in the words of the composition that a writer is writing; instead, meaning is created through the transaction between readers and what they are reading or between writers and what they are writing.

In this chapter, you will read about the reading and writing processes and see how teachers use these processes in organizing language arts instruction. As you read, think about these questions:

- ◆ What are the stages in the reading process?
- ◘ How do children comprehend what they're reading?
- ◆ What are the stages in the writing process?
- ◢ How do teachers use these two processes in teaching language arts?

THE READING PROCESS

Reading is a process in which readers negotiate meaning in order to comprehend, or create an interpretation. During reading, the meaning does not go from the page to the readers. Instead, it involves a complex negotiation between the text and readers that is shaped by many factors: readers' knowledge about the topic; readers' purpose for reading; the language community readers belong to and how closely that language matches the language used in the text; readers' culturally based expectations about reading; and readers' expectations about reading based on their previous experiences.

Aesthetic and Efferent Reading

Readers read for different purposes, and the way they approach the reading process varies according to their purpose. Often they read for enjoyment, but at other times, they read for information. When reading to be entertained, readers assume an *aesthetic* stance and focus on the lived-through experience of reading. They concentrate on the thoughts, images, feelings, and associations evoked during reading. Readers also respond to these thoughts, images, feelings, and associations. For example, as students read *Princess Academy* (Hale, 2005), they may imagine themselves in Miri's village on the isolated Mt. Eskel. When reading to carry away information, readers assume an *efferent* stance: They concentrate on the public, common referents of the words and symbols in the text. For example, as children read *Sea Horse: The Shyest Fish in the Sea* (Butterworth, 2006), their focus is on the information in the text and illustrations, not on the experience of reading.

Almost every reading experience calls for a balance between aesthetic and efferent reading (Rosenblatt, 2005); readers do not simply read stories and poems aesthetically and informational books efferently. As they read, readers move back and forth between the aesthetic and efferent stances. Literature, however, should be read primarily from the aesthetic stance.

Readers move through the five stages of the reading process: prereading, reading, responding, exploring, and applying. The key features of each stage are summarized in the LA Essentials box on the next page.

KEY FEATURES OF THE READING PROCESS

- **Stage 1: Prereading**

  Activate or build background knowledge.
  Set purposes for reading.
  Preview the text.

- **Stage 2: Reading**

  Read independently, with a buddy, using shared reading, or through guided reading, or listen to the text read aloud.
  Read the entire text from beginning to end or read one or more sections to learn specific information.
  Apply strategies and skills.
  Read the illustrations, charts, and diagrams.

- **Stage 3: Responding**

  Respond in reading logs.
  Discuss the text with classmates and the teacher.

- **Stage 4: Exploring**

  Reread and think more deeply about the text.
  Examine the author's craft.
  Learn vocabulary words.
  Participate in minilessons.

- **Stage 5: Applying**

  Create a project.
  Connect with related books.
  Value the reading experience.

Stage 1: Prereading

The reading process begins before readers open a book to read. The first stage is prereading. As readers prepare to read, they do the following:

- Activate background knowledge
- Set purposes
- Plan for reading

Activating Background Knowledge. Readers activate their background knowledge or schemata about the book before beginning to read; the topic of the book, the

title, the author, the genre, the cover illustration, a comment someone makes about the book, or something else may trigger this activation. When students are reading independently—during reading workshop, for example—they choose the books they will read and activate their background knowledge themselves. At other times, such as during literature focus units, teachers help students activate and build their background knowledge. They share information on a topic related to the book or introduce a book box with a collection of objects connected to the book. Or, they show a video or film, tell about the author, read the first paragraph aloud, or ask students to make a prediction about the book. For example, before reading *The Giver* (Lowry, 2006), teachers build a concept of what a "perfect" society might be like by having students brainstorm a list of problems in today's society and think of possible remedies.

Setting Purposes. Readers are more successful when they have a purpose for reading the selection (Blanton, Wood, & Moorman, 1990). During literature focus units, purpose setting is usually directed by the teacher, but in reading workshop, students set their own purposes because everyone is reading different books. For teacher-directed purpose setting, teachers explain how students are expected to read and what they will do after reading. The goal of teacher-directed purpose setting is to help students learn how to set personally relevant purposes when they are reading independently.

When readers have a purpose for reading, comprehension of the selection they are reading is enhanced in several ways (Blanton et al., 1990). First, the purpose guides the reading process that students use. Having a purpose provides motivation and direction for reading as well as a mechanism that students use to monitor their reading. As they monitor their reading, students ask themselves whether they are fulfilling their purpose. Second, purpose setting activates a plan for teachers to use in teaching reading. They help students draw on background knowledge as they set purposes, consider strategies they might use as they read, and think about the structure of the text they are reading. Third, when students have a purpose in mind, they are better able to identify important information to remember as they read.

Planning for Reading. Students often preview the reading selection, especially articles and nonfiction books, as they prepare to read. They examine illustrations, read the table of contents, and determine the reading difficulty of the selection. For longer books, they also decide how much to read each day. Previewing serves an important function as students connect their background knowledge, identify their purpose for reading, and take their first look at the selection.

Stage 2: Reading

Students do the actual reading in the second stage. Sometimes they read independently, but at other times, they listen to the teacher read aloud or read with classmates and the teacher. There are five types of reading that take place in classrooms:

- Shared reading
- Guided reading
- Independent reading
- Buddy reading
- Reading aloud to students

FIGURE 3–1

The Five Types of Reading

Type	Advantages	Disadvantages
Shared Reading Teachers read aloud while students follow along using individual copies of a book, a class chart, or a big book.	• Students have access to books they could not read independently. • Teachers model fluent reading. • Teachers model reading strategies. • A community of readers is developed.	• Multiple copies, a class chart, or a big book version of the text is needed. • Text may not be appropriate for all students. • Some students may not be interested in the text.
Guided Reading Teachers support students as they read texts at their reading levels. Students are grouped homogeneously.	• Teachers provide direction and scaffolding. • Students practice reading strategies. • Students read independently. • Students practice the prediction cycle.	• Multiple copies of the text are needed. • Teachers control the reading experience. • Some students may not be interested in the text.
Independent Reading Students read a text independently and often choose the text themselves.	• Students develop responsibility and ownership. • Students self-select texts. • Readers have a more authentic experience.	• Students may need assistance to read the text. • Teachers have little involvement or control.
Buddy Reading Two students read or reread a text together.	• Students are encouraged to collaborate. • Students reread familiar texts. • Students develop reading fluency. • Students talk about texts to deepen comprehension.	• Teachers' involvement and control are limited. • One student may depend on the other to do the reading.
Reading Aloud to Students Teachers or other fluent readers read aloud to students.	• Students have access to books they could not read independently. • Teachers model fluent reading. • Teachers model reading strategies. • A community of readers is developed. • Only one copy of the text is required.	• Students have no opportunity to read. • Text may not be appropriate for some students. • Some students may not be interested in the text.

The type of reading that teachers choose depends on the difficulty level of the text, students' reading levels, and the teacher's purpose. The advantages and disadvantages of each type of reading are outlined in Figure 3–1.

Shared Reading. Students follow along as the teacher reads the selection aloud. Kindergarten and first-grade teachers often use big books—enlarged versions of the selection—for shared reading (Holdaway, 1979). Children sit so that they can see the book, and they listen to the teacher read aloud and read along as the teacher reads refrains and other familiar words. The teacher or a child points to each line of text as it is read to draw children's attention to the words, to show the direction of print on a page, and to highlight important concepts about letters, words, and sentences.

Teachers in other grades also use shared reading when students have individual copies of the reading selection but it's too difficult for them to read independently (Fisher & Medvic, 2000). The teacher reads aloud as students follow along in their copies. Sometimes teachers read the first chapter or two of a chapter book together with the class, using shared reading, and then students use other types of reading as they read the rest of the book. Only those students for whom the book is too difficult continue to use shared reading and read along with the teacher.

Guided Reading. Teachers read with small groups of students who read at the same level or who use similar reading strategies and skills. They scaffold students' reading to enable them to develop and use reading strategies and skills in guided reading (Fountas & Pinnell, 1996, 2001). Selections used for guided reading should be written at students' instructional reading levels, that is, slightly beyond their ability to read the text independently. Teachers usually read the first page or two with students, and then the students read the rest of the selection silently. Teachers often group and regroup students for guided reading so that the book selected is appropriate for all students in a group.

Independent Reading. Students read silently by themselves and at their own pace (Taylor, 1993). Independent reading is the most authentic type of reading. This is what most people do when they read, and it's the way students develop a love of reading and come to think of themselves as readers. It's essential that the reading selection is either at an appropriate level of difficulty or very familiar so that students can read it independently. Otherwise, teachers use one of the other types of reading to support students and make it possible for them to participate in the reading experience.

Buddy Reading. Students read or reread a selection with a classmate in buddy reading. Sometimes students read with buddies because it's an enjoyable social

Anthony Magnacca/Merrill

Buddy Reading

These two good friends like to read chapter books together during DEAR time (Drop Everything And Read, a 20-minute daily independent reading time). They choose the books that interest them and are at their reading level from the classroom library and take turns doing the reading. Their teacher has taught them several strategies for cooperative reading, so they are able to help each other with unfamiliar words, stop reading when necessary to ask clarifying questions, and often make personal, world, and literary connections to the story. Buddy reading is a good alternative to independent reading for students who are very social or students who don't like to read.

activity, and sometimes they read together to help each other. Often students can read selections together that neither one could read individually. By working together, they are often able to figure out unfamiliar words and talk out comprehension problems. Teachers show students how to support each other as they read together. Unless students know how to work collaboratively, buddy reading often deteriorates into the better reader reading aloud to the other student, but that isn't the intention of this type of reading. Students need to take turns reading aloud to each other or read in unison. They often stop and help each other identify an unfamiliar word or take a minute or two at the end of each page to talk about what they have read. It's a valuable way of providing the practice that beginning readers need to become fluent readers.

Reading Aloud to Students. At every grade level, teachers read aloud to children for a variety of purposes each day. Teachers read aloud books that are appropriate for students' interest level but too difficult for them to read by themselves. When they read aloud, teachers do two things: They model what good readers do and how good readers use reading strategies, and they actively involve students in the reading experience by asking them to make predictions and use other comprehension strategies.

Reading aloud to students is not the same as round-robin reading, in which children take turns reading paragraphs aloud as the rest of the class listens. Round-robin reading has been used for reading chapter books aloud, but it is more commonly used for reading chapters in content-area textbooks, even though there are more effective ways to teach content-area information and read textbooks. Round-robin reading is no longer recommended, for several reasons (Opitz & Rasinski, 1998). First, students should read fluently if they are going to read aloud to the class. When less capable readers read, their reading is often difficult to listen to and embarrassing to them personally. Less capable readers need reading practice, but performing in front of the entire class is not the most productive way for them to practice. They can read with

How the Types of Reading Fit Into the Four Patterns of Practice

Literature Focus Units

Teachers usually read featured selections aloud or use shared reading because the books are often difficult for students to read on their own, even though the content is grade-level appropriate. Students should read independently, when they can.

Literature Circles

Students usually read books independently, but students read more difficult books with buddies. Teachers also use guided reading procedures when they're introducing literature circles to primary-grade students.

Reading and Writing Workshop

Reading workshop is designed to provide opportunities for students to read self-selected books independently, and teachers also read books aloud to the class and use them to teach minilessons about reading strategies and the author's craft.

Thematic Units

Teachers read many informational books aloud to students during thematic units, and students use shared reading, buddy reading, and independent reading to read other books and content-area textbooks.

buddies and in small groups during guided reading. Second, if the selection is easy enough for students to read aloud, they should read independently instead. During round-robin reading, many students follow along only just before it is their turn to read, so they don't do much reading. Third, round-robin reading is often tedious and boring, so students lose interest in reading.

Stage 3: Responding

Readers respond to their reading and continue to negotiate meaning to deepen their comprehension. They make tentative and exploratory comments by writing in reading logs and participating in grand conversations immediately after reading.

Writing in Reading Logs. Students write and draw thoughts and feelings about what they have read in reading logs. Rosenblatt (2005) explains that as readers write about what they have read, they unravel their thinking and at the same time elaborate on and clarify their responses. Students often choose their own topics for reading log entries, but many teachers hang a list of open-ended prompts in the classroom to guide students' responses. Possible prompts include the following:

> I really don't understand . . .
> I like/dislike (character) because . . .
> This book reminds me of . . .
> (Character) reminds me of myself because . . .
> I think (character) is feeling . . .
> I wonder why . . .
> (Event) makes me think about the time I . . .
> If I were (character), I'd . . .
> I noticed that (the author) is . . .
> I predict that . . .

These open-ended prompts allow students to make connections to their own lives, the world, and other literature. At other times, teachers ask specific questions to direct students' attention to some aspect of a book, as Ms. Kakutani did in the vignette at the beginning of the chapter.

Participating in Grand Conversations. Students talk about the text with classmates in discussions called *grand conversations*. Peterson and Eeds (1990) explain that in this type of discussion, students share their personal responses and tell what they liked about the selection. After sharing personal reactions, they shift the focus to "puzzle over what the author has written and . . . share what it is they find revealed" (p. 61). Often students make connections between the selection and their own lives, the world around them, or other literature they have read. If they are reading a chapter book, they also make predictions about what will happen in the next chapter. Teachers often participate in grand conversations, but they act as interested participants, not as leaders.

Grand conversations can be held with the whole class or with small groups. Young children usually meet as a class, but older students often prefer to talk with classmates in small groups. When students get together as a class, there is a feeling of community, and the teacher can be part of the group. When students meet in small groups, students have more opportunities to participate in the discussion and share their responses, but fewer viewpoints are expressed in each group and teachers must move around, spending only a few minutes with each group. Some teachers compromise and have students begin their discussions in small groups and then come together as a class and have the groups share what they discussed.

Stage 4: Exploring

Teachers lead students back into the text to explore it more analytically in this stage. They are involved in these activities:

- Rereading the selection
- Examining the author's craft
- Focusing on new vocabulary words
- Participating in minilessons

Rereading the Selection. Students often reread picture books, articles, and other brief selections several times. If the teacher used shared reading to read the selection, then students might reread it once or twice with a buddy or read it with their parents, and after these experiences, read it independently. Each time they reread, students benefit in specific ways (Yaden, 1988): They enrich their comprehension and make deeper connections between the selection and their own lives or between the selection and other literature they have read.

Examining the Author's Craft. Teachers plan exploring activities to focus students' attention on the genre, the structure of the text, and the literary language that authors use (Eeds & Peterson, 1995). Students sequence events in the story using storyboards (pages of a picture book cut apart and glued on tagboard cards) and make story maps to visually represent the plot and other story elements (Bromley, 1996). To focus on literary language, students often reread favorite excerpts in a read-around and write memorable quotes on story quilts that they create. Teachers also share information about the author and introduce other books by that author. Sometimes teachers have students compare several books written by a particular author.

Focusing on Words. Students add "important" words related to the book to word walls posted in the classroom, and then they refer to the word walls for a variety of activities during the exploring stage. Researchers emphasize the importance of immersing students in words, teaching strategies for learning words, and personalizing word learning (Blachowicz & Fisher, 2006). Students make word clusters and posters to highlight particular words. They also make word chains, sort words, create a semantic feature analysis to analyze related words, and play word games.

Teaching Minilessons. Teachers present minilessons on reading procedures, concepts, strategies, and skills during the exploring stage. They introduce the topic and make connections between the topic and examples in the featured selection so that students can connect the information with their own reading process. A list of topics for minilessons about the reading process is presented on page 98.

Stage 5: Applying

Readers continue to deepen their interpretations and value the reading experience in this last stage of the reading process. Students build on their reading experiences, the responses they made immediately after reading, and the exploring activities as they create projects. These projects can involve reading, writing, talk and drama, viewing, visually representing, or research, and can take many forms, including murals, readers theatre scripts, oral presentations, and individual books and reports, as well as reading other books. A list of projects is presented in Figure 3–2. Providing a variety of project options takes into account Howard Gardner's (2000) theory of multiple intelligences, that students have preferred ways of learning and showing knowledge. Usually students choose which projects they will do rather than working as a class on the same project. Sometimes, however, the class works together on a project.

Teaching the Reading Process

Teachers apply the five-stage reading process in the reading lessons they teach, whether they organize instruction into literature focus units, literature circles, reading workshop, or thematic units. Successful language arts instruction doesn't just happen; teachers bring students together as a community of learners and teach them the procedures for various language arts activities. Each pattern of practice requires that teachers carefully structure activities, provide appropriate books and other materials, present instruction, create time and space for students to work, and plan for assessment.

What's Important in Reading? Everyone—parents, teachers, and politicians—has an opinion about what's important in reading instruction. Often the debate centers on phonics: Some people believe that phonics is the most important factor

How the Reading Process Fits Into the Four Patterns of Practice

Literature Focus Units

Students use the reading process as they read a featured book. Teachers build background knowledge before reading, and afterward students respond, explore, and apply what they've learned.

Literature Circles

Students use the reading process as they read self-selected books in literature circles. More emphasis is placed on reading and responding, but students also participate in other activities, too.

Reading and Writing Workshop

Although the focus in reading workshop is on reading, students activate background knowledge before reading and are involved in other stages afterward, but to a lesser degree.

Thematic Units

Students often read stories and informational books as part of thematic units, and teachers incorporate activities representing all five stages in the reading process.

FIGURE 3–2

Projects for the Applying Stage of the Reading Process

Visually Representing Projects

Create a collage to represent the theme of a book.

Make a story can or box. Decorate a coffee can or cardboard box using scenes from a book. Fill the can with objects and quotes related to the book.

Construct a shoe box or other miniature scene of an episode for a favorite book.

Make a set of storyboards with one card for each episode or chapter. Include an illustration and a paragraph describing the section of the book.

Make a map or relief map of a book's setting or something related to the book.

Prepare bookmarks for a book and distribute them to classmates.

Use or prepare illustrations of the events in the story for clothesline props to use in retelling the story.

Create a quilt about a book.

Draw a graphic organizer of the big ideas in an informational book.

Writing Projects

Write a review of a favorite book for a class review file.

Write a postcard or letter about a book to a classmate, friend, or pen pal.

Write another episode or a sequel for a book.

Write and mail a letter to a favorite author.

Write a simulated letter from one book character to another.

Copy five quotable quotes from a book and list them on a poster.

Make a scrapbook about the book.

Create a found poem, or write a poem related to the book.

Keep a simulated journal from the perspective of one character in the book.

Rewrite the story from another point of view.

Prepare a multigenre project.

Reading Projects

Read another book by the same author.

Read and compare two versions of a story.

Read a biography about the author or illustrator of the book.

Viewing Projects

View a film version of the book.

Analyze the illustrator's craft.

Talk and Drama Projects

Present a book talk about the book to the class.

Create a song about a book, or choose a tune for a poem and sing the song for the class.

Dress as a character from the book and answer questions from classmates about the character.

Videotape a commercial for a book.

Research Projects

Research the author or illustrator of the book on the Internet and compile information in a chart or summary.

Research a topic related to the book. Present the information in an oral or written report.

because students need to be able to decode the words they're reading, but others consider phonics to be less important than comprehension because the purpose of reading is to make meaning from text. The view taken in this text is that there are four important factors in developing capable readers:

- Word identification
- Fluency
- Vocabulary
- Comprehension

Teachers address all of these factors through direct instruction, by reading aloud to students every day, and by providing daily opportunities for students to read books at their own reading level.

◆ **Word identification** Capable readers have a large bank of words that they recognize instantly and automatically because they can't stop and analyze every word as they read. Students learn to read phonetically regular words, such as *baking* and *first,* and high-frequency words, such as *there* and *said.* In addition, they learn word-identification strategies to figure out unfamiliar words they encounter while reading. They use phonic analysis to read *raid, strap,* and other phonetically regular words, syllabic analysis to read *jungle, election,* and other multisyllabic words, and morphemic analysis to read *omnivorous, millennium,* and other words with Latin and Greek word parts. Through a combination of instruction and reading practice, students' knowledge of words continues to grow.

Phonics, the set of phoneme-grapheme relationships, is an important part of word-identification instruction in the primary grades, but it's only one part of word identification because English is not an entirely phonetic language. During the primary grades, children also learn to recognize at least 300 high-frequency words, such as *what* and *come,* that can't be sounded out. Older students learn more sophisticated word-identification strategies about dividing words into syllables and recognizing root words and affixes.

◆ **Fluency** Capable readers have learned to read fluently—quickly and with expression. Three components of fluency are reading speed, word recognition, and prosody (Rasinski, 2004). Students need to read at least 100 words per minute to be considered fluent readers, and most children reach this speed by third grade. Speed is important because it's hard for students to remember what they're reading when they read slowly. Word recognition is related to speed because readers who automatically recognize most of the words they're reading read more quickly than those who don't. Prosody, the ability to read sentences with appropriate phrasing and intonation, is important because when readers read expressively, the text is easier to understand (Dowhower, 1991).

Developing fluency is important because readers don't have unlimited cognitive resources, and both word identification and comprehension require a great deal of mental energy. During the primary grades, the focus is on word identification, and students learn to recognize hundreds of words, but in fourth grade—after most students have become fluent readers—the focus changes to comprehension. Students who are fluent readers have the cognitive resources available for comprehension, but students who are still word-by-word readers are focusing on word identification.

◆ **Vocabulary** Capable readers have larger vocabularies than less capable readers do (National Reading Panel, 2000). They learn words at the amazing rate of

7 to 10 per day. Learning a word is developmental: Children move from recognizing that they've seen or heard the word before to learning one meaning, and then to knowing several ways to use the word (Allen, 1999). Vocabulary knowledge is important in reading because it's easier to decode words that you've heard before, and it's easier to comprehend what you're reading when you're already familiar with some words related to the topic.

Reading is the most effective way that students expand their vocabularies. Capable readers do more reading than less capable students, so they learn more words. Not only do they do more reading, but the books capable students read contain more age-appropriate vocabulary than the easier books that lower-performing students read (Stahl, 1999).

◆ *Comprehension* Readers use their past experiences and the text to construct comprehension, a meaning that's useful for a specific purpose (Irwin, 1991). Comprehension is a complex process that involves both reader and text factors (Sweet & Snow, 2003). While they're reading, readers are actively involved in thinking about what they already know about a topic. They set a purpose for reading, read strategically, and

FIGURE 3–3

How the Reading Process Nurtures Capable Readers

Stages	Word Identification	Fluency	Vocabulary	Comprehension
Stage 1 *Prereading*	Teachers introduce new words and teach word-identification strategies.		Teachers introduce key vocabulary words as they build background knowledge.	Students activate their background knowledge, and teachers build knowledge when necessary. Also, students set purposes for reading.
Stage 2 *Reading*	Students use phonics and other word-identification strategies as they read.	Students read texts at their reading levels independently.	Teachers read aloud books that students can't read independently.	Students use comprehension strategies as they read.
Stage 3 *Responding*				Students deepen their comprehension as they write in reading logs and talk about books.
Stage 4 *Exploring*	Teachers teach phonics, high-frequency words, and word-identification strategies.	Students reread familiar texts.	Students post words on word walls and participate in vocabulary activities.	Teachers teach students about comprehension strategies, genres, and the structure of texts.
Stage 5 *Applying*		Students create choral reading projects.	Students independently read texts at their reading levels.	Students extend their comprehension as they create projects.

make inferences using clues in the text. Readers also use their knowledge about texts. They think about the genre and the topic of the text, and they use their knowledge of text structure to guide their reading.

Capable readers are strategic: They use predicting, visualizing, connecting, questioning, summarizing, and other strategies to think about and understand what they're reading (Pressley, 2002). They also learn to monitor whether they're comprehending and learn how to take action to solve problems and clarify confusions when they occur. Teaching comprehension involves introducing strategies through mini-lessons, demonstrating how capable readers use them, and involving students in supervised practice activities.

Through these activities, teachers scaffold students and then gradually release responsibility for comprehending to students (Pearson & Gallagher, 1983). Teachers withdraw support slowly once students show that they can use strategies independently while they're reading. Of course, even when students are using strategies independently, they may need increased scaffolding when they're reading more difficult text, texts about unfamiliar topics, or different genres (Pardo, 2004).

Students develop into capable readers as they use the reading process. Activities are included in each stage to develop these four factors. Figure 3–3 shows how word identification, fluency, vocabulary, and comprehension are developed through the reading process.

THE WRITING PROCESS

The focus in the writing process is on what students think and do as they write; it is writer centered (Gillet & Beverly, 2001). The five stages are prewriting, drafting, revising, editing, and publishing, and the key features of each stage are shown in the box on page 85. The labeling and numbering of the stages does not mean, however, that the writing process is a linear series of neatly packaged categories. Research has shown that the process involves recurring cycles, and labeling is only an aid to identifying and discussing writing activities (Barnes, Morgan, & Weinhold, 1997; Graves, 1994; Perl, 1994). In the classroom, the stages merge and recur as students write.

Stage 1: Prewriting

Prewriting is the getting-ready-to-write stage. Writers begin the writing process before they have their topic completely thought out. They begin tentatively—talking, reading, writing—to discover what they know and decide what direction they want to take (Flower & Hayes, 1994). Prewriting has probably been the most neglected stage in the writing process; however, it is as crucial to writers as a warm-up is to athletes. Murray (1982) believes that at least 70% of writing time should be spent in prewriting. During the prewriting stage, students

- choose a topic;
- consider purpose, form, and audience;
- generate and organize ideas for writing.

KEY FEATURES OF THE WRITING PROCESS

- **Stage 1: Prewriting**
  Students engage in rehearsal activities.
  Students identify the audience and the purpose of the writing activity.
  Students choose an appropriate genre or form based on audience and purpose.

- **Stage 2: Drafting**
  Students write a rough draft.
  Students mark their writing as a rough draft.
  Students emphasize content rather than mechanics.

- **Stage 3: Revising**
  Students reread their own writing.
  Students share their writing in writing groups.
  Students participate constructively in discussions about classmates' writing.
  Students make changes in their compositions to reflect the reactions and comments of both teacher and classmates.
  Students make substantive rather than minor changes.

- **Stage 4: Editing**
  Students proofread their own compositions.
  Students help proofread classmates' compositions.
  Students increasingly identify and correct their own mechanical errors.
  Students meet with the teacher for a final editing.

- **Stage 5: Publishing**
  Students make the final copy of their writing, often using word processing.
  Students publish their writing in an appropriate form.
  Students sit in the author's chair to share their writing.

Choosing a Topic. Students often choose their own topics so that they write about things they're interested in and knowledgeable about. It's the first step in helping students become responsible for their own writing. At other times, however, teachers assign topics for writing assignments. They may ask students to write in response to a book they've read in a literature focus unit, for example, as Ms. Kakutani did in the vignette at the beginning of the chapter, or to do a writing project as part of a thematic unit. Whenever possible, teachers keep the topics general so that students can narrow them in a way that interests them.

Considering Purpose. As students prepare to write, they think about their purpose for writing. Are they writing to entertain? to inform? to persuade? Understanding the purpose of a piece of writing is important because it influences other decisions students make about audience and form. When students have no purpose in mind other than to complete the assignment, their writing is usually lackluster—without a strong voice or controlling idea.

Considering Audience. Students' writing is influenced by their sense of audience. Britton, Burgess, Martin, McLeod, and Rosen (1975) define sense of audience as "the manner in which the writer expresses a relationship with the reader in respect to the writer's understanding" (pp. 65–66). Students may write primarily for themselves or for others. Possible audiences include classmates, younger children, parents, children's authors, and pen pals. Other audiences are more distant and less well known, such as when students write letters to businesses to request information. Students adapt their writing to fit their audience, just as they vary their speech to meet the needs of the people who are listening to them.

Considering Form. One of the most important considerations is the form the writing will take: a story? a letter? a poem? a report? Five genres that students learn to use are informational writing, journals and letters, persuasive writing, poetry, and stories. Figure 3–4 reviews these genres and lists some writing activities exemplifying each one. Through reading and writing, students develop a strong sense of these genres and how they are structured. Langer (1985) found that by third grade, children responded in distinctly different ways to story- and report-writing assignments; they organized the writing differently and included varied kinds of information and elaboration. Because children are clarifying the distinctions between various genres, it is important that teachers use the correct terminology and not label all children's writing "stories."

Gathering and Organizing Ideas. Students engage in activities to gather and organize ideas for writing. Graves (1994) calls what writers do to prepare for writing "rehearsal" activities. When students read books, take field trips, view videos and DVDs, and dramatize stories, for example, they are participating in rehearsal activities because they are building and activating background knowledge. Young children use drawing to gather and organize ideas for writing, and older students prepare for writing by making graphic organizers.

Stage 2: Drafting

Students get their ideas down on paper during the drafting stage (Gillet & Beverly, 2001). They write on every other line to leave space for revisions. Teachers often make a small *x* on every other line of students' papers as a reminder to skip lines as students draft their compositions. Students label their drafts by writing "Rough Draft" in ink at the top of the paper or by stamping them with a ROUGH DRAFT stamp; this label indicates to the writer, other students, parents, and administrators that the composition is a draft in which the emphasis is on content, not mechanics. It also explains why the teacher has not graded the paper or marked mechanical errors.

Drafting is messy. Students write quickly, trying to capture the ideas they're thinking. It's not uncommon for them to leave out a word here and there and make careless spelling errors. They cross out sentences that aren't working, use carets to

FIGURE 3–4

Writing Genres

Genre	Purpose	Activities
Informational Writing	Students collect and synthesize information for informational writing. This writing is objective, and reports are the most common type of informational writing. Students use informational writing to give directions, sequence steps, compare one thing to another, explain causes and effects, or describe problems and solutions.	Alphabet books Autobiographies Biographies Directions Interviews Reports
Journals and Letters	Students write to themselves and to specific, known audiences in journals and letters. Their writing is personal and often less formal than for other genres. They share news, explore new ideas, and record notes. Letters and envelopes require special formatting, and children learn these formats during the primary grades.	Business letters E-mail messages Friendly letters Learning logs Postcards Reading logs
Persuasive Writing	Persuasion is winning someone to your viewpoint or cause. The three ways people are persuaded are by appeals to logic, moral character, and emotion. Students present their position clearly and then support it with examples and evidence.	Advertisements Book and movie reviews Persuasive letters Persuasive posters
Poetry Writing	Students create word pictures and play with rhyme and other stylistic devices as they create poems. As students experiment with poetry, they learn that poetic language is vivid and powerful but concise, and they learn that poems can be arranged in different ways on a page.	Diamante poems Five-senses poems Found poems Free verse Haiku "I am" poems
Story Writing	Students retell familiar stories, develop sequels for stories they have read, write stories called *personal narratives* about events in their own lives, and create original stories. They organize their stories into three parts: beginning, middle, and end.	Original short stories Personal narratives Retellings of stories Sequels to stories Scripts of stories

insert new ideas, and draw arrows to rearrange text. As students write rough drafts, it is important not to emphasize correct spelling and neatness. In fact, pointing out mechanical errors during the drafting stage sends students a message that mechanical correctness is more important than content (Sommers, 1994). Later, during editing, students can clean up mechanical errors and put their composition into a neat, final form.

Stage 3: Revising

Revising is the time when writers clarify and refine the ideas in their compositions (Angelillo, 2005). Novice writers often break the writing process cycle as soon as they complete a rough draft, believing that once they have jotted down their ideas, the writing task is complete. Experienced writers, however, know that they must turn to others for reactions and revise on the basis of these comments (Sommers, 1994).

Revision is not just polishing; it is meeting the needs of readers by adding, substituting, deleting, and rearranging material. The word *revision* means "seeing again," and in this stage, writers see their compositions again with the help of their classmates and teacher. Here are activities in the revising stage:

- Rereading the rough draft
- Sharing the rough draft in a writing group
- Revising on the basis of feedback
- Conferencing with the teacher

Rereading the Rough Draft. After finishing the rough draft, writers need to distance themselves from it for a day or two, then reread it from a fresh perspective, as a reader might. As they reread, students make changes—adding, substituting, deleting, and moving—and place question marks by sections that need work. It is these trouble spots that students ask for help with in their writing groups.

Writing Groups

1 The writer reads. Students take turns reading their compositions aloud. Classmates listen politely, thinking about compliments they will make after the writer finishes reading. Only the writer looks at the composition, because when others look at it, they quickly notice and comment on mechanical errors, even though the emphasis during revising is on content. Listening to the writing read aloud keeps the focus on content.

2 Listeners offer compliments. Writing-group members say what they liked about the writing. These positive comments should be specific, rather than the often heard "I liked it" or "It was good."

3 The writer asks questions. Writers ask for assistance with trouble spots they identified earlier when rereading their writing, or they ask questions that reflect more general concerns about how well they are communicating.

4 Listeners offer suggestions. Members of the writing group ask questions about things that were unclear to them and make revision suggestions. Because it's difficult for students to appreciate suggestions, it's important to teach them what kinds of suggestions are acceptable and how to word their comments in helpful ways.

5 The process is repeated. Students repeat the first four steps as they share their rough drafts.

6 Writers plan for revision. At the end of the writing-group session, students make a commitment to revise their writing. When students verbalize their planned revisions, they are more likely to complete the revision stage. After the group disbands, students make the revisions.

Sharing in Writing Groups. Students meet in writing groups to share their compositions with classmates. Because writing must meet the needs of readers, feedback is crucial. Writing groups provide a scaffold in which teachers and classmates talk about plans and strategies for writing and revising (Calkins, 1994). The Step by Step feature on page 88 describes the procedure for writing groups.

Teaching students how to work in writing groups takes patience and practice. Teachers explain the purpose of writing groups and the steps in the procedure, and next, they model the steps using a rough draft they have written. Then small groups of students model the steps while their classmates watch, and teachers point out how to provide useful feedback to writers. Teachers often have students develop a list of meaningful comments and post it in the classroom for students to refer to during this stage. Figure 3–5 shows a sixth-grade class list of compliments, questions, and suggestions that students can offer to classmates. Teachers also coach students

---

FIGURE 3–5

Sixth Graders' List of Writing-Group Comments

Compliments	Questions	Suggestions
I liked the part where _____.	Did my introduction grab your attention?	Could you add more about _____ ?
Your lead grabbed my attention because _____ .	What do you want to know more about?	I think the part about _____ is long, and you could delete some of that.
My favorite sentence is _____ .	Did you understand my organization?	
I like the way you described _____ .	What do you think the best part of my paper is?	Which part is your conclusion?
I noticed this metaphor: _____ .	Are there some words that I need to change?	I think you should substitute a better word for _____ , such as _____ .
I could hear your "voice" when you wrote _____ .	Did you like my title?	Your organization isn't clear because _____ .
I like your conclusion because _____ .	Does my dialogue sound "real" to you?	I think you might try moving the part about _____ to _____ .
I liked your organization because _____ .	Is there something that isn't clear to you?	
Your sequence is _____ .	Is there something that I need to delete?	I think you used _____ too many times. Can you combine some sentences?
Your writing is powerful because it made me feel _____ .	Is there something I should move from one part of my writing to another part?	

on how to accept their classmates' compliments and suggestions for revision without getting upset.

Writing groups can form spontaneously when several students are ready to share their compositions, or they can be formal groupings with identified leaders. In some classrooms, writing groups form when four or five students finish their rough drafts. The students gather around a conference table or in a corner of the classroom. They take turns reading their rough drafts aloud, and classmates in the group listen and respond, offering compliments and suggestions for revision. Sometimes the teacher joins the writing group, but if the teacher is involved in something else, students work independently. In other classrooms, the writing groups are established. Students get together to share their writing when everyone in the group is ready. Sometimes the teacher participates in these groups, providing feedback along with the students. At other times, the writing groups can function independently. Four or five students are assigned to each group, and a list of groups and their members is posted in the classroom. Students take turns serving as group leader.

Making Revisions. Students make four types of changes—additions, substitutions, deletions, and moves—as they revise (Faigley & Witte, 1981). They add words, substitute sentences, delete paragraphs, and move phrases. Students often use a blue pen to cross out, draw arrows, and write in the space left between the double-spaced lines of their rough drafts so that revisions will show clearly. This way teachers can examine the types of revisions students make. Revisions are an important gauge of students' growth as writers.

Conferencing With the Teacher. Sometimes the teacher participates in the writing groups and provides revision suggestions along with the students, and at other times, the teacher conferences individually with students about their rough drafts. The teacher's role during conferences is to help students make choices and define directions for revision. Barry Lane (1993, 1999) offers these suggestions for talking with students about their papers:

- Have students come to a conference prepared to begin talking about their concerns. Students should talk first in a conference.
- Ask questions rather than give answers. Ask students what is working well for them, what problems they are having, and what questions they have.
- React to students' writing as a reader, not as a teacher. Offer compliments first; give suggestions later.
- Keep the conference short, and recognize that not all problem areas or concerns can be discussed.
- Limit the number of revision suggestions, and make all suggestions specific.
- Have students meet in writing groups before conferencing. Then students can share the feedback they received from classmates.
- To conclude the conference, ask students to identify the revisions they plan to make.
- Take notes during conferences and summarize students' revision plans. These notes are a record of the conference, and the revision plans can be used in assessing students' revisions.

It is time-consuming to meet with every student, but it's worth the time (Calkins, Hartman, & White, 2005). In a 5-minute conference, teachers listen to students talk about their writing processes, guide students as they make revision plans, and offer feedback during the writing process, when it is most usable.

Stage 4: Editing

Editing is putting the piece of writing into its final form. Until this stage, the focus has been primarily on the content of students' writing. Now the focus changes to mechanics. Students polish their writing by correcting misspellings and other mechanical errors. The goal here is to make the writing "optimally readable" (Smith, 1982). Writers who write for readers understand that if their compositions aren't readable, they have written in vain because their ideas will never be read.

Mechanics are the commonly accepted conventions of written Standard English; they include capitalization, punctuation, spelling, sentence structure, usage, and formatting considerations specific to poems, scripts, letters, and other writing forms. The use of these commonly accepted conventions is a courtesy to those who will read the composition.

Mechanical skills are best taught during the editing stage. When editing a composition that will be shared with a genuine audience, students are more interested in using mechanical skills correctly so that they can communicate effectively. In a study of two third-grade classes, Calkins (1980) found that the students in the class who learned punctuation marks as a part of editing could define or explain more marks than the students in the other class, who were taught punctuation skills in a traditional manner, with instruction and practice exercises on each punctuation mark. In other words, the results of this research, as well as other studies (Graves, 1994; Routman, 1996; Weaver, 1996), suggest that students learn mechanical skills better as part of the writing process than through practice exercises.

Students move through these activities during editing:

- Getting distance from the composition
- Proofreading to locate errors
- Correcting errors

Getting Distance. Students are more efficient editors if they set the composition aside for a few days before beginning to edit. After working so closely with a piece of writing during drafting and revising, they're too familiar with it to be able to locate many mechanical errors. With the distance gained by waiting a few days, children are better able to approach editing with a fresh perspective and gather the enthusiasm necessary to finish the writing process by making the paper optimally readable.

Proofreading. Students proofread their compositions to locate and mark possible errors. Proofreading is a unique type of reading in which students read slowly, word by word, hunting for errors rather than reading quickly for meaning. Concentrating on mechanics is difficult because our natural inclination is to read for meaning. Even experienced proofreaders often find themselves reading for meaning and overlooking errors that don't inhibit meaning. It's important, therefore, to take time to explain proofreading and demonstrate how it differs from regular reading.

To demonstrate proofreading, the teacher copies a piece of student writing on the chalkboard or displays it on an overhead projector. The teacher reads it several times, each time hunting for a particular type of error. During each reading, the teacher reads the composition slowly, softly pronouncing each word and touching the word with a pencil or pen to focus attention on it. The teacher circles possible errors as they are located.

Errors are marked or corrected with special proofreaders' marks. Students enjoy using these marks, the same ones that adult authors and editors use. Proofreaders' marks that children can learn to use in editing their writing are presented in Figure 3–6. Editing checklists help students focus on particular types of errors. Teachers develop checklists with two to six items appropriate for the grade level. A first-grade checklist, for example, might contain only two items—one about capital letters at the beginning of sentences and another about periods at the end of sentences. In contrast, a middle-grade checklist might have items such as using commas in a series, indenting paragraphs, capitalizing proper nouns, and spelling homonyms correctly. Teachers can revise the checklist during the school year to focus attention on skills that have recently been taught.

A third-grade editing checklist is presented in Figure 3–7. First, children proof-read their own compositions, searching for errors in each category on the checklist; after proofreading, they check off each item. Then, after completing the checklist, children sign their names and trade checklists and compositions with a classmate. Now they become editors and complete each other's checklists. Having both writer and editor sign the checklist helps them take the activity seriously.

FIGURE 3–6

Proofreaders' Marks

Delete	ℰ	There were cots to sleep on and food to eat on at the shelter.
Insert	∧	Mrs. Kim's cat is the color of carrots.
Indent paragraph	⌐P	Riots are bad. People can get hurt and buildings can get burned down but good things can happen too. People can learn to be friends.
Capitalize	≡	Daniel and his mom didn't like mrs. Kim or her cat.
Change to lowercase	/	People were Rioting because they were angry.
Add period	⊙	I think Daniel's mom and Mrs. Kim will become friends⊙
Add comma	∧	People hurt other people,they steal things,and they burn down buildings in a riot.
Add apostrophe	∨	Daniel's cat was named Jasmine.

FIGURE 3–7

A Third-Grade Editing Checklist

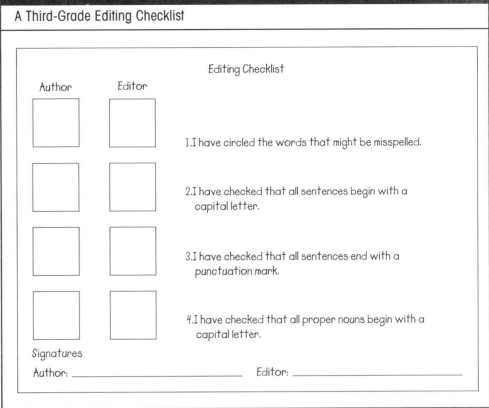

Editing Checklist

Author   Editor

1. I have circled the words that might be misspelled.

2. I have checked that all sentences begin with a capital letter.

3. I have checked that all sentences end with a punctuation mark.

4. I have checked that all proper nouns begin with a capital letter.

Signatures

Author: _____   Editor: _____

Correcting Errors. After students proofread their compositions, they correct the errors they've found individually or with an editor's assistance. Some errors are easy to correct, some require use of a dictionary, and others involve instruction from the teacher. It's unrealistic to expect students to locate and correct every mechanical error in their compositions. Not even published books are error free! Once in a while, students change a correct spelling and make it incorrect, but they correct far more errors than they create.

Editing can end after students and their editors correct as many mechanical errors as possible, or after students conference with the teacher for a final editing. When mechanical correctness is crucial, this conference is important. Teachers proofread the composition with the student, and they make the remaining corrections together, or the teacher makes checkmarks in the margin to note errors for the student to correct independently.

Stage 5: Publishing

During this stage, students bring their compositions to life by publishing them or sharing them orally with an appropriate audience. When they share their writing with classmates, other students, parents, and community members, students come to think of themselves as authors. In this stage, students

- make final copies of their writing;

- read from the author's chair;
- share their writing.

Making Final Copies. One of the most popular ways for students to publish their writing is by making books. Simple booklets can be made by folding a sheet of paper into quarters, like a greeting card. Students write the title on the front and use the three remaining sides for their compositions. They can also construct booklets by stapling sheets of writing paper together and adding construction paper covers. These stapled booklets can be cut into various shapes, too. Students can make more sophisticated books by covering cardboard covers with contact paper, wallpaper, or cloth; pages are sewn or stapled together, and the first

Meeting the Needs of English Learners

How Do Teachers Adapt the Writing Process for English Learners?

Stage 1: Prewriting

- Use drawing as a rehearsal activity.
- Have students "talk out" their compositions with a classmate before beginning to write.
- Brainstorm ideas and vocabulary words with students.

Stage 2: Drafting

- Have students dictate their rough drafts.
- Reassure students that spelling and other mechanical skills aren't important in this stage.

Stage 3: Revising

- Have students share their rough drafts with a trusted classmate before meeting in a writing group.
- Expect students to make only one or two revisions at first.

Stage 4: Editing

- Focus on one type of grammar/usage error at a time.
- Have students mark possible errors; then correct errors with them.
- Have students identify and correct errors on the first page of their compositions; then correct the remaining errors with students.

Stage 5: Publishing

- Provide opportunities for students to share their writing with classmates.
- Don't correct any remaining errors on the final copy.

and last pages (endpapers) are glued to the cardboard covers to hold the book together.

The Author's Chair. Teachers designate a special chair in their classroom as "the author's chair" (Graves & Hansen, 1983). This chair might be a rocking chair, a lawn chair with a padded seat, a wooden stool, or a director's chair, and it should be labeled "Author's Chair." Students sit in the chair to read aloud books they have written, and this is the only time anyone sits there.

When students share their writing, one student sits in the author's chair, and a group of classmates sit on the floor or in chairs in front of the author's chair (Karelitz, 1993). The student sitting in the author's chair reads the writing aloud and shows the accompanying illustrations. After the reading, classmates who want to comment raise their hands, and the author chooses several classmates to ask questions and give compliments. Then the author chooses another student to share and takes a seat in the audience.

Most students really enjoy reading their writing aloud to their classmates, and they learn about the importance of audience as they watch for their classmates' reactions. And classmates benefit from the experience as well: They get ideas for their own writing as they listen to how other students use sentence patterns and vocabulary that they might not be familiar with. The process of sharing their writing brings closure to the writing process and energizes students for their next writing project.

Sharing Writing. In addition to reading their writing to classmates, students share their writing in other ways, too. They may share it with larger audiences through hardcover books placed in the class or school library, plays performed for classmates, or letters sent to authors, businesses, and other correspondents. Here are other ways to share writing:

- Submit the piece to writing contests
- Display the writing as a mobile
- Contribute to a class anthology
- Submit it to a literary magazine
- Read it at a school assembly
- Share at a read-aloud party
- Share with parents and siblings
- Send it to a pen pal
- Post it on an e-zine
- Design a poster about the writing
- Read it to children in other classes

Through this sharing, students communicate with audiences who respond to their writing in meaningful ways.

Sharing writing is a social activity that helps students develop sensitivity to audiences and confidence in themselves as authors. Dyson (1985) advises that teachers consider the social interpretations of sharing—students' behavior, teacher's behavior, and interaction between students and teacher—within the classroom context. Individual students interpret sharing differently. More than just providing the opportunity for students to share writing, teachers need to teach students how to respond to their classmates. Teachers themselves serve as a model for responding to students' writing without dominating the sharing.

Teaching the Writing Process

Students learn to use the writing process as they write compositions in literature focus units and thematic units and as they participate in writing workshop. Learning to use the writing process is more important than any particular writing projects students might be involved in, because the writing process is a tool.

One way to introduce the writing process is to write a collaborative or group composition. The teacher models the writing process and provides an opportunity for students to practice the process approach to writing in a supportive environment. As students and teacher write a composition together, they move through the five stages of the writing process, just as writers do when they work independently. The teacher demonstrates the strategies writers use and clarifies misconceptions during the group composition, and students offer ideas for writing as well as suggestions for tackling common writing problems.

The teacher begins by introducing the idea of writing a group composition and reviewing the project. Students dictate a rough draft, which the teacher records on the chalkboard or on chart paper. The teacher notes any misunderstandings students have about the writing assignment or process and, when necessary, reviews concepts and offers suggestions. Then the teacher and students read the composition and identify ways to revise it. Some parts of the composition will need reworking, and other parts may be deleted or moved. More specific words will be substituted for less specific ones, and redundant words and sentences will be deleted. Students may also want to add new parts to the composition. After making the necessary content changes, students proofread the composition, checking for mechanical errors, for paragraph breaks, and for sentences to combine. They correct errors and make changes. Then the teacher or a student copies the completed composition on chart paper or on a sheet of notebook paper. Copies can be made and given to each student. Collaborative compositions are an essential part of many writing experiences,

---

How the Writing Process Fits Into the Four Patterns of Practice

Literature Focus Units

Students use the writing process as they create projects during the applying stage of the reading process.

Literature Circles

The writing process is not usually associated with literature circles because the focus is on reading, not writing.

Reading and Writing Workshop

Students regularly move through the stages of the writing process as they write stories, informational books, and other compositions.

Thematic Units

Students often create writing projects as part of thematic units, and they use the writing process to develop and refine their projects.

especially when students are learning to use the writing process because they serve as a dry run during which students' questions and misconceptions can be clarified.

Teachers also use minilessons to teach students how to gather and organize ideas for writing, how to participate in writing groups, how to proofread, and how to share their writing. Teachers teach these procedures, concepts, and strategies and skills during minilessons. Minilessons can be taught as part of class collaborations, during literature focus units and thematic units, and in writing workshop. Topics for minilessons on the writing process are listed on page 98, and a minilesson on one of the topics, revising, is presented on page 99. Many teachers use the editing stage as a time to informally assess students' spelling, capitalization, punctuation, and other mechanical skills and to give minilessons on a skill that students are having trouble with.

The Qualities of Effective Writing

Vicki Spandel (2005, 2008) and her colleagues at the Northwest Regional Educational Laboratory examined student writing to identify the traits or qualities of effective writing. Through their research, they identified these six traits: ideas, organization, voice, word choice, sentence fluency, and conventions. When students learn about these traits, they grow in their understanding of what effective writing looks like and develop a vocabulary to talk about writing. In a multiyear study, Culham (2003) found that teaching students about the six traits improves the quality of their writing.

◈ *Trait 1: Ideas* Ideas are the "heart of the message" (Culham, 2003, p. 11). When ideas are well developed, the writing is clear and focused. Effective details elaborate the big ideas and create images in readers' minds. As students examine this trait, they develop these abilities:

- Choosing original and interesting ideas
- Narrowing and focusing ideas
- Choosing details to develop an idea
- Using the senses to add imagery

Esperanza Rising (Ryan, 2000), the story of a girl and her mother who flee from Mexico and find work in California as migrant workers, demonstrates how effective authors develop ideas. The book's title emphasizes the theme: The main character's name is Esperanza, the Spanish word for *hope*, and she rises above her difficult circumstances. At the beginning of the book, Pam Muñoz Ryan paints a vivid picture of Esperanza's comfortable life on her family's ranch in Mexico, and later in the story, she creates a powerful contrast as she describes Esperanza's harsh existence in a migrant labor camp. As the story ends, Esperanza remains hopeful, telling her good friend Isabel never to be afraid of starting over.

◈ *Trait 2: Organization* Organization is the internal structure of a composition; its function is to enhance the central idea. Spandel (2001) explains that organization is putting "information together in an order than informs, persuades, or entertains" (p. 39). The logical pattern of the ideas varies according to genre; stories, for example, are organized differently than nonfiction or poetry. As students learn about organization, they develop these abilities:

- Using structural patterns in their writing
- Crafting leads to grab the readers' attention

What Students Need to Learn About the Reading and Writing Processes

Topics

Procedures	Concepts	Strategies and Skills
The Reading Process		
Do shared reading	**The reading process**	Predict
Do buddy reading		Visualize
Do guided reading	Aesthetic reading	Make connections
Do independent reading	Efferent reading	Make inferences
Respond in reading logs	Comprehension	Summarize
Participate in grand conversations		Monitor
Create projects		
The Writing Process		
Choose a topic	**The writing process**	Gather ideas
Cluster	Functions of writing	Organize ideas
Quickwrite	Writing forms	Draft
Participate in writing groups	Audience	*Revise*
Write "All About the Author" pages	Proofreaders' marks	Proofread
Share published writing	Author's chair	

I invite you to explore some of these topics by visiting MyEducationLab. To examine how a sixth-grade teacher involves students in a prewriting activity and how fourth graders participate in editing, go to the topic "Writing" and click on the videos "Prewriting" and "Editing." If you'd like to see how third graders create charts about the writing process, go to the topic "Visually Representing" and click on the video "Charts: The Writing Process."

Minilesson

Ms. Yarborough Introduces Revising to Third Graders

1 Introduce the topic

Ms. Yarborough names the five stages of the writing process as she points to the writing process charts hanging in the classroom. She explains that the focus today is on revising and points to that chart. She reminds children that the purpose of revising is to make their writing better and explains that writers add, delete, substitute, and move words and sentences as they revise.

2 Share examples

Ms. Yarborough shares this paragraph on the chalkboard and explains that she wrote it because they are studying about amphibians:

> *Amphibians live in water and on land. They live in water when they are babies. They live on land when they grow up. Frogs are some amphibians.*

She reads the paragraph aloud and asks the class to help her make it better by adding, deleting, substituting, and moving words and sentences.

3 Provide information

Children work with Ms. Yarborough to revise the paragraph. They add words and sentences and reorder sentences in the paragraph. As children make suggestions, Ms. Yarborough writes the changes on the chalkboard. Here is the revised paragraph:

> *Amphibians live part of their lives in water and part on land. Frogs, toads and salamanders are amphibians. They hatch from eggs in water, grow up, and live on land when they are adults. This process of changing is called metamorphosis.*

4 Supervise practice

Ms. Yarborough divides children into small groups and gives each group another paragraph about amphibians to revise. Children work together to make revisions, using blue pens and making marks as Ms. Yarborough demonstrated. Ms. Yarborough circulates as they work, and then children share their rough drafts and revised paragraphs with the class.

5 Reflect on learning

Ms. Yarborough asks children to compare the rough drafts and revised paragraphs and decide which are better. Then children brainstorm a list of reasons why revision is important. Their list includes: "The writing is more interesting," "It's more fun to read," and "The words are more scientific."

- Using transition words to link ideas together
- Writing satisfying endings

Louis Sachar's award-winning novel *Holes* (1998) is a well-organized story about a hapless boy named Stanley Yelnats who is wrongly convicted of theft and sent to Camp Green Lake, a juvenile detention facility where he spends every day digging holes. The beginning, middle, and end of the story are easy to pick out: The beginning is before Stanley arrives at Camp Green Lake, the middle is while he's there, and the end is when he escapes and redeems himself. What makes this book unique is the second plot about a curse that has followed the Yelnats family for generations. As the book ends, Stanley fulfills his destiny by digging up the truth and unraveling the family curse.

◆ **Trait 3: Voice** Voice is the writer's style; it's what breathes life into writing. Culham (2003) calls it "the soul of the piece" (p. 12). The writer's voice can be humorous or compelling, reflective or persuasive. What matters most is that the author connects with readers. Students develop their own voices in these ways:

- Retelling familiar stories from the viewpoints of different characters
- Assuming a persona and writing from that person's viewpoint
- Using strong verbs
- Avoiding redundancy and vague wording

Catherine, Called Birdy (Cushman, 1994), the fictional diary of a rebellious teenager in medieval England, has a compelling voice that keeps you reading from the first page to the last. In this witty first-person account of daily life, Birdy recounts how she avoids marrying any of the rich suitors that her father brings to meet her. Her journal entries have an authentic ring because they're infused with period details and sprinkled with exclamations, such as "corpus bones" and "God's thumbs," that sound plausible.

◆ **Trait 4: Word choice** Carefully chosen words have the power to clarify meaning or to create a mood. It's important for writers to choose words that fit both their purpose and the audience to whom their writing is directed. Students increase their word knowledge through literature focus units and lots of reading. As students experiment with word choice, develop these abilities:

- Using precise nouns, vivid verbs, and colorful modifiers
- Consulting a thesaurus to consider options
- Avoiding tired words and phrases
- Using wordplay

Readers appreciate the importance of careful word choice in Pamela Duncan Edwards's collection of alliterative stories, including *Clara Caterpillar* (2001), *Some Smug Slug* (1996), and *The Worrywarts* (2003). These tongue-twister books are fun to read aloud.

◆ **Trait 5: Sentence fluency** Sentence fluency is "the rhythm and flow of carefully structured language that makes it both easy and pleasurable to read aloud" (Spandel, 2001, p. 101). Effective sentences vary in structure and length, and students are now encouraged to include some sentence fragments to add rhythm and energy to their writing (Culham, 2003). Teachers teach students about sentence structure so that they develop these abilities:

- Varying sentence structure and length
- Including some sentence fragments

- Beginning sentences in different ways
- Combining or expanding sentences

In *Old Black Fly* (Aylesworth, 1992), a pesky fly goes on an alphabetical rampage until he is finally stopped by a fly swatter. The rhythm and flow of the snappy couplets make this a popular read-aloud book, and after reading, students are eager to try their hand at creating an imitative poem featuring an old grinning grasshopper or an old slippery seal.

◆ *Trait 6: Conventions* Conventions guide readers through the writing. Mechanics, paragraphing, and design elements are three types. Writers check that they've used Standard English mechanics—spelling, punctuation, capitalization, and grammar—as a courtesy to readers. They verify that their division of the text into paragraphs enhances the organization of the ideas. They also create a design for their compositions and arrange the text on the page to enhance readability. Students learn to apply these conventions during the editing and publishing stages of the writing process:

- Proofreading to identify mechanical errors
- Using a dictionary to correct spelling errors
- Checking paragraphing
- Adding design elements to the final copy

The importance of punctuation is highlighted in *Punctuation Takes a Vacation* (Pulver, 2003). After reading the book, teachers can remove the punctuation in excerpts from a familiar book so students can see what happens when "punctuation takes a vacation." The page layout is important in many picture books. In Jan Brett's *The Umbrella* (2004), a story set in the rain forest, and in many of her other books, illustrations on the edge of the left-hand pages show what happened on the previous page, and illustrations on the edge of the right-hand pages show what will happen next.

Teaching the Six Traits. A good way to introduce the six traits is by having students examine what makes a favorite book effective. For example, in Janet Stevens and Susan Stevens Crummel's *Jackalope* (2003), the story of a jackrabbit who wishes to be feared so his fairy godrabbit gives him horns, there's a lot to like. A class of fourth graders identified these qualities:

- The story is told by an armadillo. (Ideas, Organization)
- Armadillo sounds like he's a cowboy. (Voice)
- The story mentions fairy tales and nursery rhymes. (Ideas)
- The beginning, middle, and end are easy to pick out. (Organization)
- Some of the sentences rhyme. (Sentence fluency)
- What the armadillo says is typed in colored boxes. (Conventions)
- The funny vegetable wordplays are italicized so you are sure to notice them. (Word choice, Conventions)
- Jack is a good character because he saved the fairy godrabbit. (Ideas)
- The theme is clear: You should be happy being yourself. (Ideas)
- We didn't find any spelling or punctuation or capitalization mistakes. (Conventions)

Later, the students reread their comments and classified them according to the traits they illustrate, and like many of the best books available for children today, *Jackalope* exemplifies all of them!

Teachers introduce the six traits one by one through a series of minilessons. They explain the characteristics of the trait using stories and other books as models. Once students have some knowledge of the trait, they examine how other students applied the trait in sample compositions, and then they revise other sample compositions to incorporate the trait. Next, they apply what they've learned in their own writing.

Linking the Six Traits to the Writing Process. The writing process is a cyclical series of activities that students use as they draft and refine their writing, but it doesn't specify how to make writing better. That's where the six traits come in: Students apply what they've learned about the traits to improve the quality of their writing, particularly during the revising and editing stages (Culham, 2003).

As students reread their rough drafts, they can check that their writing exemplifies each of the traits. Teachers can develop rubrics that focus on one or more traits that students can use to self-assess their writing. Students also ask classmates in a revising group for feedback about how they might improve their sentence fluency, organization, or another trait. The six traits provide another reason for students to carefully proofread their rough drafts. They learn that they correct mechanical errors and check paragraphing to improve the readability of their compositions. Students also think about the design for their published compositions. They decide how to arrange the text on the page in order to make their writing more understandable, and with word processing, students can make their writing look very professional.

Connections Between Reading and Writing

Reading and writing are both meaning-making processes, and readers and writers are involved in remarkably similar activities. Tierney (1983) explains that reading and writing involve concurrent, complex transactions between readers and writers. Writers participate in several types of reading activities; for example, they read other authors' works to obtain ideas and to learn about the structure of stories and other texts, but they also read and reread their own work to discover, monitor, and clarify. The quality of these reading experiences seems closely tied to success in writing. Readers are writers, too: They participate in many of the same activities that writers use—generating ideas, organizing, monitoring, problem solving, and revising.

The reading and writing processes have comparable stages (Butler & Turbill, 1984). Figure 3–8 shows the stages of reading and writing and the similar activities at each stage. For example, notice the similarities between the activities listed for the third stage of reading and writing—responding and revising, respectively. Fitzgerald (1989) analyzed these activities and concluded that they draw on similar processes of author-reader-text interactions. Similar analyses can be made for activities in the other stages as well.

Readers and writers use similar strategies for constructing meaning as they interact with print. As readers, we use a variety of problem-solving strategies to make decisions about an author's meaning and to construct meaning for ourselves. As writers, we also use problem-solving strategies to decide what our readers need as we construct meaning for them and for ourselves. Tierney and Pearson (1983) compare reading to writing by describing reading as a composing process because readers compose and refine meaning through reading, much as writers do.

FIGURE 3–8

A Comparison of the Reading and Writing Processes

	What Readers Do	**What Writers Do**
Stage 1	*Prereading*	*Prewriting*
	Readers use knowledge about • the topic • reading • literature • language systems	Writers use knowledge about • the topic • writing • literature • language systems
	Readers' expectations are cued by • previous reading/writing experiences • genre • purpose for reading • audience for reading	Writers' expectations are cued by • previous reading/writing experiences • genre • purpose for writing • audience for writing
	Readers preview the text and make predictions.	Writers gather and organize ideas.
Stage 2	*Reading*	*Drafting*
	Readers • use word-identification strategies • use comprehension strategies • monitor reading • create meaning	Writers • use spelling strategies • use writing strategies • monitor writing • create meaning
Stage 3	*Responding*	*Revising*
	Readers • respond to the text • clarify misunderstandings • develop interpretations	Writers • respond to the text • clarify misunderstandings • develop interpretations
Stage 4	*Exploring*	*Editing*
	Readers examine the text by • considering the impact of words and literary language • exploring structural elements • comparing the text to others	Writers examine the text by • correcting mechanical errors • reviewing paragraph and sentence structure
Stage 5	*Applying*	*Publishing*
	Readers • develop projects to extend knowledge • share projects with classmates • reflect on the reading process • value the piece of literature • feel success • want to read again	Writers • produce the finished copy of their compositions • share their compositions with genuine audiences • reflect on the writing process • value the composition • feel success • want to write again

Adapted from Butler & Turbill, 1984.

Teachers can help students appreciate the similarities between reading and writing and understand the importance of connecting the two language arts when they follow these guidelines:

- Involve students in daily reading and writing activities.
- Introduce the reading and writing processes in kindergarten.
- Talk with students about the similarities between the reading and writing processes.
- Teach students about the reading and writing strategies.
- Emphasize both the processes and the products of reading and writing.
- Emphasize the purposes for which students use reading and writing.
- Teach reading and writing using genuine literacy experiences.

Tierney explains: "What we need are reading teachers who act as if their students were developing writers and writing teachers who act as if their students were readers" (1983, p. 151). Reading contributes to students' writing development, and writing contributes to students' reading development (Schulze, 2006; Shanahan, 1988).

Review

Reading and writing are similar processes of constructing meaning. Teachers organize reading and writing instruction using the five stages of the reading and writing processes. Students learn to use the reading and writing processes through literature focus units, literature circles, reading and writing workshop, and thematic units. Here are the key concepts presented in this chapter:

- Students use aesthetic reading when they read for enjoyment and efferent reading when they read for information.
- Four factors in developing capable readers are word identification, fluency, vocabulary, and comprehension.
- The five stages of the reading process are prereading, reading, responding, exploring, and applying.
- Five ways to read a selection are shared reading, guided reading, independent reading, buddy reading, and listening as it is read aloud.
- Students use the reading process during literature focus units, literature circles, reading workshop, and thematic units.
- The five stages of the writing process are prewriting, drafting, revising, editing, and publishing.
- Purpose, form, and audience influence students' compositions.
- Students use the writing process as they write during literature focus units, writing workshop, and thematic units.
- Teachers present minilessons on procedures, concepts, and strategies and skills in the reading and writing processes.
- The goal of both reading and writing is to construct meaning, and the two processes have comparable activities at each stage.

Professional References

Allen, J. (1999). *Words, words, words.* Portsmouth, NH: Heinemann.

Angelillo, J. (2005). *Making revision matter.* New York: Scholastic.

Barnes, D., Morgan, K., & Weinhold, K. (Eds.). (1997). *Writing process revisited: Sharing our stories.* Urbana, IL: National Council of Teachers of English.

Blachowicz, C., & Fisher, P. (2006). *Teaching vocabulary in all classrooms* (3rd ed.). Upper Saddle River, NJ: Merrill/Prentice Hall.

Blanton, W. E., Wood, K. D., & Moorman, G. B. (1990). The role of purpose in reading instruction. *The Reading Teacher, 43,* 486–493.

Britton, J., Burgess, T., Martin, N., McLeod, A., & Rosen, H. (1975). *The development of writing abilities, 11–18.* London: Schools Council Publications.

Bromley, K. D. (1996). *Webbing with literature: Creating story maps with children's books* (2nd ed.). Boston: Allyn & Bacon.

Butler, A., & Turbill, J. (1984). *Towards a reading-writing classroom.* Portsmouth, NH: Heinemann.

Calkins, L. M. (1980). When children want to punctuate: Basic skills belong in context. *Language Arts, 57,* 567–573.

Calkins, L. M. (1994). *The art of teaching writing* (2nd ed.). Portsmouth, NH: Heinemann.

Calkins, L., Hartman, A., & White, Z. (2005). *One to one: The art of conferring with young writers.* Portsmouth, NH: Heinemann.

Culham, R. (2003). *6 + 1 traits of writing: The complete guide, grades 3 and up.* New York: Scholastic.

Dowhower, S. L. (1991). Speaking of prosody. Fluency's unattended bedfellow. *Theory Into Practice, 30,* 165–173.

Dyson, A. H. (1985). Second graders sharing writing: The multiple social realities of a literacy event. *Written Communication, 2,* 189–215.

Dyson, A. H. (1986). The imaginary worlds of childhood: A multimedia presentation. *Language Arts, 63,* 799–808.

Eeds, M., & Peterson, R. L. (1995). What teachers need to know about the literary craft. In N. L. Roser & M. G. Martinez (Eds.), *Book talk and beyond: Children and teachers respond to literature* (pp. 10–23). Newark, DE: International Reading Association.

Faigley, L., & Witte, S. (1981). Analyzing revision. *College Composition and Communication, 32,* 400–410.

Fisher, B., & Medvic, E. F. (2000). *Perspectives on shared reading: Planning and practice.* Portsmouth, NH: Heinemann.

Fitzgerald, J. (1989). Enhancing two related thought processes: Revision in writing and critical thinking. *The Reading Teacher, 43,* 42–48.

Flower, L., & Hayes, J. R. (1994). The cognition of discovery: Defining a rhetorical problem. In S. Perl (Ed.), *Landmark essays on writing process* (pp. 63–74). Davis, CA: Heragoras Press.

Fountas, I. C., & Pinnell, G. S. (1996). *Guided reading: Good first teaching for all children.* Portsmouth, NH: Heinemann.

Fountas, I. C, & Pinnell, G. S. (2001). *Guiding readers and writers, grades 3–6.* Portsmouth, NH: Heinemann.

Gardner, H. (2000). *Intelligence reframed: Multiple intelligences for the 21st century.* New York: Basic Books.

Gillet, J. W., & Beverly, L. (2001). *Directing the writing workshop: An elementary teacher's handbook.* New York: Guilford Press.

Graves, D. H. (1994). *A fresh look at writing.* Portsmouth, NH: Heinemann.

Graves, D. H., & Hansen, J. (1983). The author's chair. *Language Arts, 60,* 176–183.

Holdaway, D. (1979). *The foundations of literacy.* Portsmouth, NH: Heinemann.

Irwin, J. W. (1993). *Teaching reading comprehension processes* (2nd ed.). Boston: Allyn & Bacon.

Karelitz, E. B. (1993). *The author's chair and beyond: Language and literacy in a primary classroom.* Portsmouth, NH: Heinemann.

Lane, B. (1993). *After the end: Teaching and learning creative revision.* Portsmouth, NH: Heinemann.

Lane, B. (1999). *The reviser's toolbox.* Shoreham, VT: Discover Writing Press.

Langer, J. A. (1985). Children's sense of genre. *Written Communication, 2,* 157–187.

Murray, D. H. (1982). *Learning by teaching.* Montclair, NJ: Boynton/Cook.

National Reading Panel. (2000). *Teaching children to read: An evidence-based assessment of the scientific research literature on reading and its implications for reading instruction, reports of the subgroups.* Washington, DC: National Institute of Child Health and Human Development.

Opitz, M. F., & Rasinski, T. V. (1998). *Good-bye round robin: Twenty-five effective oral reading strategies.* Portsmouth, NH: Heinemann.

Pardo, L. W. (2004). What every teacher needs to know about comprehension. *The Reading Teacher, 58,* 272–280.

Pearson, P. D., & Gallagher, M. (1983). The instruction of reading comprehension. *Contemporary Educational Psychology, 8,* 317–344.

Perl, S. (1994). Understanding composing. In S. Perl (Ed.), *Landmark essays on writing process* (pp. 99–106). Davis, CA: Heragoras Press.

Peterson, R., & Eeds, M. (1990). *Grand conversations: Literature groups in action.* New York: Scholastic.

Pressley, M. (2002). Comprehension strategies instruction: A turn-of-the-century status report. In C. C. Block & M. Pressley (Eds.), *Comprehension instruction: Research-based practices* (pp. 11–27). New York: Guilford Press.

Rasinski, T. V. (2004). Creating fluent readers. *Educational Leadership, 61*(6), 46–51.

Rosenblatt, L. M. (2005). *Making meaning with texts: Selected essays.* Portsmouth, NH: Heinemann.

Routman, R. (1996). *Literacy at the crossroads: Crucial talk about reading, writing, and other teaching dilemmas.* Portsmouth, NH: Heinemann.

Schulze, A. C. (2006). *Helping children become readers through writing.* Newark DE: International Reading Association.

Shanahan, T. (1988). The reading-writing relationship: Seven instructional principles. *The Reading Teacher, 41,* 636–647.

Smith, F. (1982). *Writing and the writer.* New York: Holt, Rinehart and Winston.

Sommers, N. (1994). Revision strategies of student writers and experienced adult writers. In S. Perl (Ed.), *Landmark essays on writing process* (pp. 75–84). Davis, CA: Heragoras Press.

Spandel, V. (2001). *Books, lessons, ideas for teaching the six traits: Writing in the elementary and middle grades.* Wilmington, MA: Great Source Education Group.

Spandel, V. (2005). *Creating writers: Through 6-trait writing assessment and instruction* (4th ed.). Boston: Allyn & Bacon.

Spandel, V. (2008). *Creating young writers: Using the six traits to enrich writing process in primary classrooms* (2nd ed.). Boston: Allyn & Bacon.

Stahl, S. A. (1999). *Vocabulary development.* Cambridge, MA: Brookline Books.

Sweet, A. P., & Snow, C. E. (2003). Reading for comprehension. In A. P. Sweet & C. E. Snow (Eds.), *Rethinking reading comprehension* (pp. 1–11). New York: Guilford Press.

Taylor, D. (1993). *From the child's point of view.* Portsmouth, NH: Heinemann.

Tierney, R. J. (1983). Writer-reader transactions: Defining the dimensions of negotiation. In P. L. Stock (Ed.), *Forum: Essays on theory and practice in the teaching of writing* (pp. 147–151). Upper Montclair, NJ: Boynton/Cook.

Tierney, R. J., & Pearson, P. D. (1983). Toward a composing model of reading. *Language Arts, 60,* 568–580.

Weaver, C. (1996). *Teaching grammar in context.* Portsmouth, NH: Heinemann.

Yaden, D. B., Jr. (1988). Understanding stories through repeated read-alouds: How many does it take? *The Reading Teacher, 41,* 556–560.

Children's Book References

Aylesworth, J. (1992). *Old black fly.* New York: Henry Holt.

Brett, J. (2004). *The umbrella.* New York: Putnam.

Butterworth, C. (2006). *Sea horse: The shyest fish in the sea.* Cambridge, MA: Candlewick Press.

Creech, S. (2003). *Granny Torrelli makes soup.* New York: HarperCollins.

Curtis, C. P. (1999). *Bud, not Buddy.* New York: Delacorte.

Cushman, K. (1994). *Catherine, called Birdy.* New York: HarperCollins.

Danziger, P. (1995). *Amber Brown goes fourth.* New York: Putnam.

Edwards, P. D. (1996). *Some smug slug.* New York: HarperCollins.

Edwards, P. D. (2001). *Clara caterpillar.* New York: HarperCollins.

Edwards, P. D. (2003). *The worrywarts.* New York: HarperCollins.

Fowler, A. (1990). *It's a good thing there are insects.* Chicago: Childrens Press.

Hale, S. (2005). *Princess academy.* New York: Bloomsbury.

Howe, D., & Howe, J. (2006). *Bunnicula: A rabbit-tale of mystery.* New York: Aladdin Books.

Lowry, L. (2006). *The giver.* New York: Delacorte.

Pulver, R. (2003). *Punctuation takes a vacation.* New York: Holiday House.

Ryan, P. M. (2000). *Esperanza rising.* New York: Scholastic.

Sachar, L. (1998). *Holes.* New York: Farrar, Straus & Giroux.

Stevens, J., & Crummel, S. S. (2003). *Jackalope.* San Diego: Harcourt Brace.

chapter four

Emerging Into Literacy

I n Mrs. Kirkpatrick's kindergarten–first grade multiage classroom, the children participate in weeklong literature focus units. She uses the featured book for shared reading and center activities that children work on while she teaches guided reading groups using leveled books at children's reading levels. This week's featured book is *If You Give a Mouse a Cookie* (Numeroff, 1985), a circular story about a mouse who, after receiving a cookie, wants a glass of milk, a straw, a napkin, other items, and finally another cookie. Mrs. Kirkpatrick has copies of both the regular-size and the big book versions of the story as well as copies of four other books by the same author that incorporate the same circular pattern, *If You Give a Moose a Muffin* (Numeroff, 1991), *If You Give a Pig a Pancake* (Numeroff, 1998), *If You Take a Mouse to the Movies* (Numeroff, 2000), and *If You Take a Mouse to School* (2002).

Mrs. Kirkpatrick teaches language arts for 2 1/2 hours each morning. Children sample cookies and talk about their favorite cookies on Monday before Mrs. Kirkpatrick begins to read the featured book using shared reading. Children read and reread the big book version of the story several times, and each time they are able to read more of the words themselves. The predictable pattern of the text and picture clues make it easier for the children to be successful. Later in the week, the children read the regular-size versions of the book individually or with buddies. Mrs. Kirkpatrick moves through the

*H*ow do teachers support children's emergence into reading and writing?

In kindergarten and first grade, children acquire phonemic awareness and phonics knowledge, learn to recognize and print the letters of the alphabet, and develop concepts about print. Literature focus units facilitate children's emergence into literacy because the book provides the foundation for a combination of direct instruction and authentic reading and writing activities. As you read this vignette, notice how Mrs. Kirkpatrick provides instruction and opportunities to nurture her students' emergence into literacy.

reading process as children respond to the story in a grand conversation, compare it to other circular stories that Laura Numeroff has written, and draw pictures and write in reading logs.

The children also participate in exploring-stage activities. Mrs. Kirkpatrick draws their attention to specific words in the story, and together they write vocabulary words on a word wall. She also teaches high-frequency words, which are posted on another word wall in the classroom. One of the high-frequency words this week is *you;* the children locate the word again and again in the story and reread all the high-frequency words that have been posted on the word wall in the classroom. Mrs. Kirkpatrick teaches minilessons on phonics concepts, using sample words from the featured book to make the connection that phonics knowledge is useful for reading and writing. She also teaches minilessons about irregular plurals after children ask whether *mouses* or *mice* is the correct plural form. They also practice reading skills at centers.

Children work on two culminating projects. They write pages for a class book following Laura Numeroff's pattern and using their own names. For example: *If you give Graciela a bag of popcorn, she will want a glass of juice.* They also make a cookie quilt to hang on the wall of the classroom. Each child makes a square for the paper quilt by designing a cookie in the center of the square and writing or dictating a sentence that is written underneath. The box on page 110 presents a stage-by-stage outline showing how Mrs. Kirkpatrick teaches the book *If You Give a Mouse a Cookie.*

Later in the morning, Mrs. Kirkpatrick meets with children in small groups for guided reading while their classmates work in centers. Two sixth graders come to the classroom to help supervise centers so Mrs. Kirkpatrick can concentrate on the reading groups. The activities at most of the centers are related to the featured book. For example, at one center, children retell the story by sequencing objects or cards with pictures of objects related to the story. A list of the centers in Mrs. Kirkpatrick's classroom is shown on page 111. Three of the centers are required, and they are marked with an asterisk in

Outline for a Literature Focus Unit on *If You Give a Mouse a Cookie*

1. **Prereading**

   - The teacher brings in several types of cookies for children to sample. Children talk about their favorite cookies, and they create a graph to chart their favorite cookies.
   - The teacher introduces the book using a big book version of the story.
   - The teacher shares a book box of objects or pictures of objects mentioned in the story (cookie, glass of milk, straw, napkin, mirror, scissors, broom, etc.), and children talk about how some of the items might be used in the story.
   - Children and the teacher begin the word wall with *cookie* and *mouse*.

2. **Reading**

   - The teacher reads the big book version of *If You Give a Mouse a Cookie* using shared reading.
   - The teacher rereads the book, and children join in when they can or they repeat each sentence after the teacher reads it.

3. **Responding**

   - The children and the teacher participate in a grand conversation about the book.
   - Children dramatize the story using objects in the book box.
   - Children draw pictures in reading logs and add words and sentences (using invented spelling) to record their reactions to the book.

4. **Exploring**

   - Children and teacher add interesting and important words to the word wall.
   - Children read regular-size versions of the book with partners and reread the book independently.
   - The teacher teaches minilessons on the /m/ sound or other phonemic awareness or phonics concepts.
   - The teacher explains the concept of a circular story, and children sequence picture cards of the events in the story to make a circle diagram.
   - The teacher presents a minilesson about the author, Laura Numeroff, and reads other books by the author.
   - Children make word posters of words on the word wall.
   - The teacher teaches a minilesson on irregular plurals (e.g., *mouse–mice, child–children*).
   - The teacher sets up centers for children to sort objects related to the phonemic awareness/phonics lesson, listen to *If You Give a Moose a Muffin* (Numeroff, 1991) and other books by the author, write books about cookies, and use cards to sequence story events.

5. **Applying**

   - Children write their own versions of the story or original circle stories.
   - Children create a cookie quilt.

The Centers in Mrs. Kirkpatrick's Classroom

Comprehension Center

Children wear a mouse hand puppet as they sequence objects and retell *If You Give a Mouse a Cookie.* Copies of the book are available at the center to use to check the order of events in the story.

Phonics Center*

Children sort a collection of objects into baskets labeled with letters. *Mm* is this week's featured letter and sound, and Mrs. Kirkpatrick has set out these *Mm* objects: toy mouse, milk carton, marble, toy monkey, macaroni, play money, mitten, and toy man. In addition, she sets out books with other phonics activities that are appropriate for children in each of the guided reading groups.

Listening Center

Children listen to books written by Laura Numeroff and write and draw pictures in their reading logs.

Writing Center*

Children make books about cookies, write a retelling of the story, or write a new version of the story. A poster with cookie labels and names of cookies and a word wall with words related to the story are posted nearby.

Quilt Center

Children make cookie blocks for the class paper quilt. A variety of art materials are available at the center for children to use.

High-Frequency Word Center

Children mark *you,* the high-frequency word of the week, and other familiar high-frequency words on charts posted at the center using Wikki-Stix (pipe cleaners covered in wax) shaped into circles. They also use magnetic letters, plastic linking letters, or foam letters to practice spelling the words.

Reading Center*

Children select and read leveled books independently. Leveled books arranged in plastic tubs are available at the center for children to choose from.

---

*Required centers

the figure. The others are free choice, and children must complete at least two of them during the week. They work at their own pace and move freely from center to center, carrying their work folders with them. Stapled inside the folders is a weekly list of centers, and the sixth-grade aides place a stamp beside the name of the center when children complete work there.

---

*I*s there a magic age when children become readers and writers? Researchers used to think that at the age of 6, most children were ready to learn to read and write, but now we know that children begin the process of becoming literate gradually during the preschool years. Very young children notice signs, logos, and other environmental print. Who hasn't observed children making scribbles on paper as they try to "write"? As children are read to, they learn how to hold a book and turn pages, and they observe how the text is read. Most children come to kindergarten and first grade

- Reading and writing letters to pen pals
- Reading and writing charts and maps

Concept of a Word. Children's understanding of the concept of a "word" is an important part of becoming literate. Young children have only vague notions of language terms, such as *word, letter, sound,* and *sentence,* that teachers use in talking about reading and writing (Invernizzi, 2003). Preschoolers equate words with the objects the words represent. As they are introduced to reading and writing experiences, children begin to differentiate between objects and words, and finally they come to appreciate that words have meanings of their own.

Several researchers have investigated children's understanding of a word as a unit of language. Papandropoulou and Sinclair (1974) identified four stages of word consciousness. At the first level, young children don't differentiate between words and things. At the next level, children describe words as labels for things. They consider words that stand for objects as words, but don't classify articles and prepositions as words because words such as *the* and *with* cannot be represented with objects. At the third level, children understand that words carry meaning and that stories are built from words. At the fourth level, more fluent readers and writers describe words as autonomous elements having meanings of their own with definite semantic and syntactic relationships. Children might say, "You make words with letters." Also, at this level, children understand that words have different appearances—they can be spoken, listened to, read, and written.

Environmental Print. Young children's "reading" experiences often begin with environmental print. Many children begin reading by recognizing logos on fast-food restaurants, department stores, grocery stores, and commonly used household items within familiar contexts (Harste, Woodward, & Burke, 1984). They recognize the golden arches of McDonald's and say "McDonald's," but when they are shown the word *McDonald's* written on a sheet of paper without the familiar sign and restaurant setting, they cannot yet read the word. Researchers have found that young emergent readers depend on context to read familiar words and memorized texts (Sulzby, 1985). Slowly, children develop relationships linking form and meaning as they learn concepts about written language and gain more experience reading and writing.

When children begin writing, they use scribbles or single letters to represent complex ideas (Clay, 1991). As they learn about letter names and phoneme-grapheme correspondences, they use one, two, or three letters to stand for a word. At first they run their writing together, but they slowly learn to segment words and leave spaces between words. They sometimes add dots or lines as markers between words, or they draw circles around words. They also move from capitalizing words randomly to using a capital letter at the beginning of a sentence and to mark proper nouns. Similarly, children move from using periods at the end of each line of writing to marking the ends of sentences with periods. Then they learn about other end-of-sentence markers and, finally, about punctuation marks that are embedded in sentences.

Literacy Play Centers. Young children learn about the functions of reading and writing as they use written language in their play. As they construct block buildings, children write signs and tape them on the buildings; as they play doctor, they write prescriptions on slips of paper; and as they play teacher, they read stories aloud to friends who are pretending to be students or to doll and stuffed-animal "students." Young children use these activities to reenact familiar, everyday activities and to

Literacy Play Centers
These kindergartners use reading and writing as they play in the housekeeping center. They read recipes and food-package labels as they cook, for example, and write telephone messages when they answer the telephone. They also leave messages for classmates who will visit this center. After "baking" clay cookies, these children wrote this message using invented spelling: GD KE R U (good cookies for you). Through these activities, young children learn to value reading and writing because of the important role literacy can play in their lives.

Anne Vega/Merrill

pretend to be someone or something else. Through these literacy-enriched play activities, children use reading and writing for a variety of functions.

Kindergarten teachers adapt play centers and add literacy materials to enhance their value for literacy learning. Housekeeping centers are probably the most common play centers in kindergarten classrooms, but teachers can transform them into grocery stores, post offices, or medical centers by changing the props (Bennett-Armistead, Duke, & Moses, 2005). Materials for reading and writing can be included in each of these centers. Food packages, price stickers, and money are props in grocery store centers; letters, stamps, and mailboxes in post office centers; and appointment books, prescription pads, and folders for patient records in medical centers. A variety of literacy play centers can be set up in classrooms to coordinate with thematic units. Ideas for literacy play centers are offered in Figure 4–1; each center includes authentic literacy materials that children can experiment with and use to learn more about the functions of written language.

Concepts About the Alphabet

Young children also develop concepts about the alphabet and how letters are used to represent phonemes. Children use this phonics knowledge to decode unfamiliar words as they read and to create spellings for words as they write. Too often it is assumed that phonics instruction is the most important component of the reading

---

FIGURE 4–1

Literacy Play Centers With Reading and Writing Materials

Post Office Center

mailboxes	wrapping paper	package seals
envelopes	tape	address labels
stamps (stickers)	packages	cash register
pens	scale	money

Hairdresser Center

hair rollers	towel	curling iron (cordless)
brush and comb	posters of hairstyles	ribbons, barrettes, clips
mirror	wig and wig stand	appointment book
empty shampoo bottle	hair dryer (cordless)	open/closed sign

Restaurant Center

tablecloth	napkins	aprons/vests for waitstaff
dishes	menus	hat and apron for chef
glasses	tray	
silverware	order pad and pencil	

Medical Center

appointment books	stethoscope	folders (for patient
white shirt/jacket	thermometer	records)
medical bag	tweezers	prescription bottles
hypodermic syringe	bandages	and labels
(play)	prescription pad	walkie-talkie

Grocery Store Center

grocery cart	price stickers	marking pen
food packages	cash register	cents-off coupons
plastic fruit and	money	advertisements
artificial foods	grocery bags	

---

program for young children, but phonics is only one of the four language systems. Emergent readers and writers use all four language systems—phonological, semantic, syntactic, and pragmatic—as well as their knowledge about written language concepts as they read and write.

The Alphabetic Principle. The one-to-one correspondence between the phonemes (or sounds) and graphemes (or letters), such that each letter consistently represents one sound, is known as the *alphabetic principle*. In phonetic languages, there is a one-to-one correspondence; however, English is not a purely phonetic language. The 26 letters represent approximately 44 phonemes, and three letters—*c*, *q*, and *x*—are superfluous because they do not represent unique phonemes. The letter *c*, for example, can represent either /k/ as in *cat* or /s/ as in *city*, and it can be joined with *h* for the digraph /ch/. To further complicate matters, there are more than 500 spellings to represent the 44 phonemes. Consonants are more consistent and predictable than vowels. Long *e*, for instance, is spelled more than 10 ways in common words.

Words are spelled phonetically approximately half the time (Hanna, Hanna, Hodges, & Rudorf, 1966). The nonphonetic spellings of many words reflect morphological information. The word *sign*, for instance, is a shortened form of *signature*, and the spelling shows this relationship. Spelling the word phonetically (i.e., *sine*) might seem simpler, but the phonetic spelling lacks semantic information (Venezky, 1999).

Letter Names. The most basic information children learn about the alphabet is to identify letter names and form the letters in handwriting. They notice letters in environmental print, and they often learn to sing the ABC song. Five-year-olds can usually recognize some letters, especially those in their own names, in names of family members and pets, and in common words in their homes and communities. They can also write some of these familiar letters.

Young children associate letters with meaningful contexts—names, signs, T-shirts, and cereal boxes. Research suggests that children do not learn alphabet letter names in any particular order or by isolating letters from meaningful written language. McGee and Richgels (2003, 2007) concluded that learning letters of the alphabet requires many, many experiences with meaningful written language. They recommend that teachers take three steps to encourage children's alphabet learning:

◆ *Capitalize on children's interests.* Teachers provide letter activities that children enjoy and talk about letters when children are interested in talking about them. Teachers know what features to comment on because they observe children during reading and writing activities to find out which letters or letter features children are exploring. Children's questions also provide insights into what they are curious about.

◆ *Talk about the role of letters in reading and writing.* Teachers talk about how letters represent sounds and how letters combine to spell words, and they point out capital and lowercase letters. Teachers often talk about the role of letters as they write with children.

◆ *Teach routines and provide opportunities for alphabet learning.* Teachers use children's names and environmental print in literacy activities, do interactive writing, encourage children to use invented spellings, share alphabet books, and play letter games to teach the letters of the alphabet.

Teachers begin teaching letters of the alphabet using two sources of words—children's own names and environmental print. They also teach children to sing the ABC song so that they will have a strategy to use to identify a particular letter: Children sing the song and point to each letter on an alphabet chart until they reach the unfamiliar letter. This is an important strategy because it gives them a real sense of independence in identifying letters. Teachers also provide routines, activities, and games for talking about and manipulating letters. During these familiar, predictable activities, teachers and children say letter names, manipulate magnetic letters, and write letters on dry-erase boards. At first the teacher structures and guides the activities, but with experience, the children internalize the routine and do it independently, often at a literacy center. Figure 4–2 presents 10 routines to teach the letters of the alphabet.

It's crucial that instruction to teach children to identify and print the letters of the alphabet be embedded in meaningful and authentic reading and writing experiences (McGee & Richgels, 2003). Instruction is meaningful when children can tie what they are learning to their own world and authentic when children can apply what they are learning to reading and writing stories and other books. Children recognize and write

FIGURE 4–2

Routines to Teach the Letters of the Alphabet

Environmental Print
Teachers collect food labels, toy traffic signs, and other environmental print for children to use in identifying letters. Children sort labels and other materials to find examples of a letter being studied.

Alphabet Books
Teachers read aloud alphabet books to build vocabulary and teach the names of words that represent each letter. Then children reread the books and consult them to think of words when making books about a letter.

Magnetic Letters
Children pick all examples of one letter from a collection of magnetic letters or match upper- and lowercase letterforms of magnetic letters. They also arrange the letters in alphabetical order and use the letters to spell their names and other familiar words.

Letter Stamps
Students use letter stamps and ink pads to stamp letters on paper or in booklets. They also use letter-shaped sponges to paint letters and letter-shaped cookie cutters to make cookies and to cut out clay letters.

Key Words
Teachers use alphabet charts with a picture of a familiar object for each letter. It is crucial that children be familiar with the objects or they won't remember the key words. Teachers recite the alphabet with children, pointing to each letter and saying, "A—apple, B—bear, C—cat," and so on.

Letter Containers
Teachers collect coffee cans or shoe boxes, one for each letter of the alphabet. They write upper- and lowercase letters on the outsides of the containers and place several familiar objects or pictures of objects that represent the letter in each one. Teachers use these containers to introduce the letters, and children use them at a center for sorting and matching activities.

Letter Frames
Teachers make circle-shaped letter frames from tagboard, collect large plastic bracelets, or shape pipe cleaners or Wikki-Stix (pipe cleaners covered in wax) into circles for students to use to highlight particular letters on charts or in big books.

Letter Books and Posters
Children make letter books with pictures of objects beginning with a particular letter on each page. They add letter stamps, stickers, or pictures cut from magazines. For posters, the teacher draws a large letterform on a chart and children add pictures, stickers, and letter stamps.

Letter Sorts
Teachers collect objects and pictures representing two or more letters. Then children sort the objects and place them in containers marked with the specific letters.

Dry-Erase Boards
Children practice writing upper- and lowercase forms of a letter and familiar words on dry-erase boards.

the letters found in environmental print and in their classmates' names, find familiar letters and words on classroom signs and in books, write letters and words as they respond to literature, and make books.

Being able to name the letters of the alphabet is a good predictor of beginning reading achievement, even though knowing the names of the letters doesn't directly affect a child's ability to read (Adams, 1990). A more likely explanation for this relationship between letter knowledge and reading is that children who have been actively involved in reading and writing activities before entering first grade know the names of the letters, and they are more likely to begin reading quickly. Simply teaching children to name the letters without the accompanying reading and writing experiences does not have this effect.

Phonemic Awareness. *Phonemic awareness* is children's basic understanding that speech is composed of a series of individual sounds, and it provides the foundation for phonics (Yopp, 1992). When children can choose a duck as the animal that begins with /d/ from a collection of toy animals, identify *duck* and *luck* as rhyming words, or blend the sounds /d/ /ŭ/ /k/ to pronounce *duck*, they're phonemically aware. (Note that the emphasis is on the sounds of spoken words, not reading letters or pronouncing letter names.) Developing phonemic awareness enables children to use sound-symbol correspondences to read and spell words. It isn't sounding out words for reading or using spelling patterns to write words; rather, it's the ability to manipulate sounds orally.

Understanding that words are composed of smaller units—phonemes—is a significant achievement for young children because phonemes are abstract language units. Phonemes carry no meaning, and children think of words according to their meanings, not their linguistic characteristics (Griffith & Olson, 1992). When children think about ducks, for example, they think of animals covered with feathers that swim in ponds and make noises we describe as "quacks"; they don't think of *duck* as a word with three phonemes or four graphemes or as a word beginning with /d/ and rhyming with *luck*. Phonemic awareness requires that children treat speech as an object. They shift their attention away from the meaning of words to the linguistic features of speech. This focus on phonemes is even more complicated because phonemes are not discrete units in speech. Often they are slurred together; think about the blended initial sound in *tree* and the ending sound in *eating*.

Children develop phonemic awareness in two ways. They learn playfully as they sing songs, chant rhymes, and listen to parents and teachers read wordplay books to them. Yopp (1995) recommends that teachers read books with wordplay aloud and encourage children to talk about the books' language. Teachers ask questions and make comments, such as "Did you notice how _____ and _____ rhyme?" and "This book is fun because of all the words beginning with the _____ sound." Once children are very familiar with the book, they can create new verses or make other variations. Books such as *Cock-a-doodle-moo!* (Most, 1996), *The Hungry Thing* (Slepian & Seidler, 2001), and *The Stuffed Animals Get Ready for Bed* (Inches, 2006) stimulate children to experiment with sounds, create nonsense words, and become enthusiastic about reading. When teachers read books with alliterative or assonant patterns, such as *Busy Buzzing Bumblebees and Other Tongue Twisters* (Schwartz, 1992), children attend to the smaller units of language.

Teachers also teach lessons to help children understand that their speech is composed of sounds (Ball & Blachman, 1991). The goal of phonemic awareness activities is

Teachers teach sound-symbol correspondences, how to blend sounds to decode words and segment sounds for spelling, and the most useful phonics generalizations, or "rules." Phonics concepts build on phonemic awareness. The most important concepts that primary-grade students learn—consonants, vowels, rimes and rhymes, phonics generalizations—are explained in the next sections.

◆ **Consonants** Letters are classified as either consonants or vowels. The consonants are *b, c, d, f, g, h, j, k, l, m, n, p, q, r, s, t, v, w, x, y,* and *z.* Most consonants represent a single sound consistently, but there are some exceptions. *C,* for example, does not represent a sound of its own: When it is followed by *a, o,* or *u,* it is pronounced /k/ (e.g., *castle, coffee, cut*), and when it is followed by *e, i,* or *y,* it is pronounced /s/ (e.g., *cell, city, cycle*). *G* represents two sounds, as the word *garbage* illustrates. It is usually pronounced /g/ (e.g., *glass, go, green, guppy*), but when *g* is followed by *e* or *i,* it is pronounced /j/, as in *giant. Gy* is not a common English spelling, but when *g* is followed by *y* (e.g., *energy, gypsy, gymnasium*), it is usually pronounced /j/. *X* is also pronounced differently according to its location in a word. When *x* is at the beginning of a word, it is often pronounced /z/, as in *xylophone,* but sometimes the letter name is used, as in *x-ray.* At the end of a word, *x* is pronounced /ks/, as in *box.*

The letters *w* and *y* are particularly interesting. At the beginning of a word or syllable, they are consonants (e.g., *wind, yard*), but when they are in the middle or at the end of a word or syllable, they are vowels (e.g., *saw, flown, day, by*).

Two kinds of combination consonants are blends and digraphs. *Consonant blends* are two or three consonants that appear next to each other in words and whose individual sounds are blended together, as in *grass, belt,* and *spring. Consonant digraphs* are letter combinations that represent single sounds. The four most common are *ch* as in *chair* and *each, sh* as in *shell* and *wish, th* as in *father* and *both,* and *wh* as in *whale.* Another consonant digraph is *ph,* as in *graph* and *photo.*

◆ **Vowels** The remaining five letters—*a, e, i, o,* and *u*—represent vowels, and *w* and *y* are also vowels when used in the middle and at the end of syllables and words. Vowels represent several sounds. The most common are short and long vowels. The short vowel sounds are /ă/ as in *cat,* /ĕ/ as in *bed,* /ĭ/ as in *win,* /ŏ/ as in *hot,* and /ŭ/ as in *cup.* The long vowel sounds are the same as the letter names, and they are illustrated in the words *make, feet, bike, coal,* and *suit.* Long vowels are usually spelled with two vowels, except when *e* or *y* is used at the end of a word or syllable (e.g., *belong, try*).

When *y* is a vowel at the end of a word, it is pronounced as long *e* or long *i,* depending on the length of the word. In one-syllable words, such as *by* and *try,* the *y* is pronounced as long *i,* but in most longer words, such as *baby* and *happy,* the *y* is pronounced as long *e.*

Vowel sounds are more complicated than consonant sounds, and many vowel combinations represent long vowels and other vowel sounds. Consider these combinations:

ai as in *nail*	*oa* as in *soap*
au as in *laugh* and *caught*	*oi* as in *oil*
aw as in *saw*	*oo* as in *cook* and *moon*
ea as in *peach* and *bread*	*ou* as in *house* and *through*
ew as in *sew* and *few*	*ow* as in *now* and *snow*
ia as in *dial*	*oy* as in *toy*
ie as in *cookie*	

Most vowel combinations are vowel digraphs or diphthongs. When two vowels represent a single sound, the combination is a vowel digraph (e.g., *nail, snow*), and when two vowels represent a glide from one sound to another, the combination is a diphthong. Two vowel combinations that are consistently diphthongs are *oi* and *oy,* but other combinations, such as *ou* in *house* (but not in *through*) and *ow* in *now* (but not in *snow*) are diphthongs when they represent a glided sound. In *through,* the *ou* represents the o͞o sound as in *moon,* and in *snow,* the *ow* represents the ō sound.

When *r* follows one or more vowels in a word, it influences the pronunciation of the vowel sound, as in *car, air, are, ear, bear, first, for, more, murder,* and *pure.* These sounds are called *r*-controlled vowels. Because they are difficult to sound out, students learn many of these words as sight words.

The vowels in the unaccented syllables of multisyllabic words are often softened and pronounced "uh," as in the first syllable of *about* and *machine* and the final syllable of *pencil, tunnel, zebra,* and *selection.* This vowel sound is called a *schwa* and is represented in dictionaries with ə, which looks like an inverted *e.*

Rimes and Rhymes. One-syllable words and syllables in longer words can be divided into two parts, the onset and the rime. The onset is the consonant sound, if any, that precedes the vowel and the rime is the vowel and any consonant sounds that follow it. For example, in *show, sh* is the onset and *ow* is the rime, and in *ball, b* is the onset and *all* is the rime. For *at* and *up,* there is no onset; the entire word is the rime. Research has shown that children make more errors decoding and spelling final consonants than initial consonants and that they make more errors on vowels than on consonants (Treiman, 1985). These problem areas correspond to rimes, and educators now speculate that teaching onsets and rimes could provide a key to developing children's phonemic awareness.

Children can focus their attention on a rime, such as *ay,* and create rhyming words, including *bay, day, lay, may, play, say,* and *way.* These words can be read and spelled by analogy because the vowel sounds are consistent in rimes. Wylie and Durrell (1970) identified 37 rimes that can be used to produce nearly 500 words that primary-grade students read and write. These rimes and some common words using them are presented in Figure 4–4.

Phonics Generalizations. Because English does not have a one-to-one correspondence between sounds and letters, both linguists and educators have created rules or generalizations to clarify English spelling patterns. One rule is that *q* is followed by *u* and pronounced /kw/ (e.g., *queen* and *earthquake*). There are very few exceptions to this rule. Another generalization that has few exceptions relates to *r*-controlled vowels: *r* influences the preceding vowel so that its sound is neither long nor short (e.g., *car, market, birth,* and *four*). There are exceptions, however; for instance, *fire.*

Many generalizations aren't very useful because there are more exceptions to the rule than words that conform (Clymer, 1996). A good example is the "when two vowels go walking" rule: When there are two vowels side by side, the long vowel sound of the first one is pronounced and the second is silent. Examples of words conforming to this rule are *meat, soap,* and *each.* There are more exceptions, however, including *food, said, head, chief, bread, look, soup, does, too, again,* and *believe.*

Only a few phonics generalizations have a high degree of utility for readers. The generalizations that work most of the time are the ones that students should learn because they are the most useful (Adams, 1990). Eight high-utility generalizations are listed in the LA Essentials box on the next page. Even though these rules are fairly reliable, very few of them approach 100% utility. The *r*-controlled vowel rule is useful in 78% of words in which the letter *r* follows the vowel (Adams, 1990). Other commonly taught, useful rules have even lower percentages of utility. The CVC pattern rule—which says that when a one-syllable word has only one vowel and the vowel comes between two consonants, it is usually short, as in *bat, land,* and *cup*—is estimated to work 62% of the time. Exceptions include *told, fall, fork,* and *birth.* The CVCe pattern rule—which says that when there are two vowels in a one-syllable word and one vowel is an *e* at the end of the word, the first vowel is long and the final *e* is silent— is estimated to work in 63% of CVCe words. Examples of conforming words are *came, hole,* and *pipe,* and two very common exceptions are *have* and *love.*

Children learn phonics as a natural part of reading and writing activities, but teachers also teach phonics directly and systematically. They explain many phonics concepts as they engage children in authentic literacy activities using children's names, titles of books, and environmental print in the classroom. During these teachable moments, teachers answer children's questions about words, model how to use phonics knowledge to decode and spell words, and have children share the strategies they use for reading and writing (Mills, O'Keefe, & Stephens, 1992). For example, as part of a literature focus unit on *The Very Hungry Caterpillar* (Carle, 2001), teachers might point out that *very* begins with *v* but that not many words start with *v.* Children might mention other *v* words, such as *valentine.* Teachers also demonstrate how to apply phonics information as they read big books with the class and do interactive writing. As they read and spell words, teachers break words apart into sounds and apply phonics rules and generalizations.

FIGURE 4–4

37 Common Rimes

Rime	Examples	Rime	Examples
-ack	black, pack, quack, stack	-ide	bride, hide, ride, side
-ail	mail, nail, sail, tail	-ight	bright, fight, light, might
-ain	brain, chain, plain, rain	-ill	fill, hill, kill, will
-ake	cake, shake, take, wake	-in	chin, grin, pin, win
-ale	male, sale, tale, whale	-ine	fine, line, mine, nine
-ame	came, flame, game, name	-ing	king, sing, thing, wing
-an	can, man, pan, than	-ink	pink, sink, think, wink
-ank	bank, drank, sank, thank	-ip	drip, hip, lip, ship
-ap	cap, clap, map, slap	-ir	fir, sir, stir
-ash	cash, dash, flash, trash	-ock	block, clock, knock, sock
-at	bat, cat, rat, that	-oke	choke, joke, poke, woke
-ate	gate, hate, late, plate	-op	chop, drop, hop, shop
-aw	claw, draw, jaw, saw	-or	for, or
-ay	day, play, say, way	-ore	chore, more, shore, store
-eat	beat, heat, meat, wheat	-uck	duck, luck, suck, truck
-ell	bell, sell, shell, well	-ug	bug, drug, hug, rug
-est	best, chest, nest, west	-ump	bump, dump, hump, lump
-ice	ice, mice, nice, rice	-unk	bunk, dunk, junk, sunk
-ick	brick, pick, sick, thick		

THE MOST USEFUL PHONICS GENERALIZATIONS

Pattern	Description	Examples	
Two sounds of *c*	The letter *c* can be pronounced as /k/ or /s/. When *c* is followed by *a, o,* or *u,* it's pronounced /k/—the hard *c* sound. When *c* is followed by *e, i,* or *y,* it's pronounced /s/—the soft *c* sound.	cat cough cut	cent city cycle
Two sounds of *g*	The sound associated with the letter *g* depends on the letter following it. When *g* is followed by *a, o,* or *u,* it's pronounced /g/—the hard *g* sound. When *g* is followed by *e, i,* or *y,* it's usually pronounced /j/—the soft *g* sound. Exceptions include *get* and *give.*	gate go guess	gentle giant gypsy
CVC pattern	When a one-syllable word has only one vowel and the vowel comes between two consonants, it's usually short. One exception is *told.*	bat cup land	
Final *e* or CVCe pattern	When there are two vowels in a one-syllable word and one of them is an *e* at the end of the word, the first vowel is long and the final *e* is silent. Two exceptions are *have* and *love.*	home safe dune	
CV pattern	When a vowel follows a consonant in a one-syllable word, the vowel is long. Exceptions include *the, to,* and *do.*	go be	
r-controlled vowels	Vowels that are followed by the letter *r* are overpowered and are neither short nor long. One exception is *fire.*	car for birthday	
-igh	When *gh* follows *i,* the *i* is long and the *gh* is silent. Two exceptions are *neighbor* and *eight.*	high night	
kn- and *wr-*	In words beginning with *kn-* and *wr-,* the first letter isn't pronounced.	knee write	

Adapted from Clymer, 1996.

Teachers also present minilessons on specific high-utility phonics concepts, skills, and generalizations as part of a systematic program. According to Shefelbine, the program should be "systematic and thorough enough to enable most students to become independent and fluent readers; yet still efficient and streamlined" (1995, p. 2). Phonics instruction is always tied to reading and writing because without meaningful reading and writing activities, children see little reason to learn phonics (Cunningham, 2005; Freppon & Dahl, 1991).

YOUNG CHILDREN EMERGE INTO READING

Children move through three stages as they learn to read: emergent reading, beginning reading, and fluent reading (Juel, 1991). In emergent reading, children gain an understanding of the communicative purpose of print. They notice environmental print, dictate stories for the teacher to record, and reread predictable books after they have memorized the pattern. From this foundation, children move into the beginning reading stage. In this stage, children learn phoneme-grapheme correspondences and begin to decode words. In the third stage, fluent reading, children have learned how to read. They recognize most words automatically and can decode unfamiliar words quickly. Children should reach this fluent stage by third grade. Once they are fluent readers, children are able to concentrate more of their cognitive energy on comprehension. This accomplishment is significant because beginning in fourth grade, children read more informational books and content-area textbooks as reading becomes a learning tool.

Primary-grade teachers organize language arts instruction into the same four patterns of practice that teachers of middle- and upper-grade students use, but they make special adaptations to accommodate young children's developing literacy abilities. Two instructional adaptations that primary-grade teachers use are shared reading and the Language Experience Approach. Through these approaches, kindergartners, first graders, and second graders read big books aloud with classmates, independently read books appropriate for their reading levels, and create texts by dictating their own words for teachers to record.

Shared Reading

Teachers and children read books together in shared reading. Usually the teacher reads aloud as children follow along in regular-size or enlarged, big book picture books. Teachers use this approach to share the enjoyment of high-quality literature when students cannot read the books independently (Fisher & Medvic, 2000; Holdaway, 1979). As they read, teachers also demonstrate how print works, provide opportunities for children to use the prediction strategy, and increase children's confidence in their ability to read. Shared reading is often used with emergent readers; however, teachers also use shared reading with older students who cannot read independently. The steps in shared reading are listed in the Step by Step feature on the next page.

Predictable Books. The stories and other books teachers use for shared reading with young children often have repeated words and sentences, rhyme, or other patterns. Books that use these patterns are known as *predictable books*. They are a valuable instructional tool because the repeated words and sentences, patterns, and sequence enable children to predict the next sentence or episode in the story

------ Shared Reading ------

Step by Step

1 Introduce the book.   Teachers introduce the book by activating children's prior knowledge about the topic or by presenting new information on a topic related to the book, and then by showing the cover of the book and reading the title and the author's name. Then children make predictions about what will happen in the book.

2 Read the book.   The teacher reads the book aloud while children follow along in individual copies or on a big book positioned on a chart rack beside the teacher. The teacher models fluent reading and uses a dramatic style to keep the children's attention. Teachers encourage children to chime in on words they know and on refrains. Periodically, teachers ask children to make predictions to redirect their attention to the text.

3 Respond to the book.   Children respond to the book by drawing and writing in reading logs and by sharing their responses in grand conversations.

4 Reread the book.   Children take turns turning pages and using the pointer to track the text as they reread the book. Teachers invite children to join in reading familiar and predictable words. Also, they take advantage of teachable moments to explain graphophonic cues and reading strategies.

5 Continue the process.   Teachers continue to reread the book with children one or two more times over a period of several days, again having them turn pages and take turns using the pointer to track the text while reading. They encourage children who can read the text to read along with them.

6 Have children read independently.   After children become familiar with the text, teachers distribute individual copies of the book for them to read independently.

---

or other book (Tompkins & Webeler, 1983). Here are four characteristics of predictable books:

◆ *Repetition.* Phrases and sentences are repeated to create a predictable pattern in many books for young children. Examples include *I Went Walking* (Williams, 1990), *Barnyard Banter* (Fleming, 1994), and *Polar Bear, Polar Bear, What Do You Hear?* (Martin, 1992). Sometimes each episode or section ends with the same words or a refrain, and in other books, the same statement or question is repeated. For example, in *The Little Red Hen* (Pinkney, 2006), the animals repeat "Not I" when the Little Red Hen asks them to help her plant the seeds, harvest the wheat, and bake the bread. After their refusals to help, the hen each time says, "Then I will."

◆ *Cumulative Sequence.* Phrases or sentences are repeated and expanded in each episode in these books. In the traditional story *The Gingerbread Boy* (Galdone, 1983), for instance, Gingerbread Boy repeats and expands his boast as he meets each character on his run away from Little Old Man and Little Old Woman. Other examples include *Jack's Garden* (Cole, 1995) and *Jump, Frog, Jump!* (Kalan, 2002).

◆ *Rhyme and Rhythm.* Rhyme and rhythm are important devices in some books. Many of the popular Dr. Seuss books, such as *Hop on Pop* (2003), are good examples. The sentences have a strong beat, and rhyme is used at the end of each line or in another poetic scheme. Also, some books have an internal rhyme—within lines rather than at the ends of lines. Other books in this category include familiar songs, such as *Shoo Fly!* (Trapani, 2000), and booklong verses, such as *Pattern Fish* (Harris, 2000).

◆ *Sequential Patterns.* Some books use a familiar sequence—such as months of the year, days of the week, numbers 1 to 10, or letters of the alphabet—to structure the text. For example, *The Very Hungry Caterpillar* (Carle, 2001) combines number and day-of-the-week sequences as the caterpillar eats through an amazing array of foods, and *Shiver Me Letters: A Pirate ABC* (Sobel, 2006) incorporates an alphabet sequence. A list of predictable books illustrating each of these patterns is presented in the Booklist below.

Big Books. Teachers use enlarged picture books called *big books* in shared reading, most commonly with primary-grade students (Ditzel, 2000). In this technique, developed in New Zealand, teachers place the enlarged picture book on an easel or chart rack where all children can see it; the teacher reads the big book with small groups of children or with the whole class (Holdaway, 1979). Trachtenburg and Ferruggia (1989) used big books with their class of transitional first graders and found that making and reading big books dramatically improved children's reading scores on standardized achievement tests. The teachers reported that children's self-concepts as readers were decidedly improved as well.

Booklist

YOUNG CHILDREN'S BOOKS WITH PREDICTABLE PATTERNS

Repetitive Sentences

Florian, D. (2000). *A pig is big.* New York: Greenwillow.
Guarino, D. (1997). *Is your mama a llama?* New York: Scholastic.
Hoberman, M. A. (2001). *"It's simple," said Simon.* New York: Knopf.

Martin, B., Jr. (1992). *Brown bear, brown bear, what do you see?* New York: Holt.
Westcott, N. B. (2003). *The lady with the alligator purse.* Boston: Little, Brown.

Cumulative Sequence

Brett, J. (2004). *The umbrella.* New York: Putnam.
Egielski, R. (1997). *The gingerbread boy.* New York: HarperCollins.
Pinkney, J. (2006). *The little red hen.* New York: Dial Books.

Taback, S. (1997). *There was an old lady who swallowed a fly.* New York: Viking.
West, C. (1996). *"I don't care!" said the bear.* Cambridge, MA: Candlewick Press.

Rhyme and Rhythm

Harris, P. (2006). *The night pirates.* New York: Scholastic.
Lies, B. (2006). *Bats at the beach.* Boston: Houghton Mifflin.

Martin, B., Jr., & Archambault, J. (1989). *Chicka chicka boom boom.* New York: Aladdin Books.
Raffi. (1999). *Down by the bay.* New York: Crown.

Sequential Patterns

Carle, E. (1984). *The very busy spider.* New York: Philomel.
Kraus, R. (1995). *Come out and play, little mouse.* New York: HarperCollins.
Numeroff, L. J. (2002). *If you take a mouse to school.* New York: HarperCollins.

Wadsworth, O. A. (2002). *Over in the meadow.* New York: North-South Books.
Wood, A. (2004). *The napping house.* San Diego: Harcourt Brace.

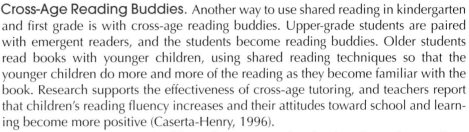

Many popular picture books, including *Silly Sally* (Wood, 1999), *How Much Is a Million?* (Schwartz, 1994), *There was an Old Lady Who Swallowed a Fly* (Taback, 1997), *Click, Clack, Moo: Cows That Type* (Cronin, 2000), and *Eating the Alphabet: Fruits and Vegetables From A to Z* (Ehlert, 2006), are available in big book editions from Scholastic. Teachers and children can also make big books themselves by printing the text of a book on large sheets of posterboard and adding illustrations.

Cross-Age Reading Buddies. Another way to use shared reading in kindergarten and first grade is with cross-age reading buddies. Upper-grade students are paired with emergent readers, and the students become reading buddies. Older students read books with younger children, using shared reading techniques so that the younger children do more and more of the reading as they become familiar with the book. Research supports the effectiveness of cross-age tutoring, and teachers report that children's reading fluency increases and their attitudes toward school and learning become more positive (Caserta-Henry, 1996).

Teachers arranging a buddy reading program decide when the students will get together, how long each session will last, and what the reading schedule will be. Primary-grade teachers explain the program to their students and talk about activities the buddies will be doing together. Upper-grade teachers teach a series of minilessons about how to work with young children, how to read aloud and encourage children to make predictions, how to use shared reading, how to select books to appeal to younger children, and how to help them respond to books. Then older students choose books to read aloud and practice reading them until they can read the books fluently.

At the first meeting, students pair off, get acquainted, and read together. They also talk about the books they have read and perhaps write in special reading logs. Buddies also may want to go to the library and choose the books they will read at the next session.

There are significant social benefits to cross-age tutoring programs. Children get acquainted with other children that they might otherwise not meet, and they learn how to work with older or younger children. As they talk about books they have read, they share personal experiences. They also talk about reading strategies, how to choose books, and their favorite authors or illustration styles. Sometimes reading buddies write notes back and forth, or they plan holiday celebrations together to strengthen the social connections between the children.

Traveling Bags of Books. Another way to encourage shared reading is to involve parents by using traveling bags of books. Teachers collect text sets of three, four, or five books on various topics for children to take home and read with their parents (Reutzel & Fawson, 1990). For example, teachers might collect copies of *The Gingerbread Boy* (Galdone, 1975), *Gingerbread Baby* (Brett, 1999), *Red Fox Dances* (Baron, 1996), and *Rosie's Walk* (Hutchins, 2005) for a traveling bag of fox stories. Then children and their parents read one or more of the books and draw or write a response to the books they have read in the reading log that accompanies the books in the traveling bag. One family's response after reading *The Gingerbread Boy* is shown in Figure 4–5. In this entry, the kindergartner drew a picture of Gingerbread Boy, an older sibling wrote the sentence the kindergartner dictated to accompany the picture, and the children's mother also wrote a comment. Children keep the bag at home for several days and then return it to school so that another child can borrow it. Teachers can also

FIGURE 4–5

A Family's Reading Log Entry Written After Reading *The Gingerbread Boy*

add small toys, stuffed animals, audiotapes of one of the books, or other related objects to the bags.

Teachers often introduce traveling bags at a special parents' meeting or an open house get-together and explain how parents use shared reading to read with their children. It is important for parents to understand that their children may not be familiar with the books and that they aren't expected to be able to read them independently. Teachers also talk about the responses that children and parents write in the reading log and show sample entries from the previous year.

Language Experience Approach

The Language Experience Approach (LEA) is based on children's language and experiences (Ashton-Warner, 1965; Stauffer, 1970). Children dictate words and sentences about their experiences, and the teacher takes down the dictation for them; the text they develop becomes the reading material. Because the language comes from the children themselves, and because the content is based on their experiences, they are usually able to read the text easily. Reading and writing are connected because children are actively involved in reading what they have written. The steps are shown in the Step by Step feature on page 131.

The Language Experience Approach is an effective way to help children emerge into reading. Even students who have not been successful with other types of reading activities can read what they have dictated. There is a drawback, however: Teachers

------------- Language Experience Approach -------------

Step by Step

1 **Provide an experience.**   A meaningful experience is identified to serve as the stimulus for the writing. For group writing, it can be a book read aloud, a field trip, or some other experience—such as having a pet or playing in the snow—that all children are familiar with. For individual writing, the stimulus can be any experience that is memorable for the particular child.

2 **Talk about the experience.**   Children and the teacher discuss the experience prior to writing. The purpose of the talk is to review the experience and generate words so that children's dictation will be more interesting and complete. Teachers often begin with an open-ended question, such as, "What are you going to write about?" As children talk about their experiences, they generate and organize ideas and brainstorm more specific vocabulary.

3 **Record the dictation.**   Teachers write down the child's dictation. Texts for individual children are written on sheets of writing paper or in small booklets, and group texts are written on chart paper. Teachers print neatly and spell words correctly, but they preserve children's language as much as possible. For individual texts, teachers continue to take the child's dictation and write until he or she hesitates. Then the teacher rereads what has been written and encourages the child to continue. For group texts, children take turns dictating sentences, and after writing each sentence, the teacher rereads it.

4 **Read the text.**   After the text has been dictated, the teacher reads it aloud, pointing to each word. This reading reminds children of the content of the text and demonstrates how to read it aloud with appropriate intonation. Then children join in the reading. After reading group texts together, individual children can take turns rereading. Group texts can also be copied so that each child has a copy to read independently.

provide a "perfect" model when they take children's dictation—they write neatly and spell all words correctly. After Language Experience activities, some young children aren't eager to do their own writing, because they prefer their teacher's "perfect" writing to their own childlike writing. To avoid this problem, teachers have young children do their own writing concurrently with the Language Experience activities so that they learn that sometimes they do their own writing, and at other times, the teacher takes their dictation.

YOUNG CHILDREN EMERGE INTO WRITING

Many young children become writers before entering kindergarten; others are introduced to writing during their first year of school (Schulze, 2006). Young children's writing development follows a pattern similar to their reading development: emergent writing, beginning writing, and fluent writing. In the first stage, emergent writing, children make scribbles to represent writing. At first, the scribbles appear randomly on a page, but with experience, children line up the letters or scribbles from left to right and from top to bottom. Children also begin to "read," or tell what their writing says. The next stage is beginning writing, and it signals children's growing awareness of the alphabetic principle. Children use invented spelling to represent words, and as they learn more about phoneme-grapheme correspondences, their writing approximates conventional spelling. They move from writing single words to writing sentences and experiment with capital letters and punctuation marks. The third stage is fluent writing, when children write in paragraphs and vary their writing according to genre. They use mainly correct spelling and other conventions of written language, including capital letters and punctuation marks.

Opportunities for writing begin on the first day of kindergarten and continue daily throughout the primary grades, regardless of whether children have already learned to read or write letters and words. Children often begin using a combination of art and scribbles or letterlike forms to express themselves (Ditzel, 2000). Their writing moves toward conventional forms as they apply concepts that they are learning about written language.

Four samples of young children's writing are shown in Figure 4–6. The first sample is a kindergartner's letter to the Great Pumpkin; the writing is at the emergent stage. The child wrote using scribbles, much like cursive, and followed the left-to-right, top-to-bottom orientation. The Great Pumpkin's comment, "I love you all," can be deciphered. The second sample is characteristic of the beginning stage. A kindergartner wrote this list of favorite foods as part of a literature focus unit on *The Very Hungry Caterpillar* (Carle, 2001). The list reads, "orange, strawberry, apple, pizza, birthday cake." The third sample is another example of beginning-stage writing, which was taken from a first grader's reading log. The child used invented spelling to list the animal characters that appear in *The Mitten* (Brett, 1989). The fifth animal from the top is a badger. The fourth sample is a page from a first grader's dinosaur book. The text reads, "No one ever saw a real dinosaur," and this child used a capital letter to begin the sentence and a period to mark the end. This sample shows the transition from beginning to fluent writing.

Introducing Young Children to Writing

Young children's writing grows out of talking and drawing (Schickedanz & Casbergue, 2004). As they begin to write, their writing is literally their talk written down, and children can usually express in writing the ideas they talk about. At the same time, children's letterlike marks develop from their drawing. With experience, children learn to differentiate between their drawing and their writing. Kindergarten teachers often explain to children that they should use crayons when they draw and pencils when they write. Teachers also differentiate where on a page children will write and draw: The drawing might go at the top of a page and the writing at the bottom, or children can use paper with space for drawing at the top and lines for writing at the bottom.

Teachers help children emerge into writing beginning on the first day of kindergarten when they give children pencils and encourage them to write. You might call

FIGURE 4–6

Four Samples of Young Children's Writing

young children's writing "kid writing" and contrast it with teachers' writing, or "adult writing." When young children understand that their writing is allowed to look different from adults' writing, they are more willing to experiment with writing. Teachers show children how to hold a pencil and do kid writing with scribbles; random, letterlike marks; or letters. During kindergarten and first grade, children's writing gradually comes more closely to approximate adult writing because teachers are modeling adult writing for children, teaching minilessons about written language, and involving them in writing activities.

Kid writing takes many different forms. Their scribbles may resemble letterlike forms, or sometimes children imitate adults' cursive writing. At first, the letters they string together don't have phoneme-grapheme correspondences, but with more experience, children invent spellings that represent more sound features of words and apply some spelling rules. A child's progressive writings of "Abbie is my dog. I love her very much" over a period of 18 months are presented in Figure 4–7. This child moves from using scribbles, to using single letters to represent words (top two entries), to spelling phonetically and misapplying a few spelling rules in the third and fourth entries. Note that in the fourth example, the child is experimenting with using periods to mark spaces between words. In the fifth example, the child's writing is more conventional, and more than half of the words are spelled correctly. The message is written as two sentences, which are marked at the beginning with capital letters and at the end with periods.

Kid writing gives young children permission to experiment with written language. Too often, children assume that they should write and spell like adults do, and they cannot. Without this ability, children do not want to write, or they ask teachers to spell every word or copy text out of books or from charts. Kid writing offers several strategies for writing and allows children to invent spellings that reflect their knowledge of written language.

Interactive Writing

Teachers use interactive writing to model conventional writing (Button, Johnson, & Furgerson, 1996; Tompkins & Collom, 2004). Children and the teacher collaborate on constructing the text to be written and then write it together. Teachers reinforce concepts about written language as they focus children's attention on individual words and on sounds within words. This procedure grew out of the Language Experience Approach, and conventional writing is used so that everyone can read the completed text.

Topics for interactive writing can come from stories students have read, classroom news, and information learned during thematic units. Children take turns holding the marking pen and doing the writing themselves. They usually sit in a circle on the carpet and take turns writing the text they construct on chart paper that is displayed on an easel. While one child is writing at the easel, the others are writing on small dry-erase boards in their laps.

Teachers begin by collecting the necessary materials. For whole-class or small-group activities, they collect chart paper, colored marking pens, white correction tape, an alphabet chart, magnetic letters, and a pointer. They also collect small

FIGURE 4–7

The Development of One Child's Kid Writing

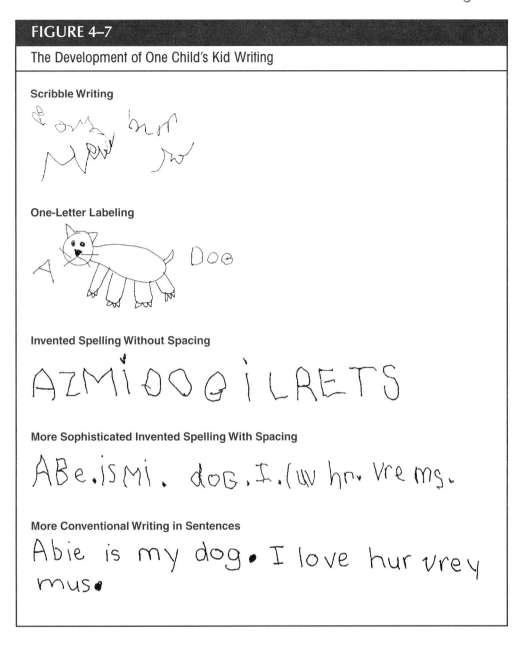

Scribble Writing

One-Letter Labeling

Doe

Invented Spelling Without Spacing

AZMIDOQiLRETS

More Sophisticated Invented Spelling With Spacing

ABe.isMi. doG.I.(uv hr. Vre ms.

More Conventional Writing in Sentences

Abie is my dog. I love hur vrey mus.

dry-erase boards, pens, and erasers for children to use. The steps in interactive writing are shown in the Step by Step feature on page 136.

When children begin interactive writing in kindergarten, they write letters to represent the beginning sounds in words and write familiar words such as *the, a,* and *is.* The first letters that children write are often the letters in their own names. As children learn more about sound-symbol correspondences and spelling patterns, they do more of the writing. Once children are writing words fluently, they can continue to do interactive writing as they work in small groups. Each child in the group uses a particular color pen, and children take turns writing letters, letter clusters, and words.

Interactive Writing

1 Collect materials. Teachers collect chart paper, colored marking pens, white correction tape, an alphabet chart, magnetic letters or letter cards, and a pointer. They also collect small dry-erase boards, pens, and erasers for individual children's writing.

2 Set a purpose. Teachers present a stimulus activity or set a purpose for the interactive writing activity. Often they read or reread a trade book, but children also write daily news, compose a letter, or brainstorm information they are learning in a thematic unit.

3 Pass out writing supplies. Teachers distribute individual dry-erase boards, pens, and erasers for children to use to write the text individually as it is written on chart paper. They periodically ask children to hold their boards up so they can see what each child is writing.

4 Choose a sentence to write. Teachers negotiate the text—often a sentence or two—with children. They repeat the sentence several times and segment it into words. The teacher also helps them remember the sentence as it is being written.

5 Write the first sentence word by word. Before writing the first word, teachers slowly pronounce the word, "stretching" it out. Then children take turns writing the letters in the first word. The teacher chooses children to write a sound or the entire word, depending on each child's knowledge of phonics and spelling. Teachers often have children use one color pen for the letters they write, and they use another color and write the parts of words that children can't spell. In that way, teachers can keep track of how much writing children are able to do. Teachers keep a poster with the upper- and lowercase letters of the alphabet to refer to when a child is unsure about a letterform, and they use white correction tape (sometimes called "boo-boo" tape) when a child writes a letter incorrectly or writes the wrong letter. After each word is written, one child serves as the "spacer" and uses his or her hand to mark the space between words and sentences. Teachers have children reread the sentence from the beginning each time a new word is completed. When appropriate, teachers call children's attention to capital letters, punctuation marks, and other conventions of print. They repeat this procedure to write additional sentences to complete the text.

6 Display the interactive writing. Teachers post the finished chart in the classroom and have children reread the text using shared or independent reading. They may also add artwork to "finish" the chart.

They also learn to use the white correction tape to correct poorly formed letters and misspelled words.

Figure 4–8 presents an interactive writing chart about brushing teeth, which was written over several days by a kindergarten class after a visit to a dentist. Notice that the children knew most beginning and ending sounds and the sight words *you* and *the.* Underlining has been added to show the letters the teacher wrote, and the boxes around letters indicate the use of correction tape.

Minilessons

Teachers teach minilessons about written language concepts and other reading and writing topics to children in kindergarten and the primary grades. Children learn about how reading and writing are used to convey messages and how children behave as readers and writers. A list of minilesson topics is presented on page 138, and a minilesson showing how to teach children to make predictions on page 139. These minilessons can be taught during literature focus units, in reading and writing workshop, and through other activities.

FIGURE 4–8

A Kindergarten Class's Interactive Writing Chart

Brushing Teeth
Brush your teeth after
You eat food.
Brush your teeth in the morning
and at night.
If You don't you will get
cavities.

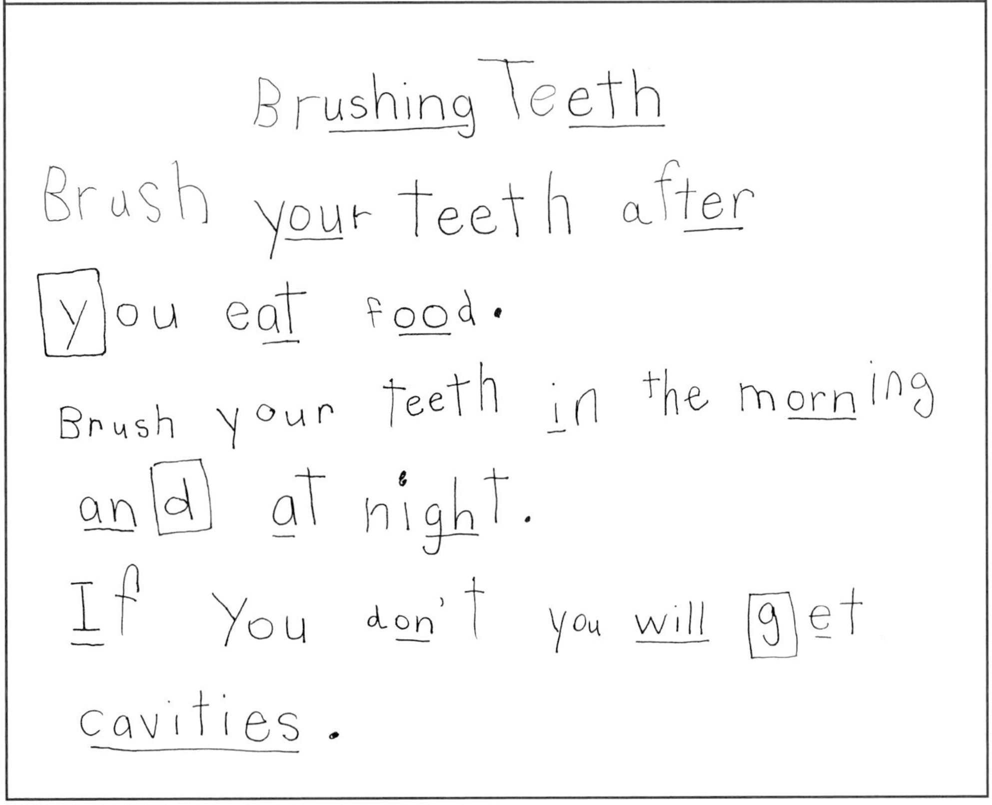

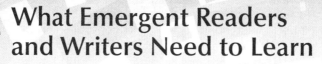

Planning for Instruction

What Emergent Readers and Writers Need to Learn

Topics

Procedures	Concepts	Strategies and Skills
Hold a book correctly	Direction of print	Identify letter names
Turn pages correctly	A word	Match upper- and lowercase
Separate words into	A sentence	letterforms
onsets and rimes	Uppercase letters	Identify phoneme-grapheme
Match printed words	Lowercase letters	correspondences
with words read aloud	Alphabetic principle	"Stretch" words
Do shared reading	Rhyming words	**Make predictions**
	The author's chair	
Dictate Language	Kid writing	Use capital letters
Experience stories		Use punctuation marks
Do interactive writing		Use invented spelling

To learn more about how teachers work with young children, please visit MyEducationLab. You can watch a first-grade teacher teach a guided reading lesson by going to the topic "Reading" and clicking on the video "Shared Reading." If you'd like to see an interactive writing lesson, go to the topic "Writing" and click on the video "Interactive Writing." And to see a first-grade teacher lead a daily news activity, click on the video "Daily News" in the topic "Viewing."

Review

Emergent literacy is based on research about how children learn to read and write. Young children learn concepts about written language as they experiment with reading and writing, and teachers demonstrate reading and writing through shared reading, interactive writing, and other teaching strategies. Children emerge into writing as they learn to use graphic symbols to represent their thoughts, and they refine their kid writing as they learn about phoneme-grapheme correspondences. Here are the key concepts presented in this chapter:

- Emergent literacy has replaced the traditional readiness approach.
- As children learn about words, they move from recognizing environmental print to reading decontextualized words in books.
- Children use phonics as well as information from the other three language systems as they learn to read.

Minilesson

Mr. Voss's Kindergartners Learn to Predict

1 Introduce the topic

Mr. Voss explains to his kindergarten class that before he begins to read a book, he thinks about it. He looks at the illustration on the book cover, reads the title, and makes a prediction or guess about the story.

2 Share examples

Mr. Voss shows the cover of *The Wolf's Chicken Stew* (Kasza, 1996) and thinks aloud about it. He says, "This book is about a wolf who is going to cook some delicious chicken stew. Yes, that makes sense because I know that wolves like to eat chickens. I think the wolf on the cover is looking for chickens to cook in the stew." Then Mr. Voss asks the kindergartners to agree or disagree. Most agree, but one child suggests that the wolf is looking for a supermarket to buy the chickens.

3 Provide information

Mr. Voss reads the book aloud, stopping several times to confirm or revise predictions. Children confirm the prediction once the hen and her chicks are introduced, but by the end, no one is surprised when the wolf befriends the chickens. After reading, they talk about how their predictions changed as they read the story.

4 Supervise practice

During story time for 5 days, the kindergartners make predictions before reading aloud. If the prediction seems far-fetched, Mr. Voss asks the child to relate it to the book or make a new prediction. Children confirm or revise predictions as they listen and discuss their predictions after reading.

5 Reflect on learning

Mr. Voss's students make a chart about predicting. The kindergartners dictate these sentences for the chart:

> *You have to turn on your brain to think before you read. You can make a prediction. Then you want to find out if you are right.*

- Both reading and writing development have three stages: emergent, beginning, and fluent.
- Teachers use shared reading to read books with young children.
- Other ways to use shared reading are cross-age reading buddies and traveling bags of books.
- Teachers use children's own language to create reading materials in the Language Experience Approach.
- Children are introduced to writing as they watch their parents and teachers write and as they experiment with writing.
- Children use "kid writing" to experiment with written language concepts and invented spelling.
- Teachers use interactive writing to teach concepts about print, phonics, spelling, high-frequency words, and written language conventions.

Professional References

Adams, M. J. (1990). *Beginning to read: Thinking and learning about print.* Cambridge, MA: MIT Press.

Ashton-Warner, S. (1965). *Teacher.* New York: Simon & Schuster.

Ball, E., & Blachman, B. (1991). Does phoneme segmentation training in kindergarten make a difference in early word recognition and developmental spelling? *Reading Research Quarterly, 26,* 49–86.

Barone, D. M., & Morrow, L. M. (2003). *Literacy and young children: Research-based practices.* New York: Guilford Press.

Bennett-Armistead, V. S., Duke, N. K., & Moses, A. M. (2005). *Literacy and the youngest learner: Best practices for educators of children from birth to 5.* New York: Scholastic.

Burns, S., Griffin, P., & Snow, C. E. (1999). *Starting out right: A guide to promoting children's reading success.* Washington, DC: National Academy Press.

Button, K., Johnson, M. J., & Furgerson, P. (1996). Interactive writing in a primary classroom. *The Reading Teacher, 49,* 446–454.

Caserta-Henry, C. (1996). Reading buddies: A first-grade intervention program. *The Reading Teacher, 49,* 500–503.

Clay, M. M. (1967). The reading behaviour of five year old children: A research report. *New Zealand Journal of Educational Studies, 2*(1), 11–31.

Clay, M. M. (1991). *Becoming literate: The construction of inner control.* Portsmouth, NH: Heinemann.

Clymer, T. (1996). The utility of phonic generalizations in the primary grades. *The Reading Teacher, 50,* 182–187.

Cunningham, P. A. (2005). *Phonics they use: Words for reading and writing* (4th ed.). Boston: Allyn & Bacon.

Ditzel, R. J. (2000). *Great beginnings: Creating a literacy-rich kindergarten.* Portsmouth, ME: Stenhouse.

Fisher, B., & Medvic, E. F. (2000). *Perspectives on shared reading: Planning and practice.* Portsmouth, NH: Heinemann.

Freppon, P. A., & Dahl, K. L. (1991). Learning about phonics in a whole language classroom. *Language Arts, 68,* 190–197.

Gillon, G. T. (2004). *Phonological awareness: From research to practice.* New York: Guilford Press.

Griffith, F., & Olson, M. (1992). Phonemic awareness helps beginning readers break the code. *The Reading Teacher, 45,* 516–523.

Hanna, P. R., Hanna, J. S., Hodges, R. E., & Rudorf, E. H. (1966). *Phoneme-grapheme correspondences as cues to spelling improvement.* Washington, DC: US Government Printing Office.

Harste, J. C., Woodward, V. A., & Burke, C. L. (1984). *Language stories and literacy lessons.* Portsmouth, NH: Heinemann.

Heath, S. B. (1983). *Ways with words: Language, life, and work in communities and classrooms.* Cambridge: Cambridge University Press.

Holdaway, D. (1979). *The foundations of literacy.* Portsmouth, NH: Heinemann.

International Reading Association and the National Association for the Education of Young Children. (1998). Learning to read and write: Developmentally appropriate practices for young children. A joint position statement of the International Reading Association and the National Association for the Education of Young Children. *Young Children, 53,* 524–546.

Invernizzi, M. (2003). Concepts, sounds, and the ABCs: A diet for a very young reader. In D. M. Barone & L. M. Morrow (Eds.), *Literacy and young children: Research-based practices* (pp. 140–156). New York: Guilford Press.

Juel, C. (1991). Beginning reading. In R. Barr, M. L. Kamil, P. Mosenthal, & P. D. Pearson (Eds.), *Handbook of reading research* (Vol. 2, pp. 759–788). New York: Longman.

Klesius, J. P., Griffith, P. L., & Zielonka, P. (1991). A whole language and traditional instruction comparison: Overall effectiveness and development of the alphabetic principle. *Reading Research and Instruction, 30,* 47–61.

Lomax, R. G., & McGee, L. M. (1987). Young children's concepts about print and meaning: Toward a model of word reading acquisition. *Reading Research Quarterly, 22,* 237–256.

McGee, L. M., & Richgels, D. J. (2003). *Designing early literacy programs.* New York: Guilford Press.

McGee, L. M., & Richgels, D. J. (2007). *Literacy's beginnings: Supporting young readers and writers* (5th ed.). Boston: Allyn & Bacon.

Mills, H., O'Keefe, T., & Stephens, D. (1992). *Looking closely: Exploring the role of phonics in one whole language classroom.* Urbana, IL: National Council of Teachers of English.

Moats, L. (1999). *Teaching reading is rocket science.* Washington, DC: American Federation of Teachers.

National Reading Panel. (2000). *Report of the National Reading Panel.* Washington, DC: National Institute of Child Health and Human Development Clearinghouse.

Papandropoulou, I., & Sinclair, H. (1974). What is a word? Experimental study of children's ideas on grammar. *Human Development, 17,* 241–258.

Perfitti, C., Beck, I., Bell, L., & Hughes, C. (1987). Phonemic knowledge and learning to read are reciprocal: A longitudinal study of first grade children. *Merrill-Palmer Quarterly, 33,* 283–319.

Reutzel, D. R., & Fawson, P. C. (1990). Traveling tales: Connecting parents and children in writing. *The Reading Teacher, 44,* 222–227.

Schickedanz, J. A., & Casbergue, R. M. (2004). *Writing in preschool: Learning to orchestrate meaning and marks.* Newark, DE: International Reading Association.

Schulze, A. C. (2006). *Helping children become readers through writing: A guide to writing workshop in kindergarten.* Newark, DE: International Reading Association.

Shefelbine, J. (1995). *Learning and using phonics in beginning reading* (Literacy research paper, vol. 10). New York: Scholastic.

Stanovich, K. E. (2000). *Progress in understanding reading: Scientific foundations and new frontiers.* New York: Guilford Press.

Stauffer, R. G. (1970). *The language experience approach to the teaching of reading.* New York: Harper & Row.

Sulzby, E. (1985). Kindergartners as readers and writers. In M. Farr (Ed.), *Advances in writing research, vol. 1: Children's early writing development* (pp. 127–199). Norwood, NJ: Ablex.

Taylor, D., & Dorsey-Gaines, C. (1987). *Growing up literate: Learning from inner-city families.* Portsmouth, NH: Heinemann.

Teale, W. H., & Sulzby, E. (1989). Emerging literacy: New perspectives. In D. S. Strickland & L. M. Morrow (Eds.), *Emerging literacy: Young children learn to read and write* (pp. 1–15). Newark, DE: International Reading Association.

Tompkins, G. E., & Collom, S. (Eds.). (2004). *Sharing the pen: Interactive writing with young children.* Upper Saddle River, NJ: Merrill/Prentice Hall.

Tompkins, G. E., & Webeler, M. B. (1983). What will happen next? Using predictable books with young children. *The Reading Teacher, 36,* 498–502.

Trachtenburg, R., & Ferruggia, A. (1989). Big books from little voices: Reaching high risk beginning readers. *The Reading Teacher, 42,* 284–289.

Treiman, R. (1985). Phonemic analysis, spelling, and reading. In T. H. Carr (Ed.), *The development of reading skills* (pp. 5–18). San Francisco: Jossey-Bass.

Venezky, R. L. (1999). *The American way of spelling: The structure and origins of American English orthography.* New York: Guilford Press.

Vukelich, C., & Christie, J. (2004). *Building a foundation for preschool literacy.* Newark, DE: International Reading Association.

Wylie, R. E., & Durrell, D. D. (1970). Teaching vowels through phonograms. *Elementary English, 47,* 787–791.

Yaden, D. B., Jr., & Templeton, S. (Eds.). (1986). *Metalinguistic awareness and beginning literacy: Conceptualizing what it means to read and write.* Portsmouth, NH: Heinemann.

Yopp, H. K. (1992). Developing phonemic awareness in young children. *The Reading Teacher, 45,* 696–703.

Yopp, H. K. (1995). Read-aloud books for developing phonemic awareness: An annotated bibliography. *The Reading Teacher, 48,* 538–542.

Children's Book References

Baron, A. (1996). *Red fox dances.* Cambridge, MA: Candlewick Press.

Brett, J. (1989). *The mitten.* New York: Putnam.

Brett, J. (1999). *Gingerbread baby.* New York: Putnam.

Carle, E. (2001). *The very hungry caterpillar.* New York: Philomel.

Cole, H. (1995). *Jack's garden.* New York: Greenwillow.

Cronin, D. (2000). *Click, clack, moo: Cows that type.* New York: Simon & Schuster.

Ehlert, L. (2006). *Eating the alphabet: Fruits and vegetables from A to Z.* San Diego: Harcourt.

Fleming, D. (1994). *Barnyard banter.* New York: Henry Holt.

Galdone, P. (1975). *The gingerbread boy.* New York: Seabury.

Harris, T. (2000). *Pattern fish.* Brookfield, CT: Millbrook Press.

Hutchins, P. (1976). *Don't forget the bacon!* New York: Mulberry Books.

Hutchins, P. (2005). *Rosie's walk.* New York: Aladdin Books.

Inches, A. (2006). *The stuffed animals get ready for bed.* San Diego: Harcourt Brace.

Kalan, R. (2002). *Jump, frog, jump!* New York: HarperFestival.

Kasza, K. (1996). *The wolf's chicken stew.* New York: Putnam.

Martin, B., Jr. (1992). *Polar bear, polar bear, what do you hear?* New York: Holt, Rinehart and Winston.

Most, B. (1996). *Cock-a-doodle-moo!* San Diego: Harcourt Brace.

Numeroff, L. J. (1985). *If you give a mouse a cookie.* New York: HarperCollins.

Numeroff, L. J. (1991). *If you give a moose a muffin.* New York: HarperCollins.

Numeroff, L. J. (1998). *If you give a pig a pancake.* New York: HarperCollins.

Numeroff, L. J. (2000). *If you take a mouse to the movies.* New York: HarperCollins.

Numeroff, L. (2002). *If you take a mouse to school.* New York: HarperCollins.

Pinkney, J. (2006). *The little red hen.* New York: Dial Books.

Schwartz, A. (1992). *Busy buzzing bumblebees and other tongue twisters.* New York: HarperCollins.

Schwartz, D. M. (1994). *How much is a million?* New York: Morrow.

Seuss, Dr. (2003). *Hop on pop.* New York: Scholastic.

Slepian, J., & Seidler, A. (2001). *The hungry thing.* New York: Scholastic.

Sobel, J. (2006). *Shiver me letters: A pirate ABC.* San Diego: Harcourt Brace.

Taback, S. (1997). *There was an old lady who swallowed a fly.* New York: Viking.

Trapani, I. (2000). *Shoo fly!* Watertown, MA: Charlesbridge.

Williams, S. (1990). *I went walking.* San Diego: Harcourt Brace.

Wood, A. (1999). *Silly Sally.* San Diego: Red Wagon Books.

chapter five

Looking Closely at Words

During a unit on the Middle Ages, Ms. Boland's eighth graders develop a word wall. They identify words to put on the word wall as they read books about the Middle Ages, including *Catherine, Called Birdy* (Cushman, 1994), *Castle Diary: The Journal of Tobias Burgess, Page* (Platt, 1999), *Ms. Frizzle's Adventures: Medieval Castle* (Cole, 2002), and *Castle* (Macaulay, 1977). Students choose 10 important words and draw word clusters on index cards, and they also write the words in their learning logs so that they can refer more easily to them during the thematic unit. The word wall is shown on page 144.

Ms. Boland uses the words on the word wall for a series of vocabulary mini-lessons. To review the meaning of the words, she uses a semantic feature analysis chart with the categories "castle," "knights," "peasants," "crusades," and "cathedral" and 20 words for students to categorize. For *villein,* the "peasants" category would be checked, and for *fortress,* the "castle" category would be checked, for example. For other words, such as *Black Death,* more than one category would be checked. She demonstrates how to fill in the chart using the first two words as examples, and then students work in small groups to complete the chart.

In the second minilesson, Ms. Boland focuses on etymology, or word history, and students learn that words about the Middle Ages come from English, French,

What is the best way to teach vocabulary?

Students are expected to learn many technical terms in thematic units, but in too many classrooms, having students look up the definition of words and write sentences using the words substitutes for teaching vocabulary. Researchers tell us that students learn many words incidentally through multiple exposures and others through word-study activities that go beyond looking up definitions. As you read this vignette, notice how Ms. Boland involves students in a variety of meaningful word-study activities.

Latin, and Greek. Ms. Boland shares some guidelines for determining the language source, such as that compound words are usually English, words in which *ch* is pronounced /sh/ are French, words that end in *-tion* are Latin, and words in which *ch* is pronounced /k/ are Greek. Then students sort these words according to language:

> English: *freeman, drawbridge, landlord, knight, forenoon, heathen, scabbard,* and *king*
>
> French: *chivalry, heraldry, garderobe, lute, troubadour,* and *tournament*
>
> Latin: *apprentice, illumination, humor, joust, entertainment, cathedral, solar, Renaissance,* and *medieval*
>
> Greek: *alchemy, monk,* and *monastery*

In the next minilesson, students examine root words and affixes to determine the meaning of *Renaissance* (rebirth), *monk* and *monastery* (alone), *manuscript* (handwritten), *medieval* (Middle Ages), *Crusades* (cross), *solar* (sun), *unicorn* (one horn). They also compare related English and Latin words—for example, *church* and *cathedral, Middle Ages* and *medieval, kingly* and *royal, sun* and *solar,* and *Black Death* and *plague*—to discover that the more common words in each pair are English and the more sophisticated ones are Latin.

In the fourth minilesson, Ms. Boland compares the English word *hand* with the Latin word *manus* ("hand") and words made from these two root words. To begin, students brainstorm a list of words with the root word *hand: handwriting, handle, handy, handmade, handshake, handsome, handicraft, right-* (or *left-*) *handed,* and *handbag.* Then Ms. Boland introduces the Latin root word *manus,* which is used in *manuscript* and a "handful" of other words, including *manufacture, manual,* and *manicure.* Students make root-word clusters for the two words in their learning logs.

In the last minilesson, Ms. Boland reviews synonyms and how to use a thesaurus. Together the students examine synonyms for *knight* and choose these five appropriate ones: *warrior, defender, protector, gallant,* and *cavalier.* Next, Ms. Boland divides students into small

Word Wall on the Middle Ages			
A archery alchemy acre archer apprentice armorer	**B** breaking fast battering ram bailey Black Death barter battlements baron bloodletting	**C** cathedral chain mail castle coat of arms constable clergy Crusades chivalry	**D** **E** dizzard estate dub entertainmentl drawbridge ear
F fairs fortress feudal system fanfare forenoon fresco flying buttresses freeman	**G** gatehouse guilds garderobe great hall	**H** heraldry harvest heathen humors heraldic arms herbs huntsman	**I** **K** illumination keep **J** kings Jerusalem knight jousts knighthood
L lance landlord lord lute leprosy	**M** manor minstrel mercenary moat medieval Magna Carta merchants monastery Middle Ages monk missionaries	**N** **O** Notre Dame nave nobles	**P** pagan pillory peasant plague parchment pilgrims pennant poacher pike portcullis
Q **R** quartering reeve quill pens royal Renaissance	**S** scabbard siege serf steward suit of armor squire shield solar	**T** tournament turrets trencher troubadours transepts twelvemonth	**U** **X** unicorn **V** **Y** vernacular yeoman villein **W** **Z** watchtower

groups, and each group investigates the synonyms for another word-wall word and chooses the five most appropriate ones.

After reading about the Middle Ages, students divide into research teams to learn more about a particular aspect of life at that time. One group researches the building of a castle, and other groups investigate medical practices; the Crusades; monks and life in a monastery; knighthood; the feudal social system; food, drink, and celebrations; the life of a serf; and the life of the nobles. The students in each group research a topic and develop a display with artifacts and a PowerPoint presentation to document what they have learned. A page from a PowerPoint presentation on the

Crusades is shown here; this excerpt shows how students incorporated the word-history information they learned about the word *Crusades*.

At the end of the thematic unit, students transform their classroom into a museum. They dress in costumes and set up their displays at stations in the classroom. Parents and other students at the school visit the displays, and students share what they have learned about the Middle Ages.

---

*S*tudents' word knowledge plays a critical role in their academic success. Reading comprehension, for instance, depends on vocabulary knowledge; when many of the words are unfamiliar, students are unlikely to grasp the text's meaning. It's not surprising that high-achieving students know many more words than low-achieving students; in fact, researchers report that the vocabularies of high-achieving third graders are equal to the lowest-achieving high school seniors (Beck, McKeown, & Kucan, 2002).

Differences in students' word knowledge are apparent in kindergarten and first grade, and these differences appear to relate to the families' socioeconomic status (SES). Researchers have noticed that children from high SES homes know twice as many words as those from low SES homes (Beck et al., 2002). How does a family's SES contribute to these differences? High SES children's vocabulary is enhanced in these ways:

◆ *Background Knowledge.* High SES children participate in a broader array of vocabulary-enriching experiences with their families.

◆ *Book Experiences.* High SES children are more likely to be read to every day, regularly visit the library and check out books, and have their own collection of books.

◆ *Parents' Vocabulary Level.* High SES parents use more sophisticated vocabulary when they talk with their children.

One way to demonstrate these differences is by comparing kindergartners' knowledge of color words. Some 5- and 6-year-olds know 25 color words or more, including *silver, magenta, turquoise, navy,* and *tan,* whereas others can't name the eight basic colors.

It's difficult for children with less vocabulary knowledge to catch up with their classmates because high achievers learn more words and they learn them more quickly than lower achievers. High SES children's vocabularies grow at an astonishing rate of 3,000 to 4,000 words a year, whereas low SES children learn words at a much slower rate. By the time children graduate from high school, high-achieving students' vocabularies reach 50,000 words or more.

As you read this chapter, think about how students develop their knowledge of words. Ask yourself these questions:

◆ How has the history of the English language affected vocabulary?

▣ What important vocabulary concepts do students learn?

◆ How do teachers develop students' vocabularies?

▰ How do teachers focus on words during the four patterns of practice?

HISTORY OF THE ENGLISH LANGUAGE

Understanding the history of English and how words entered the language contributes greatly to understanding words and their meanings. English is a historical language, which accounts for word meanings and some spelling inconsistencies (Tompkins & Yaden, 1986). English has a variety of words for a single concept, and the etymology of the words explains many apparent duplications. Consider these words related to water: *aquatic, hydrant, aquamarine, waterfall, hydroelectric, watercress, watery, aquarium, waterproof, hydraulic, aqualung,* and *hydrogen.* These words come from three root words, each meaning "water": *water* is English, of course, whereas *aqua* is Latin and *hydro* is Greek. The root word used depends on the people who created the word, the purpose of the word, and when the word entered English.

The development of the English language is divided into three periods: Old English, Middle English, and Modern English (Stevenson, 1999). The beginning and end of each period are marked by a significant event, such as an invasion or an invention.

Old English (A.D. 450–1100)

The recorded history of English begins in A.D. 449, when Germanic tribes, including the Angles and Saxons, invaded Britain. The invaders pushed the original inhabitants, the Celts, to the northern and western corners of the island. This annexation is romanticized in the King Arthur legends. Arthur is believed to have been a Celtic military leader who fought bravely against the Germanic invaders.

The English language began as an intermingling of the dialects spoken by the Germanic tribes in Britain. Many people assume that English is based on Latin, but it has Germanic roots and was brought to Britain by these invaders. Although 85% of Old English words are no longer used, many everyday words remain (e.g., *child, foot, hand, house, man, mother, old,* and *sun*). In contrast to Modern English, Old English had a highly developed inflectional system for indicating number, gender, and verb tense. The Anglo-Saxons added affixes to existing words, including *be-, for-, -ly, -dom,* and *-hood*. They also invented vividly descriptive compound words; the Old English word for "music," for example, was *ear-sport*. The folk epic *Beowulf,* the great literary work of the period, illustrates the poetic use of words; for instance, the sea is described as a "whale-path" and a "swan's road."

Foreign words also made their way into the predominantly Germanic word stock. The borrowed words came from two main sources: Romans and Vikings. Contact between the Roman soldiers and traders and the Germanic tribes on the continent, before they had invaded England, contributed some words, including *cheese, mile, street,* and *wine*. The missionaries who reintroduced Christianity to Britain in 597 also brought with them a number of religious words (e.g., *angel, candle, hymn*). In 787, the Vikings began a series of raids against English villages, and for several centuries, they occupied much of England. The Vikings' contributions to the English language were significant. They provided the pronouns *they, their, them;* introduced the /g/ and /k/ sounds (e.g., *get, kid*); contributed most of our *sk-* words (e.g., *skin, sky*) and some of our *sc-* words (e.g., *scalp, score*); and enriched our vocabulary with more than 500 everyday words, including *husband* and *window*.

The structure, spelling, and pronunciation of Old English were significantly different from those of Modern English, so much so that we would not be able to read an Old English text or understand someone speaking Old English. Some consonant combinations were pronounced that are not heard today, including the /k/ in words such as *knee*. The letter *f* represented both /f/ and /v/, resulting in the Modern English spelling pattern of *wolf* and *wolves*. The pronunciation of the vowel sounds was very different, too; for example, the Old English *stan* (*a* as in *father*) became our word *stone*.

Middle English (1100–1500)

The Norman Conquest in 1066 changed the course of the English language and ushered in the Middle English period. William, Duke of Normandy defeated King Harold at the Battle of Hastings and claimed the English throne. For more than 200 years, French was the official language in England, spoken by the nobility, even though the lower classes continued to speak English, but before the end of the 14th century, English was restored as the official language. Chaucer's *Canterbury Tales,* written in the late 1300s, provides evidence that English was replacing French. Political, social, and economic changes contributed to this reversal.

The Middle English period was one of tremendous change. Many Old English words were lost as 10,000 French words were added to the language, reflecting the Norman impact on English life, including military words (e.g., *soldier, victory*), political words (e.g., *government, princess*), medical words (e.g., *physician, surgeon*), and words related to the arts (e.g., *comedy, music, poet*) (Baugh & Cable, 2002). Many of the new loan words duplicated Old English words. Typically, one word was eventually lost; often, it was the Old English word that disappeared. If both words remained, they developed slightly different meanings. For example, *hearty* (Old English) and *cordial* (French) were originally synonyms, both meaning "from the heart," but in time they differentiated, and they now have different but related meanings.

During this period, there was a significant reduction in the use of inflections, or word endings. Many irregular verbs were lost, and others developed regular past and past-participle forms (e.g., *climb, talk*), although Modern English still retains some irregular verbs (e.g., *sing, fly, be, have*) that contribute to our usage problems. By 1000, *-s* had become the accepted plural marker, although the Old English plural form *-en* was used in some words. This artifact remains in a few plurals, such as *children*.

Modern English (1500–Present)

William Caxton's introduction of the printing press in England marks the beginning of the Modern English period. It was a powerful force in standardizing English spelling, and from this point the lag between pronunciation and spelling began to widen. The tremendous increase in travel to many parts of the world during the 1600s and 1700s resulted in a wide borrowing of words from more than 50 languages. Borrowings include *alcohol* (Arabic), *chocolate* (Spanish), *cookie* (Dutch), *czar* (Russian), *hallelujah* (Hebrew), *hurricane* (Spanish), *kindergarten* (German), *smorgasbord* (Swedish), *tycoon* (Chinese), and *violin* (Italian).

Many Latin and Greek words were added to English during the Renaissance to increase the language's prestige; for example, *congratulate, democracy,* and *education* came from Latin, and *catastrophe, encyclopedia,* and *thermometer* from Greek. Many modern Latin and Greek borrowings are scientific words (e.g., *aspirin, vaccinate*), and some of the more recently borrowed forms (e.g., *criterion, focus*) have retained their native plural forms, adding confusion about how to spell these forms in English. Also, some recent loan words from French have retained their native spellings and pronunciations, such as *hors d'oeuvre* and *cul-de-sac.*

In addition to the vocabulary expansion during this period, there have been extensive sound changes. The short vowels have remained relatively stable, but there was a striking change in the pronunciation of long vowels. This change, known as the Great Vowel Shift, was gradual, occurring during the 1500s. Because spelling had become fixed before the shift, the vowel letter symbols no longer corresponded to the sounds. For example, the word *name* had two syllables and rhymed with *comma* during the Middle English period, but during the Great Vowel Shift, the pronunciation of *name* shifted to rhyme with *game* (Hook, 1975).

The Modern English period brought changes in syntax, particularly the disappearance of double negatives and double comparatives and superlatives. Eliminations came about slowly; for instance, Shakespeare still wrote, "the most unkindest cut of all." Also, the practice of using *-er* or *-est* to form comparatives and superlatives in shorter words and *more* or *most* with longer words was not standardized until after Shakespeare's time.

Learning About Word Histories

The best source of information about word histories is an unabridged dictionary, which provides etymological information about words: the language the word was borrowed from, the spelling of the word in that language or the transliteration of the word into the Latin alphabet, and the original meaning of the word. Etymologies are enclosed in square brackets and appear at the end of a dictionary entry. They are written in a shortened form to save space, using abbreviations for language names, such as *Ar* for *Arabic* and *L* for *Latin*. Let's look at etymologies for three words derived from very different sources: *king, kimono,* and *thermometer.* Each etymology is elaborated, beginning with *king:*

> **king** [bef. 900; ME, OE *cyng*]
>
> *Elaboration:* The word *king* is an Old English word originally spelled *cyng.* It was used in English before the year 900. In the Middle English period, the spelling changed to its current form.

Next, let's consider *kimono:*

> **kimono** [1885–1890; < Japn clothing, garb, equiv. to *ki* wear + *mono* thing]
>
> *Elaboration:* Our word *kimono* comes from Japanese, and it entered English between 1885 and 1890. *Kimono* means "clothing" or "garb," and it is equivalent to the Japanese words *ki,* meaning "wear," and *mono,* meaning "thing."

Finally, we examine *thermometer:*

> **thermometer** [1615–1625; thermo < Gr *thermos,* hot + meter < *metron,* measure]
>
> *Elaboration:* The first recorded use of the word *thermometer* in English was between 1615 and 1625. Our word was created from two Greek words meaning "hot" and "measure."

A list of recommended books about the history of English is shown in the box below. The books include fascinating stories about how words grew and changed because of historical events and linguistic accidents.

Booklist

BOOKS ABOUT THE HISTORY OF ENGLISH

American Heritage editors. (2004). *Word histories and mysteries: From abracadabra to Zeus.* Boston: Houghton Mifflin. (U)

American Heritage editors. (2006). *More word histories and mysteries: From aardvark to zombie.* Boston: Houghton Mifflin. (U)

Brook, D. (1998). *The journey of English.* New York: Clarion Books. (M)

Claiborne, R. (2001). *Loose cannons, red herrings, and other lost metaphors.* New York: Norton. (U)

Clements, A. (1996). *Frindle.* New York: Simon & Schuster. (M)

Collins, H. (1987). *101 American English idioms.* New York: McGraw-Hill. (M–U)

Collins, H. (1990). *101 American English proverbs.* New York: McGraw-Hill. (M–U)

Funk, C. E. (2002). *Heavens to Betsy! And other curious sayings.* New York: Collins. (U)

Funk, C. E. (2002). *Horsefeathers and other curious words.* New York: Collins. (U)

Funk, C. E. (2002). *Thereby hangs a tale: Stories of curious word origins.* New York: Collins. (U)

Merriam-Webster editors. (1995). *Merriam-Webster new book of word histories.* Springfield, MA: Merriam-Webster. (U)

Metcalf, A. (1997). *America in so many words: Words that have shaped America.* Boston: Houghton Mifflin. (U)

Metcalf, A. (1999). *The world in so many words: A country-by-country tour of words that have shaped our language.* Boston: Houghton Mifflin. (U)

Morris, E. (2004). *From altoids to zima: The surprising stories behind 125 famous brand names.* Palmer, AK: Fireside Books. (U)

Terban, M. (1983). *In a pickle and other funny idioms.* Boston: Houghton Mifflin. (M)

Terban, M. (1988). *Guppies in tuxedos: Funny eponyms.* New York: Clarion Books. (M)

Terban, M. (2006). *Scholastic dictionary of idioms.* New York: Scholastic. (M–U)

Towle, W. (1993). *The real McCoy: The life of an African-American inventor.* New York: Scholastic. (M)

P = primary grades (K–2); M = middle grades (3–5); U = upper grades (6–8)

WORDS AND THEIR MEANINGS

Children begin kindergarten with approximately 5,000 words in their vocabularies, and their vocabularies grow at a rate of about 3,000 words a year (Graves, 2006). Through literature focus units, literature circles, reading and writing workshop, and thematic units, children experiment with words and concepts, and their knowledge of words and meanings grows. Young children assume that every word has only one meaning, and words that sound alike, such as *son* and *sun,* are confusing to them. Through continuing experiences with language, children become more sophisticated about words and their literal and figurative meanings. Children learn about words and word parts, words that mean the same thing as and the opposite of other words, words that sound alike, words with multiple meanings, the figurative language of idioms, and how words have been borrowed from languages around the world. They also learn about how words are created and have fun playing with words.

Root Words and Affixes

A root word is a morpheme, the basic part of a word to which affixes are added. Many words are developed from a single root word; for example, the Latin word *portare* ("to carry") is the source of at least nine Modern English words: *deport, export, import, port, portable, porter, report, support,* and *transportation.* Latin is one source of English root words, and Greek and Old English are two other sources.

Some root words are whole words, and others are parts of words. Some root words have become free morphemes and can be used as separate words, but others cannot. For instance, the word *act* comes from the Latin word *actus,* meaning "doing." English uses part of the word and treats it as a root word that can be used independently or in combination with affixes, as in *actor, activate, react,* and *enact.* In the words *alias, alien, inalienable,* and *alienate,* the root word *ali* comes from the Latin word *alius,* meaning "other"; it is not used as an independent root word in English. A list of English, Latin, and Greek root words appears in the LA Essentials box on the next page. Students can compile lists of words developed from these root words, and they can draw root word clusters to illustrate the relationship of the root word to the words developed from it. Figure 5–1 shows a root word cluster for the Greek root *graph,* meaning "write," made by a seventh-grade class. Recognizing basic elements from word to word helps students cut down on the amount of memorizing necessary to learn meanings and spellings.

Affixes are bound morphemes that are added to words and root words. Affixes can be prefixes or suffixes: Prefixes are added to the beginnings of words, such as *re-* in *reread,* and suffixes are added to the ends of words, such as *-ing* in *singing* and *-er* in *player.* Like root words, affixes come from English, Latin, and Greek. They often change a word's meaning, such as adding *un-* to *happy* to form *unhappy.* Sometimes they change the part of speech: For example, when *-tion* is added to *attract* to form *attraction,* the verb *attract* becomes a noun.

When an affix is "peeled off," or removed from a word, the remaining word is usually a real word. For example, when the prefix *pre-* is removed from *preview,* the word *view* can stand alone; and when the suffix *-able* is removed from *lovable,* the word *love* can stand alone (when the final *e* is added, anyway). Some words include letter sequences that might be affixes, but because the remaining word cannot stand

ROOT WORDS

Root	Language	Meaning	Sample Words
ann/enn	Latin	year	anniversary, annual, centennial, millennium, perennial
arch	Greek	ruler	anarchy, archbishop, architecture, hierarchy, monarchy,
astro	Greek	star	aster, asterisk, astrology, astronaut, astronomy, disaster
auto	Greek	self	autobiography, automatic, automobile, autopsy
bio	Greek	life	biography, biohazard, biology, biodegradable, bionic
capit/capt	Latin	head	capital, capitalize, capitol, captain, decapitate, per capita
cent	Latin	hundred	bicentennial, cent, centigrade, centipede, century, percent
circ	Latin	around	circle, circular, circus, circuit, circumference, circumstance
corp	Latin	body	corporal, corporation, corps, corpuscle
cosmo	Greek	universe	cosmic, cosmopolitan, microcosm
cred	Latin	believe	credit, creditable, creed, discredit, incredulity
cycl	Greek	wheel	bicycle, cycle, cyclist, cyclone, recycle, tricycle
dict	Latin	speak	contradict, dictate, dictator, prediction, verdict
graph	Greek	write	autobiography, biographer, cryptograph, graphic, paragraph
gram	Greek	letter	cardiogram, diagram, grammar, monogram, telegram
jus/jud/jur	Latin	law	injury, injustice, judge, juror, jury, justice, justify, prejudice
lum/lus/luc	Latin	light	illuminate, lucid, luminous, luster
man	Latin	hand	maneuver, manicure, manipulate, manual, manufacture
mar/mer	Latin	sea	aquamarine, Margaret, marine, marshy, mermaid, submarine
meter	Greek	measure	centimeter, diameter, speedometer, thermometer
mini	Latin	small	miniature, minimize, minor, minimum, minuscule, minute
mort	Latin	death	immortal, mortality, mortuary, postmortem
nym	Greek	name	anonymous, antonym, homonym, pseudonym, synonym
ped	Latin	foot	biped, pedal, pedestrian, pedicure
phono	Greek	sound	earphone, microphone, phonics, saxophone, symphony
photo	Greek	light	photograph, photographer, photosensitive, photosynthesis
pod/pus	Greek	foot	octopus, podiatry, podium, tripod
port	Latin	carry	exporter, import, port, portable, reporter, support, transportation
quer/ques/quis	Latin	seek	inquisitive, query, quest, question
scope	Latin	see	horoscope, kaleidoscope, microscope, periscope, telescope
scrib/scrip	Latin	write	describe, inscription, postscript, prescribe, scribble, script
sphere	Greek	ball	atmosphere, atmospheric, hemisphere, sphere, stratosphere
struct	Latin	build	construction, destruction, indestructible, instruct, reconstruct
tele	Greek	far	telecast, telegram, telephone, telescope, telethon, television
terr	Latin	land	subterranean, terrace, terrain, terrarium, terrier, territory
vers/vert	Latin	turn	advertise, anniversary, controversial, divert, reversible, versus
vict/vinc	Latin	conquer	convict, convince, evict, invincible, victim, victory
vis/vid	Latin	see	improvise, invisible, revise, television, video, visitor
viv/vit	Latin	live	revive, survive, vital, vitamin, vivacious, vivid, viviparous
volv	Latin	roll	convolutions, evolution, involve, revolutionary, revolver, volume

FIGURE 5–1

A Cluster for the Root Word *Graph*

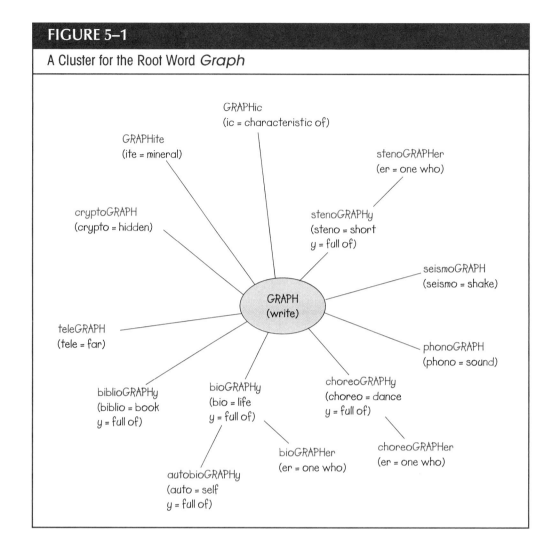

GRAPHic
(ic = characteristic of)

GRAPHite
(ite = mineral)

stenoGRAPHer
(er = one who)

cryptoGRAPH
(crypto = hidden)

stenoGRAPHy
(steno = short
y = full of)

seismoGRAPH
(seismo = shake)

GRAPH
(write)

teleGRAPH
(tele = far)

phonoGRAPH
(phono = sound)

biblioGRAPHy
(biblio = book
y = full of)

bioGRAPHy
(bio = life
y = full of)

choreoGRAPHy
(choreo = dance
y = full of)

choreoGRAPHer
(er = one who)

bioGRAPHer
(er = one who)

autobioGRAPHy
(auto = self
y = full of)

---

alone, they are not affixes. For example, the *in-* at the beginning of *include* isn't a prefix because *clude* isn't a word, and the *-ic* at the end of *magic* isn't a suffix because *mag* can't stand alone as a word, but the *-ic* at the end of *atomic* is a suffix because *atom* is a word. Sometimes, however, the root word can't stand alone. One example is *legible:* The *-ible* is a suffix and *leg-* is the root word even though it can't stand alone.

Some affixes have more than one form. For example, the prefixes *il- im-* and *ir-* are forms of the prefix *in-*, with the meanings of "in," "into," and "on"; these prefixes are used with verbs and nouns. The prefixes *il-, im-, ir-,* and *ig-* are also forms of the prefix *in-*, with the meaning "not"; these prefixes are used with adjectives. Both *in-* prefixes are borrowed from Latin. The prefix *a-* and its alternate form *an-* are borrowed from Greek and also mean "not"; the alternate form is used when the word it is being added to begins with a vowel. Similarly, some suffixes have alternate forms; for example, the suffix *-ible* is an alternate form of *-able*. The alternate form is used in words, such as *legible,* whose root words can't stand alone. There are exceptions, however, such as *collectible.*

A list of prefixes and suffixes is presented in the LA Essentials box on page 153. White, Sowell, and Yanagihara (1989) identified the affixes most commonly used in

AFFIXES

Language	Prefixes	Suffixes
English	*over-* (too much): overflow self- (by oneself): self-employed *un-* (not): unhappy *un-* (reversal): untie under- (beneath): underground	-ed (past tense): played -ful (full of): hopeful -ing (participle): eating, building -ish (like): reddish -less (without): hopeless -ling (young): duckling *-ly (in the manner of): slowly *-ness (state or quality): kindness -s/-es (plural): cats, boxes *-y (full of): sleepy
Greek	a-/an- (not): atheist, anaerobic amphi- (both): amphibian anti- (against): antiseptic di- (two): dioxide hemi- (half): hemisphere hyper- (over): hyperactive hypo- (under): hypodermic micro- (small): microfilm mono- (one): monarch omni- (all): omnivorous poly- (many): polygon sym-/syn-/sys- (together): synonym	-ism (doctrine of): communism -ist (one who): artist -logy (the study of): zoology
Latin	bi- (two, twice): bifocal, biannual de- (away): detract *dis- (not): disapprove *dis- (reversal): disinfect ex- (out): export *il-/im-/in-/ir- (not): illegible, impolite, inexpensive, irrational *in- (in, into): indoor inter- (between): intermission milli- (thousandth): millisecond *mis- (wrong): mistake multi- (many): multimillionaire post- (after): postwar pre- (before): precede quad-/quart- (four): quadruple, quarter re- (again): repay *re-/retro- (back): replace, retroactive *sub- (under): submarine trans- (across): transport tri- (three): triangle	-able/-ible (worthy of, can be): lovable, audible *-al/-ial (action, process): arrival, denial -ance/-ence (state or quality): annoyance, absence -ant (one who): servant -ary/-ory (person, place): secretary, laboratory -cule (very small): molecule -ee (one who is): trustee *-er/-or/-ar (one who): teacher, actor, liar -ic (characterized by): angelic -ify (to make): simplify -ment (state or quality): enjoyment -ous (full of): nervous *-sion/-tion (state or quality): tension, attraction -ure (state or quality): failure

*= most common affixes

English words; these are marked with an asterisk in the LA Essentials feature. White and his colleagues recommend that the commonly used affixes be taught to middle- and upper-grade students because of their usefulness. Some of the most commonly used prefixes can be confusing because they have more than one meaning. The prefix *in-*, for instance, can mean either "not" or "again," and *un-* can mean "not" or it can reverse the meaning of the word (e.g., *tie–untie*).

Synonyms and Antonyms

Synonyms are words that have the same or nearly the same meaning. English has many synonyms because so many words have been borrowed from other languages. Synonyms provide options, allowing us to express ourselves precisely. Think of all the synonyms for the word *cold: cool, chilly, frigid, icy, frosty,* and *freezing,* for example. Each word has a different shade of meaning: *Cool* means moderately cold; *chilly* is uncomfortably cold; *frigid* is intensely cold; *icy* means very cold; *frosty* means covered with frost; and *freezing* is so cold that water changes into ice. Our language would be limited if we had only the word *cold*.

Many synonyms entered English during the Norman occupation of Britain. Compare these pairs of synonyms: *end–finish, clothing–garments, forgive–pardon, buy–purchase, deadly–mortal.* The first word in each pair comes from Old English; the second was borrowed from the Normans. The Old English words are more basic words, and the French loan words are more sophisticated. Perhaps that's why both words in each pair have survived—they express slightly different ideas. Other pairs of synonyms come from different languages. For example, in the pair *comfortable* and *cozy, comfortable* is a Latin loan word, whereas *cozy* is English, probably of Scandinavian origin.

Students can check a dictionary or thesaurus to locate synonyms for words. A fifth-grade class examined the word *wretched* after reading Chris Van Allsburg's picture-book fantasy *The Wretched Stone* (1991), the story of a strange, glowing stone picked up on a sea voyage that captivates a ship's crew and has a terrible transforming effect on them. They guessed from context clues that the word meant something "bad" or "evil," but they didn't know the exact meaning. One student checked a dictionary and found three meanings for the word—"unfortunate," "causing misery," and "of poor quality." He reported back to his classmates, and they immediately recognized that the second meaning—"causing misery"—was the most appropriate. Then they checked the word in a thesaurus and found seven synonyms. The students divided into seven groups and each group studied one of the synonyms, checking its meaning in a dictionary and thinking about how the word was used in the story. Then the groups reported back that *terrible, miserable,* and *dreadful* were the three most appropriate synonyms. Finally, the students collaborated to make a class chart for *wretched,* which is shown in Figure 5–2. The word being studied is written at the top of the chart, the word is used in a sentence in the middle section, and the synonyms are listed in a T chart in the bottom section to indicate their appropriateness in this context.

Antonyms are words that express opposite meanings. Antonyms for *loud* include *soft, subdued, quiet, silent, inaudible, sedate, somber, dull,* and *colorless.* These words express shades of meaning, just as synonyms do, and some opposites are more appropriate for one meaning of *loud* than for another. When *loud* means *gaudy,* for instance, appropriate opposites might be *somber, dull,* and *colorless.*

FIGURE 5–2

Students' T-Chart of Synonyms for *Wretched*

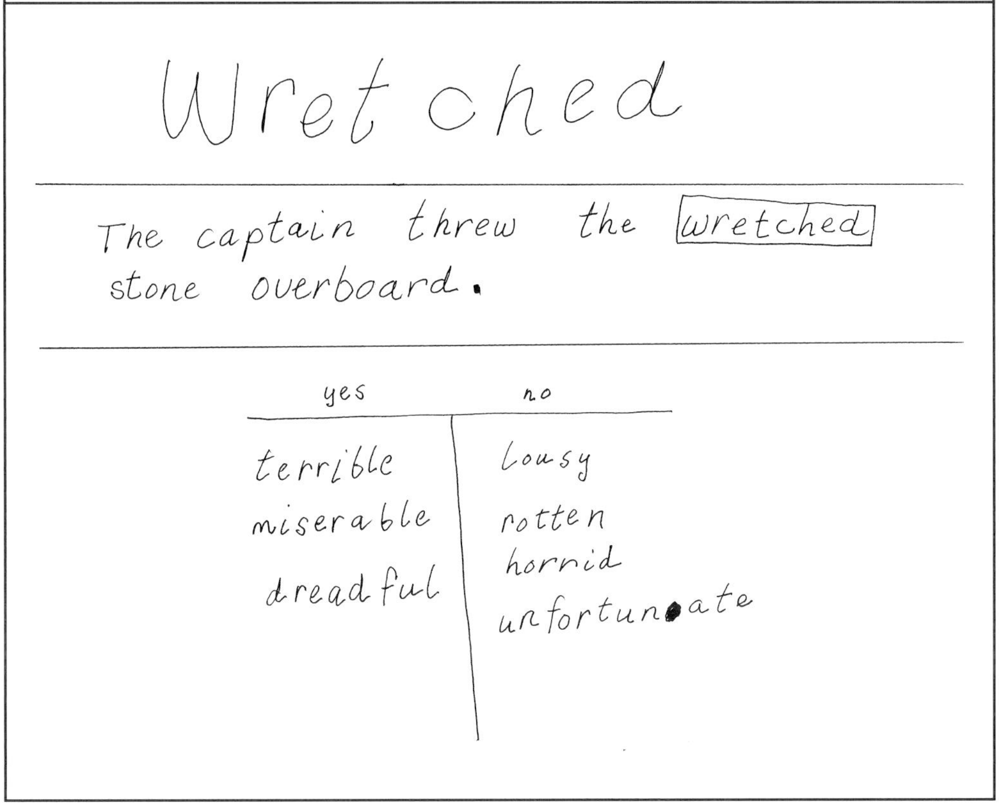

Wretched

The captain threw the [wretched] stone overboard.

yes	no
terrible	lousy
miserable	rotten
dreadful	horrid
	unfortunate

Two important reference books for examining the meanings of words are dictionaries and thesauri. Both list synonyms and antonyms, but dictionaries also explain the shades of meaning of related words. Series of dictionaries published by American Heritage, Merriam-Webster, and other publishing companies are available for children. Most series include a first dictionary for primary-grade (K–2) students, a children's dictionary for middle-grade (3–5) students, and a student's dictionary for upper-grade (6–8) students. The *Merriam-Webster Children's Dictionary* (2006), with more then 32,000 entries and 3,000 illustrations, is an excellent reference. This dictionary takes into account children's interests and was designed with visually exciting illustrations and diagrams that expand word definitions. In addition, synonym boxes suggest word choices, and word-history boxes present interesting information about how words entered English and have changed in meaning over the centuries.

An easy-to-use thesaurus is *A First Thesaurus* (Wittels & Greisman, 2001), which contains more than 2,000 entry words. Synonyms are printed in black type for each entry word, and the antonyms follow in red type. Another good thesaurus is the *Scholastic Children's Thesaurus* (Bollard, 2006). More than 2,500 synonyms are grouped under 500 entries in the thesaurus. Under the entry *common,* for example, the synonyms *ordinary, typical, familiar, everyday,* and *widespread* are listed along with a brief definition and sample sentence for each. These and other reference books are annotated in the Booklist on page 156.

Booklist

REFERENCE BOOKS

Dictionaries

The American Heritage children's dictionary. (2006). Boston: Houghton Mifflin. (M) This appealing hardcover dictionary contains 14,000 entries and more than 600 color photos and illustrations. Word history, language detective, synonym, and vocabulary-builder boxes provide additional interesting information. A phonics guide and thesaurus are also included. It's available on CD-ROM, too.

The American Heritage first dictionary. (2006). Boston: Houghton Mifflin. (P) More than 2,000 entries and 650 color photographs and graphics are presented in this attractive reference book. A clearly stated definition and an easy-to-read sentence are provided for each entry.

The American Heritage picture dictionary. (2006). Boston: Houghton Mifflin. (P) The 900 common words in this book designed for kindergartners and first graders are listed alphabetically and illustrated with lively color drawings.

The American Heritage student dictionary. (2006). Boston: Houghton Mifflin. (U) This comprehensive dictionary for middle school students has 65,000 detailed entries with sentence examples and etymologies and more than 2,000 photographs. Synonym lists, word-history boxes, and word-building features are highlighted in the text. Charts on the periodic table, geological eras, and weights and measures add to the book's usefulness.

Levey, J. S. (2006). *Scholastic first dictionary.* New York: Scholastic. (P) More than 1,500 entries are in this visually appealing dictionary for beginning readers. Each entry word is highlighted, defined, and used in a sentence.

Merriam-Webster children's dictionary. (2006). New York: Dorling Kindersley. (M–U) This stunning volume pairs the 32,000 entries from *Merriam-Webster's Elementary Dictionary* with the striking design and color illustrations that DK is famous for. This visually appealing book includes more than 3,000 photos and charts.

Scholastic children's dictionary. (2002). New York: Scholastic. (M) More than 30,000 entries are presented with color illustrations and bright page decorations. Attractively designed boxes with information about synonyms, affixes, and word histories are featured throughout the book.

Thesauri

Bollard, J. K. (2006). *Scholastic children's thesaurus.* New York: Scholastic. (M) This attractive reference book for middle-grade students contains 500 entries and 2,500 synonyms grouped under the entries. All synonyms are defined and used in sample sentences. Antonyms are not listed.

Hellweg, P. (2006). *The American Heritage children's thesaurus.* Boston: Houghton Mifflin. (M–U) This well-designed and attractive reference book contains more than 4,000 entries and 36,000 synonyms. For each entry, synonyms are listed with the best matches first, and each is used in a sentence to clarify its meaning. Antonym and word-group boxes provide additional information and extend the book's usefulness.

Hellweg, P. (2006). *The American Heritage student thesaurus.* Boston: Houghton Mifflin. (U) This comprehensive, dictionary-style thesaurus with 6,000 entries and more than 70,000 synonyms is designed for middle school and high school students. Clear sample sentences are provided for each synonym. In addition, word-group features list related vocabulary for words with no true synonyms.

Wittels, H., & Greisman, J. (2001). *A first thesaurus.* Racine, WI: Golden Books. (P–M) More than 2,000 entries are listed, with the main words printed in bold type in this easy-to-read reference. Synonyms are printed in regular type and antonyms in red.

Homonyms

Homonyms, words that have sound and spelling similarities, are divided into three categories: homophones, homographs, and homographic homophones. *Homophones* are words that sound alike but are spelled differently. Most homophones developed from entirely different root words, and it is only by accident that they have come to sound alike; for example, the homophones *right* and *write* entered English before the year 900 and were pronounced differently. *Right* was spelled *riht* in Old English; during the Middle

English period, the spelling was changed by French scribes to the current spelling. The verb *write* was spelled *writan* in Old English and *writen* in Middle English. *Write* is an irregular verb, suggesting its Old English heritage, and the silent *w* was pronounced hundreds of years ago. In contrast, a few words were derived from the same root words, such as *flea–flee, flower–flour, stationary–stationery,* and *metal–medal–mettle,* and the similar spellings have been retained to demonstrate the semantic relationships.

Homographs are words that are spelled the same but pronounced differently. Examples of homographs are *bow, close, lead, minute, record, read,* and *wind. Bow* is a homograph that has three unrelated meanings. The verb form, meaning "to bend in respect," was spelled *bugan* in Old English; the noun form, meaning "a gathering of ribbon" or "a weapon for propelling an arrow," is of Old English origin and was spelled *boga.* The other noun form of *bow,* meaning "forward end of a ship," did not enter English until the 1600s from German.

Homographic homophones are words that are both spelled and pronounced alike, such as *bark, bat, bill, box, fair, fly, hide, jet, mine, pen, ring, row, spell, toast,* and *yard.* Some are related words; others are linguistic accidents. The different meanings of *toast,* for example, came from the same Latin source word, *torrere,* meaning "to parch or bake." The derivation of the noun *toast* as heated and browned slices of bread is obvious. However, the relationship between the source word and *toast* as a verb, "drinking to someone's honor or health," is not immediately apparent; the connection is that toasted, spiced bread flavored the drinks used in making toasts. In contrast, *bat* is a linguistic accident: *Bat* as a cudgel comes from the Old English word *batt;* the verb *to bat* is derived from the Old French word *batre;* and the nocturnal *bat* derives its name from an unknown Viking word and was spelled *bakke* in Middle English. Not only do the three forms of *bat* have unrelated etymologies, but they were borrowed from three languages!

There are many books of homonyms for children, including Gwynne's *The King Who Rained* (1988b), *A Chocolate Moose for Dinner* (1988a), and *A Little Pigeon Toad* (1998). Children enjoy reading these books and making their own word books. Figure 5–3 shows a page from a second grader's homophone book.

FIGURE 5–3

A Page From a Second Grader's Homophone Book

hare   hair

Multiple Meanings

Many words have more than one meaning. The word *bank,* for example, may refer to a piled-up mass of snow or clouds, the slope of land beside a lake or river, the slope of a road on a turn, the lateral tilting of an airplane in a turn, to cover a fire with ashes for slow burning, a business establishment that receives and lends money, a container in which money is saved, a supply for use in emergencies (e.g., blood bank), a place for storage (e.g., computer's memory bank), to count on, similar things arranged in a row (e.g., a bank of elevators), or to arrange things in a row. You may be surprised that there are at least 12 meanings for the common word *bank.* Why does this happen? The meanings of *bank* just listed come from three sources. The first five meanings come from a Viking word, and they are related because they all deal with something slanted or making a slanted motion. The next five meanings come from the Italian word *banca,* a money changer's table. All these meanings deal with financial banking except for the 10th meaning, "to count on," which requires a bit more thought. We use the saying "to bank on" figuratively to mean "to depend on," but it began more literally from the actual counting of money on a table. The last two meanings come from the Old French word *banc,* meaning "bench." Words acquired multiple meanings as society became more complex and finer shades of meaning were necessary; for example, the meanings of *bank* as an emergency supply and a storage place are fairly new. As with many words with multiple meanings, it is a linguistic accident that three original words from three languages, with unrelated meanings, came to be spelled the same way.

Students can create posters with word clusters to show multiple meanings of words (Bromley, 1996). Figure 5–4 shows a cluster with 10 meanings for the word *hot* sketched on a poster made by three seventh graders. The students drew rays and wrote the meanings, listed examples, and drew illustrations.

Words assume additional meanings when an affix is added or when they are combined with another word, or compounded. Consider the word *fire* and the variety of words and phrases that incorporate *fire: fire hydrant, firebomb, fireproof, fireplace, firearm, fire drill, under fire, set the world on fire, fire away,* and *open fire.* Students can compile a list of words or make a booklet illustrating the words. Other common words with many variations include *short, key, water, book, rain, shoe, head, make, walk, cat,* and *side.*

Figurative Language

Many words have both literal and figurative meanings; literal meanings are the explicit, dictionary meanings, and figurative meanings are metaphorical or use figures of speech. For example, to describe winter as the coldest season of the year is literal, but to say that winter has icy breath is figurative. Two types of figurative language are idioms and metaphors.

Idioms are groups of words, such as "spill the beans," that have a special meaning. Idioms can be confusing to students because they must be interpreted figuratively rather than literally. "Spill the beans" dates back to ancient Greece when many Greek men belonged to secret clubs, and the members took a vote to decide whether to admit new members. They wanted the vote to remain secret, so they voted by each placing a white or brown bean in a special jar; a white bean indicated a yes vote, and a brown bean was a no vote. The club leader would then examine

FIGURE 5–4

FIGURE 5–4

Seventh Graders' Poster of 10 Meanings for *Hot*

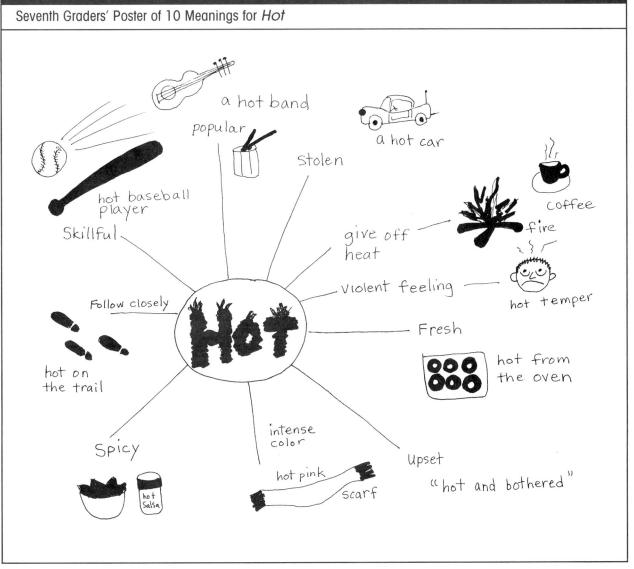

the beans, and if they were all white, the person was admitted to the club. The vote was kept secret to avoid hurting the person's feelings in case the members voted not to admit him to the club. Sometimes during the voting, one member would accidentally (or not so accidentally) knock the jar over, spilling the beans, and the vote would no longer be a secret. The Greeks turned this real happening into a saying that we still use today. Another idiom with a different history but a similar meaning is "let the cat out of the bag."

There are hundreds of idioms in English, and we use them every day to create word pictures that make language more colorful. Some examples are "out in left field," "a skeleton in the closet," "stick your neck out," "a chip off the old block," and "don't cry over spilt milk." Some of these idioms are new, and others are hundreds or thousands of years old; some are American in origin, and others come from around the world.

Three excellent books of idioms for students are the *Scholastic Dictionary of Idioms, Phrases, Sayings, and Expressions* (Terban, 2006), *Punching the Clock: Funny Action Idioms* (Terban, 1990), and *In a Pickle and Other Funny Idioms* (Terban, 1983). Because idioms are figurative sayings, many children—especially those who are English learners—have difficulty using them. It is crucial that children move beyond the literal meanings, thus learning flexibility in using language. One way for children to learn flexibility is to create idiom posters showing the literal and figurative meanings of the sayings. A fourth grader's drawing of the literal meaning of "hold your horses" is shown in Figure 5–5.

Metaphors and similes compare something to something else. A *simile* is a comparison signaled by the use of *like* or *as:* "The crowd was as rowdy as a bunch of marauding monkeys" and "In the moonlight, the dead tree looked like a skeleton" are two examples. In contrast, a *metaphor* compares two things by implying that one is something else, without using *like* or *as.* "The children were frisky puppies playing in the yard" is an example. Metaphors are a stronger comparison, as these examples show:

Simile: *The two old men crossed the street as slowly as snails.*
Metaphor: *The two old men were snails crossing the street.*

Simile: *In the moonlight, the dead tree looked like a skeleton.*
Metaphor: *In the moonlight, the dead tree was a skeleton.*

FIGURE 5–5

A Fourth Grader's Idiom Poster

Differentiating between the terms *simile* and *metaphor* is less important than understanding the meaning of comparisons in books students are reading and having students use comparisons to make their writing more vivid.

Students begin by learning traditional comparisons, such as "happy as a clam" and "high as a kite," and then they learn to notice and invent fresh, unexpected comparisons. To introduce traditional comparisons to primary-grade students, teachers use Audrey Wood's *Quick as a Cricket* (1994). Middle- and upper-grade students locate comparisons in books they are reading and invent their own as they write poems, stories, and other types of writing.

Borrowed Words

The most common way of expanding vocabulary is to borrow words from other languages. Perhaps as many as 75% of our words have been borrowed from other languages and incorporated into English. Word borrowing has occurred during every period of language development, beginning when the Angles and Saxons borrowed more than 400 words from the Romans. During the eighth and ninth centuries, the Vikings contributed approximately 900 words. The Norman conquerors introduced thousands of French words into English, reflecting every aspect of life; for example, *adventure, fork, juggler,* and *quilt.* Later, during the Renaissance, when scholars translated Greek and Latin classics into English, they borrowed many words from Latin and Greek to enrich the language, including *chaos, encyclopedia, pneumonia,* and *skeleton.* More recently, words from at least 50 languages have been added to English through exploration, colonization, and trade. These are some of the loan words from other languages (Tompkins & Yaden, 1986, p. 31):

Aboriginal Australian: *kangaroo, kiwi*
African (many languages): *banjo, cola, gumbo, safari, zombie*
Arabic: *alcohol, apricot, assassin, magazine*
Chinese: *chop suey, kowtow, tea, wok*
Dutch: *caboose, easel, pickle, waffle*
French: *ballet, beige, chauffeur*
German: *kindergarten, poodle, pretzel, waltz*
Greek: *atom, cyclone, hydrogen*
Hebrew: *cherub, kosher, rabbi*
Hindi: *dungaree, juggernaut, jungle, shampoo*
Italian: *broccoli, carnival, macaroni, opera, pizza*
Japanese: *honcho, judo, kimono, origami*
Persian: *bazaar, divan, khaki, shawl*
Portuguese: *cobra, coconut, molasses*
Russian: *czar, sputnik, steppe, troika, vodka*
Scandinavian: *egg, fjord, husband, ski, sky*
Spanish: *alligator, guitar, mosquito, potato*
Turkish: *caviar, horde, khan, kiosk, yogurt*

Native Americans have also contributed a number of words to English. The early American colonists encountered many unfamiliar animals, plants, foods, and aspects of Native American life in North America; they borrowed the Native

American terms for these objects or events and tried to spell them phonetically. Native American loan words include *chipmunk, hickory, moccasin, moose, muskrat, opossum, papoose, powwow, raccoon, skunk, toboggan, tomahawk,* and *tepee.*

TEACHING STUDENTS ABOUT WORDS

Learning a word isn't as simple as you might think. It's not that you either know a word or you don't; instead, there's a continuum of word knowledge, moving from never having seen or heard the word before to knowing it well and being able to use it effectively in a variety of contexts (Allen, 1999). Beck and her colleagues (2002) suggest that there's a continuum of word knowledge that moves from not knowing a word to knowing it well:

> *No Knowledge.* Students are not familiar with the word.
>
> *Incidental Knowledge.* Students have seen or heard the word, but they don't know its meaning.
>
> *Partial Knowledge.* Students know one definition for the word or can use it in one context.
>
> *Full Knowledge.* Students have a deep understanding of the word's multiple meanings and are able to use it effectively in multiple contexts.

It takes time for students to move from having little or no knowledge of a word to full knowledge. During a week's study of a word, for example, students may move from the no knowledge or incidental knowledge level to partial knowledge, but it's

Meeting the Needs of English Learners

How Can Teachers Develop Students' Vocabularies?

Many English learners have small vocabularies, and their limited understanding of words impedes their school success. As you continue reading, you'll learn about three ways to help English learners enrich their vocabularies. However, it's wrong to assume that all English learners have limited vocabularies because when students have rich vocabularies in their first language, they learn English words fairly easily because translating words from one language to another is much easier than learning new words.

Provide Meaningful Contexts for Learning

Graves and Fitzgerald (2006) advise teachers to provide a variety of rich, meaningful language experiences for English learners so that they can acquire new vocabulary just like native English speakers do. One way to accomplish this is by reading aloud stories, informational books, and books of poetry. Another way is through independent reading of interesting, age-appropriate books at students' reading levels (Akhavan, 2006). A third way is through thematic units where students expand their background knowledge as they develop concepts and related words (Peregoy & Boyle, 2005).

Teach Useful Words

English learners need explicit instruction to rapidly expand their vocabularies and to develop both conversational English and academic English (Graves, 2006). Teachers must be selective in choosing words to teach because they can't possibly teach all unfamiliar words related to a book students are reading or to a thematic unit. Akhavan (2006) recommends using the word's usefulness as a guide in determining which words to teach. Whenever possible, teachers group the words they've chosen to teach thematically and focus on related words and the concepts underlying the words. Words are posted on the wall so students can read and think about them.

Teaching a word involves more than looking it up in a dictionary and explaining its meanings. Teachers also focus on how to pronounce the word, use it in sentences, and spell it. English learners learn best when they're actively engaged in learning words using all six language arts (Peregoy & Boyle, 2005). They can use improvisation, for example, to dramatize how they would use a word in informal conversation, or they can create a diagram to explain its relationship to related words.

Foster Word-Learning Strategies

Word-learning strategies are especially important for English learners because they have so many words to learn (Graves & Fitzgerald, 2006). Students learn to use these strategies so that they can independently unlock the meaning of unfamiliar words:

- *Context Clues.* Students use context to infer the meaning of an unfamiliar word.
- *Morphology.* Students apply knowledge of root words and affixes to deduce the meaning of a word.
- *Multiple Meanings.* Students consider alternative meanings of a word.
- *Dictionaries.* Students use the dictionary to check the meaning of an unfamiliar word.
- *Cognates.* Students recognize that an English word is similar to a word in their native language. (Carlo, August, McGlaughlin, Snow, Dressler, Lippman, Lively, & White, 2004). Cognates are especially useful for English learners who are native Spanish speakers because so many English words have Spanish cognates.

What's Not Recommended

Too often, vocabulary instruction is equated with giving students lists of words to look up in the dictionary, but this isn't a worthwhile instructional practice. Instead, Beck, McKeown, and Kucan (2002) emphasize that teaching vocabulary to English learners involves teaching concepts about words so students can make sense of the new information and expand their background knowledge.

unlikely they'll reach the full knowledge level. In fact, it may take several years of using a word to develop a rich, decontextualized understanding of its meaning and related words.

To reach the full knowledge level, students develop "ownership" of the word, meaning that they know or can do these things:

- Pronounce the word correctly
- Understand the word's multiple meanings
- Use the word appropriately in sentences
- Identify related noun, verb, and adjective forms
- Recognize other words that come from the same root word
- Name synonyms and antonyms

With this knowledge, students will be able to understand the word when they are listening and reading and use it to express ideas in talk and writing.

Direct and Indirect Instruction

Even though students learn hundreds or thousands of words incidentally through reading and content-area study each year, teaching vocabulary directly is an essential part of language arts instruction for all students and especially for struggling students and English learners (Graves, 2006). Blachowicz and Fisher (2006) have reviewed the research on effective vocabulary instruction and identified these guidelines for teaching vocabulary:

- Teachers immerse students in vocabulary by creating a word-rich environment in the classroom. When teachers post words on word walls, students are more likely to learn them incidentally and through direct instruction.
- Teachers prepare students to become independent word learners. When teachers involve students in choosing some of the words they will study and teach word-learning tools, such as how to use root words to analyze words and how to use a dictionary, students are more likely to take control of their own learning.

- Teachers model word-learning strategies while teaching vocabulary. When teachers demonstrate ways, such as making clusters and sorting words, to become actively involved in learning word meanings and students participate in these activities, they are more likely to personalize the words and remember their meanings.
- Teachers assess both the depth and the breadth of vocabulary knowledge. When teachers choose assessment techniques based on their instructional goals, they can evaluate both how well students understand the words they've studied and the range of words they learned.

Vocabulary instruction fits into all four patterns of practice, as shown in the box on the next page. Teachers apply Blachowicz and Fisher's guidelines as they teach vocabulary. During thematic units, for example, teachers, like Ms. Boland in the vignette at the beginning of the chapter, highlight important words on word walls and teach minilessons using these words.

How Vocabulary Fits Into the Four Patterns of Practice

Literature Focus Units

Students post important words on the word wall and participate in a variety of vocabulary activities, including word maps and word sorts, during the exploring stage of the reading process.

Literature Circles

Students identify important words in books they're reading, check the meanings of these words in a dictionary, and talk about them as they participate in literature circle discussions.

Reading and Writing Workshop

Students learn hundreds, if not thousands, of new words incidentally as they use word-learning strategies while reading books independently and listening to the teacher read books aloud.

Thematic Units

Students post words on a word wall during thematic units and participate in a variety of vocabulary activities, including tea party, word chains, and semantic feature analysis.

Choosing Words to Teach

Teachers often feel overwhelmed when they think about all of the unfamiliar words in a book students are reading or in a thematic unit they're teaching. Of course, it's not possible to teach every unfamiliar word. Teachers need to choose the words that are most useful—those that are most important to understand the book or the big ideas in the unit. In addition, the words chosen for instruction should be common enough that students can use them in other contexts.

Words have different levels of usefulness. Some words, such as *comfortable* and *lonely,* are words that we use frequently, whereas words such as *brawny, frolic,* and *tolerate* are less common but still useful. Other words, such as *bailey* and *nebula,* are specialized and used infrequently. Beck, McKeown, and Kucan (2002) classified words into three tiers:

Tier 1 Words: Basic, everyday words that don't usually have to be taught in school.
Tier 2 Words: Useful words that students need to learn in school.
Tier 3 Words: Less common, specialized words that not all students need to learn before high school.

The Tier 2 words are those that teachers should post on word walls and use for instruction. They're part of academic language—the words that students need to learn to be successful in school.

Instead of teaching 50 or more unfamiliar words from a book or a thematic unit, teachers identify the Tier 2 words to focus on. There are some questions to consider when choosing words:

- Is the word important to understand the book or the big idea?
- Do students already understand the concept?
- Can students explain the unfamiliar word using words they already know?
- Can students use the word in other contexts?

After considering these questions, teachers can choose 5 to 10 words or more, depending on the grade level, for direct instruction.

Word Walls

The most important way to focus students' attention on words is to write important words on word-wall charts and post them in the classroom. Before beginning instruction, teachers hang up blank word walls made from large sheets of butcher paper that have been divided into alphabetized sections. Students and the teacher write on the word wall interesting, confusing, and important words from books they are reading and concepts they are learning during thematic units. Usually students choose the words to write on the word wall during the exploring stage of the reading process, and they may even do the writing themselves. Teachers add any key words students have not chosen. Words are added to the word wall as they come up—in books students are reading during literature focus units or during thematic units— usually not in advance; also, separate charts are used for each unit. The procedure for creating a word wall is described in the Step by Step feature below.

Step by Step

Word Walls

1 Prepare the word wall. Teachers hang a long sheet of butcher paper on a blank wall in the classroom, divide it into 12 to 16 boxes, and label with letters of the alphabet.

2 Introduce the word wall. Teachers introduce the word wall and write several key words on it during preparing activities before reading.

3 Add words to the word wall. After reading a picture book or after reading each chapter of a chapter book, students suggest "important" words for the word wall. Students and the teacher write the words on the word wall, making sure to write large enough so that most students can see the words. If a word is misspelled, it should be corrected because students will be reading and using the word in various activities. Sometimes the teacher adds a small picture or writes a synonym for a difficult word, puts a box around the root word, or writes the plural form or other related words nearby.

4 Use the word wall for exploring activities. Students use the words for a variety of activities, and teachers expect them to spell the words correctly. During literature focus units, students refer to the word wall when they are making words, writing in reading logs, doing word sorts, or working on projects. During thematic units, students use the word wall in similar ways.

5 Write the words on word cards. Teachers transfer the words from the word wall to word cards at the end of the unit. They can write the words on index cards, sentence strips, or small sheets of decorated paper that correspond to the topic of the unit. They punch holes in one corner of the cards and use metal rings or yarn to make a booklet. They place the word booklets in the writing center for students to refer to as needed.

Teachers choose the most important words from books to teach. Important words include words that are essential to understanding the text, words that may confuse students, and words students will use as they read other books. As teachers choose words for word walls and other vocabulary activities, they consider the book being read as well as the instructional context. Even though all these words and perhaps more will be added to the word wall, not all will be directly taught to students. As they plan, teachers create lists of words that they anticipate will be written on word walls during the unit. They try to identify which words will be recognizable sight words for their students and which words represent new concepts, new words, and new meanings for them. From this list, teachers choose the key words—the ones that are critical to understanding the book or the theme—and these are the words they plan to highlight or include in minilessons. They also choose any words that must be introduced before reading. According to Vygotsky's notion of a "zone of proximal development," teachers need to be alert to individual students and what words they are learning so that they can provide instruction when students are most interested in learning more about a word.

Identifying some words on the word wall as key words doesn't mean that the other words are unimportant. Students have many opportunities to use all the word wall words as they write and talk about what they are reading and studying. For example, students often use the word wall to locate a specific word they want to use to make a point during a discussion or to check the spelling of a word they are writing in a reading log or in a report. Teachers also use the words listed on the word wall for word-study activities.

Word-Study Activities

Word-study activities provide opportunities for students to explore the meanings of words listed on word walls, other words related to books they are reading, and words they are learning during social studies or science units. Through these activities, they explore the word meanings and make associations among words. None of these activities ask students to simply write words and their definitions or to use the words in sentences or a contrived story. Here are eight types of activities:

◆ **Word Posters.** Students choose a word from the word wall and write it on a small poster. Then they draw and color a picture to illustrate the word. They may also want to use the word in a sentence.

◆ **Word Maps.** Students create diagrams called *word maps* to highlight a word they're studying and its meanings. They incorporate different kinds of information about the word, including its etymology, word forms, related words, and ways to use the word in a sentence. The information that's included depends on students' knowledge of words and the word itself. Figure 5–6 shows two word maps; a fourth grader created the *alien* word map when she was learning that *alien* can mean "a person who isn't a citizen," and a fifth grader created the *repel* word map to focus on the four meanings of that word.

◆ **Dramatizing Words.** Students choose a word from the word wall and dramatize it for classmates to guess. Teachers might also want to choose a word from the word wall for a "word of the day."

◆ **Word Sorts.** Students sort a collection of words taken from the word wall into two or more categories (Bear, Invernizzi, Templeton, & Johnston, 2008). Usually students choose which categories they will use for the sort, but sometimes the teacher chooses. For example, words from a story might be sorted by character, or words from a theme on machines might be sorted according to whether they are machines or according to type of machine. The words can be written on cards, and then students sort a pack of word cards into piles. Or, students can cut apart a list of words, sort the words into categories, and then paste each group on a sheet of paper. Figure 5–7 shows a word sort done by a small group of fifth graders during a theme on the colonies. Students chose the three categories—New England colonies, middle colonies, and Southern colonies—and sorted word cards for each category. Then they glued the word cards onto a large sheet of paper.

◆ **Books About Words.** A variety of books for children are collections of words or explain words related to particular concepts. *Zin! Zin! Zin! A Violin* (Moss, 2005), for instance, explains words for groups of musicians (e.g., *solo, duo, trio, quartet*), and Ruth Heller introduces *batch, school, fleet, bevy,* and *flock* in *A Cache of Jewels and Other Collective Nouns* (1987). Marvin Terban, the author of more than a dozen books about words, explains *hocus-pocus, razzmatazz, hodgepodge, knickknack,* and 103 other words in *Superdupers! Really Funny Real Words* (1989). These and other recommended books about words are listed in the box on page 171.

◆ **Tea Party.** Teachers prepare a set of cards with text (sentences or paragraphs) from a story or informational book students are reading. At least one "important" word from the word wall is included in each excerpt, and the word is highlighted. Students have a "tea party" and read the cards to classmates. They also talk about the highlighted word and its meaning. Sometimes teachers write the definition of the word or a synonym on the back of the card.

◆ **Word Chains.** Students choose a word from the word wall and then identify three or four words to sequence before or after the word to make a chain. For example, the word *tadpole* can be chained this way: *egg, tadpole, frog;* and the word *aggravate* can be chained like this: *irritate, bother, aggravate, annoy.* Students can draw and write their chains on a sheet of paper, or they can make a construction paper chain and write the words on each link.

FIGURE 5–6

Two Students' Word Maps

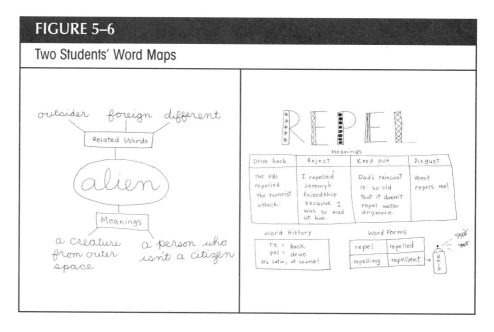

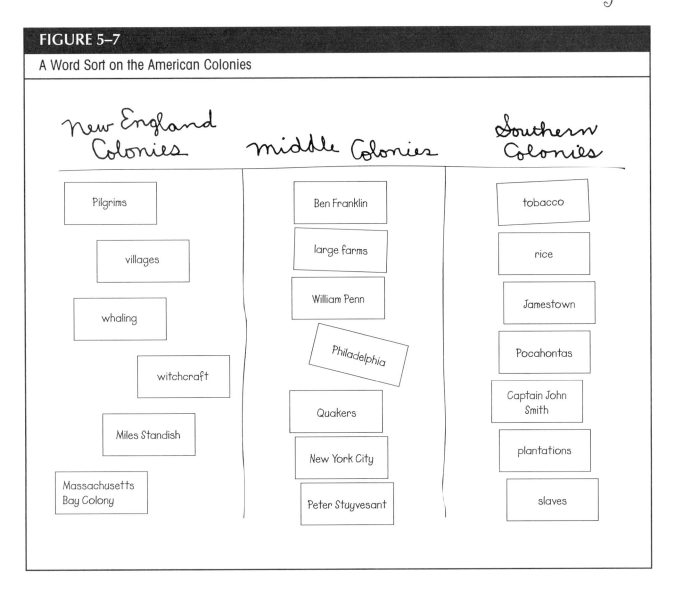

FIGURE 5–7

A Word Sort on the American Colonies

New England Colonies

- Pilgrims
- villages
- whaling
- witchcraft
- Miles Standish
- Massachusetts Bay Colony

Middle Colonies

- Ben Franklin
- large farms
- William Penn
- Philadelphia
- Quakers
- New York City
- Peter Stuyvesant

Southern Colonies

- tobacco
- rice
- Jamestown
- Pocahontas
- Captain John Smith
- plantations
- slaves

◆ *Semantic Feature Analysis.* Students select a group of related words, such as names of different kinds of birds, and then make a grid or chart to classify them according to distinguishing characteristics. A semantic feature analysis that Ms. Boland's class created during their thematic unit on medieval life is presented in Figure 5–8. This activity reinforces students' organization of knowledge and related words into schemata (Pittelman, Heimlich, Berglund, & French, 1991).

Minilessons

Traditionally, vocabulary instruction involved assigning students to look up the definitions of a list of words in a dictionary and use the words in sentences, but this approach often failed to produce in-depth understanding. Instead, teachers should teach minilessons about specific words as well as word-learning strategies

FIGURE 5–8

A Semantic Feature Analysis on Medieval Life

	castle	knights	peasants	Crusades	cathedral
apprentice	○	✓	○	○	○
bailey	✓	○	○	○	○
Black Death	○	✓	✓	○	○
chivalry	○	✓	○	○	○
clergy	○	○	○	?	✓
dub	○	✓	○	○	○
flying buttress	○	○	○	○	✓
fortress	✓	○	○	○	○
garderobe	✓	○	○	○	○
jousts	○	✓	○	○	○
keep	✓	○	○	○	○
mercenary	○	?	○	✓	○
moat	✓	○	○	○	○
pilgrims	○	?	○	✓	○
portcullis	✓	○	○	○	○
serf	○	○	✓	○	○
siege	✓	○	○	○	○
tournament	○	✓	○	○	○
villein	○	○	✓	○	○

Code: ✓ = yes

○ = no

? = don't know

Scott Cunningham/Merrill

Minilessons

This teacher is reviewing how to take notes using key vocabulary words. She taught the minilesson to the whole class, and then students were to continue to take notes as they read the next chapter. These four students were unsure how to proceed, so the teacher reviewed the steps in taking notes and next will work with students as they read, make a cluster, and take notes on the next chapter together. Teachers provide direct instruction through minilessons and are then available to give additional assistance to students who need more support.

Booklist

BOOKS ABOUT WORDS AND WORDPLAY

Agee, J. (2002). *Palindromania!* New York: Farrar, Straus & Giroux. (See other wordplay books by the same author.) (M–U)

Cleary, B. P. (2005). *How much can a bare bear bear? What are homonyms and homophones?* Brookfield, CT: Millbrook Press. (M)

Clements, A. (1996). *Frindle.* New York: Simon & Schuster. (M–U)

DeGross, M. (1998). *Donavan's word jar.* New York: HarperCollins. (M)

Evans, D. (2004). *MVP*.* Blodgett, OR: Hand Print Press. (U)

Falwell, C. (1998). *Word wizard.* New York: Clarion Books. (M)

Fine, E. H. (2004). *Cryptomania: Teleporting into Greek and Latin with cryptokids.* Berkeley, CA: Triangle Press. (M–U)

Frasier, D. (2000). *Miss Alaineus: A vocabulary disaster.* San Diego: Harcourt Brace. (M)

Heller, R. (1998). *A cache of jewels and other collective nouns.* New York: Putnam. (M–U)

Mammano, J. (2001). *Rhinos who play soccer.* San Francisco: Chronicle Books. (See other books in the series.) (P–M)

Moss, L. (2005). *Zin! Zin! Zin! A violin.* New York: Aladdin Books. (P–M)

Most, B. (1992). *There's an ant in Anthony.* New York: HarperCollins. (P–M)

Pallotta, J. (2006). *The construction alphabet book.* Watertown, MA: Charlesbridge. (See other alphabet books by the same author.) (M)

Terban, M. (1988). *Guppies in tuxedos: Funny eponyms.* New York: Clarion Books. (M–U)

Terban, M. (1993). *It figures! Fun figures of speech.* New York: Clarion Books. (M)

Terban, M. (2006). *Building your vocabulary and making it great!* New York: Scholastic. (U)

Terban, M. (2006). *The Scholastic dictionary of idioms.* New York: Scholastic. (M–U)

Planning for Instruction

What Students Need to Learn About Vocabulary

Topics

Procedures	Concepts	Strategies and Skills
Choose words for word walls	***Word Histories***	Use phonics to pronounce a word
Extrapolate the etymology	Root words	Use structural analysis to identify a word
"Peel off" affixes	Prefixes	Use context clues to identify a word
Make a word poster	Suffixes	Consider shades of meaning in
Make a word map	Synonyms	selecting a word
Do a word sort	Antonyms	Use a thesaurus to choose a better word
Make a word chain	Homophones	Use a dictionary to identify a word
Do a semantic feature analysis	Homographs	Consider multiple meanings of
Locate a word in a dictionary	Homographic homophones	words
Locate a word in a thesaurus	Idioms	
	Literal meanings	
	Figurative meanings	

I invite you to learn more about teaching vocabulary by visiting MyEducationLab. To see how sixth graders examine root words and affixes, go to the topic "Vocabulary" and click on the video "Apply Affixes."

(Baumann & Kame'enui, 2004). To teach specific words, they provide in-depth information about words, provide multiple opportunities to learn a word, and get students to actively investigate words in order to deepen their level of knowledge. To teach word-learning strategies, teachers explain and demonstrate strategies for unlocking word meanings, such as peeling off affixes or using the root word to determine the word's meaning. A list of topics for minilessons and a sample minilesson showing how a sixth-grade teacher explains to her students how related words develop from English, Latin, and Greek root words presented are here and on page 173.

Minilesson

Mrs. Monroe Teaches Her Sixth Graders About Word Histories

1 Introduce the topic

Mrs. Monroe asks her sixth-grade students to brainstorm a list of words about teeth, and students suggest words, including *teeth, toothbrush, floss, dentist, cavities, cleaning, tooth fairy, dental, orthodontist, braces,* and *dentures.* She points out that it seems unusual that words such as *toothbrush, dentist,* and *orthodontist* all relate to teeth, but look so different.

2 Share examples

Mrs. Monroe explains that many words dealing with teeth come from three root words—*tooth* (English), *dent* (Latin), and *dont* (Greek). They sort the words from the brainstormed list into four columns:

tooth	dent	dont	other
teeth	dentist	orthodontist	floss
toothbrush	dental		cavities
tooth fairy	dentures		braces

She points out that Latin and Greek words are likely to be medical or scientific.

3 Provide information

Mrs. Monroe explains that there are other trios of related words:

star (E), *stell* (L), and *astr* (Gr)
sound (E), *sono* (L), and *phon* (Gr)
people (E), *pop* (L), and *demo* (Gr)
foot (E), *ped* (L), and *pod* (Gr)
water (E), *aqua* (L), and *hydro* (Gr)

The students brainstorm some examples of the trios and ask why words come from different root words. The teacher explains that many words in English come from different languages because people wanted to be able to express various ideas, and that at different historical times, the English liked to invent new words from other languages, especially Latin and Greek.

4 Supervise practice

Mrs. Monroe divides the class into five groups and gives each group a set of word cards representing a different trio of words. The students read the word cards, check the meanings of any unfamiliar words, sort the words, glue the sorted words on a poster, and add other related words.

5 Reflect on learning

Students share their posters with the class and marvel at the complexity of English.

Assessing Students' Vocabulary Knowledge

Teachers assess students' word knowledge in a variety of ways. They listen while students talk during the unit, examine students' writing and projects, and ask students to talk or write about what they have learned. Here are some specific strategies to determine whether students have learned and are applying new words:

- Check reading logs, learning logs, or simulated journals for newly taught words.
- Listen for new vocabulary words when students give an oral report.

- Ask students to draw a word map or other diagram highlighting a word.
- Check students' reports, biographies, poems, stories, or other writings for unit-related words.
- Check students' projects for these words.
- Ask students to write a letter to you, telling what they have learned in the unit.

It's probably not very useful to give tests on the vocabulary words because a correct answer on a test does not indicate whether students have ownership of a word or whether they are applying it in meaningful and genuine ways.

Review

Learning about words is an important part of language arts. Few words have only one meaning, and students gradually learn about multiple meanings as well as about root words and affixes; homonyms, synonyms, and antonyms; and figurative meanings of words, such as idioms and metaphors. The best measure of students' learning of words is their ability to use the words in meaningful ways. Here are the key points in this chapter:

- English is a historical language, and its diverse origins account for word meanings and some spelling inconsistencies.
- The fact that children's vocabularies grow at a rate of about 3,000 to 4,000 words a year suggests that they learn many words incidentally.
- Students use their knowledge of root words and affixes to unlock the meaning of unfamiliar words.
- Many words have more than one meaning, and students learn additional word meanings through the four patterns of practice.
- Idioms and metaphors can be confusing because they must be interpreted figuratively rather than literally.
- Reading and writing are the most important ways students learn vocabulary, but direct instruction is also important.
- Students need to use a word many times in order to learn it well.
- Words are not all equally difficult or easy to learn; the degree of difficulty depends on what students already know about a word.
- Students use reference books, including dictionaries and thesauri, to expand their knowledge of words.
- Word-study activities include word walls, word posters, word clusters, word sorts, word chains, and semantic feature analysis.

Professional References

Akhavan, N. (2006). *Help! My kids don't all speak English: How to set up a language workshop in your linguistically diverse classroom.* Portsmouth, NH: Heinemann.

Allen, J. (1999). *Words, words, words.* Portsmouth, NH: Heinemann.

Baugh, A. C., & Cable, T. (2002). *The history of the English language.* Oxford, UK: Routledge Books.

Baumann, J. F., & Kame'enui, E. J. (Eds.). (2004). *Vocabulary instruction: Research to practice.* New York: Guilford Press.

Bear, D. R., Invernizzi, M., Templeton, S., & Johnston, F. (2008). *Words their way: Word study for phonics, vocabulary, and spelling instruction* (4th ed.). Upper Saddle River, NJ: Merrill/Prentice Hall.

Beck, I. L., McKeown, M. G., & Kucan, L. (2002). *Bringing words to life: Robust vocabulary instruction.* New York: Guilford Press.

Blachowicz, C., & Fisher, P. (2006). *Teaching vocabulary in all classrooms* (3rd ed.). Upper Saddle River, NJ: Merrill/Prentice Hall.

Bromley, K. D. (1996). *Webbing with literature: Creating story maps with children's books* (2nd ed.). Boston: Allyn & Bacon.

Carlo, M. S., August, D., McGlaughlin, B., Snow, C. E., Dressler, C., Lippman, D. N., Lively, T. J., & White, C. E. (2004). Closing the gap: Addressing the vocabulary needs of English-language learners in bilingual and mainstream classes. *Reading Research Quarterly, 39,* 188–215.

Graves, M. F. (2006). *The vocabulary book: Learning and instruction.* New York: Teachers College Press.

Graves, M. F., & Fitzgerald, J. (2006). Effective vocabulary instruction for English language learners. In C. C. Block & J. N. Mangieri (Eds.), *The vocabulary-enriched classroom: Practices for improving the reading performance of all students in grades 3 and up* (pp. 118–137). New York: Scholastic.

Hook, J. N. (1975). *History of the English language.* New York: Ronald Press.

Nagy, W. E. (1988). *Teaching vocabulary to improve reading comprehension.* Urbana, IL: ERIC Clearinghouse on Reading and Communication Skills and the National Council of Teachers of English and the International Reading Association.

Nagy, W. E., & Herman, P. (1985). Incidental vs. instructional approaches to increasing reading vocabulary. *Educational Perspectives, 23,* 16–21.

Peregoy, S. F., & Boyle, O. F. (2005). *Reading, writing, and learning in ESL: A resource book for K–12 teachers* (4th ed.). Boston: Allyn & Bacon.

Pittelman, S. D., Heimlich, J. E., Berglund, R. L., & French, M. P. (1991). *Semantic feature analysis: Classroom applications.* Newark, DE: International Reading Association.

Stevenson, V. (1999). *The world of words.* New York: Sterling.

Tompkins, G. E. (2008). *Teaching writing: Balancing process and product* (5th ed.). Upper Saddle River, NJ: Merrill/Prentice Hall.

Tompkins, G. E., & Yaden, D. B., Jr. (1986). *Answering students' questions about words.* Urbana, IL: National Council of Teachers of English.

White, T. G., Sowell, J., & Yanagihara, A. (1989). Teaching elementary students to use word-part clues. *The Reading Teacher, 42,* 302–308.

Children's Book References

Bollard, J. K. (2006). *Scholastic children's thesaurus.* New York: Scholastic.

Cole, J. (2002). *Ms. Frizzle's adventures: Medieval castle.* New York: Scholastic.

Cushman, K. (1994). *Catherine, called Birdy.* New York: HarperCollins.

Gwynne, F. (1988a). *A chocolate moose for dinner.* New York: Aladdin Books.

Gwynne, F. (1988b). *The king who rained.* New York: Aladdin Books.

Gwynne, F. (1998). *A little pigeon toad.* New York: Aladdin Books.

Heller, R. (1987). *A cache of jewels and other collective nouns.* New York: Grosset & Dunlap.

Macaulay, D. (1977). *Castle.* Boston: Houghton Mifflin.

Merriam-Webster children's dictionary. (2006). New York: Dorling Kindersley.

Moss, L. (2005). *Zin! Zin! Zin! A violin.* New York: Aladdin Books.

Platt, R. (1999). *Castle diary: The journal of Tobias Burgess, page.* Cambridge, MA: Candlewick Press.

Terban, M. (1983). *In a pickle and other funny idioms.* New York: Clarion Books.

Terban, M. (1989). *Superdupers! Really funny real words.* New York: Clarion Books.

Terban, M. (1990). *Punching the clock: Funny action idioms.* New York: Clarion Books.

Terban, M. (1996). *Scholastic dictionary of idioms, phrases, sayings, and expressions.* New York: Scholastic.

Van Allsburg, C. (1991). *The wretched stone.* Boston: Houghton Mifflin.

Wittels, H., & Greisman, J. (2001). *A first thesaurus.* Racine, WI: Golden Books.

Wood, A. (1994). *Quick as a cricket.* New York: Scholastic.

chapter six

Personal Writing

Ms. Meinke teaches seventh-grade language arts, and her students often participate in literature circles. One group of six students is reading *The Great Gilly Hopkins* (Paterson, 1987), the story of Gilly, an angry, mistrustful, disrespectful foster child who eventually finds love and acceptance. To begin their 3-week period of literature circles, the students sign up to read one of the six books that Ms. Meinke has introduced. The students divide into groups, after which each group selects a group leader and sets its schedule for reading and discussing the book. Students also construct reading logs by stapling paper into booklets and adding construction paper covers.

Ms. Meinke meets with *The Great Gilly Hopkins* group to talk about the book. She explains that the story is about a girl named Gilly Hopkins who is a foster child. They talk about foster care and how children become foster children. Several students mention that they know someone who is a foster child. She also passes out a list of topics for reading log entries, and students place the sheet in their reading logs. A copy of the topics sheet is shown on page 178.

Ms. Meinke varies the types of entries that she asks students to write in reading logs. She does this for two reasons. First of all, she believes that each chapter is different and that the content of the chapter should determine the type of response. Also, she has found that students tire of writing regular reading log entries because of their repetitiveness and predictability.

The students read in class and at home, and every two days, they meet to discuss their reading. Often Ms. Meinke sits in on at least part of their discussions.

Sometimes students choose their own topics for reading log entries, and sometimes teachers provide topics for students. There are benefits to each approach. When students choose their own topics, they assume more responsibility and probe the ideas that interest them, but when teachers provide the topics, students explore ideas that they might otherwise miss. As you continue reading, think about why Ms. Meinke provides questions to direct her students' thinking and their writing.

During the discussions, students ask questions and clarify misunderstandings, share their favorite excerpts, and make predictions about what will happen next. Sometimes, too, they share their reading log entries or talk about how they will write their entries.

Timothy wrote this simulated-journal entry after reading Chapter 2:

Dear Diary,

I can't live here, it's a dump. I have to live with Miss Trotter and that colored (or black) man Mr. Randolph. I will have to get out of this dump and fast. Today was the first day Mr. Randolph came and I can't escort him every day to dinner. I don't belong here, even Mrs. Nevin's house was better than here.

I cannot believe Miss Ellis took me to this awful place. I got to find a way to call Courtney Hopkins. She'll take me outta this place. Everyone's trying to be nice to me but I'll show them who's the boss, and I bet there is something wrong with W. E.

After reading Chapter 6, about how mean Gilly is to her teacher, Miss Harris, Steven wrote this simulated letter to Gilly:

Hey Gilly,

That was the best note you have ever written. That was cool because you actually made Miss Harris curse. I bet you none of the kids at this school could ever make a teacher do that. I wish I could write cards like that and make teachers curse. You are also very brave because you wrote that to a teacher. No kid is crazy enough to do something like that. That is how crazy I think you are.

Your classmate,

Steven

Johanna wrote this response about whether it is ever right to lie and steal after reading Chapter 7:

I think she shouldn't be forgiven. I know she has

Reading Log Assignments for *The Great Gilly Hopkins*

Chapter 1 "Welcome to Thompson Park"
What is a foster child? How do foster children feel and behave? Why?

Chapter 2 "The Man Who Comes to Supper"
Write a diary entry from Gilly's viewpoint.

Chapter 3 "More Unpleasant Surprises"
Write a double entry with a quote from the chapter and your response.

Chapter 4 "Sarsaparilla to Sorcery"
Write a diary entry from Gilly's viewpoint.

Chapter 5 "William Ernest and Other Mean Flowers"
Do a character study on Maime Trotter. Identify and list three characteristics. Then locate and copy two quotes as evidence for each characteristic.

Chapter 6 "Harassing Miss Harris"
Write a letter to Gilly telling her what you think of what she did to Miss Harris.

Chapter 7 "Dust and Desperation"
Gilly does two things that are considered immoral: she lies and she steals. She has had a rough life, so maybe doing these things is excusable. Perhaps, however, lying and stealing are wrong under any circumstances. Take a position and support it with evidence from the book.

Chapter 8 "The One Way Ticket"
Draw a scene from the chapter and write a brief description of the scene.

Chapter 9 "Pow"
There is a definite change in Gilly's behavior and feelings in this chapter. Describe how she changes and then describe the causes of these changes using examples from the book.

Chapter 10 "The Visitor"
Draw a picture of Gilly and her family at Thanksgiving dinner. Then, in a paragraph, describe Gilly's foster family and how they make each other feel needed. Or, draw Nonnie, Gilly's grandmother. Then, in a paragraph, tell what she looks like, what kind of person she seems to be, how she behaves, and how she gets along with her daughter, Courtney.

Chapter 11 "Never and Other Canceled Promises"
So where should Gilly go? List three reasons why she should stay with Trotter and list three reasons why she should go with her grandmother Nonnie. Then write a short paragraph telling where you would like her to go and why.

Chapters 12 and 13 "The Going" and "Jackson, Virginia"
Select eight to ten images, details, interesting phrases, or parts of sentences from the book and arrange the "found" parts into a poem.

Chapters 14 and 15 "She'll Be Riding Six White Horses" and "Homecoming"
In this final response, write about your feelings. What did you like? dislike? Why?

---

had a horrible life, but it's never right. It is one thing to steal and it's another to steal from a blind man. That is just mean. I kind of feel bad for her because of everything she's been through. She lies, cheats, and steals. I am not sure which side to take because in one way she should be forgiven but on another side she shouldn't be because she's done too many bad things. Especially stealing from Mr. Randolph.

Sarah wrote about how Gilly has changed after reading Chapter 9:

> *Gilly changes because she sees that Trotter really cares for her. Trotter got in an argument about what Gilly did. Miss Ellis wanted to take Gilly back but Trotter wouldn't let her. Gilly becomes more liking toward Trotter. Gilly even starts liking W. E. Gilly doesn't think he is dumb any more. Another example is "Look, W. E.," she bent over close to his ear and whispered hoarsely into it, "I'm going to teach you how to fight. No charge or anything. Then when some big punk comes up to you and tries to start something, you can just let them have it," said Gilly.*

After reading Chapters 12 and 13, Timothy wrote this found poem:

> *He tore a piece of him and gave it to you.*
> *Don't make it harder for us, baby.*
> *This was supposed to be a party, not a funeral.*
> *Sometimes it's best not to go visiting.*
> *You make me proud.*
> *Why would anybody leave peace for war?*
> *Stop hovering over me.*
> *Inside her head, she was screaming.*

Steven reflects on the book in his last entry:

> *I thought that at the end Gilly was going to go with her mom. I also thought Gilly's mom was going to be nice and sweet. I thought this was very good because it had an unexpected ending. I didn't think that Gilly's mom would be so rude and mean. Now I wish that Gilly would go back with Trotter because Courtney is mean. Those are my reasons why she should be with Trotter.*

Ms. Meinke is especially interested in the students' responses in this last entry. She finds that many students, like Steven, want Gilly to stay with Trotter, but she is pleased when they realize that Nonnie, who never even knew of Gilly's existence, is family and is delighted to provide a home for her only granddaughter.

Ms. Meinke collects the students' reading logs twice—once halfway through the literature circle and again at the end—to grade them. She has found that students appreciate the opportunity to pace themselves as they read and write the entries. She awards points for each journal entry, and these points are part of students' grades for the literature circle.

---

*A*ll kinds of people—artists, scientists, dancers, politicians, writers, and assassins—do personal writing. They write letters and keep journals. People record the everyday events of their lives and the issues that concern them. The personal writing of some public figures has survived for hundreds of years and provides a fascinating glimpse of their authors and the times in which they lived. For example, the Renaissance genius Leonardo da Vinci recorded his daily activities, dreams, and plans for his

Journal writing gives students valuable writing practice. Kindergartners use a combination of drawing and writing in their journal entries (McGee & Richgels, 2007). They write scribbles, random letters and numbers, simple captions, or extended texts using invented spelling. Their invented spellings often seem bizarre by adult standards, but they are reasonable in terms of children's knowledge of phoneme-grapheme correspondences and spelling patterns. In first and second grades, children gain fluency and confidence that they can write through journal writing. Older children experiment with writing conventions that must be considered in more public writing. If they decide to make an entry "public," they can later revise and edit their writing.

Personal Journals

Personal journals are usually the first type of journal writing that young children do. Kindergartners begin writing in journals early in the school year, and their writing becomes more conventional as they learn concepts about print, letters of the alphabet, and phonics skills. Hannon (1999) recommends beginning with personal or dialogue journals. Two kindergartners' journal entries are presented in Figure 6–1. In the left entry, a 5-year-old draws a detailed picture of a football game (note that the player in the middle-right position has the ball) and adds five letters for the text so that his entry will have some writing. In the entry on the right, another child writes, "I spent the night at my dad's house."

FIGURE 6–1

Two Kindergartners' Journal Entries

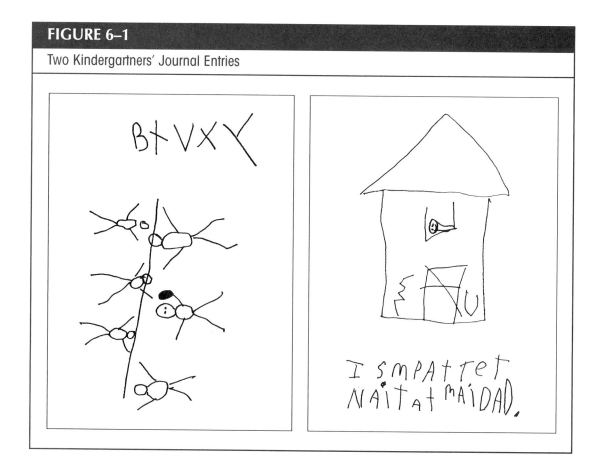

FIGURE 6–2

Fourth and Fifth Graders' List of Writing Topics

Things to Write About in Personal Journals

my favorite place in town	if I had three wishes
boyfriends/girlfriends	my teacher
things that make me happy or sad	TV shows I watch
music	my favorite holiday
an imaginary planet	if I were stranded on an island
cars	what I want to be when I grow up
magazines I like to read	private thoughts
what if snow were hot	how to be a superhero
cartoons	dinosaurs
places I've been	my mom/my dad
favorite movies	my friends
if I were a movie/rock star	my next vacation
poems	if I were an animal or something else
pets	books I've read
football	favorite things to do
astronauts	my hobbies
the president	if I were a skydiver
jokes	when I get a car
motorcycles	if I had a lot of money
things that happen in my school	if I were rich
current events	wrestling and other sports
things I do on weekends	favorite colors

or ANYTHING else I want to write about

Students often keep personal journals in which they recount events in their lives and write about topics of their choosing. They choose to write about a variety of topics and explore their feelings in these entries. It's normal for students to misspell a few words in their entries; when they write in personal journals, the emphasis is on what they say, not how correctly they write. It's helpful to develop a list of possible journal-writing topics on a chart in the classroom or make copies for students to clip inside their journal notebooks. Students choose their own topics for personal journals. Although they can write about almost anything, some students will complain that they don't know what to write about, so a list of topics gives them a crutch. Figure 6–2 shows a list of possible journal-writing topics developed by a class of fourth and fifth graders. They continue to add topics to their list so that it may include more than 100 topics by the end of the school year. Referring students to the list or asking them to brainstorm a list of topics encourages them to become more independent writers.

Privacy becomes an important issue as students grow older. Most young children are willing to share what they have written, but by third or fourth grade, they grow less willing to read their journal entries aloud to the class, although they are usually willing to share the entries with a trusted teacher. Teachers must be scrupulous about respecting students' privacy and not insist that they share their writing when they are unwilling to do so. It is important to talk with students about respecting classmates' privacy and not reading each other's journals. Also, many teachers keep personal journals on an out-of-the-way shelf when they are not in use.

When students share personal information with teachers through their journals, a second issue arises: Sometimes teachers learn details about students' problems and family life that they don't know how to deal with. Entries about child abuse, suicide, or drug use may be a student's way of asking for help. Although teachers are not counselors, they have a legal obligation to protect their students and to report possible problems to appropriate school personnel. Occasionally a student invents a personal problem as an attention-getting tactic; however, asking about the journal entry or having a school counselor do so will help to ensure that the student's safety is fully considered.

Dialogue Journals

Students converse in writing with the teacher or with a classmate through dialogue journals. These journals are interactive and conversational in tone. Most important, dialogue journals are an authentic writing activity and provide the opportunity for real communication between students or between a student and the teacher. Students write informally about something of interest, a concern, a book they are reading, or what they are learning in a thematic unit. They choose their own topics and usually control the direction the writing takes.

When teachers or classmates respond to students' entries, they answer as they would in an oral conversation. They react to their comments, ask questions, and offer suggestions. Teachers acknowledge students' ideas and encourage them to continue to write about their interests. They also provide new information about topics, so that students will want to read their responses. Teachers try to avoid unspecific comments, such as "good idea" or "very interesting." Their responses don't need to be lengthy; a sentence or two is often enough. Even so, it's time-consuming to respond to 25, 30, or more journal entries every day. To solve this problem, many teachers read and respond to students' journal entries on a rotating basis; they might respond to one group one week and another group the next week.

In this fifth grader's dialogue journal, Daniel shares the events and problems in his life with his teacher, and she responds sympathetically. Daniel writes:

> *Over spring break I went down to my grandma's house and played basketball in their backyard and while we were there we went to see some of my uncles who are all Indians. Out of my whole family down there they are all Indians except Grandpa Russell.*

And Daniel's teacher responds:

> *What a fun spring break! That is so interesting to have Indians in your family. I think I might have some Indian ancestors too. Do you still plan to go to Padre Island for the summer?*

The next day Daniel writes:

> *My family and I plan to go to Padre Island in June and I imagine we will stay there for quite a while. I think the funnest part will probably be swimming or camping or something like that. When we get there my mom says we will probably stay in a nice motel.*

Daniel's teacher responds:

> *That really sounds like a fun vacation. I think swimming is the most fun, too. Who will go with you?*

Daniel continues to talk about his family, now focusing on the problems he and his family are facing:

> Well, my mom and dad are divorced so that is why I am going to court to testify on Tuesday but my mom, me, and my sister and brother are all going and that kind of makes me sad because a couple of years ago when my mom and dad were together we used to go a lot of places like camping and hiking but now after what happened we hardly go anywhere.

His teacher responds:

> I am so sorry your family is having problems. It sounds as if your mom and dad are having problems with each other, but they both love you and want to be with you. Be sure to keep talking to them about how you feel.

Daniel replies:

> I wish my mom and dad did not have problems because I would have a lot more fun and get to go and do a lot more things together, but since my mom and dad are divorced I have to take turns spending time with both of them.

This journal is not a series of teacher questions and student answers; instead, the student and teacher are having a conversation, and the interchange is built on mutual trust and respect.

Dialogue journals are especially effective in promoting the writing development of children who are English learners. Researchers have found that these students are more successful writers when they choose their own topics for writing and when their teachers contribute to the dialogue with requests for a reply, statements, and other comments (Reyes, 1991). Not surprisingly, researchers found that students wrote more when teachers requested a reply than when teachers made comments that did not require a response. Also, when a student was particularly interested in a topic, it was less important what the teacher did, and when the teacher and the student were both interested in a topic, the topic seemed to take over as they shared and built on each other's writing. Reyes also found that English learners were much more successful in writing dialogue journal entries than in writing in response to books they had read.

Students use dialogue journals to write to classmates or the teacher about books they are reading (Nash, 1995). In these journal entries, students write about the books they are reading, compare the books to others by the same author or books by other authors they have read, and offer opinions about the book and whether a classmate or the teacher might enjoy reading it. They also write about their book-selection strategies and their reading behavior. This approach is especially effective in reading workshop classrooms when students are reading different books. They're often paired and write back and forth to their reading buddies. This activity provides the socialization that independent reading does not. Depending on whether students are reading relatively short picture books or longer chapter books, they can write dialogue journal entries every other day or once a week, and then classmates write back.

Reading Logs

Students write in reading logs about the stories and other books they are reading or listening to the teacher read aloud during literature focus units, literature circles, and reading workshop. Rather than simply summarize their reading, students delve into important ideas and relate their reading to their own lives or to other literature they

FIGURE 6–5

Excerpts From a Fifth Grader's Double-Entry Journal About *The Lion, the Witch and the Wardrobe*

In the Text	My Response
Chapter 1 I tell you this is the sort of house where no one is going to mind what we do.	I remember the time that I went to Beaumont, Texas to stay with my aunt. My aunt's house was very large. She had a piano and she let us play it. She told us that we could do whatever we wanted to.
Chapter 5 "How do you know?" he asked, "that your sister's story is not true?"	It reminds me of when I was little and I had an imaginary place. I would go there in my mind. I made up all kinds of make-believe stories about myself in this imaginary place. One time I told my big brother about my imaginary place. He laughed at me and told me I was silly. But it didn't bother me because nobody can stop me from thinking what I want.
Chapter 15 Still they could see the shape of the great lion lying dead in his bonds. They're nibbling at the cords.	When Aslan died I thought about when my Uncle Carl died. This reminds me of the story where the lion lets the mouse go and the mouse helps the lion.

By recording this information in a notebook, students create a permanent reference book to use during language arts activities. Older students often divide their language arts notebooks into several sections, and they add information to sections on authors, words, spelling, parts of speech, sentences, strategies, poetry, stories, and study skills.

Learning Logs

Students write entries in learning logs to record and think about what they are learning in math, science, social studies, or other content areas. As they write in these journals, students reflect on their learning, discover gaps in their knowledge, and explore relationships between what they are learning and their past experiences. For example, in math class, they record explanations and examples of concepts presented in class and react to the mathematical concepts they are learning and any problems they may be having. Figure 6–6 presents an entry from a sixth grader's learning log in which she describes how to change improper fractions. Notice that after she describes the steps in sequence, she includes a review of the six steps. In addition, some upper-grade teachers allow students the last 5 minutes of math class to summarize the day's lesson and react to it in their learning logs.

Students can make daily entries in science logs to track the growth of plants or animals. For instance, a second-grade class observed caterpillars as they changed from caterpillars to chrysalides to butterflies over a period of 4 to 6 weeks. They each kept a log with daily entries, in which they noted the changes they observed using words describing shape, color, size, and other properties. Two pages from a second grader's log documenting the caterpillars' growth and change are presented in Figure 6–7.

FIGURE 6–6

A Sixth Grader's Math Learning Log Entry

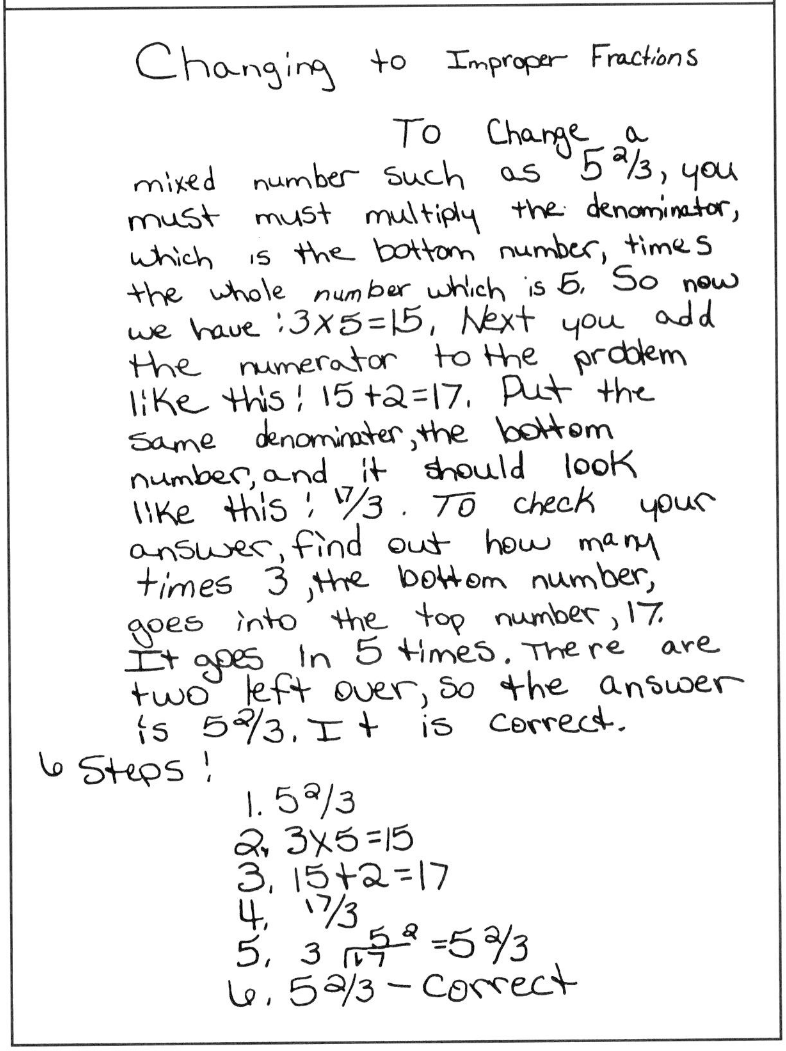

Changing to Improper Fractions

To Change a mixed number such as $5\frac{2}{3}$, you must must multiply the denominator, which is the bottom number, times the whole number which is 5. So now we have : 3×5=15. Next you add the numerator to the problem like this : 15+2=17. Put the same denominater, the bottom number, and it should look like this : $\frac{17}{3}$. To check your answer, find out how many times 3, the bottom number, goes into the top number, 17. It goes in 5 times. There are two left over, so the answer is $5\frac{2}{3}$. It is correct.

6 Steps !

1. $5\frac{2}{3}$
2. 3×5=15
3. 15+2=17
4. $\frac{17}{3}$
5. $3\overline{)17}^{\,5\,2}=5\frac{2}{3}$
6. $5\frac{2}{3}$ – correct

Simulated Journals

Some children's books, such as *Catherine, Called Birdy* (Cushman, 1994), the story of a disenchanted English noble woman of the 13th century, are written as journals; authors research the time period, assume the role of a character, and write from the character's point of view. These books might be considered simulated journals. They are rich with historical details and incorporate both the words and phrasing of the period. At the end of these books, authors often include information about how they researched the period and explanations about the liberties they took with the character, setting, or events that are recorded. Scholastic Books publishes historical journals appropriate for fourth through eighth graders. The books include *I Walk in Dread: The Diary of Deliverance Trembley, Witness to the Salem Witch Trials* (Fraustino, 2004), which recounts events during the Salem witch hunts of 1692; *The Journal of Jesse Smoke: A Cherokee*

Anthony Magnacca/Merrill

old one's place something bad would happen. But I'm happy because I am the maker of the first American flag and I'm only 25 years old!

Students can use simulated journals in two ways: as a tool for learning or as a project. When students use simulated journals as a tool for learning, they write the entries as they are reading a book in order to get to know the character better or during a thematic unit as they are learning about the historical period. In these entries, students are exploring concepts and making connections between what they are learning and what they already know. These journal entries are less polished than when students write a simulated journal as a project. Students might choose to write a simulated journal as a culminating project for a literature focus unit or a thematic unit. For a project, students plan out their journals carefully, choose important dates, and use the writing process to draft, revise, edit, and publish their journals.

Teaching Students to Write in Journals

Journals are typically written in notebooks or booklets. Spiral-bound notebooks are useful for long-term personal and dialogue journals and for language arts notebooks, whereas small booklets of paper stapled together are more often used for reading logs, learning logs, and simulated journals that are used for one literature focus unit, literature circle, or thematic unit. Most teachers prefer to keep the journals in the classroom so that they will be available for students to write in each day, but students could write at home, too.

Students usually write at a particular time each day. Many teachers have students make personal or dialogue journal entries while they take attendance or immediately after recess. Language arts notebooks are often used during minilessons to record information about topics being studied. Teachers may assign the same types of journals throughout the school year, or they may alternate them, starting and stopping with particular literature focus units and thematic units.

How Journals Fit Into the Four Patterns of Practice

Literature Focus Units

Students usually write in reading logs, but sometimes they keep simulated journals where they write from one character's viewpoint as they read each chapter. They also write in language arts notebooks about information presented during minilessons.

Literature Circles

Students create reading logs for each book they read and discuss in a literature circle. They write notes while they're reading and take notes as classmates share information during the small-group discussions.

Reading and Writing Workshop

During reading workshop, students keep reading logs where they list books they've read and write responses, and during writing workshop, they can write lists of writing topics and first drafts in personal journals.

Thematic Units

Students write in learning logs. They can also keep double-entry journals where they write information in one column and their responses in the other, or they write simulated journals from the viewpoint of a historical personality or scientist.

Booklist

BOOKS IN WHICH CHARACTERS AND HISTORICAL PERSONALITIES KEEP JOURNALS

Cronin, D. (2005). *Diary of a spider*. New York: HarperCollins. (P)

Cruise, R. (1998). *The top-secret journal of Fiona Claire Jardin*. San Diego: Harcourt Brace. (M)

Cunningham, L. S. (2005). *The midnight diary of Zoya Blume*. New York: HarperCollins. (M–U).

Danticat, E. (2005). *Anacaona: Golden flower*. New York: Scholastic. (M–U)

Garland, S. (1998). *A line in the sand: The Alamo diary of Lucinda Lawrence*. New York: Scholastic. (M–U)

George, J. C. (2001). *My side of the mountain*. New York: Puffin Books. (M–U)

Hesse, K. (2000). *Stowaway*. New York: McElderry. (M–U)

Hite, S. (2003). *Journal of Rufus Rowe, witness to the battle of Fredericksburg*. New York: Scholastic. (M–U)

Lewis, C. C. (1998). *Dilly's big sister diary*. New York: Millbrook Press. (P)

Ma, Y. (2005). *The diary of Ma Yan: The struggles and hopes of a Chinese schoolgirl*. New York: HarperCollins. (M–U)

McKissack, P. C. (2000). *Nzingha: Warrior queen of Matamba*. New York: Scholastic. (M–U)

Morpurgo, M. (2006). *The amazing story of Adolphus Tips*. New York: Scholastic. (M–U)

Moss, M. (2002). *Galen: My life in imperial Rome*. San Diego: Harcourt Brace. (M–U)

Myers, W. D. (1999). *The journal of Scott Pendleton Collins: A World War II soldier*. New York: Scholastic. (M–U)

Parker, S. (1999). *It's a frog's life*. Pleasantville, NY: Reader's Digest. (P)

Perez, A. I. (2002). *My diary from here to there/Mi diario de aquí hasta allá*. San Francisco: Children's Book Press. (P)

Philbrick, R. (2001). *The journal of Douglas Allen Deeds: The Donner party expedition*. New York: Scholastic. (M–U)

Platt, R. (2005). *Egyptian diary: The journal of Nakht*. New York: Candlewick Press. (M)

Veciana-Suarez, A. (2002). *Flight to freedom*. New York: Scholastic. (U)

Watts, L. (2002). *Stonecutter*. San Diego: Harcourt Brace. (U)

P = primary grades (K–2); M = middle grades (3–5); U = upper grades (6–8)

Teachers introduce students to journal writing using minilessons in which they explain the purpose of the journal-writing activity and the procedures for gathering ideas, writing the entry, and sharing it with classmates. Teachers often model the procedure by writing a sample entry on chart paper as students observe. This sample demonstrates that the writing is to be informal, with ideas emphasized over correctness. Then students make their own first entries, and several read their entries aloud. Through this sharing, students who are still unclear about the activity have additional models on which to base their own writing. Similar minilessons are used to introduce each type of journal. Even though most types of journals are similar, the purpose of the journal, the information included in the entries, and the writer's viewpoint vary according to type.

Students write in journals on a regular schedule, usually daily. After they know how to write the appropriate type of entry, they can write independently, and some students usually read their journal entries aloud afterward. If the sharing becomes too time-consuming, they can share in small groups or with partners. Then, after everyone has had a chance to share, several students can be selected to share with the entire class.

The Reading-Writing Connection. Journal writing can also be introduced with examples from literature. Characters in children's literature, such as Amelia in *Amelia's Notebook* (Moss, 2006) and Birdy in *Catherine, Called Birdy* (Cushman, 1994), keep journals in which they record events in their lives and their thoughts and dreams. A list of books in which characters and historical personalities keep journals is presented in the Booklist on page 195. In these books, the characters demonstrate the process of journal writing and illustrate both the pleasures and the difficulties of keeping a journal.

Minilessons. Teachers teach minilessons on procedures, concepts, strategies, and skills about writing in journals. A list of minilesson topics is presented in the box on pages 204. It is especially important to teach a minilesson when students are learning a new type of journal or when they are having difficulty with a particular procedure or strategy, such as changing point of view for simulated journals or writing in two columns in double-entry journals.

Assessing Students' Journal Entries

Students can write in journals independently with little or no sharing with the teacher, or they can make daily entries that the teacher monitors or reads regularly. Typically, students are accustomed to having teachers read all or most of their writing, but the quantity of writing students produce in journals is often too great for teachers to keep up with. Some teachers rarely check students' journals; others read selected entries and monitor the remaining ones; still others try to read all entries. These three management approaches can be termed *private journals, monitored journals*, and *shared journals*. When students write private journals, they write primarily for themselves, and sharing with classmates or the teacher is voluntary; the teacher does not read the journals unless invited to. When students write monitored journals, they write primarily for themselves, but the teacher monitors the writing to ensure that entries are being made regularly. The teacher simply checks that entries have been made and does not read the entries unless they are marked "Read me." Students write shared journals primarily for the teacher; the teacher regularly reads all entries, except those marked "private," and offers encouragement and suggestions.

Many teachers have concerns about how to grade journal entries. Because the writing is usually not revised and edited, teachers should not grade the quality of the entries. One option is to give points for each entry made, especially in personal journals. However, some teachers grade the content in learning logs and simulated journals because they can check to see whether the entries include particular pieces of information. For example, if students are writing simulated journals about the Crusades, they may be asked to include five pieces of historically accurate information in their entries. (It is helpful to ask students to identify the five pieces of information by underlining and numbering them.) Rough-draft journal entries should not be graded for mechanical correctness. Students need to complete the writing process and revise and edit their entries if they are to be graded for mechanical correctness.

LETTER WRITING

Letters are a way of talking to people who live too far away to visit. Audience and purpose are important considerations, but form is also important in letter writing. Although letters may be personal, they involve a genuine audience of one or more persons. Through letter writing, students have the opportunity not only to sharpen their writing skills, but also to increase their awareness of audience. Because letters are written to communicate with a specific and important audience, students

Meeting the Needs of English Learners

How Can Teachers Use Journals With English Learners?

Writing can be difficult for English learners, and journals are the best way to introduce writing. It's essential that English learners have daily opportunities to practice writing because they need to develop writing fluency, the ability to get words down on paper. Through sustained writing, their handwriting skills improve, and their ability to spell high-frequency English words increases. In addition, there's less pressure because when students write in journals, the emphasis is on ideas rather than on correctness and neatness.

Students usually write about events in their own lives before writing about books they're reading and the content they're learning in thematic units. Peregoy and Boyle (2005) recommend that English learners write in buddy journals, which are a lot like dialogue journals: Students write back and forth to other English learners, and in these entries that are like written conversations, they write about topics that interest them, sharing ideas and asking questions. And as they're developing writing fluency, students are also learning that the purpose of writing is communicating ideas.

Many English learners write brief entries, often using and reusing familiar words and sentence patterns, and their entries are typically sprinkled with grammatical errors and misspelled words. Too often, teachers conclude that their English learners just can't write, but they can help these students write better journal entries. The first step involves examining students' entries to determine whether the problems center on undeveloped ideas, limited vocabulary, nonstandard grammar, or spelling errors. Often teachers notice problems in all four areas, but they prioritize the problem areas and then work to resolve them.

Ideas and Vocabulary

Ideas and vocabulary usually go hand in hand. Teachers model how to brainstorm ideas and related words before beginning to write, and they also demonstrate how to write entries with interesting, well-developed ideas. Teachers can also help individual students talk out their ideas and brainstorm a bank of words before they begin writing.

Grammar

To focus on correcting nonstandard grammar errors, teachers teach minilessons on particular grammar concepts and then have students locate examples of the concept in their journal entries and make any needed corrections.

Spelling

Even though students usually misspell some words in their journals entries, they should be expected to spell most high-frequency words correctly. Teachers explain how useful high-frequency words are to writers, and they demonstrate how to locate high-frequency words on the classroom word wall or on individual word walls that students keep in their journals. English learners can also return to a previously written journal entry and check for misspelled words using the word wall as a resource.

take more care to think through what they want to say, to write legibly, and to use spelling, capitalization, and punctuation conventions correctly.

Children's letters are typically classified as friendly or business letters. Formats for friendly and business letters are shown in the LA Essentials box on page 199. The choice of format depends on the purpose of the letter. Friendly letters might be informal, chatty letters to pen pals or thank-you notes to a television newscaster who has visited the classroom. When students write to the National Park Service requesting information about the Grand Canyon or another park or send letters to the president expressing an opinion about current events, they use the more formal, business-letter style. Before students write both types of letters, they need to learn how to format them.

Friendly Letters

After teachers have introduced the format for friendly letters, students need to choose a "real" someone to write to. Writing authentic letters that will be delivered is much more valuable than writing practice letters to be graded by the teacher. Students write friendly letters to classmates, friends who live out of town, relatives, and pen pals. They may want to keep a list of addresses of people to write friendly letters to on a special page in their journals or in address booklets. In these casual letters, they share news about events in their lives and ask questions to learn more about the person they are writing to and to encourage that person to write back. Receiving mail is the real reward of letter writing!

Robinson, Crawford, and Hall (1991) examined the effects of personal letter writing on young children's writing development. In the study, a group of 20 kindergartners wrote back and forth to the researchers over a 2-year period. In their early letters, the children told about themselves, promised to be friends with their correspondent, and asked the correspondent questions. Over the 2-year period, they matured as letter writers and continued to be eager correspondents. Their letters became more sophisticated, and they developed letter-writing strategies that took their readers into account. The researchers concluded that authentic, purposeful, and sustained letter-writing experiences are extremely valuable for children.

Pen Pal Letters. Teachers can arrange for their students to exchange letters with students in another class by contacting a teacher in a nearby school or local educational associations, or by answering advertisements online or in educational magazines. Another possible arrangement is to have your class become pen pals with college students in a language arts methods class. Over a semester, the children and the preservice teachers can write back and forth four, five, or six times, and perhaps even meet at the end of the semester. The children have the opportunity to be pen pals with college students, and the preservice teachers have the opportunity to get to know a student and examine his or her writing development.

Courtesy Letters. Invitations and thank-you notes are two other types of friendly letters that students write. They may write to parents to invite them to an after-school program, to the class across the hall to invite them to visit a classroom exhibit, or to a person in the community to invite him or her to be interviewed as part of a thematic unit. Students also write letters to thank people who have been helpful.

FORMS FOR FRIENDLY AND BUSINESS LETTERS

Friendly Letter

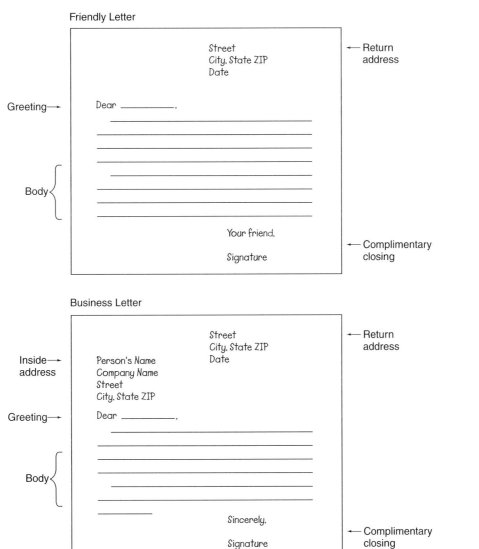

Street
City, State ZIP
Date
⟵ Return address

Greeting⟶ Dear _____,

Body

Your friend,

Signature
⟵ Complimentary closing

Business Letter

Street
City, State ZIP
Date
⟵ Return address

Inside⟶ address
Person's Name
Company Name
Street
City, State ZIP

Greeting⟶ Dear _____,

Body

Sincerely,

Signature
⟵ Complimentary closing

E-mail Messages. The Internet has created a completely new way for students to send messages electronically to correspondents anywhere in the world. It's a fast and simple way to send and reply to mail, and messages can be saved and stored on the computer, too. Students can use e-mail message forms. They type the correspondent's e-mail address in the top window, specify a topic in the subject window, and then write their message in the large window. They begin by greeting their correspondent, and then they write their message. Students should keep their messages short—no longer than one or two screens—so that they can easily be read on the computer screen. They end their messages with a closing, much as in other types of letters. McKeon (1999) studied the e-mail messages that a class of third graders wrote about the books they were reading and concluded that e-mail is a constructive way to enhance students' learning as well as an effective strategy for teachers to personalize their interaction with students.

Letters to Authors and Illustrators. Students write letters to favorite authors and illustrators to share their ideas and feelings about the books they have read. They ask questions about how a particular character was developed or why the illustrator used a certain art medium. Students also describe the books they have written. Here's a letter that a fourth grader wrote to Eve Bunting at the end of an author study, after the class had read and responded to eight of her books.

> *Dear Eve Bunting,*
>
> *I have read some of your books. All of them had friendship in them. My favorite book is Smoky Night. I think the theme is get along and respect each other. My family needs to learn to respect each other and to get along because I fight with my brother and he fights with my sister.*
>
> *How many picture books have you written? I have read eight of them. Have you ever met Chris Van Allsburg because we did an author study on him also. Why do you write your books?*
>
> *Sincerely,*
>
> *Jeffrey*

Most authors and illustrators reply to children's letters when possible, and Eve Bunting answered this fourth grader's letters. However, they receive thousands of letters from children every year and cannot be pen pals with students. Beverly Cleary's award-winning book *Dear Mr. Henshaw* (1983) offers a worthwhile lesson about what students (and their teachers) can realistically expect from authors and illustrators. Here are some guidelines for writing to authors and illustrators:

- Follow the correct letter format with return address, greeting, body, closing, and signature.
- Use the process approach to write, revise, and edit the letter.
- Recopy the letter so that it will be neat and easy to read.
- Write the return address on both envelope and letter.
- Include a stamped, self-addressed envelope for a reply.
- Be polite in the letter.

Students should write genuine letters to share their thoughts and feelings about the author's writing or the illustrator's artwork, and they should write only to authors and illustrators whose work they are familiar with. In their letters, students should avoid asking personal questions, such as how much money the author or illustrator earns. They should not ask for free books, because authors and illustrators usually don't have copies of their books to give away. Students send their letters to the author or illustrator in care of the publisher (the publisher's name appears on the book's title page, and the address usually appears on the copyright page, the page following the title page). If students cannot find the complete mailing address, they can check online.

Business Letters

Students write business letters to seek information, to complain and compliment, and to transact business. They use this more formal letter style and format (as shown in the LA Essentials box on page 199) to communicate with businesses, local newspapers, and government agencies. Students may write to businesses to order products, to ask questions, and to complain about or compliment specific products; they write letters to the editors of local newspapers and magazines to comment on articles and to express their opinions. It is important that students support their comments and opinions with facts if they hope to have their letters published. Students can also write to local, state, and national government officials to express concerns, make suggestions, or seek information.

Simulated Letters

Students can write simulated letters, in which they assume the identity of a historical or literary figure (Roop, 1995). Simulated letters are similar to simulated journals except that they are formatted as letters. Students can write letters as though they were Davy Crockett or another of the men defending the Alamo, or Thomas Edison, describing his invention of the lightbulb. They can write from one book character to another; for example, after reading *Sarah, Plain and Tall* (MacLachlan, 2004), students can assume the persona of Sarah and write a letter to her brother William, as a third grader did in this letter:

> *Dear William,*
>
> *I'm having fun here. There was a very big storm here. It was so big it looked like the sea. Sometimes I am very lonesome for home but sometimes it is very fun here in Ohio. We swam in the cow pond and I taught Caleb how to swim. They were afraid I would leave. Maggie and Matthew brought some chickens.*
>
> *Love,*
>
> *Sarah*

Even though these letters are never mailed, they are written to a specific audience. Classmates can assume the role of the person to whom the letter is addressed and respond to the letter from that point of view. Also, these letters show clearly how well students comprehend the story, and teachers can use them to monitor students' learning.

Teaching Students to Write Letters

Students use the process approach to write letters so that they can make their letters interesting, complete, and readable. The steps are shown in the Step by Step feature below.

The Reading-Writing Connection. A variety of books that include letters have been published for children. Some of these are stories with letters that children can take out of envelopes and read. *With Love, Little Red Hen* (Ada, 2001) is a collection of letters that tells a story, and Ann Turner's *Nettie's Trip South* (1987) is a book-length letter about the inhumanity of slavery in the antebellum South. Other books are epistolary novels in which the story is told through a collection of letters, such as *Dear Whiskers* (Nagda, 2000), the story of a fourth grader who befriends her second-grade pen pal, a Saudi Arabian girl who has recently come to the United States. The Booklist on the next page lists books that teachers can share as part of letter-writing activities.

Minilessons. Teachers present minilessons about letters, including how they are formatted and how to craft letters to encourage correspondents to respond. A list of minilesson topics and a sample minilesson on writing letters to favorite authors are presented in the box on pages 204 and 205. These lessons are sometimes presented as part of language arts, but at other times teachers teach minilessons on letter writing as part of social studies or science lessons because students often write letters as part of thematic units. For example, students write business letters to request information during a science unit on ecology or write simulated letters as part of a history-based thematic unit.

-------- Writing Letters ------------------------------

1 **Gather and organize information for the letter.** Students participate in prewriting activities, such as brainstorming or clustering, to decide what information to include in their letters. If they are writing friendly letters, particularly to pen pals, they also identify several questions to ask.

2 **Review the friendly- or business-letter form.** Before writing the rough drafts of their letters, students review the friendly- or business-letter form.

3 **Draft the letter.** Students write a rough draft, incorporating the information developed during prewriting and following either the friendly- or the business-letter style.

4 **Revise and edit the letter.** Students meet in a writing group to share their rough drafts and get feedback to use in revising their letters. They also edit their letters with a partner, proofreading to identify errors and correcting as many as possible.

5 **Make the final copy of the letter.** Students recopy their letters and address envelopes. Teachers often review how to address an envelope during this step, too.

6 **Mail the letter.** The crucial last step is to mail the letters and wait for a reply.

Booklist

BOOKS THAT INCLUDE LETTERS

Ada, A. F. (1998). *Yours truly, Goldilocks.* New York: Atheneum. (P)

Ada, A. F. (2001). *With love, Little Red Hen.* New York: Atheneum. (P)

Avi. (2003). *Nothing but the truth.* New York: Orchard Books. (U)

Ayres, K. (1998). *North by night: A story of the Underground Railroad.* New York: Delacorte. (M–U)

Bonners, S. (2000). *Edwina victorious.* New York: Farrar, Straus & Giroux. (M)

Cherry, L. (1994). *The armadillo from Amarillo.* New York: Gulliver Green. (M)

Danziger, P., & Martin, A. M. (1998). *P. S. Longer letter later.* New York: Scholastic. (M)

Danziger, P., & Martin, A. M. (2000). *Snail mail no more.* New York: Scholastic. (M)

Klise, K. (1999). *Letters from camp.* New York: Avon. (U)

Klise, K. (2006). *Regarding the bathrooms: A privy to the past.* San Diego: Harcourt. (U)

Lyons, M. E. (1992). *Letters from a slave girl: The story of Harriet Jacobs.* New York: Scribner. (U)

Nagda, A. W. (2000). *Dear Whiskers.* New York: Holiday House. (M)

Nolen, J. (2002). *Plantzilla.* San Diego: Harcourt Brace. (P–M)

Olson, M. W. (2000). *Nice try, tooth fairy.* New York: Simon & Schuster. (P)

Pak, S. (1999). *Dear Juno.* New York: Viking. (P)

Pinkney, A. D. (1994). *Dear Benjamin Banneker.* San Diego: Gulliver/Harcourt Brace. (M)

Stewart, S. (1997). *The gardener.* New York: Farrar, Straus & Giroux. (P)

Teague, M. (2002). *Dear Mrs. LaRue: Letters from obedience school.* New York: Scholastic. (P)

Teague, M. (2004). *Detective LaRue: Letters from the investigation.* New York: Scholastic. (P)

Woodruff, E. (1994). *Dear Levi: Letters from the Overland Trail.* New York: Knopf. (M–U)

Assessing Students' Letters

Traditionally, students wrote letters and turned them in for the teacher to grade. The letters were returned to the students after they were graded, but they were never mailed. Teachers now recognize the importance of having an audience for student writing, and research suggests that students write better when they know that their writing will be read by someone other than the teacher. Although it's often necessary to assess student writing, it would be inappropriate for the teacher to put a grade on the letter if it's going to be mailed to someone. Teachers can instead develop a checklist or rubric for evaluating students' letters without marking on them.

A third-grade teacher developed the checklist in the Weaving Assessment Into Practice feature on page 206; the checklist identifies specific behaviors and measurable products. The teacher shares the checklist with students before they begin to write so that they know what is expected of them and how they will be graded. At an evaluation conference before the letters are mailed, the teacher reviews the checklist with each student. The letters are mailed without evaluative comments or grades written on them, but the completed checklist goes into students' writing folders. A grading scale can be developed from the checklist; for example, points can be awarded for each checkmark in the Yes column so that five checkmarks can equal a grade of A, four checkmarks a B, and so on.

What Students Need to Learn About Personal Writing

Topics

Procedures	Concepts	Strategies and Skills
Journals		
Write a journal entry	Personal journals	Choose a topic
Share entries	Dialogue journals	Generate
Respond in dialogue journals	Language arts notebooks	Organize
Write in language arts notebooks	**Reading logs**	Predict
Write reading log entries	Double-entry journals	Incorporate key vocabulary
Write double-entry journals	Learning logs	Assume another viewpoint
Use learning logs	Simulated journals	
Write simulated journals		
Letters		
Write pen pal letters	Friendly-letter format	Use letter formats correctly
Write courtesy letters	Business-letter format	Ask questions to elicit information
Write e-mail messages		Respond to correspondent's questions
Write letters to authors and illustrators		
Write business letters		
Write simulated letters		

To learn more about personal writing, please visit MyEducationLab. You can watch fourth graders responding in reading logs to the books their teacher is reading aloud by going to the topic "Writing" and clicking on the video "Reading Logs."

Minilesson

Mr. Rinaldi's Eighth Graders Write Simulated Letters

1 Introduce the topic

Mr. Rinaldi's eighth graders are studying the American Civil War, and each student has assumed the persona of someone who lived in that period. Many students have become Union or Confederate soldiers and given themselves names and identities. Today, Mr. Rinaldi asks his students to think about the war as their persona would. He explains that they will write simulated letters to Abraham Lincoln or Jefferson Davis, arguing an issue as their persona might. He explains that a simulated letter is a letter that is written as if the writer were someone else.

2 Share examples

Mr. Rinaldi assumed the persona of a Confederate bugle boy when his students assumed personas, and he reads a letter he has written to Abraham Lincoln as that bugle boy, begging Lincoln to end the war. He gives three reasons why the war should end: the South has the right to choose its own destiny; the South is being destroyed by the war; and too many boys are dying. He ends his emotional letter this way: *I 'spect I'ma gonna die, too, Mr. President. What ya' gonna do when there be no more of us to shoot? No more Johnny Rebs to die. When the South has all died away, will you be a-smilin' then?* The students are stunned by the power of their teacher's simulated letter.

3 Provide information

Mr. Rinaldi explains that he did three things in his simulated letter to make it powerful: He wrote in persona—the way a scared, uneducated boy might write—he included vocabulary words about the war, and he argued his point of view persuasively. Together they brainstorm a list of arguments or persuasive appeals—for better food and clothing for soldiers and to end the war or to continue the war. He passes out a prewriting form that students use to plan their simulated letters.

4 Supervise practice

The students write their letters using the writing process. The planning sheet serves as prewriting, and students draft, revise, and edit their letters as Mr. Rinaldi conferences with students, encouraging them to develop the voice of their personas. Afterward, students share their letters with the class.

5 Reflect on learning

After the lesson, Mr. Rinaldi talks with his students about their simulated letters. He asks them to reflect on what they have learned, and the students emphasize that what they learned was about the inhumanity of war, even though they thought they were learning about letters.

Weaving Assessment Into Practice

A CHECKLIST FOR ASSESSING STUDENTS' PEN PAL LETTERS

Pen Pal Letter Checklist

	Yes	No
Name _____		
1. Did you complete the cluster?	☐	☐
2. Did you include questions in your letter?	☐	☐
3. Did you put your letter in the friendly letter form?	☐	☐
_____ return address		
_____ greeting		
_____ 3 or more paragraphs		
_____ closing		
_____ salutation and name		
4. Did you write a rough draft of your letter?	☐	☐
5. Did you revise your letter with suggestions from people in your writing group?	☐	☐
6. Did you proofread your letter and correct as many errors as possible?	☐	☐

Review

Two types of personal writing are journals and letters. Journals are an important learning tool that students at all grade levels can use effectively. Students use journal writing to share events in their lives and to record what they are learning in literature focus units, literature circles, and thematic units. Students write three kinds of letters: friendly letters, business letters, and simulated letters. Here are the key concepts presented in this chapter:

- Students write in seven kinds of journals: personal journals, dialogue journals, reading logs, double-entry journals, language arts notebooks, learning logs, and simulated journals.
- Dialogue journals are especially useful for English learners.
- Reading logs, double-entry journals, and simulated journals are often used during literature focus units and literature circles.
- Learning logs and simulated journals are used for thematic units.
- Even young children can draw and write in personal journals and reading logs.
- Teachers teach minilessons about how to write in journals.
- Students often share entries with classmates, although personal journal entries are usually private.
- The friendly and business letters that children write should be mailed to authentic audiences.

- Students write simulated letters in connection with literature focus units, literature circles, and thematic units.
- The focus in personal writing is on developing writing fluency and using writing for authentic purposes.

Professional References

Berthoff, A. E. (1981). *The making of meaning.* Montclair, NJ: Boynton/Cook.

Bode, B. A. (1989). Dialogue journal writing. *The Reading Teacher, 42,* 568–571.

Britton, J., Burgess, T., Martin, N., McLeod, A., & Rosen, H. (1975). *The development of writing abilities, 11–18.* London: Schools Council Publications.

Hancock, M. R. (2007). *Language arts: Extending the possibilities.* Upper Saddle River, NJ: Merrill/Prentice Hall.

Hannon, J. (1999). Talking back: Kindergarten dialogue journals. *The Reading Teacher, 53,* 200–203.

Macon, J. M., Bewell, D., & Vogt, M. E. (1991). *Responses to literature, grades K–8.* Newark, DE: International Reading Association.

McGee, L. M., & Richgels, D. J. (2007). *Literacy's beginnings: Supporting young readers and writers* (5th ed.). Boston: Allyn & Bacon.

McKeon, C. A. (1999). The nature of children's e-mail in one classroom. *The Reading Teacher, 52,* 698–706.

Nash, M. F. (1995). "Leading from behind": Dialogue response journals. In N. L. Roser & M. G. Martinez (Eds.), *Book talk and beyond: Children and teachers respond to literature* (pp. 217–225). Newark, DE: International Reading Association.

Peregoy, S. F., & Boyle, W. F. (2005). *Reading, writing, and learning in ESL: A resource book for K–12 teachers* (4th ed.). Boston: Allyn & Bacon.

Reyes, M. de la Luz. (1991). A process approach to literacy using dialogue journals and literature logs with second language learners. *Research in the Teaching of English, 25,* 291–313.

Robinson, A., Crawford, L., & Hall, N. (1991). *Someday you will no (sic) all about me: Young children's explorations in the world of letters.* Portsmouth, NH: Heinemann.

Roop, P. (1995). Keep the reading lights burning. In M. Sorensen & B. Lehman (Eds.), *Teaching with children's books: Paths to literature-based instruction* (pp. 197–202). Urbana, IL: National Council of Teachers of English.

Children's Book References

Ada, A. F. (2001). *With love, Little Red Hen.* New York: Atheneum.

Ahlberg, J., & Ahlberg, A. (2006). *The jolly postman, or other people's letters.* New York: LB Kids.

Bruchac, J. (2001). *The journal of Jesse Smoke: A Cherokee boy.* New York: Scholastic.

Bunting, E. (1999). *Smoky night.* San Diego: Harcourt Brace.

Cleary, B. (1983). *Dear Mr. Henshaw.* New York: Morrow.

Cushman, K. (1994). *Catherine, called Birdy.* New York: HarperCollins.

Finch, M. (2001). *The three billy goats Gruff.* Cambridge, MA: Barefoot Books.

Fraustino, L. R. (2004). *I walk in dread: The diary of Deliverance Trembley, Witness to the Salem witch trials.* New York: Scholastic.

Gregory, K. (2005). *Catherine: The great journey.* New York: Scholastic.

Lewis, C. S. (2005). *The lion, the witch and the wardrobe.* New York: HarperCollins.

Lowry, L. (2006). *The giver.* New York: Delacorte.

MacLachlan, P. (2004). *Sarah, plain and tall.* New York: HarperCollins.

Moss, M. (2006). *Amelia's notebook.* New York: Simon & Schuster.

Nagda, A. W. (2000). *Dear Whiskers.* New York: Holiday House.

Paterson, K. (1987). *The great Gilly Hopkins.* New York: Harper & Row.

Turner, A. (1987). *Nettie's trip south.* New York: Macmillan.

chapter seven

Listening to Learn

The second graders in Mr. Hernandez's classroom are involved in a monthlong study of folktales, and this week they're comparing several versions of "The Little Red Hen." On Monday, Mr. Hernandez read aloud Paul Galdone's *Little Red Hen* (2006), and the children reread it with buddies the next day. Next, he read aloud Jerry Pinkney's *The Little Red Hen* (2006), and they compared it to Galdone's version. On Wednesday and Thursday, the children read "The Little Red Hen" in their reading textbooks and compared this version with the others.

Parent volunteers came into the classroom on Wednesday to make bread with the students. The second graders learned how to read a recipe and use measuring cups and other cooking tools as they made the bread. They baked the bread in the school kitchen, and what they enjoyed was eating freshly baked bread—still warm from the oven—dripping with butter and jam.

The next day, Mr. Hernandez read aloud *Bread, Bread, Bread* (Morris, 1993), an informational book about the breads that people eat around the world, and parents brought in different kinds of bread for the children to sample, including tortillas, rye bread, corn bread, bagels, Jewish matzoh, blueberry muffins, Indian chapatty, and Italian breadsticks. As they sampled them, the children took turns talking about the kinds of bread their families eat.

Today, Mr. Hernandez is reading aloud *Cook-a-Doodle-Doo!* (Stevens & Crummel, 1999), the story of the Little Red Hen's great-grandson, Big Brown Rooster, who manages to bake a strawberry shortcake with the help of three friends—Turtle, Iguana, and Pig. He sets out a story box of objects related to the story: a chef's hat,

Should teachers encourage discussion *during a read-aloud or postpone it until afterward?*

Some teachers ask children to listen quietly while they read aloud and then talk about it afterward. Other teachers, however, invite children to become actively involved as they read aloud. These teachers stop reading periodically to pose questions to stimulate discussion, ask them to make predictions, and encourage children to offer spontaneous comments while they are listening. As you read this vignette, notice how Mr. Hernandez uses discussion to support his second graders' comprehension.

a flour sifter, an egg beater, a plastic strawberry, an oven mitt, a shortcake pan, a timer, a pastry blender, and measuring cups and spoons. The students identify the objects, and Mr. Hernandez prepares a word card for each one so that they can practice matching objects and word cards at a center. Almost immediately, Mikey guesses, "I know what the story is about! Little Red Hen is going to cook something, but it isn't bread. Um . . . Maybe it is strawberry jam to put on the bread."

"That's a good prediction, Mikey, but let me get one more clue for this story box," Mr. Hernandez says, as he reaches over to a nearby rack of puppets. He selects a rooster puppet and adds it to the box. He looks at the students expectantly, and Mallory asks, "Is that a hen?" "No, it isn't," Mr. Hernandez replies. Again he waits until Cristina offers, "I think it's a rooster." "You're right! A rooster is a male chicken, and a hen is a female chicken," he explains. Then Mikey revises his prediction, "Now I know! It's a story about a rooster who cooks something with strawberries."

Mr. Hernandez shows the cover of *Cook-a-Doodle-Doo!* and reads the title. At first the children laugh at the title, and then several of them repeat it aloud. "What does the title make you think of?" Mr. Hernandez asks. Jesus jumps up and imitates a rooster as he calls, "Cock-a-doodle-doo! Cock-a-doodle-doo!" The children compare the sound a rooster makes to the book's title and conclude that the rooster in this book is going to do some cooking.

The teacher draws the students' attention back to the book and asks, "What do you think the rooster is going to cook?" Lacey and Connor both answer "strawberry pancakes," and everyone agrees. Mr. Hernandez asks if anyone has ever tasted strawberry shortcake, but no one has. He explains what it is and tells the class it's his favorite dessert. Then he looks back at the cover illustration and says, "I keep looking at this picture, and I think it looks just like strawberry shortcake."

"Let's start reading," Mr. Hernandez says, and he reads the first two pages of the story that introduce the Little Red Hen's great-grandson, Big Brown Rooster, who is the main character. The children point out the similarity between Little Red Hen's and Big Brown Rooster's names: They are each three words long, they each have a size word, a color word, and an animal name, and words are in the same order in each name.

Mr. Hernandez continues reading, and they learn that the Rooster does plan to make strawberry shortcake—their teacher's favorite dessert. "What's shortcake?" Larry asks. "Is it the opposite of long cake?" Everyone laughs, including Mr. Hernandez. He explains that shortcake is flatter than cake, more like a biscuit. Mikey asks, "Is it like a brownie? Brownies are flatter than chocolate cake." "That's a good comparison," Mr. Hernandez says. Sammy offers: "A tortilla is flatter than a piece of bread." "Good! That's another good comparison," the teacher responds. "All this talk about food is making me hungry."

"Look at this," Mr. Hernandez says, and he points to the cookbook that Big Brown Rooster is holding in the illustration. "That's Little Red Hen's cookbook—*The Joy of Cooking Alone,*" he laughs. "My wife's favorite cookbook is called *The Joy of Cooking,*" he explains. "I wonder why the illustrator added the word *alone* to the title of her cookbook?" "That's because no one would help her make bread," Mallory explains.

The teacher continues reading the story. He turns the page and shows the illustration, a picture of Big Brown Rooster talking to a dog, a cat, and a goose, and the children, remembering the events from "Little Red Hen," spontaneously call out to Rooster, "No, don't ask them. They won't help you!" Big Brown Rooster does ask the three animals to help him, and as the children predicted, they refuse. As Mr. Hernandez reads the "Not I" refrain, everyone joins in. Sondra comments on the similarities to the "Little Red Hen" story: "There's a dog, a cat, and a goose like in the other story, and they won't listen to the Big Brown Rooster either." Then the children predict that Big Brown Rooster, like Little Red Hen, will have to cook alone.

On the next several pages, they learn that three other animals—Turtle, who can read recipes, Iguana, who can get "stuff," and Pig, who is a tasting expert—offer to help. The children get excited. "I think this story is going to be different. It's better," Cristina comments. Mr. Hernandez wonders aloud if these three animals will be good helpers, and the children agree that they will be.

The rooster calls the four of them a "team" on the next page, and Mr. Hernandez asks, "What is a team?" The second graders mention basketball teams, so the teacher rephrases his question: "What makes a group of basketball players a team? What do they do when they are a team?" Students respond that players work together to make a score and win a game. "So, what kind of team are the rooster, the turtle, the iguana, and the pig?" Connor explains, "They are a cooking team. I predict they will work together to cook strawberry shortcake." Then Raymond adds, "And Mr. Hernandez is the captain of the team!"

Mr. Hernandez continues reading, as Turtle reads the recipe and Iguana collects the ingredients for strawberry shortcake. In the story, Iguana doesn't know the difference between a *flower* and *flour* and because the children seem confused, too, the teacher explains the homophones. Iguana doesn't know about cooking tools and procedures either. He wants to use a ruler instead of a measuring cup to measure flour and he looks for teaspoons in a teapot, for example. Because the children recently used measuring cups and spoons when they baked bread, they are more knowledgeable than Iguana, and Sammy says, "That iguana is silly. He's not very smart either." On the next page,

Iguana misunderstands "stick of butter." He breaks a stick from a tree branch, and Lacey calls out, "No, Iguana, that's the wrong kind of stick."

As each ingredient is added, Pig offers to taste the batter, but Big Brown Rooster replies "not yet." Mr. Hernandez pauses after he reads this and reflects, "Pig is eager to taste the shortcake batter. I wonder how long he'll wait patiently for his turn to taste." "Maybe Big Brown Rooster should give him something else to do," Sondra offers. "I'd tell him to go in the living room and watch a video because that's what my mama tells my brother," says Connor. Mr. Hernandez continues reading, and in the story, Pig is getting more desperate to taste the batter. Jesus calls out, "Oh no! Now Pig really, really wants to taste it. Something bad is going to happen." Everyone agrees.

The teacher continues reading. The characters finish mixing the ingredients and put the batter in the oven to bake. "Wow! I'm surprised that Pig is being so good," Mallory offers. "I thought he would gobble up all the shortcake from the mixing bowl." The others agree. "So, now you think the shortcake is going to turn out right?" Mr. Hernandez asks. Most of the children think that it will, but Jesus and Mikey predict trouble ahead.

Mr. Hernandez continues reading. The characters cut the strawberries in half and make whipped cream while the shortcake is in the oven. As he reads, some of the children spontaneously pretend to cut strawberries or pretend to use the egg beater to whip the cream. They dramatize cooking activities again as the teacher reads. The next several pages tell how Rooster takes the shortcake out of

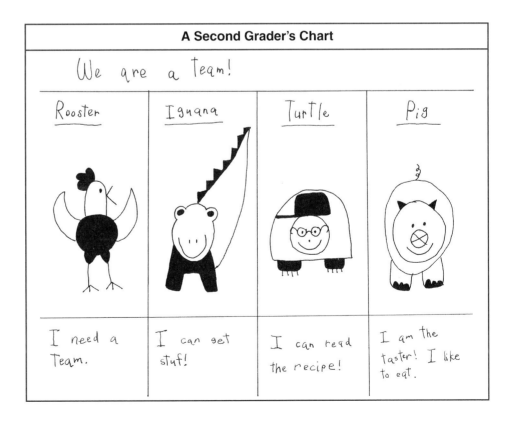

A Second Grader's Chart

the oven, lets it cool, and slices it in half, and assembles the layers of cake, whipped cream, and strawberries. Mikey notices that Pig smells the shortcake when it comes out of the oven and really wants to taste it. "I still think that Pig is bad news," he says.

Finally, the strawberry shortcake is ready to eat, and Rooster says, "If Great-Granny could see me now!" Mr. Hernandez asks what the sentence means. Connor answers, "Rooster wants her to know he is a good cook, too!" Lacey suggests, "Rooster is really proud of himself." Raymond says, "I think Rooster wants Little Red Hen to know that he has a team to help him cook."

Mr. Hernandez turns the page and the students gasp. The illustration shows the strawberry shortcake falling off the plate as Iguana carries it to the table. "Oh no, it's ruined!" Mallory says. "They can't eat it because it's on the floor." "Pig can! Yes, Pig can. Now it really is his turn," Mikey says gleefully. Jesus cheers. "Well, I guess pigs can eat food on the floor," Mallory allows.

"What about the other animals?" Mr. Hernandez asks. "Won't they get to eat strawberry shortcake?" At first the children guess that they won't, and then Jacob offers, "Well, they could go to the store and buy more food and make another strawberry shortcake." Most of the children agree that Jacob has a good idea, but Larry disagrees, "No way. 'Snip, snap, snout. This story's told out,' said Pig." Everyone laughs as Larry suggests an alternative ending using the final words from the "Gingerbread Man" story they read several weeks before.

Mr. Hernandez reads the last few pages in the book, and the children learn that the animals do make another delicious strawberry shortcake for everyone to eat. They're satisfied with how the story turned out. "I'm really glad everyone got to eat some strawberry shortcake," Cristina says. "It's a really good story," Sammy reflects, "because it's funny and serious, too." "What's funny in the story?" the teacher asks. The children say that Iguana is the funniest character, and the funniest part is when the shortcake falls on the floor and Pig gobbles it up. Then Mr. Hernandez asks, "What's serious in the story?" The students recognize the authors' message and identify it as the serious part of the book. They say that the book's message is that a job is easier to do when you work together as a team. "I'm glad Rooster had a team," said Sondra. "What about us?" Mr. Hernandez asks, "Do we have a team?" Mikey says, "I think that our class is a team." Mr. Hernandez responds, "What do you think makes us a team?" "We help each other learn and do our work," Larry answers. The other children agree.

Finally, Mr. Hernandez shows the last page with Little Red Hen's recipe for strawberry shortcake, and he surprises everyone by announcing that he brought the ingredients and that they'll make strawberry shortcake after lunch.

The second graders regularly make charts in their reading logs to help them remember an important idea about each story they read or listen to read aloud. After reading *Cook-a-Doodle-Doo!*, they make charts about how the characters in the story were a team. One child's chart about the team is shown in the box on page 211. Mr. Hernandez helps them brainstorm a list of words to use on their charts and writes the words on the chalkboard so that the children can spell them correctly. The words they brainstorm include *team, Big Brown Rooster, Turtle, Iguana, Pig, Little Red Hen, strawberry shortcake, helper, recipe,* and *taster.*

*W*hy do people listen? Children often say that they listen to learn or to avoid punishment, but according to Wolvin and Coakley (1996), people listen differently according to their purpose. They've identified these purposes:

◆ *Discriminative Listening.* People use discriminative listening to distinguish sounds. Young children use discriminative listening as they develop phonemic awareness, the ability to blend and segment the sounds in spoken words. Children also "listen" to nonverbal messages. They learn the meanings of more sophisticated forms of body language and recognize how teachers emphasize that something they are teaching is important, such as by writing it on the chalkboard, speaking more loudly, or repeating information.

◻ *Aesthetic Listening.* People listen aesthetically when they're listening for enjoyment to stories read aloud, as Mr. Hernandez's students did in the vignette at the beginning of the chapter. The focus is on the lived-through experience of the literature and the connections children make to their own lives, the world around them, and other literature. Viewing film, DVD, and videotape versions of stories are other examples of aesthetic listening.

◻ *Efferent Listening.* People listen efferently to understand a message and remember important information. This is the type of listening required in many instructional activities, including minilessons. Children use efferent listening as they listen to teachers present information or read informational books aloud. They determine the speaker's purpose, identify the main ideas, and organize the information in order to remember it.

◻ *Critical Listening.* People listen critically to evaluate a message. Critical listening is an extension of efferent listening. Children listen to understand a message, but they also filter the message to detect propaganda devices, persuasive language, and emotional appeals. It's used when people listen to debates, commercials, political speeches, and other arguments.

The four types of listening are reviewed in Figure 7–1.

As you continue reading, you will learn about these four kinds of listening. Keep these points in mind as you read:

◆   How do children listen aesthetically?
◻   How do children listen efferently?
◆   How do children listen critically?
◻   How is each type of listening taught and assessed?

AESTHETIC LISTENING

Louise Rosenblatt (2005) coined the term *aesthetic reading* to describe the stance readers take when they are concerned with the experience they are living through and with their relationship to the literature they are reading. The focus is on their experience during reading, not on the information they will carry away from the experience. Similarly, the term *aesthetic listening* can be used to describe the type of listening children and adults do as they listen to teachers read aloud stories, poets recite poems, actors perform a play, and singers sing songs, and as they view films and videotape versions of stories. Children also use aesthetic listening as they listen

---

FIGURE 7–1

Overview of the Four Types of Listening

Types	Characteristics	Examples
Discriminative	Distinguish among sounds	Participate in phonemic awareness activities Notice rhyming words in poems and songs Recognize alliteration and onomatopoeia Experiment with tongue twisters
Aesthetic	Listen for pleasure or enjoyment	Listen to stories and poems read aloud View video versions of stories Listen to stories at a listening center Watch students perform a play or readers theatre reading Participate in grand conversations Participate in tea party activities
Efferent	Listen to understand messages	Listen to informational books read aloud or at a listening center Use anticipation guides Listen to oral reports Use clusters and graphic organizers View informational videos Listen to book talks Participate in instructional conversations Participate in writing groups Do note taking/note making Listen during minilessons Listen to students share projects
Critical	Evaluate messages	Listen to debates and political speeches View commercials and other advertisements Evaluate themes and arguments in books read aloud

---

to stories at the listening center. The focus of this type of listening is on the lived-through experience and the connections the listeners are making to the literature they are listening to. More traditional names for aesthetic listening are appreciative listening and listening for pleasure.

Interactive Read-Alouds

Reading aloud to children is a cherished classroom routine. In a recent study of sixth graders' reading preferences, an overwhelming 62% of students reported that they enjoy listening to the teacher read aloud (Ivey & Broaddus, 2001). Children's author Mem Fox (2001) and reading-aloud guru Jim Trelease (2006) both urge teachers to make time to read aloud every day because as students listen, they gain valuable experiences with books, enrich their background knowledge and vocabulary, and develop a love of reading. Reading aloud is an art; effective readers are familiar with the book they're reading, and they read fluently and with expression, changing the tone of their voices and using pauses to enhance students' listening experience.

Reading aloud has been an informal activity in most classrooms: Teachers pick up a book, read the title aloud, and begin reading while children listen quietly. Often young children sit in a group on the floor around the teacher, and older students sit attentively at their desks. The children are passive as they listen, but afterward, they become more engaged as they talk briefly about the story and perhaps participate in a follow-up activity. The focus is on the sharing of literature with little or no student involvement until after the reading is over. Researchers who have studied reading aloud, however, have concluded that children are better listeners when they are involved while the teacher is reading, not afterward (Dickinson & Tabors, 2001). This conclusion has led to the development of the interactive read-aloud procedure (Barrentine, 1996).

In an interactive read-aloud, teachers introduce the book and activate students' background knowledge before they begin to read. They model listening strategies and fluent oral reading as they read aloud, and they engage students while they're reading. Then after reading, they provide opportunities for students to respond to the book. The most important component, however, is how teachers involve students while they're reading aloud (Fisher, Flood, Lapp, & Frey, 2004). The steps in an interactive read-aloud are described on page 216.

One way that teachers engage students is to stop reading periodically to discuss what has just been read. What matters is when teachers stop reading: When they're reading stories aloud, it's more effective to stop at points where students can make predictions and suggest connections, after reading episodes that students might find confusing, and just before it becomes clear how the story will end. When they're reading poems, teachers often read the entire poem once, and then stop as they read the poem a second time for students to play with words, notice poetic

Laima Druskis/PH College

Using Listening Centers

These two first graders enjoy rereading a familiar story at the listening center. After their teacher reads aloud stories, she places two or more copies of the book at the listening center along with the tape she made as she read the book aloud. As students listen to the tape and follow along in the book, they notice high-frequency words, learn vocabulary, and gain valuable reading experience. Listening centers promote students' learning when teachers teach them how to work effectively in the center.

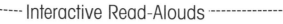

Interactive Read-Alouds

1 Pick a book   Teaches choose award-winning and other high-quality books that are appropriate for students and that fit into their instructional programs.

2 Preview the book   Teachers practice reading the book to ensure that they can read it fluently and to decide where to pause and engage the class with the text; they write prompts on self-stick notes to mark these pages. Teachers also think about how they will introduce the book and select difficult vocabulary words to highlight.

3 Introduce the book   Teachers activate students' background knowledge, set a clear purpose for listening, and preview the text.

4 Read the book interactively   Teachers read the book aloud, modeling fluent and expressive reading. They stop periodically to ask questions to focus students on specific points in the text and involve them in other activities.

5 Involve students in after-reading activities   Students participate in discussions and other types of response activities.

devices, and repeat favorite words and lines. Deciding how often to stop for discussion and knowing when to end the discussion and continue reading develop through practice and vary from one group of students to another. When they're reading informational books aloud, teachers stop to talk about big ideas as they're presented, briefly explain technical terms, and emphasize connections among the big ideas. Figure 7–2 presents additional ways to actively involve students with read-aloud books.

Choosing Books to Read Aloud. Guidelines for choosing stories to read aloud are simple: Choose books that you like and that you think will appeal to your students. Trelease (2006) makes these suggestions: Stories should be fast-paced to hook students' interest as quickly as possible; contain well-developed characters; include easy-to-read dialogue; and keep long descriptive passages to a minimum. Books that have received awards or other acclaim from teachers, librarians, and children make good choices. Two of the most prestigious awards are the Caldecott Medal and the Newbery Medal. Lists of outstanding books are prepared annually by the National Council of Teachers of English and other professional groups. In many states, children read and vote for books to receive recognition, such as the Buckeye Book Award in Ohio and the Sequoyah Book Award in Oklahoma. The International Reading Association sponsors a Children's Choices competition, in which children read and select their favorite books, and a similar Teachers' Choices competition; lists of these books are published annually in *The Reading Teacher*. Some of my favorite read-aloud stories are included in the booklist on page 217.

Teachers choose grade-appropriate books for read-alouds that are too difficult for students to read independently. The idea is that even if students can't read the words, they can understand the ideas presented in the book. This read-aloud strategy works for many students, but for others, it doesn't. For example, students may lack sufficient background knowledge on the topic or may be overwhelmed by unfamiliar

Booklist

RECOMMENDED READ-ALOUD STORIES

Kindergarten ------------------------------------

McCloskey, R. (2001). *Make way for ducklings*. New York: Viking.

Sendak, M. (2003). *Where the wild things are*. New York: HarperCollins.

Grade 1 ------------------------------------

Brett, J. (1989). *The mitten*. New York: Putnam.

Rathmann, P. (1995). *Officer Buckle and Gloria*. New York: Putnam.

Grade 2 ------------------------------------

Meddaugh, S. (1995). *Hog-eye*. Boston: Houghton Mifflin.

Polacco, P. (1996). *Rechenka's eggs*. New York: Putnam.

Grade 3 ------------------------------------

MacLachlan, P. (2004). *Sarah, plain and tall*. New York: HarperCollins.

White, E. B. (2006). *Charlotte's web*. New York: HarperCollins.

Grade 4 ------------------------------------

Ryan, P. M. (2000). *Esperanza rising*. New York: Scholastic.

Cohen, B. (2005). *Molly's pilgrim*. New York: HarperCollins.

Grade 5 ------------------------------------

Curtis, C. P. (2000). *The Watsons go to Birmingham—1963*. New York: Delacorte.

Lowry, L. (2005). *Number the stars*. New York: Yearling.

Grade 6 ------------------------------------

Babbitt, N. (2002). *Tuck everlasting*. New York: Farrar, Straus & Giroux.

Paulsen, G. (2006). *Hatchet*. New York: Aladdin Books.

Grade 7 ------------------------------------

Cushman, K. (1994). *Catherine, called Birdy*. New York: HarperCollins.

Sachar, L. (1998). *Holes*. New York: Farrar, Straus & Giroux.

Grade 8 ------------------------------------

Lowry, L. (2006). *The giver*. New York: Delacorte.

Whelan, G. (2000). *Homeless bird*. New York: Scholastic.

FIGURE 7–2

Ways to Actively Involve Students With Books

Stories	• Make and revise predictions at pivotal points in the story • Share personal, world, and literary connections • Talk about what they're visualizing or how they're using other strategies • Draw a picture of a character or an event • Assume the persona of a character and share what the character might be thinking • Reenact a scene from the story
Poems	• Add sound effects • Mumble-read along with the teacher as the poem is read • Repeat lines after the teacher • Clap or snap fingers when they hear rhyming words, alliterations, onomatopoeia, or other poetic devices
Informational Books	• Ask questions or share information • Raise their hands when they hear specific information • Restate headings as questions • Take notes • Complete graphic organizers

vocabulary in the book. They may not listen strategically, or they may not be interested in the book.

Teachers can solve these problems. First, they can build background knowledge before reading by showing a video, reading a picture book, or sharing a story box of objects related to the book. At the same time they're building background knowledge, they introduce key vocabulary words, and while reading, they briefly explain unfamiliar words—sometimes providing a synonym is enough. In addition, struggling students may not know how to listen. It's important to teach listening strategies. Finally, struggling students often complain that a book is "boring," but what they generally mean is that they don't understand it. Making sure that students understand often takes care of their seeming lack of interest; however, if the book really doesn't interest students, teachers need to create interest by making connections with students' lives, showing the video version of the story, or asking students to assume a role as a character and dramatize events from the story. If none of these strategies work, then teachers should choose a different book to read.

It's not unusual for primary-grade students to listen to their teacher read aloud several books during the school day. If children are read to only once a day, they will listen to fewer than 200 books during the school year, and this isn't enough! More than 50,000 books are available for children, and reading aloud is an important way to share this literature with children. Older students should also listen to chapter books read aloud as part of literature focus units.

What About Rereading Books? Children—especially kindergartners and first graders—often beg to have familiar stories reread. Although it's important to share a wide variety of books with children, researchers have found that children benefit in specific ways from repeated readings (Yaden, 1988). Through repetition, children gain control over the parts of a story and are better able to synthesize those parts into a whole. The quality of children's responses to a repeated story changes, too.

Martinez and Roser (1985) examined young children's responses to stories and found that as stories became increasingly familiar, children's responses indicated a greater depth of understanding. They found that children talked almost twice as much about familiar books that had been reread many times as they did about unfamiliar books that had been read only once or twice. The form and focus of children's talk changed, too: Children tended to ask questions about unfamiliar stories, but they made comments about familiar ones. Children's talk about unfamiliar stories focused on characters; the focus changed to details and word meanings when they talked about familiar stories.

The researchers also found that children's comments after repeated readings were more probing and more specific, suggesting that they had greater insight into the story. Researchers investigating the value of repeated readings have focused mainly on preschool and primary-grade students, but rereading favorite stories and other books may have similar benefits for older students as well.

Benefits of Reading Aloud. It's easy to take reading aloud for granted, assuming that it's something teachers do for fun in between instructional activities. However, reading aloud to students is an important instructional activity with numerous benefits, including the following:

- Students' interest in reading is stimulated.
- Students' reading interests and their taste for quality literature are broadened.

- Students are introduced to the sounds of written language.
- Students' knowledge of vocabulary and sentence patterns is expanded.
- Students are introduced to books that are "too good to miss."
- Students listen to books that are too difficult for them to read on their own or that are "hard to get into."
- Students see their teachers model what capable readers do.
- Students' background knowledge is expanded.
- Students are introduced to genres and elements of text structure.

And, most important, students who regularly listen to stories read aloud are more likely to become lifelong readers.

Responding to Stories

In the vignette, Mr. Hernandez actively involved his second graders in listening by encouraging them to talk about the story as he read it aloud. Barrentine (1996) recommends that teachers invite brief conversations so that students can talk about their use of listening strategies, notice literary elements and other aspects of the story, and make predictions and connections. Sipe (2002) found that students make five types of responses as they interact with stories; Mr. Hernandez's second graders made these responses in the vignette:

Dramatizing. Students spontaneously act out the story in both nonverbal and verbal ways. Mr. Hernandez's second graders, for example, dramatized cutting strawberries and beating cream as their teacher read aloud.

Talking Back. Students talk back to the characters, giving them advice or criticizing and complimenting them. At the beginning of the story, for example, Mr. Hernandez's students tell the Rooster not to ask the cat, the dog, and the goose for help, and later in the story, they tell Iguana that he has the wrong kind of stick.

Critiquing/Controlling. Students suggest alternative plots, characters, or settings to personalize the story. For example, several of Mr. Hernandez's students suggest ways that Rooster could handle Pig more effectively.

Inserting. Students insert themselves or their friends into the story. One of Mr. Hernandez's students, for example, inserts Mr. Hernandez into the story and says that he is the team captain.

Taking Over. Students take over the text and manipulate it to express their own creativity. These responses are usually humorous and provide an opportunity for students to show off. For example, after Mr. Hernandez's students suggest several possible endings for the story after the pig eats the first strawberry shortcake, Larry gets a big laugh when he suggests a different ending using words from "Gingerbread Man."

Students make these types of responses when teachers encourage their active participation in the story, but the tricky part is to balance the time spent reading and talking.

Listening and Viewing

Students often view high-quality videos of children's literature as part of literature focus units and thematic units, and it's important that teachers take advantage of the unique capabilities of this technology. Teachers use videos in connection with books children are reading or books they're listening to the teacher read aloud. Teachers decide whether students view the video before or after reading, or how much of the video they watch, depending on the students' needs and interests. Those with limited background knowledge often benefit from viewing before reading or listening to the book read aloud, but for other students, watching a video before reading would curtail their interest in reading the book.

Students often make comparisons between the book and video versions of a story and choose the one they like better. Interestingly, less capable students who don't visualize the story in their minds often prefer the video version, whereas more capable listeners often prefer the book version because the video doesn't meet their expectations. They can also examine some of the conventions used in video productions, such as narration, music and sound effects, the visual representation of characters and the setting, the camera's perspective, and any changes from the book version. Guidelines for using videos in the classroom are listed in the LA Essentials box on page 221.

Teaching Aesthetic Listening

Listening is something most people take for granted. It's an invisible process by which spoken messages are received and converted to meaning in the mind (Lundsteen, 1979; National Communication Association, 1998). Children are often admonished to listen, but few teachers teach them how to improve their ability to listen. Instead, teachers usually assume that children already know how to listen. Also, some teachers feel that it's more important to spend instructional time on reading and writing instruction. Despite these concerns, most teachers agree that children need to more about how to listen because it's essential for learning (Opitz & Zbaracki, 2004).

When reading stories aloud, teachers have three responsibilities. First, they help students activate their background knowledge before reading. Students need to become actively involved in books they listen to read aloud, and the first step in active involvement is to connect the book to their background knowledge. Second, teachers model and teach aesthetic listening strategies as they read aloud and provide opportunities for students to practice using the strategies as they listen. And third, teachers provide opportunities for students to respond to the book after reading. Students need opportunities to share their ideas, ask questions, and bring closure to the listening experience.

Aesthetic Listening Strategies. Three of the most important strategies that students use for aesthetic listening are predicting, visualizing, and connecting.

Predicting. As students listen, they're predicting what will happen next, and they revise their predictions as they continue listening. When they read aloud, teachers encourage students to predict by stopping and asking them what they think will happen next.

Visualizing. Students create an image or picture in their minds while listening to a story that has strong visual images. They practice this strategy by closing their

GUIDELINES FOR USING VIDEOS IN THE CLASSROOM

- **Preview the Video**

  Before showing the video to students, teachers make sure it's suitable for them to view. It may be necessary to skip some portions because of excessive length or unsuitable content.

- **Plan How to Use the Video**

  Students who have little background knowledge on the topic or students for whom the sentence structure or vocabulary is difficult may benefit from viewing the video before reading or listening to the book read aloud.

- **Set the Purpose**

  Teachers explain the purpose for viewing the video and explain whether students should use primarily aesthetic, efferent, or critical listening.

- **Use the Pause Function**

  Teachers stop the video periodically for students to make predictions, reflect on their use of a listening strategy, talk about the video, or compare the book and video versions. When students are listening to an informational video, teachers can stop the video periodically to allow students to take notes.

- **Re-view the Video**

  Teachers consider showing the video more than once because re-viewing is as beneficial as rereading. Use the rewind function to show particular scenes twice during the first viewing, or show the video without interruption the first time and later play it a second time.

- **Vary the Procedure Used to Show Videos**

  Teachers sometimes show the beginning of a story on the videotape and then read aloud the entire book. Afterward, students can view the entire video. Or, teachers can alternate reading and viewing chapters of a longer book.

- **Compare the Author's and Camera's Views**

  Students can examine the impact of the narration, music and sound effects, the visual representation of the characters and setting, and camera angles.

- **Respond to the Video**

  Teachers provide opportunities for students to respond to videos after viewing. They can respond by participating in grand conversations or instructional conversations and writing in reading logs.

eyes, thinking about descriptive words and phrases, and trying to draw mental pictures while they're listening.

🔲 **Connecting.** Students make three types of connections when they are listening to a story read aloud. First, they make text-to-self connections between the story and events in their own lives. Next, they make text-to-world connections between the story and familiar current events. Third, they make text-to-text connections between the story and other stories they've read or television shows and movies they've watched. Teachers help students use this strategy by asking them to talk about connections they've made as they discuss the story.

The second graders in the vignette at the beginning of this chapter used these strategies as they listened to their teacher read aloud *Cook-a-Doodle-Doo!* (Stevens & Crummel, 1999). Mikey offered predictions spontaneously, and at key points in the story, Mr. Hernandez asked the children to make additional predictions. They made personal connections to their families' cooking experiences and literary connections to the "Little Red Hen" stories they had read. The children also made literary connections when they noticed the similarity between the names *Big Brown Rooster* and *Little Red Hen* and the "not I" refrain from "The Little Red Hen." The children used visualizing when they made character charts after listening to Mr. Hernandez read the story. Students don't always use every strategy as they listen to a story, but this story provided many opportunities, and Mr. Hernandez knew how to take advantage of them.

Minilessons. Researchers have repeatedly cited the need to teach listening strategies to help children become more effective listeners (Optiz & Zbaracki, 2004; Wolvin & Coakley, 1996). There are added benefits, too: Children use the same strategies when they're listening, reading, and viewing because these three language arts are receptive processes, and sometimes teachers are more successful when they teach strategies while students are listening to stories instead of when they're reading stories. Teachers teach minilessons to introduce, practice, and review strategies, as well as procedures, concepts, and skills related to aesthetic listening. See page 232 for a list of topics for minilessons related to aesthetic listening.

Assessing Students' Aesthetic Listening

Students need to learn how to listen aesthetically so that they can engage more fully in the lived-through experience of literature. Teachers assess whether students are listening aesthetically in several ways. First, they judge the predictions students make to see that they are actively involved in listening to and thinking about the story being read aloud. Teachers also listen to the comments students make as they talk about stories and read entries in students' reading logs to see whether they are using aesthetic listening strategies. Teachers can also check that students are transferring their use of these listening strategies to reading and viewing.

EFFERENT LISTENING

Efferent listening is practical listening to understand a message. The term *efferent,* first applied to language arts by Louise Rosenblatt (2005), means "carrying away." It's the most common type of listening students do in school. They listen efferently when teachers present information and give directions. Students may be learning about homonyms during language arts, for example, the water cycle during a science unit,

or the Bill of Rights during a social studies unit. No matter the topic, teachers want students to remember the big ideas and understand the relationships among them. They can use these five techniques to improve students' listening:

- Activating students' background knowledge
- Setting a clear purpose for listening
- Using manipulatives
- Creating graphic organizers
- Having students take notes

Teachers make their oral presentations more like interactive read-alouds when they incorporate these techniques, and students' curiosity is piqued and they are likely to become more actively involved in listening.

Meeting the Needs of English Learners

Why Is Listening Crucial for English Learners?

Listening is a key to language development because children learn English as they listen to the teacher and classmates talk and read aloud.

Reason 1: Language Models

When teachers read aloud, the books provide language models. English learners acquire new vocabulary and more sophisticated language patterns and sentence structures through listening. Gibbons (2002) warns, however, that classrooms are noisy places and the background buzz may make it harder for English learners to hear, understand, and learn. Teachers can alleviate this problem by sitting English learners close to where they often talk and read to the whole class and by insisting that classmates be courteous listeners.

Reason 2: Expanding Knowledge

Students also develop background knowledge through listening. They learn new information and the vocabulary to express ideas, and they also make new connections between the ideas and past experiences. This contribution is especially important for children of poverty, including English learners, who have limited background knowledge.

Reason 3: Transfer to Reading

Listening is an important instructional tool because it's a receptive process, like reading. Students can transfer the listening strategies they learn to reading, and both listening and reading involve the active construction of meaning.

Effective listening can be very challenging for English learners because it depends on expectations and predictions about the content, language, and genre that listeners bring to the text (Rothenberg & Fisher, 2007). In addition, whether students are successful listeners depends on their background knowledge and familiarity with the topic teachers are talking or reading about.

🔖 *Activate Background Knowledge.* Teachers encourage students to activate background knowledge and build on that knowledge by having them explore the topic. They can brainstorm ideas while the teacher takes notes on chart paper, in list or cluster format. As students share ideas, the teacher asks them to elaborate, and the teacher clarifies any misconceptions. Or, students can quickwrite on the topic and then share their writing with the class. Teachers also use anticipation guides to stimulate students' interest in a topic and activate their background knowledge. They present a set of statements related to the topic, some of which are true and will be confirmed by the presentation, and others that are false and will be corrected by the presentation. Before the presentation, students read and discuss each statement and mark whether they think it's true or false. Then they listen to the presentation and mark each statement again after listening (Readence, Bean, & Baldwin, 2004). An eighth-grade anticipation guide on the Crusades is presented in Figure 7–3. Notice that students mark whether they agree or disagree before listening on the left side of the paper and after listening on the right side of the paper. The steps in preparing anticipation guides are shown in the Step by Step feature on page 225.

🔖 **Set a Clear Purpose.** Teachers explain the purpose for listening and tell students to listen efferently, to remember information. For example, their purpose might be to learn how to identify prefixes or to identify the reasons why pioneers traveled west in covered wagons.

🔖 **Use Manipulatives.** Teachers choose objects, pictures, and photos, or word cards for students to examine or use in activities during the presentation. Using manipulatives increases students' interest and makes abstract ideas more concrete.

🔖 **Create Graphic Organizers.** Teachers create diagrams using circles, boxes, lines, and arrows to show the relationships among the big ideas, and students complete the graphic organizers by adding words during the presentation.

FIGURE 7–3

An Eighth-Grade Anticipation Guide

Anticipation Guide on the Crusades

Before			After	
T	F		T	F
		1. The Crusaders wanted to go to the Holy Land to meet Jesus.		
		2. The Crusades took place between 1096 and 1270.		
		3. The Crusaders fought the Muslims to recapture the Holy Land.		
		4. Only noblemen and rich people were allowed to go on the Crusades.		
		5. The Crusaders traveled to the Holy Land for religious reasons.		
		6. Because of the Crusades, Europeans were introduced to many luxuries, including sugar, silk, and glass mirrors.		

-------------- Anticipation Guides ---------------

Step by Step

1 Identify several major concepts. Teachers consider their students' knowledge about the topic and any misconceptions students might have as they identify concepts related to their presentation.

2 Develop a list of three to six statements. Teachers write a statement about each major concept they identified on a chart, or individual copies can be made for each student. These statements should be general enough to stimulate discussion, present major concepts, and help clarify misconceptions.

3 Discuss the statements on the anticipation guide. Teachers introduce the anticipation guide and have students respond to the statements. Students think about the statements and mark whether they are true or false.

4 Listen to the presentation. Students listen to the oral presentation and think about information that relates to the statements on the anticipation guide.

5 Discuss the statements again. After listening, students reconsider their earlier responses to each statement and again mark whether the statements are true or false. Then students share their responses with the class. Sometimes they also revise the false statements to make them true.

◙ **Have Students Take Notes.** Students are more active listeners when they take notes to help them remember the big ideas while they listen to an oral presentation. Teachers introduce note taking by demonstrating the procedure. They set a clear purpose, and during the oral presentation, they stop periodically and ask students to identify the idea being presented and its relationship to other ideas that have been presented. Then teachers list students' responses on the chalkboard. Teachers often begin by writing notes in a list format, but the notes can also be written in an outline or diagram.

Upper-grade students often use a special kind of note taking in which they divide their papers into two columns, labeling the left column *Take Notes* and the right column *Make Notes*. They write notes in the left column, but, more important, they think about the notes, make connections, and personalize the notes in the right column (Berthoff, 1981). The right column should be more extensive than the left one because this column shows students' thinking. A fifth grader's note-taking and note-making sheet about illegal drugs is presented in Figure 7–4. The student's comments in the "Make Notes" column are especially interesting because they show the connections she was making.

Reading Aloud Informational Books

Teachers use the interactive read-aloud procedure to actively involve students in the informational books they're reading aloud. Informational books have the power to intrigue and excite students, and students use a combination of efferent and aesthetic listening because informational books provide both a literary and a learning experience. High-quality informational books cover a wide range of topics, including *Wildfire* (Morrison, 2006), which explains why forest fires have been increasing and how firefighters use cutting-edge technologies to control the devastation; *Mosquito Bite* (Siy, 2005), which presents photomicrograph close-ups of mosquito anatomy; *Reaching for the Moon* (Aldrin, 2005), which describes the author's lifelong interest in space and his history-making trip to the moon; *Now and Ben: The Modern Inventions of Benjamin Franklin* (Barretta, 2006), which humorously explains how 22 of his inventions are still used today; and *Aliens Are Coming! The True Account of the 1938 War of the Worlds Radio Broadcast* (McCarthy, 2006), which recounts the real-life panic that ensued when the radio play convinced many listeners there was a real alien invasion. Teachers often think about the instructional value of informational books when they read them aloud, but the books also captivate students' imaginations while they are listening. Guidelines for using informational books are listed in the LA Essentials box on page 227.

After reading, students need to talk about the book: They share interesting information, ask questions, clarify confusions, and respond to the listening experience. Teachers often have students complete graphic organizers, write in learning logs, and apply what they have learned. Students apply what they have learned as

---

FIGURE 7–4

A Fifth Grader's Note-Taking and Note-Making Sheet

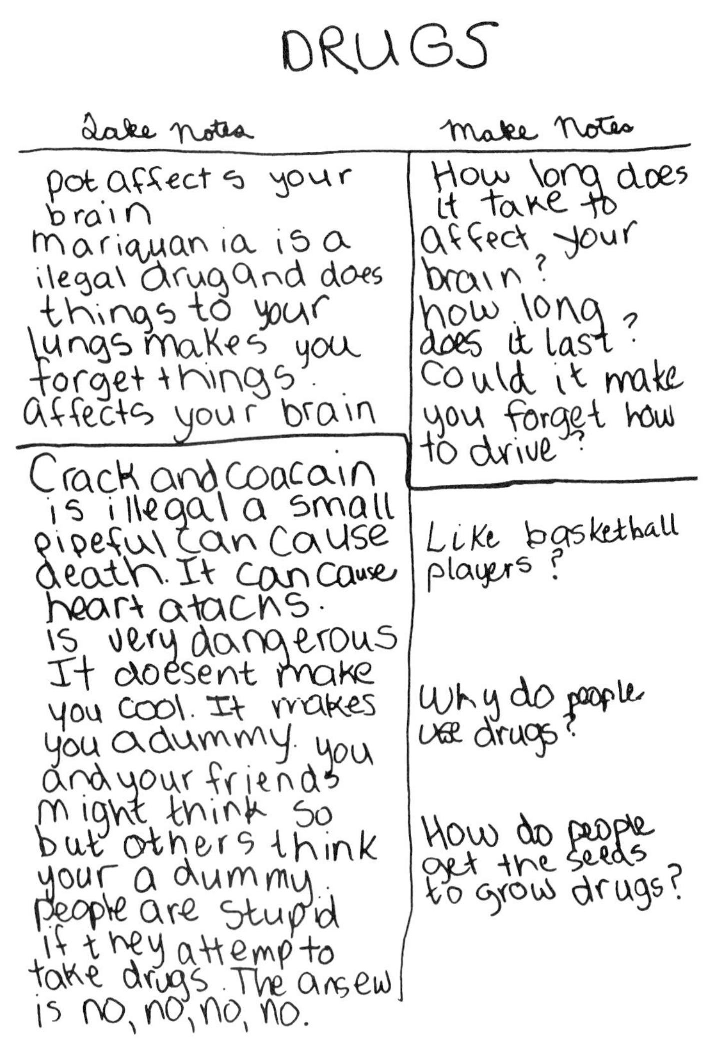

DRUGS

Take notes	Make notes
pot affects your brain mariguania is a ilegal drug and does things to your lungs makes you forget things. Affects your brain	How long does it take to affect your brain? how long? does it last? Could it make you forget how to drive?
Crack and coacain is illegal a small pipeful can cause death. It can cause heart atacks. is very dangerous It doesent make you cool. It makes you a dummy. you and your friends might think so but others think your a dummy. people are stupid if they attempt to take drugs. The ansew is no, no, no, no.	Like basketball players? Why do people use drugs? How do people get the seeds to grow drugs?

GUIDELINES FOR READING ALOUD INFORMATIONAL BOOKS

- **Choose High-Quality Books**

  Teachers choose high-quality informational books for thematic-unit text sets. Books should have visual appeal and relevance to the unit.

- **Actively Involve Children in the Reading Experience**

  Teachers increase children's involvement in the book when they ask questions and set purposes, use manipulatives and graphic organizers, and have students raise their hands when they hear important information or answers to questions that have been asked.

- **Point Out Features of Informational Books**

  As teachers read aloud, they point out the unique features of informational books, including the table of contents, glossary, illustrations and diagrams, and index, and they demonstrate how to use them.

- **Teach Efferent Listening Strategies**

  Teachers model and teach note taking and other efferent listening strategies when reading aloud informational books.

- **Use Graphic Organizers**

  Teachers give students copies of a chart to complete while they listen or draw a diagram on the chalkboard to organize students' thinking before reading.

- **Plan Oral Performances**

  Teachers and students adapt informational books for readers theatre performances, choral reading, puppet shows, and other presentations.

they create projects, including posters, oral reports, and found poems. They can also write their own informational books and create information quilts—like story quilts, but with facts students have learned written and illustrated on each square.

Teaching Efferent Listening

Teachers can improve students' efferent listening. They enhance students' interest in the topic and increase their active involvement during listening. They use minilessons to explain the differences between aesthetic and efferent listening and teach students how to use the efferent listening strategies.

Pg. 321

Efferent Listening Strategies. Students use a variety of strategies as they listen efferently; some of the strategies are the same as for reading and viewing, and others are unique to efferent listening. The purpose of each strategy is to help listeners organize and remember the information. Four of the most important strategies that students use for efferent listening are organizing, summarizing, getting clues from the speaker, and monitoring.

▪ *Organizing* Informational presentations are usually organized in special ways called *expository text structures*. The five most common patterns are description, sequence, comparison, cause and effect, and problem and solution. Students learn to recognize these patterns and use them to understand and remember a speaker's message more easily. Speakers often use certain words to signal the organizational structures they are following; signal words include *first, second, third, next, in contrast,* and *in summary.* Students can learn to attend to these signals to identify the organizational pattern the speaker is using. To learn more about the expository text structures, turn to Chapter 10, "Reading and Writing Information."

Students often use graphic organizers to visualize the organization of oral presentations, informational videos, or informational books (Yopp & Yopp, 2006). When students listen to a presentation comparing amphibians and reptiles, for example, students make T-charts or Venn diagrams to organize the information. They can draw a two-column T-chart, labeling one column "Amphibians" and the other "Reptiles," then they write notes in the columns while they listen to the presentation or immediately after listening. A sixth grader's T-chart comparing amphibians and reptiles is shown in Figure 7–5.

FIGURE 7–5

A Sixth Grader's T-Chart Comparing Amphibians and Reptiles

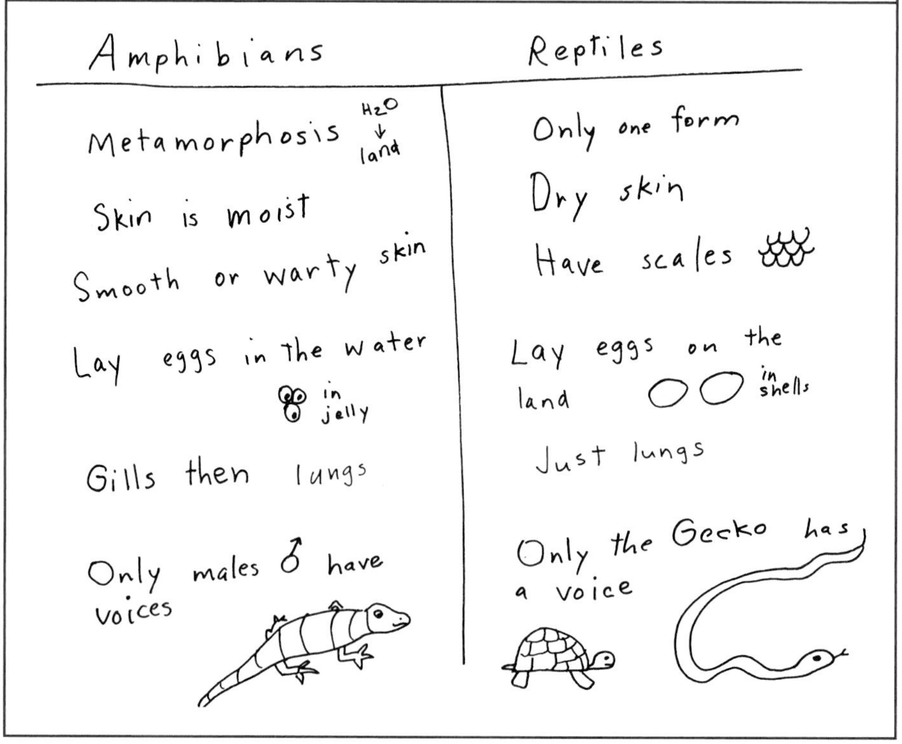

FIGURE 7–6

Cluster Diagram on Simple Machines

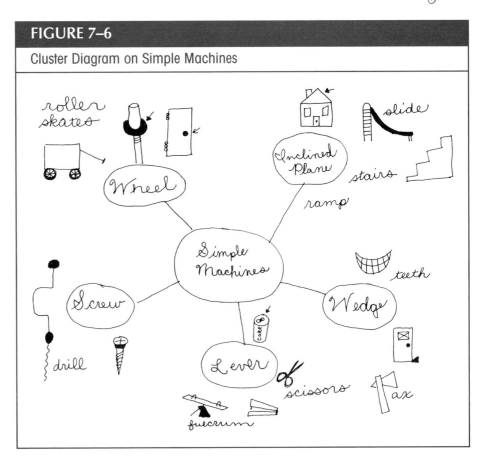

When students are listening to a presentation or an informational book that contains information on more than two or three categories, they can make a cluster diagram, write each category on a ray, and then add descriptive information. For example, when students are listening to a presentation on simple machines, they make a cluster with five rays, one for each type of simple machine. Then students add words and drawings to take notes about each type of simple machine. A fifth grader's cluster is shown in Figure 7–6.

◤ *Summarizing* Speakers present several main ideas and many details during oral presentations, so students need to learn to focus on the main ideas in order to summarize; otherwise, they try to remember everything and quickly feel overwhelmed. Once students can identify the main ideas, they can chunk the details to the main idea.

When teachers introduce the summarizing strategy, they ask students to listen for two or three main ideas; they write these ideas on the chalkboard and draw boxes around them. Then teachers give an oral presentation, having students raise their hands when they hear the first main idea stated. Students then raise their hands when they hear the second main idea, and again for the third main idea. After students gain practice in detecting already-stated main ideas, teachers give a very brief presentation with one main idea and ask students to identify it. Once students can identify the main idea, teachers give longer oral presentations and ask students to identify two or three main ideas. A teacher might make these points when giving an oral presentation on simple machines:

There are five kinds of simple machines.
Simple machines are combined in specialized machines.

Machines make work easier.

Almost everything we do involves machines.

After students identify the main ideas during an oral presentation, they can chunk details to the main ideas. This hierarchical organization is the most economical way to remember information, and students need to understand that they can remember more information when they use the summarizing strategy.

▶ *Getting clues from the speaker* Speakers use both visual and verbal clues to convey their messages and direct their listeners' attention. Visual clues include gesturing, writing or underlining important information on the chalkboard, and changing facial expressions. Verbal clues include pausing, raising or lowering the voice, slowing down speech to stress key points, and repeating important information. Surprisingly, many children are not aware of these attention-directing behaviors, so teachers must point them out. Once children are aware of these clues, they can use them to increase their understanding of a message.

▶ *Monitoring* Students monitor whether they're understanding while they're actively involved in listening. It's an important strategy because students need to know when they're not listening successfully or when a listening strategy isn't working so that they can correct the situation. Students can use these self-questions as they begin to listen:

- Why am I listening to this message?
- Will I need to take notes?
- Does this information make sense to me?

These are possible questions to use as students continue listening:

- Is my strategy still working?
- Am I organizing the information effectively?
- Is the speaker giving me clues about the organization of the message?
- Is the speaker giving me nonverbal clues, such as gestures and facial expressions?

Monitoring is an important strategy for all sorts of language arts activities because students always need to be aware of whether what they're doing is effective and meets their purposes.

Minilessons. Because efferent listening is so important in school, teachers shouldn't assume that students already know how to listen to oral presentations of information. In addition to helping students with brainstorming ideas, using anticipation guides and graphic organizers, and note taking, teachers also teach minilessons about efferent listening. A list of minilesson topics for efferent listening is presented in the box on page 232, followed by a sample minilesson about getting clues from the speaker.

Assessing Students' Efferent Listening

Teachers often use objective tests to measure students' efferent listening. For example, if teachers have provided information about the causes of the American Revolution or the greenhouse effect, they can check students' understanding of the information and infer whether students listened. However, teachers should assess students' listening more directly. Specifically, they should check how well students understand efferent listening strategies and how they apply them when they're listening. Asking students to reflect on and talk about the strategies they use provides insights into students' thinking in a way that objective tests can't.

CRITICAL LISTENING

Students—even those in the primary grades—need to become critical listeners because they're exposed to persuasion and propaganda all around. Interpreting books and films requires critical thinking and listening. And social studies and science lessons on topics such as the Ku Klux Klan, illegal drugs, gangs, and global warming demand that students listen and think critically. Television commercials are another form of persuasion and source of propaganda, and because many commercials are directed at children, it is essential that they listen critically and learn to judge the advertising claims. For example, do the jogging shoes actually help you run faster? Will the breakfast cereal make you a better football player? Will a particular video game make you more popular?

Persuasion and Propaganda

There are three ways to persuade people. The first is by reason. We seek logical conclusions, whether from absolute facts or from strong possibilities; for example, we can be persuaded to practice more healthful living as the result of medical research. It's necessary, of course, to distinguish between reasonable arguments and illogical appeals. To suggest that diet pills will bring about extraordinary weight loss is illogical.

A second way is an appeal to character. We can be persuaded by what another person recommends if we trust that person. Trust comes from personal knowledge or the reputation of the person who is trying to persuade. We can believe what scientists say about the dangers of nuclear waste, but can we believe what a sports personality says about the taste of a particular brand of coffee?

The third way is by appealing to people's emotions. Emotional appeals can be as strong as intellectual appeals. We have strong feelings and concern for ourselves and other people and animals. Fear, a need for peer acceptance, and a desire for freedom of expression are all potent feelings that influence our opinions and beliefs.

Any of the three types of appeals can be used to try to persuade someone. For example, when a child wishes to convince her parents that her bedtime should be delayed by 30 minutes, she might argue that neighbors allow their children to stay up later—an appeal to character. It's an appeal to reason when the argument focuses on the amount of sleep a 10-year-old needs. And when the child announces that she has the earliest bedtime of anyone in her class and it makes her feel like a baby, the appeal is to emotion. The same three appeals apply to in-school persuasion. To persuade classmates to read a particular book in a book report "commercial," a student might argue that classmates should read the book because it's written by a favorite author (reason); because it's hilarious (emotion); or because it's the most popular book in the seventh grade and everyone else is reading it (character).

It's essential that students become critical consumers of commercials and advertisements because they're bombarded with them (Brownell, 2006; Lutz, 1997). Advertisers use appeals to reason, character, and emotion just as other persuaders

What Students Need to Learn About Listening

Topics

Procedures	*Concepts*	*Strategies and Skills*
Aesthetic Listening Listen to a story read aloud Listen to a poem read aloud Write a response in a reading log Choose favorite quotations from a story	**Aesthetic listening** Difference between aesthetic and efferent listening Concept of story	Activate background knowledge Predict Visualize Make connections
Efferent Listening Take notes Do note taking/note making Use graphic organizers Participate in instructional conversations	**Efferent listening** Organizational patterns of informational texts Features of informational books	Activate background knowledge Set purpose Organize ideas Summarize Monitor understanding Ask questions **Get clues from the speaker**
Critical Listening Analyze propaganda Create advertisements	Critical listening Types of persuasion Propaganda Deceptive language Propaganda devices	Evaluate the message Determine the speaker's purpose Recognize appeals Recognize deceptive language Identify propaganda devices

If you'd like to learn more about teaching listening, visit MyEducationLab. To view sixth graders listening to their teacher read a novel aloud, look in the topic "Listening" and click on the video "Aesthetic Listening;" and to watch sixth graders listen while a classmate reads aloud a composition from the author's chair, go again to the topic "Listening" and click on the video "Efferent Listening."

Minilesson

Mrs. Rodriquez's Students Watch for Clues

1 Introduce the topic

Mrs. Rodriquez explains to her second graders that she often does some special things to get their attention and to tell them what information is most important when she teaches a lesson.

2 Share examples

Mrs. Rodriquez asks her students to watch her carefully as she begins a lesson about the body of an insect as part of a thematic unit on insects. She begins to speak, and she holds up three fingers as she explains that insects have three body parts. Next, she points to the three body parts on a nearby chart and names them, tapping each part with a pointer. Then she writes the names of the body parts on the chalkboard. Afterward, Mrs. Rodriquez asks children to recall what she did during the presentation, and they correctly point out the three clues she used.

3 Provide information

Mrs. Rodriquez explains to children that teachers or other presenters often use clues to help listeners understand what is most important in a lesson. She explains that teachers use a variety of clues and asks her students to look for more clues as she continues the lesson. She demonstrates several more clues, including repeating an important fact and raising her voice for emphasis. Afterward, Mrs. Rodriquez asks the class to identify the clues.

4 Supervise practice

The next day, Mrs. Rodriquez presents a lesson comparing insects and spiders, and she asks children to watch for her clues and to raise their hands to indicate that they noticed them. Afterward, she reviews the clues she used. She repeats this step for several additional lessons about insects.

5 Reflect on learning

Mrs. Rodriquez and her second graders make a list of clues she uses during a lesson, and children draw pictures to illustrate each clue they add to the list. Then they post the list in the classroom.

do to promote products, ideas, and services; however, advertisers may also use propaganda to influence our beliefs and actions. Propaganda suggests something shady or underhanded. Like persuasion, propaganda is designed to influence people's beliefs and actions, but propagandists may use certain techniques to distort, conceal, and exaggerate. Two of these techniques are deceptive language and propaganda devices.

People seeking to influence us often use words that evoke a variety of responses. They claim that something is "improved," "more natural," or "50% better"—loaded words and phrases that are deceptive because they are suggestive. When a product is advertised as 50% better, for example, consumers need to ask, "50% better than what?" Advertisements rarely answer that question.

Doublespeak is another type of deceptive language characterized as evasive, euphemistic, confusing, and self-contradictory. It is language that only pretends to communicate (Lutz, 1997). Two kinds of doublespeak that children can understand are euphemisms and inflated language. Euphemisms are words or phrases (e.g., "passed away") that are used to avoid a harsh or distasteful reality, often out of concern for someone's feelings rather than to deceive. Inflated language includes words intended to make the ordinary seem extraordinary. Thus, car mechanics become "automotive internists," and used cars become "pre-owned" or even "experienced."

Students need to learn that people sometimes use words that only pretend to communicate; sometimes they use words to intentionally misrepresent, as when someone advertises a vinyl wallet as "genuine imitation leather" or a ring with a glass stone as a "faux diamond." When students can interpret deceptive language, they can avoid being deceived.

To sell products, advertisers use propaganda devices, such as testimonials, the bandwagon effect, and rewards. Six devices that students can identify are listed in Figure 7–7. Students can listen to commercials to find examples of each propaganda device and discuss the effect the device has on them. They can also investigate how the same devices vary in commercials directed toward youngsters, teenagers, and adults. For instance, a commercial for a snack food with a sticker or toy in the package will appeal to a youngster, and an advertisement for DVD player offering a factory rebate will appeal to an adult. The same propaganda device—a reward—is used in both ads. Propaganda devices can be used to sell ideas as well as products; public service announcements as well as political advertisements use these devices.

Critical listening strategies The most important strategy for critical listening is evaluating because students need to judge the message (Lundsteen, 1979). As they listen, students consider these questions simultaneously:

- What's the speaker's (or author's) purpose?
- Is there an intellectual appeal? a character appeal? an emotional appeal?
- Are propaganda devices being used?
- Are deceptive words or inflated language used?

As students listen to books read aloud, view commercials and advertisements, and listen to speakers, they ask themselves these questions in order to critically evaluate the message. They also use efferent listening strategies because critical listening is an extension of efferent listening.

FIGURE 7–7

Propaganda Devices

Device	Description
Glittering Generality	Propagandists use generalities such as "environmentally safe" to enhance the quality of a product. Even though the generality is powerful, listeners need to think beyond it to assess the product.
Name Calling	Persuaders try to pin a bad label on someone or something they want listeners to dislike, such as calling a person "unpatriotic." Listeners then consider the effect of the label.
Bandwagon	Advertisers claim that everyone is using their product; for example, "four of five physicians recommend this medicine." Listeners must consider whether everyone really does use this product.
Testimonial	Advertisers associate a product with an athlete or movie star. Listeners must consider whether the person offering the endorsement has the expertise to judge the quality of the product.
Card Stacking	Propagandists often use only items that favor one side of an issue; unfavorable facts are ignored. To be objective, listeners seek information about other viewpoints.
Rewards	Propagandists offer rewards for buying their products— children are lured by toys and adults by discounts or rebates. Listeners need to ask whether the reward makes the product worth buying.

Teaching Critical Listening

The steps in teaching students to be critical listeners are similar to those in teaching aesthetic and efferent listening strategies. In this teaching strategy, students view commercials to examine propaganda devices and persuasive language. Later, they can create their own commercials and advertisements. The steps are shown in the Step by Step feature on page 236.

Students use the same procedures and activities with advertisements they collect from magazines and product packages. Have them collect advertisements and display them on a bulletin board. They examine advertisements and then decide how the writer is trying to persuade them to purchase the product. Students can also compare the amount of space devoted to text and illustrations. Not surprisingly, toy advertisements feature large, colorful pictures and cosmetic advertisements feature pictures of beautiful women, but advertisements for medicines devote more space to text. Students may also point out sports stars and entertainment personalities in many advertisements. Even young children recognize intellectual, character, and emotional appeals in these advertisements. Students apply what they have learned about persuasion by creating advertisements. Figure 7–8 shows the "Wanted" poster a second grader made after reading *Sylvester and the Magic Pebble* (Steig, 2005), the story of a donkey who is lost after magically turning into a stone. The student featured a large picture of the missing donkey with an emotional appeal and a reward offer.

Step by Step

---- Creating Commercials and Advertisements ----

1 **Introduce commercials.** Talk about commercials, and ask students about familiar commercials. Videotape some commercials and share them with your class. Use these questions to probe students' thinking about persuasion and propaganda:

- What is the speaker's purpose?
- What are the speaker's credentials?
- Is there evidence of bias?
- Does the speaker use deceptive language?
- Does the speaker make sweeping generalizations or unsupported inferences?
- Do opinions predominate the talk?
- Does the speaker use any propaganda devices?
- Do you accept the message? (Devine, 1982, pp. 41–42)

2 **Explain deceptive language.** Introduce the propaganda devices, and view the commercials again, looking for examples of each device. Explain deceptive language, and view the commercials a third time to look for examples of doublespeak.

3 **Analyze deceptive language.** Have students work in small groups to critique a commercial as to type of persuasion, propaganda devices, and deceptive language. They might also want to test the claims made in the commercial.

4 **Review concepts.** Review the concepts about persuasion and propaganda introduced in the first three steps. It's often helpful for students to make charts about these concepts.

5 **Provide practice.** Have students work in small groups to critique a new set of videotaped commercials. Ask them to identify persuasion, propaganda devices, and deceptive language in them.

6 **Create commercials.** Have students apply what they have learned by creating their own products and writing and producing their own commercials to advertise them. Possible products include breakfast cereals, toys, beauty and diet products, and sports equipment. They might also create homework and house-sitting services to advertise, or they can choose community or environmental issues to campaign for or against.

Teaching With Trade Books. Many stories and informational books that teachers read aloud encourage critical thinking. Students use a combination of aesthetic and critical listening as they listen to stories such as *Flush* (Hiaasen, 2005) and *The True Story of the 3 Little Pigs!* (Scieszka, 1999). They use critical listening to evaluate the environmental theme and to determine whether the wolf's story is believable. When students listen to informational books such as *Rosa* (2005), in which Nikki Giovanni recounts Rosa Parks's act of civil disobedience, they confront important social issues. Through these activities, students think more deeply about

FIGURE 7–8

A Second Grader's "Wanted" Poster

controversial issues and challenge and expand their own beliefs. A list of recommended books that encourage critical listening is presented in the Booklist on page 238.

Minilessons. Teachers also teach minilessons to introduce, practice, and review procedures, concepts, and strategies and skills related to critical listening. See page 232 for a list of topics for minilessons on critical listening.

Assessing Students' Critical Listening

After teaching about persuasion and propaganda, teachers can assess students' knowledge of critical listening by having them view and critique commercials, advertisements, and other oral presentations. They can note the critical listening procedures, strategies, and skills their students use. A second way to assess students' understanding of critical listening is to have them develop their own commercials and advertisements. Critical listening goes beyond one unit, however, and is something that teachers should return to again and again during the school year.

Booklist

BOOKS THAT ENCOURAGE CRITICAL LISTENING

Avi. (2003). *Nothing but the truth.* New York: Orchard Books. (U)

Babbitt, N. (2002). *Tuck everlasting.* New York: Farrar, Straus & Giroux. (U)

Bunting, E. (1999). *Smoky night.* San Diego: Harcourt Brace. (M)

Cohen, B. (1998). *Molly's pilgrim.* New York: Lothrop, Lee & Shepard. (M)

Cowcher, H. (1990). *Antarctica.* New York: Farrar, Straus & Giroux. (P–M)

Creech, S. (2004). *Heartbeat.* New York: HarperCollins. (M–U)

Gantos, J. (2000). *Joey Pigza loses control.* New York: Farrar, Straus & Giroux. (M–U)

Giovanni, N. (2005). *Rosa.* New York: Henry Holt. (M)

Haddix, M. P. (1998). *Among the hidden.* New York: Aladdin Books. (U)

Hesse, K. (2001). *Witness.* New York: Scholastic. (U)

Hiaasen, C. (2002). *Hoot.* New York: Knopf. (M–U)

Hiaasen, C. (2005). *Flush.* New York: Knopf. (M–U)

Jeffers, S. (2002). *Brother eagle, sister sky.* New York: Dial Books. (M)

Lobel, A. (2004). *Potatoes, potatoes.* New York: Greenwillow. (P–M)

Naylor, P. R. (2000). *Shiloh.* New York: Aladdin Books. (M–U)

Scieszka, J. (1999). *The true story of the 3 little pigs!* New York: Viking. (P–M)

Spinelli, J. (1997). *Wringer.* New York: HarperCollins. (M–U)

Turner, A. (1987). *Nettie's trip south.* New York: Macmillan. (M)

Whelan, G. (2000). *Homeless bird.* New York: HarperCollins. (U)

Woodson, J. (2005). *Show way.* New York: Putnam. (M–U)

P = primary grades (K–2); M = middle grades (3–5); U = upper grades (6–8).

Review

Listening is the most basic and most used of the language arts. Despite its importance, listening instruction is often neglected because teachers assume that students already know how to listen. This chapter focused on four types of listening—discriminative, aesthetic, efferent, and critical—and you read about how to help students become more effective listeners. Here are the key concepts presented in this chapter:

- Students use discriminative listening as they develop phonemic awareness.
- Students listen aesthetically as teachers read stories aloud and while viewing puppet shows, plays, and movie versions of stories.
- Teachers use interactive read-alouds to share stories with students.
- Students are more successful listeners when they're responding to the stories that the teacher reads aloud.
- Students learn strategies to become more effective listeners.
- Students use efferent listening to remember information.
- Students are more effective listeners when they're actively involved in listening.
- Students use critical listening to evaluate a message.
- Students need to learn to listen critically because they are exposed to many types of persuasion.
- Students apply what they learn about persuasion as they create commercials and advertisements.

Professional References

Barrentine, S. J. (1996). Engaging with reading through interactive read-alouds. *The Reading Teacher, 50,* 36–43.

Berthoff, A. E. (1981). *The making of meaning.* Montclair, NJ: Boynton/Cook.

Brownell, J. (2006). *Listening: Attitudes, principles, and skills.* Boston: Allyn & Bacon.

Devine, T. G. (1982). *Listening skills schoolwide: Activities and programs.* Urbana, IL: ERIC Clearinghouse on Reading and Communication Skills and the National Council of Teachers of English.

Dickinson, D. K., & Tabors, P. O. (2001). *Beginning literacy with language.* Baltimore: Brookes.

Fisher, D., Flood, J., Lapp, D., & Frey, N. (2004). Interactive read-alouds: Is there a common set of implementation practices? *The Reading Teacher, 58,* 8–17.

Fox, M. (2001). *Reading magic: Why reading aloud to our children will change their lives forever.* San Diego: Harcourt Brace.

Gibbons, P. (2002). *Scaffolding language, scaffolding learning: Teaching second language learners in the mainstream classroom.* Portsmouth, NH: Heinemann.

Ivey, G., & Broaddus, K. (2001). "Just plain reading": A survey of what makes students want to read in middle school classrooms. *Reading Research Quarterly, 36,* 350–377.

Lundsteen, S. W. (1979). *Listening: Its impact on reading and the other language arts* (Rev. ed.). Urbana, IL: National Council of Teachers of English.

Lutz, W. (1997). *The new doublespeak: Why no one knows what anyone's saying anymore.* New York: HarperCollins.

Martinez, M. G., & Roser, N. L. (1985). Read it again: The value of repeated readings during storytime. *The Reading Teacher, 38,* 782–786.

National Communication Association. (1998). *Competent communicators: K–12 speaking, listening, and media literacy standards and competencies.* Washington, DC: Author.

Opitz, M. F., & Zbaracki, M. D. (2004). *Listen hear! 25 effective comprehension strategies.* Portsmouth, NH: Heinemann.

Readence, J. E., Bean, T. W., & Baldwin, R. S. (2004). *Content area reading: An integrated approach* (8th ed.). Dubuque, IA: Kendall/Hunt.

Rosenblatt, L. (2005). *Making meaning with texts: Selected essays.* Portsmouth, NH: Heinemann.

Rothenberg, C., & Fisher, D. (2007). *Teaching English language learners: A differentiated approach.* Upper Saddle River, NJ: Merrill/Prentice Hall.

Sipe, L. R. (2002). Talking back and taking over: Young children's expressive engagement during storybook read-alouds. *The Reading Teacher, 55,* 476–483.

Trelease, J. (2006). *The read-aloud handbook* (6th ed.). New York: Penguin.

Wolvin, A. D., & Coakley, C. G. (1996). *Listening* (5th ed.). New York: McGraw-Hill.

Yaden, D. B., Jr. (1988). Understanding stories through repeated read-alouds: How many does it take? *The Reading Teacher, 41,* 556–560.

Yopp, H. K., & Yopp, R. H. (2006). *Literature-based reading activities* (4th ed.). Boston: Allyn & Bacon.

Children's Book References

Aldrin, B. (2005). *Reaching for the moon.* New York: HarperCollins.

Barretta, G. (2006). *Now and Ben: The modern inventions of Benjamin Franklin.* New York: Holt.

Galdone, P. (2006). *The Little Red Hen.* New York: Clarion Books.

Giovanni, N. (2005). *Rosa.* New York: Henry Holt.

Hiaasen, C. (2005). *Flush.* New York: Knopf.

McCarthy, M. (2006). *Aliens are coming! The true account of the 1938 War of the Worlds radio broadcast.* New York: Knopf.

Morris, A. (1993). *Bread, bread, bread.* New York: HarperCollins.

Morrison, T. (2006). *Wildfire.* Boston: Houghton Mifflin.

Pinkney, J. (2006). *The little red hen.* New York: Dial Books.

Scieszka, J. (1999). *The true story of the 3 little pigs!* New York: Viking.

Siy, A. (2005). *Mosquito bite.* Watertown, MA: Charlesbridge.

Steig, W. (2005). *Sylvester and the magic pebble.* New York: Simon & Schuster.

Stevens, J., & Crummel, S. S. (1999). *Cook-a-doodle-doo!* San Diego: Harcourt Brace.

chapter eight

Sustaining Talk in the Classroom

In addition to guided reading lessons, the students in Mrs. Zumwalt's third-grade class participate in literature circles each day because she knows that these children need lots of reading practice and opportunities to talk about books. For 30 minutes each day, they read or talk about the easy chapter books they are reading in small groups. Most of her students are English learners who read a year below grade level, so Mrs. Zumwalt works hard to find easy-to-read chapter books that will interest them. The box on page 242 lists 20 of the books that Mrs. Zumwalt has in her classroom.

One small group of children is reading *The Cat's Meow* (Soto, 1997), the story of a white cat named Pip who speaks Spanish to Graciela, the little girl who owns him. Spanish words are included in the text. All but one of the children in this group speak Spanish at home, so they feel very comfortable with the inclusion of the Spanish words.

Yesterday, the five children in the group read the first chapter, and now they're talking about the story. Mrs. Zumwalt joins the group for a few minutes. The discussion focuses on whether the cat can really speak Spanish or whether it's just Graciela's imagination at work.

---

*W*hat can you learn by listening to students talk about a book?

Teachers know that they can learn a great deal through observing students as they work, listening to students participate in discussions, and talking with students during conferences. As you read this vignette about a small group of third graders discussing a book they're reading, notice Armando's role in the discussion and how the children use talk to clarify their understanding. In addition, think about how they talk about their use of reading strategies.

Armando: That girl knows Spanish, so it could be that she is just pretending. She really could be just thinking those Spanish words. And it says that her mom and dad are weird. Maybe she comes from a weird family. That's what I think.

Maricela: I think Pip can speak Spanish, but she will just speak to that girl and no one else.

Marcos: Yeah, I think Pip can talk in Spanish. That would be cool.

Ruben: No, Armando. It's for real, man. The cat—what's his name?

Linda: Pip, and she's a girl, not a boy.

Ruben: Yeah, Pip. I think he, I mean she, can talk. And Linda, how do you know it's a girl cat?

Linda: Look, I'll show you. (She turns to the first page of the first chapter, scanning for a word.) Look, on page 1, here it is. It says "looked at *her* empty bowl." Her. That's how I know.

Mrs. Zumwalt redirects the conversation and asks, "Do you think you'll find out for sure whether Pip can talk by the time you finish reading the book?" The children are sure they will find out. Then she asks them to consider possible story lines: "So, what do you think might happen in the story?"

Linda: I think the story might be like the one about Martha the talking dog that we read last year. Martha got in trouble for talking too much so she stopped talking, but then at the end when some robbers came, she called the police and was a hero.

Mrs. Zumwalt: I know that story! It's called *Martha Speaks,* right? (The children agree.)

Armando: I don't think Pip will talk in front of anyone except for Graciela. Not that Juanita. Pip doesn't

Twenty Easy-to-Read Chapter Books

Bang-Campbell, M. (2002). *Little rat sets sail.* San Diego: Harcourt Brace.

Benchley, P. (1994). *Small wolf.* New York: HarperCollins.

Cazet, D. (2005). *The octopus.* New York: HarperCollins.

Coerr, E. (1993). *Chang's paper pony.* New York: HarperCollins.

Coerr, E. (1999). *Buffalo Bill and the Pony Express.* New York: HarperCollins.

Coerr, E. (1999). *The Josefina story quilt.* New York: HarperCollins.

Cushman, D. (2000). *Inspector Hopper.* New York: HarperCollins.

Dahl, R. (1999). *Esio trot.* New York: Puffin Books.

Danziger, P. (2006). *Amber Brown is not a crayon.* New York: Puffin Books.

Haas, J. (2001). *Runaway radish.* New York: Greenwillow.

Horowitz, R. (2001). *Breakout at the bug lab.* New York: Dial Books.

Laurence, D. (2001). *Captain and matey set sail.* New York: HarperCollins.

Livingstone, S. (2001). *Harley.* New York: North-South Books.

Lottridge, C. B. (2003). *Berta: A remarkable dog.* Toronto: Groundwood Books.

Lowry, L. (2002). *Gooney bird Greene.* Boston: Houghton Mifflin.

McDonald, M. (2002). *Judy Moody.* Cambridge, MA: Candlewick Press.

Rylant, C. (2005). *The high-rise private eyes: The case of the desperate duck.* New York: Greenwillow.

Seuling, B. (2001). *Robert and the great pepperoni.* Chicago: Cricket Books.

Turner, A. (1997). *Dust for dinner.* New York: HarperCollins.

Yee, W. H. (2005). *Upstairs mouse, downstairs mole.* Boston: Houghton Mifflin.

---

want to be sent to be in a circus because she's a freak. She wants to be a normal white cat. I think maybe it will stay her secret.

Ruben: I think people will find out about Pip and she will be famous. Then she'll win a million dollars on *Who Wants to Be a Millionaire?*

After everyone laughs at Ruben's comment, Mrs. Zumwalt asks about Juanita, and the children respond.

Armando: Juanita is the girl that Graciela talks to and tells that Pip can talk Spanish. She doesn't believe her, but she could still gossip about it at school.

Mrs. Zumwalt: Is Juanita a friend of Graciela's?

Linda: I think so.

Maricela: They play together.

Armando: No, I don't think they're friends. They just know each other and maybe they play together, but they are not friends. They don't act like friends.

Maricela: I think Graciela *wants* to be friends. That's what I think.

Mrs. Zumwalt moves the conversation around to Juanita because the children seemed unaware of her when Armando mentioned her and because she will figure prominently in the book. As several of the children suggested, people will find out about Pip the talking cat, and a big problem develops.

The children continue reading and talking about the book as they learn that Graciela's neighbor, Sr. Medina, is the one who taught Pip to speak Spanish. In Chapter 6, they read that Sr. Medina's nosy neighbor has called the television stations and told them about Pip and her special ability. During their discussion, the children talk about the television news crews coming to interview Sr. Medina and Pip. The children are angry that the neighbor called the television stations.

Linda:	It's not fair that that lady across the street was so nosy and she ruined everything. It got so bad that Sr. Medina had to move away.
Maricela:	I like that Graciela sprayed that lady with the hose and she got all wet. And Graciela called her a "sour old snoop." That's funny.
Mrs. Zumwalt:	In the book, it says that Graciela hoped the lady would "shrink into a puddle of nothing like the evil witch in *The Wizard of Oz.*" What does that mean?
Armando:	That's what happened in *The Wizard of Oz.* I saw the movie so I know.
Ruben:	This chapter reminds me of when my neighbor's son got killed. His name was Manuel. He was 16, I think. He got killed by some gang bangers. They were in a car and they came by his house and they shot him. He was in the house and the bullet came in through the window. Then the ambulance came but he was dead. So the police came and they put up this yellow ribbon all around the house. My mom and dad made me stay in the house but I wanted to go outside and watch. Then the television reporters came and it was crowded with people. Just like in this chapter.
Marcos:	Sr. Medina had to move away and he took Pip with him.
Linda:	No, he didn't take Pip. She's Graciela's cat.
Marcos:	Look on page 69. It says, "He moved out last night and took his cat with him."
Linda:	Well, it's not *his* cat.

Mrs. Zumwalt asks the children to predict whether Graciela will get her cat back, and then they read the last chapter of the book and learn that Pip does come back, and now she's black, not white, and she speaks French, not Spanish! They talk about the ending.

Linda:	I'm happy. I knew Pip would come back. I would be so, so, so sad if anyone stole my cat.
Marcos:	I liked this book. It was funny.
Ruben:	I wish it would happen to me.
Maricela:	I would like to be Graciela.
Mrs. Zumwalt:	Why?
Maricela:	Well, her parents are weird; that's for sure. But, she does some interesting things. And I wish I had a cat who could talk to me in Spanish or in English.
Armando:	I liked the Spanish words. I'm going to write a story and put Spanish words in it. Those Spanish words made it fun to read this book.

Mrs. Zumwalt moves from group to group as they discuss the books they're reading. Her focus in these conversations is that children should use talk to deepen their comprehension. She watches to make sure that all children are participating and that the conversation explores important elements of plot, character, and theme. She asks questions to probe their thinking or redirect their attention. She also watches children's growing involvement with the story. Mrs. Zumwalt is pleased that Ruben became more involved with *The Cat's Meow*; after reading the first chapter, he didn't seem interested in the story, but by the end, he was hooked. Mrs. Zumwalt believes that it is the conversation that brings about the change.

---

*N*oted researcher Shirley Brice Heath (1983) explored the value of talk in classrooms and concluded that students' talk is an essential part of language arts and is necessary for academic success. Quiet classrooms were once considered the most conducive to learning, but research now emphasizes that talk is a necessary ingredient for learning. Talk is often thwarted in classrooms because of large class size and the mistaken assumption that silence facilitates learning; instead, teachers must make an extra effort to provide opportunities for students to use talk for both socialization and learning.

As you continue reading, you will learn ways to encourage talk in your classroom. Think about these questions as you read:

- How do students participate in conversations?
- How do students use talk to respond to literature?
- How do students use talk as a learning tool?
- What types of dramatic activities are appropriate for students?

CONVERSATIONS

Students get together to respond to literature they're reading, talk about each other's writing, work on projects, and share information they've learned. The most important feature of talk activities is that they promote higher-level thinking. Teachers take students' ideas seriously, and students are validated as thinkers (Nystrand, Gamoran, & Heck, 1993). As they converse with classmates, students use talk for different purposes: to control classmates' behavior, maintain social relationships, convey information, and share personal experiences and opinions.

Small-Group Conversations

Students learn and refine their strategies for conversing with classmates as they participate in small-group conversations (Kaufman, 2000). They learn how to begin conversations, take turns, keep the conversation moving forward, support comments and questions that classmates make, deal with conflicts, and bring the conversation to a close. And, they learn how powerful talk is in making meaning and creating knowledge. The characteristics of small-group conversations are listed in Figure 8–1.

To begin the conversation, students gather in groups at tables or other areas in the classroom, bringing with them any necessary materials. One student in each group begins the conversation with a question or comment; classmates then take turns making

FIGURE 8–1

Characteristics of Small-Group Conversations

- Each group has three to six members. These groups may be permanent, or they may be established for specific activities. It's important that group members be a cohesive group and courteous to and supportive of each other. Students in established groups often choose names for their groups.
- The purpose of the small-group conversation or work session is to develop interpretations and create knowledge.
- Students' talk is meaningful, functional, and genuine. Students use talk to solve problems and discover answers to authentic questions—questions that require interpretation and critical thinking.
- The teacher clearly defines the goal of the group work and outlines the activities to be completed. Activities require cooperation and collaboration and could not be done as effectively through independent work.
- Group members have assigned jobs. Sometimes students keep the same jobs over a period of time, and at other times, specific jobs are identified for a particular purpose.
- Students use strategies to begin the conversation, keep it moving forward and on task, and end it.
- Students feel ownership of and responsibility for the activities they are involved in and the projects they create.

comments and asking questions and support the other group members as they elaborate on and expand their comments. The tone is exploratory, and throughout the conversation, the group is progressing toward a common goal. The goal may be deepening students' understanding of a book they have read, responding to a question the teacher has asked, or creating a project. From time to time, the conversation slows down and there may be a few minutes of silence. Then a group member asks a question or makes a comment that sends the conversation in a new direction.

Students try to support one another in groups, and two of the most important ways they do this are by calling each other by name and maintaining eye contact. They also cultivate a climate of trust in the group by expressing agreement, sharing feelings, voicing approval, and referring to comments that group members made earlier. Conflict is inevitable, but students need to learn how to deal with it so that it doesn't get out of control. They learn to accept that there will be differing viewpoints and to make compromises. Cintorino (1993) reported that her eighth graders used humor to defuse disagreements in small-group conversations.

At the end of a conversation, students reach consensus and conclude that they have finished sharing ideas, explored all dimensions of a question, or completed a project. Sometimes they produce a product during the conversation; the product may be a brainstormed list, a chart, or something more elaborate, such as a set of puppets. Group members are responsible for collecting and storing materials they have used and for reporting on the group's work.

Students participate in small-group conversations as part of all four patterns of practice, as shown in the box on page 246. Teachers play an important role in making the conversations successful, beginning with creating a community of learners in the classroom so that students understand that they are responsible group members

How Small-Group Conversations Fit Into the Four Patterns of Practice

Literature Focus Units

Students often participate in small-group conversations as they talk about the book they're reading. They also work in small groups as they create projects during the applying stage.

Literature Circles

Literature circles are essentially small-group conversations. Students work in small groups as they read and respond to a book.

Reading and Writing Workshop

Students don't usually participate in small-group conversations during reading workshop because they are reading different books, but they do meet in small groups to share their rough drafts during writing workshop.

Thematic Units

Students often get into small groups to read an informational book or content-area textbook chapter and to work on projects. They also participate in small-group conversations to talk about their reading.

(Kaufman, 2000). Teachers create a climate of trust by demonstrating to students that they trust them and their ability to learn. Similarly, students learn to socialize with classmates and to respect one another as they work together in small groups.

Grand Conversations

To dig deeper into a story and deepen their comprehension, students talk about stories they are reading in literature focus units and literature circles; these conversations are often called *grand conversations* (Peterson & Eeds, 1990). They're different from traditional discussions because students take responsibility for their own learning as they voice their opinions and support their views with examples from the story. They talk about what puzzles them, what they find interesting, their personal connections to the story, and connections they see between this story and others they have read. Students also encourage their classmates to contribute to the conversation. Even though teachers often sit in on conversations as a participant, not as a judge, the talk is primarily among the students.

Teachers often use a combination of small-group and whole-class groupings for grand conversations, but they can be held with the whole class or in small groups. When students meet in small groups, they have more opportunities to talk, and when they meet as a class, there is a feeling of community. Young children usually meet as a class, but students participating in literature circles meet in small groups because they are reading different books. When the teacher is reading aloud a novel, students often meet first in small groups and then come together as a class to respond to the book.

Grand conversations have two parts. The first part is open-ended: Students talk about their reactions to the book, and their comments determine the direction of the conversation. Teachers do participate, however, and share their responses, ask questions, and provide information. In the second part, the teacher focuses students' attention on one or two aspects of the book that they did not talk about in the first part of the conversation. The steps are shown in the Step by Step feature below.

After the grand conversation, students often write in their reading logs, or write again if they wrote before the grand conversation. Then they continue reading the book if they have read only part of it. Both participating in grand conversations and writing entries in reading logs help students think about and respond to what they have read.

From their observational study of fifth and sixth graders conducting grand conversations, Eeds and Wells (1989) found that students extend their individual interpretations of books through talk and even create a better understanding of them. Students talk about their understanding of the story and can change their opinions after listening to classmates' alternative views. They share personal stories related to their reading in

Step by Step

------- Grand Conversations -------

1 **Read the book.**   Students read a picture book or a chapter in a novel or listen to the teacher read a story aloud.

2 **Prepare for the conversation.**   Students think about the story by drawing pictures or writing in reading logs. This step is especially important when students don't talk much because with this preparation, they are more likely to have ideas to share.

3 **Have small-group conversations.**   Students form small groups to talk about the story before getting together as a class. This step is optional and is generally used when students don't talk much.

4 **Begin the class conversation.**   Students form a circle for the class conversation so that everyone can see each other. Teachers begin by asking, "Who would like to begin?" or "What are you thinking about?" One student makes a comment, and classmates take turns talking about the idea that the first student introduced.

5 **Continue the class conversation.**   A student introduces a new idea, and classmates talk about it, making connections, providing details, and reading excerpts from the story to make a point. Students limit their comments to the idea being discussed, and after they finish discussing this idea, a new one is introduced. To ensure that everyone participates, teachers often ask students not to make more than three comments until everyone has spoken at least once.

6 **Ask questions.**   Teachers ask questions to direct students to an aspect of the story that has been missed; for example, they might focus on an element of story structure or the author's craft. Or, they may ask students to compare the books to the film version of the story, or to other books by the same author.

7 **Conclude the conversation.**   After all of the big ideas have been explored, teachers end the conversation by summarizing and drawing conclusions about the story.

8 **Reflect on the conversation.**   Students often write in reading logs to reflect on the ideas discussed in the grand conversation.

poignant ways that trigger other students to identify with them. Students also gain insights about how authors use the elements of story structure to develop their message.

Martinez and Roser (1995) researched the content of students' grand conversations, and they found that students often talk about story events and characters or explore the themes of the story but delve less often into the author's craft to explore the way he or she structured the book, the arrangement of text and illustrations on the page, or the author's use of figurative or repetitive language. The researchers called these three conversation directions *experience, message,* and *object.* They suggest that stories help to shape students' talk about books and that some books lend themselves to conversation about message and others to talk about experience or object. Stories with dramatic plots or stories that present a problem to which students can relate, such as *Chrysanthemum* (Henkes, 1991) and *The Tale of Despereaux* (DiCamillo, 2003), focus the conversation on the book as experience. Multilayered stories or books in which main characters deal with dilemmas, such as *Smoky Night* (Bunting, 1999) and *Princess Academy* (Hale, 2005), focus the conversation on the message. Books with distinctive structures or language features, such as *Flotsam* (Wiesner, 2006) and *Witness* (Hesse, 2001), focus the conversation on the object.

Drawing students' attention to the "object" is important because they apply what they've learned about the author's craft when they write their own stories. Students who know more about leads, pacing, figurative language, point of view, imagery, surprise endings, voice, and flashbacks write better stories than those who don't. One way teachers can help students examine the author's craft is through the questions they ask during grand conversations.

An additional benefit of grand conversations is that when students talk in depth about stories, their writing shows the same level of inferential comprehension

Gail E. Tompkins

Grand Conversation

These sixth graders are participating in a literature circle, and they meet with their teacher twice a week to talk about the novel they are reading. Their discussion is a grand conversation because it's authentic; the students share ideas, make connections, ask questions, offer predictions, and talk about the author's use of story elements and literary devices. Their teacher also participates in the grand conversation, modeling how to talk about literature, scaffolding students' comments, and asking questions to help them think more critically about the novel.

(Sorenson, 1993). Students seem to be more successful in grand conversations if they have written in reading logs first, and they are more successful in writing entries if they've talked about the story first.

Instructional Conversations

Instructional conversations provide opportunities for students to talk about the main ideas they are learning in thematic units; through these conversations, students enhance their academic language proficiency (Goldenberg, 1992/1993). As in grand conversations, students are active participants, sharing ideas and building on classmates' ideas with their own comments. Teachers are participants, too, making comments much as the students do, but they also clarify misconceptions, ask questions, and provide instruction.

Instructional conversations deepen students' content-area knowledge and develop their academic language proficiency in these ways:

- Students deepen their knowledge about the topic.
- Students use technical and precise vocabulary and more complex sentence structures to express the ideas being discussed.
- Students learn to provide support for the ideas they present with information found in informational books, content-area textbooks, and other resources in the classroom.
- Students ask inference and critical-level questions, those with more than one answer.
- Students participate actively and make comments that build on and expand classmates' comments.

Students use talk in instructional conversations to accomplish goals, learn information, and work out problems in thematic units. As they talk, students pose hypotheses, ask questions, provide information, and clarify ideas; recall ideas presented earlier; make personal, world, and literary connections; make inferences; and evaluate the text and the information presented in it (Roser & Keehn, 2002). In contrast to grand conversations about stories in which students use primarily aesthetic talk to create and deepen their interpretations, here students use primarily efferent talk to create knowledge and understand relationships among the big ideas they're learning.

Researchers have compared the effectiveness of small-group conversations with other instructional approaches and have found that students' learning is enhanced when they relate what they are learning to their own experiences—especially when they do so in their own words (Wittrock & Alesandrini, 1990). Similarly, Pressley (1992) reported that students' learning was promoted when they had opportunities to elaborate ideas through talk. The steps in an instructional conversation are explained in the Step by Step feature on page 250.

Instructional conversations are useful for helping students grapple with important ideas they are learning in social studies, science, and other content areas. When students are discussing literature, they use generally grand conversations, which facilitate response to literature. An exception is when students focus on analyzing plot, characters, theme, and other elements of story structure; then they are thinking efferently and are participating in an instructional conversation, not a grand conversation.

--- Instructional Conversations ---

1 Choose a focus. Teachers choose a focus that's related to the goals of a thematic unit.

2 Present information. Teachers present information or read an informational book or an excerpt from a content-area textbook in preparation for the discussion.

3 Prepare for the instructional conversation. Sometimes teachers have students complete a graphic organizer together as a class or in small groups before beginning the conversation.

4 Have small-group conversations. Sometimes students respond to a question in small groups before beginning the whole-class conversation.

5 Begin the conversation. Teachers begin by asking a question related to the focus they identified in the first step. Students take turns sharing information, asking questions, and making connections. Teachers often write students' comments on chart paper in a list or create a graphic organizer.

6 Continue the conversation. Teachers continue the conversations by asking additional questions, and students take turns responding to the questions and reexploring the big ideas.

7 Conclude the conversation. Teachers bring the conversation to an end by reviewing the big ideas that were discussed using the charts they've developed.

8 Reflect on the conversation. Students record the ideas discussed during the conversation by writing and drawing in learning logs.

TALK AS A LEARNING TOOL

Asking Questions

Asking and answering questions are common types of talk in classrooms. Researchers have found that teachers ask as many as 50,000 questions a year, whereas students ask as few as 10 (Watson & Young, 2003). The most common questions are literal questions, those that require simple recall, even though the most useful questions require students to analyze, interpret, evaluate, and offer opinions.

After reading *Amber Brown Is Not a Crayon* (Danziger, 2006), the story of two best friends and what happens as one of them moves to another state, a group of third graders in Mrs. Zumwalt's class wrote their own questions. The group spent a few minutes considering the questions and deciding which ones to actually use. Their questions included the following:

Why do you think Amber and Justin are best friends?
Do you think Mr. Cohn is sort of like Ms. Frizzle [in the Magic School Bus series]?
Do you think Mr. Cohn is a good teacher?

Meeting the Needs of English Learners

How Do English Learners Use Talk as a Learning Tool?

Talk facilitates learning for all students, but it's especially important for English learners who are struggling to learn English at the same time they're grappling with grade-level content-area learning (Gibbons, 2002; Rothenberg & Fisher, 2007). In addition, school is the only place where some English learners have opportunities to hear and speak English. How does talk facilitate learning? As they talk, students focus on the big ideas, questioning, clarifying, and elaborating their thinking. They organize these big ideas, relate them to their background knowledge, and practice using newly introduced vocabulary words. English learners benefit from daily opportunities to talk in large groups, in small groups, and one-on-one with a classmate or the teacher (Fay & Whaley, 2004).

English learners use talk as a learning tool in all four patterns of practice. In thematic unit, for example, students use talk as they are involved in meaningful oral, written, and visual activities and broaden their knowledge of the world. Teachers support English learners in these ways during thematic units and the other patterns of practice:

- Involve students in hands-on, active learning opportunities
- Have students work with classmates in small groups
- Link lessons to students' prior experiences, or build needed background knowledge
- Clarify meaning with objects, photos, and demonstrations
- Teach technical vocabulary related to the topic
- Use graphic organizers to emphasize the relationships among the big ideas
- Have students talk, read, create visuals, and write about the topic
- Teach students to recognize when they're confused and how to take action to solve the problem
- Demonstrate how to ask and answer higher-level questions
- Teach students how to listen to informational books and content-area textbooks
- Involve students in making small-group projects to demonstrate their learning

With these instructional supports in place, students are better able to learn age-appropriate content knowledge along with their classmates.

Did you know from the beginning that Justin was going to move away?
How can best friends fight and still be best friends?
Is Justin happy or sad about moving to Alabama?
Why is Amber so mean to Justin?
What do you think will happen to the friendship after Justin moves away?
Can they still be best friends after Justin moves away?

These questions involve higher-level thinking and delve into the "best friends" theme of the book. They require students to think deeply about the story and even to go back and reread portions to support their answers. If students are not going this deeply into a story, teachers should pose questions like these.

Questions can be grouped into three levels: literal, inferential, and critical. Literal or "on the page" questions have a single factual answer and can usually be answered with a few words or "yes" or "no." When the questions refer to a story or other book that students are reading, the answers are directly stated in the text. The second level of questions is inferential or "between the lines." To answer these questions, students synthesize information and form interpretations using both their background knowledge and clues in the text. The answers are implicitly stated in the text. The third, most complex level of questioning is critical or "beyond the page." These questions are open-ended; they require students to go beyond the text and think creatively and abstractly about global ideas, issues, and concerns. At this level, students apply information, make connections, evaluate and value the text, and express opinions. The LA Essentials box below reviews the three levels of questioning.

Teachers use these three levels of questions for different purposes. They use literal questions to check that students have basic information and understand the meaning of words. Literal questions are easy to ask and to answer, but, because they are the most frequently asked questions, teachers need to be careful not to use too many of them.

LEVELS OF QUESTIONING

Level	Category	Description
3	Critical or "Beyond the Page" Questions	Critical questions go beyond the text and focus on global issues, ideas, and problems. Often there are no correct answers. To answer these questions, students think creatively; make personal connections, world connections, and literary connections; evaluate the text; and express opinions.
2	Inferential or "Between the Lines" Questions	Inferential questions require analysis and interpretation. The answers are implicitly stated in the text. To answer these questions, students use a combination of background knowledge and clues in the text.
1	Literal or "On the Page" Questions	Literal questions are factual. The answers to these questions are stated explicitly in the text. Students answer these questions with "yes" or "no" or with a few words taken directly from the text.

To help students think more deeply and to challenge their thinking, teachers use inferential and critical questions. When they are talking about literature, teachers ask inferential questions to probe students' understanding of a story and make interpretations, and when they ask students to analyze the ideas, make comparisons, and summarize information. Teachers ask critical questions to challenge students' thinking to go beyond the story to make connections, evaluate the story, reflect on the overall theme, and delve into the author's craft. They ask critical questions during thematic units for similar purposes: to consider different viewpoints, examine issues, and draw conclusions.

Teachers commonly use the IRF (Initiate-Response-Feedback) cycle when they ask questions:

- *Initiate:* The teacher asks a question.
- *Response:* The student answers the question.
- *Feedback:* The teacher responds to the student's answer.

This cycle is teacher centered because teachers do most of the talking and control the flow of the conversation. It's the primary way teachers involve students in discussion; in fact, researchers report that more than half the instructional talk in classrooms occurs in IRF cycles (Watson & Young, 2003). Teachers often use this cycle for assessment, to check on students' attention and understanding rather than to promote learning. Even though the IRF cycle is common, it's less conducive to learning than other procedures that involve students in asking questions and doing more of the talk.

K-W-L Charts

Teachers use K-W-L charts (Ogle, 1989) to activate and build students' background knowledge during thematic units. The letters *K, W,* and *L* stand for "What I/We Know," "What I/We Want to Learn" or "What I/We Wonder," and "What I/We Learned." Students share what they know and ask questions about a topic, and teachers write students' comments and questions on a chart. Through this activity, students become curious and more engaged in the learning process, and teachers have opportunities to introduce complex ideas and technical vocabulary in a nonthreatening way.

Teachers divide a large chart into three columns and label them "K—What We Know," "W—What We wonder," and "L—What We learned." At the beginning of a unit, teachers introduce the chart and complete the first two columns as students think about the topic, share information, and ask questions. Then at the end of the unit, teachers complete the third column of the chart to summarize and review students' learning. The Step by Step box on page 258 lists the steps in the procedure.

Teachers direct, scribe, and monitor the development of the K-W-L chart, but it's the students' talk that makes this such a powerful activity. Students use talk to explore and question ideas as they complete the K and W columns and to share new knowledge as they complete the L column.

K-W-L charts are very adaptable; they can be used in several ways. Teachers can make class K-W-L charts with their students, students can work in small groups to make charts, and students can make individual charts in journals or on drawing paper. Class charts work best for younger children or for older students who have not made K-W-L charts before. Middle- and upper-grade students often work with classmates to make group charts on chart paper, or they can make individual K-W-L charts. Figure 8–2 shows a K-W-L chart that a second-grade class developed as they studied penguins, and

FIGURE 8–2

A Second-Grade Class's K-W-L Chart on Penguins

K What We Know	W What We Wonder	L What We Learned
Penguins are black and white.	Are penguins fish or birds?	Some penguins can swim real fast—25 miles an hour.
Penguins are good swimmers and divers.	Do penguins live in California?	They have feathers on their bodies.
We saw penguins at the zoo.	What do penguin babies look like?	Penguins live at the South Pole. It is called Antarctica.
They eat fish.	Do polar bears hunt and kill penguins?	They don't get cold because they have fat and feathers on their bodies to keep warm.
Penguins like to play on ice and snow.	Do penguins have enemies?	Penguins have flippers that look like little wings but they can't fly.
Penguins look funny when they walk on little feet.	Do penguins ever get cold?	The emperor penguin is the largest penguin. It's almost as big as us.
	How long do penguins live?	Babies hatch from eggs. They're chicks.
	Can you have a penguin for a pet?	The fathers care for eggs until they hatch.
		The penguin's enemies are leopard seals, killer whales, sharks, and people.

Figure 8–3 shows an individual K-W-L chart on spiders. The individual chart was made by folding a sheet of paper in half vertically. Next, the student cut three flaps and labeled them "K," "W," and "L," as shown in the top drawing in the figure. Then the student flipped up the flaps to write on the chart, as shown in the lower drawing.

Minilessons

So that children can grow in their knowledge of and use of academic language, Courtney Cazden (2001) challenges teachers to make changes in classroom language use and to incorporate more academic language. Finding ways to help all children develop academic language has become more urgent because of the enactment of the No Child Left Behind Act of 2001. It's essential that teachers set high standards for themselves and for their students. The activities they organize should challenge students to use higher-order thinking as they listen, talk, read, and write. Whether students use higher-order thinking is dependent on the level of questions teachers ask and on the types of activities in which students are involved. Teachers should incorporate academic language into their instruction, even with young children and English learners. Too often, in an attempt to be kind, they simplify the words and sentence structures they use. What happens,

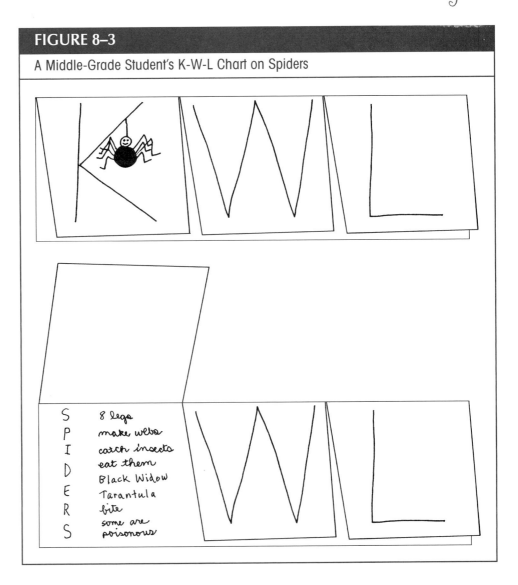

FIGURE 8–3

A Middle-Grade Student's K-W-L Chart on Spiders

however, is that students don't have the opportunity to learn the technical vocabulary and sophisticated sentence patterns that are part of academic language.

Teachers teach minilessons about academic language and a variety of talk-related procedures, concepts, strategies, and skills. A list of minilesson topics related to talk is presented on page 256, along with a sample minilesson on how to sustain a conversation.

Oral Reports

Learning how to prepare and present an oral report is an important efferent talk activity for middle- and upper-grade students. However, students are often assigned an oral report without any guidance about how to prepare and give one. Too many students simply copy the report verbatim from an encyclopedia and then read it aloud. The result is that students learn to fear speaking in front of a group rather than gain confidence in their oral language abilities.

What Students Need to Learn About Talk

Topics

Procedures	Concepts	Strategies and Skills
Begin a conversation	Academic language	Refer to previous comments
Take turns	Higher-level questions	Extend a comment
Sustain a conversation	Roles of speakers and listeners	Call classmates by name
	Small-group conversations	Look at classmates while speaking
End a conversation		Vary tone of voice
Tell a story	**Grand conversations**	Vary pace of speech
Make K-W-L charts		Ask questions
Present an oral report	**Instructional conversations**	Express a viewpoint
Conduct an interview		Maintain the audience's interest
Participate in a debate	Levels of questions	Present main ideas coherently
Create a puppet	Interviews	
Perform a puppet show	Oral presentations	
Write a script	Debates	

I invite you to learn more about sustaining talk in the classroom by visiting MyEducationLab. To see sixth graders participate in a grand conversation, go to the topic "Talking" and click on the video "Grand Conversations," and to watch fourth graders participate in an instructional conversation, go to the topic "Talking" and click on the video "Instructional Conversations."

Minilesson

Ms. Shapiro Teaches Her Second Graders About Sustaining Conversations

1 Introduce the topic

Ms. Shapiro explains to her second graders that she wants them to think about how they behave during grand conversations. She asks them to observe a grand conversation that she has planned with four students in the class. "We will be doing some good things to help the conversation and some bad things that hurt the conversation," she says. "Watch carefully so you will notice them."

2 Share examples

Ms. Shapiro and four chidlren have a grand conversation about a familiar story, *Hey, Al* (Yorinks, 1986). She chose a familiar story so that students could focus on the conversation itself and not get caught up in the story. The students participating in the conversation take turns making comments, but they don't expand on each other's comments, nor do they call each other by name or look at classmates as they are talking. Also, some children are looking away from the group as though they are not listening.

3 Provide information

Ms. Shapiro's students are eager to identify the strengths and weaknesses of the grand conversation they have observed. The "good things" were that "everyone talked about the story and nothing else" and "everybody was nice." The

"bad things" included that "some people didn't pay attention and look at the person talking," "some people didn't say other people's names," and "some people just said things but they didn't go next to what other people said." Ms. Shapiro agrees that the children have identified the problems, and she explains that she's seen some of these same problems in their conversations. Together they make a chart of "Good Things to Do in a Grand Conversation."

4 Supervise practice

Ms. Shapiro's students participate in grand conversations as part of literature circles and after she reads a book aloud to the class. She explains that she will observe their grand conversations to make sure they are doing all the good things they listed on their chart. For the next 2 weeks, Ms. Shapiro briefly reviews the chart with them before each grand conversation and takes a few minutes afterward to talk about the changes in behavior she has observed.

5 Reflect on learning

After 2 weeks of practice, Ms. Shapiro brings the children together to talk about their grand conversations, and she asks the second graders which of the good things from the chart they're doing better now. The children mention various points and conclude that their grand conversations have improved.

1 **Create a large chart.** Teachers post a large sheet of paper on the classroom wall, divide it into three columns, and label the columns *K* (or "What We *K*now"), *W* (or "*W*hat We *W*onder"), and *L* (or "What We *L*earned").

2 **Complete the K column.** At the beginning of the thematic unit, teachers have students brainstorm what they know about the topic and then record their responses in this column. If students suggest any incorrect information, teachers help them reword the information as a question and add it to the W column.

3 **Complete the W column.** Teachers write the questions that students ask in the W column. They continue to add questions to the W column throughout the unit.

4 **Complete the L column.** At the end of the unit, students reflect on what they've learned, and then teachers record this information in the L column. Teachers don't expect students to answer each of the questions posted in the W column; instead, students focus on the most important and interesting information they've learned.

Students prepare and give reports about topics they are studying in social studies and science. Giving a report orally helps students to learn about topics in specific content areas as well as to develop their speaking abilities. Students need more than just an assignment to prepare a report for presentation on a particular date; they need to learn how to prepare and present an oral report. The steps in giving reports are listed in the Step by Step feature on the next page.

Students are usually the audience for the oral reports, and members of the audience have responsibilities: They should be attentive, listen to the speaker, ask questions, and applaud the speaker. Sometimes they also provide feedback to speakers about their presentations using a checklist or rubric, but at other times, students self-assess the process they used to prepare and give their presentations. The Weaving Assessment Into Practice feature on page 260 presents a self-assessment rubric developed by a fourth-grade class; it lists questions about the students' preparation for the presentation and about the presentation itself.

Interviews

Almost all students see interviews on television news programs and are familiar with the interviewing techniques reporters use. Interviewing is an exciting language arts activity that helps students refine questioning skills and use oral and written language for authentic purposes. Interviewing is an important language tool that can be integrated effectively in literature focus units and thematic units. As part of a unit on school, for example, a class of first graders invited the local high school principal to visit their class to be interviewed. The principal, who had been blinded several years earlier, brought his guide dog with him. The children asked him questions about how visually impaired people manage everyday tasks as well as how he performed his job as a principal. They also asked questions about his guide dog. After the interview, students drew pictures and wrote summaries of the interview. A first grader's report is shown in Figure 8–4.

One way to introduce interviewing is to watch interviews conducted on a television newscast and discuss what the purpose of the interview is, what a reporter does before and after an interview, and what types of questions are asked. Interviewers use a variety of questions, some to elicit facts and others to probe for feelings and opinions, but all questions are open-ended. Rarely do interviewers ask questions that require only a *yes* or *no* answer.

Interviewing involves far more than simply conducting the actual interview. Students prepare for the interview by generating a list of questions and follow up after the interview by using what they have learned in some way. For example, they might write a biography about the person who was interviewed or use the information in a report they're writing.

Hot Seat. Children assume the persona of a character from a story or biography they're reading and sit in the "hot seat" to be interviewed by classmates. It's called the "hot seat" because they're expected to respond to their classmates' questions. Students aren't intimidated by the activity; in fact, in most classrooms, it's very popular. Students are usually eager for their turn to sit in the hot seat. They answer the

Oral Reports

Step by Step

1 Choose a topic. Students begin by brainstorming a list of possible topics related to the thematic unit, and then each student chooses a topic for the report. Next, students inventory, or think over, what they know about their topic and decide what they need to learn about it. Teachers often help students identify several key questions to focus the report.

2 Gather and organize information. Students gather information to answer the key questions using a variety of resources, including informational books, content-area textbooks, the Internet, and encyclopedias. In addition, students can view videotapes and interview people in the community who have special expertise on the topic.

3 Develop the report. Students review the information they have gathered and decide how best to present it so that the report will be both interesting and well organized. Students can transfer the notes they want to use for their reports from the cluster or data chart onto note cards. Only key words—not sentences or paragraphs— should be written on the cards.

4 Create visuals. Students develop visuals, such as charts, diagrams, maps, pictures, models, and time lines. Visuals provide a crutch for the speaker and add an element of interest for the listeners.

5 Rehearse the presentation. Students choose an interesting fact to begin their presentation, review key points, and read over their note cards; however, they don't read the report verbatim from the note cards. Then they rehearse their presentations.

6 Give the presentation. Before the presentations begin, teachers teach minilessons on the characteristics of successful presentations. For instance, speakers should talk loudly enough for all to hear, look at the audience, keep to the key points, refer to note cards for important facts, and use the visuals they have prepared.

FIGURE 8–4

A First Grader's Interview Report

Mr. Kirtley came down. We asked him questions. He answered them. He is blind. His dog's name is Milo.

Weaving Assessment Into Practice

A SELF-ASSESSMENT RUBRIC FOR ORAL REPORTS

Name _____ Date _____

Topic _____

	no	1	2	3	4	yes
1. Did you collect enough information on a cluster or data chart?	—	—	—	—	—	—
2. Did you make a useful chart or visual to show during your presentation?	—	—	—	—	—	—
3. Did you rehearse your presentation?	—	—	—	—	—	—
4. Did you speak loudly so everyone could hear?	—	—	—	—	—	—
5. Did you look at the audience?	—	—	—	—	—	—
6. Did you use your visuals?	—	—	—	—	—	—
7. Did you make your main points?	—	—	—	—	—	—
8. How pleased were you with your report?	—	—	—	—	—	—
9. How did the audience respond?	—	—	—	—	—	—

questions they're asked from the viewpoint of the character; through this activity, they deepen their comprehension as well as their classmates'. The steps in the procedure are listed in the box below. Students often wear a costume they've created when they assume the character's persona and share information about the character with classmates. They also collect objects and make artifacts to share.

Debates

Students participate in debates when they are excited about an issue and when most of the students have taken positions on one side of the issue or the other. Students can debate issues related to social studies and science topics, community issues, and current events. Middle- and upper-grade students can also debate topics related to books they are reading. For example, after reading *Tuck Everlasting* (Babbitt, 2002), they might debate whether people should live forever. Books that spark debates are listed in the Booklist on page 262. Students have strong feelings about the issues raised in many of these books, and debating provides a forum for thinking about important issues.

As they participate in debates, students learn how to use oral language to persuade their classmates. They must be able to articulate their viewpoints clearly, use information and emotional appeals to support their viewpoints, and think on their feet to respond to the opposing team's questions. The steps in a debate are listed in the Step by Step feature on page 262.

Students who are not participating in the debate often assess their classmates' performance in the debate and determine the winning team. The students can develop an assessment form and award points to each team based on the effectiveness of the team's arguments and manner of presentation.

Step by Step

---- Hot Seat ----

1 Learn about the character. Students prepare for the hot seat activity by reading a story or a biography to learn about the character they will impersonate.

2 Create a costume. Students design a costume appropriate for the character. In addition, they often collect objects or create artifacts to use in their presentation.

3 Prepare opening remarks. Students think about the most important things they'd like to share about the character and plan what they will say at the beginning of the activity.

4 Introduce the character. The student sits in front of classmates in a chair designated as the "hot seat," tells a little about the character he or she is role-playing using a first-person viewpoint (e.g., "I was the first person to step onto the moon's surface"), and shares artifacts.

5 Ask questions. Classmates ask thoughtful, higher-level questions to learn more about the character, and the student remains in the role to answer them.

6 Summarize the ideas. The student doing the role play selects a classmate to summarize the important ideas that have been presented and adds any big ideas that the classmate doesn't mention.

Booklist

BOOKS THAT SPARK DEBATES

Avi. (2003). *Nothing but the truth.* New York: Orchard Books. (U)

Babbitt, N. (2002). *Tuck everlasting.* New York: Farrar, Straus & Giroux. (U)

Bunting, E. (1997). *A day's work.* New York: Clarion Books. (M)

Bunting, E. (1999). *Smoky night.* San Diego: Harcourt Brace. (M)

Clements, A. (1998). *Frindle.* New York: Aladdin Books. (M–U)

Curtis, C. P. (2000). *The Watsons go to Birmingham— 1963.* New York: Delacorte. (M–U)

Fox, P. (2003). *One-eyed cat.* New York: Simon & Schuster. (M–U)

Gantos, J. (2000). *Joey Pigza loses control.* New York: Farrar, Straus & Giroux. (U)

Haddix, M. P. (1998). *Among the hidden.* New York: Aladdin Books. (U)

Lowry, L. (2005). *Number the stars.* New York: Yearling. (M–U)

Lowry, L. (2006). *The giver.* New York: Delacorte. (U)

Naylor, P. R. (2000). *Shiloh.* New York: Aladdin Books. (M)

Ryan, P. M. (1998). *Riding Freedom.* New York: Scholastic. (M–U)

Sachar, L. (1998). *Holes.* New York: Farrar, Straus & Giroux. (U)

Staples, S. F. (1989). *Shabanu: Daughter of the wind.* New York: Knopf. (U)

Steig, W. (1990). *Doctor DeSoto.* New York: Farrar, Straus & Giroux. (M)

P = primary grades (K–2); M = middle grades (3–5); U = upper grades (6–8).

Debates

Step by Step

1 Identify a topic. The class decides on an issue, clarifies it, and identifies positions that support or oppose the issue.

2 Prepare for the debate. Students form supporting and opposing teams. Then students in each team prepare for the debate by deciding on their arguments and how they will respond to the other team's arguments.

3 Conduct the debate. A podium is set up in the front of the classroom, and the teacher initiates the debate by asking a student from the supporting side to state that position on the issue. After this opening statement, a student on the opposing side makes a statement. From this point, students take turns going to the podium and speaking in support of or in opposition to the issue. Students who have just made a statement are often asked a question before a student for the other side makes a return statement.

4 Conclude the debate. After students on both sides have presented their viewpoints, one member from each team makes a final statement to sum up that team's position.

THE POWER OF DRAMA

Drama provides a medium for students to use language—both verbal and nonverbal— in a meaningful context. Drama is not only a powerful form of communication but also a valuable way of knowing. When students participate in dramatic activities, they interact with classmates, share experiences, and explore their own understanding.

According to Dorothy Heathcote, a highly acclaimed British drama teacher, drama "cracks the code" so that the message can be understood (Wagner, 1999). Drama has this power for three reasons: It involves a combination of logical and creative thinking, it requires active experience, and it integrates the language arts. Research confirms that drama has a positive effect on both students' oral language development and their literacy learning (Wagner, 2003). Too often, however, teachers ignore drama because it seems unimportant compared to reading and writing.

Dramatic activities range from quick improvisations that are student centered to polished theatrical performances that are audience centered. Instead of encouraging students to be spontaneous and use drama to explore ideas, theatrical performances require that students memorize lines and rehearse their presentations. Our focus here is on student-centered dramatizations that are used to enhance learning.

Improvisation

Students step into someone else's shoes and view the world from that perspective as they reenact stories. These activities are usually quick and informal because the emphasis is on learning, not performance. Students assume the role of a character and then role-play as the teacher narrates or guides the dramatization. Students usually don't wear costumes, and there's little or no rehearsal; it's the spontaneity that makes improvisation so effective.

Students often reenact stories during literature focus units. Sometimes they dramatize episodes while they are reading to examine a character, understand the sequence of events, or clarify a misunderstanding. As students dramatize an episode, teachers often direct the class's attention by asking questions, such as "What's (*character's name*) thinking?" and "Why is (*character's name*) making him do this?" For example, while seventh graders read *Holes* (Sachar, 2002), the story of a boy named Stanley Yelnats who is sent to a juvenile detention center for a crime he didn't commit, they often reenact Stanley digging a hole on his first day at Camp Green Lake to analyze the effect the experience had on him. Later, as they continue reading, they focus on pivotal points in the story: when Stanley finds the small gold lipstick tube while he's digging a hole, when he claims he stole a bag of sunflower seeds and is taken to the Warden's office, when he escapes from the camp and meets up with another escaped boy nicknamed "Zero," and finally, when the two boys return to camp and find the "treasure" suitcase. Through these improvisations, students understand individual episodes better as well as the overall structure of the story.

At other times, students, especially young children, dramatize an entire story after they finish reading it or listening to the teacher read it aloud. Teachers often break stories into three parts—beginning, middle, and end—to organize the dramatization and provide more opportunities for children to participate in the activity. Through improvisation, children review and sequence the events in a story and develop their concept of story. Folktales, such as *One Grain of Rice: A Mathematical Folktale* (Demi, 1997) and *The Empty Pot* (Demi, 1996), are easy for younger children to dramatize.

Process Drama

British educator Dorothy Heathcote has developed an imaginative and spontaneous dramatic activity called *process drama* to help students explore stories they're reading, social studies topics, and current events (Tierney & Readence, 2005; Wagner,

1999). Teachers create an unscripted dramatic context about a story episode or a historical event, and the students in the class assume roles to experience and reflect on the episode or event (Schneider & Jackson, 2000).

For example, if the class is studying the Underground Railroad, the teacher might create a dramatic context on the moment when the escaped slaves reach the Ohio River. They'll be safe once they cross the river, but they're not safe yet. It's important that the teacher focuses on a particular critical moment—one that is tension filled or that creates challenges. Most of the students would play the role of escaped slaves, but others would be conductors guiding the slaves to safety or the Quakers who risked their lives to hide the slaves. Either the teacher or other students would be bounty hunters or plantation owners trying to capture the escaped slaves.

With everyone participating in a role, the class dramatizes the event, examining the critical moment from their viewpoint. The teacher moves the action forward by recounting the event and asking questions. After reliving the experience, students reflect on it by writing a simulated journal entry or a simulated letter; they write in the persona of their character, sharing information about the experience and reflecting on it. Afterward, students step out of their roles to discuss the experience and share what they have learned. The steps in process drama are summarized in the Step by Step box below.

Process drama goes beyond improvisation: Not only do the students reenact the episode or event, but they explore the topic from the viewpoint of their character as they respond to the teacher's questions and when they write simulated journal entries or letters. The discussion that follows the reenactment also deepens students' understanding. Heathcote believes that process drama is a valuable activity because it stimulates students' curiosity and makes them want to read books and learn more about historical or current events.

Step by Step ----- Process Drama -----

1 Set the purpose. Teachers identify the purpose for the dramatic activity.

2 Create the dramatic context. Teachers explain the dramatic context for the activity, and everyone assumes a role. Sometimes teachers share artifacts they have collected that relate to the characters and the event.

3 Dramatize the event. Students participate in the dramatization, staying in the role of the character they have chosen and building on the experience. Teachers create tension or present a challenge during the dramatization.

4 Ask questions. Teachers ask questions or they invite students to ask questions about the dramatic context, and then students respond to them, usually from the viewpoint of their characters.

5 Prompt reflection. Students write simulated journal entries or letters in the persona of their characters. They include details and insights they've gained through the dramatization.

6 Discuss the activity. Teachers and students talk about the dramatization, reflecting on the experience and sharing their writing to gain new insights about the event.

Playing With Puppets

Students become characters from their favorite stories when they put puppets on their hands. A second grader pulls a green sock on one hand and a brown sock on the other, and with these simple puppets that have buttons sewn on for eyes, the characters of Frog and Toad from Arnold Lobel's award-winning books *Frog and Toad Are Friends* (1979) and *Frog and Toad Together* (1999) come to life. The child talks in the voices of the two characters and uses the puppets to retell events from the stories. Even though many adults feel self-conscious with puppets, children don't.

Students can create puppet shows with commercially manufactured puppets, or they can construct their own. When students create their own puppets, they are limited only by their imaginations, their ability to construct things, and the materials at hand. Simple puppets provide students with the opportunity to develop both creative and dramatic ability. The simpler the puppet, the more is left to the imagination of the audience and the puppeteer. Six kinds of hand and finger puppets that students can make are shown in Figure 8–5.

After students have made their puppets, they can create and perform puppet shows almost anywhere; they don't even need a script or a stage. Several students can sit together on the floor holding their puppets and invent a story that they tell to other classmates who sit nearby, listening intently. Or, students can make a stage from an empty appliance packing crate and climb inside to present their puppet show. What matters is that students can use their puppets to share a story with an appreciative audience. Simple puppets provide children with the opportunity to develop both creative and dramatic ability.

Theatrical Productions

Scripts are a unique written language form that students need opportunities to explore. Scriptwriting often grows out of informal dramatic activities. Soon students recognize the need to write notes when they prepare for plays, puppet shows, readers theatre, and other dramatic productions. This need provides the impetus for introducing students to the unique dramatic conventions and for encouraging them to write scripts to present as theatrical productions.

Scriptwriting. Once students want to write scripts, they'll recognize the need to add the structures unique to dramatic writing to their repertoire of written language conventions. Students begin by examining scripts. It's especially effective to have them compare narrative and script versions of the same story; for example, Richard George has adapted two of Roald Dahl's fantastic stories, *Charlie and the Chocolate Factory* (2004) and *James and the Giant Peach* (2007), into scripts. Then students discuss their observations and compile a list of the unique characteristics of scripts. An upper-grade class compiled the list of unique dramatic conventions presented in Figure 8–6.

The next step is to have students apply what they have learned about scripts by writing a class collaboration script. The whole class develops a script by adapting a familiar story. As the script is being written, the teacher refers to the chart of dramatic conventions and asks students to check that they are using these conventions. Collaborative writing affords unique teaching opportunities and needed practice for students before they must write individually. After the script is completed, students produce it as a puppet show or play.

Once students are aware of the dramatic conventions and have participated in writing a class collaboration script, they can write scripts individually or in small

FIGURE 8–5

Types of Puppets

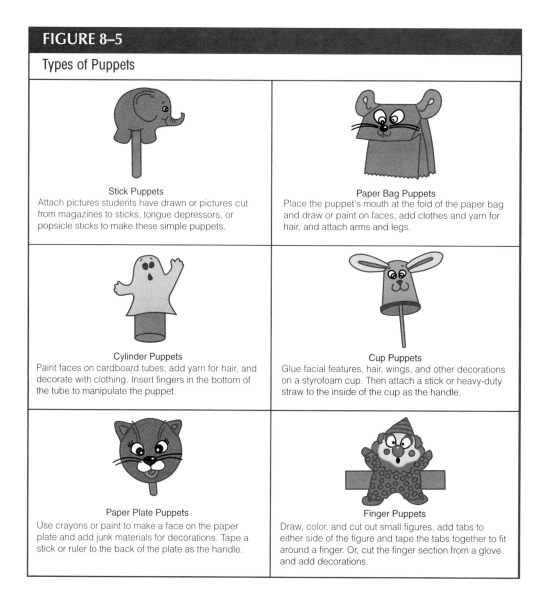

Stick Puppets
Attach pictures students have drawn or pictures cut from magazines to sticks, tongue depressors, or popsicle sticks to make these simple puppets.

Paper Bag Puppets
Place the puppet's mouth at the fold of the paper bag and draw or paint on faces, add clothes and yarn for hair, and attach arms and legs.

Cylinder Puppets
Paint faces on cardboard tubes, add yarn for hair, and decorate with clothing. Insert fingers in the bottom of the tube to manipulate the puppet.

Cup Puppets
Glue facial features, hair, wings, and other decorations on a styrofoam cup. Then attach a stick or heavy-duty straw to the inside of the cup as the handle.

Paper Plate Puppets
Use crayons or paint to make a face on the paper plate and add junk materials for decorations. Tape a stick or ruler to the back of the plate as the handle.

Finger Puppets
Draw, color, and cut out small figures, add tabs to either side of the figure and tape the tabs together to fit around a finger. Or, cut the finger section from a glove and add decorations.

groups. Students often adapt familiar stories for their first scripts; later, they will want to create original scripts. An excerpt from "The Lonely Troll," a script written by a small group of sixth graders, appears in Figure 8–7 as an example of the type of scripts older students can compose. Although most of the scripts they write are narrative, students also create biographical scripts about famous people or informational scripts about science or social studies topics.

Producing Video Scripts. Students use a similar approach in writing scripts that will be videotaped, but they must now consider the visual component of the film as well as the written script. They often compose their scripts on storyboards, which focus their attention on the camera's view and how the story they are creating will be filmed (Cox, 1985). Storyboards—sheets of paper divided into three sections—are used to sketch in scenes. Students place a series of three or four large squares in a row down the center of the paper, with space for dialogue and narration on the left and shooting directions

FIGURE 8–6

An Upper-Grade-Class List of Dramatic Conventions

Everything You Ever Wanted to Know About Scripts

1. Scripts are divided into acts and scenes.
2. Scripts have four parts:
   a. a list of characters (or cast)
   b. the setting at the beginning of each act or scene
   c. stage directions written in parentheses
   d. dialogue
3. The dialogue carries the action.
4. Descriptions and other information are set apart in the setting or in stage directions.
5. Stage directions give actors important information about how to act and how to feel.
6. The dialogue is written like this:
   Character's Name: Dialogue
7. Sometimes a narrator is used to quickly fill in parts of the story.

FIGURE 8–7

An Excerpt From a Script Written by Upper-Grade Students

The Lonely Troll

NARRATOR: Once upon a time, in a far, far away land, there was a troll named Pippin who lived all alone in his little corner of the woods. The troll hated all the creatures of the woods and was very lonely because he didn't have anyone to talk to since he scared everyone away. One day, a dwarf named Sam wandered into Pippin's yard and . . .

PIPPIN: Grrr. What are you doing here?

SAM: Ahhhhh! A troll! Please don't eat me!

PIPPIN: Why shouldn't I?

SAM: (Begging) Look, I'm all skin and bones. I won't make a good meal.

PIPPIN: You look fat enough for me. (Turns to audience) Do you think I should eat him? (Sam jumps off stage and hides in the audience.)

PIPPIN: Where did he go? (Pippin jumps off stage and looks for Sam. When he finds Sam, he takes him back on stage, laughing; then he ties Sam up.) Ha, ha, ha. Boy, that sure did tire me out. (Yawn) I'll take a nap. Then I'll eat him later. (Pippin falls asleep. Lights dim. Sam escapes and runs behind a tree. Lights return, and Pippin wakens.)

PIPPIN: (To audience) Where's my breakfast? (Sam peeps out from behind a tree and cautions the audience to be quiet.) Huh? Did someone say he was behind that tree? (Points to tree. Pippin walks around. Sam kicks him in the rear. Pippin falls and is knocked out.)

SAM: I must get out of here, and warn the queen about this short, small, mean, ugly troll. (Sam leaves. Curtains close.)

NARRATOR: So Sam went to tell Queen Muffy about the troll. Meanwhile, in the forest, Pippin awakens, and decides to set a trap for Sam. (Open curtains to forest scene, showing Pippin making a box trap.)

on the right. Cox compares storyboards to road maps because they provide directions for filming the script. The scene renderings and the shooting directions help students tie the dialogue to the visual images that will appear on the videotape.

The script can be produced several ways—as a live-action play, as a puppet show, or through animation. After writing the script on the storyboards or transferring a previously written script to storyboards, students collect or construct the props they will need to produce the script. They design a backdrop and collect clothes for costumes. Teachers should encourage students to keep the production details simple. Students should also print the title and credits on large posters to appear at the beginning of the film. After several rehearsals, the students film the script using a video camera.

Review

Talk is a valuable instructional tool. Children talk about stories they're reading and information they're learning in thematic units. They learn and use academic language as they participate in conversations, give oral reports, and participate in other types of talk activities. Here are the key points in this chapter:

- Academic language, the language of schooling, is more cognitively demanding and decontextualized than social language.
- Questions can be classified as literal, inferential, or critical.
- Students use K-W-L charts to talk about what they are learning in a thematic unit.
- Students participate in small-group conversations as part of all four instructional patterns.
- Students use talk to respond to stories in grand conversations.
- Students participate in instructional conversations to discuss what they're learning in thematic units.
- Students share what they've learned and develop presentational skills when they give oral reports.
- Students develop their abilities to persuade when they participate in debates.
- Students use improvisation and process drama as a tool for learning.
- Students integrate the language arts when they write scripts and present them as plays or videos.

Professional References

Cazden, C. D. (2001). *Classroom discourse: The language of teaching and learning* (2nd ed.). Portsmouth, NH: Heinemann.

Cintorino, M. A. (1993). Getting together, getting along, getting to the business of teaching and learning. *English Journal, 82,* 23–32.

Cox, C. (1985). Filmmaking as a composing process. *Language Arts, 62,* 60–69.

Eeds, M., & Wells, D. (1989). Grand conversations: An exploration of meaning construction in literature study groups. *Research in the Teaching of English, 23,* 4–29.

Fay, K., & Whaley, S. (2004). *Becoming one community: Reading and writing with English language learners.* Portland, ME: Stenhouse.

Gibbons, P. (2002). *Scaffolding language, scaffolding learning: Teaching second language learners in the mainstream classroom.* Portsmouth, NH: Heinemann.

Goldenberg, C. (1992/1993). Instructional conversations: Promoting comprehension through discussion. *The Reading Teacher, 46,* 316–326.

Heath, S. B. (1983). Research currents: A lot of talk about nothing. *Language Arts, 60,* 999–1007.

Kaufman, D. (2000). *Conferences and conversations: Listening to the literate classroom.* Portsmouth, NH: Heinemann.

Martinez, M. G., & Roser, N. L. (1995). The books make a difference in story talk. In N. L. Roser & M. G. Martinez (Eds.), *Book talk and beyond: Children and teachers respond to literature* (pp. 32–41). Newark, DE: International Reading Association.

Nystrand, M., Gamoran, A., & Heck, M. J. (1993). Using small groups for response to and thinking about literature. *English Journal, 82,* 14–22.

Ogle, D. M. (1989). The know, want to know, learn strategy. In K. D. Muth (Ed.), *Children's comprehension of text: Research into practice* (pp. 205–223). Newark, DE: International Reading Association.

Peterson, R., & Eeds, M. (1990). *Grand conversations: Literature groups in action.* New York: Scholastic.

Pressley, M. (1992). Encouraging mindful use of prior knowledge: Attempting to construct explanatory answers facilitates learning. *Educational Psychologist, 27,* 91–109.

Roser, N. L., & Keehn, S. (2002). Fostering thought, talk, and inquiry: Linking literature and social studies. *The Reading Teacher, 55,* 416–426.

Rothenberg, C., & Fisher, D. (2007). *Teaching English learners: A differentiated approach.* Upper Saddle River, NJ: Merrill/Prentice Hall.

Schneider, J. J., & Jackson, S. A. W. (2000). Process drama: A special space and place for writing. *The Reading Teacher, 54,* 38–51.

Sorenson, M. (1993). Teach each other: Connecting talking and writing. *English Journal, 82,* 42–47.

Tierney, R. J., & Readence, J. E. (2005). *Reading strategies and practices: A compendium* (6th ed.). Boston: Allyn & Bacon.

Wagner, B. J. (1999). *Dorothy Heathcote: Drama as a learning medium* (Rev. ed.). Portsmouth, NH: Heinemann.

Wagner, B. J. (2003). Imaginative expression. In J. Flood, D. Lapp, J. R. Squire, & J. M. Jensen (Eds.), *Handbook of research on teaching the English language arts* (2nd ed., pp. 1008–1025). Mahwah, NJ: Erlbaum.

Watson, K., & Young, B. (2003). Discourse for learning in the classroom. In S. Murphy, & C. Dudley-Marling (Eds.), *Literacy through language arts: Teaching and learning in context* (pp. 39–49). Urbana, IL: National Council of Teachers of English.

Wittrock, M. C., & Alesandrini, K. (1990). Generation of summaries and analogies and analytic and holistic abilities. *American Research Journal, 27,* 489–502.

Children's Book References

Babbitt, N. (2002). *Tuck everlasting.* New York: Farrar, Straus & Giroux.

Bunting, E. (1999). *Smoky night.* San Diego: Harcourt Brace.

Danziger, P. (2006). *Amber Brown is not a crayon.* New York: Puffin Books.

Dahl, R. (2004). *Charlie and the chocolate factory.* New York: Knopf.

Dahl, R. (2007). *James and the giant peach.* New York: Puffin Books.

Demi. (1996). *The empty pot.* New York: Henry Holt.

Demi. (1997). *One grain of rice: A mathematical folktale.* New York: Scholastic.

DiCamillo, K. (2003). *The tale of Despereaux.* Cambridge, MA: Candlewick Press.

Hale, S. (2005). *Princess academy.* New York: Bloomsbury.

Henkes, K. (1991). *Chrysanthemum.* New York: Greenwillow.

Hesse, K. (2001). *Witness.* New York: Scholastic.

Lobel, A. (1979). *Frog and Toad are friends.* New York: HarperCollins.

Lobel, A. (1999). *Frog and Toad together.* New York: Harper-Collins.

Meddaugh, S. (1995). *Martha speaks.* Boston: Houghton Mifflin.

Sachar, L. (2002). *Holes.* Austin, TX: Holt, Rinehart & Winston.

Soto, G. (1997). *The cat's meow.* New York: Scholastic.

Wiesner, D. (2006). *Flotsam.* New York: Clarion Books.

Yorinks, A. (1986). *Hey, Al.* New York: Farrar, Straus & Giroux.

chapter nine

Reading and Writing Stories

Mrs. Ochs teaches a literature focus unit on *Number the Stars* (Lowry, 2005), a Newbery award–winning story of two girls, one Christian and one Jewish, set in Denmark during World War II. In her unit, she wants to help her fifth-grade students use their knowledge of genre and story structure to deepen their comprehension of the story. She rereads the story, analyzes the elements of story structure in the book, and considers how she wants to teach the unit. She makes the chart shown on page 272.

To begin the unit, Mrs. Ochs asks about friendship: "Would you help your friend if he or she needed help?" The students talk about friendship and what it means to them. They agree that they would help their friends in any way they could—helping them get medical treatment if they were ill, and sharing their lunch if they were hungry, for example. One student volunteers that he is sure that his mom would let his friend's family stay at his house if the friend's house burned down. Then Mrs. Ochs asks, "What if your friend asked you to hold something for him or her, something so dangerous that 60 years ago you could be imprisoned or killed for having it?" Many say they would, but doubt they would ever be called to do that. Then she shows them a broken Star of David necklace, similar to the one on the cover of *Number the Stars,* and one student says, "You're talking about the Nazis and the Jews in World War II."

*H*ow can teachers facilitate students' comprehension of stories?

Teachers include activities at each stage of the reading process in literature focus units to ensure that everyone comprehends what they're reading. This attention to comprehension is essential because when students don't understand what they are reading, the experience has been wasted. As you read this vignette, notice how Mrs. Ochs involves her fifth graders in language arts activities to deepen their understanding of World War II and facilitate their comprehension of *Number the Stars*.

The prereading stage continues for 2 more days as students share what they know about the war, and Mrs. Ochs presents information, reads several picture-book stories about the war, and shows a video.

Mrs. Ochs reads the first chapter of *Number the Stars* aloud to students as they follow along in individual copies of the book. She almost always starts a book this way because she wants to get all students off to a good start and because so many concepts and key vocabulary words are introduced in the beginning of a book. After the first chapter, students continue reading the second chapter. Most of the students read independently, but some read with buddies, and Mrs. Ochs continues reading with a group of the six lowest readers.

Then Mrs. Ochs brings the class together for a grand conversation. The students make connections between the information they have learned about World War II and the story events. Mrs. Ochs reads aloud *The Yellow Star: The Legend of King Christian X of Denmark* (Deedy, 2000), a picture-book story about the Danish king who defies the Nazis, because the king is the focus of the second chapter. The students predict that the Nazis will take Ellen and her family to a concentration camp even though Annemarie and her family try to hide them. After the grand conversation, the students write in reading logs. For this entry, Mrs. Ochs asks students to write predictions about what will happen in the story based on what they know about World War II and what they read in the first two chapters.

Mrs. Ochs continues having the students read and respond to the chapters. Some students read independently, but many of them form reading groups so that they can read and talk about the story as they are reading. Mrs. Ochs continues reading with the lowest readers. The whole class comes together after reading each day to talk about the story in a grand conversation. Afterward, they write in journals.

During the grand conversations, Mrs. Ochs probes students' understanding of the story and asks them to think about the role in the story of plot, characters, setting, and other elements of story structure. Mrs. Ochs has taught the students about the elements,

	Mrs. Ochs's Story Analysis	
Element	**Story Analysis**	**Teaching Ideas**
Plot	The beginning is before Ellen goes into hiding; the middle is while Ellen is hiding; and the end is after Ellen and her family leave for the safety of Sweden. The problem is saving Ellen's life.	Build background knowledge about World War II, the Nazis, Jews and the holocaust, and Resistance fighters before reading. There are many details, so it is important to focus on the problem and how to solve it.
Characters	Annemarie and Ellen are the main characters, and through their actions and beliefs, readers learn that these two girls are much more alike than different. They're both courageous, one because she has to be, the other because she chooses to be.	Even though one girl is Christian and one is Jewish, the girls are more alike than they are different. Use a Venn diagram to emphasize this point. Students might make open-mind portraits from one girl's viewpoint.
Setting	The story is set in Denmark during World War II. The setting is integral to the plot and based on actual events, including fishermen ferrying Jews to safety in Sweden.	Use maps of Europe to locate the setting of the story. Students can draw maps and mark story locations, and they can also mark the spread of the German (and Japanese) forces during the war on a world map.
Point of View	The story is limited omniscient. It is told from the third-person viewpoint, and readers know only what Annemarie is thinking.	Have students retell important events from one of the girls' perspectives or from the parents' or the Nazis' viewpoints.
Theme	This story deals with courage and bravery: the Jews, the fishermen, the Resistance fighters, King Christian X and Danes who wore six-pointed, yellow stars on their clothes, and Annemarie and her family. One theme is that people choose to be courageous when they see others mistreated.	Ask students to focus on the theme as they talk in grand conversations and collect favorite quotes from the story. Students might also read about other people who have been courageous to examine the qualities of courage.

so they are able to apply their knowledge to the story they are reading. One day, she asks about the conflict situation in the story. At first the students say that the conflict is between people—Nazis and Danes—but as they continue talking, they realize that the conflict is not between individual people, but within society.

Another day, Mrs. Ochs talks about the setting. She asks if this story could have happened in the United States. At first the students say no, because the Nazis never invaded the United States, and they use maps to make their point. But as they continue to talk, students broaden their discussion to the persecution of minorities and conclude that persecution can happen anywhere. They cite two examples—the mistreatment of Native Americans and internment of Japanese Americans during World War II.

During the grand conversation after students finish reading *Number the Stars,* Mrs. Ochs asks about the theme. "Did Lois Lowry have a message in her book? What do you think about the theme?" Several students comment that the theme was that the Nazis were bad people. Others said "innocent people get killed in wars" and "peace is better than war." To move the students forward in their thinking, Mrs. Ochs suggests that one theme is about courage or being brave. She reads two sentences from the book: "That's all that *brave* means—not thinking about the dangers. Just thinking about what you must do" (p. 123). The students agree that both girls and their families were brave. Mrs. Ochs asks students to think back through the story and help her brainstorm a list of all the times they were brave. They brainstormed more than 30 instances of bravery!

Mrs. Ochs and her students continue their discussion about the theme for several more days. Finally, she asks them, "Do you think you're brave? Would you be brave if you were Annemarie or Ellen?" They talk about war and having to be brave in a war. "What about Ellen?" Mrs. Ochs asks. "Did she *have* to be brave?" The students agree that she did. "But what about Annemarie? Couldn't she and her family have stayed safely in Copenhagen?" The students are surprised at first by the question, but through their talk, they realize that Annemarie, her family, and the other Resistance fighters had chosen to be brave.

As the students read *Number the Stars,* Mrs. Ochs also involves them in several exploring-stage activities focusing on the story structure. They mark areas of Nazi and Japanese occupation on world maps and draw maps of Denmark. To compare Annemarie and Ellen, they make Venn diagrams and conclude that the girls are more alike than they are different; one student's Venn diagram is shown here. They also make open-mind portraits of one of the girls, showing what the girl is thinking at several pivotal points in the story. The cover and one page from one student's open-mind portrait of Ellen are shown on page 274.

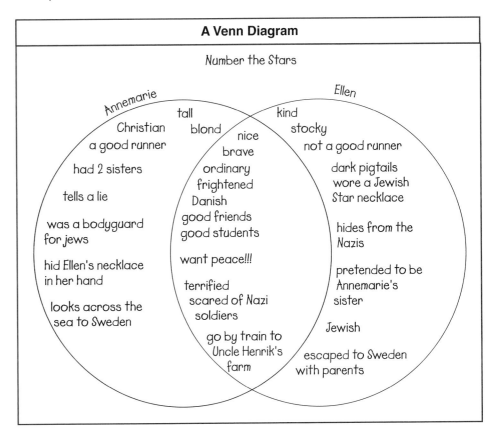

A Venn Diagram

Number the Stars

Annemarie — Ellen

tall, blond, nice, brave, ordinary, frightened, Danish, good friends, good students, want peace!!!, terrified, scared of Nazi soldiers, go by train to Uncle Henrik's farm

Annemarie: Christian, a good runner, had 2 sisters, tells a lie, was a bodyguard for jews, hid Ellen's necklace in her hand, looks across the sea to Sweden

Ellen: kind, stocky, not a good runner, dark pigtails, wore a Jewish Star necklace, hides from the Nazis, pretended to be Annemarie's sister, Jewish, escaped to Sweden with parents

The students plan an applying-stage activity after the great-grandfather of one of the students comes for a visit. This student brings his great-grandfather to school to talk about his remembrances of World War II, and then the students decide to each interview a great-grandparent or an elderly neighbor who was alive during the war. They develop this set of interview questions:

- ♦ What did you do during the war?
- ▣ How old were you?
- ♦ Were you on the home front or the war front?
- ▣ Did you know about the Holocaust then?
- ♦ What do you remember most from World War II?

Then each student conducts an interview and writes an essay about the person's wartime experiences using the writing process. They word-process their essays so that they have a professional look. Here is one student's essay:

> My great-grandfather Arnold Ott was in college at the time the war started. All of a sudden after Pearl Harbor was attacked, all his classmates started to join the army. He did also and became an engineer that worked on B-24 and B-25 bombers. The military kept sending him to different schools so he would be able to fix all the bombers. He never had to fight because of that. He earned some medals, but he said the real ones were only given to those who fought. He said that he was glad that he did not fight because he had friends that never came back.

Then Mrs. Ochs duplicates the essays and binds them into books. She also makes extra copies for the interviewees. The students are so excited about the people they interviewed and the essays they wrote that they decide to have a party. They invite the interviewees and introduce them to their classmates, and they ask the interviewees to autograph the essays they've written about them.

---

*S*tories give meaning to the human experience, and they're a powerful way of knowing and learning. Preschoolers listen to family members tell and read stories aloud, and they have developed an understanding or concept about stories by the time they come to school. Students refine this knowledge as they read and write stories. Many educators, including Jerome Bruner (1986), recommend using stories as a way into literacy.

Students write stories about events in their lives, such as a birthday party, a fishing trip, or a car accident; retell familiar stories, including "Gingerbread Man"; and write sequels for favorite stories. The stories that students write reflect what they've read. De Ford (1981) and Eckhoff (1983) found that when students read stories in traditional basal reading textbooks, they write stories that reflect the short, choppy linguistic style of the textbooks, but when students read trade-book stories, their writing reflects the more sophisticated language structures and literary style of the trade books. Dressel (1990) also found that the quality of fifth graders' writing was dependent on the quality of the stories they read or listened to someone read aloud, regardless of their reading levels.

As you read this chapter, think about these questions:

- How do students develop a concept of story?
- What kinds of reading activities are available for students?
- What kinds of writing activities are available for students?
- How do students read and write stories as part of the four instructional patterns?

CHILDREN'S CONCEPT OF STORY

Researchers have documented that children's concept of story begins in the preschool years (Applebee, 1978). Children acquire this concept of story gradually, by listening to stories read to them, by reading stories themselves, and by telling and writing stories. Not surprisingly, older children have a better understanding of story structure than do younger children. Similarly, the stories older children tell and write are increasingly more complex; the plot structures are more tightly organized, and the characters are more fully developed. Yet, Applebee found that by the time children who have been read to begin kindergarten, they have already developed a basic concept of what a story is, and these expectations guide them in responding to stories and telling their own stories. He found, for example, that kindergartners could use three story markers: "Once upon a time . . . " to begin a story; the past tense in telling a story; and formal endings such as "The End" or " . . . and they lived happily ever after."

Meeting the Needs of English Learners

How Do Teachers Scaffold English Learners' Knowledge of Stories?

When English learners understand about how stories are structured, their comprehension improves, and they're better able to write well-crafted, entertaining stories. Three ways that teachers help English learners learn about stories are through providing opportunities for students to do extensive reading, teaching them about the elements of story structure, and nurturing their responses to literature.

Extensive Reading

All students need daily opportunities to enjoy good literature. Teachers regularly read stories to students using interactive read-aloud procedures, and students read stories themselves as they participate in guided reading, literature circles, and reading workshop. As they listen and read, students expand their background knowledge, build their vocabularies, and become more interested in literature. It's essential that teachers put together a large collection of multicultural books at a variety of reading levels that their students will find interesting. Students need to know how to select books at their reading levels; if older students read at lower levels, then books at those levels need to be age-appropriate.

Elements of Story Structure

To deepen their understanding of stories, English learners need to learn about the elements of story structure (Peregoy & Boyle, 2005). They will acquire some basic understanding about the structure of stories through reading, but they also need direct instruction about the story elements. In addition to minilessons, English learners benefit from activities that include nonverbal components. Graphic organizers, such as diagrams of the beginning, middle, and end of a story or an open-mind portrait, help students visually represent the structure of a story. Dramatic activities are also useful: To examine the plot of story, students can reenact beginning, middle, and end events; to explore a character, they can participate in a hot seat activity; and to understand the importance of setting, they can draw a setting map.

Response to Literature

English learners negotiate meaning through social interaction, just like their classmates do (Samway & McKeon, 1999). As they share their own reactions to a story and listen to their classmates' ideas about plot, characters, and setting, they deepen their comprehension. It's important that English learners know how to talk about the stories they're reading and that they're able to apply what they've learned about story structure through conversation. They need to learn how to reflect on stories they're reading, write in reading logs, and participate in grand conversations in small, comfortable groups with their classmates.

Because stories are often at the center of the language arts program, it's crucial that English learners develop their knowledge of stories so that they can read and write them more successfully.

Students' concept of story plays an important role in their comprehension of the stories they read, and it is just as important in their writing (Golden, Meiners, Lewis, 1992; Rumelhart, 1975). Story meaning is dynamic, growing continuously in readers' minds, and as they respond to and explore stories they are reading and writing, students learn about elements of story structure.

Elements of Story Structure

Stories have unique structural elements that distinguish them from other forms of literature. In fact, the structure of stories is quite complex—plot, characters, setting, and other elements interact to produce a story. Authors manipulate the elements to make their stories complex and interesting. The five most important elements of story structure are *plot, characters, setting, point of view,* and *theme.* In the following sections, you'll read about each element and how students examine the element using familiar and award-winning trade books.

Plot. The sequence of events involving characters in conflict situations is the *plot.* The plot is based on the goals of one or more characters and the processes they go through to attain these goals (Lukens, 2006). The main characters want to achieve a goal, and other characters are introduced to oppose the main characters or prevent them from being successful. The story events are put in motion by characters as they attempt to overcome conflict, reach their goals, and solve their problems.

The most basic aspect of plot is the division of the main events of a story into three parts—beginning, middle, and end. Upper-grade students may substitute the terms *introduction, development* or *complication,* and *resolution.* In *The Tale of Peter Rabbit* (Potter, 2002), for instance, one can easily pick out the three story parts: As the story begins, Mrs. Rabbit sends her children out to play after warning them not to go into Mr. McGregor's garden; in the middle, Peter goes to Mr. McGregor's garden and is almost caught; then Peter finds his way out of the garden and gets home safely—the end of the story. Students can cluster the beginning-middle-end of a story using words or pictures, as the cluster for *The Tale of Peter Rabbit* in Figure 9–1 shows.

Specific information is included in each story part. In the beginning, the author introduces the characters, describes the setting, and presents a problem. Together, the characters, setting, and events develop the plot and sustain the theme throughout the story. In the middle, the author adds to events presented in the beginning, with each event preparing readers for what comes next. Conflict heightens as the characters face roadblocks that keep them from solving their problems. Seeing how the characters tackle these problems adds suspense to keep readers interested. In the end, the author reconciles all that has happened in the story, and readers learn whether the characters' struggles are successful. Recommended stories exemplifying plot and other elements of story structure are presented in the Booklist on page 279.

The plot is developed through the problem that's introduced in the beginning of a story, expanded in the middle, and finally resolved at the end. Plot development involves four components:

- **A Problem.** A problem is presented at the beginning of a story.
- **Roadblocks.** In the middle of the story, characters face roadblocks in attempting to solve the problem.

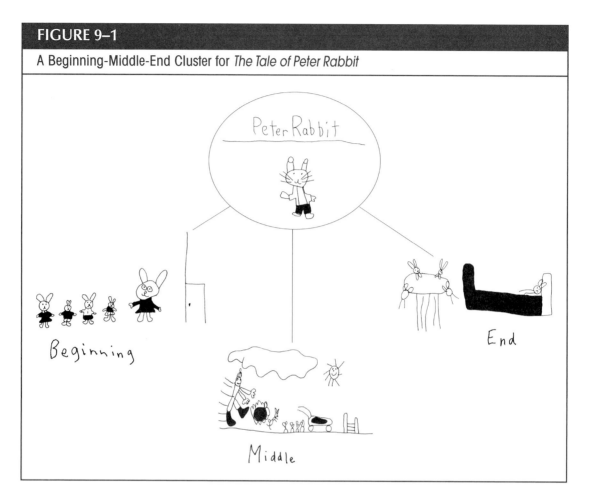

FIGURE 9–1

A Beginning-Middle-End Cluster for *The Tale of Peter Rabbit*

- **The High Point.** The high point in the action occurs when the problem is about to be solved. It separates the middle and end of the story.
- **Solution.** The problem is solved and the roadblocks are overcome at the end of the story.

The problem is introduced at the beginning of the story, and the main character is faced with trying to solve it. The problem determines the conflict. For example, the problem in Hans Christian Andersen's heartfelt story *The Ugly Duckling* (Pinkney, 1999) is that the big, gray duckling does not fit in with the other ducklings, and conflict develops between the ugly duckling and the other ducks.

After the problem has been introduced, authors use conflict to throw roadblocks in the way of an easy solution. As characters remove one roadblock, the author devises another to further thwart the characters. Postponing the solution by introducing road-blocks is the core of plot development. In *The Ugly Duckling*, the first conflict comes in the yard when the ducks make fun of the main character. The conflict is so great that the duckling goes out into the world and spends a miserable, cold winter in the marsh.

The high point of the action occurs when the solution of the problem hangs in the balance. Tension is high, and readers continue reading to learn whether the main characters solve the problem. With *The Ugly Duckling*, readers are relieved that the duckling has survived the winter, but tension continues because he's still an outcast. Then he flies to a pond and sees some beautiful swans. He flies near to them even though he expects to be scorned.

As the story ends, the problem is solved and the goal is achieved. When he joins the other swans at the garden pond, they welcome him. He sees his reflection in the water and realizes that he is no longer an ugly duckling. Children come to feed the swans and praise the new swan's beauty. The young swan is happy at last!

Students make a chart called a *plot profile* to track the tension in a story (Johnson & Louis, 1987). Figure 9–2 presents a plot profile for *Stone Fox* (Gardiner, 2003), a story about a boy who wins a dogsled race to save his grandfather's farm. A class of fourth graders met in small groups to talk about each chapter, and after these discussions, the whole class came together to decide how to mark the chart. At the end of the story, students analyzed the chart and rationalized the tension dips in Chapters 3 and 7: They decided that the story would be too stressful without these dips. Also, students were upset about the abrupt ending to the story and wished the story had continued a chapter or two longer so that their tension would have been reduced.

Booklist

STORIES EXEMPLIFYING THE STORY ELEMENTS

Plot

Bunting, E. (1999). *Smoky night*. San Diego: Harcourt Brace. (P–M)

Dahl, R. (2004). *Charlie and the chocolate factory*. New York: Knopf. (M)

Sachar, L. (1998). *Holes*. New York: Farrar, Straus & Giroux. (U)

Soto, G. (1993). *Too many tamales*. New York: Putnam. (P)

Characters

Avi. (2005). *Poppy*. New York: HarperCollins. (M)

Cushman, K. (1994). *Catherine, called Birdy*. New York: HarperCollins. (U)

Henkes, K. (1991). *Chrysanthemum*. New York: Greenwillow. (P)

Spinelli, J. (2002). *Maniac Magee*. New York: Scholastic. (U)

Setting

Curtis, C. P. (2000). *The Watsons go to Birmingham—1963*. New York: Delacorte. (M–U)

Lowry, L. (2006). *The giver*. New York: Delacorte. (U)

Hale, S. (2005). *Princess academy*. New York: Bloomsbury. (M–U)

Whelan, G. (2000). *Homeless bird*. New York: Scholastic. (U)

Point of View

Babbitt, N. (2002). *Tuck everlasting*. New York: Farrar, Straus & Giroux. (U)

Creech, S. (2000). *The wanderer*. New York: Scholastic. (M–U)

Meddaugh, S. (1995). *Hog-eye*. Boston: Houghton Mifflin. (P)

Ryan, P. M. (2000). *Esperanza rising*. New York: Scholastic. (M)

Theme

Avi. (2003). *Nothing but the truth: A documentary novel*. New York: Orchard Books. (U)

Hesse, K. (2001). *Witness*. New York: Scholastic. (U)

Pinkney, J. (1999). *The ugly duckling*. New York: Morrow. (P)

White, E. B. (2006). *Charlotte's web*. New York: HarperCollins. (M)

P = primary grades (K–2); M = middle grades (3–5); U = upper grades (6–8).

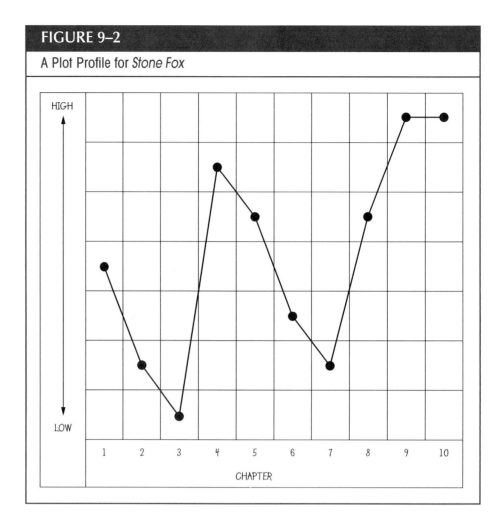

FIGURE 9–2

A Plot Profile for *Stone Fox*

Characters. Characters, the people or personified animals who are involved in the story, are often the most important element of story structure because many stories are centered on a character. In *Catherine, Called Birdy* (Cushman, 1994), for example, the story focuses on Birdy and her determination to outwit her father and not be married off to a revolting, shaggy-bearded suitor. Usually, one or two well-rounded characters and several supporting characters are created in a story. Fully developed main characters have many personality traits, both good and bad—that is to say, they have all the characteristics of real people, and it's essential to understand these traits to comprehend a story. Smith (2005) emphasizes that teachers should introduce their students to character-rich stories. The Booklist on page 279 includes stories with fully developed main characters.

Birdy is the main character in *Catherine, Called Birdy,* and readers get to know her as a real person. Although she is shaped by the culture of medieval England, she challenges the traditional role of "a lady" and is determined to marry someone she cares for, not some rich lord of her father's choosing. Through Birdy's journal entries, readers learn about her activities at the manor, how she helps her mother care for sick and injured people, and her beliefs and superstitions. Readers view events in the story through her eyes and sense her wit as she recounts her daily activities. In contrast, the author tells us little about the supporting characters in the story: Birdy's parents, her brothers, the servants, and the peasants who live and work on her father's lands.

Characters are developed in four ways—through appearance, action, dialogue, and monologue. Authors present the characters to involve readers in the story's experiences. Similarly, readers notice these four types of information as they read in order to understand the characters. Authors generally provide some physical description of the characters when they are introduced. Readers learn about characters by the description of their facial features, body shapes, habits of dress, mannerisms, and gestures. Little emphasis is placed on Birdy's appearance, but Birdy writes that she is unattractive. She squints because of poor eyesight and describes herself as tanned and with gray eyes. She often blackens her teeth and crosses her eyes to make herself more unattractive when her father introduces her to potential suitors.

The second way to learn about characters is through their actions, and what a character does is often the best way to know about him or her. Birdy writes about picking fleas off her body, making soap and remedies for the sick, doctoring with her mother, keeping birds as pets, traveling to a fair and to a friend's castle, and learning how to sew and embroider. She tells how she prefers being outside and how she sneaks away to visit the goat-boy and other friends who work at the manor.

Dialogue is the third way characters are developed. What characters say is important, but so is how they speak. The register of the characters' language is determined by the social situation: A character might speak less formally with friends than with respected elders or characters in positions of authority. The geographic location of the story, the historical period, and the characters' socioeconomic status also determine how characters speak. The language in Birdy's journal entries is often archaic:

> *"Mayhap I could be a hermit."* (p. 130)
>
> *"I am full weary tonight . . . "* (p. 131)
>
> *"Corpus bones. I utterly loathe my life."* (p. 133)

Authors also provide insight into characters by revealing their thoughts through monologue. Birdy shares her innermost thoughts in her journal. Readers know how she attempts to thwart her father's plans to marry her off to a rich lord, her worries about her mother's miscarriages, her love for the goat-boy, and her guilt over meddling in Uncle George's love life.

As students examine the main character of a story, they draw conclusions about his or her defining traits. Birdy, for example, is witty, defiant, determined, clever, kindhearted, and superstitious. Teachers work with students to develop a list of character traits, and then students write about one or more of the traits, providing examples from the story to show how the character exemplified the trait. Students can write about character traits in a reading log entry or make a chart. Figure 9–3 shows an eighth grader's chart about Birdy's character traits. Another way students can examine characters and reflect on story events from the character's viewpoint is to draw open-mind portraits, as Mrs. Ochs's students did in the vignette at the beginning of the chapter. These portraits have two parts: The face of the character is on one page, and his or her mind is on the second page. The two pages are stapled together, with the mind page under the face page.

FIGURE 9–3

An Eighth Grader's Character Traits Chart

Will the Real Birdy Please Stand Up?

Trait	Explanation
Defiant	Birdy is defiant because she does not obey her parents. She doesn't want to marry any of the rich men that her father wants her to marry. She does not want to do the needlework that her mother wants her to do. Because she is rebellious, disobedient, and obstinate, she is defiant.
Kindhearted	Birdy is very kindhearted. She is compassionate to the servants and the peasants who are her friends. She treats them like they are as good as her. She is humane because she is like a doctor making medicines and treating sick people. Birdy has a charitable manner; therefore she is kindhearted.
Clever	Birdy is a clever girl. She manages to get rid of her suitors with ingenious plans. She avoids her mother because she is quick-witted. She is smart for someone in the Middle Ages, but not for someone now. She can even read and write which is unusual for a girl back then. Because she gets her way most of the time, I think she is clever.

Setting. In some stories, the setting is barely sketched; these settings are *backdrop settings*. The setting in many folktales, for example, is relatively unimportant, and these tales may simply use the convention "Once upon a time . . ." to set the stage. In other stories, the setting is elaborated and is integral to the story's effectiveness. These settings are *integral settings* (Lukens, 2006). Stories with integral settings are included in the Booklist on page 279. The setting is specific, and authors take care to ensure the authenticity of the historical period or geographic location in which the story is set. Four dimensions of setting are location, weather, time period, and time.

Location is an important dimension in many stories. For example, the Boston Public Garden in *Make Way for Ducklings* (McCloskey, 2001) and the Alaskan North Slope in *Julie of the Wolves* (George, 2005) are integral to the effectiveness of those stories. The settings are artfully described and add something unique to the story. In contrast, many stories take place in predictable settings that do not contribute to their effectiveness.

Weather is a second dimension of setting and, like location, is crucial in some stories. A rainstorm is essential to the plot development in *Bridge to Terabithia* (Paterson, 2006), but at other times, weather isn't mentioned because it doesn't affect the outcome of the story. Many stories take place on warm, sunny days. Think about the impact weather can have on a story; for example, what might have happened if a snowstorm had prevented Little Red Riding Hood from reaching her grandmother's house?

The third dimension of setting is the time period, an important element in stories set in the past or future. If *The Witch of Blackbird Pond* (Speare, 2003) were set in a different era, for example, it would lose much of its impact. Today, few people would believe that Kit Tyler is a witch. In stories that take place in the future, such as *A Wrinkle in Time* (L'Engle, 2007), things are possible that are not possible today.

The fourth dimension, time, includes both time of day and the passage of time. Most stories ignore time of day, except for scary stories that take place after dark. In nighttime stories, time is a more important dimension than in stories that take place during the day, because night makes things scarier. Many short stories span a brief period of time, often less than a day, and sometimes less than an hour. Other stories, such as *Charlotte's Web* (White, 2006) and *The Ugly Duckling* (Pinkney, 1999), span a long enough period for the main character to grow to maturity.

Students can draw maps to show the setting of a story; these maps may show the path a character traveled or the passage of time in a story. Figure 9–4 shows a setting map for *Number the Stars* (Lowry, 2005) that indicates where the families lived in Copenhagen, their trip to a fishing village in northern Denmark, and the ship they hid away on for the trip to Sweden.

FIGURE 9–4

A Setting Map for *Number the Stars*

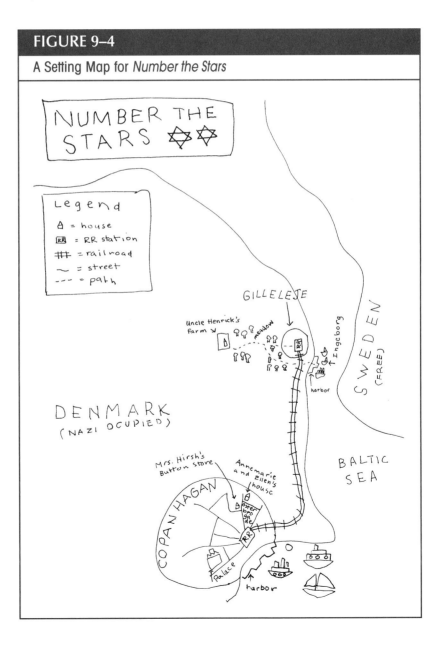

Point of View. Stories are written from a particular viewpoint, and this focus determines to a great extent readers' understanding of the characters and the events of the story. The four points of view are first-person viewpoint, omniscient viewpoint, limited omniscient viewpoint, and objective viewpoint (Lukens, 2006). The Booklist on page 279 includes stories written from different viewpoints.

The first-person viewpoint tells a story through the eyes of one character using the first-person pronoun *I.* In this point of view, the reader experiences the story as the narrator tells it. The narrator, usually the main character, speaks as an eyewitness to and a participant in the events. For example, in *Shiloh* (Naylor, 2000), Marty tells how he works for Judd Travers in order to buy the puppy Travers has mistreated, and in *Abuela* (Dorros, 1991) and the sequel, *Isla* (Dorros, 1995), a girl describes magical flying adventures with her grandmother. Many children's books are written from the first-person viewpoint, and the narrator's voice is usually very effective. However, one limitation is that the narrator must remain an eyewitness.

In the omniscient viewpoint, the author is godlike, knowing all. The author tells readers about the thought processes of each character without worrying about how the information is obtained. Most stories told from the omniscient viewpoint are chapter books, because revealing the thought processes of each character makes a story longer. One notable exception is *Doctor De Soto* (Steig, 1990), a picture-book story about a mouse dentist who outwits a fox with a toothache. Steig lets readers know that the fox wants to eat the dentist as soon as his toothache is cured and that the mouse dentist is planning to trick the fox.

The limited omniscient viewpoint is used so that readers can know the thoughts of one character. The story is told in the third person, and the author concentrates on the thoughts, feelings, and significant past experiences of the main character or another important character. Many stories are told from this viewpoint. Lois Lowry uses this viewpoint in *The Giver* (2006). She concentrates on the main character, Jonas, using his thoughts to explain the "perfect" community to readers. Later in the story, Jonas's thoughts reveal his growing dissatisfaction with the community and his decision to escape with the baby Gabriel.

In the objective viewpoint, readers are eyewitnesses to the story and are confined to the immediate scene. They learn only what they can see and hear, without knowing what any character thinks. Many folktales, such as *The Three Little Pigs* (Galdone, 2006) and *The Little Red Hen* (Pinkney, 2006), are told from this viewpoint. Other picture-book stories, such as *Martha Speaks* (Meddaugh, 1992), are also told from this viewpoint. The focus is on recounting events, not on developing the personalities of the characters.

Most teachers postpone introducing the four viewpoints until the upper grades, but younger children can experiment with point of view to understand how the author's viewpoint affects a story. One way to demonstrate point of view is to contrast *The Three Little Pigs* (Galdone, 2006), the traditional version told from an objective viewpoint, with *The True Story of the 3 Little Pigs!* (Scieszka, 1999), a self-serving narrative told by Mr. A. Wolf from a first-person viewpoint. In this satirical retelling, the wolf tries to explain away his bad image. Even first graders are struck by how different the two versions are and how the narrator filters the information.

Theme. The underlying meaning of a story is the *theme,* and it embodies general truths about human nature (Lehr, 1991). It usually deals with the characters' emotions and values. Themes can be stated either explicitly or implicitly. Explicit themes are stated openly and clearly in the story. Lukens (2006) uses *Charlotte's Web* to point out how one theme of friendship—the giving of oneself for a friend—is expressed as an explicit theme:

> Charlotte has encouraged, protected, and mothered Wilbur, bargained and sacrificed for him, and Wilbur, the grateful receiver, realizes that "Friendship is one of the most satisfying things in the world." And Charlotte says later, "By helping you perhaps I was trying to lift up my life a little. Anyone's life can stand a little of that." Because these quoted sentences are exact statements from the text they are called explicit themes. (p. 94)

Implicit themes are suggested rather than explicitly stated in the story. They are developed as the characters attempt to overcome the obstacles that prevent them from reaching their goals. The theme emerges through the thoughts, speech, and actions of the characters as they seek to resolve their conflicts. Lukens also uses *Charlotte's Web* to illustrate implicit themes:

> Charlotte's selflessness—working late at night to finish a new word, expending her last energies for her friend—is evidence that friendship is giving oneself. Wilbur's protection of Charlotte's egg sac, his sacrifice of first turn at the slops, and his devotion to Charlotte's babies—giving without any need to stay even or to pay back—leads us to another theme: True friendship is naturally reciprocal. As the two become fond of each other, still another theme emerges: One's best friend can do no wrong. In fact, a best friend is sensational! Both Charlotte and Wilbur believe in these ideas; their experiences verify them. (p. 95)

Charlotte's Web has several friendship themes, one explicitly stated and others inferred from the text. Stories generally have more than one theme, and their themes generally cannot be articulated with a single word. Friendship is a multidimensional theme. Teachers can ask questions during conversations about literature to guide students' thinking as they work to construct a theme (Au, 1992). Students must go beyond one-word labels in describing the theme and construct their own ideas about it.

Sketch-to-stretch is a visually representing activity that moves students beyond literal comprehension to think more deeply about the theme of a story (Harste, Short, & Burke, 1988; Whitin, 1996). Students work in small groups or individually to draw pictures or diagrams to represent what the story means to them, not pictures of their favorite character or episode. In their sketches, students use lines, shapes, colors, symbols, and words to express their interpretations and feelings. Because students work in a social setting with the support of classmates, they share ideas, extend their understanding, and generate new insights. Students make sketch-to-stretch drawings in reading logs or on posters. The steps in sketch-to-stretch are given in the Step by Step feature on page 286.

Students need many opportunities to experiment with this activity before they can think symbolically. It's helpful to introduce this teaching strategy through a minilesson and draw several sketches together as a class before students do their own sketches. As they create symbolic illustrations of books, students probe their understanding of the story and what it means to them (Whitin, 2002). *The Ballad of Lucy Whipple* (Cushman, 1996), for example, is the story of a girl who reluctantly comes with her family to Lucky Diggins, California, during the 1849 Gold Rush. Even though she wants nothing more than to return home to Massachusetts, Lucy makes a new home for herself and finally becomes a "happy citizen" (p. 187) in Lucky Diggins. Figure 9–5 shows a fourth grader's sketch-to-stretch drawing about *The Ballad of Lucy Whipple* that reflects the "home" theme.

In a yearlong study of two seventh-grade language arts classes, Whitin (1996) found that students' use of sketching helped deepen their understanding of theme; however, she warns that some upper-grade students view this strategy as an easy form of response and suggests that teachers clarify this misconception early in the school year. Students explored new avenues of expression, such as using color to signify meaning and pie charts to signify feelings. Whitin also had her students write reflections to accompany the sketches.

Students also examine the theme as they create quilts. As students design class quilts, the symbols, colors, and quotes they choose reflect their understanding of theme. For example, after reading *Chrysanthemum* (Henkes, 1991), the story of a little girl mouse who is made fun of at school because of her name, and discussing the theme of the story, a second-grade class made a names quilt using construction paper. They decided to emphasize the importance of honoring one another's names in their quilt. The children researched their names, and then each child wrote his or her name and its meaning in a square for the quilt. The teacher also added a square about her first name, and because one more square was needed to finish the quilt, one child made a square about Chrysanthemum, the mouse in the story, and her name. They placed the squares next to each other, and

---

-------- Sketch-to-Stretch --------------------------------

1 **Read a story.** Students read a story or several chapters of a longer book.

2 **Discuss the story.** Students discuss the story in a grand conversation and talk about ways to symbolize the theme using lines, colors, shapes, and words.

3 **Draw sketches.** Students draw sketches that reflect what the story means to them. Rather than drawing a picture of their favorite part, they focus on using symbols to represent what the story means to them.

4 **Share the sketches.** Students meet in small groups to share their sketches and talk about the symbols they used. Teachers encourage classmates to study each student's sketch and tell what they think he or she is trying to convey.

5 **Share some sketches with the class.** Each group chooses one sketch to share with the class.

FIGURE 9–5

A Fourth Grader's Sketch-to-Stretch Drawing for *The Ballad of Lucy Whipple*

around the outside border of the quilt they wrote "Our names are very important to us. We never make fun of anyone's name. Everyone has a beautiful and special name with a story behind it."

Genres

Stories can be categorized in different ways, one of which is according to genres (Buss & Karnowski, 2000). Three broad categories are *folklore, fantasies*, and *realism*. Traditional stories, including fables, fairy tales, myths, and legends, are folklore. Many of these stories, such as "Gingerbread Man," "The Tortoise and the Hare," and "Cinderella," were told and retold for centuries before they were written down. Fantasies are make-believe stories. They may be set in imaginary worlds or in future worlds where characters do impossible things. In some fantasies, such as *Bunnicula: A Rabbit-Tale of Mystery* (Howe & Howe, 2006), animals can talk, and in others, the characters travel through time. In *King of Shadows* (Cooper, 1999), for instance, modern-day Nat Field travels to London as part of a drama troupe to perform in the newly built replica of the famous Globe Theatre. After arriving in England, Nat goes to bed ill and awakens after being transported back 400 years to Elizabethan times to perform in the original Globe Theatre with William Shakespeare. Realistic stories, in contrast, are believable. Some stories take place in the past, such as *Crispin: The Cross of Lead* (Avi, 2002), set in medieval England, and *Rodzina* (Cushman, 2003), an orphan train story set in the 1800s. Other stories are set in the contemporary world, such as *Joey Pigza*

Anne Vega/Merill

Conferencing With Students

This teacher asks students to think about the elements of story structure in the stories they are reading. Students come together to talk about how the author of their particular book crafted the story using plot, characters, setting, point of view, and theme. This conversation is more than a check to make sure students understand what they are reading; it's important because students deepen their comprehension and gain new insights as they think and talk about the story.

Loses Control (Gantos, 2000) and *Amber Brown Is Not a Crayon* (Danziger, 2006). Figure 9–6 presents an overview of the story genres. Poetry, biography, and nonfiction are genres, too, and you will learn more about them in upcoming chapters.

Some researchers are currently looking at genres in a much broader way: They have moved beyond the idea of genres as simply categories of children's literature to examine the different patterns or genres of text that young children interact with at home or at school. These genres include magazines, lists, recipes, children's books, workbooks, newspapers, and letters and greeting cards. Through their examination of young children's interaction with genres, Duke and Purcell-Gates (2003) concluded that during the preschool years, children develop the understanding that texts have different patterns or genres. Duke and Kays (1998) also found that kindergartners demonstrate their knowledge of genres when they vary how they pretend-read unfamiliar wordless books—these young children pretend-read information books differently than stories. These studies suggest that students come to school with a concept of genre and that through reading and writing experiences and minilessons, they refine and apply their understanding of genres.

Literary Devices

Authors use literary devices to make their writing more vivid and memorable. Without these devices, writing can be dull (Lukens, 2006). A list of six literary devices that students learn about is presented in Figure 9–7. Imagery is probably the most commonly used literary device; many authors use imagery as they paint rich word pictures that bring their characters and settings to life. Authors use metaphors and similes to compare one thing to another, personification to endow animals and objects with human qualities, and hyperbole to exaggerate or stretch the truth. They also create symbols as they use one thing to represent something else. In Chris Van Allsburg's *The Wretched Stone* (1991), for example, the glowing stone that distracts the crew from reading, from spending time with their friends, and from doing their jobs symbolizes television or computers. For students to understand the theme of the story, they need to recognize symbols. The author's style conveys the tone or overall feeling in a story. Some stories are humorous, some are uplifting celebrations of life, and others are sobering commentaries on society.

FIGURE 9–6

Story Genres

Category	Genre	Description and Examples
Folklore	Fables	Brief tales told to point out a moral. For example: *Aesop's Fables* (Pinkney, 2000) and *Head, Body, Legs: A Story From Liberia* (Paye & Lippert, 2002).
	Folk- and Fairy Tales	Stories in which heroes and heroines demonstrate virtues to triumph over adversity. For example: *Beautiful Blackbird* (Bryan, 2003), *The Girl Who Spun Gold* (Hamilton, 2000), and *The Sleeping Beauty* (Hyman, 2000).
	Myths	Stories created by ancient peoples to explain natural phenomena. For example: *King Midas: The Golden Touch* (Demi, 2002), *A Gift From Zeus: Sixteen Favorite Myths* (Steig, 2001), and *The Star-Bearer: A Creation Myth From Ancient Egypt* (Hofmeyr, 2001).
	Legends	Stories, including tall tales, that recount the courageous deeds of people as they struggled against each other or against gods and monsters. For example: *Mystic Horse* (Goble, 2003), *Mike Fink* (Kellogg, 1998), *The Boy Who Drew Cats* (Hodges, 2002), and *Master Man: A Tall Tale of Nigeria* (Shepard, 2001).
Fantasy	Modern Literary Tales	Stories written by modern authors that exemplify the characteristics of folktales. For example: *The Runaway Tortilla* (Kimmel, 2000), *Gingerbread Baby* (Brett, 1999), and *Sylvester and the Magic Pebble* (Steig, 2006).
	Fantastic Stories	Imaginative stories that explore alternate realities and contain one or more elements not found in the natural world. For example: *Princess Academy* (Hale, 2005) and *Charlotte's Web* (White, 2006).
	Science Fiction	Stories that explore scientific possibilities. For example: *Commander Toad in Space* (Yolen, 1980), *The Giver* (Lowry, 2006), and *Stinker From Space* (Service, 1988).
	High Fantasy	These stories focus on the conflict between good and evil and often involve quests. For example: *The Lion, the Witch and the Wardrobe* (Lewis, 2005) and *Harry Potter and the Chamber of Secrets* (Rowling, 1999).
Realism	Contemporary Stories	Stories that portray the real world and contemporary society. For example: *Hatchet* (Paulsen, 2006), *Joey Pigza Loses Control* (Gantos, 2000), and *Locomotion* (Woodson, 2003).
	Historical Fiction	Realistic stories set in the past. For example: *The Watsons Go to Birmingham—1963* (Curtis, 2000), *Sarah, Plain and Tall* (MacLachlan, 2004), and *A Single Shard* (Park, 2001).

FIGURE 9–7

Literary Devices

Comparison	Authors compare one thing to another. When the comparison uses the word *like* or *as*, it's a simile; when the comparison is stated directly, it's a metaphor. For example, "the ocean is like a playground for whales" is a simile; "the ocean is a playground for whales" is a metaphor. Metaphors are stronger comparisons because they're more direct.
Hyperbole	Authors use hyperbole when they overstate or stretch the truth to make obvious and intentional exaggerations. "It's raining cats and dogs" and "my feet are killing me" are two. American tall tales also have rich examples of hyperbole.
Imagery	Authors use descriptive or sensory words and phrases to create imagery or a picture in the reader's mind. Sensory language stirs the reader's imagination. Instead of saying "the kitchen smelled good as Grandmother cooked Thanksgiving dinner," authors create imagery when they write "the aroma of a turkey roasting in the oven filled Grandmother's kitchen on Thanksgiving."
Personification	Authors use personification when they attribute human characteristics to animals or objects. For example, "the moss crept across the sidewalk" is personification.
Symbolism	Authors often use a person, place, or thing as a symbol to represent something else. For example, a dove symbolizes peace, the Statue of Liberty symbolizes freedom, and books symbolize knowledge.
Tone	Authors create an overall feeling or effect in the story through their choice of words and use of other literary devices. For example, *Bunnicula: A Rabbit-Tale of Mystery* (Howe & Howe, 2006) and *Catherine, Called Birdy* (Cushman, 1994) are humorous stories, and *Babe the Gallant Pig* (King-Smith, 2005) and *Sarah, Plain and Tall* (MacLachlan, 2004) are uplifting, feel-good stories.

Young children focus on events and characters as they read and discuss a story, but gradually students become more sophisticated readers. They learn to notice both what the author says and how he or she says it. Teachers facilitate students' growth in reading and evaluating stories by directing their attention to literary devices and the author's style during the responding and exploring stages of the reading process.

Teaching Students About Stories

The most important way that students refine their concept of story is by reading and writing stories, but teachers help students expand their concepts through a variety of activities. As they talk about stories during grand conversations, teachers often draw students' attention to theme and other elements of story structure, genres, and literary devices. And as students develop open-mind portraits, beginning-middle-end clusters, and other diagrams and charts, they're examining stories more closely. In addition, teachers teach minilessons that focus on story elements, genres, and literary devices.

Minilessons. Teachers adapt the teaching strategy set out in Chapter 2 to teach minilessons about story structure, genres, and literary devices as well as other procedures, concepts, and strategies and skills related to reading and writing stories. A list of topics for minilessons about stories is presented on pages 292 and 293, as well as a minilesson that a second-grade teacher taught on theme.

Minilessons about story structure, genres, and literary devices are usually taught during the exploring stage of the reading process, after students have had an opportunity to read and respond to a story and share their reactions. This sequence is important because students need to understand the events of the story before they try to analyze the story at a more abstract level.

READING STORIES

Students read stories as they participate in literature focus units, literature circles, reading workshop, and thematic units, and as they read stories, their concept of story informs and supports their reading. Teachers provide guidance and support for students as they participate in a variety of reading activities, including guided reading and readers theatre, and they can assess students' comprehension through retelling stories.

Guided Reading

Teachers scaffold students' reading to enable them to develop and use reading strategies and skills in guided reading (Fountas & Pinnell, 1996, 2001). This type of reading is teacher directed and is usually done in small groups with students who read at the same level or who use similar reading strategies and skills. Teachers listen to individual students read during guided reading, noticing how they use meaning, structure, and phonological cues. When a student makes an error, the teacher quickly determines the source of the error and decides what type of immediate instruction or other support to use so that the student can be successful (Schwartz, 2005). Teachers often use guided reading with young children and with other students who need direct instruction.

Selections used for guided reading should be written at students' instructional reading levels, that is, slightly beyond their ability to read the text independently, or at their level of proximal development. They usually read the selection silently so if the selection is too difficult, shared reading is a better procedure. If the selection is too easy, then independent reading is a better choice because teacher support isn't needed. Teachers often group and regroup students for guided reading so that the book selected is appropriate for all students in a group. The steps in guided reading are shown in the Step by Step feature on page 294.

Readers Theatre

Readers theatre is a dramatic presentation of a story by a group of readers. Stories are usually rewritten as scripts, and students each assume a role and read that character's lines. Students develop reading fluency and increased motivation for reading through

What Students Need to Learn About Stories

Topics

Procedures	Concepts	Strategies and Skills
Make a beginning-middle-end cluster	**Concept of story**	Visualize
Make a setting map		Predict and confirm
Make a plot profile	Beginning-middle-end	Empathize with characters
Make an open-mind portrait	Plot	Identify with characters
Do a sketch-to-stretch drawing	Characters	Write dialogue for characters
Design a story quilt	Setting	**Rereading**
Do a readers theatre presentation	**Theme**	Retell a story
Use the Goldilocks strategy	Point of view	Respond to stories
Participate in SSR	Genres	Monitor understanding
Make a class collaboration book	Literary devices	Connect to one's own life
Write an innovation	Metaphor	Connect to the world
Write a sequel	Simile	Connect to previously read literature
Write original stories		Value the story
		Evaluate the story

To investigate about how students learn about stories, please visit MyEducationLab. You can watch second graders use their knowledge of story structure as they "read" a wordless book by going to the topic "Viewing" and clicking on the video "Concept of Story," or see an eighth-grade teacher review story structure by going to the topic "Reading" and clicking on the video "Literary Elements." And if you'd like to see second graders rereading a story, go again to the topic "Reading" and click on the video "Rereading."

Minilesson

Mrs. Levin's Second Graders Learn About Theme

1 Introduce the topic

Mrs. Levin's second-grade class has just read *Martha Speaks* (Meddaugh, 1992), the story of a talking dog. Mrs. Levin rereads the last paragraph of the story, which exemplifies the theme, and says, "I think this is what the author, Susan Meddaugh, is trying to tell us—that sometimes we should talk and sometimes we should be quiet. What do you think?" The children agree, and Mrs. Levin explains that the author's message or lesson about life is called the *theme*.

2 Share examples

Mrs. Levin shows the class *Little Red Riding Hood* (Galdone, 1974), a story they read earlier in the year, and after briefly reviewing the story, she asks children about the theme of this story. One child quickly responds, "I think the author means that you shouldn't talk to strangers." Another child explains, "Little Red Riding Hood's mom probably tried to teach her to not talk to strangers but Little Red Riding Hood must have forgotten because she talked to the wolf and he was like a stranger." It is a message every child has heard, but they agree that they, too, sometimes forget, just like Little Red Riding Hood.

3 Provide information

The next day, Mrs. Levin shares three other familiar books and asks children to identify the theme. The first book is *The Three Bears* (Galdone, 1972), and children easily identify the "don't intrude" theme. The second book is *Chrysanthemum* (Henkes, 1991), the story of a young mouse named Chrysanthemum who doesn't like herself after her classmates make fun of her name. The children identify two variations of the theme: "you should be nice to everyone and not hurt their feelings," and "kids who aren't nice get in trouble." The third book is *Miss Nelson Is Missing!* (Allard, 1977), the story of a sweet teacher who transforms herself into a mean teacher after her students refuse to behave. The children identify the theme as "teachers are nice when you behave but they are mean when you are bad."

4 Supervise practice

Mrs. Levin asks children to choose one of the five stories they have examined and to draw pictures showing the theme. For example, they could draw a picture of Martha using the telephone to report burglars in the house or a picture of themselves ringing the doorbell at a friend's house. Mrs. Levin walks around as children work, helping them add titles to their pictures that focus on the theme of the story.

5 Reflect on learning

Children share their pictures with the class and explain how they illustrate the theme of the various stories.

1 Choose a book.   Teachers choose a book that students in a small group can read with 90–94% accuracy and collect copies of the book for each student in the group.

2 Introduce the book.   Teachers show the cover, reading the title and author's name, and activate students' background knowledge on a related topic. They use key vocabulary words as they talk about the book but don't directly teach them. Students also "picture walk" through the book, examining the illustrations.

3 Have students read the book.   Teachers have students read the book independently and ask individual students to take turns reading aloud. They help individual students decode unfamiliar words, deal with unfamiliar sentence structures, and comprehend ideas whenever assistance is needed.

4 Respond to the book.   Students talk about the book and relate it to others they have read, as in a grand conversation.

5 Teach concepts.   Teachers teach a comprehension strategy or a phonics skill, review vocabulary words, or examine an element of story structure.

6 Provide opportunities for independent reading.   Teachers have students reread the book several more times to develop fluency. They often place the book in students' book baskets so they can reread it independently.

this dramatic activity (Black & Stave, 2007; Worthy & Prater, 2002). The reader's responsibility is to interpret a story without using much action. Students may stand or sit, but they must carry the whole communication of the plot, characterization, mood, and theme through their voices, gestures, and facial expressions.

A few collections of readers theatre scripts are available for young children, including *Getting Ready to Read With Readers Theatre* (Barchers & Pfeffinger, 2007) and *Nonfiction Readers Theatre for Beginning Readers* (Fredericks, 2007). However, very few quality scripts are available for older students, so they usually prepare their own scripts from books they have read, such as *Amber Brown Is Not a Crayon* (Danziger, 2006) and *The Giver* (Lowry, 2006). Karen Hesse's *Witness* (2001), a story told from multiple voices, is very powerful when performed as a readers theatre presentation. Students begin by reading the book and thinking about its theme, characters, and plot. Next, they choose an episode to script, make copies of it, and use felt-tip pens to highlight the dialogue. They then adapt the scene by adding narrators' lines to bridge gaps, set the scene, and summarize. Students assume roles and read the script aloud, revising and experimenting with new text until they are satisfied with the script. The final version is typed, duplicated, and stapled into booklets. The steps in developing readers theatre performances are shown in the Step by Step feature on the next page.

Independent Reading

One way to provide daily opportunities for recreational reading is what Stephen Krashen (1993) calls *free voluntary reading* (FVR). Researchers have confirmed again and again that children, including English learners, who do more reading become more capable readers (Cohen, 1999; Krashen, 1993, 2001). Two ways to provide independent reading at school are Sustained Silent Reading and reading workshop. No matter which program teachers use to provide students with independent reading, these guidelines are followed:

- Students choose the books they read.
- Students have access to a large collection of books from which to choose those they want to read and are able to read.
- Students have daily uninterrupted time to read.
- Students have a comfortable, quiet location in which to read.
- Students receive encouragement from their teachers.

The Goldilocks Strategy. Students need to learn to choose books for independent reading that they really can read. Ohlhausen and Jepsen (1992) developed a strategy for choosing books called the "Goldilocks strategy." These teachers developed three categories of books—"too easy," "too hard," and "just right" using "The Three Bears" folktale as their model. The books in the "too easy" category were books students had read before or could read fluently. "Too hard" books were unfamiliar and confusing, and books in the "just right" category were interesting and had just a few unfamiliar words. The books in each category vary according to the students' reading levels. This approach was developed with second graders, but the categorization scheme can work at any grade level. Figure 9–8 presents a chart developed by a third-grade class about choosing books for independent reading using the Goldilocks strategy.

Readers Theatre

Step by Step

1 Select a script.   Teachers select a script for students to use, or they work with students to craft a script from a familiar picture-book story or an episode from a chapter book.

2 Rehearse the performance.   Students choose their parts and read through the script once or twice. Then they stop to talk about the story and deepen their understanding of the characters they're playing. They decide how to use their voices, gestures, and facial expressions to interpret the characters and read the script one or two more times, striving for accurate pronunciation, strong voice projection, and appropriate inflection.

3 Decide on props.   Students often collect props and prepare simple costumes to enhance their presentation, but students shouldn't get so involved in props that it interferes with the interpretive quality of the reading.

4 Stage the performance.   Students usually do the readers theatre performance at the front of the classroom. They stand or sit in a row and read their lines, staying in position throughout the performance. If readers are sitting, they may stand to read their lines; if they are standing, they may step forward to read. The emphasis isn't on production quality; rather, it's on the interpretive quality of the readers' voices and expressions.

FIGURE 9–8

A Third-Grade Chart Applying the Goldilocks Strategy

How to Choose the Best Books for YOU

"Too Easy" Books

1. The book is short.
2. The print is big.
3. You have read the book before.
4. You know all the words in the book.
5. The book has a lot of pictures.
6. You are an expert on this topic.

"Just Right" Books

1. The book looks interesting.
2. You can decode most of the words in the book.
3. Mrs. Donnelly has read this book aloud to you.
4. You have read other books by this author.
5. There's someone to give you help if you need it.
6. You know something about this topic.

"Too Hard" Books

1. The book is long.
2. The print is small.
3. There aren't many pictures in the book.
4. There are a lot of words that you can't decode.
5. There's no one to help you read this book.
6. You don't know much about this topic.

Sustained Silent Reading. In Sustained Silent Reading (SSR), students read independently for 10 to 15 minutes or more in books they've chosen themselves that are at their reading level, and teachers model independent reading at the same time (Pilgreen, 2000). Children don't write book reports, and teachers don't keep records of which books children read; instead, the emphasis is on reading for pleasure. This popular reading activity goes by a variety of names, including "drop everything and read" (DEAR), "sustained quiet reading time" (SQUIRT), and "our time to enjoy reading" (OTTER). In contrast, reading workshop is different; it's not a short block of time. Students usually spend more time reading, and students participate in other types of activities (Atwell, 1998). Students conference with the teacher about books they're reading, and they share the books they've read with the class. The teacher's role is different, too, because teachers monitor and assess students' reading during reading workshop.

Teachers often have concerns that students won't use the reading time productively or that they'll always choose books that are too easy for them, but that doesn't seem to be the case (Von Sprecken & Krashen, 1998). Most students actually read during SSR, and students' reading tastes do mature gradually.

Responding to Stories

When you're reading a novel, do you imagine yourself as one of the characters? Do you laugh out loud or cry while you're reading? Do you wish the story wouldn't end because you're enjoying it so much? If so, it's because you're having a dynamic engagement with literature. This powerful feeling of pleasure and desire to do more reading is reader response, and it's what teachers want their students to experience. Marjorie Hancock (2004) describes response to literature as "the unique interaction that occurs within the mind and heart of the individual reader through the literature event" (p. 9).

The three components of response are the reader, the text, and the context for response (Galda, 1988). Readers bring their background knowledge, past literary experiences, ability to use reading strategies and skills, and desire to read to the reading experience; these characteristics are part of the reason why students' responses are unique and personal. Text characteristics are topic, genre, structural patterns, and literary elements, and students' awareness of these characteristics affects their comprehension. The context is the setting for the response. Students' responses reflect their sociocultural background, their family's income level, their religious beliefs, and the classroom climate. When teachers involve students with literature through literature focus units, literature circles, and reading workshop, they provide opportunities for response and celebrate students' responses. Not surprisingly, children respond differently than when teachers don't highlight literature in their language arts programs.

Many of the responses that students make are spontaneous, but others are planned by teachers. For example, kindergartners laugh (spontaneous response) while listening to their teacher read Thacher Hurd's hilarious picture book, *Moo Cow Kaboom!* (2003). In the story, Moo Cow is cownapped by a space cowboy named Zork and taken to Planet 246 for the InterGalactic Rodeo. Afterward, children take turns dressing up as Farmer George (wearing a nightshirt), Moo Cow (wearing a cow mask), and Zork (wearing a black cowboy hat) while classmates become a cast of supporting characters to reenact the story. This is a planned response. As eighth graders read *Crispin: The Cross of Lead* (Avi, 2002), the story of Crispin, a 13-year-old peasant boy who is falsely accused of being a thief and declared a "wolf's head" (which gives everyone in the country permission to kill him on sight), they compare Crispin's life to their own and comment on their compassion for him. This is a spontaneous response. Students also make entries in their reading logs to explore the ideas in the story and make connections to what they're learning about the Middle Ages—a planned response. And when students reach the end of the story, where Crispin redeems himself, they cheer loudly. This is another spontaneous response.

Spontaneous responses are those that students make without prompting by the teacher. They make these responses because the story is so engaging. Young children, for example, clap their hands and tap their feet to the rhythm of Bill Martin and John Archambault's *Chicka Chicka Boom Boom* (1989) and chant along as the teacher reads and rereads the book. They spot the dangers facing two bugs named Frieda and Gloria in the illustrations in *Absolutely Not!* (McElligott, 2004) and call

Weaving Assessment Into Practice

RETELLING STORIES SCORING GUIDE

Name *Cassie* Date *Mar. 10*

Book *Ruby Lu, Brave and True*

4	__ Names and describes all characters.
	__ Includes specific details about the setting.
	__ Explains the problem.
	__ Describes attempts to solve the problem.
	__ Explains the solution.
	__ Identifies the theme.
③	✓ Names all characters and <u>describes</u> some of them. *P*
	__ Identifies more than one detail about the setting (location, weather, time).
	✓ Recalls events in order.
	✓ Identifies the problem.
	✓ Includes the beginning, <u>middle</u>, and end. *P*
2	__ Names all characters.
	✓ Mentions the setting.
	__ Recalls most events in order.
	__ Includes the beginning and end.
1	__ Names some characters.
	__ Recalls events haphazardly.
	__ Includes only beginning or end.

P = prompted

Teachers can't assume that students already know how to retell stories, even though many do. Through a series of minilessons on retelling strategies and demonstrations of the procedure, students will understand what's expected of them. They need to practice retelling stories before they'll be good at it. They can retell stories with a classmate and to their parents at home. Students who continue to have difficulty retelling stories may need to learn more about story structure, especially beginning, middle, and end. It's often helpful to have them draw pictures to scaffold their retellings. As their comprehension improves, so will their retelling abilities.

Judging Students' Retellings. Most students enjoy retelling stories, and their rubric scores provide a useful measure of their comprehension. A rubric for scoring third graders' retellings is shown in the Weaving Assessment Into Practice box above. Some students, however, are shy or uncomfortable talking with teachers, so their scores may underestimate how well they comprehend (McKenna & Stahl, 2003). The same is true for English learners.

WRITING STORIES

As students read and talk about stories, they learn how writers craft stories. They also draw from stories they've read as they create their own stories, intertwining several story ideas and adapting story elements and genres to meet their own needs (Atwell, 1998). Cairney (1990) found that students weave bits of the stories they've read into the stories they write; they share their compositions, and then bits of these compositions make their way into classmates' compositions. Students make intertextual links in different ways:

- Use specific story ideas without copying the plot
- Copy the plot from a story, but add new events, characters, and settings
- Use a specific genre they have studied for a story
- Use a character borrowed from a story read previously
- Write a retelling of the story
- Incorporate content from an informational book into a story
- Combine several stories into a new story

The first two strategies were the ones most commonly used in Cairney's study of sixth graders. The next-to-the-last strategy was used only by less capable readers, and the last one only by more capable readers.

When students write stories, they incorporate what they have learned about stories, and they use the writing process to draft and refine their stories. They write stories as part of literature focus units, during thematic units, and in writing workshop. Stories are probably the most complex writing form that students use. It is difficult—even for adults—to craft well-formed stories incorporating plot and character development and other elements of story structure.

Writing Retellings of Stories

Students often write retellings of stories they've read and enjoyed. As they retell a story, they internalize the structure of the story and play with the language the author used. Sometimes students work together to write a collaborative retelling, and at other times, they write their own individual retellings. Students can work together as a group to write or dictate the retelling, or they can divide the story into sections or chapters and have each student or pair of students write a small part. Then the parts are compiled. A class of second graders worked together to dictate their retelling of *I, Doko: The Tale of a Basket* (Young, 2004), which they published as a big book.

Page 1: *I am a basket, and my name is Doko. A good man named Yeh-yeh bought me at a market many years ago.*

Page 2: *Yeh-yeh's wife used to carry her precious baby inside me. I was a safe basket.*

Page 3: *In the blink of an eye the baby grew and became a boy. I was always with him and I helped him carry the wood for the cooking fire. I was a protective basket.*

Page 4: *Then a bad time came and Yeh-yeh's wife died. Yeh-yeh put her dead body in my basket, and I carried her to the grave. I was a trusted basket.*

Page 5: *By now the boy was all grown up and he got married. I got a good scrubbing before the wedding, and I got to carry the bride's presents to her new home. I was a handsome basket.*

Page 6: *Next the boy and his wife had a baby. They called him Wangal and I carried him in my basket. I was a proud basket.*

Page 7: *Finally Yeh-yeh got old and so did I. We stayed home by the fire, and Yeh-yeh told me wonderful stories. I was a listening basket.*

Page 8: *One day Yeh-yeh let the fire go out of the fireplace and almost burned down the house. People said it was time to get rid of Yeh-yeh. They told Yeh-yeh's son to take him to the temple steps and leave him there for the priests to take care of. I was a worried basket.*

Page 9: *The next day Yeh-yeh's son put the old man in my basket to take him to the temple steps, but Wangal said something very important. He said, "Don't forget to bring Doko back home because I will need it to get rid of you when you get old." That made Yeh-yeh's son understand that he was doing something very bad. I was a sad basket.*

Page 10: *Yeh-yeh's son learned a good lesson: He learned to respect old people and not want to get rid of them. So Yeh-yeh lived at home with his son and Wangal and me for many happy years. I was a respectful basket.*

As the second graders dictated the retelling, their teacher wrote it on chart paper. Then they read the story over several times, making revisions. Next, the children divided the text into sections for each page. Then they recopied the text onto each page for the big book, drew pictures to illustrate each page, and added a cover and a title page. Children also wrote their own books, including the major points at the beginning, middle, and end of the story.

Sometimes students change the point of view in their retellings and tell the story from a particular character's viewpoint. A fourth grader wrote this retelling of "Goldilocks and the Three Bears" from Baby Bear's perspective:

One day mom got me up. I had to take a bath. I hate to take baths, but I had to. While I was taking my bath, Mom was making breakfast. When I got out of the tub breakfast was ready. But Dad got mad because his breakfast porridge was too hot to eat. So Mom said, "Let's go for a walk and let it cool." I thought, "Oh boy, we get to go for a walk!" My porridge was just right, but I could eat it later.

When we got back our front door was open. Dad thought it was an animal so he started to growl. I hate it when Dad growls. It really scares me. Anyway, there was no animal anywhere so I rushed to the table. Everybody was sitting down to eat. I said, "Someone ate my porridge." Then Dad noticed someone had tasted his porridge. He got really mad.

Then I went into the living room because I did not want to get yelled at. I noticed my rocking chair was broken. I told Dad and he got even madder.

Then I went into my bedroom. I said, "Someone has been sleeping in my bed and she's still in it." So this little girl with long blond hair raises up and starts to scream. Dad plugged his ears. She jumped up like she was scared of us and ran out of the house. We never saw that little girl again.

Writing Innovations

Many stories have a repetitive pattern or refrain, and students can use this structure to write their own stories. As part of a literature focus unit, a first-grade class read *If You Give a Mouse a Cookie* (Numeroff, 1985) and talked about the circular structure of the story: The story begins with giving a mouse a cookie and ends with the mouse getting a second cookie. Then the first graders wrote stories about what they would do if they were given a cookie. A child named Michelle drew the circle diagram shown in Figure 9–9 to organize her story, and then she wrote this story, which has been transcribed into conventional English spelling:

If you gave Michelle a cookie she would probably want some pop. Then she would want a napkin to clean her face. That would make her tired and she would go to bed to take a nap. Before you know it, she will be awake and she would like to take a swim in a swimming pool. Then she would watch cartoons on T.V. And she would be getting hungry again so she would probably want another cookie.

FIGURE 9–9

A Circle Diagram for *If You Give Michelle a Cookie*

Judith Viorst's *Alexander and the Terrible, Horrible, No Good, Very Bad Day* (1987) is a more sophisticated pattern story. After reading the book, students often write about their own bad days. A fifth grader named Jacob wrote his version, entitled "Jacob and the Crummy, Stupid, Very Bad Day":

> *One day I was riding my bike and I fell off and broke my arm and sprained my foot. I had to go to the hospital in an ambulance and get my arm set in a cast and my foot wrapped up real tight in a bandage. I knew it was going to be a crummy, stupid, very bad day. I think I'll swim to China.*
>
> *Then I had to go to the dentist with my sister Melissa. My sister had no cavities, but guess who had two cavities. I knew it was going to be a crummy, stupid, very bad day. I think I'll swim to China.*
>
> *My mom felt bad for me because it was such a bad day so she went and bought me a present—two Nintendo games. But my sister started fighting with me and my mom blamed me for it even though it wasn't my fault. So my mom took the games away. I wonder if there are better sisters in China?*
>
> *Then I went outside and found out that someone had stolen my bike. It was gone without a trace. It really was a crummy, stupid, very bad day. Now I am going to swim to China for sure.*

Writing Sequels

Students often choose to write sequels as projects during literature focus units. For example, after reading *The Sign of the Beaver* (Speare, 2005), students can write sequels in which Matt and Attean meet again. They write additional adventures about the boa constrictor after reading *The Day Jimmy's Boa Ate the Wash* (Noble, 1992). Many stories lend themselves to sequels, and students enjoy extending a favorite story.

Writing Genre Stories

During some literature focus units, students read books and learn about a particular genre, such as folktales, historical fiction, myths, or fables. After learning about the genre, they try their hand at writing stories that incorporate its characteristics. After reading gingerbread man stories, a class of kindergartners dictated this story, which their teacher wrote on chart paper. Interestingly, the children asked their teacher to write the story in two columns. In the left column, the teacher wrote the story, and in the right column, she wrote the refrain:

THE RUNAWAY HORSE

Once upon a time	*Run, run,*
there was a horse.	*as fast as you can,*
He jumped over the	*you can't catch me!*
stable gate and ran away.	
He meets a farmer.	*Run, run,*
The farmer chases him	*as fast as you can,*
but the horse runs	*you can't catch me!*
as fast as the wind.	
The horse meets a dog.	*Run, run,*

The dog chases him.	*as fast as you can,*
The horse runs	*you can't catch me!*
as fast as the wind.	
Then the horse meets a fox.	*Snip, snap, snout,*
And the fox gobbles him up.	*This tale is told out.*

A seventh-grade class read and examined myths and compared myths from various cultures. Then they applied what they had learned about myths in this class collaboration myth, "Suntaria and Lunaria: Rulers of the Earth," about the origin of the sun and the moon:

> *Long ago when gods still ruled the earth, there lived two brothers, Suntaria and Lunaria. Both brothers were wise and powerful men. People from all over the earth sought their wisdom and counsel. Each man, in his own way, was good and just, yet the two were as different as gold and coal. Suntaria was large and strong with blue eyes and brilliantly golden hair. Lunaria's hair and eyes were the blackest black.*
>
> *One day Zeus, looking down from Mount Olympus, decided that Earth needed a ruler—someone to watch over his people whenever he became too tired or too busy to do his job. His eyes fell upon Suntaria and Lunaria. Both men were wise and honest. Both men would be good rulers. Which man would be the first ruler of the earth?*
>
> *Zeus decided there was only one fair way to solve his problem. He sent his messenger, Postlet, down to earth with ballots instructing the mortals to vote for a king. There were only two names on the ballot—Suntaria and Lunaria.*
>
> *Each mortal voted and after the ballots were placed in a secure box, Postlet returned them to Zeus. For seven years Zeus and Postlet counted and recounted the ballots. Each time they came up with the same results: 50% of the votes were for Suntaria and 50% were for Lunaria. There was only one thing Zeus could do. He declared that both men would rule over the earth.*
>
> *This is how it was, and this is how it is. Suntaria still spreads his warm golden rays to rule over our days. At night he steps down from his throne, and Lunaria's dark, soft night watches and protects us while we dream.*

The students incorporated three characteristics of myths in their story. First, their myth explained a phenomenon that has more recently been explained scientifically. Second, the setting is backdrop and barely sketched, and finally, the characters in their myth are heroes with supernatural powers.

Writing Original Stories

Students move into writing original stories through writing personal narratives and writing retellings of familiar stories they've read, movies and television programs they've watched, and video games they've played. Their first stories are typically action-driven. Jorgensen (2001) explains that many children's stories resemble a fast-paced television commercial: There's action, more action, and still more action; sometimes with a high point, but other times without one. Other young writers' stories lack focus; they're either endless conversations or a series of unrelated events.

In contrast, more knowledgeable writers craft character-driven stories that exemplify these characteristics:

- The plot is logical with a beginning, middle, and end, and the focus is on the conflict between the characters.
- The characters seem like real people: They come to life through their appearance, dialogue, and actions.
- The setting is carefully described so that readers can visualize it, and it's usually important to the story.
- The narrator's viewpoint is consistent throughout the story.
- A worthwhile theme or message is expressed through the story's characters and events.

Students learn to write more effective stories by examining the elements of story structure, reading lots of stories, and writing stories themselves.

Students' stories represent a variety of genres, especially realistic stories based on events drawn from their own lives and fantasy stories describing imaginary worlds, talking animals, and events that couldn't really happen in today's world. Books, such as the Harry Potter series (Rowling, 2007), give students ideas for their fantasies. Increasingly, both boys and girls include violence in their stories, and it's essential that teachers set guidelines to avoid offensive language and gratuitous bloodthirstiness and brutality.

Karen Jorgensen (2001) taught her fifth graders to write well-crafted stories through a writing workshop approach she calls "fiction workshop." They spend time writing stories independently, and they also conference with classmates and the teacher to get feedback on their stories. When students finish writing a story, they publish it by making a book and reading it to classmates. Then they ceremoniously place the book in the classroom library. She also teaches minilessons about the elements of story structure and how to solve common fiction-writing problems, such as an ineffective setting and excessive dialogue.

Assessing Students' Stories

Teachers consider four components in assessing students' stories: their knowledge of the elements of story structure, their application of the elements in writing, their use of the writing process, and the quality of the finished stories. Determining whether students learned about the element and applied what they learned in their stories is crucial in assessing their stories. Consider the following points:

- Can the student define or identify the characteristics of the element?
- Can the student explain how the element was used in a particular story?
- Did the student apply the element in the story he or she has written?

The quality of students' stories is difficult to measure. Students who write high-quality and interesting stories use the story structure, genre, and literary devices to their advantage. The assessment and grading of students' stories, however, should reflect more than simply the quality of the finished product; they should reflect all four components of students' involvement with stories.

Review

Students develop their concept of stories as they learn about story structure, genres, and literary devices. Students apply this knowledge as they read and write stories. Here are the key concepts presented in this chapter:

- Students acquire a concept of story by reading and writing stories and by learning about story structure, genres, and literary devices.
- Stories have unique structural elements that distinguish them from other forms of writing: plot, characters, setting, point of view, and theme.
- Stories can be categorized according to genres, such as fairy tales and science fiction, and each genre has distinguishing characteristics.
- Literary devices, including comparison, hyperbole, imagery, personification, symbolism, and tone, make stories more vivid and memorable.
- Teachers use guided reading to teach reading to small groups of students who read at the same level.
- As students perform readers theatre presentations, they demonstrate their interpretations of a story.
- Teachers promote reading through free voluntary reading.
- When students respond to literature in both spontaneous and planned ways, their comprehension and interest in reading are enhanced.
- Students retell stories to demonstrate their comprehension.
- Students use intertextuality as they incorporate ideas from the stories they have read into the stories they write.

Professional References

Applebee, A. N. (1978). *The child's concept of story: Ages 2 to 17*. Chicago: University of Chicago Press.

Atwell, N. (1998). *In the middle: New understandings about writing, reading, and learning*. Portsmouth, NH: Heinemann.

Au, K. H. (1992). Constructing the theme of a story. *Language Arts, 69,* 106–111.

Barchers, S. I., & Pfeffinger, C. R. (2007). *Getting ready to read with readers theatre*. Portsmouth, NH: Teacher Ideas Press.

Black, A., & Stave, A. M. (2007). *A comprehensive guide to readers theatre*. Newark, DE: International Reading Association.

Bruner, J. (1980). *Actual minds, possible worlds*. Cambridge, MA: Harvard University Press.

Buss, K., & Karnowski, L. (2000). *Reading and writing literary genres*. Newark, DE: International Reading Association.

Cairney, T. (1990). Intertextuality: Infectious echoes from the past. *The Reading Teacher, 43,* 478–484.

Cohen, K. (1999). Reluctant eighth grade readers enjoy Sustained Silent Reading. *California Reader, 33*(1), 22–25.

De Ford, D. (1981). Literacy: Reading, writing, and other essentials. *Language Arts, 58,* 652–658.

Dressel, J. H. (1990). The effects of listening to and discussing different qualities of children's literature on the narrative writing of fifth graders. *Research in the Teaching of English, 24,* 397–414.

Duke, N. K., & Kays, J. (1998). "Can I say 'Once upon a time'?": Kindergarten children's developing knowledge of information book language. *Early Childhood Research Quarterly, 13,* 295–318.

Duke, N. K., & Purcell-Gates, V. (2003). Genres at home and at school: Bridging the known to the new. *The Reading Teacher, 57,* 30–37.

Eckhoff, B. (1983). How reading affects children's writing. *Language Arts, 60,* 607–616.

Fountas, I. C., & Pinnell, G. S. (1996). *Guided reading: Good first teaching for all children*. Portsmouth, NH: Heinemann.

Fountas, I. C., & Pinnell, G. S. (2001). *Guided readers and writers, grades 3–6*. Portsmouth, NH: Heinemann.

Fredericks, A. D. (2007). *Nonfiction readers theatre for beginning readers*. Portsmouth, NH: Teacher Ideas Press.

Galda, L. (1998). Readers, texts, and contexts: A response-based view of literature in the classroom. *The New Advocate, 1,* 92–102.

Golden, J. M., Meiners, A., & Lewis, S. (1992). The growth of story meaning. *Language Arts, 69,* 22–27.

Hancock, M. R. (2004). *A celebration of literature and response: Children, books, and teachers in K–8 classrooms* (2nd ed.). Upper Saddle River, NJ: Merrill/Prentice Hall.

Harste, J. C., Short, K. G., & Burke, C. (1988). *Creating classrooms for authors: The reading-writing connection.* Portsmouth, NH: Heinemann.

Hickman, J. (1980). Children's responses to literature: What happens in the classroom. *Language Arts, 57,* 524–529.

Hoyt, L. (1999). *Revisit, reflect, retell: Strategies for improving reading comprehension.* Portsmouth, NH: Heinemann.

Johnson, T. D., & Louis, D. R. (1987). *Literacy through literature.* Portsmouth, NH: Heinemann.

Jorgensen, K. (2001). *The whole story: Crafting fiction in the upper elementary grades.* Portsmouth, NH: Heinemann.

Krashen, S. (1993). *The power of reading: Insights from the research.* Englewood, CO: Libraries Unlimited.

Krashen, S. (2001). More smoke and mirrors: A critique of the National Reading Panel report on fluency. *Phi Delta Kappan, 83,* 119–123.

Lehr, S. S. (1991). *The child's developing sense of theme: Responses to literature.* New York: Teachers College Press.

Lukens, R. J. (2006). *A critical handbook of children's literature* (8th ed.). New York: Allyn & Bacon.

McKenna, M., & Stahl, S. (2003). *Assessment for reading instruction.* New York: Guilford Press.

Ohlhausen, M. M., & Jepsen, M. (1992). Lessons from Goldilocks: "Somebody's been choosing my books but I can make my own choices now!" *The New Advocate, 5,* 31–46.

O'Malley, J. M., & Pierce, L. V. (1996). *Authentic assessment for English language learners: Practical approaches for teachers.* Reading, MA: Addison-Wesley.

Peregoy, S. F., & Boyle, O. F. (2005). *Reading, writing, and learning in ESL: A resource book for K–12 teachers* (4th ed.). Boston: Allyn & Bacon.

Pilgreen, J. (2000). *The SSR handbook: How to organize and maintain a Sustained Silent Reading program.* Portsmouth, NH: Heinemann.

Rumelhart, D. (1975). Notes on a schema for stories. In D. G. Bobrow (Ed.), *Representation and understanding: Studies in cognitive science* (pp. 99–135). New York: Academic Press.

Samway, K. D., & McKeon, D. (1999). *Myths and realities: Best practices for language minority students.* Portsmouth, NH: Heinemann.

Schwartz, R. M. (2005). Decisions, decisions: Responding to primary students during guided reading. *The Reading Teacher, 58,* 436–443.

Smith, K. (2005). Enhancing the literature experience through deep discussions of character. In N. L. Roser & M. G. Martinez (Eds.), *What a character! Character study as a guide to literary meaning making in grades K–8* (pp. 124–132). Newark, DE: International Reading Association.

Spiegel, D. L. (1998). Reader response approaches and the growth of readers. *Language Arts, 76,* 41–48.

Von Sprecken, D., & Krashen, S. (1998). Do students read during sustained silent reading? *California Reader, 32*(1), 11–13.

Whitin, P. E. (1996). Exploring visual response to literature. *Research in the Teaching of English, 30,* 114–140.

Whitin, P. E. (2002). Leading into literature circles through the sketch-to-stretch strategy. *The Reading Teacher, 55,* 444–450.

Worthy, J., & Prater, K. (2002). "I thought about it all night": Readers theatre for reading fluency and motivation. *The Reading Teacher, 50,* 204–212.

Children's Book References

Allard, H. (1977). *Miss Nelson is missing!* Boston: Houghton Mifflin.

Avi. (2002). *Crispin: The cross of lead.* New York: Hyperion Books.

Brett, J. (1999). *Gingerbread baby.* New York: Putnam.

Bryan, A. (2003). *Beautiful blackbird.* New York: Atheneum.

Cooper, S. (1999). *King of shadows.* New York: Aladdin Books.

Curtis, C. P. (2000). *The Watsons go to Birmingham—1963.* New York: Delacorte.

Cushman, K. (1994). *Catherine, called Birdy.* New York: HarperCollins.

Cushman, K. (1996). *The ballad of Lucy Whipple.* New York: Clarion Books.

Cushman, K. (2003). *Rodzina.* New York: Clarion Books.

Danziger, P. (2006). *Amber Brown is not a crayon.* New York: Puffin Books.

Deedy, C. A. (2000). *The yellow star: The legend of King Christian X of Denmark.* Atlanta: Peachtree.

Demi. (2002). *King Midas: The golden touch.* New York: McElderry.

Dorros, A. (1991). *Abuela.* New York: Dutton.

Dorros, A. (1995). *Isla.* New York: Dutton.

Fleischman, P. (2004). *Seedfolks.* New York: HarperTrophy.

Galdone, P. (1972). *The three bears.* New York: Clarion Books.

Galdone, P. (1974). *Little red riding hood.* New York: McGraw-Hill.

Galdone, P. (2006). *The three little pigs.* New York: Clarion Books.

Gantos, J. (2000). *Joey Pigza loses control.* New York: Farrar, Straus & Giroux.

Gardiner, J. R. (2003). *Stone Fox.* New York: HarperTrophy.

George, J. C. (2005). *Julie of the wolves.* New York: HarperTrophy.

Gobel, P. (2002). *Mystic horse.* New York: HarperCollins.

Hamilton, V. (2000). *The girl who spun gold.* New York: Scholastic.

Henkes, K. (1991). *Chrysanthemum.* New York: Morrow.

Hesse, K. (2001). *Witness.* New York: Scholastic.

Hodges, M. (2002). *The boy who drew cats.* New York: Holiday House.

Hofmeyr, D. (2001). *The star-bearer: A creation myth from ancient Egypt.* New York: Farrar, Straus & Giroux.

Howe, D., & Howe, J. (2006). *Bunnicula: A rabbit-tale of mystery.* New York: Aladdin Books.

Hurd, T. (2003). *Moo cow kaboom!* New York: HarperCollins.

Hyman, T. S. (2000). *The sleeping beauty.* Boston: Little, Brown.

Kellogg, S. (1998). *Mike Fink.* New York: Aladdin Books.

Kimmel, E. A. (2000). *The runaway tortilla.* Delray Beach, FL: Winslow Press.

King-Smith, D. (2005). *Babe the gallant pig.* New York: Random House.

L'Engle, M. (2007). *A wrinkle in time.* Shoreham, VT: Square Fish.

Lewis, C. S. (2005). *The lion, the witch and the wardrobe.* New York: HarperCollins.

Lowry, L. (2005). *Number the stars.* New York: Yearling.

Lowry, L. (2006). *The giver.* Boston: Delacorte.

MacLachlan, P. (2004). *Sarah, plain and tall.* New York: HarperCollins.

Martin, B., Jr., & Archambault, J. (1998). *Chicka chicka boom boom.* New York: Simon & Schuster.

McCloskey, R. (2001). *Make way for ducklings.* New York: Viking.

McElligott, M. (2004). *Absolutely not!* New York: Walker.

Meddaugh, S. (1992). *Martha speaks.* Boston: Houghton Mifflin.

Naylor, P. R. (2000). *Shiloh.* New York: Aladdin Books.

Noble, T. H. (1992). *The day Jimmy's boa ate the wash.* New York: Dial Books.

Numeroff, L. J. (1985). *If you give a mouse a cookie.* New York: HarperCollins.

Park, L. S. (2001). *A single shard.* New York: Clarion Books.

Paterson, K. (2006). *Bridge to Terabithia.* New York: HarperCollins.

Paulsen, G. (2006). *Hatchet.* New York: Aladdin Books.

Paye, W., & Lippert, M. H. (2002). *Head, body, legs: A story from Liberia.* New York: Holt.

Pinkney, J. (1999). *The ugly duckling.* New York: Morrow.

Pinkney, J. (2000). *Aesop's fables.* New York: North-South.

Pinkney, J. (2006). *The little red hen.* New York: Dial Books.

Potter, B. (2002). *The tale of Peter Rabbit.* New York: Warne.

Rowling, J. K. (1999). *Harry Potter and the chamber of secrets.* New York: Scholastic.

Rowling, J. K. (2007). *Harry Potter and the deathly hallows.* New York: Scholastic.

Scieszka, J. (1999). *The true story of the 3 little pigs!* New York: Viking.

Sendak, M. (2003). *Where the wild things are.* New York: HarperCollins.

Service, P. (1988). *Stinker from space.* New York: Scribner.

Shepard, A. (2001). *Master man: A tall tale of Nigeria.* New York: HarperCollins.

Speare, E. G. (2003). *The witch of Blackbird Pond.* Boston: Houghton Mifflin.

Speare, E. G. (2005). *The sign of the beaver.* New York: Yearling.

Steig, W. (1990). *Doctor De Soto.* New York: Farrar, Straus & Giroux.

Steig, J. (2001). *A gift from Zeus: Sixteen favorite myths.* New York: HarperCollins.

Steig, W. (2006). *Sylvester and the magic pebble.* New York: Aladdin Books.

Yolen, J. (1980). *Commander Toad in space.* New York: Coward, McCann.

Yorinks, A. (1986). *Hey, Al.* New York: Farrar, Straus & Giroux.

Young, E. (2004). *I, Doko: The tale of a basket.* New York: Philomel.

Van Allsburg, C. (1991). *The wretched stone.* Boston: Houghton Mifflin.

Viorst, J. (1987). *Alexander and the terrible, horrible, no good, very bad day.* New York: Atheneum.

White, E. B. (2006). *Charlotte's web.* New York: HarperCollins.

Woodson, J. (2003). *Locomotion.* New York: Putnam.

chapter ten

Reading and Writing Information

M rs. LaRue's kindergartners are studying fish. The thematic unit began when the teacher brought in two goldfish to be class pets. The children were excited and immediately named them; they named the orange one Goldie and the white one Moon. So that the children would know how to care for them, the teacher read aloud *Pet Fish* (Nelson, 2002). After listening to the book, the class wrote about their new pets using interactive writing. The children usually write one sentence on chart paper, but because they had more to write, they wrote the first sentence interactively and then Mrs. LaRue wrote their dictated sentences. Here's their completed chart about "Our New Pets":

> *We have 2 goldfish named Goldie and Moon. We will take good care of them. We will feed them goldfish food and keep their bowl clean. We will look at them but not touch them.*

They posted the chart near the fish bowl and reread it each day. With practice, the children learned to pick out some familiar words on the chart, such as *we, good, goldfish, Goldie,* and *Moon.*

Can kindergartners read and write information?

Some teachers think that stories are more appropriate for young children and that reading and writing information should be postponed until the middle grades. Nothing could be further from the truth! Many kindergartners, especially boys, are very curious about science topics. In fact, they prefer to read and write about information. As you read this vignette, notice how Mrs. La Rue's students listened to informational books read aloud and wrote their own informational books.

Mrs. LaRue began a K-W-L chart at the beginning of the unit to record what the children knew about fish and what they wanted to learn. Looking for answers to their questions helped direct the children's attention as they participated in unit-related activities. Today, they are completing the right column of the chart about what they have learned. They have learned so much information to list on the chart that it takes Mrs. LaRue 30 minutes to write their dictated sentences. The completed chart is shown on page 314.

Mrs. LaRue has a text set of stories and informational books about fish that she has been reading aloud to the kindergartners, and she uses the books as springboards to language arts activities. The children are curious about the parts of a fish, so Mrs. LaRue shows them an illustration of a goldfish in *Fish: Pet Care Guides for Kids* (Evans & Caras, 2001), and they identify the fish's body parts—mouth, eyes, scales, gills, fins, tail. Afterward, she draws a picture of goldfish on chart paper, and the children use interactive writing to label the parts. Later, many of the children draw or paint their own pictures of fish, and Mrs. LaRue helps them label two or more body parts on their pictures.

Each day, Mrs. LaRue reads a story or informational book about fish. The kindergartners' favorite book is *The Rainbow Fish* (Pfister, 2002), the story of a vain and selfish fish who learns the value of friendship. The children talk about this book in a grand conversation, and later they draw pictures about their favorite part of the story and dictate a sentence for Mrs. LaRue to add to their pictures. The children share their pictures from the author's chair, and then the teacher binds the pictures into a book that's placed in the classroom library for children to "read."

The next day, this question is posted on their sign-in chart: *What did the rainbow fish learn?* The children choose from among these three answers: *To be selfish. To be a friend. To look pretty.* Mrs. LaRue reads the three possible answers to the first few children who ar-rive in the classroom, and then they read them to the next group and so on until everyone has signed in. The teacher uses the sign-in chart to check her students' comprehension as well as to take attendance and encourage socialization and sharing.

The children learn more about fish at learning centers. They spend 30 minutes each day working at centers. Mrs. LaRue has set up these eight centers in the classroom:

Science center Children use magnifying glasses to observe the goldfish and draw pictures of them in their science journals. Charts about fish and several informational books about fish are also available for children to examine.

Book-making center After reading Lois Ehlert's *Fish Eyes: A Book You Can Count On* (2001), the children make their own fish counting books. Some kindergartners make books to count to 5, and others with more interest in writing and knowledge about numbers make books to count to 10. They use a familiar sentence starter, "I see . . . ," and Mrs. LaRue has introduced the words *big* and *little*. Children choose a word card with one of the words to add to their sentence. They write the other words themselves with the assistance of a parent volunteer. One page from a child's book is shown in the box on the next page.

The Kindergartners' K-W-L Chart About Fish		
What We Know About Fish	What We Wonder About Fish	What We Learned About Fish
Fish live in water.	Are sharks fish?	Sharks are fish.
Fish can swim.	How does a fish breathe underwater?	Eels are fish.
Tuna is a fish.	How long does a fish live?	Sea horses are fish, too.
My Grandpa likes to fish.	Why don't fish have arms and legs?	Whales are not fish.
There are different kinds of fish.	Are whales fish?	Jellyfish and starfish are not fish either.
Fish are slippery if you hold them.	Where do fish live?	Fish breathe through gills.
You can eat fish.	Do fish sleep?	Fish live any place there is water.
Fish are pretty.	What do they eat?	Fish eat little animals they find in the water.
	Can fish hear me talk?	Fish eyes don't have eyelids.
		Fish swim by moving their tails.
		Fish will die if they are not in the water because they cannot breathe.
		Fish hatch from eggs in the water.
		Fish have all the colors of the rainbow.
		Fishes' skin is covered with scales.
		Yes, fish can hear.

A Page From a Child's Fish Counting Book

I see 8 | little | Fish.

🐟 *Listening center* Children listen to cassette tapes of Dr. Seuss's *One Fish Two Fish Red Fish Blue Fish* (1960) and *Fish Is Fish* (Lionni, 2005) and follow along in individual copies of the books.

🐟 *Storytelling center* Children use storyboards (pictures from the story backed with cardboard and laminated) from *The Rainbow Fish* (Pfister, 2002) and puppets of the rainbow fish and other fish to retell the story and create new adventures for the rainbow fish.

🐟 *Sequencing center* Kindergartners arrange a set of life-cycle photos in order from egg to adult fish.

🐟 *Sorting center* Children sort picture cards of fish and other water animals and place the cards with pictures of fish in one pocket chart labeled "Fish," and pictures of other animals in the "Not Fish" pocket chart. Fish pictures include goldfish, swordfish, trout, shark, eel, catfish, and seahorse; other animal pictures include dolphin, octopus, crab, turtle, whale, jellyfish, lobster, sea otter, and starfish. Mrs. LaRue introduced this center after teaching that fish have backbones and breathe with gills. The children practiced identifying and sorting the picture cards with the teacher before working at the center.

🐟 *Word work center* Mrs. LaRue teaches phonemic awareness, phonics, and spelling lessons here. The children read and recite rhymes about fish, match objects that rhyme, such as *fish* and *dish,* and sort pictures and objects that begin with /f/, such as a fish, a fan, and a feather. They also write letters and words on dry-erase boards as Mrs. LaRue teaches handwriting skills at the same time she is teaching phonics and spelling.

🐟 *Library center* Children look at fish books from the text set. Each day, a fifth-grade student comes to help out at the center. This student rereads one of the books Mrs. LaRue has already read to interested children while other kindergartners look at books independently.

The highlight of the unit is the day that the children take a field trip to a nearby aquarium to observe the fish they've been learning about. Mrs. LaRue takes many

books about specific people are biographies and autobiographies: Biographies are accounts of a person's life written by someone else, such *as Leonardo: Beautiful Dreamer* (Byrd, 2003), and autobiographies are written by the featured person. Many authors of children's books, including Gary Paulsen (1999, 2001), Stan and Jan Berenstain (2002), Tomie dePaola (2006), Lois Lowry (1998), and Dick King-Smith (2002), have written autobiographies that appeal to children who enjoy their books. In addition, many upper-grade students read Francisco Jiménez's moving books about his family's experiences as migrant farm workers, *The Circuit* (1997) and *Breaking Through* (2001). Other books about animals, places, and things are referred to simply as nonfiction. Figure 10–1 lists the types of informational books.

Many nonfiction books are concept books—they explore a topic, such as *Hurricanes* (Simon, 2003) or *Mosque* (Macaulay, 2003). When the concept is explored mainly using photos, the book is a photo essay. Others are arranged in special ways. For example, in alphabet books, such as *America: A Patriotic Primer* (Cheney, 2002), the information is organized around key words beginning with each letter of the alphabet. Information is organized sequentially in how-to books, and the question-and-answer format is used in others, including . . . *If You Lived When There Was Slavery in America* (Kamma, 2004). Journals and collections of letters, such as *Searching for Anne Frank: Letters From Amsterdam to Iowa* (Rubin, 2003), are informational books, too.

Multigenre Books Present Information Using More Than One Genre. The Magic School Bus series of science-related books, including *The Magic School Bus in the Rain Forest* (Cole, 1998), and the social studies–related books in the Ms. Frizzle's Adventures series, including *Ms. Frizzle's Adventures: Medieval Castle* (Cole, 2003), are the best-known multigenre books. The main text is presented as a narrative, and the side panels and other special boxes provide additional information. This information is presented as questions and answers, notes, and brief reports written by Ms. Frizzle's students as well as charts, maps, and other diagrams. *The 5,000-Year-Old Puzzle: Solving a Mystery of Ancient Egypt* (Logan, 2002) presents information about the discovery of King Tut's tomb through journal entries, photos, maps, postcards, sidebars, and newspaper articles. By using a combination of genres, the author and illustrator provide multiple viewpoints and enrich their presentation of information in the book. In *Leonardo: Beautiful Dreamer* (Byrd, 2003), boxes with notes, explanations, and excerpts from Leonardo da Vinci's own notes amplify the text. Multigenre books are richly layered texts, often presented in picture-book form. Because of the complexity of the page layout, Chapman and Sopko (2003) compare reading multigenre books to peeling an onion. They recommend that teachers read such books three or four times over a period of several days so that students can fully comprehend and appreciate them. First, they suggest taking a picture walk to examine the illustrations. Then teachers read the book, focusing on the informational text, and for the second reading, they focus on the narrative text. Finally, they focus on the sketches and borders. Of course, the number of rereadings depends on the students' interests and the complexity of the book.

Differences Between Stories and Informational Books. Stories and informational books are different; they're written and read differently. It's important that children learn about these differences so that they can recognize whether a book is a story or nonfiction in order to read it effectively. To examine these differences, pick up a story and a nonfiction book on the same topic; Mary Pope Osborne's popular Magic Tree House series, for example, includes both stories and accompanying nonfiction research

FIGURE 10–1

Types of Informational Books

Type	Description	Examples
Concept books	A topic is delineated using a combination of text and illustrations.	Ballard, C. (2004). *How we use water.* Cambridge, MA: Candlewick Press. (P–M) McWhorter, D. (2004). *A dream of freedom: The civil rights movement from 1954 to 1968.* New York: Scholastic. (U)
Photo essays	A photo display with minimal accompanying text.	Goodman, S. E. (2004). *Skyscraper: From the ground up.* New York: Knopf. (M) Sobol, R. (2004). *An elephant in the backyard.* New York: Dutton. (P–M)
Alphabet books	Facts are presented in alphabetical order.	Grodin, E. (2004). *D is for democracy: A citizen's alphabet.* Chelsea, MI: Sleeping Bear Press. (M)
Directions	The steps in making or doing something are described.	LaFosse, M. G. (2004). *Origami activities: Asian arts and crafts for creative kids.* North Clarendon, VT: Tuttle. (M–U)
Question-and-answer books	A question-and-answer format is used to share information.	Crisp, M. (2004). *Everything dolphin: What kids really want to know about dolphins.* Minnetonka, MN: NorthWord. (M)
Biographies	An account of a person's life, written by someone else.	Krull, K. (2004). *The boy on Fairfield Street: How Ted Geisel grew up to become Dr. Seuss.* New York: Random House. (M) Robinson, S. (2004). *Promises to keep: How Jackie Robinson changed America.* New York: Scholastic. (M–U)
Autobiographies	An account of a person's life, written by that person.	Weber, E. N. R. (2004). *Rattlesnake mesa: Stories from a Native American childhood.* New York: Lee & Low. (U)
Journals, letters, and speeches	A collection of documents.	Al-Windawi, T. (2004). *Thura's diary: My life in wartime Iraq.* New York: Viking. (U)
Reference books	A comprehensive collection of articles on a topic.	Ransford, S. (2004). *The Kingfisher illustrated horse and pony encyclopedia.* Boston: Kingfisher. (M–U)
Blended story/ informational books	A book that combines narrative and expository elements.	Warren, A. (2004). *Escape from Saigon: How a Vietnam War orphan became an American boy.* New York: Farrar, Straus & Giroux. (U)

P = primary grades (K–2); M = middle grades (3–5); U = upper grades (6–8).

guides. The differences are easy to pick out when you read *Hour of the Olympics* (Osborne, 1998) and *Ancient Greece and the Olympics* (Osborne, 2004). Here is a list of differences that a class of fourth graders noticed after reading these two books:

- Informational books are true, but stories are invented.
- You can start reading anywhere in an informational book, but you read stories from beginning to end.

- Informational books have photos and drawings, but stories just have drawings.
- Informational books have a table of contents, but only some stories have it.
- Informational books have indexes at the back, but stories don't.
- Informational books have extra things: notes in the margin, highlighted words, pronunciation guides, and diagrams with labels.
- At the end of informational books, the author tells you how to learn more.

As they examine informational books, children learn how to use the special features to enhance their comprehension. They learn to use an index to locate specific information, to use diagrams and margin notes to learn more about topics presented in the regular text, and to notice the vocabulary terms that are highlighted in the text.

Why Use Informational Books? According to Kristo and Bamford (2004), the most compelling reason for using informational books is the impact that they have on students. As they read and listen to the teacher read informational books, students expand their background knowledge and enrich their vocabulary. Many of the words they're learning are academic English. The students often become more interested in reading and learning through nonfiction. Teachers notice that they participate more actively in class projects and show initiative in researching topics. More than just learning facts, students are often more motivated and better prepared for school success when they read informational books.

Expository Text Structures

Informational books are organized in particular ways called *expository text structures.* Five of the most common organizational patterns are *description, sequence, comparison, cause and effect,* and *problem and solution* (Meyer & Freedle, 1984). Figure 10–2 gives an overview of these patterns and lists informational books illustrating each one. Some informational books are organized around a single pattern, but often they use a combination of patterns. Gail Gibbons's picture book *Owls* (2006), for example, is basically a book that describes owls, their behavior, and their habitat (descriptive), but the book also includes information on their life cycle (sequence), different species (comparison), and environmental hazards threatening some species (cause and effect).

     Description Writers describe a topic by listing characteristics, features, and examples in this organizational pattern. Phrases such as *for example* and *characteristics are* cue this structure. When students delineate any topic, such as tigers, submarines, or Alaska, they use description.

     Sequence Writers list items or events in numerical or chronological order in this pattern. Cue words include *first, second, third, next, then,* and *finally.* Students use sequence to write directions for completing a math problem, the stages in an animal's life cycle, or events in a biography.

     Comparison Writers explain how two or more things are alike or different in this structure. *Different, in contrast, alike, same as,* and *on the other hand* are cue words and phrases that signal this structure. When students compare and contrast book and video versions of a story, reptiles and amphibians, or life in ancient Greece with life in ancient Egypt, they use this organizational pattern.

     Cause and effect Writers describe one or more causes and the resulting effect or effects in this pattern. *Reasons why, if . . . then, as a result, therefore,* and *because* are words and phrases that cue this structure. Explanations of why dinosaurs

---

FIGURE 10–2

The Expository Text Structures

Structure	Description	Examples
Description	A topic is delineated using attributes and examples.	Arnosky, J. (2002). *All about frogs.* New York: Scholastic. (P–M) Gibbons, G. (2007). *Vegetables we eat.* New York: Holiday House. (P) Simon, S. (2000). *Gorillas.* New York: HarperCollins. (M–U)
Sequence	Steps, events, or directions are presented in numerical or chronological order.	Hibbert, C. (2004). *The life of a grasshopper.* Chicago: Raintree. (P–M) Steltzer, U. (1995). *Building an igloo.* New York: Holt. (P–M) Zemlicka, S. (2004). *From fruit to jelly.* Minneapolis: Lerner. (P)
Comparison	Two or more things are compared or contrasted.	Markle, S. (1993). *Outside and inside trees.* New York: Bradbury Press. (M) Robinson, F. (1995). *Solid, liquid, or gas?* Chicago: Childrens Press. (P) Spier, P. (1991). *We the people.* New York: Doubleday. (M–U)
Cause and effect	Causes and the resulting effects are described.	Heller, R. (1999). *The reason for a flower.* New York: Grosset & Dunlap. (M) Lauber, P. (1995). *Who eats what? Food chains and food webs.* New York: HarperCollins. (M) Pfeffer, W. (2004). *Wiggling worms at work.* New York: HarperCollins. (P–M)
Problem and solution	A problem and one or more solutions are presented. Also includes question-and-answer format.	Allen, T. B. (2004). *George Washington, spymaster: How the Americans outspied the British and won the Revolutionary War.* Washington, DC: National Geographic Association. (M–U) Geisert, B. (1995). *Haystack.* Boston: Houghton Mifflin. (P) Schanzer, R. (2003). *How Ben Franklin stole the lightning.* New York: HarperCollins. (M)

became extinct, the effects of pollution on the environment, or the causes of the Civil War use the cause-and-effect pattern.

🖋 ***Problem and solution*** Writers present a problem and offer one or more solutions in this expository structure. A variation is the question-and-answer format, in which the writer poses a question and then answers it. Cue words and phrases include *the problem is, the puzzle is, solve,* and *question . . . answer.* Students use this structure when they write about why money was invented, saving endangered animals, and building dams to stop flooding. They often use the problem-solution pattern in writing advertisements and in other persuasive writing.

Graphic organizers can help students organize and visually represent ideas for the five organizational patterns. Students might use a cluster for description, a Venn diagram or T-chart for comparison, or a series of boxes and arrows for cause and effect (Yopp & Yopp, 2005). Most of the research on expository text structures has focused on older students' use of these patterns in reading; however, children also use the patterns and cue words in their writing (Raphael, Englert, & Kirschner, 1989).

Even though the expository text structures are used with informational texts, some books that are classified as stories also involve sequence, cause and effect, or one of the other expository text structures. Teachers can point out these structures or use graphic organizers to help students look more closely at the story. The popular *The Very Hungry Caterpillar* (Carle, 2002), for example, involves two sequences: Eric Carle uses sequence to show the development of the caterpillar from egg to butterfly and to list what the caterpillar ate each day. In *The Blue and the Gray* (2001), a story about the construction of a modern interracial community on the site of a Civil War battlefield, Eve Bunting contrasts the misery of the war with the harmony of the neighborhood. Bunting's Caldecott Medal book about the riots in Los Angeles, *Smoky Night* (1999), demonstrates cause and effect. Anger causes the riots, and the riots bring hope and understanding.

Teaching Students About Informational Books

Teachers infuse informational books into their classrooms and incorporate them into instruction throughout the school day. They read aloud informational books and often pair them with stories or with content-area textbooks. Teachers also teach students how to read and understand nonfiction and about the unique structures and features of these books.

Scott Cunningham/Merrill

Graphic Organizers

These second graders are working with their teacher to create a cluster to record information they are learning during a unit on animals. They are beginning the cluster after reading a book about different types of animal homes, and as they continue to read books and learn more about animal homes, they will add more information to the cluster. Later they will use the information on the cluster to make posters and write reports. Clusters and other graphic organizers are important note-taking tools for all students, even primary-grade students.

How to Read Informational Books. To take full advantage of informational books, students need to know how to read them and how to use their special features to locate information, how to read pages that combine textual and visual information, and how to use text structure to comprehend and remember what they've read. Kristo and Bamford (2004) call this "navigating" informational books. Teachers teach students how to navigate informational books through minilessons and demonstrations as they read books aloud.

Reading nonfiction begins in kindergarten; it shouldn't be postponed until students are older. Young children can distinguish fact from fiction and learn information from informational books that teachers read aloud (Richgels, 2002). Primary-grade teachers often use informational big books for read-alouds, and children are actively engaged in the reading experience. They listen intently, ask questions, share experiences, and notice nonfiction features in the text. In addition, the collections of leveled books that teachers use in guided reading in the primary grades include many nonfiction titles.

Teachers use the same reading process to read stories, informational books, and poems, but some of the activities vary because informational books are different from other types of texts and place different demands on readers. When students read informational books, activating and building their background knowledge and introducing key vocabulary words become more important. Teachers often spend more time during the prereading stage to ensure that students are prepared to begin reading. Students also examine the special features of nonfiction texts so that they're prepared to use the features as comprehension aids while they're reading.

During reading, the focus is on helping students identify and remember the big ideas. Sometimes students read an informational book one section at a time. They turn the heading of the section into a question to set a purpose for reading, and then they read to find the answer. Students often stop to discuss each section of text after they've read it, rather than reading the entire book before talking about it. Their discussions are instructional conversations, not grand conversations.

After reading, the focus is on deepening students' understanding of the big ideas. They reread sentences with the big ideas, add vocabulary to the word wall, complete graphic organizers to emphasize the relationships among the big ideas, draw visual representations of the big ideas, and create projects to apply what they've learned.

Examining Expository Text Structures. Just as teachers teach students about the elements of story structure, they point out how authors structure informational books. When students recognize the five expository text structures in books they are reading, they are better able to comprehend what they are reading, and when they structure their own informational writing according to these structures, the writing is easier to understand. Research over the past 20 years has confirmed the importance of teaching students to recognize expository text structures as an aid to reading comprehension and to improve writing effectiveness (Harvey, 1998; Robb, 2003).

Many informational books are clearly organized using one of the expository text structures, and students can identify the pattern because it is signaled by the title, topic sentences, or cue words. Other books, however, use a combination of two or more structures or may have no apparent structure at all. Sometimes the title of a book incorrectly signals an organizational pattern. When the book doesn't have a clear structure or falsely signals a structure, students are likely to have trouble

What Students Need to Learn About Informational Books

Topics

Procedures	Concepts	Strategies and Skills
Expository Text Structures Topics		
Make clusters	Description	Vary reading according to purpose
Make Venn diagrams	Sequence	Locate information in resources
Make flowcharts	Comparison	Interpret information
	Cause and effect	Identify expository text structures
	Problem and solution	Note cue words
		Use graphic organizers
Report-Writing Topics		
Read charts, diagrams, and maps	Reports versus stories	Design questions
Make K-W-L charts	Alphabet books	Gather information
Draw clusters	Introductions	Organize information
Draw diagrams	Big ideas	Take a stand
Write data charts	Conclusions	Summarize
	Transitions	
Draw time lines		
Make cubes		

I invite you to learn more about reading and writing information by visiting MyEducationLab. To see how first graders create a chart about the ocean food chain, go to the topic "Visually Representing" and click on the video "Graphic Organizers."

comprehending and remembering big ideas. Whenever there isn't a clear structure, teachers should provide one through the purpose they set for reading the book.

As teachers share informational books with students, they teach them to identify the expository text structures. Being able to identify the expository structures is not the goal, but when students recognize how a text is structured, they're better able to comprehend what they're reading. Similarly, students learn to diagram each expository text structure using a specific graphic organizer so they'll be able to use

Minilesson

Mr. Uchida Teaches His Fifth Graders How to Write Data Charts

1 Introduce the topic

Mr. Uchida's fifth graders are preparing to write state reports. They have each chosen a state to research, and they developed a list of five research questions:

Who are the people in the state?
What are the physical features of the state?
What are the key events in the state's history?
What is the economy of the state?
What places should you visit in the state?

Mr. Uchida explains that students need to collect information to answer each of these five questions, and he has a neat tool to use to collect the data: It's called a *data chart*.

2 Share examples

Mr. Uchida shares three sample data charts that his students made to collect information for their state reports last year. He unfolds the large sheets of white construction paper that have been folded into many cells or sections. Each cell is filled with information. The students examine the data charts and read the information in each cell.

3 Provide information

Mr. Uchida folds a clean sheet of construction paper into four rows and five columns to create 20 cells. Then he unfolds the paper, shows it to the students, and counts the 20 cells. He explains how he folded the paper and traces over the folded lines so that students can see the cells.

Then he writes the five research questions in the cells in the top row. He explains that students will write the information they locate to answer each question in the cells under that question. He demonstrates how to paraphrase information and take notes in the cells.

4 Supervise practice

Mr. Uchida passes out large sheets of white construction paper and assists students as they divide the sheet into 20 cells and write the research questions in the top row. Then the fifth graders begin to take notes using resources they have collected. Mr. Uchida circulates in the classroom, helping students to locate information and take notes.

5 Reflect on learning

After several days, Mr. Uchida brings the class together to check on the progress students are making with their data charts. Students show their partially completed charts and talk about their data collection. They ask what to do when they can't find information or when the information won't all fit into one box. Several students comment that they know how they will use their data charts when they begin writing their reports: They will use all the information in one column for one chapter of the report. They are amazed to have made this discovery!

the structure to help them pick out the main ideas when they are reading. This knowledge pays off as well when students are writing: They apply what they have learned as they organize their writing.

Minilessons. Teachers present minilessons about the five expository text structures and show students how to use the organizational patterns to improve their reading comprehension as well as to organize their writing. A list of minilesson topics related to expository text structures is presented on the preceding page.

RESEARCHING AND WRITING REPORTS

Isn't researching too difficult for children? Not according to Paula Rogovin (2001), who points out that children are naturally inquisitive. They enthusiastically pursue special interests and show genuine engagement with learning as they participate in research workshop. They identify an important question that drives the research (McMackin & Siegel, 2002). Asking and answering questions seem to be as empowering for children as for adults and help children become more thoughtful adults. As children explore topics they're passionate about and search for answers to questions that puzzle them, they learn the inquiry process. Their understanding of the world deepens as they uncover answers, write reports, and share what they've learned with classmates (Harvey, 1998).

Visual Reports

Students can report the answers they've found in charts, maps, flowcharts, and other diagrams (Stead, 2006). Visual reports are used when the information can be presented more effectively through a diagram than through a written report. Formats for visual reports include clusters, diagrams, data charts, maps, time lines, and cubes. Moline (1995) explains that visual presentations are sophisticated, multilayered reports. At first thought, these formats might seem easier to produce than written reports, but if they are done properly, they're just as challenging.

The diagrams used for visual reports can be used as learning tools as well as for reports. When students make a flowchart in their learning logs, for example, they are using the flowchart as a graphic organizer to better understand a concept they're learning. Students' diagrams are quickly sketched when they are being used as part of the learning process. In contrast, when students use diagrams for visual reports, they use the writing process to draft, revise, edit, and make a final copy. As reports, visual reports are as formal as other types of reports.

As students develop their visual reports, they consider the layout, how the words and drawings are integrated, and the typography, the type styles they use to communicate meaning (Moline, 1995). As they plan their layout, students consider the arrangement of the diagram on the page; the use of lines, boxes, and headings to organize information; and the drawings and colors to highlight key points. Students also consider how they use type styles: They might print some words in all capital letters or highlight key terms, or they might choose a type style for the title that emphasizes the concept. For example, when students make a visual report on ancient Egypt, they use a type style that resembles hieroglyphics for the title. Word processing programs allow students to experiment with a variety of fonts and to use italics and boldface to add emphasis.

Two types of visual reports are *clusters* and *cubes*. Clusters are weblike diagrams that students use to gather and organize information (Bromley, Irvin-Devitis, Hires, 1999; Rico, 1983). The topic is written in a circle centered on a sheet of paper or poster. Main ideas are written on rays drawn out from the circle, and branches with details and examples are added to complete each main idea.

Two clusters are presented in Figure 10–3. The top cluster was developed by a sixth-grade teacher during a thematic unit on birds. The purpose of the cluster was to assist students in categorizing birds such as cardinals, penguins, vultures,

How Do English Learners Use Writing as a Learning Tool?

Writing is a learning tool for all students, and it's an essential tool for helping English learners remember the big ideas and important details that they've read in informational books. Students are more apt to understand connections among big ideas when they write about them, both in learning logs and through projects. Peregoy and Boyle (2005) recommend that teachers have English learners use writing to facilitate learning in these ways: write in learning logs, conduct research, and create projects. They've found that even young English learners can use writing as a learning tool and to report their learning.

Writing in Learning Logs

As English learners make entries in learning logs, they use the technical vocabulary that teachers have introduced and posted on word walls. They learn the meanings of these words and how to spell them. They practice stringing words together and manipulating sentences to clarify and extend the meaning. As they write, students summarize the big ideas they're learning, make connections to their background knowledge and personal experiences, and think about ways to apply the information. Sometimes students self-select topics for journal entries, but teachers often provide prompts to direct students' attention to the big ideas and technical vocabulary words.

Conducting Research

English learners often participate in small groups to conduct research on nonfiction topics related to thematic units. Like their classmates, English learners should select and shape their own research topics. They work together to learn about a topic using informational books, the Internet, and other classroom resources. The benefit of working together with their classmates is that English learners can share the work and learn from each other. Students use writing as they take notes and record information on graphic organizers and drawings.

Creating Projects

English learners create projects to share the results of their research. They can work with classmates to create traditional written reports, but multigenre reports are often more successful because they integrate written and visual reports of information. Peregoy and Boyle (2005) suggest that English learners create photo essays by organizing a set of photographs into a useful sequence and adding captions. Or, students can draw a series of pictures and use them in creating a pictorial essay. Afterward, students do brief oral presentations to share their projects with classmates.

All three of these ways to use writing as a learning tool are effective because they encourage students to think about the big ideas they're studying. As an added benefit, teachers can monitor students' writing to assess what they understand.

FIGURE 10–3

Two Clusters About Birds

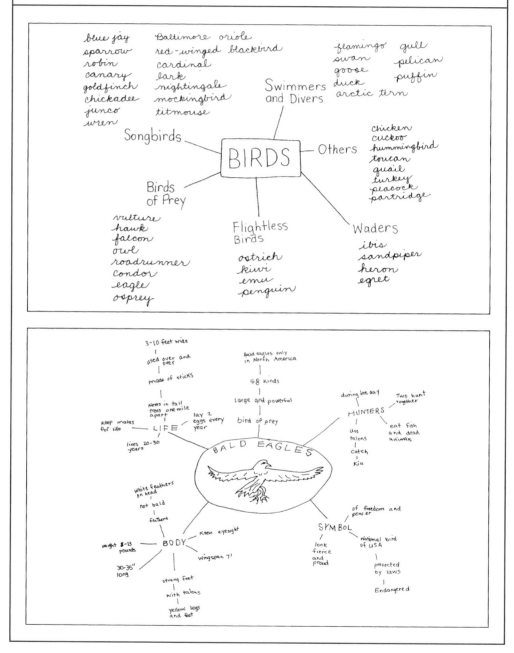

chickens, and ducks. As the class talked about the categories, students wrote the names of examples beside each category to complete the cluster. Later in the unit, students each chose one bird to research, and then they presented the results of their research in cluster form. The bottom cluster presents the results of one student's research on bald eagles. The information in the cluster is divided into four categories: life, hunters, symbol, and body; other, more general, information is listed at the top of the figure.

Cubing is a useful procedure for thematic units; middle- and upper-grade students can cube topics such as Antarctica, the United States Constitution, tigers or other endangered animals, the Underground Railroad, and the Nile River. In cubing, students explore a topic they have studied from six dimensions or viewpoints (Neeld, 1990). The name *cubing* comes from the fact that cubes have six sides and students explore the topic from six perspectives in this activity:

🖋 *Description.* Students describe the topic, including its colors, shapes, and sizes.

🖋 *Comparison.* Students compare the topic to something else. They consider how it is similar to or different from this other thing.

🖋 *Association.* Students associate the topic to something else and explain why the topic makes them think of this other thing.

🖋 *Analysis.* Students analyze the topic and tell how it is made or what it is composed of.

🖋 *Application.* Students apply the topic and tell how it can be used or what can be done with it.

🖋 *Argumentation.* Students argue for or against the topic. They take a stand and list reasons to support it.

The steps in cubing are described in the Step by Step feature below.

What's especially valuable about cubing is that students apply the information they've been learning about a topic in new ways as they analyze, associate, and consider the other perspectives. Figure 10–4 presents a cubing written by small groups of fifth graders at the end of a thematic unit on the American Revolution.

--------- Cubing ---------

Step by Step

1 Choose a topic. Students choose a familiar topic related to a social studies or science unit.

2 Examine the topic from each perspective. Students divide into six small groups, and each group examines the topic from one of the perspectives.

3 Draft a paragraph. Students brainstorm ideas and use them to develop a paragraph that explores the perspective.

4 Share drafts with the class. Students read their paragraphs to the class, and classmates react to the ideas and novel connections they've made and suggest possible revisions.

5 Revise and edit the paragraphs. Students revise, edit, and then make a final copy of their paragraphs.

6 Construct the cube. Students attach the final copies of their paragraphs to a box or cube.

7 Display the cube. Students display the cube in the classroom.

FIGURE 10–4

A Cubing on the American Revolution

Describe	The American Revolution was fought from 1775 to 1783 between Britain's Lobster Backs and the young American patriots. From the first major battle of Bunker Hill in 1775 to the battle of Yorktown in 1781, there were many hardships and deaths. The brave Americans continued on in spite of Britain's better supplied army because they wanted freedom, justice, and independence from King George.
Compare	The American Revolution and the Civil War were alike in many ways. They were both fought on American soil. Both wars were fought for people's rights and freedoms. With families fighting against families, these wars were very emotional. The winning side of each war had commanding generals who became presidents of the United States: George Washington and Ulysses S. Grant. The soldiers in the war rallied to the song "Yankee Doodle."
Associate	We celebrate the American Revolution on the 4th of July with fireworks and parades. Fireworks are spectacular things for spectacular days! Rockets shoot into the air like cannonballs! Great big booms and sparkles fall from the sky as people celebrate! Parades remind us of soldiers marching into battle led by flutes, drums, and flags! The 4th of July is a celebration of history.
Analyze	The American Revolution began when King George taxed the colonists too much and did not ask them if they wanted to pay or not. In five years, the Stamp Act, the Townsend Act, the Quartering Act, and the Intolerable Acts were forced on the colonists. This money was to pay for the French and Indian War. This made the colonists angry. One time the colonists dressed up like Indians and threw tea into the Boston Harbor. King George kept on pushing until the colonists revolted and started a war.
Apply	The most important outcome of the American Revolution was the beginning of our 200-year-old country. We enjoy the freedom of speech, religion, and the press. The Constitution grants us a lot of other freedoms, too. This living document has given us the opportunity to be anything we want to be.
Argue for	If we had not fought and won the American Revolution, there would be no United States of America. We would not have the right to speak our minds. We might all have to go to the same church. We would not have freedom or equality. There would be no Liberty Bell or Statue of Liberty. Although war is scary, painful, and violent, if we had the chance to go back, we would go and fight with all our might. We would rather do math problems all day than be ruled by a king.

"All About . . ." Books

Children write or dictate "All About . . . " books on a single topic. Usually one piece of information and an illustration appear on each page. A second grader wrote the "All About . . ." book, "Snowy Thoughts," shown in Figure 10–5, as part of a unit on the four seasons. Even though the child omitted some capital letters and punctuation

FIGURE 10–5

A Second Grader's "All About . . . " Book

marks and used invented spelling for a few words in his book, the information can be easily deciphered.

Young children can dictate reports to their teacher, who serves as scribe to record them. After listening to a guest speaker, viewing a film, or reading several books about a particular topic, kindergartners and first graders can dictate brief reports. A class of kindergartners compiled this book-length report on police officers:

Page 1: *Police officers help people who are in trouble. They are nice to kids. They are only mean to robbers and bad people. Police officers make people obey the laws. They give tickets to people who drive cars too fast.*

Page 2: *Men and women can be police officers. They wear blue uniforms like Officer Jerry's. But sometimes police officers wear regular clothes when they work undercover. They wear badges on their uniforms and on their hats. Officer Jerry's badge number is 3407. Police officers have guns, handcuffs, whistles, sticks, and two-way radios. They have to carry all these things.*

Page 3: *Police officers drive police cars with flashing lights and loud sirens. The cars have radios so the officers can talk to other police officers at the police station. Sometimes they ride on police motorcycles or on police horses or in police helicopters or in police boats.*

Page 4: *Police officers work at police stations. The jail for the bad people that they catch is right next door. One police officer sits at the radio to talk to the police officers who are driving their cars. The police chief works at the police station, too.*

Page 5: *Police officers are your friends. They want to help you so you shouldn't be afraid of them. You can ask them if you need some help.*

Page 6: *How We Learned About Police Officers for Our Report*

    1. We read these books:
    Police by Ray Broekel
    What Do They Do? Policemen and Firemen by Carla Greene
    2. We interviewed Officer Jerry.
    3. We visited the police station.

The teacher read two books aloud to the children, and Officer Jerry visited the classroom and talked to the class about his job. The children also took a field trip to the police station. The teacher took photos of Officer Jerry, his police car, and the police station to illustrate the report. With this background, the children and the teacher together developed a cluster with these five main ideas: what police officers do, what equipment police officers have, how police officers travel, where police officers work, and police officers are your friends. The children added details to each main idea until each one developed into one page of the report. The background of experiences and the clustering activity prepared children to compose their report. After they completed the report, included a bibliography called "How We Learned About Police Officers for Our Report," and inserted the photographs, it was ceremoniously presented to the school library to be enjoyed by all students in the school.

Collaborative Reports

An effective way to introduce report writing is to write a collaborative report. The teacher presents a broad "umbrella" topic, and then students brainstorm subtopics and identify questions related to them. Students choose questions, and those who are interested in the same questions gather in small groups to work together. Before they begin working, however, the teacher chooses one of the questions that no one chose and the class researches that question and writes the answer collaboratively. Then the groups work together to research their questions and write their sections of the report. Afterward, the teacher collects the completed sections, compiles them, and makes copies for each student. The steps are listed in the Step by Step feature below.

A class of second graders researched crabs as part of a thematic unit about the seashore. First they wrote this chapter as a collaborative report:

How Are Crabs Like Us?

We don't look anything like crabs, but we are alike in some ways. The most important thing is that crabs and people are both alive. Crabs eat, but they eat different food than we do. Crabs have arms but they look different. They have pincers instead of fingers. They have legs, but they have 6 more legs than we do. We can walk, run, and swim, and that's what crabs can do.

Step by Step

Collaborative Reports

1 Choose a question.   Teachers identify an "umbrella" topic, and then students identify related questions to research.

2 Model how to write a section.   The teacher chooses a different question to research and works with students to gather information, organize it in a graphic organizer, and write the section of the report on chart paper. Often the teacher takes the students' dictation to speed up the process.

3 Gather and organize information.   Students working in small groups research their questions using books, the Internet, and other resources. They take notes and organize the information in a graphic organizer.

4 Write the sections.   Students write and refine their sections using the writing process. Then the class comes together and reads the entire report aloud, checking for errors or redundancies. Finally, students word-process the final copy of their sections.

5 Compile the report.   Students compile their sections, and as a class, they design the cover, make the title page and table of contents, and compile the bibliography.

6 Publish the report.   The teacher duplicates and binds a copy for each student.

Then the second graders divided into small groups and wrote answers to these questions:

Where Do Crabs Live?

Crabs live in lots of different places. Some crabs live in shallow pools. They also like to live under the sand and in the ocean. Each place is just perfect for the crabs to live and grow.

How Do Crabs Move?

Crabs have eight legs. There are four on each side. We think that so many legs probably makes it hard to move. Crabs don't walk or run like we do. They actually move sideways.

Do You Know Why Crabs Have Pincers?

Crabs have two claws called pincers. They use their pincers to catch food, and they use their pincers to fight predators like seagulls. The pincers are powerful.

How Do Crabs Grow?

Crabs have hard shells. They grow and grow inside their shells. When they outgrow their shells, crabs shed it and grow a new one.

Can Crabs Grow New Legs?

Yes! Crabs really can grow new legs. They can get new claws and new antennas, too. So if an animal bites off their leg, crabs grow new ones. They are small at first but they keep growing until they are normal. It's just remarkable!

Students can organize reports in a variety of formats—formats they see used in informational books. One possibility is a question-and-answer format; another possibility is an alphabet book. A group of fourth-grade students wrote an alphabet book about the California missions, with one page for each letter of the alphabet. The "U" page appears in Figure 10–6.

Individual Reports

After students learn to conduct research and share what they learn in a collaborative report, they're ready to write individual reports. Writing an individual report is similar to writing a collaborative report, except that students assume the entire responsibility themselves. To begin, students identify several research questions or an umbrella question with several subtopics, and then they research the answers. Each question and answer usually becomes a chapter in the report. Students use a variety of techniques as they conduct research: They interview experts, collect data through surveys, conduct experiments, make observations, consult Internet sources, and read

FIGURE 10–6

The "U" Page From an Alphabet Book on California Missions

Some of the Indians thought life was UNBEARABLE at the missions. They thought this because they couldn't hunt or do the things they were used to. Once they were at the missions they couldn't leave. They were sometimes beaten if they did.

informational books (Kristo & Bamford, 2004). They learn to choose the techniques that are most appropriate for their questions (Harvey, 1998).

As students consult the books and other resources, they collect lots of information that they need to remember. Students often use self-stick notes to mark important information in books as they're reading. Then they go back and write short phrases, usually paraphrasing the information, on note cards, or they complete graphic organizers. They don't try to take notes about everything they read, only about the big ideas. In addition, they're careful not to get distracted by other interesting information in the resources they're reading.

Next, students need to create categories to organize it. Choosing an appropriate organizational structure is important because it's reflected in the students' writing. The structure also influences which information is most important. Sometimes students complete graphic organizers, design charts, or write informal outlines.

As students begin to draft, they write sentences and paragraphs to present the information they collected. They also think about which special features to include to aid readers, such as chapter titles and headings. As they write, they summarize and synthesize the big ideas, being careful to distinguish between fact and opinion. They write leads to engage readers and summarize the big ideas in the conclusion. Students also create visuals to display other information, and sometimes they identify additional information to highlight in sidebars (Kristo & Bamford, 2004).

When students revise their rough drafts, their first concern is whether they've answered their questions. They share their rough drafts with classmates and get feedback on how well they're communicating. They also double-check their notes to ensure the accuracy of their information and statistics, add details, revise their leads, and check transitions. Next, students finish the writing process by editing their reports to correct misspelled words, capitalization and punctuation errors, and nonstandard English usage.

Students usually word-process the final copies of their reports, and they carefully format them, taking advantage of what they know about nonfiction features. They include a title page, a table of contents, chapter titles, illustrations with captions, photos downloaded from the Internet, a bibliography, and an index. They compile the pages and bind them into a book or display them on a chart. The steps in writing individual reports are reviewed in the Step by Step feature below.

A fourth-grade class began a unit on birds by brainstorming questions they wanted to answer. The teacher encouraged them to search for answers in the books they had checked out of the school and community libraries and during an interview with an ornithologist from the local zoo. Once they learned the answers to their

Step by Step

Individual Reports

1 Choose a topic. Students choose a topic for a report that's related to a thematic unit, hobby, or other interest.

2 Design research questions. Students brainstorm a list of questions related to the topic that they'd like to research. They review the list, combine some questions, delete others, and finally arrive at four to six questions that they think they can answer and that will be interesting to readers.

3 Gather and organize information. Students read books, consult Internet sources, and use other resources to gather information, and then they use graphic organizers to organize information they've collected.

4 Draft the report. Students write a rough draft using the information they've gathered. Each research question becomes a section or a chapter in students' reports.

5 Revise and edit the report. Students meet in writing groups to share their rough drafts, and then they make revisions based on the feedback they receive from their classmates. Afterward, they proofread and correct mechanical errors in their reports.

6 Publish the report. Students recopy their reports in book format and add illustrations, a title page, a table of contents, and bibliographic information.

FIGURE 10–7

An Excerpt From a Fourth Grader's Report on Egrets

How to Recognize an Egret!

An egret is a bird with white feathers. Some egrets have black and red feathers but the egrets around Marysville are white. They have very long necks and long beaks because they stick their heads under water to catch fish. An egret can be from 20 to 41 inches tall. When they are just standing, they look like in the picture but when they are flying their wing spand can stretch to one-and-a-half feet.

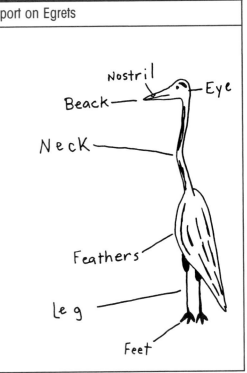

questions, the students were eager to share their new knowledge and decided to write reports and publish them as books. Each student's book began with a table of contents and contained four or five chapters, a glossary, a bibliography, and an index. An excerpt from a fourth grader's book on egrets is presented in Figure 10–7. The text was word processed, and then the student added the illustrations.

Multigenre Projects

A new approach to report writing is the multigenre project (Allen, 2001; Romano, 2000), in which students explore a topic through several genres. Tom Romano (1995) explains, "Each genre offers me ways of seeing and understanding that others do not" (p. 109). Grierson, Anson, and Baird (2002) explain that "research comes alive when students explore a range of alternate genres instead of writing the traditional research report" (p. 51). Students collect a variety of informational materials, including books, textbooks, Internet articles, charts, diagrams, and photos, and then they study the materials. Students write several pieces, including essays, letters, journal entries, stories, and poems; collect photos, charts, and other visual representations; and compile them in a book or display them on a poster. For example, for a multigenre project on the planet Mars, students might include the following pieces:

- An informational essay describing the planet
- A data chart comparing Mars to other planets taken from an informational book students have read

- A photograph of the planet downloaded from the NASA website
- A found poem about Mars with words and phrases taken from a book students have read
- A simulated journal written from the perspective of an astronaut who is exploring the planet

Through these five pieces, students present different kinds of information about the planet, and the project is much more complete than it would have been with just one genre. The LA Essentials box on the next page lists different genres that can be used for multigenre projects.

Teaching Students to Write Reports

For students to become capable researchers, teachers need to establish a climate of inquiry in their classrooms and teach students how to conduct research and write reports. They scaffold students' first report-writing experiences to help them develop the knowledge, strategies, and skills to be successful. Perry and Drummond (2002) describe this process as moving from teacher-regulated to student self-regulated report writing. They have identified these characteristics of classrooms that promote responsible, independent writers:

- The classroom is a community of learners where students collaborate and cooperate with classmates.
- Students are involved in meaningful research activities that require them to think strategically and reflectively.
- Students increasingly assume responsibility for their learning by making choices, dealing constructively with challenges, and evaluating their work.
- The evaluation emphasizes both research and the writing process that students use as well as the quality of their finished products.
- The teacher scaffolds students' learning by providing direct instruction about doing research, modeling the process, having students do research in groups, and gradually releasing responsibility to the students to work independently.

It's essential that teachers establish a climate of inquiry in their classrooms and teach students how to conduct research and write reports rather than just assigning students to write reports as homework. Nor is it enough for students to complete one research project during the school year.

The Inquiry Process. Inquiry is a way of learning (Berghoff, Egawa, Harste, & Hoonan, 2000). Students use the inquiry process as they ask questions and collect information to answer their questions in preparation for writing reports and sharing learning (McMackin & Siegel, 2002). Here are the steps:

1. *Questioning:* Students identify a question that interests them to research.
2. *Planning:* Students think about how they will be able to find answers to their questions. They identify people to interview, plan surveys and observations, and locate books, magazine articles, and Internet resources to use.
3. *Collecting:* Students gather information from a variety of resources and organize the information using a graphic organizer or outline.
4. *Synthesizing:* Students combine the big ideas to create a coherent report or other project.

GENRES FOR MULTIGENRE PROJECTS

Bibliography	Students list the resources they consulted in preparing the paper or poster or list suggested readings related to a topic.
Biographical sketch	Students write a biographical sketch of a person related to the topic being studied.
Cartoons	Students draw a cartoon or copy a published cartoon from a book or Internet article.
Clusters	Students draw clusters or other diagrams to display information concisely.
Cubes	Students examine a topic from six perspectives.
Data charts	Students create a data chart to list and compare information.
Found poems	Students collect words and phrases from a book or article and arrange them to make a poem.
Graffiti	Students write words and draw designs to represent the topic visually.
Letters	Students write simulated letters or make copies of real letters related to the topic.
Lifelines	Students draw lifelines and mark important dates related to a person's life.
Maps	Students make copies of actual maps or draw maps related to the topic.
Newspaper articles	Students make copies of actual newspaper articles or write simulated articles related to the topic.
Open-mind portraits	Students draw open-mind portraits of people related to the topic.
Photos	Students download photos from the Internet or make copies of photos in books.
Quotes	Students collect quotes about the topic from materials they are reading.
Simulated journals	Students write simulated-journal entries from the viewpoint of a person related to the topic.
Sketch-to-stretch	Students make sketch-to-stretch drawings to emphasize the theme or key points related to the topic.
Stories	Students write stories related to the topic.
Time lines	Students draw time lines to sequence events related to the topic.
Venn diagrams	Students draw Venn diagrams to compare the topic with something else.
Word wall	Students make an alphabetized word wall of key words related to the topic.

5. *Evaluating:* Students examine their reports to judge the accuracy of their information, the completeness of their answers, and the effectiveness of their writing.

6. *Reporting:* Students share their completed reports with classmates and other audiences.

This process, which is similar to the writing process, nurtures students' curiosity, promotes questioning, and develops students' ownership of their research projects.

Plagiarism isn't a big problem when students use the inquiry process, but they still need to understand what plagiarism is and why it's wrong. Students are less likely to plagiarize because they've collected information to answer questions that they care about, and because they have developed their compositions step by step—from prewriting and drafting to revising and editing. The two best ways to avoid having students copy from another source and pass it off as their own are to teach the inquiry process and to have students write reports at school using the writing process rather than assigning reports as homework.

Research Workshop. Research workshop is a 60- to 90-minute period where students identify questions and conduct research to find answers to the questions they've posed. It's a unique combination of reading workshop and writing workshop that can fit into all the patterns of practice, as shown in the box below. Sometimes students choose questions that interest them; at other times, research workshop is connected to thematic units. In this case, the teacher identifies an umbrella topic, and students choose subtopic questions. In addition to providing a large chunk of time for students to read, research, and write, teachers teach minilessons on research procedures and model how to do research as the class works together on collaborative projects. At the end of the workshop, students come together as a class to share what they've been working on and what they've learned.

When Rogovin (2001) conducts research workshops, she chooses broad topics, such as people at work or immigration, for her students to study, and then they choose subtopics, ask questions, and do research in small groups. The students collect information and share what they've learned by writing reports and giving oral

How Research Workshop Fits Into the Four Patterns of Practice

Literature Focus Units

After the students read a featured book during a literature focus unit, they may then participate in research workshop to learn more about the historical period in which the book was set or another related topic.

Literature Circles

Research workshop doesn't fit into literature circles, but after students read an informational book during a literature circle, they may decide to form an inquiry group to learn more about the topic.

Reading and Writing Workshop

Research workshop fits naturally because it's a combination of reading and writing workshop. Students read books to find answers to their questions and then share what they've learned by writing reports and other books.

Thematic Units

Students often use research workshop to delve more deeply into topics related to thematic units. They conduct research to find answers to questions and then write reports to share what they've learned.

presentations. Christine Duthie (1996) also has her primary-grade students conduct research during their writing workshop periods.

Minilessons. Teachers teach minilessons about nonfiction writing and to prepare students for writing reports (Portalupi & Fletcher, 2001). Students learn how to pose questions, search for answers, and share what they've learned. A list of minilesson topics related to report writing is presented on page 324. Included with the list is a description of Mr. Uchida's minilesson on data charts.

Assessing Students' Reports

Students need to understand what they're expected to do when they're asked to write a report and how they'll be assessed. Many teachers distribute a checklist before students begin working so that they can take responsibility for completing the assignment. The checklist for an individual report might include these observable behaviors and products:

- Identify four or five questions to research.
- Use a graphic organizer to gather and organize information to answer each question.
- Write a rough draft with a section or a chapter to answer each question.
- Meet in writing groups to get feedback about your rough draft.
- Make at least three changes in your rough draft.
- Complete an editing checklist with a partner.
- Add a bibliography.
- Write the final copy.

The checklist can be simpler or more complex, depending on students' ages and experiences. Students staple the checklist to the inside cover of the folder in which they keep all the work for the project and check off each requirement as they complete it.

Other teachers use rubrics. Sometimes they use commercially prepared rubrics, but it's more effective when teachers create a rubric with students before they begin to work. This way they'll know what's expected of them. The focus of the rubric is whether students answered their research questions clearly and completely. Teachers often specify these points in the rubric:

- Ideas are fully developed.
- Details elaborate ideas.
- Organization clarifies ideas.
- Transitions between paragraphs are effective.
- Style is captivating.
- Mechanics are used appropriately.

Sometimes teachers use the rubric to provide feedback during revising and editing as well as after the report has been completed.

LIFE STORIES

Children often wonder what it would be like to be someone else—an Olympic athlete, a test pilot, a knight in shining armor, a dancer, or the president, for example. One of the best ways to learn about other people's lives is by reading biographies and

autobiographies. There are so many life-story books available today that children can read about a wide range of contemporary and historical personalities, including Mohammed, Annie Oakley, J. K. Rowling, Dizzy Gillespie, Harriet Tubman, and Houdini. At the same time children are reading about these people's lives, they also are learning about personal qualities such as courage and determination that they can apply to their own lives to help them reach their dreams and deal with the realities of both success and failure. As they read life stories and listen to them read aloud, children learn about this genre and examine its structure. These books also serve as models for children's own writing.

Reading Biographies

Authors use several approaches in writing biographies (Fleming & McGinnis, 1985). The most common approach is historical: The writer focuses on dates and events and presents them chronologically. Many biographies that span the person's entire life follow this pattern, including *Theodore Roosevelt: Champion of the American Spirit* (Kraft, 2003) and *Martin's Big Words: The Life of Dr. Martin Luther King, Jr.* (Rappaport, 2001).

Next is the sociological approach, in which the writer describes life during a historical period, providing information about family life, food, clothing, education, economics, transportation, and so on. For instance, in *Woody Guthrie: Poet of the People* (Christensen, 2001), readers learn about the hard life many Americans faced during the Depression as they learn about the folk legend.

A third approach is psychological: The writer focuses on conflicts the central figure faces. Conflicts may be with oneself, others, nature, or society. The psychological approach has many elements in common with stories and is most often used in shorter autobiographies and biographies that revolve around particular events or phases in the person's life. One example is *John Muir: America's First Environmentalist* (Lasky, 2006), which describes Muir's reverence for the natural world and his drive to preserve it.

Biographies are accounts of a person's life written by someone else, and autobiographies are written by the featured person himself or herself. Contemporary biographies are written about a living person, whereas historical biographies are about people who are no longer alive. To make the account as accurate and authentic as possible, writers consult a variety of sources of information during their research. The best source, of course, is the biography's subject, and writers can learn many things about the person through an interview. Other primary sources include diaries and letters, photographs, mementos, historical records, and recollections of people who know the person. Examples of secondary sources are books and newspaper articles written by someone other than the biographical subject.

Recommended autobiographies and biographies appear in the Booklist on the next page . These life stories feature well-known people such as astronauts, prophets, and entertainers, as well as "common" people who have endured hardship and shown exceptional courage.

Booklist

LIFE STORIES

Autobiographies

Aldrin, B. (2005). *Reaching for the moon.* New York: HarperCollins. (P–M)

dePaola, T. (2006). *I'm still scared: The war years.* New York: Putnam. (P)

Fletcher, R. (2005). *Marshfield dreams: When I was a kid.* New York: Henry Holt. (M)

Gantos, J. (2002). *Hole in my life.* New York: Farrar, Straus & Giroux. (M–U)

Kimmel, E. A. (2005). *Tuning up: A visit with Eric A. Kimmel.* Katonah, NY: Richard C. Owen.

Jiménez, F. (2001). *Breaking through.* Boston: Houghton Mifflin. (M–U)

Ma, Y. (2005). *The diary of Ma Yan: The struggles and hopes of a Chinese schoolgirl.* New York: HarperCollins. (U)

Numeroff, L. (2003). *If you give an author a pencil.* Katonah, NY: Richard C. Owen. (P)

Russo, M. (2005). *Always remember me.* New York: Atheneum. (M–U)

Steig, W. (2003). *When everybody wore a hat.* New York: HarperCollins. (P–M)

Biographies

Cohn, A. L., & Schmidt, S. (2002). *Abraham Lincoln.* New York: Scholastic. (P–M)

Demi. (2003). *Muhammad.* New York: McElderry. (M)

Fleischman, S. (2006). *Escape! The story of the great Houdini.* New York: Greenwillow. (M–U)

Freedman, R. (2002). *Confucius: The golden rule.* New York: Scholastic. (M–U)

Mitchell, D. (2006). *Liftoff: A photobiography of John Glenn.* Washington, DC: National Geographic Society. (M–U)

Pinkney, A. D. (2002). *Ella Fitzgerald: The tale of a vocal virtuosa.* New York: Hyperion Books. (P–M)

Poole, J. (2005). *Joan of Arc.* New York: Knopf. (M–U)

St. George, J. (2004). *You're on your way, Teddy Roosevelt.* New York: Philomel. (M)

Weatherford, C. B. (2006). *Moses: When Harriet Tubman led her people to freedom.* New York: Hyperion Books. (P–M)

Winter, J. (2006). *Dizzy.* New York: Scholastic. (P–M)

Teaching Students to Write Autobiographies

When students write autobiographies, they relive and document their lives, usually in chronological order. They describe the memorable events that are important to know about in order to understand them. Autobiographical writing grows out of children's personal journal entries and "All About Me" books that they write in kindergarten and first grade. Students' own experiences and memories are their primary sources of information for writing.

"Me" Boxes. One way for students to focus on their own lives is to make a "me" box (Duthie, 1996). Students collect objects and pictures representing events in their lives, their families, their hobbies, and special accomplishments. Next, they write explanations to accompany each object. Then students decorate the outside of a shoe box, coffee can, or other container and put all the objects in it. They can use the same approach to make character boxes about a character in a book they are reading or about a historical figure as part of a biography project.

Lifeline Clotheslines. Another way students gather and organize information for an autobiography is to collect objects that symbolize their life and hang them on a lifeline clothesline (Fleming & McGinnis, 1985). Next, they write briefly about each object, explaining what the object is and how it relates to their lives, and then they add their explanations to the clothesline, too.

"All About Me" Books. Children in kindergarten and first grade often compile "All About Me" books. These autobiographies usually list information such as the child's birthday, family members, friends, and favorite activities, with drawings as well as text. Figure 10–8 shows two pages from a first grader's "All About Me" book. To write these books, the children first decide on a topic for each page; then, after brainstorming possible ideas for the topic, they draw a picture and write about it. Children may also need to ask their parents for information about their birth and events during their preschool years.

Teaching Students to Write Biographies

When students study someone else's life in preparation for writing a biography, they need to become personally involved in the project (Zarnowski, 1988). There are several ways to engage students in biographical study, that is, to help them walk in the subject's footsteps. For contemporary biographies, meeting and interviewing the

---

FIGURE 10–8

Two Pages From a First Grader's "All About Me" Book

This is me wen I'm five. I'm reading a book. My mom comes in and puts out my cloths for me to wear but I didn't, wat to wear them. I became very picky about my cloths my dad said.

This is my Grammy's house. I have my own room in it. Sometimes I sleep on the love seat. I like to see papa. Sometimes my papa takes me fishing. I love to go fishing. My Grammy makes me feel special.

person are best; for other projects, students read books about the person, view videos, dramatize events from the person's life, and write about the person. An especially valuable activity is writing simulated journals, in which students assume the role of the person they are studying and write journal entries just as that person might have.

Students write biographies about living people they know personally as well as about famous personalities. In contrast to the primary sources available for gathering information about local people, students may have to depend on secondary sources (e.g., books, magazines, newspapers, Internet sources) for information about well-known and geographically more distant people. Sometimes, however, students can write letters to well-known personalities or perhaps arrange conference telephone calls.

Lifelines. Students sequence the information they gather—about either their life or someone else's—on a lifeline, a person's time line. This activity helps students identify and sequence milestones and other events. They can use the information on the lifeline to identify topics for a biography.

Biography Boxes. Students can make biography boxes similar to "me" boxes. They begin by identifying items that represent the person, then collect them and put them in a box they have decorated. They also write papers to put with each object, explaining its significance to the person. A fifth grader created a biography box for Paul Revere and decorated it with aluminum foil, explaining that it looked like silver and Paul Revere was a silversmith. Inside the box, he placed the following items:

- A spoon (to represent his career as a silversmith)
- A toy horse (to represent his famous midnight ride)
- A tea bag (to represent his involvement in the Boston Tea Party)
- A copy of Longfellow's poem "The Midnight Ride of Paul Revere"
- An advertisement for Revere pots and pans (along with an explanation that Paul Revere is credited with inventing the process of layering metals)
- A portrait of the patriot
- Photos of Boston, Lexington, and Concord that were downloaded from the Internet
- A lifeline the student had drawn marking important events in Paul Revere's life

The student wrote a card describing the relationship of each object to Paul Revere and attached it to the item.

Biography Posters. Students present the information they've learned about the subject of their biography project on a poster. Posters can include a portrait of the person and information about the person's life and accomplishments. Students in an eighth-grade class made a biography quilt with paper squares, and each square was modeled after the illustrations in *My Fellow Americans,* by Alice Provensen (1995). One student's square about Martin Luther King Jr. is presented in Figure 10–9. This student drew a portrait of the civil rights leader set in Washington, D.C., on August 28, 1963, the day he delivered his famous "I Have a Dream" speech. The student also added well-known sayings and other phrases related to Martin Luther King Jr. around the outside.

FIGURE 10–9

A Biography Poster About Martin Luther King Jr.

Multigenre Biography Projects. Students write and draw a variety of pieces about a person to create a multigenre biography, which is like a multigenre report. Students collect and create some of the following items for a multigenre biography:

lifeline	*collection of objects*
quotations	*simulated journal*
photographs	*found poem or other poem*
open-mind portrait	*story*
report	*poster*

Each item is a complete piece by itself and contributes to the overall impact of the biography. Students compile their biographies on posters or in notebooks.

A seventh-grade class created multigenre biographies. To begin, students read a biography and located additional information about the person from two other sources. Then they created the following pieces for their biography project:

- A lifeline: Students made a lifeline of the person's life, indicating the dates of the person's birth and death and at least 10 key events in his or her life.
- A simulated journal: Students wrote 10 entries spanning the person's entire life.
- An open-mind portrait: Students drew a portrait of the person and on separate pages showed what the person was thinking about three key events in his or her life.
- Quotes: Students collected at least three quotes that best illustrated how the person spoke or what he or she believed.
- A heart map: Students drew a heart and filled it with pictures and words representing things that really mattered to the person.

Figure 10–10 presents excerpts from a seventh grader's multigenre biography project on Maya Angelou.

Assessing Students' Life Stories

Students need to know the requirements for their autobiography or biography project, as well as how they will be assessed or graded. A checklist for an autobiography might include the following components:

- Make a lifeline showing at least one important event for each year of your life.
- Draw a cluster showing at least three main-idea topics and at least five details for each topic.
- Write a rough draft with an introduction, three or more chapters, and a conclusion.
- Meet in a writing group to share your autobiography.
- Make at least three changes in your rough draft.
- Complete an editing checklist with a partner.
- Write a final copy with photos or drawings as illustrations.
- Compile your autobiography as a book.
- Decorate the cover.

The checklist for a biography might include the following requirements:

- Learn about the person's life from at least three sources (including Internet websites as well as books).
- Make a lifeline listing at least 10 important events.
- Write at least 10 simulated-journal entries as the person you are studying.
- Make a cluster with at least three main-idea topics and at least five details for each topic.
- Write a rough draft with at least three chapters and a bibliography.
- Meet in a writing group to share your biography.
- Make at least three changes in your rough draft.
- Complete an editing checklist with a partner.
- Recopy the biography.

FIGURE 10–10

Excerpts From a Seventh Grader's Multigenre Biography Project on Maya Angelou

Maya Angelou

In Maya's Heart

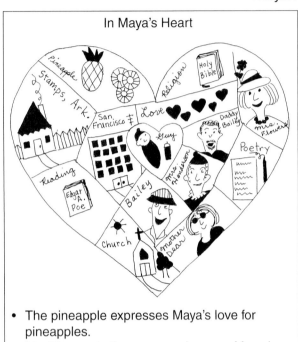

- The pineapple expresses Maya's love for pineapples.
- Ms. Flowers is the woman who gave Maya her first book of poetry.
- Mother Dear is Maya's mother and even though she didn't really raise her, Maya looked up to her.
- Bailey was Maya's brother and they had a strong bond being that they were only one year apart in age.
- Guy is her son and her entire life.

Dear Diary,
One night I was scared and momma let me sleep in the bed with her and Mr. Freeman. Then when momma left early to run an errand, I felt a strange pressure on my left leg. I knew it wasn't a hand because it was much too soft. I was afraid to move and I didn't budge. Mr. Freeman's eyes were wide open with both hands above the covers. He then said, "Stay right here, Rite, I'm not gonna hurt you." I really wasn't afraid, a little curious, but not afraid. Then he left and came back with a glass of water and poured it on the bed. He said, "see how you done peed in the bed." Afterwards, I was confused and didn't understand why Mr. Freeman had held me so gently, then accused me of peeing in the bed. Marguerite

Dear Diary,
While I was sitting talking to Miss Glory, Mrs. Cullinan called for someone. She said, "Mary P." We didn't know who she was calling, but my name is Marguerite. Now I settled for Margaret, but Mary was a whole nother name. Bailey told me bout Whites and how they felt like they had the power to shorten our names for their convenience. Miss Glory told me her name used to be Hallelujah and Mrs. Cullinan shortened it to Glory. Mrs. Cullinan sent me on an errand, which was a good idea because I was upset and anything was bound to come out of my mouth at the time.
Marguerite

Dear Diary,
Graduation day was a big event in Stamps. The high school seniors received most of the glory. I'm just a twelve year old 8th grader. I'm pretty high-ranked in my class along with Henry Reed. Henry is also our class valedictorian. The tenth grade teacher helped him with his speech. Momma was even going to close the store. Our graduation dresses are a lemon yellow, but momma added ruffles and cuffs with a crocheted collar. She added daisy embroideries around the trim before she considered herself finished. I just knew all eyes were going to be on me when graduation day came.
Marguerite

Quotes

"Cleanliness is next to Godliness."

"God blessed everyone with an intelligent mind. Only we can decide how we use it."

Students keep the checklist in their project folders and check off each item as it is completed; at the end of the project, they submit the folders to be assessed or graded. Teachers can award credit for each item on the checklist, as discussed in the section on assessing students' research reports. This approach helps students assume greater responsibility for their own learning and gives them a better understanding of why they receive a particular grade.

Review

Recent research suggests that reading and writing information may be as important for kindergarten through eighth-grade students as reading and writing stories. Students enjoy reading informational books, and they learn This knowledge about text structure supports students' reading and writing. Students write a variety of reports of information, including visual reports, collaborative books, and individual reports. Students also read biographies and autobiographies, and they write their own life stories. Here are some of the important concepts presented in this chapter:

- Students read informational books to learn information, and they write informational books to share information with others.
- Students may use either efferent or aesthetic reading when reading informational books, depending on their purpose for reading.
- Informational writing is organized into five expository text patterns: description, sequence, comparison, cause and effect, and problem and solution.
- Students use their knowledge of expository text structures when reading and writing informational books.
- Students create visual reports using clusters, diagrams, flowcharts, data charts, maps, time lines, and cubes.
- Students write collaborative reports to learn how to write reports before writing individual reports.
- Students prepare multigenre projects using a combination of reports, stories, poems, photographs and other illustrations, and other materials.
- Students make boxes, lifelines, and posters to document events in their own lives and in other people's lives.
- Students write autobiographies about events in their own lives and write biographies about both historical and contemporary personalities.
- Students use the writing process to write reports, autobiographies, and biographies.

Professional References

Allen, C. A. (2001). *The multigenre research paper: Voice, passion, and discovery in grades 4–6.* Portsmouth, NH: Heinemann.

Berghoff, B., Egawa, K. A., Harste, J. C., & Hoonan, B. T. (2000). *Beyond reading and writing: Inquiry, curriculum, and multiple ways of knowing.* Urbana, IL: National Council of Teachers of English.

Bromley, K., Irwin-Devitis, L., & Hires, D. (1999). *Graphic organizers.* New York: Scholastic.

Chapman, V. G., & Sopko, D. (2003). Developing strategic use of combined-text trade books. *The Reading Teacher, 57,* 236–239.

Duthie, C. (1996). *True stories: Nonfiction literacy in the primary classroom.* York, ME: Stenhouse.

Fleming, M., & McGinnis, J. (Eds.). (1985). *Portraits: Biography and autobiography in the secondary school.* Urbana, IL: National Council of Teachers of English.

Freeman, E. B. (1991). Informational books: Models for student report writing. *Language Arts, 68,* 470–473.

Grierson, S. T., Anson, A., & Baird, J. (2002). Exploring the past through multigenre writing. *Language Arts, 80,* 51–59.

Harvey, S. (1998). *Nonfiction matters: Reading, writing, and research in grades 3–8.* York, ME: Stenhouse.

Kristo, J. V., & Bamford, R. A. (2004). *Nonfiction in focus.* New York: Scholastic.

McMackin, M. C., & Siegel, B. S. (2002). *Knowing how: Researching and writing nonfiction, 3–8.* Portland, ME: Stenhouse.

Meyer, B. J., & Freedle, R. O. (1984). Effects of discourse type on recall. *American Educational Research Journal, 21,* 121–143.

Moline, S. (1995). *I see what you mean: Children at work with visual information.* York, ME: Stenhouse.

Moss, B., & Hendershot, J. (2002). Exploring sixth graders' selection of nonfiction trade books. *The Reading Teacher, 56,* 6–17.

Neeld, E. C. (1990). *Writing* (3rd ed.). Glenview, IL: Scott Foresman.

Palmer, R. G., & Stewart, R. A. (2003). Nonfiction trade book use in primary grades. *The Reading Teacher, 57,* 38–48.

Peregoy, S. F., & Boyle, O. F. (2005). *Reading, writing, and learning in ESL: A resource book for K–12 teachers* (4th ed.). Boston: Allyn & Bacon.

Perry, N., & Drummond, L. (2002). Helping young students become self-regulated researchers and writers. *The Reading Teacher, 56,* 298–310.

Portalupi, J., & Fletcher, R. (2001). *Nonfiction craft lessons: Teaching information writing K–8.* York, ME: Stenhouse.

Raphael, T. E., Englert, C. S., & Kirschner, B. W. (1989). Acquisition of expository writing skills. In J. M. Mason (Ed.), *Reading and writing connections* (pp. 261–290). Boston: Allyn & Bacon.

Read, S. (2001). "Kid mice hunt for their selfs": First and second graders writing research. *Language Arts, 78,* 333–342.

Richgels, D. J. (2002). Informational texts in kindergarten. *The Reading Teacher, 55,* 586–595.

Rico, G. L. (1983). *Writing the natural way.* Los Angeles: Tarcher.

Robb, L. (2003). *Teaching reading in social studies, science, and math.* New York: Scholastic.

Robb, L. (2004). *Nonfiction writing: From the inside out.* New York: Scholastic.

Rogovin, P. (2001). *The research workshop: Bringing the world into your classroom.* Portsmouth, NH: Heinemann.

Romano, T. (1995). *Writing with passion: Life stories, multiple genres.* Portsmouth, NH: Boynton/Cook.

Romano, T. (2000). *Blending genre, altering style: Writing multigenre papers.* Portsmouth, NH: Boynton/Cook.

Rosenblatt, L. M. (2005). *Making meaning with texts: Selected essays.* Portsmouth, NH: Heinemann.

Stead, T. (2002). *Is that a fact? Teaching nonfiction writing K–3.* Portland, ME: Stenhouse.

Stead, T. (2006). *Reality checks: Teaching reading comprehension with nonfiction K–5.* Portland, ME: Stenhouse.

Yopp, H. K., & Yopp, R. H. (2005). *Literature-based reading activities* (4th ed.). Boston: Allyn & Bacon.

Zarnowski, M. (1988, February). The middle school student as biographer. *Middle School Journal, 19,* 25–27.

Children's Book References

Berenstain, S., & Berenstain, J. (2002). *Down a sunny dirt road.* New York: Random House.

Bunting, E. (1999). *Smoky night.* San Diego: Harcourt Brace.

Bunting, E. (2001). *The blue and the gray.* New York: Scholastic.

Byrd, R. (2003). *Leonardo: Beautiful dreamer.* New York: Dutton.

Carle, E. (2002). *The very hungry caterpillar.* New York: Puffin Books.

Cheney, L. (2002). *America: A patriotic primer.* New York: Simon & Schuster.

Christensen, B. (2001). *Woody Guthrie: Poet of the people.* New York: Knopf.

Cole, J. (1998). *The magic school bus in the rain forest.* New York: Scholastic.

Cole, J. (2003). *Ms. Frizzle's adventures: Medieval castle.* New York: Scholastic.

dePaola, T. (2006). *I'm still scared: A 26 Fairmount Avenue book.* New York: Putnam.

Ehlert, L. (2001). *Fish eyes: A book you can count on.* New York: Red Wagon Books.

Evans, M., & Caras, R. A. (2001). *Fish: Pet care guides for kids.* New York: Dorling Kindersley.

Gibbons, G. (2006). *Owls.* New York: Holiday House.

Jiménez, F. (1997). *The circuit.* Albuquerque: University of New Mexico Press.

Jiménez, F. (2001). *Breaking through.* Boston: Houghton Mifflin.

Kamma, A. (2004). *. . . If you lived when there was slavery in America.* New York: Scholastic.

King-Smith, D. (2002). *Chewing the cud: An extraordinary life remembered by the author of* Babe: The gallant pig. New York: Knopf.

Kraft, B. H. (2003). *Theodore Roosevelt: Champion of the American spirit.* New York: Clarion Books.

Lasky, K. (2006). *John Muir: America's first environmentalist.* Cambridge, MA: Candlewick Press.

Lionni, L. (2005). *Fish is fish.* New York: Scholastic.

Logan, C. (2002). *The 5,000-year-old puzzle: Solving a mystery of ancient Egypt.* New York: Farrar, Straus & Giroux.

Longfellow, H. W. (1996). *Hiawatha.* New York: Puffin Books.

Longfellow, H. W. (2000). *The midnight ride of Paul Revere.* Washington, DC: National Geographic Society.

Lowry, L. (1998). *Looking back: A book of memories.* Boston: Houghton Mifflin.

Macaulay, D. (2003). *Mosque.* Boston: Houghton Mifflin.

Moore, C. (1998). *The night before Christmas.* New York: Putnam.

Nelson, R. (2002). *Pet fish.* Minneapolis: Lerner.

Osborne, M. P. (1998). *Hour of the Olympics.* New York: Random House.

Osborne, M. P. (2004). *Ancient Greece and the Olympics.* New York: Random House.

Paulsen, G. (1999). *My life in dog years.* New York: Yearling.

Paulsen, G. (2001). *Guts: The true stories behind Hatchet and the Brian books.* New York: Delacorte.

Pfister, M. (2002). *The rainbow fish.* New York: North-South Books.

Provensen, A. (1995). *My fellow Americans: A family album.* San Diego: Browndeer Press.

Rappaport, D. (2001). *Martin's big words: The life of Dr. Martin Luther King, Jr.* New York: Hyperion Books.

Rubin, S. G. (2003). *Searching for Anne Frank: Letters from Amsterdam to Iowa.* New York: Abrams.

Seuss, Dr. (1960). *One fish two fish red fish blue fish.* New York: Random House.

Simon, S. (2003). *Hurricanes.* New York: HarperCollins.

chapter eleven

Reading and Writing Poetry

Mrs. Harris holds a weeklong poetry workshop in her sixth-grade classroom several times each year. It lasts 2 hours each day; the first hour is devoted to reading poetry and the second to writing poetry. Her students read and respond to poems during the reading workshop component and write poems during the writing workshop component. Her schedule is shown in the box on page 354.

During class meetings this week, Mrs. Harris draws students' attention to poetic devices. On Monday, she asks students to think about their favorite poems. What makes a poem a good poem? She reads aloud some favorite poems, and the students mention these poetic elements: rhyme, alliteration, repetition, and onomatopoeia, which they call "sound effects."

On Tuesday, Mrs. Harris focuses on metaphors and similes. She reads aloud these poems from *The Random House Book of Poetry for Children* (Prelutsky, 2000): "The Toaster," "Steam Shovel," "The Dandelion," and "The Eagle." She reads each poem aloud to students, and they notice these comparisons: The toaster is compared to a dragon, the steam shovel to a dinosaur, the dandelion to a soldier, and the eagle's dive to a bolt of lightning. The next day, students come to the class meeting to share poems they have found that have comparisons. Their classmates identify the comparisons. After they discuss the poems, Mrs. Harris explains the terms *metaphor*

How does poetry fit into the four patterns of practice?

Teachers incorporate poetry into all four instructional patterns. They share poems with students on topics related to literature focus units and thematic units, and in literature circles and reading workshops, students read books of poetry as well as other books. Students write poems as projects, and once students learn how to write poetry, they often choose to do so during writing workshop. As you continue reading, notice how Mrs. Harris adapts reading and writing workshop for her poetry workshop.

and *simile* and asks students to classify the comparisons in the poems they've shared.

On Thursday, Mrs. Harris reads aloud "The Night Is a Big Black Cat" (Prelutsky, 2000), a brief, four-line poem comparing night to a black cat, the moon to the cat's eye, and the stars to mice she is hunting in the sky. The students draw pictures illustrating the poem and add the lines or paraphrases of the lines to their pictures. One student's drawing is shown on page 355. On Friday, students finish their pictures and share them with the class.

Mrs. Harris points out the poetry section of the classroom library that's been infused with 75 more books of poetry. Students select books of poetry from the library to read during the independent reading time. Next, she introduces some recently published books about poetry. *Love That Dog* (Creech, 2001), *Locomotion* (Woodson, 2003), and *A Bird About to Sing* (Montenegro, 2003) are stories written in poetic form about how children use poetry to write about their feelings. She also shares Janet Wong's book of poetry with advice about writing poems, *You Have to Write* (2002), and three informational books, *Poetry Matters: Writing a Poem From the Inside Out* (Fletcher, 2002), *A Kick in the Head: An Everyday Guide to Poetic Forms* (Janeczko, 2005), and *Troy Thompson's Excellent Peotry* [sic] *Book* (Crew, 1998), books about how to write poetry. She has several copies of each book, and students choose one to read during the week.

During independent reading time, students also read poems and pick their favorites to share with classmates. They list the books they read in their poetry folders. They also choose their three favorite poems, and Mrs. Harris makes copies of them for their poetry folders. For each poem, students write a brief reflection explaining why they like the poem, mentioning poetic elements whenever possible in their explanations.

After reading, students get into small groups to share their favorite poems, and they rehearse the poem they'll read to the whole class. Five or six students read one poem aloud each day. During a previous poetry workshop, Mrs. Harris taught the students how to read poetry expressively, or as she says, "like a

Poetry Workshop Schedule	
15 minutes	**Class Meeting** Mrs. Harris leads a whole-class meeting to give a book talk on a new poetry book, talk about a poet, read several favorite poems using choral reading, or talk about a difficult or confusing poem.
30 minutes	**Independent Reading** Students choose books of poetry from the classroom library and read poems independently. As they read, students choose favorite poems and mark them with small self-stick notes.
15 minutes	**Sharing** Students form small groups and share favorite poems with class mates. Then several students read their favorite poems aloud to the whole class. They rehearse before reading to the class and try to "read like a poet" with good expression.
15 minutes	**Minilesson** Mrs. Harris teaches minilessons on poetry-writing strategies, such as how to use poetic devices, how to arrange the lines of a poem on a page, and how to use "unwriting" to revise poems. She also introduces and reviews poetry formulas during minilessons.
45 minutes	**Writing** Students write lots of rough-draft poems and choose the ones they like best to take through the writing process and publish. Students meet in revising groups and editing conferences with Mrs. Harris and classmates as they polish their poems. On Friday, the students have a poetry reading and they read aloud one of the poems they have written.

poet." They know how to vary the speed and loudness of their voices, how to emphasize the rhyme or other important words, and how to pause at the ends of lines or within lines. Mrs. Harris expects her students to apply what they've learned when they read poetry aloud.

During the writing workshop minilessons this week, Mrs. Harris focuses on "unwriting," a strategy students use to revise their poems. On Monday, she shares the rough draft of a color poem she's written, which she displays on an overhead projector. She explains that she thinks it has too many unnecessary words and asks the students to help her unwrite it. The students make suggestions, and she crosses out words and substitutes stronger words for long phrases. Together they revise the poem to make it tighter. Mrs. Harris explains that poems are powerful because they say so much using only a few words and encourages students to use unwriting as they revise their poems.

On Tuesday and Wednesday, Mrs. Harris shares students' rough-draft poems, which she has copied onto transparencies. Then students suggest ways to unwrite their classmates' poems using the same procedure they used on Monday.

Several students ask to learn more about limericks, so on Thursday, Mrs. Harris reviews the limerick form and shares limericks from a book in the classroom library and other limericks that her students wrote in previous years. Then on Friday, students

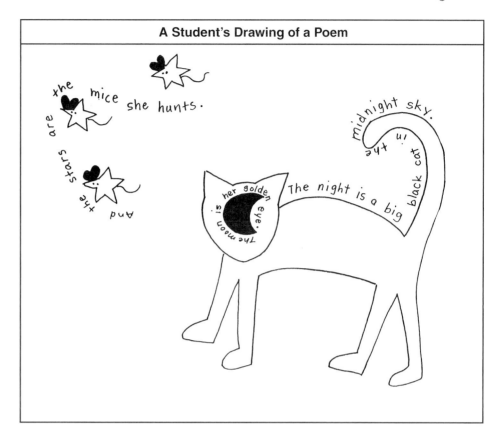

A Student's Drawing of a Poem

divide into small groups to try their hand at writing limericks. Mrs. Harris moves from group to group, providing assistance as needed. Afterward, they share their limericks with classmates.

Mrs. Harris's students keep writing notebooks in which they record collections of words, quotes from books they've read, interesting sentences and descriptions, lists of writing topics, and rough drafts of stories, poems, and other writings. They also have a paper describing the different types of poems that Mrs. Harris has taught them. During the independent writing time, they often use ideas, words and sentences, or even rough-draft poems in their writing notebooks. Students write lots of rough drafts and then choose the most promising ones to take through the writing process and publish. During the week, they meet in revising groups and editing conferences with Mrs. Harris and a small group of classmates. During the first half of the writing time, Mrs. Harris holds a revising group, and during the second half, she holds an editing group. Students sign up for the groups in advance. They keep all their drafts of the poems they publish to document their use of the writing process and to trace the development of their poems.

On the last day of the poetry workshop, the students type final copies of their poems, which they contribute to the class book of poetry that Mrs. Harris compiles. The students move their desks into a circle and have a poetry reading. They read around, each taking a turn to read aloud one of the poems he or she has written.

Mrs. Harris posts the schedule for poetry workshop in the classroom so that students know what they're doing during the 2-hour time block. She also sets out her expectations for students at the beginning of the poetry workshop: They are to read and

write lots of poems. She wants them to choose at least three favorite poems from the ones that they read and to take at least one poem that they write through the writing process. She passes out copies of the grading sheet they'll use that week, and they place them in their writing folders. This way students know from the first day of the workshop what they're expected to accomplish. A copy of Mrs. Harris's poetry workshop grading sheet is shown here.

Poetry Workshop Grading Sheet

Name _____   Date _____

Student's Check   Teacher's Grade

_____ 1. Read lots of poems. Keep a list of poetry books that you read. (15)   _____

_____ 2. Make copies of three favorite poems and write why you like the poems. (15)   _____

_____ 3. Read one poem aloud to the class. Be sure to read like a poet. (10)   _____

_____ 4. Write rough drafts of at least five poems. (25)   _____

_____ 5. Take one poem through the writing process to publication. (15)   _____

_____ 6. Read one of your poems during the poetry reading on Friday. (10)   _____

_____ 7. Other (10)   _____
       Draw a "night cat" picture.
       Write a limerick in a small group.

As students complete the assignments, they add checkmarks in the lefthand column. After they finish the unit, they turn in their writing folders with the grading sheet and the papers they completed during the workshop. Mrs. Harris reviews their assignments and awards points to determine the grade using a 100-point grading scale.

Poetry **"brings sound and sense together in words and lines,"** according to Donald Graves, "ordering them on the page in such a way that both the writer and reader get a different view of life" (1992, p. 3). Our concept of poetry has broadened to include songs and raps, word pictures, memories, riddles, observations, questions, odes, and rhymes. Adult and child poets write about every imaginable subject—grasshoppers, fire trucks, boa constrictors, spaghetti and meatballs, Jupiter, and grandfathers. These poems tell stories, create images and moods, make us laugh or cry, develop our sense of wonder, and show us the world in a new way (Cullinan, Scala, & Schroder, 1995; Glover, 1999).

In an article in *Language Arts*, Lisa Siemens (1996) describes how her primary-grade students are immersed in reading and writing poetry. She makes poetry the core of her language arts program, and her students respond enthusiastically. She shares three of her students' descriptions of poetry. One child writes:

> *A poem is like a big green dragon waiting to blow fire at the knight who seeks the treasure. (p. 239)*

Another child shares:

> *Poems are words that you feel and mumble jumble words too, also words that float around in your head. (p. 239)*

A third child explains:

> *I think poetry is when you wake up and see the sun racing above from the clouds. Poetry is when sunlight and moon shines up together. Poetry is when you go to Claude Monet's garden for the first time and everything is breathtaking. That is what I think poetry is. (p. 239)*

With the current emphasis on standards, poetry is sometimes considered to be a frill, but for these young children, it's essential! Other teachers, too, know that reading and writing poetry can be an effective way to meet content-area standards (Holbrook, 2005).

The focus of this chapter is on involving students with poetry. As you read, think about these questions:

- ◈ How do teachers encourage students to play with words and express ideas using figurative language?
- ◈ How do students read and respond to poems?
- ◈ What kinds of poems do students write?
- ◈ How can teachers incorporate poetry activities into the four patterns of practice?

PLAYING WITH WORDS

As children experiment with words, they create images, play with words, and evoke feelings. They laugh with language, experiment with rhyme, and invent new words. These activities provide a rich background of experiences for reading and writing poetry, and children gain confidence in choosing the "right" word to express an idea, emphasizing the sounds of words, and expressing familiar ideas with fresh comparisons. The Booklist on page 358 presents a collection of wordplay books.

Laughing With Language

As children learn that words have the power to amuse, they enjoy reading, telling, and writing riddles and jokes. Geller (1985) researched children's humorous language and identified two stages of riddle play: Primary-grade children experiment with the riddle form and its content, and beginning in third or fourth grade, students explore the paradoxical constructions in riddles. Riddles are written in a question-and-answer format,

Booklist

WORDPLAY BOOKS

Agee, J. (1994). *Go hang a salami! I'm a lasagna hog! and other palindromes.* New York: Farrar, Straus & Giroux. (U)

Agee, J. (2002). *Palindromania!* New York: Farrar, Straus & Giroux. (M–U)

Bayer, J. (1992). *A my name is Alice.* New York: Dial Books. (P–M)

Carroll, L. (2003). *Jabberwocky.* Cambridge, MA: Candlewick Press. (M–U)

Cerf, B. (1999). *Riddles and more riddles.* New York: Random House. (P)

Cobb, R. (2006). *Tongue twisters to tangle your tongue.* London: Marion Boyars. (M)

Cole, J. (1994). *Why did the chicken cross the road?* New York: HarperCollins. (P–M)

Eiting, M., & Folsom, M. (2005). *Q is for duck: An alphabet guessing game.* New York: Clarion Books. (P–M)

Ernst, L. C. (2004). *The turn-around, upside-down alphabet book.* New York: Simon & Schuster. (P)

Gwynne, F. (2005). *A chocolate moose for dinner.* New York: Aladdin Books. (M–U)

Gwynne, F. (2006). *The king who rained.* New York: Aladdin Books. (M–U)

Hall, K., & Eisenberg, L. (2002). *Kitty riddles.* New York: Puffin. (P)

Schwartz, A. (1992). *Busy buzzing bumblebees and other tongue twisters.* New York: HarperCollins. (P–M)

Terban, M. (1992). *Funny you should ask: How to make up jokes and riddles with wordplay.* New York: Clarion Books. (M–U)

Terban, M. (1997). *Time to rhyme: A rhyming dictionary.* Honesdale, PA: Wordsong. (M)

Terban, M. (2007). *Eight ate: A feast of homonym riddles.* New York: Clarion Books. (P–M)

Terban, M. (2007). *In a pickle and other funny idioms.* New York: Clarion Books. (M)

Wilbur, R. (2006). *Opposites, more opposites, and a few differences.* San Diego: Harcourt. (M–U)

P = primary grades (K–2); M = middle grades (3–5); U = upper grades (6–8)

but young children at first may only ask questions, or ask questions and offer unrelated answers. As they gain experience, children learn to provide questions and give related answers, and their answers may be either descriptive or nonsensical. Here is an example of a descriptive answer:

> *Why did the turtle go out of his shell?*
> *Because he was getting too big for it.*

A nonsensical answer might involve an invented word. For example:

> *Why did the cat want to catch a snake?*
> *Because he wanted to turn into a rattlecat. (Geller, 1981, p. 672)*

Children's riddles seem foolish by adult standards, but wordplay is an important precursor to creating true riddles.

Riddles depend on using metaphors and on manipulating words with multiple meanings or similar sounds. The Opies (1967) identified five riddle strategies that children learn to use:

- Using multiple referents for a noun: What has an eye but cannot see? A needle.
- Combining literal and figurative interpretations for a single phrase: Why did the kid throw the clock out the window? Because he wanted to see time fly.
- Shifting word boundaries to suggest another meaning: Why did the cookie cry? Because its mother was a wafer (away for) so long.

- Separating a word into syllables to suggest another meaning: When is a door not a door? When it's ajar (a jar).
- Creating a metaphor: What are polka dots on your face? Pimples.

Children begin riddle play by telling familiar riddles and reading riddles written by others, and soon they're composing their own by adapting riddles they've read and turning jokes into riddles. A third grader wrote this riddle using two meanings for Milky Way:

> *Why did the astronaut go to the Milky Way?*
> *Because he wanted a Milky Way Bar.*

A fifth grader wrote this riddle using the homophones *hair* and *hare:*

> *What is gray and jumpy and on your head? A gray hare!*

The juxtaposition of words is important in many jokes and riddles.

Creating Word Pictures

Children create word pictures by arranging words to make a picture. These word pictures can be single-word pictures or a string of words or a sentence arranged in a picture. Figure 11–1 shows two word pictures. In the box on the left, the word *nervous* is written concretely, and on the right, descriptive sentences about an ice cream cone have been arranged in that shape. An asterisk indicates where to start reading the sentence picture. To make word pictures, students sketch a picture. Next, they place a second sheet of paper over the drawing and replace all or most of the lines with descriptive words so that the arrangement, size, and intensity of the letters illustrate the meaning.

Experimenting With Rhyme

Because of their experience with Dr. Seuss stories and nursery rhymes, children enjoy creating rhymes. When it comes naturally, rhyme adds a delightful quality to children's writing, but when it is equated with poetry, it can get in the way of wordplay and vivid images. The following three-line poem, "Thoughts After a 40-Mile Bike Ride," shows a fifth grader's effective use of rhyme:

> My feet
> And seat
> Are beat.

A small group of first graders created their own version of *Oh, A-Hunting We Will Go* (Langstaff, 1991). They identified the refrain (lines 1, 2, and 5) and added their own rhyming couplets. Here is an excerpt:

> Oh, a-hunting we will go,
> a-hunting we will go.
> We'll catch a little bear
> and curl his hair,
> and never let him go.
> Oh, a-hunting we will go,
> a-hunting we will go.
> We'll catch a little bug
> and give him a big hug
> and never let him go.
> Oh, a-hunting we will go,
> a-hunting we will go.
> We'll catch a little bunny
> and fill her full of honey,
> and never let her go.
> Oh, we'll put them in a ring
> and listen to them sing
> and then we'll let them go.

FIGURE 11–1

Students' Word Pictures

The first graders wrote this collaboration with the teacher taking dictation on a large chart. Next, each child chose a stanza to copy and illustrate. The pages were collected and compiled to make a book. Finally, they shared the book with their classmates, with each child reading aloud his or her own page.

Hink-pinks are short rhymes that take the form of an answer to a riddle or describe something. These rhymes are composed with two one-syllable rhyming words; they're called *hinky-pinkies* when two two-syllable words are used, and *hinkity-pinkities* with two three-syllable words (Geller, 1981). Here are two examples:

Ghost
White
Fright

What do you call an astronaut?
A sky guy.

Poetic Devices

Poets choose words carefully. They craft powerful images when they use unexpected comparisons, repeat sounds within a line or stanza, imitate sounds, and repeat words and phrases; these techniques are *poetic devices*. As students learn about them, they appreciate the poet's ability to manipulate an element in poems they read and apply it in their own writing (Cullinan et al., 1995). The terminology is also helpful when students talk about poems they've read and in writing groups when they want to compliment classmates on the use of a device or suggest that they try a particular element when they revise their writing.

◗ **Comparison** One way to describe something is to compare it to something else. Students compare images, feelings, and actions to other things using two types of comparisons—*similes* and *metaphors*. A simile is an explicit comparison of one thing to another—a statement that one thing is like something else. Similes are signaled by the use of *like* or *as*. In contrast, a metaphor compares two things by implying that one is something else, without using *like* or *as*. Differentiating between the two terms is less important than using comparisons to make writing more vivid; for example, children can compare anger to an occurrence in nature. Using a simile, they might say, "Anger is like a thunderstorm, screaming with thunder-feelings and lightning-words." Or, as a metaphor, they might say, "Anger is a volcano, erupting with poisonous words and hot-lava actions."

Students begin by learning traditional comparisons and idioms, and they learn to avoid stale comparisons, such as "high as a kite," "butterflies in your stomach," and "light as a feather." Then they invent fresh, unexpected comparisons. A sixth grader uses a combination of expected and unexpected comparisons in this poem, "People":

> People are like birds
> who are constantly getting their feathers ruffled.
> People are like alligators
> who find pleasure in evil cleverness.
> People are like bees
> who are always busy.
> People are like penguins
> who want to have fun.
> People are like platypuses—unexplainable!

🖎 *Alliteration* Alliteration is the repetition of the initial consonant sound in consecutive words or in words in close proximity. Repeating the initial sound makes poetry fun to read, and children enjoy reading and reciting alliterative verses, such as *A My Name Is Alice* (Bayer, 1992) and *The Z Was Zapped* (Van Allsburg, 1998). After reading one of these books, children can create their own versions. A fourth-grade class created its own version of Van Allsburg's book, which they called *The Z Was Zipped*. Students divided into pairs, and each pair composed two pages for the class book. Students illustrated their letter on the front of the paper and wrote a sentence on the back to describe their illustration, following Van Allsburg's pattern. Two pages from the book are shown in Figure 11–2. Before reading the sentences, examine the illustrations and try to figure out the sentences. These are the students' alliterative sentences:

> *The D got dunked by the duck.*
> *The T was totally terrified.*

Tongue twisters are an exaggerated type of alliteration in which every word (or almost every word) in the twister begins with the same letter. Dr. Seuss compiled an easy-to-read collection of tongue twisters for primary-grade students in *Oh Say Can You Say?* (2004). *Tongue Twisters to Tangle Your Tongue* (Cobb, 2006) and *Alison's Zinnia* (Lobel, 1996) are two good books of tongue twisters for middle-grade students. Practice with tongue twisters and alliterative books increases children's awareness of the poetic device in poems they read and write. Few students consciously think about adding alliteration to a poem they are writing, but they get high praise in writing groups when classmates notice an alliteration and compliment the writer on it.

🖎 *Onomatopoeia* Onomatopoeia is a device in which poets use sound words to make their writing more sensory and more vivid. Sound words (e.g., *crash, slurp, varoom, meow*) sound like their meanings. Two books of sound words are *Slop Goes the Soup: A Noisy Warthog Word Book* (Edwards, 2001) and *Achoo! Bang! Crash! The Noisy Alphabet* (MacDonald, 2003). Children can compile a list of sound words they find in stories, poems, and wordplay books and display the list on a classroom chart or in their language arts notebooks to refer to when they write their own poems.

In *Wishes, Lies, and Dreams* (2000), Kenneth Koch recommends having children write noise poems that include a noise or sound word in each line. These first poems often sound contrived (e.g., "A dog barks bow-wow"), but the experience helps children learn to use onomatopoeia, as this poem, "Elephant Noses," dictated by a kindergartner, illustrates:

ELEPHANT NOSES

Elephant noses
Elephants have big noses
Big noses

Big noses
Elephants have big noses
through which they drink
SCHLURRP

🖋 ***Repetition*** Repetition of words and phrases is another device writers use to structure their writing as well as to add interest. Poe's use of the word *nevermore* in "The Raven" is one example, as is the Gingerbread Boy's boastful refrain in "Gingerbread Boy." In this riddle, a fourth grader uses a refrain effectively:

I am a little man standing all alone
In the deep, dark wood.
I am standing on one foot
In the deep, dark wood.
Tell me quickly, if you can,

What to call this little man
Standing all alone
In the deep, dark wood.
Who am I?
(Answer: a mushroom)

FIGURE 11–2

Two Pages From a Fourth-Grade Class Book of Alliterations

READING POEMS

Children have a natural affinity to verse, songs, riddles, jokes, chants, and puns. Preschoolers are introduced to poetry when their parents repeat Mother Goose rhymes, read *The House at Pooh Corner* (Milne, 2001) and the Dr. Seuss books, and sing songs to them. And, children often create jump-rope rhymes and other ditties on the playground.

Types of Poems

Poems for children assume many different forms. The most common type of poetry is rhymed verse, such as Christina Rossetti's "Who Has Seen the Wind" and John Ciardi's "Mummy Slept Late and Daddy Fixed Breakfast" (Prelutsky, 2000). Poems that tell a story are narrative poems; examples are Clement Moore's *The Night Before Christmas* (1998) and Henry Wadsworth Longfellow's "Hiawatha" (1996). A Japanese form, haiku, is popular in anthologies of poetry for children. Haiku is a three-line poem that contains just 17 syllables. Because of its brevity, it has been considered an appropriate form of poetry for children to read and write. Free verse has lines that don't rhyme, and rhythm is less important than in other types of poetry; images take on greater importance in free-form verse. Carl Sandburg's "Fog" and William Carlos Williams's "This Is Just to Say" (Prelutsky, 2004) are two examples of free verse. Other forms of poetry include limericks, a short, five-line, rhymed verse form popularized by Edward Lear (1995), and concrete poems, which are arranged on the page to create a picture or an image. These forms are summarized in Figure 11–3.

There are three types of poetry books. A number of picture-book versions of single poems (in which each line or stanza is illustrated on a page) are available, such as *The Midnight Ride of Paul Revere* (Longfellow, 2001). Others are specialized collections, either written by a single poet or related to a single theme, such as dinosaurs or Halloween. Comprehensive anthologies are the third type, and they feature 50 to 500 or more poems arranged by category. One of the best anthologies is *The Random House Book of Poetry for Children* (Prelutsky, 2000). Poetry books representing each type are included in the Booklist on page 365.

Children have definite preferences about which poems they like best. Fisher and Natarella (1982) surveyed the poetry preferences of first, second, and third graders; Terry (1974) investigated fourth, fifth, and sixth graders' preferences; and Kutiper (1985) researched seventh, eighth, and ninth graders' preferences. The results of the three studies are important for teachers to consider when they select poems. The most popular forms of poetry were limericks and narrative poems; least popular were haiku and free verse. In addition, children preferred funny poems, poems about animals, and poems about familiar experiences; they disliked poems with visual imagery and figurative language. The most important elements were rhyme, rhythm, and sound. Primary-grade students preferred traditional poetry, middle graders preferred modern poetry, and upper-grade students preferred rhyming verse. The researchers found that children in all three studies liked poetry, enjoyed listening to poetry read aloud, and could give reasons why they liked or disliked particular poems.

Researchers have also used school library circulation figures to examine children's poetry preferences. Kutiper and Wilson (1993) found that the humorous poetry of Shel Silverstein (2004) and Jack Prelutsky (1984) was the most popular. Both poets

FIGURE 11–3

Forms of Poetry

Type	Description	Examples
Rhymed verse	Poems with a rhyme scheme so that some lines end with the same sound.	Kirk, D. (2003). *Dogs rule!* New York: Hyperion Books. (M) Shields, C. D. (2003). *Almost late to school: And more school poems.* New York: Dutton. (P–M)
Free verse	Poems that don't rhyme; images take on greater importance.	Medina, J. (2004). *The dream on Blanca's wall. Poems in English and Spanish.* Honesdale, PA: Boyds Mills Press. (M–U) Wong, J. S. (2002). *You have to write.* New York: McElderry. (M)
Haiku	Japanese three-line nature poems containing 17 syllables.	Mannis, C. D. (2002). *One leaf rides the wind: Counting in a Japanese garden.* New York: Viking. (P) Prelutsky, J. (2004). *If not for the cat.* New York: Greenwillow. (P)
Limerick	A five-line, rhymed verse form popularized by Edward Lear.	Ciardi, J. (1992). *The hopeful trout and other limericks.* Boston: Houghton Mifflin. (M–U) Livingston, M. C. (1991). *Lots of limericks.* New York: McElderry. (M)
Concrete	Poems arranged on the page to create a picture or image.	Janeczko, P. B. (2001). *A poke in the I: A collection of concrete poems.* Cambridge, MA: Candlewick Press. (M–U) Roemer, H. B. (2004). *Come to my party and other shape poems.* New York: Holt. (P–M)
Acrostic	Lines in a poem arranged so the first letter of each line spells a word when read vertically.	Powell, C. (2003). *Amazing apples.* New York: Whitman. (P–M) Schnur, S. (2001). *Summer: An alphabet acrostic.* New York: Clarion Books. (P–M)

use rhyme and rhythm effectively in their humorous narrative poems about familiar, everyday occurrences; these are the same qualities that children liked in the earlier poetry preference studies.

Reading and Responding to Poems

In her poem "How to Eat a Poem," Eve Merriam (American Poetry and Literacy Project, 2006) provides useful advice for students who are reading poems: She compares reading a poem to eating a piece of fruit and advises biting right in and letting the juice run down your chin. The focus is on enjoyment: Children read poems and listen to them read aloud because they're pleasurable activities. With so many poems available for children today, it's easy to find poems that appeal to every child and poems that teachers like, too. Guidelines for reading and responding to poems are presented in the LA Essentials feature on page 366.

How to Read a Poem. Poetry is intended to be shared orally because the words and phrases lose much of their music when they're read with the eyes and not with the voice. As teachers and students read poems aloud, they read expressively, stressing and elongating words, adjusting reading speeds, and using musical instruments or props to accompany the reading (Elster & Hanauer, 2002). Readers consider these four aspects of expressive reading:

- Tempo—how fast or slowly to read the lines
- Rhythm—which words to stress or say loudest

- Pitch—when to raise or lower the voice
- Juncture—when and how long to pause

Students experiment with tempo, rhythm, pitch, and juncture as they read poems in different ways and learn how to vary their reading to make their presentations more interpretive. They also learn that in some poems, reading speed may be more important and that in others, pausing is more important. These considerations reinforce the need to rehearse a poem several times before reading it aloud for classmates.

Making Sense of Poems. Some poems are very approachable, and students grasp their meaning during the first reading. For example, Jack Prelutsky's poem "The New Kid on the Block" (1984) is about a bully, and in the last line of the poem, students learn that the bully is a girl. What a kicker! Students laugh as they realize that they'd assumed the bully was a boy. They reread the poem to figure out how the poet set

Booklist

POETRY BOOKS

Picture-Book Versions of Single Poems

Bates, K. L. (2003). *America the beautiful*. New York: Putnam. (M)

Carroll, L. (2003). *Jabberwocky*. Cambridge, MA: Candlewick Press. (M–U)

Frost, R. (2002). *Birches* (E. Young, Illus.). New York: Henry Holt. (U)

Hoberman, M. A. (2003). *The lady with the alligator purse*. Boston: Little, Brown. (P)

Howitt, M. (2002). *The spider and the fly*. New York: Simon & Schuster. (P)

Thayer, E. L. (2000). *Casey at the bat: A ballad of the republic sung in the year 1888*. (C. Bing, Illus.). New York: Handprint Books. (M–U)

Specialized Collections

Adoff, J. (2002). *Song shoots out of my mouth: A celebration of music*. New York: Dutton. (U)

Carlson, L. M. (Ed.). (1998). *Sol a sol: Bilingual poems*. New York: Henry Holt. (P–M)

Demi. (1994). *In the eyes of the cat: Japanese poetry for all seasons*. New York: Henry Holt. (M)

Fleischman, P. (2004). *Joyful noise: Poems for two voices*. New York: HarperCollins. (M–U)

Florian, D. (2003). *Bow wow meow meow: It's rhyming cats and dogs*. San Diego: Harcourt Brace. (P)

Herrera, J. F. (1998). *Laughing out loud, I fly*. New York: HarperCollins. (M–U)

Hopkins, L. B. (Ed.). (2002). *Hoofbeats, claws and rippled fins: Creature poems*. New York: HarperCollins. (P)

Kennedy, X. J. (2002). *Exploding gray: Poems to make you laugh*. Boston: Little, Brown. (M–U)

Kuskin, K. (2003). *Moon, have you met my mother? The collected poems of Karla Kuskin*. New York: HarperCollins. (M)

Myers, W. D. (2003). *blues journey*. New York: Holiday House. (M–U)

Prelutsky, J. (2006). *Behold the bold umbrellaphant*. New York: Greenwillow. (M)

Swados, E. (2002). *Hey you! C'mere: A poetry slam*. New York: Scholastic. (M–U)

Comprehensive Anthologies

Hall, D. (2001). *The Oxford illustrated book of American children's poems*. New York: Oxford University Press. (P–M–U)

Prelutsky, J. (Compiler). (2000). *The Random House book of poetry for children*. New York: Random House. (P–M–U)

GUIDELINES FOR READING POEMS

- **Reading Aloud**

  Read poetry aloud, not silently, in order to appreciate the cadence of the words. Even if students are reading independently, they should speak each word, albeit softly or in an undertone.

- **Expression**

  Teach students how to read a poem expressively, how to emphasize the rhythm and feel of the words, and where to pause.

- **Song Tunes**

  Have children sing poems to familiar tunes, such as "Twinkle, Twinkle Little Star" or "I've Been Working on the Railroad," that fit the line structure of the poem.

- **Rehearsal**

  Have readers rehearse poems several times before reading aloud so that they can read fluently and with expression. In other words, encourage students to read "poetically."

- **Poetry Books**

  Include a collection of poetry books in the classroom library for children to read during reading workshop and other independent reading times.

- **Memorization**

  Rarely assign students a particular poem to memorize; rather, encourage students who are interested in learning a favorite poem to do so and to share it with class members.

- **Author Units**

  Teach author units to focus on a poet, such as Dr. Seuss, Jack Prelutsky, or Gary Soto. Have students read the poet's poems and learn about his or her life through biographies and Internet resources.

- **Display Poems**

  Copy and display poems on chart paper or on sentence strips in pocket charts for students to read and enjoy.

them up, and they pick out the words in the poem that created the image of a boy bully in their minds. As they talk about the poem, students discuss their assumptions about bullies and point out words in the text that led them astray. Some students also insist that the poet used the words *and boy* as an interjection early in the poem to intentionally mislead them.

Other poems are more difficult to understand. It might be helpful to think that understanding a poem is like peeling an onion. It requires multiple readings (Wood, 2006). From the first reading, students come away with an initial impression. Words and images stick in their minds: They giggle over silly rhymes, repeat alliterations and refrains, and ask questions about things that puzzle them.

Students' comprehension grows as they explore the poem. In the primary grades, students often explore poems together as a class, but Dias (1996) recommends that older students work in small groups to reread and talk about a poem. At this point, it's important that students remain flexible and recognize that a fuller meaning is possible. They reread the poem, drawing on their personal experiences and their knowledge of poetry to look for clues to meaning. Sometimes they wonder about the title of the poem and why the poet chose it. They also identify favorite lines, divide the poem into parts to understand its organization, examine line breaks, or discuss one of these points:

- Structure of the poem
- Order of words in a line
- Rhythm and rhyme
- Shape of the poem
- Imagery in the poem

They share their ideas, and as they listen to classmates' comments, their understanding grows. Teachers support students as they delve into a poem; they don't simply tell them what it means. They do provide information and ask questions to nudge students toward becoming independent, responsible readers. Poems often mean different things to students because they approach the poem with individual background knowledge and past experiences. Even so, a poem can't mean just anything; students' interpretations must be supported by the words in the text.

Reading Poems

These children are rereading a poem their teacher recently introduced to the class. Through this reading practice, these first graders learn high-frequency words and develop reading fluency as well as an awareness of various poetic devices. After reading the poem, the children take the sentence strips out of the pocket chart, shuffle them, and then resequence them on the chart. Sometimes they decide that they prefer their new arrangement to the poet's. In another week of practice, their teacher will cut apart the words on each strip, and children can again practice resequencing the words in each line.

Gail E. Tompkins

Performing Poems. Students share their understanding of a poem as they perform it for classmates. One way is using choral reading, in which students take turns reading a poem together. Students arrange the poem for choral reading so that individual students, pairs of students, and small groups read particular lines or stanzas. Here are four possible arrangements:

Echo Reading. The leader reads each line, and the group repeats it.
Leader and Chorus Reading. The leader reads the main part of the poem, and the group reads the refrain or chorus in unison.
Small-Group Reading. The class divides into two or more groups, and each group reads one part of the poem.
Cumulative Reading. One student or one group reads the first line or stanza, and another student or group joins in as each line or stanza is read so that a cumulative effect is created.

Then students rehearse their parts and, finally, they read the poem as an oral presentation. Students also can add props or play music in the background to enhance their presentation. The procedure for choral reading is shown in the Step by Step feature below.

Spanish speakers enjoy reading poems that incorporate some Spanish words, such as Gary Soto's *Neighborhood Odes* (2005) and Juan Felipe Herrera's *Laughing Out Loud, I Fly* (1998). The Spanish words are translated in a glossary, so even non-Spanish speakers can understand the poems. Other books of poetry are bilingual; the poems are printed side by side in Spanish and English, such as *Sol a Sol: Bilingual Poems* (Carlson, 1998), *Poems to Dream Together/Poemas para Soñar Juntos* (Alarcón, 2005), and *The Tree Is Older Than You Are* (Nye, 1998). Students can read these poems in either language, or alternate reading one line in English and the next in Spanish.

--------- Choral Reading ---------

1 Select a poem. Teachers choose a poem and copy it onto a chart or make multiple copies for students to read.

2 Create the arrangement. Teachers work with students to decide how to read the poem. They divide the poem into parts and identify who will read each part. Then the teacher adds marks to the chart, or students mark their copies so that they can follow the arrangement.

3 Rehearse the poem. Teachers read the poem with students several times at a natural speed, pronouncing words carefully. Individual students and small groups are careful to read only their own parts.

4 Perform the poem. Students read the poem expressively, following the arrangement they have rehearsed. Teachers often tape-record students' reading so that they can listen to their presentation.

5 Revise the arrangement. Teachers work with students to fine-tune the arrangement to make it more effective, or they create another arrangement and perform it again.

FIGURE 11–4

Ways to Respond to a Poem

Oral Activities

- Read the poem expressively to classmates.
- Sing the poem.
- Arrange the poem for choral reading and have classmates read it aloud.

Reading and Writing Activities

- Choose a favorite line and use it in a poem the student is writing.
- Read other poems written by the same poet.
- Write a poem on the same topic or following the format of the poem the student has read.
- Research the poet by reading a biography and consulting Internet resources.

Visual Activities

- Dramatize the poem with classmates as a tape recording of the poem is played aloud.
- Draw or paint a picture of an image the poem brings to mind and write a favorite line or two from the poem on the picture.
- Write the poem on sentence strips and then "build" the poem, sequencing the strips in a pocket chart.
- Make a picture book with lines or a stanza of the poem written on each page and illustrated.
- "Can," "box," or "bag" the poem by decorating a container and inserting a copy of the poem and two related items.

Response Activities. As children read poems or listen to them read aloud, they participate spontaneously in response actions: They move their bodies, tap their feet, or clap to the poem's rhythm, and they often repeat words, rhymes, and refrains, savoring the word choice and rhyme. Teachers also plan response activities that involve oral, reading and writing, and visual activities to enhance students' appreciation of the poems they're reading. Some activities are listed in Figure 11–4.

One way students explore a poem is by sequencing the lines. Teachers copy the lines of the poem on long strips of chart paper, and students sequence the lines in a pocket chart or by lining up around the classroom. Through this sequencing activity, students investigate the syntactic structure of poems and get ideas for poems they write.

A second way children respond to poems is by singing them. They pick a tune that fits the rhythm of the poem and sing it instead of reading it. Many teachers report that children quickly memorize poems when they sing them again and again. Alan Katz's hilarious book *Take Me Out of the Bathtub and Other Silly Dilly Songs* (2001) shows children how to fit new words to familiar tunes.

Children can celebrate a favorite poem by creating a class collaboration book of the poem. They each prepare one page by writing a line or stanza of the poem on it and then add an illustration to complement the text. One student also makes a cover for the book with the title of the poem and the poet's name. The teacher compiles the pages and binds the book, and then the book is placed in the classroom library. Children enjoy rereading their illustrated version of the poem. A page from a third-grade class book illustrating Shel Silverstein's "Hug O' War" (2004) is shown in Figure 11–5.

FIGURE 11–5

An Excerpt From a Third-Grade Book Illustrating Shel Silverstein's "Hug O' War"

Instead of tugs,

Writing is another way students respond to poems. They can write new poems following the format of the poem they've read. In this poem, a second grader uses "My Teacher" (Dakos, 1995) as a model:

MY MOM

She loves to exercise at the gym
And watch romantic movies
And eat Mexican food
And get flowers painted on her nails
And sing in the choir at church
And most of all
ME!

Students also write poems by choosing a favorite line from a poem and incorporating it in a poem they write.

What About Memorizing Poems? Memorization is a useful mental exercise, but it's probably not a good idea to assign a particular poem for students to learn. Children vary in their poetry preferences, and requiring them to memorize a poem that they don't like risks killing their interest in poetry. A better approach is to encourage students who are interested in memorizing a favorite poem to do so and then recite it for the class; soon memorizing poems will become a popular response activity. In addition, as children rehearse for choral reading presentations, they often memorize the poem without even trying.

Teaching Minilessons. Teachers present minilessons to teach students about how to read and respond to poems. Minilessons cover procedures, concepts, and strategies and skills related to reading poetry. They also teach students to identify and appreciate comparisons, alliteration, and other types of wordplay in poems. A list of topics for minilessons is presented on page 372. Also included is a minilesson about how to read a poem expressively.

Assessing Students' Experiences With Poems

Teachers assess students' experiences with poetry in several ways. They observe students as they participate in poetry-reading activities, and they keep anecdotal notes of students as they read and respond to poems and share poems they like with classmates. Teachers can also conference with students and ask them about favorite poems to assess their interest in poetry. Students can write reflections about their learning and work habits during the poetry activities, and these reflections provide valuable assessment information.

WRITING POEMS

Children can write poetry! They write funny verses, vivid word pictures, powerful comparisons, and expressions of deep sentiment. The key to successful poetry is poetic formulas, which serve as scaffolds, or temporary writing frameworks, so that students focus on ideas rather than on the mechanics of writing poems (Cecil, 1997). In some formula poems, students begin each line with particular words, as with color poems; in some, they count syllables, as in haiku; and in others, they follow rhyming patterns, as in limericks. Many types of poetry do not use rhyme, and rhyme is the sticking point for many would-be poets. In searching for a rhyming word, children often create inane verse, for example:

> I see a funny little goat
> Wearing a blue sailor's coat
> Sitting in an old motorboat.

Of course, children should be allowed to write rhyming poetry, but rhyme should never be imposed as a criterion for acceptable poetry. Children should use rhyme when it fits naturally into their writing. When children write poetry, they are searching for their own voices, and they need freedom to do that.

Five types of poetic forms are formula poems, free-form poems, syllable- and word-count poems, rhymed poems, and model poems. They're discussed in the upcoming sections, and students' poems illustrate each poetic form. Kindergartners' and first graders' poems may seem little more than lists of sentences compared with the more sophisticated poems of older students, but the range of poems shows how students in kindergarten through eighth grade grow in their ability to write poetry.

What Students Need to Learn About Poetry

Topics

Procedures	Concepts	Strategies and Skills
Reading Poetry		
Read a poem expressively	Poetry	Vary tempo
Do choral reading	Rhymed verse	Emphasize rhythm
	Narrative poems	Vary pitch
Share poems	Free verse	Stress juncture
Respond to poems	Concrete poems	
Do a project	Poetic elements	
Compile an anthology	Information about poets	
Writing Poetry Topics		
Write formula poems	Poetic forms	Use poetic forms
Write preposition poems		Create sensory images
Craft found poem		Paint word pictures
Write free-form poems		Unwrite
Design concrete poems		Use model poems
Write word-count poems		Write rhymes
Write limericks		Punctuate poems
Write model poems		Capitalize poems
		Arrange poems on the page

If you'd like to learn more about teaching poetry, visit MyEducationLab. To watch first graders perform a choral reading presentation of a poem, go to the topic "Reading" and click on the video "Choral Reading."

Formula Poems

The poetic forms may seem like recipes, but they're not intended to be followed rigidly (Janeczko, 2005). Rather, they provide a scaffold, organization, or skeleton for students' poetry-writing activities. After collecting words, images, and comparisons through brainstorming or another prewriting strategy, students craft their poems, choosing words and arranging them to create a message. Meaning is always most important, and form follows the search for meaning.

Minilesson

Mr. Johnston Teaches His Third Graders How to Read Poems Expressively

1 Introduce the topic

Mr. Johnston places a transparency of "A Pizza the Size of the Sun" by Jack Prelutsky (1996) on the overhead projector and reads it aloud in a monotone voice. He asks his third graders if he did a good job reading the poem, and they tell him that his reading was boring.

2 Share examples

Mr. Johnston asks what he could do to make his reading better, and they suggest that he read with more expression. He asks the children to tell him which words he should read more expressively and marks their changes on the transparency. He reads the poem again, and the children agree that it is better. Then they suggest he vary his reading speed, and he marks their changes on the transparency. He reads the poem a third time, incorporating more changes. The children agree that his third reading is the best!

3 Provide information

Mr. Johnston praises his students for their suggestions; they did help him make this reading better. Then he asks what he can do to make his reading more interesting, and they make these suggestions:

- Read some parts loud and some parts soft.
- Read some parts fast and some parts slow.
- Change your voice for some words.

4 Supervise practice

Mr. Johnston divides the class into small groups and passes out transparencies of other poems. Children in each group decide how to read the poem and mark parts they will read in special ways. Mr. Johnston circulates around the classroom as children work, providing assistance as needed. Then children display their poems on the overhead projector and read them aloud with expression.

5 Reflect on learning

Mr. Johnston asks the third graders to talk about what they have learned. One child explains that there are two ways of reading: One is boring and the other is fun. They have learned how to read the fun way so that they can share their enjoyment of poems with others.

Poet Kenneth Koch (2000) developed some simple formulas that make it easy for nearly every student to become a successful poet. These formulas call for students to begin every line the same way or to insert a particular kind of word in every line. The formulas use repetition, a stylistic device that is more effective for young poets than rhyme. Some forms may seem more like sentences than poems, but the dividing line between poetry and prose is a blurry one, and these poetry experiences help students move toward poetic expression.

Meeting the Needs of English Learners

Shouldn't English Learners Be Doing Something More Important Than Reading and Writing Poetry?

You might argue that there is so much language arts instruction that English learners need that they don't have time for poetry, but that's just plain wrong. Poetry offers English learners a unique opportunity for success, and when they're successful, their self-confidence increases, and they're more willing to take risks with other language arts activities.

There are specific benefits for reading, too. Students develop reading fluency and learn vocabulary words as they practice reading a favorite poem in preparation for choral reading performance (Peregoy & Boyle, 2005). Students refine their oral language and presentational skills as they read and respond to poetry: They might memorize a favorite poem and recite it expressively, adding background music or pictures to accompany it. Or, they might share a poem written in their native language and then translate it for the class.

There are benefits for writing as well. Many English learners have difficulty with long writing assignments. Because poems are short, they're often easier to write. English learners' poems are usually better organized than other compositions because they structure their writing with familiar poetic forms, and the quality of their poems is often remarkable. They draw images with words, combine words in fresh, unexpected ways, and create a strong voice through their writing; in fact, students often surprise themselves with the poems they write.

"I Wish . . . " Poems. Students begin each line of their poems with the words "I wish" and complete the line with a wish (Koch, 2000). In a second-grade class collaboration, children simply listed their wishes:

> I wish I had all the money in the world.
> I wish I was a star fallen down from Mars.
> I wish I were a butterfly.
> I wish I were a teddy bear.
> I wish I had a cat.
> I wish I were a pink rose.
> I wish it wouldn't rain today.
> I wish I didn't have to wash a dish.
> I wish I had a flying carpet.
> I wish I could go to Disney World.
> I wish school was out.
> I wish I could go outside and play.

After this experience, students choose one of their wishes and expand on the idea in another poem. Brandi expanded her wish this way:

> I wish I were a teddy bear
> Who sat on a beautiful bed
> Who got a hug every night
> By a little girl or boy

Maybe tonight I'll get my wish
And wake up on a little girl's bed
And then I'll be as happy as can be.

Color Poems. Students begin each line of their poems with a color. They can use the same color in each line or choose a different color (Koch, 2000). For example, a class of seventh graders wrote about yellow:

Yellow is shiny galoshes
splashing through mud puddles.
Yellow is a street lamp
beaming through a dark, black night.
Yellow is the egg yolk
bubbling in a frying pan.
Yellow is the lemon cake
that makes you pucker your lips.
Yellow is the sunset
and the warm summer breeze.
Yellow is the tingling in your mouth
after a lemon drop melts.

Students can also write more complex poems by expanding each idea into a stanza, as this poem about black illustrates:

Black is a deep hole
sitting in the ground
waiting for animals
that live inside.
Black is a beautiful horse
standing on a high hill
with the wind
swirling its mane.
Black is a winter night sky
without stars
to keep it
company.
Black is a panther
creeping around a jungle
searching for
its prey.

Yellow Elephant: A Bright Bestiary (Larios, 2006) is one source of color poems, and *Hailstones and Halibut Bones* (O'Neill, 1990) is another. However, poets often use rhyme as a poetic device so it's important to emphasize that students' poems need not rhyme.

Five-Senses Poems. Students write about a topic using the five senses. These poems are usually five lines long, with one line for each sense, as this poem, "Being Heartbroken," written by a sixth grader, demonstrates:

Sounds like thunder and lightning
Looks like a carrot going through a blender

Tastes like sour milk
Feels like a splinter in your finger
Smells like a dead fish
It must be horrible!

It is often helpful to have students develop a five-senses cluster and collect ideas for each sense before beginning to write. Then they select the most vivid idea for each sense to use in a line of the poem.

"If I Were . . . " Poems. Students write about how they would feel and what they would do if they were something else—a Tyrannosaurus rex, a hamburger, or sunshine (Koch, 2000). They begin each poem with "If I were" and tell what it would be like to be that thing. Students can also write poems from the viewpoint of a book character. Fifth graders, for example, wrote this short poem after reading *Number the Stars* (Lowry, 2005):

If I were Annemarie,   I would lie if I had to.
I'd be brave.   If I were Annemarie,
I'd hide my friends,   I'd be brave.
and trick those Nazi soldiers.

Comparison Poems. Students compare something to something else and then expand on the comparison in the rest of the poem (Koch, 2000). A third grader wrote this poem after brainstorming a list of possible explanations for thunder:

Thunder is a brontosaurus sneezing,
that's all it is.
Nothing to frighten you—
just a dinosaur with a cold.

This child's comparison is a metaphor. She could have written "Thunder is like a brontosaurus sneezing," a simile, but her metaphor is a much stronger comparison.

"I Am . . . " Poems. Children write "I Am . . . " poems from the viewpoint of a book character or historical figure. They use repetition by beginning and ending each stanza with "I am" and beginning the lines in between with "I." First graders wrote this class collaboration poem after reading *Where the Wild Things Are* (Sendak, 2003), the story of a boy who imagines that he travels to the land of the wild things after being sent to his bedroom for misbehaving:

I am Max   But I got homesick
wearing my wolf suit   so I sailed home.
and making mischief.   I am Max,
I turned into a Wild Thing.   a hungry little boy
I became the king of the Wild Things.   who wants his mommy.

Preposition Poems. Students begin each line of their poems with a preposition. This pattern often produces a delightful poetic effect. A seventh grader wrote this preposition poem about Superman:

Within the city   Through the walls
In a phone booth   Until the crime
Into his clothes   Among us
Like a bird   Is defeated!
In the sky

It's helpful to have a list of prepositions available for students to refer to when they write preposition poems. Students may find that they need to ignore the formula for a line or two to give the content of their poems top priority, or they may mistakenly begin a line with an infinitive (e.g., *to say*) rather than a preposition. These forms provide a structure for students' writing that should be adapted as necessary.

Acrostic Poems. Students write acrostic poems using key words. They choose a key word and write it vertically on a sheet of paper. Then they create lines of poetry, each one beginning with a letter of the word they've written (Janeczko, 2005). Students can use their names during a unit on autobiography or names of characters during a literature focus unit. For example, after reading *Officer Buckle and Gloria* (Rathmann, 1995), the story of a police officer and his dog who give safety speeches at schools, a group of first graders wrote this acrostic using the dog's name, Gloria, as the key word:

> **G**loria
> **L**oves to do tricks.
> **O**fficer Buckle tells safety
> **R**ules at schools.
> **I** wish I had
> **A** dog like Gloria.

Other children composed this acrostic using the same key word:

> **G**ood dog Gloria
> **L**ikes to help
> **O**fficer Buckle teach safety
> **R**ules to boys and girls.
> **I** promise to remember
> **A**ll the lessons.

Free-Form Poems

Students choose words to describe something and put the words together to express a thought or tell a story, without concern for rhyme or other arrangements. The number of words per line and the use of punctuation vary. In the following poem, an eighth grader poignantly describes loneliness concisely, using only 15 well-chosen words:

> A lifetime
> Of broken dreams
> And promises
> Lost love
> Hurt
> My heart
> Cries
> In silence

Students can use several methods for writing free-form poems: They can select words and phrases from brainstormed lists and clusters, or they can write a paragraph and then "unwrite" it to create the poem by deleting unnecessary words. They arrange the remaining words to look like a poem.

Concrete Poems. Students create concrete poems through art and the careful arrangement of words on a page (Fletcher, 2002). Words, phrases, and sentences can

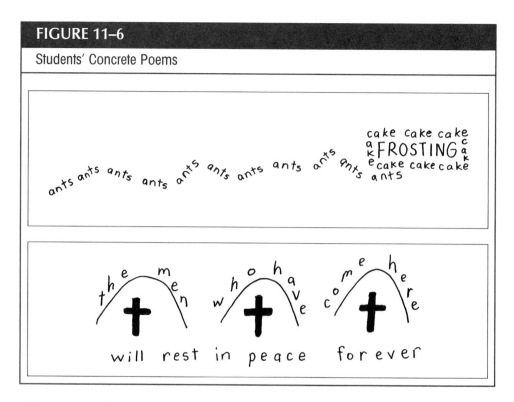

FIGURE 11–6

Students' Concrete Poems

be written in the shape of an object, or word pictures can be inserted within poems written left to right and top to bottom (Janeczko, 2005). Concrete poems are extensions of the word pictures discussed earlier. Two concrete poems are shown in Figure 11–6. In "Ants," the words *ants, cake,* and *frosting* create the image of a familiar picnic scene, and in "Cemetery," repetition and form create a reflection of peace. Three books of concrete poems are *Meow Ruff: A Story in Concrete Poetry* (Sidman, 2006), *Technically, It's Not My Fault: Concrete Poems* (Grandits, 2004), and *A Poke in the I* (Janeczko, 2001).

Found Poems. Students create poems by culling words from other sources, such as stories, songs, and informational books (Fletcher, 2002). They collect words and phrases and then arrange them to make a poem (Janeczko, 2005). A sixth grader wrote this poem after reading *Hatchet* (Paulsen, 2006), the story of a boy who survives for months in the wilderness after his plane crashes:

> He was 13.
> Always started with a single word:
> Divorce.
> An ugly word,
> A breaking word, an ugly breaking word.
> A tearing ugly word that meant fights and yelling.
> Secrets.
> Visitation rights.
> A hatchet on his belt.
> His plane.
> The pilot had been sighted.
> He rubbed his shoulder.
> Aches and pains.

A heart attack.
The engine droned.
A survival pack which had emergency supplies.
Brian Robeson
Alone.
Help, p-l-e-a-s-e.

When they write found poems, students experiment with more sophisticated words and language structures than they might write themselves, and they also document their understanding of the stories and other texts they've read.

Poems for Two Voices. A unique type of free verse is poems for two voices. These poems are written in two columns, side by side, and the columns are read together by two readers or groups of readers: one reader reads the left column, and the other reads the right column. Sometimes readers alternate when they read, but when readers both have words—either the same words or different words—written on the same line, they read them simultaneously so that the poem sounds like a musical duet. Two books of poems for two readers are Paul Fleischman's *I Am Phoenix: Poems for Two Voices* (1985), which is about birds, and the Newbery Medal–winning *Joyful Noise: Poems for Two Voices* (2004), which is about insects. And, if two voices aren't enough, Fleischman has also written *Big Talk: Poems for Four Voices* (2000).

Lorraine Wilson (1994) suggests that topics with contrasting viewpoints are the most effective. Students can also write poems from two characters' viewpoints. For example, after reading *Officer Buckle and Gloria* (Rathmann, 1995), a second-grade class wrote this poem for two voices. The voice on the left is Officer Buckle's and the voice on the right is Gloria the dog's:

I am Officer Buckle	
	I am Gloria,
	a police dog in the K-9.
I teach safety tips	I teach safety tips
to boys and girls.	to boys and girls.
I say,	
"Keep your shoelaces tied."	
	I do a trick.
I say,	
"Do not go swimming	
during electrical storms."	
	I do a trick.
I say,	
"Stay away from guns."	
	I do a trick.
Bravo!	Bravo!
Everyone claps.	Everyone claps.
Do the kids love me?	
	Yes, they do.
No, the kids love you more.	
	The kids love both of us.
We're buddies!	We're buddies!
Always stick with your buddy.	Always stick with your buddy.

Syllable- and Word-Count Poems

Haiku and other syllable- and word-count poems provide a structure that helps students succeed in writing; however, the need to adhere to these poems' formulas may restrict freedom of expression. In other words, the poetic structure may both help and hinder. The exact syllable counts force students to search for just the right words to express their ideas and feelings and provide a valuable opportunity for them to use thesauri and dictionaries.

Haiku. The most familiar syllable-count poem is *haiku* (high-KOO), a Japanese poetic form consisting of 17 syllables arranged in three lines of 5, 7, and 5 syllables. Haiku poems deal with nature and present a single, clear image. Haiku is a concise form, much like a telegram. A fourth grader wrote this haiku poem about a spider web she saw one morning:

> Spider web shining
> Tangled on the grass with dew
> Waiting quietly.

Books of haiku to share with students include *Cool Melons—Turn to Frogs!* (Gollub, 1998), *Fold Me a Poem* (George, 2005), and *In the Eyes of the Cat: Japanese Poetry for All Seasons* (Demi, 1994). The photographs and artwork in these trade books may give students ideas for illustrating their haiku poems.

Cinquain. A cinquain (SIN-cane) is a five-line poem containing 22 syllables in a 2-4-6-8-2 syllable pattern. They usually describe something but may also tell a story. This is the formula:

> Line 1: a one-word subject with two syllables
> Line 2: four syllables describing the subject
> Line 3: six syllables showing action
> Line 4: eight syllables expressing a feeling or an observation about the subject
> Line 5: two syllables describing or renaming the subject

A seventh-grade student wrote this cinquain poem:

> Wrestling
> skinny, fat
> coaching, arguing, pinning
> trying hard to win
> tournament

If you compare this poem to the cinquain formula, you'll notice that some lines are short a syllable or two. The student bent some of the guidelines in choosing words to create a powerful image of wrestling; however, the message of the poem is always more important than adhering to the formula.

Diamante. Iris Tiedt (2002) invented the *diamante* (dee-ah-MAHN-tay), a seven-line contrast poem written in the shape of a diamond. This poetic form helps students apply their knowledge of opposites and parts of speech. The formula is as follows:

> Line 1: one noun as the subject
> Line 2: two adjectives describing the subject

Line 3: three participles (ending in -*ing*) telling about the subject
Line 4: four nouns (the first two related to the subject and the second two related to the opposite)
Line 5: three participles telling about the opposite
Line 6: two adjectives describing the opposite
Line 7: one noun that is the opposite of the subject

A third-grade class wrote this diamante poem about the stages of life:

Baby
wrinkled tiny
crying wetting sleeping
rattles diapers money house
caring working loving
smart helpful
Adult

The students created a contrast between *baby,* the subject represented by the noun in the first line, and *adult,* the opposite in the last line. This contrast gives students the opportunity to play with words and apply their understanding of opposites. The third word in the fourth line, *money,* begins the transition from *baby* to its opposite, *adult.*

Rhymed Verse Forms

Several rhymed verse forms, such as limericks and clerihews, can be used effectively with middle- and upper-grade students. However, it is important that teachers try to prevent the forms and rhyme schemes from restricting students' creative and imaginative expression.

Limericks. The limerick is a form of light verse that uses both rhyme and rhythm. The poem consists of five lines; the first, second, and fifth lines rhyme, and the third and fourth lines rhyme with each other and are shorter than the other three (Janeczko, 2005). The last line often contains a funny or surprise ending, as in this limerick written by an eighth grader:

There once was a frog named Pete
Who did nothing but sit and eat.
He examined each fly
With so careful an eye
And then said, "You're dead meat."

Writing limericks can be a challenging assignment for many upper-grade students, but middle-grade students can also be successful with this poetic form, especially if they write a collaborative poem first.

Limericks are believed to have originated in Limerick, Ireland, and were first popularized by Edward Lear (1812–1888). Poet X. J. Kennedy (1999) describes limericks as the most popular type of poem in the English language and recommends introducing students to limericks by reading aloud some of Lear's verses so they can appreciate the rhythm of the verse. Two collections of Lear's limericks are *Daffy Down Dillies: Silly Limericks by Edward Lear* (Lear, 1995) and *Lots of Limericks* (Livingston,

1991). Children also enjoy the playfulness of John Ciardi's verses in *The Hopeful Trout and Other Limericks* (1992).

Clerihews. *Clerihews* (KLER-i-hyoos), four-line rhymed verses that describe a person (Janeczko, 2005). They're named for Edmund Clerihew Bentley (1875–1956), a British detective writer who invented the form. This is the formula:

    Line 1: the person's name

    Line 2: the last word rhymes with the last word in the first line

    Lines 3 and 4: the last words in these lines rhyme with each other

Clerihews can be written about anyone—historical figures, characters in stories, and even the students themselves. A sixth grader wrote this clerihew about Albert Einstein:

    Albert Einstein
    His genius did shine.
    Of relativity and energy did he dream
    And scientists today hold him in high esteem.

Model Poems

Students model their poems on poems composed by adult poets, as Kenneth Koch suggested in *Rose, Where Did You Get That Red?* (1990). In this approach, students read a poem and write their own, using some of the words and the theme expressed in the model poem. For other examples of model poems, see Paul Janeczko's *Poetry From A to Z: A Guide for Young Writers* (1994) and Nancy Cecil's *For the Love of Language* (1994).

Apologies. Using William Carlos Williams's "This Is Just to Say" as the model, children write a poem in which they apologize for something they are secretly glad they did (Koch, 1990). Middle- and upper-grade students are familiar with offering apologies and enjoy writing humorous apologies. A seventh grader wrote this apology poem, "The Truck," to his dad:

    Dad,   I knew it
    I'm sorry   was wrong.
    that I took   But . . .
    the truck   the exhilarating
    out for   motion was
    a spin.   AWESOME!

Apology poems don't have to be humorous; they may be sensitive, genuine apologies, as another seventh grader's poem, "Open Up," demonstrates:

    I didn't   a death
    open my   had caused.
    immature eyes   Forgive me,
    to see   I misunderstood
    the pain   your anguished
    within you   broken heart.

Invitations. Students write poems in which they invite someone to a magical, beautiful place full of sounds and colors and where all kinds of marvelous things happen.

The model is Shakespeare's "Come Unto These Yellow Sands" (Koch, 1990). A seventh grader wrote this invitation poem, "The Golden Shore":

> Come unto the golden shore
> Where days are filled with laughter,
> And nights filled with whispering winds.
> Where sunflowers and sun
> Are filled with love.
> Come take my hand
> As we walk into the sun.

Teaching Students to Write Poems

Students use what they have learned about poetry through reading poems and mini-lessons as they write poems. Too often they have misconceptions that interfere with their ability to write poems. It's important that teachers help students develop a concept of poetry and experiment with poetic elements as they begin writing poems.

Introducing Students to Writing Poetry. One way to introduce students to writing poetry is to read excerpts from the first chapter of *Anastasia Krupnik* (Lowry, 1995), in which 10-year-old Anastasia, the main character, is excited when her teacher, Mrs. Westvessel, announces that the class will write poems. Anastasia works at home for eight nights to write a poem. Lowry does an excellent job of describing how poets search long and hard for words to express meaning and the delight that comes when they realize their poems are finished. Then Anastasia and her classmates bring their poems to class to read aloud. One student reads his four-line rhymed verse:

> I have a dog whose name is Spot.
> He likes to eat and drink a lot.
> When I put water in his dish,
> He laps it up just like a fish. (p. 10)

Anastasia is not impressed. She knows the child who wrote the poem has a dog named Sputnik, not Spot! But Mrs. Westvessel gives it an A and hangs it on the bulletin board. Soon it is Anastasia's turn, and she is nervous because her poem is very different. She reads her poem about tiny creatures that move about in tidepools at night:

> hush   hush   the sea-soft night is aswim
>   with wrinklesquirm creatures
>   listen (!)
> to them   move   smooth   in the moistly dark
>   here in the   whisperwarm   (pp. 11–12)

In this free-form poem without rhyme or capital letters, Anastasia has created a marvelous picture with invented words. Regrettably, Mrs. Westvessel has an antiquated view that poems should be about only serious subjects, be composed of rhyming sentences, and use conventional capitalization and punctuation. She doesn't understand Anastasia's poem and gives her an F because she didn't follow directions.

Although this first chapter presents a depressing picture of teachers and their lack of knowledge about poetry, it's a dramatic introduction about what poetry is and what it isn't. After reading excerpts from the chapter, develop a chart with your students comparing what poetry is in Mrs. Westvessel's class and what poetry is in your class. A seventh-grade class developed the chart in Figure 11–7

After this introduction to writing poetry, teachers teach minilessons about the poetic formulas and how to write poems, and they provide opportunities for students to write poems. Jack Prelutsky's *Read a Rhyme, Write a Rhyme* (2005) also provides "poemstarts" to help children start writing their own poems. A list of guidelines for writing poetry is shown in the LA Essentials box on the next page.

Minilessons. Teachers use minilessons to introduce students to poetic forms and write collaborative poems for practice before students write poems independently. Class collaborations are crucial because they are a practice run for students who aren't sure what to do. The 5 minutes it takes to write a class collaboration poem can be the difference between success and failure for students. Teachers also teach other topics related to writing poetry. They teach minilessons on the poetic elements and how to incorporate them into the poems that students write, how to arrange lines of poetry for the greatest impact, and how to punctuate and capitalize poems, for example. A list of topics for minilessons related to writing poetry is presented on page 372

Teaching minilessons about writing poetry is important; it is not enough simply to provide opportunities for students to experiment with poetry. Georgia Heard (1999) emphasizes the importance of teaching students about line breaks and white space on the page. Young children often write poems with the same page arrangement as stories, but as they experiment with line breaks, they shape their poems to emphasize rhythm and rhyme, images, and poetic elements. Students learn that the way the lines are broken affects both how the poem looks and how it sounds when read aloud.

FIGURE 11–7

A Comparison Chart Created After Reading *Anastasia Krupnik*

Rules About Writing Poetry

Mrs. Westvessel's Rules	Our Rules
1. Poems must rhyme.	1. Poems do not have to rhyme.
2. The first letter in each line must be capitalized.	2. The first letter in each line does not have to be capitalized.
3. Each line must start at the left margin.	3. Poems can take different shapes and be anywhere on a page.
4. Poems must have a certain rhythm.	4. You hear the writer's voice in a poem—with or without rhythm.
5. Poems should be written about serious things.	5. Poems can be about anything—serious or silly things.
6. Poems should be punctuated like other types of writing.	6. Poems can be punctuated in different ways or not be punctuated at all.
7. Poems are failures if they don't follow these rules.	7. There are no real rules for poems, and no poem is a failure.

GUIDELINES FOR WRITING POEMS

- **Concept of Poetry**

  Explain what poetry is and what makes a good poem. Too often, students assume that all poems must rhyme, are written on topics such as love and flowers, must be punctuated in a particular way, or have other restrictions.

- **Poetry Books**

  Set out books of poetry in a special section of the classroom library. Students learn about poetry through reading, and some poems can serve as models for the poems they write.

- **Model Poems**

  Encourage students to write poems that model or incorporate a line from a poem they've read.

- **Formulas**

  Teach students 5 to 10 poetic formulas so that they have options when they write poems. At the same time, it's important that students know that they can break the formulas in order to express themselves more effectively.

- **Class Collaboration Poems**

  Write a collaborative poem with students to ensure that everyone understands how to write a poem before they write poems on their own.

- **Minilessons**

  Present minilessons on poetic devices, formulas, and other topics.

- **Wordplay**

  Encourage students to play with words, invent new words, and create word pictures as they write poems.

- **Anthologies**

  Create a class anthology of students' poems, and make copies of the anthology for each student. Students can also make collections of the poems they've written.

Publishing Students' Poems. Students use the writing process to draft and refine their poems; the final stage of the writing process is publishing. It's important because it brings closure to the writing process, and students are motivated by sharing and by receiving their classmates' approval. They also collect ideas they can use in their own writing as they listen to and read their classmates' poems. Students share their poetry in two ways—by reading it aloud to classmates and by sharing written copies of their poems for classmates to read.

The most common way that students share their poems is by reading them aloud—and with expression—from the author's chair. Classmates listen and then offer compliments about what they liked about the poem—word choice, topic, or poetic element. Another way that students share their poems with classmates is through a read-around, as Mrs. Harris's students did in the vignette at the beginning of the chapter.

Students compile their poems into anthologies that they place in the classroom library for classmates to read. Teachers also display copies of students' poems, often accompanied by an illustration, on a wall of the classroom and then have a gallery walk for students to read and respond to the poems. If there isn't enough classroom space to display the students' work, teachers can post them in the hallway or on students' desks. Students move from poem to poem and read and respond using small self-stick notes that they attach to the edge of the student's paper. The steps in conducting a gallery walk are shown in the Step by Step feature below. This activity is quick; it can be completed much more quickly than if each student were to share his or her poem in front of the class.

Step by Step

---- Gallery Walks ----

1 Display the work. Students post their work on classroom walls or place it on desks so classmates can read it.

2 Provide comment sheets. Teachers give students small self-stick notes on which to write comments about each student's work. Students will attach notes with their comments to the edge of classmates' work.

3 Give directions. Teachers explain the purpose of the gallery walk, how to view and/or read the work, and what comments to make to classmates. Teachers also set time limits and direct students to visit three, five, eight, or more students' work, if there isn't time to read everyone's work.

4 Model behavior. The teacher models how to view, read, and respond during the gallery walk using one or two students' work as examples.

5 Direct the flow of traffic. Teachers direct students as they move around the classroom, making sure that everyone's work is read and that comments are supportive and useful.

6 Bring closure. Students move to their own work and look at the comments, questions, or other responses they've received. One or two students may share their responses or comment on the gallery walk experience.

Incorporating Poetry Into the Patterns of Practice. Teachers share poems and invite students to write poems as part of most of the patterns of practice. It's easy to find poems to accompany most featured books for literature focus units and topics for thematic units, and many students often choose to write poetry, when they're given a choice. The box below shows how poetry fits into the four patterns of practice. Teachers can also create a poetry workshop as Mrs. Harris did in the vignette at the beginning of the chapter.

Assessing the Poems Students Write

Donald Graves (1992) recommends that teachers focus on the passion and wonder in students' writing and on their unique ability to make the common seem uncommon. Teachers notice the specific details, strong images, wordplay, comparisons, onomatopoeia, alliteration, and repetitions of words and lines that students incorporate in their poems. Assessing the quality of students' poems is especially difficult, because poems are creative combinations of wordplay, poetic forms, and poetic devices. Instead of trying to give a grade for quality, teachers can ask these questions:

- Has the student experimented with the poetic form presented in a minilesson?
- Has the student used the process approach in writing, revising, and editing the poem?
- Has the student used wordplay or another poetic device in the poem?

Teachers also ask students to assess their own poems. Students choose their best efforts and poems that show promise. They can explain which writing strategies they used in particular poems and which poetic forms they used.

How Poetry Fits Into the Four Patterns of Practice

Literature Focus Units

Teachers often share poems in conjunction with featured books, and students often choose to write poems as projects during the extending stage of the reading process.

Literature Circles

Poetry isn't used very often in literature circles, but sometimes students do choose to read books of poetry in a literature circle.

Reading and Writing Workshop

Sometimes students choose books of poetry to read during reading workshop, especially when teachers frequently read poetry aloud to students. Many students write poems during writing workshop, especially when they've learned to use various poetic formulas.

Thematic Units

Teachers and students often read aloud poems related to the thematic unit, and they also write poems. Sometimes they use the poems they've read as models, incorporate a line from a familiar poem, or choose a formula they've learned for the poems they write.

Review

Students read and respond to poems, and they write their own poems. They participate in wordplay activities and read and write poetry as part of the four patterns of practice. Here are some of the important concepts about reading and writing poetry presented in this chapter:

- Wordplay activities with riddles, comparisons, rhyme, and other poetic devices provide the background of experiences students need for reading and writing poetry.
- Three types of poetry books published for children are picture-book versions of single poems, specialized collections of poems, and comprehensive anthologies of poems.
- Students have definite opinions about the types of poems they like best.
- Poems should be read aloud and with expression.
- Tempo, rhythm, pitch, and juncture are four considerations when reading poetry aloud.
- Choral reading is an effective way for students to perform a poem.
- Students participate in oral, reading and writing, and visual response activities to explore favorite poems.
- Students can write poems successfully using poetic formulas in which they begin each line with particular words, count syllables, or create word pictures.
- Because rhyme is a sticking point for many, students should be encouraged to experiment with other poetic elements in their writing.
- Reading and writing poetry aren't frills; they're an important part of the language arts program.

Professional References

Cecil, N. L. (1994). *For the love of language: Poetry for every learner.* Winnipeg, MB: Peguis.

Cullinan, B. E., Scala, M. C., & Schroder, V. C. (1995). *Three voices: An invitation to poetry across the curriculum.* York, ME: Stenhouse.

Dias, P. X. (1996). *Reading and responding to poetry: Patterns in the process.* Portsmouth, NH: Boynton/Cook.

Elster, C. A., & Hanauer, D. I. (2002). Voicing texts, voices around texts: Reading poems in elementary school classrooms. *Research in the Teaching of English, 37,* 89–134.

Fisher, C. J., & Natarella, M. A. (1982). Young children's preferences in poetry: A national survey of first, second, and third graders. *Research in the Teaching of English, 16,* 339–354.

Fletcher, R. (2002). *Poetry matters: Writing a poem from the inside out.* New York: HarperCollins.

Geller, L. G. (1981). Riddling: A playful way to explore language. *Language Arts, 58,* 669–674.

Geller, L. G. (1985). *Word play and language learning for children.* Urbana, IL: National Council of Teachers of English.

Glover, M. K. (1999). *A garden of poets: Poetry writing in the elementary classroom.* Urbana, IL: National Council of Teachers of English.

Graves, D. H. (1992). *Explore poetry.* Portsmouth, NH: Heinemann.

Heard, G. (1999). *Awakening the heart: Exploring poetry in elementary and middle school.* Portsmouth, NH: Heinemann.

Holbrook, S. (2005). *Practical poetry: A nonstandard approach to meeting content-area standards.* Portsmouth, NH: Heinemann.

Janeczko, P. B. (2005). *A kick in the head: An everyday guide to poetic forms.* Cambridge, MA: Candlewick Press.

Koch, K. (2000). *Wishes, lies, and dreams.* New York: Harper-Perennial.

Koch, K. (1990). *Rose, where did you get that red?* New York: Vintage.

Kutiper, K. (1985). *A survey of the poetry preferences of seventh, eighth, and ninth graders.* Unpublished doctoral dissertation, University of Houston.

Kutiper, K., & Wilson, P. (1993). Updating poetry preferences: A look at the poetry children really like. *The Reading Teacher, 47,* 28–35.

Opie, I., & Opie, P. (1967). *The lore and language of school children.* Oxford: Oxford University Press.

Peregoy, S. F., & Boyle, O. F. (2005). *Reading, writing, and learning in ESL: A resource book for K–12 teachers* (4th ed.). Boston: Allyn & Bacon.

Siemens, L. (1996). "Walking through the time of kids": Going places with poetry. *Language Arts, 73,* 234–240.

Terry, A. (1974). *Children's poetry preferences: A national survey of upper elementary grades* (NCTE Research Report No. 16). Urbana, IL: National Council of Teachers of English.

Tiedt, I. (2002). *Tiger lilies, toadstools, and thunderbolts: Engaging K–8 students with poetry.* Newark, DE: International Reading Association.

Wilson, L. (1994). *Write me a poem: Reading, writing, and performing poetry.* Portsmouth, NH: Heinemann.

Wood, J. R. (2006). *Living voices: Multicultural poetry in the middle school classroom.* Urbana, IL: National Council of Teachers of English.

Children's Book References

Alarcón, F. X. (2006). *Poems to dream together/poemas para soñar juntos.* New York: Greenwillow.

American Poetry and Literacy Project. (2006). *How to eat a poem: A smorgasbord of tasty and delicious poems for young readers.* Mineola, NY: Dover.

Bayer, J. (1992). *A my name is Alice.* New York: Dial Books.

Carlson, L. M. (Ed.). (1998). *Sol a sol: Bilingual poems.* New York: Henry Holt.

Ciardi, J. (1992). *The hopeful trout and other limericks.* Boston: Houghton Mifflin.

Cobb, R. (2006). *Tongue twisters to tangle your tongue.* London: Marion Boyars.

Creech, S. (2001). *Love that dog.* New York: HarperCollins.

Crew, G. (1998). *Troy Thompson's excellent peotry* [*sic*] *book.* Victoria, Australia: Lothian.

Dakos, K. (1995). *Mrs. Cole on an onion roll and other school poems.* New York: Aladdin Books.

Demi. (1994). *In the eyes of the cat: Japanese poetry for all seasons.* New York: Henry Holt.

Edwards, P. D. (2001). *Slop goes the soup: A noisy warthog word book.* New York: Hyperion Books.

Fleischman, P. (1985). *I am phoenix: Poems for two voices.* New York: HarperCollins.

Fleischman, P. (2000). *Big talk: Poems for four voices.* Cambridge, MA: Candlewick Press.

Fleischman, P. (2004). *Joyful noise: Poems for two voices.* New York: HarperCollins.

Fletcher, R. (2002). *Poetry matters: Writing a poem from the inside out.* New York: HarperCollins.

George, K. O. (2005). *Fold me a poem.* San Diego: Harcourt.

Grandits, J. (2004). *Technically it's not my fault: Concrete poems.* New York: Clarion Books.

Gollub, M. (1998). *Cool melons—turn to frogs!* New York: Lee & Low.

Herrera, J. F. (1998). *Laughing out loud, I fly.* New York: HarperCollins.

Janeczko, P. B. (1994). *Poetry from A to Z: A guide for young writers.* New York: Bradbury Press.

Janeczko, P. B. (2001). *A poke in the I.* Cambridge, MA: Candlewick Press.

Katz, A. (2001). *Take me out of the bathtub and other silly dilly songs.* New York: McElderry.

Kennedy, X. J., & Kennedy, D. M. (1999). *Knock at a star: A child's introduction to poetry* (rev. ed.). Boston: Little, Brown.

Langstaff, J. (1991). *Oh, a-hunting we will go.* New York: Aladdin Books.

Larios, J. (2006). *Yellow elephant: A bright bestiary.* San Diego: Harcourt.

Lear, E. (1995). *Daffy down dillies: Silly limericks by Edward Lear.* Honesdale, PA: Wordsong.

Livingston, M. C. (1991). *Lots of limericks.* New York: McElderry.

Lobel, A. (1996). *Alison's zinnia.* New York: Greenwillow.

Longfellow, H. W. (1996). *Hiawatha.* New York: Puffin Books.

Longfellow, H. W. (2001). *The midnight ride of Paul Revere* (C. Bing, Illus.). New York: Handprint Books.

Lowry, L. (1995). *Anastasia Krupnik.* New York: HarperCollins.

Lowry, L. (2005). *Number the stars.* New York: Yearling.

MacDonald, R. (2003). *Achoo! Bang! Crash! The noisy alphabet.* New York: Roaring Brook Press.

Milne, A. A. (2001). *The house at Pooh Corner.* New York: Dutton.

Montenegro, L. N. (2003). *A bird about to sing.* Boston: Houghton Mifflin.

Moore, C. C. (1998). *The night before Christmas.* New York: Putnam.

Nye, N. S. (1998). *The tree is older than you are.* New York: Simon & Schuster.

O'Neill, M. (1990). *Hailstones and halibut bones: Adventures in color.* Garden City, NJ: Doubleday.

Paulsen, G. (2006). *Hatchet.* New York: Aladdin Books.

Prelutsky, J. (1984). *The new kid on the block*. New York: Greenwillow.

Prelutsky, J. (1996). *A pizza the size of the sun*. New York: Greenwillow.

Prelutsky, J. (Sel.). (2000). *The Random House book of poetry for children*. New York: Random House.

Prelutsky, J. (2005). *Read a rhyme, write a rhyme*. New York: Knopf.

Rathmann, P. (1995). *Officer Buckle and Gloria*. New York: Putnam.

Sendak, M. (2003). *Where the wild things are*. New York: HarperCollins.

Seuss, Dr. (2004). *Oh say can you say?* New York: Beginner Books.

Sidman, J. (2006). *Meow ruff: A story in concrete poetry*. Boston: Houghton Mifflin.

Silverstein, S. (2004). *Where the sidewalk ends*. New York: HarperCollins.

Soto, G. (2005). *Neighborhood odes*. San Diego: Harcourt.

Van Allsburg, C. (1998). *The Z was zapped*. Boston: Houghton Mifflin.

Wong, J. S. (2002). *You have to write*. New York: McElderry.

Woodson, J. (2003). *Locomotion*. New York: Putnam.

Learning to Spell Conventionally

The 28 students in Mr. Martinez's fourth-grade classroom participate in a 30-minute spelling lesson sandwiched between reading and writing workshop. During this time, the teacher assigns spelling words, and students practice them for the Friday test. Mr. Martinez uses the words from a textbook spelling program, and each week's list of words focuses on a topic—*r*-controlled vowels or compound words, for example. Mr. Martinez introduces the topic through a series of lessons a week in advance so that his students will understand the topic and be familiar with the words before they study them for the spelling test.

During the first semester, students studied vowel patterns (e.g., *strike, each*), *r*-controlled vowels (e.g., *first*), diphthongs (e.g., *soil*), more sophisticated consonant spellings (e.g., *edge, catch*), words with silent letters (e.g., *climb*), and homophones (e.g., *one–won*). Now in the second semester, they are learning two-syllable words. They've studied compound words (e.g., *headache*) and words with inflectional suffixes (e.g., *get–getting*), and now the topic is irregular verbs. It's a difficult topic because students need to know the verb forms as well as how to spell the words.

Because the students' spelling levels range from second to sixth grade, Mr. Martinez has divided them into three groups. Each month, the groups choose

How can teachers incorporate textbooks into their spelling programs?

Teaching spelling is more than having students memorize a list of words and take a test on Friday. Students need to learn spelling concepts—not just practice words—in order to become competent spellers. Also, a single list of words usually isn't appropriate for everyone. As you read this vignette about Mr. Martinez's spelling program, notice how he teaches spelling concepts, incorporates the textbook's weekly lists of spelling words, and takes into account students' levels of spelling development.

new food-related names for themselves. This month, the names are types of pizza; earlier in the year, they chose fruit names, Mexican food names, vegetable names, cookie names, and snack names. Of course, at the end of the month, they sample the foods. Mr. Martinez calls these food names his "secret classroom management tool" because students behave and work hard in order to participate in the tasting.

Students in the Pepperoni Pizza group spell at the second-grade level, and they're studying *r*-controlled vowels. They have already studied two-letter spelling patterns, and now they are learning three-letter patterns. This week, the focus is on *ear* and *eer* patterns. Students in the Sausage Pizza group are at and almost at grade level; they're reviewing ways to spell /ou/. Students in the Hawaiian Pizza group are above-grade-level spellers; they're studying Latin root words and examining noun and verb forms of these words. This week's focus is spelling /shun/. Mr. Martinez meets with each group twice a week, and each group has a folder of activities to work on between meetings. Some of these group meetings are held during the spelling period (usually on Thursdays), and others are squeezed into reading and writing workshop. The teacher also encourages students to look for words they're studying in the books they're reading and to use them in their writing. They bring their examples to share at these meetings.

This week's spelling list is shown on page 394. The irregular verbs in the "All Pizzas" column are taken from the spelling textbook. All students study the words in the "All Pizzas" column, and students in each group also study their own list of words. Students study between 15 and 20 words each week, and they spell 15 words on the Friday test. When they are studying more than 15 words, as they are this week, students don't know which words will be on the test, but the asterisks in the box indicate which words Mr. Martinez plans to use.

Mr. Martinez and his students are involved in three types of activities during the 30-minute

This Week's Spelling List			
All Pizzas	Pepperoni Pizzas	Sausage Pizzas	Hawaiian Pizzas
*forget	*year	*smooth	educate
*forgot	fear	*group	*education
*forgotten	deer	soup	observe
*know	beard	*moving	*observation
*knew	*cheer	wood	admit
*known	*hear	would	*admission
*throw			
*threw			
*thrown			
*break			
*broke			
*broken			

* = words on the spelling test

spelling period: He teaches lessons on the weekly topic, students study words for the weekly spelling test, and they meet in small groups to study other spelling topics. Here is the schedule:

Monday	15 min.	Introduce the topic for the week
	15 min.	Have students take the pretest and self-check it
Tuesday	20 min.	Teach a lesson on the week's topic
	10 min.	Have students practice spelling words
Wednesday	15 min.	Teach a lesson on the week's topic
	15 min.	Have students take the practice test and self-check it
Thursday	20 min.	Work with small groups on other spelling topics
	10 min.	Have students practice spelling words
Friday	10 min.	Give spelling test
	20 min.	Review topic for the week and/or meet with small groups

This is the fourth week that Mr. Martinez has been teaching verbs. During the first week, students brainstormed verbs and Mr. Martinez listed them on one of four charts: verbs that don't change form (e.g., *set, hurt*), regular verbs (e.g., *walk–walked*), irregular verbs with three forms (e.g., *do–did–done*), and irregular verbs with two forms (e.g., *sell–sold*). The students reviewed verbs that don't change form and regular verbs whose past and past participle forms are created by adding -*ed*. That week, students were tested on words with inflectional suffixes, the topic taught the previous week. Regular verbs were tested the week after they were taught. For the next 2 weeks, students studied irregular verbs with three forms; because it was a difficult concept for many of the students, Mr. Martinez took 2 weeks to teach it. Students sorted the words into present, past, and past participle columns, practiced spelling the words on dry-erase boards, and created posters using the words in sentences. One student chose *eat–ate–eaten* and wrote this paragraph:

> *I like to EAT m & ms. They are my favorite candy. I ATE a whole bag of m & ms yesterday. Now I have a stomachache because I have EATEN too much candy.*

The students created their posters during writing workshop. They used the writing process to draft and refine their sentences, word-processed them, enlarged them to fit their posters, and printed them out. After sharing them during a spelling lesson, the students posted them on a wall in the classroom.

This week, the focus changes to irregular verbs with two forms, such as *sleep–slept, leave–left,* and *buy–bought.* On Monday, they review the list of verbs they created several weeks ago that is shown below. Mr. Martinez observes that students are already familiar with these irregular verbs; the only difficult one is *wind–wound.* The students know the nouns *wind* and *wound,* but not the verbs *wind* and *wound.* Mr. Martinez explains each word:

Wind (noun; pronounced with a short i): air in motion

Wind (verb; pronounced with a long i): to coil or wrap something or to take a bending course

Wound (verb—past tense of wind; the ou is pronounced as in cow): having coiled or wrapped something or to have taken a bending course

Wound (noun; the ou is pronounced as in moon): an injury

He sets out these objects to clarify the words: a small alarm clock to wind, a map showing a road that winds around a mountain, wind chimes to show the wind's motion, a skein of yarn to wind, and an elastic bandage to wind around a wound. The students examine each item and talk about how it relates to one or more of the words. Clayton explains the bandage and manages to include all four words:

> *OK. Let's say it is a windy day. The wind could blow you over and you could sprain your ankle. I know because it happened to me. A sprain is an injury like a wound but there's no blood. Well, then you get a bandage and you put it around your ankle like this [he demonstrates as he talks]: You wind it around and around to give your ankle some support. Now [he says triumphantly], I have wound the bandage over the wound.*

Irregular Verbs With Two Forms			
*sleep-slept	meet-met	*leave-left	*bring-brought
shine-shone	fight-fought	*wind-wound	*buy-bought
*catch-caught	pay-paid	mean-meant	hang-hung
bleed-bled	*teach-taught	creep-crept	*build-built
dig-dug	tell-told	*think-thought	sell-sold
make-made	keep-kept	*sweep-swept	say-said

* = word (past-tense form) on next week's spelling list

On Tuesday, the students play the "I'm thinking of . . . " game to practice the words on the Irregular Verbs With Two Forms chart. They are familiar with the game and eager to play it. Mr. Martinez begins, "I'm thinking of a word where you delete one vowel to change the spelling from present to past tense." The students identify *bleed–bled* and *meet–met*. Next, he says, "I'm thinking of a word where you add one letter to the present-tense verb to spell the past-tense form," and the students identify *mean–meant*.

Then the students take turns being the leader. Simone begins, "I'm thinking of a word where you change one vowel for the past tense." The students identify *dig–dug, hang–hung,* and *shine–shone*. Next, Erika says, "I'm thinking of a word where you change one consonant to make past tense," and the students answer *build–built* and *make–made*. Joey offers, "I'm thinking of a verb where you change the *i* to *ou* to get the past tense." The students identify four pairs: *wind–wound, think–thought, bring–brought,* and *fight–fought*. Then, Camille says, "I'm thinking of a verb where you take away an *e* and add a *t* to make the past tense," and the students reply *keep–kept, sweep–swept, sleep–slept,* and *creep–crept*. The students continue the game until they have practiced all the verbs.

Today Mr. Martinez distributes dry-erase boards to the class. He says the past-tense form of an irregular verb, and students write both the present- and past-tense forms, without looking at the chart, unless they need help: *slept, taught, paid, bought, built,* and *left*. Many of the words he chooses are the ones that will be on next week's spelling list, but he also includes other words from the list. After they write each pair of words, the students hold up their boards so that Mr. Martinez can check their work. When necessary, he reviews how to form a letter or points out an illegible letter.

After 15 minutes of practice, the students return to their desks to take the practice test on this week's words. Mr. Martinez reads the list aloud while the students write using blue pens, and then he places a transparency with the words on the overhead projector so students can check their own tests. The students put away their blue pens and get out red pens to check their papers, so cheating is rarely a problem. Mr. Martinez walks around the classroom to monitor students' progress.

Spelling is a tool for writers that allows them to communicate conventionally with readers. As Graves explains: "Spelling is for writing. Children may achieve high scores on phonic inventories or weekly spelling tests, but the ultimate test is what the child does under 'game conditions,' within the process of moving toward meaning" (1983, pp. 193–194). Rather than equating spelling instruction with weekly spelling tests, students need to learn to spell words conventionally so that they can communicate effectively through writing. English spelling is complex, and attempts to teach spelling through weekly lists have not been very successful. Many students spell the words correctly on the weekly test, but they continue to misspell them in their writing.

As you continue reading this chapter, consider these questions:

- How do children learn to spell?
- How can teachers determine students' level of spelling development?
- How should spelling be taught?
- How can teachers make weekly spelling tests more effective?

STUDENTS' SPELLING DEVELOPMENT

The alphabetic principle suggests a one-to-one correspondence between phonemes and graphemes, but English spelling is phonetic only about half the time. Other spellings reflect the language from which a word was borrowed. For example, *alcohol,* like most words beginning with *al-*, is an Arabic word, and *homonym,* like most words with *y* where *i* would work, is a Greek word. Other words are spelled to reflect semantic relationships, not phonological ones. The spelling of *national* and *nation* and of *grade* and *gradual* indicates related meanings even though there are vowel or consonant changes in the pronunciations of the word pairs. If English were a purely phonetic language, it would be easier to spell, but at the same time, it would lose much of its sophistication.

Students learn to spell the phonetic elements of English as they learn about phoneme-grapheme correspondences, and they continue to refine their spelling knowledge through reading and writing. Children's spelling reflects their growing awareness of English orthography, and they move from using scribbles and single letters to represent words through a series of stages until they adopt conventional spellings.

What Is Invented Spelling?

Children create unique spellings, called *invented spellings*, based on their knowledge of English orthography. Charles Read (1975), one of the first researchers to study preschoolers' efforts to spell words, discovered that they used their knowledge of phonology to invent spellings. These children used letter names to spell words, such as U (*you*) and R (*are*), and they used consonant sounds rather consistently: GRL (*girl*), TIGR (*tiger*), and NIT (*night*). The preschoolers used several unusual but phonetically based spelling patterns to represent affricates: They spelled *tr* with *chr* (e.g., CHRIBLES for *troubles*) and *dr* with *jr* (e.g., JRAGIN for *dragon*), and they substituted *d* for *t* (e.g., PREDE for *pretty*). Words with long vowels were spelled using letter names: MI (*my*), LADE (*lady*), and FEL (*feel*). The children used several ingenious strategies to spell words with short vowels. The 3-, 4-, and 5-year-olds rather consistently selected letters to represent short vowels on the basis of place of articulation in the mouth. Short *i* was represented with *e* as in FES (*fish*), short *e* with *a* as in LAFFT (*left*), and short *o* with *i* as in CLIK (*clock*). These spellings may seem odd to adults, but they are based on phonetic relationships. The children often omitted nasals within words (e.g., ED for *end*) and substituted *-eg* or *-ig* for *-ing* (e.g., CUMIG for *coming* and GOWEG for *going*). Also, they often ignored the vowel in unaccented syllables, as in AFTR (*after*) and MUTHR (*mother*).

These children developed strategies for their spellings based on their knowledge of the phonological system and of letter names, their judgments of phonetic similarities and differences, and their ability to abstract phonetic information from letter names. Read suggested that from among the many phonetic properties in the phonological system, children abstract certain phonetic details and preserve others in their invented spellings.

Stages of Spelling Development

Based on Read's seminal work, other researchers began to systematically study how children learn to spell. After examining students' spelling errors and determining that their errors reflected their knowledge of English orthography, Bear, Invernizzi, Templeton, and Johnston (2007b) identified these five stages of spelling development that students move through as they learn to read and write: emergent spelling, letter-name spelling, within-word spelling, syllables and affixes spelling, and derivational relations spelling. The characteristics of each of the stages are summarized in this LA Essentials box on page 399.

As they continued to study students' spelling development, Bear and his colleagues also noticed three principles of English orthography that children master as they move through the stages of spelling development:

- Alphabetic Principle: Letters represent sounds.
- Pattern Principle: Letters are combined in predictable ways to spell sounds.
- Meaning Principle: Related words have similar spellings even when they are pronounced differently.

Young children focus on the alphabetic principle as they learn to represent sounds with letters. They pronounce words and record letters to represent sounds they hear, spelling *are* as *r* and *bed* as *bad*, for example. Children learn the pattern principle next, as they study phonics. They learn to spell consonant and vowel patterns; for example, they learn to spell the /k/ at the end of short-vowel words with *ck* so that they spell *luck* correctly, not as *luk*, and they learn the CVCe pattern, as in *shine*. They also learn the pattern for adding inflectional suffixes, so that they spell the plural of *baby* as *babies*, not *babys*. The third principle is meaning; students learn, for example, that the words *oppose* and *opposition* are related in both spelling and meaning. Once students understand this principle, they are less confused by irregular spellings because they don't expect words to be phonetically regular.

Emergent Spelling. Children string scribbles, letters, and letterlike forms together, but they don't associate the marks they make with any specific phonemes. Emergent spelling represents a natural, early expression of the alphabet and other concepts about writing. Children may write from left to right, right to left, top to bottom, or randomly across the page. Some emergent spellers have a large repertoire of letterforms to use in writing, whereas others repeat a small number of letters over and over. Children use both upper- and lowercase letters, but they show a distinct preference for uppercase letters. Toward the end of this stage, children are beginning to discover how spelling works and that letters represent sounds in words. This stage is typical of preschoolers, ages 3 to 5. During the emergent stage, children learn these concepts:

- The distinction between drawing and writing
- The formation of upper- and lowercase letters
- The direction of writing on a page
- Some letter-sound matches

CHARACTERISTICS OF THE STAGES OF SPELLING DEVELOPMENT

Stage 1: Emergent Spelling

Children string scribbles, letters, and letterlike forms together, but they do not associate the marks they make with any specific phonemes. This stage is typical of 3- to 5-year-olds who learn these concepts:

- The difference between drawing and writing
- The direction of writing on a page
- Some letter-sound matches
- The formation of letters

Stage 2: Letter-Name Spelling

Children represent phonemes in words with letters. At first, their spellings are quite abbreviated, but they learn to use consonant blends and digraphs and short-vowel patterns to spell words. Spellers are 5- to 7-year-olds who learn these concepts:

- The alphabetic principle
- Short vowel sounds
- Consonant sounds
- Consonant blends and digraphs

Stage 3: Within-Word Spelling

Students learn long-vowel patterns and *r*-controlled vowels, but they may confuse spelling patterns and spell *meet* as *mete* and reverse the order of letters, such as *form* for *from* and *gril* for *girl.* Spellers are 7- to 9-year-olds who learn these concepts:

- Long-vowel spelling patterns
- Complex consonant patterns
- *r*-controlled vowels
- Diphthongs

Stage 4: Syllables and Affixes Spelling

Students learn to spell multisyllabic words. They also add inflectional endings, use apostrophes in contractions, and differentiate between homophones, such as *your–you're.* Spellers are often 9- to 11-year-olds who learn these concepts:

- Inflectional endings
- Homophones
- Syllabication
- Possessives

Stage 5: Derivational Relations Spelling

Students explore the relationship between spelling and meaning and learn that words with related meanings are often related in spelling despite sound changes (e.g., *wise–wisdom*). They also learn Latin and Greek root words and derivational affixes (e.g., *amphi-, -tion*). Spellers are 11- to 14-year-olds who learn these concepts:

- Consonant and vowel alternations
- Greek affixes and root words
- Latin affixes and root words
- Etymologies

Adapted from Bear, Invernizzi, Templeton, & Johnston, 2007b.

Letter-Name Spelling. Children learn to represent phonemes in words with letters, indicating that they have a rudimentary understanding of the alphabetic principle—that a link exists between letters and sounds. Spellings are quite abbreviated and represent only the most prominent features in words. Examples of stage 2 spelling are DA (*day*), KLZ (*closed*), BAD (*bed*), and CLEN (*clean*). Many children continue to write mainly with capital letters. These spellers use a letter-name strategy: They slowly pronounce words they want to write, listening for familiar letter names and sounds. Spellers at this stage are 5- to 7-year-olds. During the letter-name stage, children learn the following concepts:

- The alphabetic principle
- Consonant sounds
- Short vowel sounds
- Consonant blends and digraphs

Within-Word Spelling. Children's understanding of the alphabetic principle is further refined in this stage as they learn how to spell long-vowel patterns, diphthongs and the less common vowel patterns, and r-controlled vowels (Henderson, 1990). Examples of within-word spelling include LIEV (*live*), SOPE (*soap*), HUOSE (*house*), and BERN (*burn*). Children experiment with long-vowel patterns and learn that words such as *come* and *bread* are exceptions that don't fit the vowel patterns. Children may confuse spelling patterns and spell *meet* as METE, and they reverse the order of letters, such as FORM for *from* and GRIL for *girl*. They also learn about complex consonant sounds, including *-tch* (*match*) and *-dge* (*judge*), and about diphthongs (*oi/oy*) and other less common vowel patterns, including *au* (*caught*), *aw* (*saw*), *ew* (*sew, few*), *ou* (*house*), and *ow* (*cow*). Children also become aware of homophones and compare long- and short-vowel combinations (*hop–hope*) as they experiment with vowel patterns. Spellers at this stage are typically 7- to 9-year-olds, and they learn these spelling concepts:

- Long-vowel spelling patterns
- *r*-controlled vowels
- More complex consonant patterns
- Diphthongs and other less common vowel patterns

Syllables and Affixes Spelling. The focus in this stage is on syllables and the spellings used where two syllables join together. Students apply what they have learned about one-syllable words to multisyllabic words, and they learn to break words into syllables. They learn about inflectional endings (*-s, -es, -ed,* and *-ing*) and rules about consonant doubling, changing the final *y* to *i*, or dropping the final *e* before adding an inflectional suffix. They also learn about homophones, compound words, possessives, and contractions, as well as some of the more common derivational prefixes and suffixes. Examples of syllables and affixes spelling include EAGUL (*eagle*), MONY (*money*), GETING (*getting*), BABYIES (*babies*), THEIR (*there*), CA'NT (*can't*), and BE CAUSE (*because*). Spellers in this stage are generally 9- to 11-year-olds. Students learn about these concepts during the syllables and affixes stage of spelling development:

- Inflectional endings (*-s, -es, -ed, -ing*)
- Syllabication
- Contractions

- Homophones
- Possessives

Derivational Relations Spelling. Students explore the relationship between spelling and meaning during the derivational relations stage, and they learn that words with related meanings are often related in spelling despite changes in vowel and consonant sounds (e.g., *wise–wisdom, sign–signal, nation–national*) (Templeton, 1983). Examples of spelling errors include CRITISIZE (*criticize*), APPEARENCE (*appearance*), and COMMITTE or COMMITEE (*committee*). The focus in this stage is on morphemes, and students learn about Greek and Latin root words and affixes. They also begin to examine etymologies and the role of history in shaping how words are spelled. They learn about eponyms (words from people's names), such as *maverick* and *sandwich.* Spellers at this stage are 11- to 14-year-olds. Students learn these concepts at this stage of spelling development:

- Consonant alternations (e.g., *soft–soften, magic–magician*)
- Vowel alternations (e.g., *please–pleasant, define–definition, explain–explanation*)
- Greek and Latin affixes and root words
- Etymologies

Teachers do many things to scaffold students' spelling development as they move through the stages of spelling development, and the kind of support they provide depends on students' stage of development. As young children scribble, for example, teachers encourage them to use pencils, not crayons, for writing, to differentiate between drawing and writing. Letter-name spellers notice words in their environment, and teachers help children use these familiar words to choose letters to represent the sounds in the words they are writing. As students enter the syllables and affixes stage, teachers teach syllabication rules, and in the derivational relations stage, they teach students about root words and the variety of words created from a single Latin or Greek root word. For example, from the Latin root word *-ann* or *-enn,* meaning "year," students learn these words: *annual, centennial, biannual, millennium, anniversary, perennial,* and *sesquicentennial.* Figure 12–1 presents a list of guidelines for supporting students' spelling development at each stage.

Analyzing Students' Spelling Development

Teachers analyze the spelling errors in students' compositions by classifying them according to the five stages of spelling development. This analysis will provide information about the student's current level of spelling development and the kinds of errors he or she makes. Knowing the stage of a student's spelling development helps teachers determine the appropriate type of instruction.

A personal journal entry written by Marc, a first grader, is presented in the Weaving Assessment Into Practice feature on page 403. He reverses *d* and *s,* and these two reversals make his writing more difficult to decipher. Here is Marc's composition using conventional spelling:

> *Today a person at home called us and said that a bomb was in our school and made us go outside and made us wait a half of an hour and it made us waste our time on learning. The end.*

FIGURE 12–1

Ways to Support Students' Spelling at Each Stage of Development

Stage 1: Emergent Spelling
Allow the child to experiment with making and placing marks on the paper.
Suggest that the child write with a pencil and draw with a crayon.
Model how adults write.
Point out the direction of print in books.
Encourage the child to notice letters in names and environmental print.
Ask the child to talk about what he or she has written.

Stage 2: Letter-Name Spelling
Sing the ABC song and name letters of the alphabet with children.
Show the child how to form letters in names and other common words.
Demonstrate how to say a word slowly, stretch it out, and isolate beginning, middle, and ending sounds in the word.
Use Elkonin boxes to segment words into beginning, middle, and ending sounds.
Post high-frequency words on a word wall.
Teach lessons on consonants, consonant digraphs, and short vowels.
Write sentences using interactive writing.

Stage 3: Within-Word Spelling
Teach lessons on long-vowel spelling rules, vowel digraphs, and *r*-controlled vowels.
Encourage students to develop visualization skills in order to recognize whether a word "looks" right.
Teach students to spell irregular high-frequency words.
Focus on silent letters in one-syllable words (e.g., *k*now, li*gh*t).
Have students sort words according to spelling patterns.
Have students make words using magnetic letters and letter cards.
Introduce proofreading so students can identify and correct misspelled words in compositions.
Write sentences using interactive writing.

Stage 4: Syllables and Affixes Spelling
Teach how to divide words into syllables and the rules for adding inflectional endings.
Teach schwa sounds and spelling patterns (e.g., *handle*).
Teach homophones, contractions, compound words, and possessives.
Sort two-syllable words and homophones.
Have students make words using letter cards.
Teach proofreading skills, and encourage students to proofread all writings.

Stage 5: Derivational Relations
Teach root words and derivational affixes.
Make clusters with a root word in the center and related words on rays.
Teach students to identify words with English, Latin, and Greek spellings.
Sort words according to roots or language of origin.
Have students check the etymologies of words in a dictionary.

Marc was writing about a traumatic event, and it was appropriate for him to use invented spelling in his journal entry. Primary-grade students should write using invented spelling, and correct spelling is appropriate when the composition will "go public." Prematurely differentiating between "kid" and "adult" spelling interferes with children's natural spelling development and makes them dependent on adults to supply the adult spelling.

Weaving Assessment Into Practice

AN ANALYSIS OF A FIRST GRADER'S SPELLING

ToBay a perezun at hone koB
uz anb seb that a bome wuz in
on skuwl anb mab uz go at zib
anb makbe uz wat a haf uf
a awn anb it mab uz wazt on
time on loren ee ing.

THE eNb

Emergent	Letter-Name	Within-Word	Syllables and Affixes	Derivational Relations
	KOB/called	BOME/bomb	TO BAY/today	
	SEB/said	OR/our	PEREZUN/person	
	WUZ/was	SKUWL/school	MAKBE/maked	
	MAB/made	AT SIB/outside		
	WAT/wait	UF/of		
	HAF/half	AWR/hour		
	MAB/made	OR/our		
	WAZT/waste	LORENEEING/learning		

Data Analysis		Conclusions
Emergent	0	Marc's spelling is at the Letter-Name and Within-Word stages. From his misspellings, he is ready for the following instruction:
Letter-Name	8	
Within-Word	8	
Syllables and Affixes	3	• high-frequency words
Derivational Relations	0	• CVCe spellings
Correctly spelled words	22	• r-controlled vowels
Total words in sample	41	• compound words

He also reverses b/d and s/z.

Spelling can be categorized on a chart, also shown in the feature on page 403, to gauge students' spelling development and to anticipate upcoming changes in their spelling strategies. Teachers write the stages of spelling development across the top of the chart and list each misspelled word in the student's composition under one of the categories, ignoring proper nouns. When teachers are scoring young children's spellings, they often ignore capitalization errors and poorly formed or reversed letters, but when scoring older students' spellings, these errors are considered.

Perhaps the most interesting thing about Marc's writing is that he spelled half the words correctly even though at first reading it might seem that he spelled very few words correctly. Marc wrote this paper in January of his first-grade year, and his spellings are typical of first graders. Of his misspellings, eight were categorized as letter-name spelling, and another eight were within-word spellings. This score suggests that he is moving into the within-word stage.

Marc is clearly using a sounding-out strategy, which is best typified by his spelling of the word *learning*. His errors suggest that he is ready to learn CVCe and other long-vowel spelling patterns and *r*-controlled vowels. Marc spells some high-frequency words phonetically, so he would benefit from more exposure to high-frequency words, such as *was* and *of*. He also spelled *today* and *outside* as separate words, so he is ready to learn about compound words.

Marc pronounced the word MAKBE as "maked," and the DE is a reversal of letters, a common characteristic of within-word spelling. Based on this categorization of Marc's spelling errors, he would benefit from instruction on high-frequency words, the CVCe long-vowel spelling pattern, *r*-controlled vowels, and compound words. His teacher should also monitor his *b*/*d* and *s*/*z* reversal problem to see if it disappears with more writing practice. It is important, of course, to base instructional recommendations on more than one writing sample. Teachers should look at three or more samples to be sure the recommendations are valid.

Older students' spelling can also be analyzed the same way. Fifth-grade Eugenio wrote the "Why My Mom Is Special" essay shown in the Weaving Assessment Into Practice feature on the next page. Eugenio is Hispanic; his native language is Spanish, but he's now fully proficient in English. His writing is more sophisticated than Marc's, and the spelling errors he makes reflect both his use of longer, more complex words and his pronunciation of English sounds.

All but one of Eugenio's spelling errors are classified at either the within-word stage or the syllables and affixes stage. His other error, classified at the letter-name stage, is probably an accident because when he was asked, he could spell the word correctly.

Eugenio's within-word stage errors involve more complex consonant and vowel spelling patterns. Eugenio has moved beyond spelling *because* as BECUZ, but he still must learn to replace the *u* with *au* and the *z* with *s*. His spelling of *shoes* as SHOSE is interesting because he has reversed the last two letters. He doesn't recognize that, however, when he is questioned. Instead, his focus is on representing the /sh/ and the /oo/ sounds correctly. His spelling of both *school* and *career* seem to be influenced by his pronunciation. The /sh/ sound is difficult for him, as it is for many children whose first language is Spanish, and he doesn't recognize that *school* begins with /sk/, not /sh/. Eugenio pronounces the first syllable of *career* as he spelled it, and he explains that it's a hard word but it looks right to him. These comments suggest that Eugenio understands that spelling has both phonetic and visual properties. In the word *policeman*, Eugenio used *s* rather than *ce* to represent the /s/. Even though it is

Weaving Assessment Into Practice

AN ANALYSIS OF A FIFTH GRADER'S SPELLING

My mom is special to me. She gave me everething when I was small. When she gets some mony she byes me pizza. My mom is specil to me becuze she taks me anywhere I want to get some nike shose. She byes me some.

My mom changed my life. She is so nice and loveble. She cares what I am doing in shool. She cares about my grades. I will do anything for mom. I would get a ceriar. Maybe I could be a polisman. That is why I think she is so nice.

Emergent	Letter-Name	Within-Word	Syllables and Affixes	Derivational Relations
	TAKS/takes	BECUZE/because SHOSE/shoes SHOOL/school CERIAR/career POLISMAN/policeman	SPECIL/special EVERETHING/everything MONY/money BYES/buys SPECIL/special BYES/buys LOVEBLE/lovable	

	Data Analysis		Conclusions
Emergent	0		Eugenio's spelling is at the syllables and affixes stage. Based on this sample, this instruction is suggested:
Letter-Name	1		
Within-Word	5		• dividing words into syllables
Syllables and Affixes	7		• compound words
Derivational Relations	0		• using y at the end of 1- and 2-syllable words
Correctly spelled words	82		• homophones
Total words in sample	95		• suffixes

444

494444494

4494

a compound word, this word is classified at this level because the error has to do with spelling a complex consonant sound.

The largest number of Eugenio's spelling errors fall into the syllables and affixes stage. Most of his errors at this stage deal with spelling multisyllabic words. In SPECIL, Eugenio has misspelled the schwa sound, the vowel sound in unaccented syllables of multisyllabic words. In *everything,* Eugenio wrote *e* instead of *y* at the end of *every.* What he did not understand is that the long *e* sound at the end of a two-syllable word is usually represented by *y.* Eugenio spelled *money* as MONY. It's interesting that he used *y* to represent the long *e* sound here, but in this case, *ey* is needed. BYES for *buys* is a homophone error, and all homophone errors are classified as this stage even though they are one-syllable words. Eugenio's other spelling error at this stage is LOVEBLE. Here he added the suffix *-able* but misspelled it. He wasn't aware that he added a suffix. When he was asked about it, he explained that he sounded it out and wrote the sounds that he heard. It is likely that he also knows about the *-ble* end-of-word spelling pattern because if he had spelled the suffix phonetically, he probably would have written LOVEBUL.

Even though Eugenio has a number of errors at both the within-word and syllables and affixes stages, his spelling can be classified at the syllables and affixes stage because most of his errors are at that stage. Based on this one writing sample, it appears that he would benefit from instruction on dividing words into syllables, compound words, using *y* at the end of one- and two-syllable words, homophones, and suffixes. These instructional recommendations should not be based on only one writing sample; they should be validated by examining several writing samples.

TEACHING SPELLING

Conventional spelling is often considered to be the hallmark of an educated person. Parents say that they view spelling as critically important, citing the relationship between reading and spelling, the need for students to be conventional spellers to be successful in the job market and in higher education, and the negative effect incorrect spellings have on compositions as reasons for its importance (Chandler & the Mapleton Teacher-Research Group, 2000). However, Bean and Bouffler (1997) claim that "standard spelling has assumed an importance beyond the function it plays in written language" (p. 67).

The goal of spelling instruction is to help students develop what Gentry (1997) and Turbill (2000) call a *spelling conscience*—a desire to spell words conventionally. Two dimensions of a spelling conscience are understanding that standard spelling is a courtesy to readers and developing the ability to proofread to spot and correct misspellings. Spelling is important to effective writing, but it's a means to an end, not the end in itself. Dull, uninspired writing, not matter how well spelled, has little communicative effect.

The question is how to best teach spelling because we know that reliance on spelling textbooks and rote memorization of words is inadequate. The widely held assumption that children learn how to spell through weekly spelling tests has been challenged by research (Rymer & Williams, 2000). Studies raise questions about the transfer of spelling skills learned through weekly spelling tests to students' writing. There's more to the development of conventional spellers than rote memorization of about a thousand words between first and eighth grades.

Learning to Spell Conventionally

Meeting the Needs of English Learners

How Do Teachers Teach Spelling to English Learners?

English learners move through the same five stages of spelling development that native English speakers do (Bear, Helman, Templeton, Invernizzi, & Johnston, 2007a). How quickly and easily they learn to spell English words depends on what they already know about how words are spelled. Students have more orthographic knowledge when their home language is similar to English, when they are literate in their home language, and when their parents are literate.

Bear and his colleagues (2007a) recommend that in addition to determining students' level of spelling development, teachers do the following as they plan spelling instruction for English learners:

◆ *Compare oral languages.* Teachers analyze the sounds and grammar structures used in students' native language and compare them to English because it's important to point out the similarities and differences to make it easier for students to learn English words.

◆ *Compare written languages.* Teachers examine the writing system—including its characters or letters and directionality—in students' native language, investigate how sounds are spelled and other spelling patterns, and compare them to English in order to explain the similarities and differences to students as they learn to spell English words.

◆ *Investigate students' language and literacy experiences.* Teachers learn about students' levels of experience using their own language and English because students come to school with a range of language and literacy experiences, and they use what they know about their native language as they learn to speak, read, and write in English.

With this information, teachers set goals for their English learners, taking into account that students' differing levels of language and literacy experiences will affect their success, and plan spelling activities to support students as they become more conventional spellers.

The best way to teach spelling to English learners is through a combination of explicit and systematic instruction, opportunities to practice new spelling concepts through word-study activities, and authentic opportunities for students to apply what they're learning about spelling through writing. First, teachers teach minilessons on spelling concepts that are appropriate for students' level of spelling development, taking care to point out similarities and differences between students' home language and English. They emphasize the pronunciation of English words because the way students pronounce a word often influences their spelling. If the words are unfamiliar to students, teachers explain their meaning and model how to use them in English sentences. Next, they involve students in interactive writing activities and have them work in small groups to participate in word-study activities, including making words and word sorts. Third, teachers involve students in a wide variety of reading and writing activities every day so that they can apply their spelling knowledge. Just like their classmates, English learners write books and other compositions in writing

workshop, read and discuss books with classmates in literature circles, and create projects as part of literature focus units and thematic units.

Weekly spelling tests aren't generally considered to be a good way to teach spelling, and they're even less effective for English learners. These students need to learn the sound, pattern, and meaning layers of words rather than simply memorize the sequence of letters in words. The words on a grade-level spelling list may be too difficult for English learners who might not be familiar with the words or understand their meaning. When teachers have to use weekly spelling tests, they should select several words from grade-level lists and others that are more appropriate for students' developmental level, including some high-frequency words.

Components of the Spelling Program

A comprehensive spelling program has a number of components, including reading and writing opportunities, making-words activities, proofreading, and using the dictionary. These components are summarized in the LA Essentials box on the next page.

◆ *Daily writing opportunities* Providing daily opportunities for students to write is an essential component of an effective spelling program. Students who write daily use their knowledge of English orthography to invent spellings for unfamiliar words, and in the process they move closer and closer toward conventional spelling (Hughes & Searle, 2000). When they write, students predict spellings using their developing knowledge of sound-symbol correspondences and spelling patterns. When students use the writing process to develop and polish their writings, emphasis on conventional spelling belongs in the editing stage. Through the process approach, students learn to recognize spelling for what it is—a courtesy to readers. As they write, revise, edit, and share their writing with genuine audiences, students understand that they need to spell conventionally so that their audience can read their compositions.

◆ *Daily reading opportunities* Reading plays an enormous role in students' learning to spell (Hughes & Searle, 1997). As they read, students store the visual shapes of words. The ability to recall how words look helps students decide when a spelling they are writing is correct. When students decide that a word doesn't look right, they can rewrite the word several ways until it does look right, ask the teacher or a classmate who knows the spelling, or check the spelling in a dictionary.

◆ *Word walls* One way to direct students' attention to words in books they're reading or in thematic units is through the use of word walls. Students and the teacher choose words to write on word walls, large sheets of paper hanging in the classroom. Then students refer to these word walls for word-study activities and when they are writing. Seeing the words posted on word walls, clusters, and other charts in the classroom and using them in their writing help students learn to spell the words. Teachers also hang word walls with high-frequency words (Cunningham, 2004). Researchers have identified the most commonly used words and recommend that children learn to spell 100 to 500 of these words because of their usefulness. The 100 most frequently used words represent more than 50% of all the words children and adults write (Horn, 1926)! Figure 12–2 lists the 100 most frequently used words, and Figure 12–3 presents a

COMPONENTS OF A COMPREHENSIVE SPELLING PROGRAM

Writing
Students write informally in journals and use the writing process to draft, revise, and edit writing every day.

Reading
Students develop visual images of words as they read a variety of books each day.

Word Walls
Students and the teacher post high-frequency words, words related to books they are reading, and words related to thematic units in alphabetized sections on word walls in the classroom.

Making Words
Students participate in making-words activities in which they arrange letter cards to spell increasingly longer and more complex words.

Word Sorts
Students sort word cards into two or more categories to focus on particular spelling patterns.

Proofreading
Students learn to proofread their own compositions to locate and then correct spelling errors.

Dictionaries
Students learn to use dictionaries to locate the spellings of unknown words.

Spelling Options
Students explore the variety of ways phonemes are spelled in English in order to know options they have for spelling sounds in words.

Root Words and Affixes
Students learn about root words and affixes and use that knowledge to spell multisyllabic words.

Spelling Strategies
Students learn strategies, including "think it out," to spell unknown words.

FIGURE 12–2

The 100 Most Frequently Used Words

A	B	C	D	E
a and about are after around all as am at an	back be because but by	came can could	day did didn't do don't down	

F	G	H	I	J
for from	get got	had his have home he house her how him	I into if is in it	just

K	L	M	N	O
know	like little	man me mother my	no not now	of our on out one over or

P	QR	S	T	U
people put		said saw school see she so some	that think the this them time then to there too they two things	up us

V	W	X	Y	Z
very	was when we who well will went with were would what		you your	

FIGURE 12–3

100 High-Frequency Words for Older Students

A	B	C	D	E
a lot	beautiful	caught	decided	either
again	because	certain	desert–dessert	embarrassed
all right	belief	close–clothes	different	enough
although	believe	committee	discussed	especially
another	beneath	complete	doesn't	etc.
anything	between			everything
around	board–bored			everywhere
	breathe			excellent
	brought			experience

F	G	H	I	J
familiar		hear–here	immediately	
favorite		heard–herd	interesting	
field		height	it's–its	
finally		herself		
foreign		himself		
friends		humorous		
frighten		hungry		

K	L	M	N	O
knew–new	language	maybe	necessary	once
know–no	lying		neighbor	ourselves
knowledge				

P	QR	S	T	U
particular	quiet–quite	safety	their–there–they're	until
people	really	school	themselves	usually
piece–peace	receive	separate	though	
please	recommend	serious	thought	
possible	remember	since	threw–through	
probably	restaurant	special	throughout	
	right–write	something	to–two–too	
		success	together	

V	W	X	Y	Z
	weight		your–you're	
	were			
	we're			
	where			
	whether			
	whole–hole			

second list of 100 useful words for students in the middle and upper grades. Some teachers type the alphabetized word list on small cards—personal word walls—that students keep at their desks to refer to when they write (Lacey, 1994).

◆ **Making words** Students arrange and rearrange a group of letter cards to spell words (Cunningham & Cunningham, 1992). Primary-grade students can use the letters *s, p, i, d, e,* and *r* to spell *is, red, dip, rip, sip, side, ride,* and *ripe.* With the letters *t, e, m, p, e, r, a, t, u, r,* and *e,* a class of fifth graders spelled these words:

2-letter words: at, up
3-letter words: pet, are, rat, eat, ate, tap, pat
4-letter words: ramp, rate, pare, pear, meat, meet, team, tree
5-letter word: treat
6-letter words: temper, tamper, mature, repeat, turret
7-letter words: trumpet, rapture
8-letter words: repeater
9-letter words: temperate, trumpeter

The procedure for making words is explained in the Step by Step feature below.

Teachers often introduce making words as a whole-class lesson and then set the cards and the word list in a center for students to use again independently or in small groups. Teachers can use almost any words for making-words activities, but words related to literature focus units and thematic units work best.

Making Words

Step by Step

1 **Make letter cards.** Teachers prepare a set of small letter cards with multiple copies of each letter, especially common letters such as *a, e, i, r, s,* and *t.* They print the lowercase letter form on one side of the letter cards and the uppercase form on the reverse. They store the cards with each letter separately in plastic trays or plastic bags.

2 **Choose a word.** Teachers choose a word or spelling pattern to use in the word-making activity, and they have a student distribute the needed letter cards to individual students or to small groups of students.

3 **Name the letter cards.** Teachers ask students to name the letter cards and to arrange consonants in one group and vowels in another.

4 **Make words.** Students use the letter cards to spell words containing two, three, four, five, and six or more letters and then list the words they've spelled on a chart. Teachers monitor students' work and encourage them to fix any misspelled words.

5 **Share words.** Teachers have students identify two-letter words they made with the letter cards and continue to report longer and longer words until they identify the chosen word using every single letter card. After students share all of the words, teachers suggest any words they missed and point out recently taught spelling patterns and other concepts.

Making Words
These second graders use small plastic letters to spell words. They benefit more by manipulating plastic letters than by writing lists of words—because making words is a fun activity and students actually do spell more words this way than through traditional spelling activities. Through making words, children examine spelling patterns and practice spelling high-frequency words. When teachers participate by asking children to switch letters or substitute one letter for another, they take advantage of teachable moments.

Anthony Magnacca/Merrill

◆ *Word sorts* Students use word sorts to compare and contrast spelling patterns as they sort a pack of word cards. Teachers prepare word cards for students to sort into two or more categories according to vowel patterns, affixes, root words, or another spelling concept (Bear et al., 2007b). Sometimes teachers tell students what categories to use, making the sort a closed sort; at other times, students determine the categories themselves, making the sort an open sort. Students can sort word cards and then return them to an envelope for future use, or they can glue the cards onto a sheet of paper. Figure 12–4 shows a word sort for *r*-controlled vowels. In this sort, students work in small groups to pronounce the words and sort them according to how the *r*-controlled vowel is spelled.

◆ *Proofreading* Proofreading is a special kind of reading that students use to locate misspelled words and other mechanical errors in their rough drafts. As students learn about the writing process, they are introduced to proofreading. In the editing stage, they receive more in-depth instruction about how to use proofreading to locate spelling errors and then correct these misspelled words (Wilde, 1996). Through a series of minilessons, students can proofread sample student papers and mark misspelled words. Then, working in pairs, students can correct the misspelled words.

Proofreading is introduced in the primary grades. Young children and their teachers proofread class collaboration and dictated stories together, and students can be encouraged to read over their own compositions and make necessary corrections soon after they begin writing. In this way, students accept proofreading as a natural part of both spelling and writing. Proofreading activities are more valuable for teaching spelling than dictation activities, in which teachers dictate sentences for students

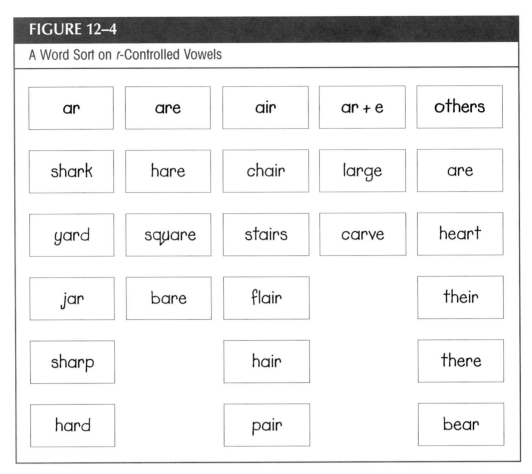

FIGURE 12–4

A Word Sort on *r*-Controlled Vowels

ar	are	air	ar + e	others
shark	hare	chair	large	are
yard	square	stairs	carve	heart
jar	bare	flair		their
sharp		hair		there
hard		pair		bear

to write and correctly capitalize and punctuate. Few people use dictation in their daily lives, but students use proofreading skills every time they polish a piece of writing.

◊ **Dictionaries** Students need to learn how to locate the spelling of unknown words in the dictionary. Of the approximately 750,000 entry words in an unabridged dictionary, students typically learn to spell 3,000 through weekly spelling tests by the end of eighth grade—leaving 747,000 words unaccounted for! Obviously, students must learn how to locate the spellings of some additional words. Although it is relatively easy to find a "known" word in the dictionary, it is hard to locate an unfamiliar word, so students need to learn what to do when they don't know how to spell a word. One approach is to predict possible spellings for unknown words, then check the most probable spellings in a dictionary. This procedure involves six steps:

1. Identify root words and affixes.
2. Consider related words (e.g., *medicine–medical*).
3. Determine the sounds in the word.

4. Generate a list of possible spellings.
5. Select the most probable alternatives.
6. Consult a dictionary to check the correct spelling.

The fourth step, during which students develop a list of possible spellings using their knowledge of both phonology and morphology, is undoubtedly the most difficult. Phoneme-grapheme relationships may rate primary consideration in generating spelling options for some words; root words and affixes or related words may be more important in determining how other words are spelled.

◆ *Spelling options* In English, there are alternative spellings for many sounds because so many words borrowed from other languages retain their native spellings. There are many more options for vowel sounds than for consonants. Even so, there are four spelling options for /f/ (*f, ff, ph, gh*). Spelling options sometimes vary according to position in a syllable or word. For example, *ff* and *gh* are used to represent /f/ only at the end of a syllable or word, as in *cuff* and *laughter*. Common spelling options for phonemes are listed in Figure 12–5.

Teachers point out spelling options as they write words on word walls and when students ask about the spelling of a word. They can also use a series of minilessons to teach upper-grade students about these options. During each minilesson, students focus on one phoneme, such as /f/ or /ar/, and as a class or small group develop a list of the various ways the sound is spelled in English, giving examples of each spelling. A sixth-grade chart on long *i* is presented in Figure 12–6 with lists of one-syllable and multisyllable words. The location of the long *i* sound in the word is also marked on the chart.

◆ *Root words and affixes* Students learn about roots and affixes as they read and spell longer, multisyllabic words. Teaching root words helps students unlock meaning when they read and spell the words correctly when they write. Consider the Latin root word *terra*, meaning "earth." Middle- and upper-grade students learn to read and spell these *terra* words and phrases: *terrarium, all-terrain vehicles, subterranean, territory, terrace,* and *terrier dogs*. Lessons about root words merge instruction about vocabulary and spelling.

Children learn to spell inflectional suffixes, such as the plural *-s* marker and the past-tense *-ed* marker, in the primary grades, and in the middle and upper grades, they learn about derivational prefixes and suffixes and how they affect meaning. They learn to recognize the related forms of a root word, for example: *educate, uneducated, educator, education, educational*.

Students also learn rules for spelling suffixes. For example, the *-able* suffix is added to *read* to spell *readable,* but the *-ible* suffix is added to *leg-* (a Latin root word that is not a word in English) to spell *legible*. The rule is that *-able* is added to complete words and *-ible* is added to word parts. In other words, such as *lovable,* the final e in *love* is dropped before adding *-able* because a serves the same function in the word, and in *huggable,* the g is doubled before adding *-able* because the u in *hug* is short. Through a combination of wide reading and minilessons, students learn about root words and affixes, and they use this knowledge to expand their vocabularies.

◆ *Spelling strategies* Students use strategies to spell unfamiliar words (Laminack & Wood, 1996). Novice spellers often use a "sound-it-out" strategy for spelling, but because English isn't a completely phonetic language, this strategy is only somewhat effective. Students identify many of the sounds they hear in a word, but they can't spell

FIGURE 12–5

Common Spelling Options for Phonemes

Sound	Spellings	Examples	Sound	Spellings	Examples
long a	a-e	date	short oo	oo	book
	a	angel		u	put
	ai	aid		ou	could
	ay	day		o	woman
ch	ch	church	ou	ou	out
	t(u)	picture		ow	cow
	tch	watch	s	s	sick
	ti	question		ce	office
long e	ea	each		c	city
	ee	feel		ss	class
	e	evil		se	else
	e-e	these		x(ks)	box
	ea-e	breathe	sh	ti	attention
short e	e	end		sh	she
	ea	head		ci	ancient
f	f	feel		ssi	admission
	ff	sheriff	t	t	teacher
	gh	cough		te	definite
	ph	photograph		ed	furnished
j	ge	strange		tt	attend
	g	general	long u	u	union
	j	job		u-e	use
	dge	bridge		ue	value
k	c	call		ew	few
	k	keep	short u	u	ugly
	ck	black		o	company
l	l	last		ou	country
	ll	allow	y	y	yes
	le	automobile		i	onion
m	m	man	z	z	zoo
	me	come		s	present
	mm	comment		se	applause
n	n	no		ze	gauze
	ne	done	syllabic l	le	able
long o	o	go		al	animal
	o-e	note		el	cancel
	ow	own		il	civil
	oa	load	syllabic n	en	written
short o	o	office		on	lesson
	a	all		an	important
	au	author		in	cousin
	aw	saw		contractions	didn't
oi	oi	oil		ain	certain
	oy	boy	r-controlled	er	her
long oo	u	cruel		ur	church
	oo	noon		ir	first
	u-e	rule		or	world
	o-e	lose		ear	heard
	ue	blue		our	courage
	o	to			
	ou	group			

FIGURE 12–6

Sixth Graders' Chart of Spelling Options for Long *i*

Spelling	Examples	Location		
		Initial	Medial	Final
i	child, climb, blind, wild, hire		x	
	idea, Friday, microwave, lion, gigantic, rhinoceros, variety, triangle, siren, liar, rabbi	x	x	x
i-e	smile, bride, drive, write		x	
	criticize, impolite, beehive, paradise, valentine, capsize, ninety, sniper, united, decide		x	x
ie	pies, lie, die		x	x
	untie			x
ei	none			
	feisty, seismograph		x	
igh	high, sight, knight, bright		x	x
	knighthood, sunlight		x	
eigh	height		x	
	none			
y	why, my, by, try, fly			x
	July, nylon, crying, xylophone, unicycle, notify, dynamite, skyscraper, hydrogen		x	x
y-e	byte, types, hype, rhyme		x	x
	paralyze, stylist		x	x
ye	dye, rye			x
	goodbye			x
eye	eye			x
	eyeball, eyelash	x		
ui	none			
	guidance		x	
ui-e	guide			x
	none			
uy	guy, buy			x
	buyer		x	

unpronounced letters or spelling patterns (e.g., SIK–sick, BABES–*babies*). The "think-it-out" strategy is much more effective. Students who have more knowledge about spelling will sound the word out and then think about what they know about English spelling patterns and meaning relationships among words to create a more conventional spelling. Specifically, they do the following:

- Break the word into syllables
- Sound out each syllable
- Add affixes to root words
- Look at the word to see if it looks correct
- Generate possible spellings based on spelling patterns and meaning relationships if the word doesn't look correct
- Choose the best alternative

Students also use other spelling strategies: They learn to proofread to identify and correct spelling errors in their writing. They also learn two ways to find the correct spelling of a word. First, they locate words they want to spell on word walls and other charts in the classroom; and second, they find the spelling of unfamiliar words in a dictionary.

Minilessons

Teachers teach students about spelling procedures, concepts, and strategies and skills during minilessons. A list of topics for spelling minilessons is presented on pages 420–421, along with a second-grade teacher's minilesson on the "think it out" strategy.

Weekly Spelling Tests

Many teachers question the use of spelling tests to teach spelling, because research on children's spelling development suggests that spelling is best learned through reading and writing (Gentry & Gillet, 1993; Wilde, 1992). In addition, teachers complain that lists of spelling words are unrelated to the words students are reading and writing, and that the 30 minutes of valuable instructional time spent each day in completing spelling textbook activities is excessive. Weekly spelling tests, when they are used, should be individualized so that children learn to spell the words they need for their writing.

In an individualized approach to spelling instruction, students choose the words they will study, and many of the words they choose are words they use in their writing projects. Students study five to eight words during the week using a specific study strategy. This approach places more responsibility on students for their own learning, and when students have responsibility, they tend to perform better. The guidelines for using individualized spelling tests are provided in the LA Essentials feature on page 422.

Teachers develop a weekly word list of 25 to 50 words of varying levels of difficulty from which students select words to study. Words for the master list are drawn from words students needed for their writing projects during the previous week, high-frequency words, and words related to literature focus units and thematic units ongoing in the classroom. Words from spelling textbooks can also be

added to the list, but they should never make up the entire list. The master word list can be used for minilessons during the week. Students can look for phoneme-grapheme correspondences, add words to charts of spelling options, and note root words and affixes.

On Monday, the teacher administers the pretest using the master list of words, and students spell as many of the words as they can. Students correct their own pretests, and from the words they misspell, each student chooses 5 to 10 words to study. They make two copies of their study list. Students number their spelling words using the numbers on the master list to make it easier to take the final test on Friday. Students keep one copy of the list to study, and the teacher keeps the second copy.

Researchers have found that the pretest is a critical component in learning to spell. The pretest eliminates words that students already know how to spell so that they can direct their study toward words that they don't know yet. More than half a century ago, Ernest Horn recommended that the best way to improve students' spelling was for them to get immediate feedback by correcting their own pretests. His advice is still sound today.

Students spend approximately 5 to 10 minutes studying the words on their study lists each day during the week. Research shows that instead of busywork activities, such as using their spelling words in sentences or gluing yarn in the shape of the words, it is more effective for students to use this strategy for practicing spelling words:

1. Look at the word and say it to yourself.
2. Say each letter in the word to yourself.
3. Close your eyes and spell the word to yourself.
4. Write the word, and check that you spelled it correctly.
5. Write the word again, and check that you spelled it correctly.

This strategy focuses on the whole word rather than breaking it apart into sounds or syllables. During a minilesson at the beginning of the school year, teachers explain how to use the strategy, and then they post a copy of the strategy in the classroom. In addition to this word-study strategy, sometimes students trade word lists with a partner on Wednesday or Thursday and give each other a practice test.

A final test is administered on Friday. The teacher reads the master list, and students write only those words they have practiced during the week. To make it easier to administer the test, students first list the numbers of the words they have practiced from their study lists on their test papers. Any words that students misspell should be included on their lists the following week.

This individualized approach is recommended instead of a textbook approach. Typically, textbooks are arranged in weeklong units, with lists of 10 to 20 words and practice activities that often require at least 30 minutes per day to complete. Research indicates that only 60 to 75 minutes per week should be spent on spelling instruction, however; greater periods of time do not result in improved spelling ability (Johnson, Langford, & Quorn, 1981). Moreover, many textbook activities focus on language arts skills that are not directly related to learning to spell.

The words in each unit are often grouped according to spelling patterns or phonetic generalizations, even though researchers question this approach unless teachers teach students about the pattern and provide practice activities, as Mr. Martinez did in the vignette at the beginning of the chapter. Otherwise, students

What Students Need to Learn About Spelling

Topics

Procedures	*Concepts*	*Strategies and Skills*
Locate words on a word wall	Alphabetic principle	Invent spellings
Locate words in a dictionary	"Kid" or invented spelling	Use placeholders
Use a thesaurus	Homophones	Sound it out
Do making words	Root words and affixes	
	Spelling options	**Think it out**
Do word sorts	High-frequency words	
Study a spelling word	Contractions	Visualize words
Analyze spelling errors	Compound words	Spell by analogy
	Possessives	Apply affixes
		Proofread
		Apply capitalization rules

I invite you to learn more about spelling by visiting MyEducationLab. To see how third graders participate in a making-words activity, go to the topic "Grammar" and click on the video "Making Words."

Minilesson

Mrs. Hamilton Teaches the "Think It Out" Strategy to Her Second Graders

1 Introduce the topic

Mrs. Hamilton asks her second graders how to spell the word *because*, and they suggest these options: *beecuz, becauz, becuse,* and *becuzz.* She asks the children to explain their spellings. Aaron explains that he sounded the word out and heard *bee* and *cuz.* Molly explains that she knows there is no *z* in *because* so she spelled it *becuse.* Other students explain that they say the word slowly, listening for all the sounds, and then write the sounds they hear. Mrs. Hamilton explains that this is a good first-grade strategy, but now she is going to teach them an even more important second-grade strategy called "think it out."

2 Share examples

Mrs. Hamilton asks the class to observe as she spells the word *make.* She says the word slowly and writes *mak* on the chalkboard. Then she explains, "I sounded the word out and wrote the sounds I heard, but I don't think the word is spelled right because it looks funny." The children agree and eagerly raise their hands to supply the right answer. "No," she says, "I want to 'think it out.' Let's see. Hmmm. Well, there are vowel rules. The *a* is long so I could add an *e* at the end of the word." The students clap, happy that she has figured out the spelling of the word. She models the process two more times, spelling *great* and *running.*

3 Provide information

Mrs. Hamilton shares a chart she has made with the steps in the "think it out" strategy:

1. Sound the word out and spell it the best you can.
2. Think about spelling rules to add.
3. Look at the word to see if it looks right.
4. If it doesn't look right, try to change some letters, ask for help, or check the dictionary.

The children talk about how Mrs. Hamilton used the strategy to spell *make, great,* and *running.*

4 Supervise practice

Mrs. Hamilton passes out dry-erase boards and pens for the children to use as they practice the strategy. They write *time, what, walked, taking, bread,* and *people* using the "think it out" strategy. As they move through each step, they hold up their boards to show Mrs. Hamilton their work.

5 Reflect on learning

Mrs. Hamilton ends the minilesson by asking children what they learned, and they explain that they learned the grown-up way to spell words. They explain the steps this way: First they sound it out, then they look it out, and then they think it out.

INDIVIDUALIZED SPELLING TESTS

Master List
Teachers prepare a master list of 20–50 words, depending on students' grade level and the range of spelling levels in the classroom. Words on the list are drawn from spelling textbooks, words students misspell in their writing, and spelling skills being taught.

Pretest
On Monday, students take a pretest of the 20–50 words on the master list, and they self-correct their pretests immediately afterward using red pens.

Words to Study
Students choose 5 to 10 words to study from the words they misspelled on the pretest.

Study Lists
Students make two study lists, one to take home and one to use at school.

Study Strategy
Students use an effective strategy to study the words each day during the week. They study their spelling words this way rather than by writing sentences or stories using the words.

Practice Test
Students work with a partner to give each other a practice test during the week to check their progress in learning to spell the words.

Posttest
On Friday, students take a posttest of the words they have practiced. Teachers collect the tests and grade them themselves.

Next Week's Words
Teachers make a list of words that students misspell to include on their master list for the following week.

memorize the rule or spelling pattern and score perfectly on the spelling test but later are unable to choose among spelling options in their writing. For example, after learning the *i-e* vowel rule and the *-igh* spelling pattern in isolation, students are often stumped about how to spell a word such as *light*. They have learned two spelling options for /i/, *i-e* and *-igh,* and *lite* is an option, one they often see in their environment. Instead of organizing words according to phonetic generalizations and spelling rules, teachers should teach minilessons and point out the rules as they occur when writing words on word walls.

Assessing Students' Progress in Spelling

Grades on weekly spelling tests are the traditional measure of progress in spelling, and the individualized approach to spelling instruction provides this convenient way to assess students. This method of assessing student progress is somewhat deceptive, however, because the goal of spelling instruction is not simply to spell words correctly on weekly tests but to use the words, spelled conventionally, in writing. Samples of student writing should be collected periodically to determine whether words that were spelled correctly on tests are being spelled correctly in writing projects. If students are not applying in their writing what they have learned through the weekly spelling instruction, they may not have learned to spell the words after all.

When students perform poorly on spelling tests, consider whether faulty pronunciation or poor handwriting is to blame. Ask students to pronounce words they habitually misspell to see if their pronunciation or dialect differences may be contributing to spelling problems. Students need to recognize that pronunciation does not always predict spelling. For example, in some parts of the United States, people pronounce the words *pin* and *pen* as though they were spelled with the same vowel, and sometimes we pronounce *better* as though it were spelled *bedder* and *going* as though it were spelled *goin'*. Also, ask students to spell orally the words they misspell in their writing to see whether handwriting difficulties are contributing to spelling problems. Sometimes a minilesson on how to connect two cursive letters (e.g., *br*) or a reminder about the importance of legible handwriting will solve the problem.

It is essential that teachers keep anecdotal information and samples of students' writing to monitor their overall progress in spelling. Teachers can examine error patterns and spelling strategies in these samples. Checking to see if students have spelled their spelling words correctly in writing samples provides one type of information, and examining writing samples for error patterns and spelling strategies provides additional information. Fewer misspellings do not necessarily indicate progress, because to learn to spell, students must experiment with spellings of unfamiliar words, which will result in errors from time to time. Students often misspell a word by misapplying a newly learned spelling pattern. The word *extension* is a good example: Middle-grade students spell the word EXTENSHUN, then change their spelling to EXTENTION after they learn the suffix *-tion*. Although they are still misspelling the word, they have moved from using sound-symbol correspondences to using a spelling pattern—from a less sophisticated spelling strategy to a more sophisticated one.

Students' behavior as they proofread and edit their compositions also provides evidence of spelling development. They should become increasingly able to spot misspelled words in their compositions and to locate the spelling of unknown words in a dictionary. It is easy for teachers to calculate the number of spelling errors students have identified in proofreading their compositions and to chart students' progress in learning to spot errors. Locating errors is the first step in proofreading; correcting the errors is the second step. It is fairly simple for students to correct the spelling of known words, but to correct unknown words, they must consider spelling options and predict possible spellings before they can locate the words in a dictionary. Teachers can document students' growth in locating unfamiliar words in a dictionary by observing their behavior when they edit their compositions.

Teachers can use the writing samples they collect to document children's spelling development. They can note primary-grade students' progression through the stages of invented spelling by analyzing writing samples using a chart such as the ones in the Weaving Assessment Into Practice Features on pages 403 and 405 to determine a general stage of development. Students in the middle and upper grades can use this chart to analyze their own spelling errors.

Review

Spelling is a language tool, and through instruction in spelling, students learn to communicate more effectively. Most students learn to spell conventionally before they enter high school. Here are the key concepts discussed in this chapter:

- Students move through a series of five stages of spelling development.
- In the first stage, emergent spelling, students string scribbles, letters, and letterlike forms together with little or no understanding of the alphabetic principle.
- In the second stage, letter-name spelling, students learn to represent phonemes in the beginning, middle, and end of words with letters.
- In the third stage, within-word spelling, students learn to spell long-vowel patterns, *r*-controlled vowels, and complex consonant combinations.
- In the fourth stage, syllables and affixes, students learn to spell two-syllable words and add inflectional endings.
- In the fifth stage, derivational relations, students learn that multisyllabic words with related meanings are often related in spelling despite changes in vowel and consonant sounds.
- Teachers can analyze students' misspellings to determine their stage of spelling development and plan appropriate instruction.
- Spelling instruction includes daily opportunities to read and write, word walls, word-making and word-sort activities, proofreading, dictionary use, and instruction in spelling options, root words and affixes, and other spelling concepts.
- Teachers teach minilessons about strategies for spelling unfamiliar words as well as other spelling procedures, concepts, and strategies and skills.
- Weekly spelling tests, when they are used, should be individualized so that students learn to spell words they don't already know how to spell.

Professional References

Bean, W., & Bouffler, C. (1997). *Read, write, spell.* York, ME: Stenhouse.

Bear, D. R., Helman, L., Templeton, S., Invernizzi, M., & Johnston, F. (2007a). *Words their way with English learners.* Upper Saddle River, NJ: Merrill/Prentice Hall.

Bear, D. R., Invernizzi, M., Templeton, S., & Johnston, F. (2007b). *Words their way: Word study for phonics, vocabulary, and spelling instruction* (4th ed.). Upper Saddle River, NJ: Merrill/Prentice Hall.

Chandler, K., & the Mapleton teacher-research group. (2000). Squaring up to spelling: A teacher-research group surveys parents. *Language Arts, 77,* 224–231.

Cunningham, P. M. (2004). *Phonics they use: Words for reading and writing* (4th ed.). Boston: Allyn & Bacon.

Cunningham, P. M., & Cunningham, J. W. (1992). Making words: Enhancing the invented spelling-decoding connection. *The Reading Teacher, 46,* 106–115.

Gentry, J. R. (1997). *My kid can't spell! Understanding and assessing your child's literacy development.* Portsmouth, NH: Heinemann.

Gentry, J. R., & Gillet, J. W. (1993). *Teaching kids to spell.* Portsmouth, NH: Heinemann.

Graves, D. H. (1983). *Writing: Teachers and children at work.* Portsmouth, NH: Heinemann.

Henderson, E. H. (1990). *Teaching spelling* (2nd ed.). Boston: Houghton Mifflin.

Horn, E. (1926). *A basic writing vocabulary.* Iowa City: University of Iowa Press.

Hughes, M., & Searle, D. (1997). *The violent "e" and other tricky sounds: Learning to spell from kindergarten through grade 6.* York, ME: Stenhouse.

Hughes, M., & Searle, D. (2000). Spelling and "the second 'R.'" *Language Arts, 77,* 203–208.

Johnson, T. D., Langford, K. G., & Quorn, K. C. (1981). Characteristics of an effective spelling program. *Language Arts, 58,* 581–588.

Lacey, C. (1994). *Moving on in spelling: Strategies and activities for the whole language classroom.* New York: Scholastic.

Laminack, L. L., & Wood, K. (1996). *Spelling in use: Looking closely at spelling in whole language classrooms.* Urbana, IL: National Council of Teachers of English.

Read, C. (1975). *Children's categorization of speech sounds in English* (NCTE Research Report No. 17). Urbana, IL: National Council of Teachers of English.

Rymer, R., & Williams, C. (2000). "Wasn't that a spelling word?" Spelling instruction and young children's writing. *Language Arts, 77,* 241–249.

Templeton, S. (1979). Spelling first, sound later: The relationship between orthography and higher order phonological knowledge in older students. *Research in the Teaching of English, 13,* 255–265.

Turbill, J. (2000). Developing a spelling conscience. *Language Arts, 77,* 209–217.

Wilde, S. (1992). *You kan red this! Spelling and punctuation for whole language classrooms, K–6.* Portsmouth, NH: Heinemann.

Wilde, S. (1996). A speller's bill of rights. *Primary Voices K–6, 4,* 7–10.

chapter thirteen

Language Tools: Grammar and Handwriting

Mr. Keogh's fifth graders are reading *Poppy* (Avi, 1995), the story of a little deer mouse named Poppy who outwits Mr. Ocax, a great horned owl. Mr. Keogh introduced the novel to the class, and they read the first chapter together. Then the students continued reading and talking about the book in small groups that operate like literature circles. The teacher brings the class back together for grammar activities and other exploring-stage activities.

The students list important words from the story on the word wall posted in the classroom after reading each chapter or two, and as the words are listed, the teacher asks them to identify their parts of speech. Even though the book is rich with adverbs, few are chosen for the word wall, so Mr. Keogh begins adding some, such as *profoundly, sufficiently,* and *ravenously.*

For the first grammar activity, Mr. Keogh has students work in small groups to list 10 nouns, 10 adjectives, 10 verbs, and 10 adverbs from the word wall. The teacher walks around the classroom, monitoring students' progress and referring them to the

How can teachers teach grammar as part of literature focus units?

Traditionally, teachers taught grammar by having their students complete exercises in a textbook. The problem was that students didn't apply what they were practicing orally or in writing. A newer approach is to teach grammar more authentically through books students are reading and through their writing. The focus on grammar fits into the exploring stage of the reading process and the editing stage of the writing process. In this vignette, you'll see how Mr. Keogh incorporates grammar instruction into a literature focus unit.

novel to see how a word was used or to the dictionary to check the part of speech. Some of the words are tricky because they are written in isolation on the word wall. An example is *fake*. It can be used in two ways: as an adjective in *the fake owl* and as a noun in *it was a fake*. Mr. Keogh allows the students to list it either way, but they have to be able to defend their choice. This activity serves as a good review.

Next, Mr. Keogh creates a word-sort activity using words from the groups' lists. Students cut the word cards apart and sort them into noun, adjective, verb, and adverb categories. Pairs of students practice several times before they glue the cards down. One student's completed word sort is shown on page 428.

The next day, the students create sentences using one or more words from each category on their word sort; they can also add words to complete the sentences. The first sentences they create, *Mr. Ocax shrieked furiously from the abandoned tree* and *Mr. Ocax shrieked harshly under the crescent moon,* are predictable. Mr. Keogh encourages the fifth graders to experiment with more creative ways to use the words, the way Avi did in *Poppy*. The students work with partners to create these sentences:

> *Delicate little Poppy swiveled nervously on one foot, searching the sky for Mr. Ocax.*

> *Harshly Mr. Ocax snatched the appetizing little mouse named Poppy from the slippery moss-covered rock.*

They write their sentences on sentence strips and post them in the classroom to reread. The next day, Mr. Keogh has them reread the sentences and mark the nouns with green crayons and the verbs with blue crayons.

After this review of the parts of speech, Mr. Keogh changes his focus to sentences. He has created a pack of word and phrase cards to use in reviewing simple sentences, sentence fragments, and compound sentences. He also includes *as* and *when* cards in the pack so his students can build complex sentences, even though they are not expected to learn this concept in fifth grade. Students cut apart a sheet of cards

to use in making sentences about Mr. Ocax. A copy of the sheet of cards is shown on page 429.

First, the fifth graders use the cards to create these simple sentences:

The great horned owl ruled Dimwood Forest.

He swiveled his head from right to left.

The great horned owl smiled into the night air.

Soundlessly, the great horned owl soared into the night air.

With his piercing gaze, Mr. Ocax ruled Dimwood Forest triumphantly.

After they create each sentence, Mr. Keogh asks them to identify the subject and the verb. To simplify the process, students color their subject cards green and their verb cards blue. They continue to sort the cards and identify the adverbs and prepositional phrases and the one conjunction card in the pack.

The students save their packs of cards in small, self-sealing plastic bags, and they continue this activity the next day. Mr. Keogh asks them to use the *and* card in their sentences, and they create these sentences with compound predicates:

Mr. Ocax swiveled his head from right to left and surveyed Dimwood Forest.

The great horned owl called a long, low cry of triumph, spread his wings, and soared back into the air.

The students identify the subjects and verbs in the sentences to figure out that these sentences have compound predicates. They try to make a sentence with a compound subject but find that they can't with the word cards they have.

Next, Mr. Keogh asks them to craft compound sentences using two subjects and two verbs, and they arrange these sentences:

The great horned owl called a long, low cry of triumph, and he soared soundlessly into the night air.

Mr. Ocax surveyed Dimwood Forest triumphantly, and he smiled.

Grammar Word Sort			
Nouns	Adjectives	Verbs	Adverbs
Mr. Ocax	crescent	shrieked	enormously
whirligig	charred	hunched	cautiously
dignity	appetizing	roosting	furiously
Poppy	motionless	luxuriating	harshly
porcupine	perplexed	saunter	desperately
notion	porcupine-quill	surveyed	deftly
Ereth	wary	skittered	stately
privacy	abandoned	swiveling	profoundly
effrontery	delicate	plunged	nervously
camouflage	fake	snatch	entirely

Cards for Making Sentences			
spread his wings	on a branch	triumphantly	with his piercing gaze
soundlessly	a long, low cry of triumph	surveyed	called
from right to left	and	of an old charred oak	he
back into the air	perched	Mr. Ocax	into the night air
swiveled his head	when	smiled	Dimwood Forest
ruled	the great horned owl	as	soared

After they share each sentence, Mr. Keogh asks the students to identify the subjects and verbs. Several students make additional word cards so that they can create the compound sentences they want:

The great horned owl spread his wings, and he flew up high into the night sky.

Mr. Ocax blinked his large round eyes, and he watched a little mouse named Poppy.

"Let's make some even more interesting sentences," Mr. Keogh suggests as he asks them to use the *as* or *when* cards in their sentences. They create these complex sentences:

Mr. Ocax smiled triumphantly as he ruled Dimwood Forest.

As the great horned owl called a long, low cry of triumph, he perched on a branch of an old charred oak.

Mr. Ocax smiled as he soundlessly spread his wings and soared back into the air.

The students identify the subjects and verbs in the sentences, and at first they assume the sentences are compound sentences. Mr. Keogh explains that these sentences are called *complex sentences*: They have one independent clause and one dependent clause. He explains that the clauses beginning with *as* or *when* are called *dependent clauses* because they cannot stand alone as sentences. The students color these two cards red so that they will stand out in a sentence.

Several days later, Mr. Keogh repeats the process with a pack of cards with words and phrases about Poppy. The students practice arranging the cards to make simple, compound, and complex sentences, and they keep a list of the sentences they make in their reading logs.

For one of the projects at the end of the book, the students write a character sketch about Mr. Ocax or Poppy. Mr. Keogh explains that in a character sketch, students do three things:

- Describe what the character looks like
- Describe what the character did
- Identify one character trait the character exemplified, such as being smart, brave, or determined

This writing project grows out of the grammar activities. The students are encouraged to use words they've been arranging as well as other words from the word wall in their character sketches. They don't plagiarize because they're using newly learned words and phrases from charts in the classroom in their writing. Here is Darla's character sketch about Poppy; the underlined words and phrases in her writing came from the novel and were collected on charts or sentence strips posted in the classroom:

> *Poppy was a <u>dainty</u> little girl mouse. She looked like a mouse. Her fur was <u>orange-brown</u>, and she had a <u>plump belly</u> that was white. She had <u>a tiny nose, pink toes</u>, and a very long <u>tail</u>. On her nose was a scar made by a <u>great horned owl</u> named Mr. Ocax. Her <u>ears were long</u>, and <u>her eyes were dark, almost round</u>.*

> *Mr. Ocax <u>ruled </u>over the entire <u>territory</u> where Poppy lived. He controlled them <u>with pure power and fury</u>. They had to get his <u>permission</u> to do anything or else they were his <u>dinner</u>. He said he protected them from the <u>vicious</u> porcupine who lived in Dimwood Forest, but he was lying. One day Poppy met Ereth, the porcupine. He told her that he eats bark, not mice. Mr. Ocax had to stop Poppy or she would tell everyone that he was <u>a liar and a bully</u>. He would not be <u>king</u> anymore. Many times the owl tried to catch Poppy, but she always escaped. Then he tricked her and caught her. <u>Bravely</u> she stuck her <u>porcupine-quill</u> sword into his <u>left claw</u>. That's how she escaped. Mr. Ocax was not so lucky. His flying was <u>totally out of control</u> because of the pain in his claw, and he <u>slammed into the salt lick</u>. It was the violent death he deserved.*

> *Poppy was a brave little mouse. I think she was a hero. That might surprise you because she <u>was trembling with fear</u> every time she confronted the owl who <u>looked like death</u> to her. What she did was she pretended to be brave. To be a coward was bad. She said it is <u>hard to be brave, but harder to be a coward</u>. She risked her life, but now her whole family was safe.*

Through these grammar activities, Darla's writing has become stronger with more sophisticated language and sentence patterns.

Children learn the structure of the English language—its grammar—intuitively as they learn to talk; the process is an unconscious one, and they have almost completed it by the time they enter kindergarten. The purpose of grammar instruction, then, is to make this intuitive knowledge about the English language explicit and to provide labels for words within sentences, parts of sentences, and types of sentences. Children speak the dialect that their parents and community members speak. Dialect, whether Standard English or nonstandard English, is informal and differs to some degree from the written Standard English, or book language, that students will read and write in school (Edelsky, 1989; Pooley, 1974).

Handwriting is a tool for writers. Students need to develop legible and fluent handwriting so that they can communicate their ideas effectively though writing. Although nearly everyone would agree that the message is more than the formation of letters, handwriting instruction can't be ignored. Donald Graves (1994) urges teachers to keep handwriting in perspective and to remember that it is a tool, best taught and applied through authentic writing activities.

As you read this chapter, think about the role of grammar and handwriting in the language arts program. Use these questions to guide your reading:

- What are the components of grammar?
- How should teachers teach grammar concepts?
- How does children's handwriting develop?
- How do teachers teach and assess handwriting?

GRAMMAR

Grammar is probably the most controversial area of language arts. Teachers, parents, and the community disagree about the content of grammar instruction, how to teach it, and when to begin teaching it. Some people believe that formal instruction in grammar is unnecessary—if not harmful—during the elementary grades; others believe that grammar instruction should be a key component of language arts instruction. Before getting into the controversy, let's clarify the terms *grammar* and *usage. Grammar* is the description of the syntax or structure of a language and prescriptions for its use (Weaver, 1996). It involves principles of word and sentence formation. In contrast, *usage* is correctness, or using the appropriate word or phrase in a sentence. It is the socially preferred way of using language within a dialect. *My friend, she; the man brung;* and *hisself* are examples of Standard English usage errors that students sometimes make.

Grammar Concepts

The five most common types of information about grammar that students learn are parts of speech, parts of sentences, types of sentences, capitalization and punctuation, and usage. These components are summarized in the LA Essentials box on page 432.

Parts of Speech. Grammarians have sorted words into eight groups, called *parts of speech*: nouns, pronouns, verbs, adjectives, adverbs, prepositions, conjunctions, and interjections. Words in each group are used in essentially the same way in all sentences. Consider this sentence: *Hey, did you know that it rains more than 200 days a year in a tropical rain forest and that as much as 240 inches of rain fall each year?* All eight parts of speech are represented in this sentence. *Rain forest, days, year, inches,* and *rain* are nouns, and *you* and *it* are pronouns. *Tropical* is an adjective describing *rain forest,* and *each* is an adjective describing *year.* The verbs are *did know, rains,* and

COMPONENTS OF GRAMMAR INSTRUCTION

Parts of Speech
The eight parts of speech are nouns, pronouns, adjectives, verbs, adverbs, prepositions, conjunctions, and interjections. Students learn to identify the parts of speech in order to understand the role of each in a sentence.

Parts of Sentences
Simple sentences can be divided into the subject and the predicate. The subject is the noun or pronoun and words or phrases that modify it, and the predicate is the verb and the words or phrases that modify it. Students learn to identify subjects and predicates to check for subject-verb agreement and to determine sentence types.

Types of Sentences
Sentences can be classified according to structure and purpose. The structure of a sentence may be simple, compound, complex, or compound-complex, according to the number and type of clauses. The purpose of a sentence can be to make a statement (declarative sentence), ask a question (interrogative sentence), make a command (imperative sentence), or express strong emotion or surprise (exclamatory sentence). Students learn to recognize the structure and purposes of sentences.

Capitalization and Punctuation
Capitalization and punctuation marks signal the structure of a sentence. The first word and other important words in the sentence are capitalized, and some punctuation marks indicate internal sentence structure whereas others mark the end of a sentence. Students learn to use capital letters and punctuation marks to indicate the structure of the sentences they write.

Usage
Standard English is used by educated people in speaking and writing; however, many people speak dialects, or nonstandard varieties of English. Children come to school speaking the language used by their families, and those children who speak nonstandard varieties learn Standard English through reading and writing activities.

fall. More than is an adverb modifying *200 days,* and *as much as* is an adverb modifying *240 inches;* they both answer the question "how much." *Of* and *in* are prepositions, and they introduce prepositional phrases. The conjunction *and* joins the two dependent clauses. The first word in the sentence, *hey,* is an interjection, and it's set off with a comma. Figure 13–1 presents an overview of the eight parts of speech.

Parts of a Sentence. A sentence is made up of one or more words to express a complete thought and, to express the thought, must have a subject and a predicate

FIGURE 13–1

The Eight Parts of Speech

Part of Speech	Definition	Examples	
Noun	A word used to name something—a person, a place, or a thing. A proper noun names a particular person, place, or thing and is capitalized. In contrast, a common noun doesn't name a particular person, place, or thing and isn't capitalized.	United States Kleenex pilot	sandwich courage
Pronoun	A word used in place of a noun.	I me	you who
Adjective	A word used to describe a noun or a pronoun. Adjectives are common or proper, and proper adjectives are capitalized. Some words can be either adjectives or pronouns; they are adjectives if they come before a noun and modify it, and they're pronouns if they stand alone.	the fastest	American slippery-fingered
Verb	A word used to show action or state of being. A verb's form varies depending on its number (singular or plural) and tense (present, past, future). Some verbs are auxiliary, or helping, verbs; they are used to help form some tenses or voice. Voice is either active or passive.	eat think will have	saw is can would
Adverb	A word used to modify a verb, an adjective, or another adverb. An adverb tells how, when, where, why, how often, and how much.	quickly outside loudly	now well
Preposition	A word or group of words used to show position, direction, or how two words or ideas are related to each other.	at to between	with from
Conjunction	A word used to connect words and groups of words. These are the three types: coordinating conjunctions, which connect equivalent words, phrases, or clauses; correlative conjunctions, which are used in pairs; and subordinating conjunctions, which connect two clauses that are not equally important.	and or because	but either-or when
Interjection	A word or phrase used to express strong emotion and set off by commas or an exclamation point.	wow hey	How are you? Cool, dude!

(one-word sentences have understood subjects—"Help!"—or predicates—"You!"). The subject names who or what the sentence is about, and the predicate includes the verb and anything that completes or modifies it. In a simple sentence with one subject and one predicate, everything that is not part of the subject is part of the predicate. Consider this sentence about the rain forest: *Most rain forests are found in warm, wet climates near the equator.* The subject is *most rain forests,* and the rest of the sentence is the predicate.

Types of Sentences. Sentences are classified in two ways. First, they're classified according to structure, or how they're put together. The structure may be simple, compound, complex, or compound-complex, according to the number and type of clauses in the sentence. A clause consists of a subject and a predicate, and there are two types of clauses. If the clause presents a complete thought and can stand alone, it's an independent clause. If the clause isn't a complete thought and can't stand alone as a sentence, it's a dependent clause because it depends on the meaning expressed in the independent clause. An example of an independent clause is *Tropical rain forests are the most complex ecosystems on earth,* and an example of a dependent clause is *Because tropical rain forests are the most complex ecosystems on earth.* This dependent clause can't stand alone as a sentence; it must be attached to an independent clause. For example: *Because tropical rain forests are the most complex ecosystems on earth, scientists are interested in studying them.* The independent clause, which could stand alone as a sentence, is *scientists are interested in studying them.*

A simple sentence contains only one independent clause, and a compound sentence has two or more independent clauses. A complex sentence contains one independent clause and one or more dependent clauses. A compound-complex sentence has two or more independent clauses and one or more dependent clauses. Can you identify which of these sentences are simple, compound, complex, and compound-complex?

Although a tropical rain forest is a single ecosystem, it is composed of four layers.
The tallest trees in the rain forest grow to be about 300 feet tall, and they form the top, emergent layer.
The next level is the canopy, and it is alive with activity as hummingbirds, woodpeckers, tree frogs, and monkeys go from flower to flower and branch to branch.
Vines, ferns, and palms grow in the understory.
Few flowers bloom in the understory because sunlight does not shine through the leaves of the canopy.
The bottom layer is the forest floor; mosses, fungi, and other parasitic plants grow here.

The fourth sentence is simple, the second and sixth sentences are compound, the first and fifth sentences are complex, and the third sentence is compound-complex.

Second, sentences are classified according to their purpose or the type of message they contain. Sentences that make statements are declarative, those that ask questions are interrogative, those that make commands are imperative, and those that communicate strong emotion or surprise are exclamatory. The purpose of a sentence is often signaled by the punctuation mark placed at the end of the sentence. Declarative sentences and some imperative sentences are marked with periods, interrogative sentences are marked with question marks, and exclamatory sentences and some imperative sentences are marked with exclamation points.

Capitalization and Punctuation. Students learn that capital letters divide sentences and signal important words within sentences (Fearn & Farnan, 1998). Consider how the use of capital letters affects the meaning of these three sentences:

> They were going to the white house for dinner.
> They were going to the White house for dinner.
> They were going to the White House for dinner. (Wilde, 1992, p. 18)

Capital letters also express loudness of speech or intensity of emotion because they stand out visually.

Children often begin writing during the preschool years using only capital letters; during kindergarten and first grade, they learn the lowercase forms of letters. They learn to capitalize *I*, the first word in a sentence, and names and other proper nouns and adjectives. By sixth grade, the most common problem is overcapitalization, or capitalizing too many words in a sentence, as in this example: *If the Tropical Rain Forest is destroyed, the Earth's climate could get warmer, and this is known as the Greenhouse Effect.* This problem persists into adolescence because students have trouble differentiating between common and proper nouns (Shaughnessy, 1977). Too often, students assume that important words in the sentence should be capitalized.

It's a common assumption that punctuation marks signal pauses in speech, but punctuation plays a greater role than that, according to Sandra Wilde (1992).

Linda Peterson/Merrill

Learning Centers

These first graders experiment with end-of-sentence punctuation marks at a learning center. The sentences they're working with were written during a minilesson several days ago. As they work collaboratively to identify the punctuation marks, reread the sentences, and choose the appropriate punctuation marks, they are learning more than they would by working individually to complete a worksheet. Teachers can make the center activities self-checking, too, so that students will know immediately if they're correct, and can get help from classmates or the teacher if they aren't correct.

Punctuation marks both signal grammatical boundaries and express meaning; some punctuation marks indicate sentence boundaries as well. Periods, question marks, and exclamation points mark sentence boundaries and indicate whether a sentence makes a statement, asks a question, or expresses an exclamation. In contrast, commas, semicolons, and colons mark grammatical units within sentences.

Quotation marks and apostrophes express meaning within sentences. Quotation marks are used most often to indicate talk, but a more sophisticated use is to express irony, as in *My son "loves" to wash the dishes*. Apostrophes are used in contractions to join two words and in possessive nouns to show relationships. Consider the different meanings of these phrases:

The monkey's howling (and it's running around the cage).

The monkey's howling (annoyed us; we wanted to kill it).

The monkeys' howling (annoyed us; we wanted to kill them).

(We listened all night to) the monkeys howling. (Wilde, 1992, p. 18)

Researchers have documented that learning to use punctuation is a developmental process. Beginning in the preschool years, children notice punctuation marks and learn to discriminate them from letters (Clay, 1991). In kindergarten and first grade, children are formally introduced to the end-of-sentence punctuation marks, and they learn to use them conventionally about half the time (Cordeiro, Giacobbe, & Cazden, 1983). Many beginning writers use punctuation marks in more idiosyncratic ways, such as between words and at the end of each line of writing, but over time, children's usage becomes more conventional. English learners exhibit similar developmental patterns.

Usage. Children come to school speaking dialects or varieties of English that their parents speak, and when these dialects differ from Standard English, they're called *nonstandard English*. Children may use double negatives rather than single negatives, so that they say *I ain't got no money* instead of *I don't have any money*. Or they may use objective pronouns instead of subjective pronouns so that they say *Me and him have dirt bikes* instead of *He and I have dirt bikes*.

Students who speak nonstandard English learn Standard English as an alternative to the forms they already know. Rather than trying to substitute standard forms for students' nonstandard forms, teachers explain that Standard English is the language of school. It is the language used in books, and students can easily locate Standard English examples in books they are reading. Calling Standard English "book language" also helps to explain the importance of proofreading to identify and correct usage errors in students' writing. Figure 13–2 lists 10 types of usage errors that older students can learn to correct.

Teaching Grammar

For many years, grammar was taught using language arts textbooks. Students read rules and definitions, copied words and sentences, and marked them to apply the concepts presented in the text, but this type of activity often seemed meaningless to students. Researchers suggest that integrating grammar study with reading and writing produces the best results (Beers, 2001; Weaver, McNally, & Moerman, 2001). They view grammar

---

FIGURE 13–2

Ten Usage Errors That Middle- and Upper-Grade Students Can Correct

Irregular Verb Forms

Students form the past tense of irregular verbs as they would a regular verb; for example, some students might use *catch + ed* to make *catched* instead of *caught,* or *swim + ed* to make *swimmed* instead of *swam.*

Past-Tense Forms

Students use present-tense or past-participle forms in place of past-tense forms, such as *I ask* for *I asked, she run* for *she ran,* or *he seen* for *he saw.*

Nonstandard Verb Forms

Students use *brung* for *brought* or *had went* for *had gone.*

Double Subjects

Students use both a noun and a pronoun in the subject, such as *My mom she.*

Nonstandard Pronoun Forms

Students use nonstandard pronoun forms, such as *hisself* for *himself, them books* for *those books*, and *hisn* for *his*

Objective Pronouns for the Subject

Students use objective pronouns instead of subjective pronouns in the subject, such as *Me and my friend went to the store* or *Her and me want to play outside.*

Lack of Subject-Verb Agreement

Students use *we was* for *we were* and *he don't* for *he doesn't.*

Double Negatives

Students use two negatives when only one is needed; for example, *I don't got none* and *Joe don't have none.*

Confusing Pairs of Words

Some students confuse word pairs, such as *learn–teach, lay–lie,* and *leave–let.* They might say *I'll learn you to read,* instead of *I'll teach you to read, go lay down* instead of *go lie down,* and *leave me do it* instead of *let me do it.* Other confusing pairs include *bring–take, among–between, fewer–less, good–well, passed–past, real–really, set–sit, than–then, who–which–that, who–whom, it's–its,* and *your–you're.*

I as an Objective Pronoun

Students incorrectly use *I* instead of *me* as an objective pronoun, saying or writing *It's for Bill and I* instead of *It's for Bill and me.*

Adapted from Pooley, 1974, and Weaver, 1996.

as a language tool and recommend integrating grammar instruction with reading and writing. Guidelines for teaching grammar are listed in the LA Essentials box on page 438. In the vignette at the beginning of the chapter, Mr. Keogh followed many of these recommendations as he taught grammar as part of a literature focus unit.

Why Teach Grammar? Teachers, parents, and the community at large cite many reasons for teaching grammar. First, using Standard English is the mark of an educated person, and students should know how to use it. Many teachers feel that

GUIDELINES FOR TEACHING GRAMMAR

- **Minilessons**

  Teachers teach minilessons on grammar concepts and have students locate examples of the grammar concepts they're learning in books they're reading and in their writing.

- **Concept Books**

  Teachers share concept books when students are studying parts of speech, and students also create their own grammar concept books.

- **Sentence Collection**

  Students collect favorite sentences from books they're reading and use the sentences for grammar activities.

- **Sentence Manipulation**

  Students use sentences from books they're reading for sentence unscrambling, sentence imitating, sentence combining, and sentence expanding activities.

- **New Versions of Books**

  Young children write innovations, or new versions of books, using sentence patterns in books they have read.

- **Posters**

  Students make grammar posters to visually represent parts of speech, sentence types, and other grammar conepts they're learning.

- **Proofreading**

  Students need to learn to proofread so that they can locate and correct grammar and usage errors in their own writing.

- **Standard English Alternative**

  Teachers explain that Standard English is the language of school and is one way of speaking and writing. It is important that students understand that the purpose of grammar instruction is to expand their repertoire of language options, not to replace their home language.

teaching grammar will help students understand sentence structure and form sentences to express their thoughts. Another reason is that parents expect that grammar will be taught, and teachers must meet these expectations. Other teachers explain that they teach grammar to prepare students for the next grade or for instruction in a foreign language. Others pragmatically rationalize grammar instruction because it is a part of norm-referenced achievement tests mandated by state departments of education.

Conventional wisdom is that knowledge about grammar and usage should improve students' oral language and writing, but research for more than 75 years hasn't confirmed this assumption. In 1936, for example, the National Council of Teachers of English (NCTE) passed a resolution against the formal teaching of grammar, and based on their review of research conducted before 1963, Braddock, Lloyd-Jones, and Schoer concluded that "the teaching of formal grammar has a negligible or, because it usually displaces some instruction and practice in actual composition, even a harmful effect on the improvement of writing" (1963, pp. 37–38). Since then, other studies have reached the same conclusion, and the NCTE resolution has been reaffirmed again and again (Hillocks & Smith, 2003).

Despite the controversy about teaching grammar and its value for students, grammar is a part of the language arts program and will undoubtedly remain so for some time. Given this fact, it is only reasonable that grammar should be taught in the most beneficial manner possible.

Teaching Grammar Through Reading. Students learn about the structure of the English language through reading. They learn more sophisticated academic language, a more formal register than they speak, and sophisticated ways of phrasing ideas and arranging words into sentences. Students often read sentences that are longer than the ones they speak and learn new ways to string words into sentences. In *Chrysanthemum* (Henkes, 1991), the story of a mouse named Chrysanthemum who loves her name until she starts school and is teased by her classmates, the author uses a combination of long and short sentences very effectively: "Chrysanthemum could scarcely believe her ears. She blushed. She beamed. She bloomed" (n.p.).

Students read sentences exemplifying all four sentence types in many books. One example is the Caldecott Medal–winning *Officer Buckle and Gloria* (Rathmann, 1995), the story of a police officer and his dog, Gloria. "Officer Buckle loved having a buddy" and "That night Officer Buckle watched himself on the 10 o'clock news" (n.p.) are statements, or declarative sentences. "How about Gloria?" and "Could she come?" (n.p.) are questions, or interrogative sentences. Officer Buckle's safety tips, such as "Keep your shoelaces tied" and "Do not go swimming during electrical storms!" (n.p.), are imperative sentences. The children loved Gloria and her tricks, and they cheered, "Bravo!" (n.p.)—an example of an exclamation, or exclamatory sentence.

Students read simple, compound, complex, and compound-complex sentences in books. On the first page of *The Giver* (Lowry, 2006), for instance, there are examples of simple, compound, and complex sentences:

Simple Sentence: *"But the aircraft a year ago had been different."*
Compound Sentence: *"It was almost December, and Jonas was beginning to be frightened."*
Complex Sentence: *"Frightened was the way he had felt a year ago when an unidentified aircraft had overflown the community twice."*

Meeting the Needs of English Learners

What's the Best Way to Teach Grammar to English Learners?

The goal of grammar instruction is to increase students' ability to structure and manipulate sentences and to expand their repertoire of sentence patterns. Teaching grammar is a controversial issue, and it is especially so for English learners, but learning Standard English is crucial for these students' success in school.

Correcting Students' Grammar Errors

The best way to promote students' language development is to encourage all students to talk freely in the classroom. In the past, researchers have recommended that teachers not correct students' talk so as not to embarrass them; however; teachers are now finding that many English learners want to be corrected so that they can learn to speak Standard English correctly in order to do well in school (Scarcella, 2003).

The same is true with writing. During the editing stage of the writing process, teachers teach proofreading and help students identify and correct grammar and usage errors. After teachers explain grammar concepts in minilessons, students should become responsible for identifying and correcting the errors themselves.

Teaching Grammar Concepts

Teachers also provide direct instruction about grammar concepts through minilessons for English learners and other students who don't speak and write Standard English. The rationale for providing direct instruction is that many English learners haven't been successful in acquiring Standard English through naturalistic approaches alone.

Topics for Minilessons

The best way to choose minilesson topics is to identify the kinds of errors students are making and then teach lessons on those topics. Also, teachers choose topics from state and district-level curriculum guides. Here are 10 of the most common topics:

Plurals	Prepositions
Verb tenses	Possessives
Irregular verbs	Negatives
Contractions	Comparatives
Subject-verb agreement	Articles

Teachers use the same approach for grammar minilessons that they use for other types of lessons.

Learning to speak, read, and write Standard English takes time, and it's unrealistic to assume that students will learn a grammar topic through a single minilesson. What's important is that teachers regularly teach Standard English to their English learners and expect them to assume responsibility for learning it.

And on the second page, there's an example of a compound-complex sentence: "His parents were both at work, and his little sister, Lily, was at the Childcare Center where she spent her after-school hours."

One way to help students focus on sentences in stories is sentence collecting (Speaker & Speaker, 1991). Students collect favorite sentences and share them with classmates. They copy the sentences on chart paper or on long strips of tagboard and post them in the classroom. Students and the teacher talk about the merits of each sentence, focus on word choice, and analyze the sentence types. Sometimes students also cut the words in the sentences apart and rebuild them, either in the author's original order or in an order that appeals to them.

Teaching the Parts of Speech. Students learn about parts of speech through reading and writing activities as well as through minilessons. They can locate examples of the parts of speech in books they're reading and experiment with words to see how the parts of speech are combined to form sentences. They read grammar concept books, including the popular books by author-illustrator Ruth Heller, and make their own books, too. These activities are described in the following sections.

◆ *Collecting parts of speech* Students work in small groups to identify words representing one part of speech or all eight parts of speech from a book they are reading. A group of fifth graders identified words representing the parts of speech in Van Allsburg's popular book *The Polar Express* (2005):

- Nouns: *train, children, Santa Claus, elves, pajamas, roller coaster, conductor, sleigh, hug, clock, Sarah*
- Pronouns: *we, they, he, it, us, you, his, I, me*
- Verbs: *filled, ate, flickered, raced, were, cheered, marched, asked, pranced, stood, shouted*
- Adjectives: *melted, white-tailed, quiet, no, first, magical, cold, dark, polar, Santa's*
- Adverbs: *soon, faster, wildly, apart, closer, alone*
- Prepositions: *in, through, over, with, of, in front of, behind, at, for, across, into*
- Conjunctions: *and, but*
- Interjections: *oh, well, now*

After identifying the parts of speech, teachers can make word cards and have students sort the words according to the part of speech. Because some words, such as *melted* and *hug,* can represent more than one part of speech, depending on how the word is used in a sentence, teachers must choose words for this activity carefully or use the words in a sentence on the word card so that students can classify them correctly.

After collecting words representing one part of speech from books they are reading or from books they have written, students can create a book using some of these words. Figure 13–3 shows the cover and a page from an alphabet book focusing on adjectives that second graders developed.

◆ *Reading and writing grammar concept books* Students examine concept books that focus on one part of speech or another grammar concept. For example, Brian Cleary describes adjectives and lists many examples in *Hairy, Scary, Ordinary: What Is an Adjective?* (2000). After students read the book and identify the adjectives, they can make posters or write their own books about the parts of speech. Useful books for teaching parts of speech are listed in the Booklist on page 444.

FIGURE 13–3

An Excerpt From a Second-Grade Class Book on Adjectives

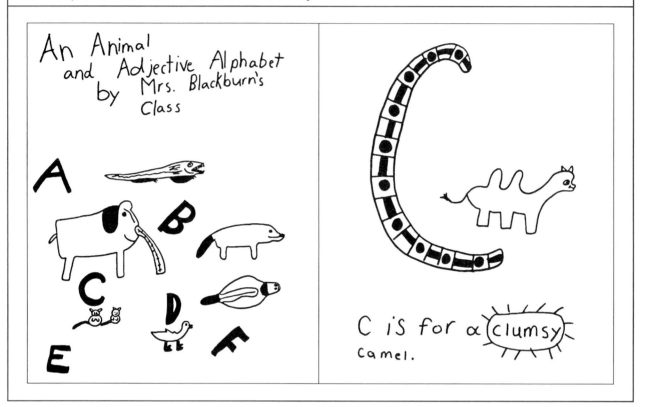

Students in an eighth-grade class divided into small groups to read Ruth Heller's books about parts of speech, including *Up, Up and Away: A Book About Adverbs* (1991), *Mine, All Mine: A Book About Pronouns* (1997), *Behind the Mask: A Book of Prepositions* (1995), and *Merry-Go-Round: A Book About Nouns* (1990). After reading one of her books, students made a poster with information about the parts of speech, which they presented to the class. The students' poster for adverbs is shown in Figure 13–4. Later, students divided into small groups to do a word sort. In this activity, students cut apart a list of words and sorted them into groups according to the part of speech. All the words had been taken from posters that students created, and they could refer to the posters if needed.

Teaching Students to Manipulate Sentences. Students experiment with or manipulate sentences when they rearrange words and phrases in a sentence, combine several sentences to make a single, stronger sentence, or write sentences based on a particular sentence pattern. Through these activities, students learn about the structure of sentences and experiment with more sophisticated sentences than they might otherwise write.

Primary-grade students often create new books or "innovations" using the sentence structure in repetitive books. For example, young children write their own versions of *Brown Bear, Brown Bear, What Do You See?* (Martin, 2007) and the sequel, *Polar*

Bear, Polar Bear, What Do You Hear? (Martin, 1992). Similarly, middle-grade students write new verses following the rhyming pattern in Laura Numeroff's *Dogs Don't Wear Sneakers* (1993) and the sequel, *Chimps Don't Wear Glasses* (1995). Third graders used Numeroff's frame to write verses, including this verse that rhymes *TV* and *bumblebee:*

> Ducks don't have tea parties,
> Lions don't watch TV,
> And you won't see a salamander
> being friends with a bumblebee.

Older students often choose a favorite sentence from a book they're reading and imitate its structure by plugging in new words, a procedure Stephen Dunning calls "copy changes" (Dunning & Stafford, 1992). For example, eighth graders chose sentences from *The Giver* (Lowry, 2006) for copy changes. One original sentence was "Dimly, from a nearly forgotten perception as blurred as the substance itself, Jonas recalled what the whiteness was" (p. 175). A student created this sentence using the sentence frame: "Softly, from a corner of the barn as cozy and warm as the kitchen, the baby kitten mewed to its mother."

FIGURE 13–4

An Eighth-Grade Poster on Adverbs

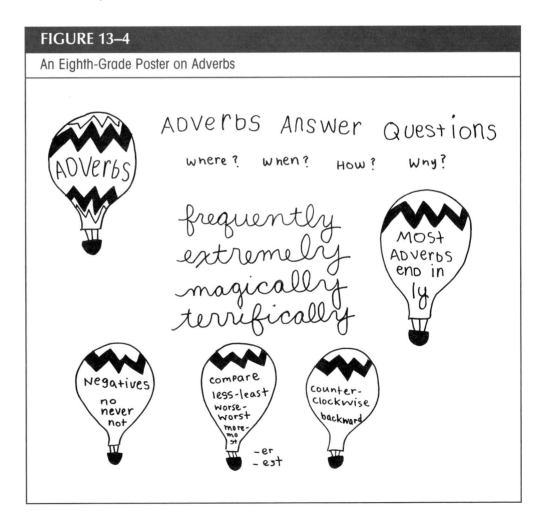

Booklist

GRAMMAR CONCEPT BOOKS

Nouns

Cleary, B. P. (1999). *A mink, a fink, a skating rink: What is a noun?* Minneapolis: Carolrhoda. (M)

Heller, R. (1990). *Merry-go-round: A book about nouns.* New York: Grosset & Dunlap. (M–U)

Terban, M. (1986). *Your foot's on my feet! and other tricky nouns.* New York: Clarion Books. (M)

Pronouns

Cleary, B. P. (2004). *I and you and don't forget who: What is a pronoun?* Minneapolis: Carolrhoda. (M)

Heller, R. (1997). *Mine, all mine: A book about pronouns.* New York: Grosset & Dunlap. (M–U)

Adjectives

Cleary, B. P. (2000). *Hairy, scary, ordinary: What is an adjective?* Minneapolis: Carolrhoda. (M)

Heller, R. (1989). *Many luscious lollipops: A book about adjectives.* New York: Grosset & Dunlap. (M–U)

Verbs

Cleary, B. P. (2001). *To root, to toot, to parachute: What is a verb?* Minneapolis: Carolrhoda. (M)

Heller, R. (1988). *Kites sail high: A book about verbs.* New York: Grosset & Dunlap. (M–U)

Schneider, R. M. (1995). *Add it, dip it, fix it: A book of verbs.* Boston: Houghton Mifflin. (M)

Adverbs

Cleary, B. P. (2003). *Dearly, nearly, insincerely: What is an adverb?* Minneapolis: Carolrhoda. (M)

Heller, R. (1991). *Up, up and away: A book about adverbs.* New York: Grosset & Dunlap. (M–U)

Prepositions

Cleary, B. P. (2002). *Under, over, by the clover: What is a preposition?* Minneapolis: Carolrhoda. (M)

Heller, R. (1995). *Behind the mask: A book of prepositions.* New York: Grosset & Dunlap. (M–U)

Conjunctions

Heller, R. (1998). *Fantastic! Wow! And unreal! A book about interjections and conjunctions.* New York: Penguin. (M–U)

Interjections

Heller, R. (1998). *Fantastic! Wow! And unreal! A book about interjections and conjunctions.* New York: Penguin. (M–U)

P = primary grades (K–2); M = middle grades (3–5); U = upper grades (6–8)

Killgallon (1997, 1998) recommends that teachers help students examine how authors write sentences through four types of activities: sentence unscrambling, sentence imitating, sentence combining, and sentence expanding. Sentence imitating is like the innovations and copy changes discussed earlier. Through sentence manipulation, students learn new syntactic structures and practice ways to vary the sentences they write. These four types of sentence manipulation are summarized in Figure 13–5.

◆ *Sentence unscrambling* Teachers choose a sentence from a book students are reading and divide it into phrases. They present the phrases in a random order,

---

FIGURE 13–5

Killgallon's Four Types of Sentence Manipulation

Sentence Unscrambling
Teachers choose a long sentence from a book students are reading and break it into phrases. Then students reassemble the sentence to examine how the author structures sentences. Sometimes students duplicate the author's sentence, but other times, they create an original sentence that they like better.

Sentence Imitating
Teachers choose a sentence with an interesting structure to imitate from a book students are reading. Then students create a new sentence on a new topic that imitates the structure and style of the original sentence.

Sentence Combining
Teachers choose a conceptually dense sentence from a book students are reading and break the sentence into three or more simple sentences. Then students combine and embed the simple sentences to re-create the author's original sentence. They compare their sentence with the original sentence.

Sentence Expanding
Teachers choose a sentence from a book students are reading and shorten the sentence to make an abridged version. Then students expand the abridged sentence, trying to re-create the author's original sentence, or write a new sentence, trying to match the author's style.

Adapted from Killgallon, 1997, 1998.

and students unscramble the sentence and rearrange the phrases, trying to duplicate the author's original order. Then students compare their rearrangement with the author's. Sometimes they discover that they've created a new sentence that they like better. Here's a sentence from E. B. White's *Charlotte's Web* (2006), broken into phrases and scrambled:

in the middle of the kitchen
teaching it to suck from the bottle
a minute later
with an infant between her knees
Fern was seated on the floor

Can you unscramble the sentence? Here's the original: "A minute later Fern was seated on the floor in the middle of the kitchen with an infant between her knees, teaching it to suck from the bottle" (pp. 6–7).

◆ *Sentence imitating* Students choose a sentence from a book they are reading and then write their own sentence imitating the structure of the one they've chosen. Here's an original sentence from *Charlotte's Web:* "Avery noticed the spider web, and coming closer, he saw Charlotte" (p. 71). Can you create a sentence on a new topic that imitates E. B. White's sentence structure, especially the "and coming closer" part? A class of sixth graders created this imitation: *The fox smelled the poultry, and coming closer, he saw five juicy chickens scratching in the dirt.* Here's another sentence from *Charlotte's Web:* "His medal still hung from his neck; by

looking out of the corner of his eye he could still see it" (p. 163). Sixth graders also created this imitation: *The message was still stuck in the keyhole; using a magnifying glass the little mouse could still read those awful words.*

◆ *Sentence combining* Students combine and rearrange words in sentences to make the sentences longer and more conceptually dense (Strong, 1996). The goal of sentence combining is for students to experiment with different ways to join and embed words. Teachers choose a sentence from a book students are reading and break it into short, simple sentences. Then students combine the sentences, trying to recapture the author's original sentence. Try your hand at combining these short sentences that were taken from a more complex sentence in *Charlotte's Web*:

No one ever had such a friend.
The friend was so affectionate.
The friend was so loyal.
The friend was so skillful.

Here is the original sentence: "No one ever had such a friend—so affectionate, so loyal, and so skillful" (p. 173). You might wonder whether the *and* before *so skillful* is necessary. Students often wonder why E. B. White added it.

◆ *Sentence expanding* Teachers choose a rich sentence from a book students are reading and present an abridged version. Then students expand the sentence, taking care that the words and phrases they add blend in with the author's sentence. Here's an abridged sentence from *Charlotte's Web*:

There is no place like home. . . .

This is the original: "There is no place like home, Wilbur thought, as he placed Charlotte's 514 unborn children carefully in a safe corner" (p. 172). A sixth grader wrote this expansion: *There is no place like home, like his home in the barn, cozy and warm straw to sleep on, the delicious smell of manure in the air, Charlotte's egg sac to guard, and his friends Templeton, the goose, and the sheep nearby.* Even though it is not the same as E. B. White's sentence, the student's sentence retains the character of White's writing style.

Minilessons Teachers teach minilessons on grammar topics. They explain grammar concepts, have students make charts and posters, and involve them in examining sentences in books they're reading and in writing their own sentences. Finally, students apply what they're learning in their own writing.

Teachers identify topics for grammar minilessons in two ways. They identify concepts by examining students' writing and noting what types of grammar errors they're making. Teachers also choose topics from state standards for their grade level. A list of minilesson topics is presented in the Planning for Instruction feature on pages 454 and 455.

Assessing Students' Knowledge About Grammar Teachers might think about administering a test to assess students' knowledge of grammar, but the best gauge is how they arrange words into sentences as part of genuine writing projects. As teachers examine students' compositions, they note errors, plan and teach minilessons based on these observed needs, note further errors, plan and teach other minilessons, and so on.

HANDWRITING

The goal in handwriting instruction is to help students develop legible forms to communicate effectively through writing. The two most important criteria in determining quality in handwriting are legibility (the writing can be easily and quickly read) and fluency (the writing can be easily and quickly written). Even though a few students take great pleasure in developing flawless handwriting skills, most feel that handwriting instruction is boring and unnecessary. It's imperative, therefore, to convey to students the importance of developing legible handwriting. Writing for genuine audiences is the best way to convey the importance of legibility. A letter sent to a favorite author that is returned by the post office because the address is not decipherable or a child's published hardcover book that sits unread on the library shelf because the handwriting is illegible makes clear the importance of legibility. Illegible writing means a failure to communicate—a harsh lesson for a writer!

Handwriting Forms

Two forms of handwriting are currently used in elementary schools: manuscript, or printing, and cursive, or connected writing. These are illustrated in Figure 13–6. Typically, young children use the manuscript form, and they switch to cursive handwriting in third grade. In the upper grades, students use both handwriting forms.

Manuscript Handwriting. Until the 1920s, students learned only cursive handwriting. Marjorie Wise is credited with introducing the manuscript form for young children in 1921 (Hildreth, 1960). Manuscript handwriting is considered better for young children because they lack the eye–hand coordination necessary for cursive handwriting. In addition, manuscript handwriting is similar to the type style in primary-level reading textbooks. Only two lowercase letters, *a* and *g*, are usually different in typed and handwritten forms. The similarity may actually facilitate young children's introduction to reading because it simplifies letter recognition (Adams, 1990).

Despite its advantages, the manuscript form has been criticized. A major complaint is the reversal problem caused by some similar lowercase letters; *b* and *d* are particularly confusing. Detractors also argue that using both the manuscript and cursive forms requires teaching students two totally different kinds of handwriting within several years. They also complain that the "circle and sticks" style of manuscript handwriting requires frequent stops and starts, thus inhibiting a smooth and rhythmic flow of writing.

Cursive Handwriting. When most people think of handwriting, the cursive or connected form comes to mind. The letters in cursive handwriting are joined together to form a word with one continuous movement. Children often view cursive handwriting as the grown-up type. Primary-grade students often attempt to imitate this form by connecting the manuscript letters in their names and other words before they are taught how to form and join the letters. Awareness of cursive handwriting and interest in imitating it are indicators that children are ready for instruction.

D'Nealian Handwriting. D'Nealian handwriting is an innovative manuscript and cursive handwriting program developed by Donald Neal Thurber, a teacher in Michigan, to mitigate some of the problems associated with the traditional manuscript

FIGURE 13–6

Manuscript and Cursive Handwriting Forms

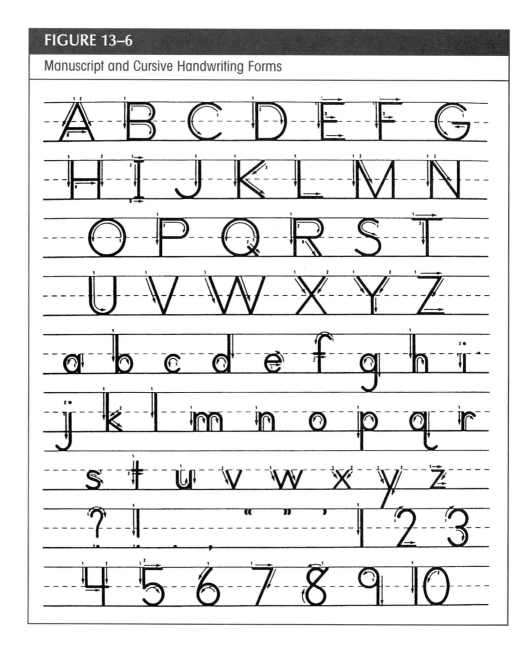

form. D'Nealian manuscript uses the same basic letter forms that students will need for cursive handwriting, as well as the slant and rhythm required for cursive. In the manuscript form, letters are slanted and formed with a continuous stroke; in the cursive form, the letters are simplified, without the flourishes of traditional cursive. Both forms were designed to increase legibility and fluency and to ease the transition from manuscript to cursive handwriting. Another advantage is that the transition from manuscript to cursive involves adding only connective strokes to most manuscript letters. Only five letters—*f, r, s, v,* and *z*—are shaped differently in the cursive form. The D'Nealian handwriting forms are shown in Figure 13–7. Research has not yet documented that D'Nealian is better than the traditional manuscript form even though many teachers prefer it (Graham, 1992).

FIGURE 13–6   (Continued)

Used with permission of the publisher, Zaner-Bloser, Inc., Columbus, OH, copyright 2003. From *Handwriting: A Way to Self-Expression,* by Clinton Hackney.

Children's Handwriting Development

Young children enter kindergarten with different backgrounds of handwriting experience. Some 5-year-olds have never held a pencil, whereas others have written cursivelike scribbles or manuscript-letter-like forms. Some preschoolers have learned to print their names and some other letters. Handwriting in kindergarten typically includes three types of activities: stimulating children's interest in writing, developing their ability to hold writing instruments, and printing letters of the alphabet. Adults are influential role models in stimulating children's interest in writing. They record children's talk and write labels on signs. They can also provide paper, pencils, and pens so that children can experiment with writing. Children learn to hold a pencil by

FIGURE 13–7

D'Nealian Manuscript and Cursive Handwriting Forms

D'Nealian manuscript and cursive alphabets and numbers from D'NEALIAN HANDWRITIING. Copyright © 2008 by Pearson Education, Inc. D'Nealian Handwriting is a registered trademark of Donald Neal Thurber. Reprinted by permission.

watching adults and through numerous opportunities to experiment with pencils, paintbrushes, and crayons. Instruction is necessary so that children don't learn bad habits that later must be broken. They often devise bizarre ways to form letters when they haven't been shown how to form them, and these bad habits can cause problems as children need to develop greater writing speed.

Formal handwriting instruction begins in first grade. Students learn how to form manuscript letters and space between them, and they develop skills related to the six elements of legibility (see pp. 452 and 456). A common handwriting activity requires students to copy short writing samples from the chalkboard, but this type of activity is not recommended. For one thing, young children have great difficulty with far-to-near copying; a piece of writing should be placed close to the child for copying. Children can recopy interactive writing compositions and Language Experience stories, but other types of copying should be avoided. It's far better for children to create their own writing than to copy words and sentences they may not even be able to read!

Special pencils and handwriting paper are often provided for handwriting instruction. Kindergartners and first graders have commonly been given "fat" beginner pencils because it has been assumed that these pencils are easier for young children to hold; however, most children prefer to use regular-sized pencils that older students and adults use. Moreover, regular pencils have erasers! Research now indicates that beginner pencils aren't better than regular-sized pencils for young children (Graham, 1992). Likewise, there's no evidence that specially shaped pencils and small writing aids that slip onto pencils to improve children's grips are effective.

Students' introduction to cursive handwriting typically occurs in the first semester of third grade. Parents and students often attach great importance to the transition from manuscript to cursive, thus adding unnecessary pressure for the students. Beverly Cleary's *Muggie Maggie* (1990) describes the pressure some children feel. The time of transition is usually dictated by tradition rather than by sound educational theory. All students in a school or school district are usually introduced to cursive handwriting at the same time, regardless of their interest in making the change.

Some students indicate an early interest in cursive handwriting by trying to connect manuscript letters or by asking their parents to demonstrate how to write their names. Because of individual differences in motor skills and levels of interest in cursive writing, it's better to introduce some students to cursive handwriting in first or second grade while providing other students with additional time to refine their manuscript skills. These students then learn cursive handwriting in third or fourth grade.

The practice of changing to cursive handwriting only a year or two after children learn the manuscript form is receiving increasing criticism. The argument has been that students need to learn cursive handwriting as early as possible because of their growing need for handwriting speed. Because of its continuous flow, cursive handwriting was thought to be faster to write than manuscript; however, research suggests that manuscript handwriting can be written as quickly as cursive handwriting (Jackson, 1971). The controversy over the benefits of the two forms and the best time to introduce cursive handwriting is likely to continue.

Students are introduced to the cursive handwriting form in third grade. Usually, the basic strokes that make up the letters (e.g., slant stroke, undercurve, downcurve) are taught first. Next, the lowercase letters are taught in isolation, and then the connecting strokes are introduced. Uppercase letters are taught later because they are used far less often and are more difficult to form. Which cursive letters are most difficult? The lowercase *r* is the most troublesome letter. The other lowercase letters students frequently form incorrectly are *k, p,* and *z*.

Cursive handwriting does not replace manuscript handwriting. Students continue to use manuscript handwriting part of the time. Because manuscript handwriting is easier for them to form and to read, many students often continue to use the manuscript form when they're writing informally, saving cursive handwriting for projects and final copies of their writing. Teachers need to review both forms periodically. By this time, too, students have firmly established handwriting habits, both good and bad. Now the emphasis is on helping students diagnose and correct their handwriting trouble spots so that they can develop a legible and fluent handwriting style. Older students both simplify their letterforms and add unique flourishes to their handwriting to develop their own trademark styles. A review of the sequence of handwriting development is presented in the LA Essentials box on the next page.

Teaching Handwriting

Handwriting is best taught in separate periods of direct instruction and teacher-supervised practice. As soon as skills are taught, students should apply them in real-life writing activities; busywork assignments, such as copying sentences from the chalkboard, aren't effective. Moreover, students often develop poor handwriting habits or learn to form letters incorrectly if they practice without direct supervision. It's much more difficult to correct bad habits and errors in letter formation than to teach correct handwriting in the first place.

Elements of Legibility. For students to develop legible handwriting, they need to know what qualities or elements determine legibility and then to analyze their own handwriting according to these elements (Hackney, 2003). Here are the six elements of legible handwriting:

◆ *Letter Formation.* Letters are formed with specific strokes. Letters in manuscript handwriting are composed of vertical, horizontal, and slanted lines plus circles or parts of circles. The letter *b*, for example, is composed of a vertical line and a circle, and *M* is composed of vertical and slanted lines. Cursive letters are composed of slanted lines, loops, and curved lines. The lowercase cursive letters *m* and *n*, for instance, are composed of a slant stroke, a loop, and an undercurve stroke. An additional component in cursive handwriting is the connecting stroke used to join letters.

◆ *Size and Proportion.* Students' handwriting gradually becomes smaller, and the proportional size of uppercase to lowercase letters increases. First graders' uppercase manuscript letters are twice the size of their lowercase letters. When second- and third-grade students begin cursive handwriting, the proportional size of letters remains 2:1; later, the proportion increases to 3:1 for middle- and upper-grade students.

◆ *Spacing.* Students should leave adequate space between letters in words and between words in sentences. Spacing between words in manuscript handwriting should equal one lowercase letter *o*, and spacing between sentences should equal two lowercase *o*'s. The most important aspect of spacing within words in cursive handwriting is consistency. To correctly space between words, the writer makes the beginning stroke of the new word directly below the end stroke of the preceding word. Spacing between sentences should equal one uppercase letter *O*, and the indent for a new paragraph should equal two uppercase letter *O*'s.

SEQUENCE OF HANDWRITING DEVELOPMENT

Handwriting Before First Grade
Teachers teach basic handwriting skills during kindergarten.

- Children learn how to hold a pencil.
- Children learn to form upper- and lowercase letters.
- Children learn to write their names and other common words.

Handwriting in the Primary Grades
Primary-grade students develop legible manuscript handwriting.

- Children learn to form upper- and lowercase manuscript letters and space between letters.
- Children often use "fat" beginner pencils even though research does not support this practice.
- Children use wide, lined paper with a dotted midline to guide them in forming lowercase letters.

Transition to Cursive Handwriting in the Middle Grades
Teachers teach students to both read and write cursive handwriting because it is a new writing system.

- Students are introduced to cursive handwriting in third grade.
- Students learn to read cursive writing.
- Students learn to form upper- and lowercase letters and to join letters.

Handwriting in the Upper Grades
Teachers expect students to use both manuscript and cursive handwriting in daily writing activities.

- Students have learned both manuscript and cursive handwriting forms.
- Students develop their own trademark styles.
- Students vary the legibility and neatness of their handwriting for private and public writing.

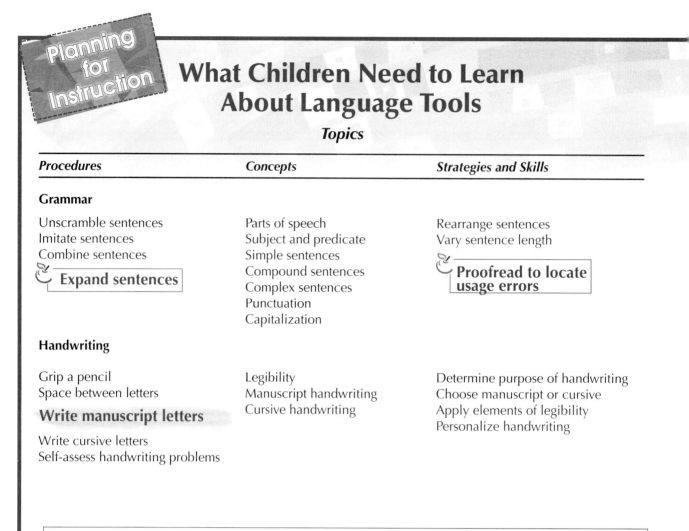

Planning for Instruction

What Children Need to Learn About Language Tools

Topics

Procedures	*Concepts*	*Strategies and Skills*
Grammar		
Unscramble sentences	Parts of speech	Rearrange sentences
Imitate sentences	Subject and predicate	Vary sentence length
Combine sentences	Simple sentences	
Expand sentences	Compound sentences	**Proofread to locate usage errors**
	Complex sentences	
	Punctuation	
	Capitalization	
Handwriting		
Grip a pencil	Legibility	Determine purpose of handwriting
Space between letters	Manuscript handwriting	Choose manuscript or cursive
Write manuscript letters	Cursive handwriting	Apply elements of legibility
Write cursive letters		Personalize handwriting
Self-assess handwriting problems		

If you'd like to learn more about teaching grammar and handwriting, visit MyEducationLab. To view third graders expanding sentences, go to the topic "Grammar" and click on the video "Expanding Sentences," and to see a student-teacher conference on writing mechanics, go to the topic "Writing" and click on the video "Proofreading."

Minilesson

Ms. Thomas Teaches Her First Graders Manuscript-Letter Formation

1 Introduce the topic

Ms. Thomas brings her first graders together on the rug for handwriting practice and passes out a small dry-erase board, pen, and eraser to each child. They begin by rereading the class news chart that they wrote the day before using interactive writing. Ms. Thomas explains that she wants to practice three lowercase letters—*m, n,* and *u*—that the children had difficulty writing the previous day.

2 Share examples

Ms. Thomas rereads the chart and asks children to point out the three letters when they notice them in the class news chart. She asks one child to underline each word the children point out. They mention these words: *and, made, not, when, never, some, then, you, your,* and *wanted.* After reading the entire chart, the children agree that these letters are important because they are used so often in their writing.

3 Provide information

Ms. Thomas demonstrates how to form each of the letters by writing the letter on a dry-erase board and verbalizing the strokes she's making.

Then the children practice writing the letters on their boards as Ms. Thomas observes them. She assists several children in holding their pencils correctly, and she demonstrates again for several children who are continuing to have trouble writing the letters.

4 Supervise practice

Once she is satisfied that each child can form the three letters and differentiate among them, Ms. Thomas asks children to write several of the underlined words on their dry-erase boards as she observes. She provides immediate feedback to those who are not forming the letters correctly or who make the letters too large.

5 Reflect on learning

After this brief review, Ms. Thomas asks children to remember what they learned about forming these letters when they are writing. The children name all the occasions they have during the day to remember how to form the letters when they are writing—when they write books at the writing center, when they write in journals, and when they do interactive writing.

◆ *Slant.* Letters should be consistently parallel. Letters in manuscript handwriting are vertical, and in the cursive form, letters slant slightly to the right. To ensure the correct slant, right-handed students tilt their papers to the left, and left-handed students tilt their papers to the right.

◆ *Alignment.* For proper alignment in both manuscript and cursive handwriting, all letters should be uniform in size and consistently touch the baseline.

◆ *Line quality.* Students should write at a consistent speed and hold their writing instruments correctly and in a relaxed manner to make steady, unwavering lines of even thickness.

Correct letter formation and spacing receive the major focus in handwriting instruction. Although the other four elements usually receive less attention, they are important in developing legible handwriting.

Minilessons. Handwriting is best taught in minilessons. Brief lessons and practice sessions taught several times a week are more effective than a single, lengthy period weekly or monthly. Regular handwriting instruction is necessary when teaching the manuscript form in kindergarten and first grade and the cursive form in third grade. In the upper grades, instruction focuses on specific handwriting problems that students demonstrate and periodic reviews of both handwriting forms. A list of minilesson topics is presented in the box on page 454, and a sample lesson on teaching manuscript-letter formation in first grade is also shown.

Research has shown the importance of the teacher's active involvement in handwriting instruction and practice. Observing "moving" models—that is, having students watch the teacher write the handwriting sample—is of far greater value than copying models that have already been written (Wright & Wright, 1980). Moving models are possible when the teacher circulates around the classroom, stopping to demonstrate a procedure, strategy, or skill for one student and moving to assist another; circling incorrectly formed letters and marking other errors with a red pen on completed handwriting sheets is of little value.

Working With Left-Handed Writers. Approximately 10% of the U.S. population is left-handed, and two or three students in most classrooms are left-handed. Until 1950 or so, teachers insisted that left-handed students use their right hands for handwriting because left-handed writers were thought to have inferior handwriting skills. Parents and teachers are more realistic now and accept children's natural tendencies for left- or right-handedness.

Most young children develop handedness—the preference for using either the right or left hand for fine-motor activities—by age 5. Teachers must help those children who haven't developed handedness to consistently use one hand for handwriting and other fine-motor activities. Teachers observe the child's behavior and hand preference over a period of days and note which hand he or she uses in activities such as building with blocks, throwing balls, cutting with scissors, holding a paintbrush, manipulating clay, and pouring water. Teachers may find that a child uses both hands interchangeably. For example, a child may first reach for several blocks with one hand and then reach for the next block with the other. During drawing activities, the child may switch hands every few minutes. In this situation, the teacher asks the child's parents to observe his or her behavior at home, noting hand preferences when the child eats, brushes teeth, turns on the television, opens drawers, and so on. Then the teacher, the child, and the child's parents confer and—based on the results of joint observations, the handedness of family members, and the child's wishes—make a tentative decision about hand preference. At school, teacher and child will work closely together so that the child uses the chosen hand. As long as the child continues to use both hands interchangeably, neither hand will develop the prerequisite fine-motor control for handwriting.

Teaching handwriting to left-handed students isn't simply the reverse of teaching handwriting to right-handed students: Left-handed students have unique handwriting problems, so special adaptations of the procedures for teaching right-handed students are necessary. In fact, many of the problems that left-handed students have can actually be made worse by using the procedures designed for right-handed writers (Harrison, 1981). Special adjustments are necessary to enable left-handed students to write legibly, fluently, and with less fatigue.

The basic difference between right- and left-handed writing is physical orientation: Right-handed students pull their arms toward their bodies as they write, whereas left-handed writers push away. As left-handed students write, they move their left hand across what they have just written, often covering it. Consequently, many children adopt a "hook" position to avoid covering and smudging what they have written. Because of their different physical orientation, left-handed writers need to make three major types of adjustments:

Holding Pencils. Left-handed writers should hold pencils an inch or more farther back from the tip than right-handed writers do. This change helps them see what they have just written and avoid smearing their writing. Left-handed writers need to work to avoid hooking their wrists: They should keep their wrists straight and elbows close to their bodies to avoid the awkward hooked position. Practicing handwriting on the chalkboard is one way to help them develop a more natural style.

Tilting Paper. Left-handed students should tilt their writing papers slightly to the right, in contrast to right-handed students, who tilt their papers to the left. Sometimes it is helpful to place a piece of masking tape on the student's desk to indicate the proper amount of tilt.

Slanting Letters. Whereas right-handed students are encouraged to slant their cursive letters to the right, left-handed writers often write vertically or even slant their letters slightly backward. Some handwriting programs recommend that left-handed writers slant their cursive letters slightly to the right as right-handed students do, but others advise teachers to permit any slant between vertical and 45 degrees to the left of vertical.

Correcting Handwriting Problems Students use the six elements of legibility to diagnose their handwriting problems. Primary-grade students, for example, can check to see that they have formed a particular letter correctly, that the round parts of letters are joined neatly, and that slanted letters are joined in sharp points. Older students can examine a piece of handwriting to see if their letters are consistently parallel and if the letters touch the baseline consistently. A checklist for evaluating manuscript handwriting is shown in the Weaving Assessment Into Practice feature on page 458. Checklists can also be developed for cursive handwriting. It is important to involve students in developing the checklists so that they appreciate the need to make their handwriting more legible.

Another reason students need to diagnose and correct their handwriting problems is that handwriting quality influences teacher evaluation and grading. Researchers have found that teachers consistently grade papers with better handwriting higher than those with poor handwriting, regardless of the content (Graham, 1992). Children aren't too young to learn that poor or illegible handwriting may lead to lower grades.

Weaving Assessment Into Practice

A CHECKLIST FOR ASSESSING MANUSCRIPT HANDWRITING

Name _____

Writing Project _____

Date _____

_____ 1.   Did I form my letters correctly?
          Did I start my line letters at the top?
          Did I start my circle letters at 1:00?
          Did I join the round parts of the letters neatly?
          Did I join the slanted strokes in sharp points?

_____ 2.   Did my lines touch the midline or top line neatly?

_____ 3.   Did I space evenly between letters?

_____ 4.   Did I leave enough space between words?

_____ 5.   Did I make my letters straight up and down?

_____ 6.   Did I make all my letters sit on the baseline?

Keyboarding: An Alternative to Handwriting

To become efficient computer users, students need to develop keyboarding skills so they can use the computer more easily for word processing, to write e-mail messages, and to create HyperStudio® projects. Keyboarding is also faster than writing by hand: By sixth or seventh grade, students can learn to type 20 to 25 words per minute, but they handwrite only 10 to 15 words in the same amount of time (National Business Education Association, 1997).

Informal keyboarding instruction begins in the primary grades. Students become familiar with the keyboard and learn basic hand positioning. They learn to keep their right hand on the right side of the keyboard and their left hand on the left side. They learn simple keyboarding skills, such as keeping their fingers on the home-row keys (*asdfghjkl;*) and typing with more than one finger. Students also learn proper posture: They sit directly in front of the computer and keep their feet on the floor.

In third or fourth grade, students receive formal keyboarding lessons. Through a series of lessons, they learn touch typing and to look mainly at the screen rather than at their fingers while typing. It is crucial that students develop good touch-typing skills and avoid bad habits that inhibit efficient use of the keyboard. Students often practice keyboarding using AlphaSmart™ or another portable keyboard because a full computer is not needed. Guidelines for teaching keyboarding skills are presented in the LA Essentials box on the next page.

Students can learn keyboarding through teacher-directed lessons or using software packages. The Kid Keys® software package, which is recommended for primary students, includes lessons on becoming familiar with the letter positions on the keyboard and games using keyboarding skills to make music. The Mavis Beacon Teaches Typing® software package is recommended for students in third grade and above; the lessons teach fundamental keyboarding skills at several levels of difficulty and offer

GUIDELINES FOR SUCCESSFUL KEYBOARDING

- **Body Position**

  Students sit up straight and directly in front of the keyboard, aligning the center of their bodies with the *j* key.

- **Foot Position**

  Students keep their feet flat on the floor, about a hand span's distance apart.

- **Back Position**

  Students keep their backs straight and lean slightly forward.

- **Arm Position**

  Students keep their arms and shoulders relaxed and their elbows close to the body.

- **Wrist Position**

  Students keep their wrists straight.

- **Home-Row Keys**

  Students anchor their fingers on the home-row keys (*asdfghjkl;*). They use their thumbs to press the space bar and their little fingers to press the shift and return keys.

- **Finger Position**

  Students keep their fingers in a well-curved position and use a snap stroke to press the keys.

- **Touch Typing**

  Students learn touch typing and other special computer-related keyboard features.

- **Eye Position**

  Students keep their eyes on the screen or the text they are typing onto the computer.

- **Speed and Accuracy**

  Students develop typing speed and accuracy through practice and using the computer for authentic writing activities.

National Business Education Association, 1997.

games to reinforce the skills. Even though voice-recognition systems may someday replace the need for computer keyboards, keyboarding skills are still essential.

Review

Grammar and handwriting are language tools. *Grammar* is the description of the structure of a language and the principles of word and sentence formation. Even though grammar is a controversial topic, the position in this text is that grammar should be taught within the context of authentic reading and writing activities. Handwriting is a tool for writers, and students learn both manuscript and cursive handwriting. The emphasis in handwriting instruction is on legibility rather than on imitating handwriting models perfectly; students need to learn how to write so that their writing can be easily read. Here are the key concepts discussed in this chapter:

- Grammar is the structure of language, whereas usage is the socially accepted way of using words in sentences.
- Teaching grammar is a controversial topic, but teachers are expected to teach grammar even though research hasn't documented its usefulness.
- Grammar should be taught in the context of reading and writing activities.
- Teachers use sentences from books students are reading and from students' own writing for grammar instruction.
- Teachers deal with students' usage errors more effectively as part of the editing stage of the writing process than by correcting their oral language.
- Students learn two handwriting forms—manuscript and cursive—within several years.
- D'Nealian handwriting simplifies students' transition from manuscript to cursive handwriting.
- The six elements of handwriting are letter formation, size and proportion, spacing, slant, alignment, and line quality.
- The most important component of handwriting instruction is that the teacher demonstrate handwriting and provide feedback during the lesson.
- Students learn keyboarding as an alternative to handwriting.

Professional References

Adams, M. J. (1990). *Beginning to read: Thinking and learning about print.* Cambridge, MA: MIT Press.

Beers, K. (2001). Contextualizing grammar. *Voices From the Middle, 8*(3), 4.

Braddock, R., Lloyd-Jones, R., & Schoer, L. (1963). *Research in written composition.* Champaign, IL: National Council of Teachers of English.

Clay, M. M. (1991). *Becoming literate: The construction of inner control.* Portsmouth, NH: Heinemann.

Cordeiro, P., Giacobbe, M. E., & Cazden, C. (1983). Apostrophes, quotation marks, and periods: Learning punctuation in the first grade. *Language Arts, 60,* 323–332.

Dunning, S., & Stafford, W. (1992). *Getting the knack: 20 poetry writing exercises.* Urbana, IL: National Council of Teachers of English.

Edelsky, C. (1989). Putting language variation to work for you. In P. Rigg & V. G. Allen (Eds.), *When they don't all speak English: Integrating the ESL student into the regular classroom* (pp. 96–107). Urbana, IL: National Council of Teachers of English.

Fearn, L., & Farnan, N. (1998). *Writing effectively: Helping children master the conventions of writing.* Boston: Allyn & Bacon.

Graham, S. (1992). Issues in handwriting instruction. *Focus on Exceptional Children, 25,* 1–14.

Graves, D. H. (1994). *A fresh look at writing*. Portsmouth, NH: Heinemann.

Hackney, C. (2003). *Handwriting: A way to self-expression*. Columbus, OH: Zaner-Bloser.

Harrison, S. (1981). Open letter from a left-handed teacher: Some sinistral ideas on the teaching of handwriting. *Teaching Exceptional Children, 13,* 116–120.

Hildreth, G. (1960). Manuscript writing after sixty years. *Elementary English, 37,* 3–13.

Hillocks, G., Jr., & Smith, M. W. (2003). Grammar and literacy learning. In J. Flood, D. Lapp, J. R. Squire, & J. M. Jensen (Eds.), *Handbook of research on teaching the English language arts* (2nd ed., pp. 721–737). Mahwah, NJ: Erlbaum.

Jackson, A. D. (1971). *A comparison of speed and legibility of manuscript and cursive handwriting of intermediate grade pupils*. Unpublished doctoral dissertation, University of Arizona. *Dissertation Abstracts, 31,* 4384A.

Killgallon, D. (1997). *Sentence composing for middle school*. Portsmouth, NH: Heinemann.

Killgallon, D. (1998). Sentence composing: Notes on a new rhetoric. In C. Weaver (Ed.), *Lessons to share: On teaching grammar in context* (pp. 169–183). Portsmouth, NH: Heinemann.

National Business Education Association. (1997). *Elementary/middle school keyboarding strategies guide* (2nd ed.). Reston, VA: Author.

Pooley, R. C. (1974). *The teaching of English usage*. Urbana, IL: National Council of Teachers of English.

Scarcella, R. C. (2003). *Accelerating academic English: A focus on the English learner*. Oakland: Regents of the University of California.

Shaughnessy, M. P. (1977). *Errors and expectations: A guide for teachers of basic writing*. New York: Oxford University Press.

Speaker, R. B., Jr., & Speaker, P. R. (1991). Sentence collecting: Authentic literacy events in the classroom. *Journal of Reading, 35,* 92–95.

Strong, W. (1996). *Writer's toolbox: A sentence-combining workshop*. New York: McGraw-Hill.

Thurber, D. N. (1999). *D'Nealian handwriting (grades K–8)*. Glenview, IL: Scott, Foresman.

Weaver, C. (1996). *Teaching grammar in context*. Portsmouth, NH: Heinemann.

Weaver, C., McNally, C., & Moerman, S. (2001). To grammar or not to grammar: That is *not* the question! *Voices From the Middle, 8*(3), 17–33.

Wilde, S. (1992). *You kan red this! Spelling and punctuation for whole language classrooms, K–6*. Portsmouth, NH: Heinemann.

Wright, C. D., & Wright, J. P. (1980). Handwriting: The effectiveness of copying from moving versus still models. *Journal of Educational Research, 74,* 95–98.

Children's Book References

Avi. (1995). *Poppy*. New York: Orchard Books.

Cleary, B. (1990). *Muggie Maggie*. New York: Morrow.

Cleary, B. P. (2000). *Hairy, scary, ordinary: What is an adjective?* Minneapolis: Carolrhoda.

Heller, R. (1990). *Merry-go-round: A book about nouns*. New York: Grosset & Dunlap.

Heller, R. (1991). *Up, up and away: A book about adverbs*. New York: Grosset & Dunlap.

Heller, R. (1995). *Behind the mask: A book of prepositions*. New York: Grosset & Dunlap.

Heller, R. (1997). *Mine, all mine: A book about pronouns*. New York: Grosset & Dunlap.

Henkes, K. (1991). *Chrysanthemum*. New York: Greenwillow.

Lowry, L. (2006). *The giver*. New York: Delacorte.

Martin, B., Jr. (1992). *Polar bear, polar bear, what do you hear?* New York: Holt.

Martin, B., Jr. (2007). *Brown bear, brown bear, what do you see?* New York: Holt.

Numeroff, L. J. (1993). *Dogs don't wear sneakers*. New York: Simon & Schuster.

Numeroff, L. J. (1995). *Chimps don't wear glasses*. New York: Simon & Schuster.

Rathmann, P. (1995). *Officer Buckle and Gloria*. New York: Putnam.

Van Allsburg, C. (2005). *The polar express*. Boston: Houghton Mifflin.

White, E. B. (2006). *Charlotte's web*. New York: HarperCollins.

chapter fourteen

Putting It All Together

Mrs. McNeal's first graders are studying the solar system. At the beginning of the thematic unit, the children listed what they knew about the planets on a K-W-L chart, and at the end of the unit, they'll finish the chart by adding what they've learned. A word wall also went up at the beginning of the unit, and children added the names of the planets, *astronaut, moon, ring, asteroid, alien, comet,* and other new words to the word wall. They also added small illustrations to make identifying the words easier.

Each morning, the first graders sign in when they arrive in the classroom. Mrs. McNeal makes daily sign-in sheets on a large sheet of drawing paper by writing a unit-related question at the top of the paper and two or three possible answers at the bottom. The children read the question and possible answers and sign in by writing their names in a column above the answer they think is correct. Today's question is *What makes the moon shine?* These are three possible answers: *The sun makes it shine, It has its own light,* and *The earth makes it shine.* Most of the students think that it has its own light, but they aren't sure. The purpose of the question is to pique the children's interest before reading, and Mrs. McNeal reads aloud Gail Gibbons's *The Moon Book* (1997). They learn, of course, that the moon reflects the sun's light.

*H*ow do students use the six language arts during thematic units?

Students use the six language arts as tools for learning and to document their learning during thematic units. For example, they talk and listen as they participate in discussions, read text sets of books, write in learning logs and create reports, view photos and maps, and make posters. As you continue reading, notice how Mrs. McNeal provides opportunities for her students to use the language arts as they learn about the solar system.

Mrs. McNeal has been reading aloud stories, informational books, and poems from a text set of books about the solar system. After they read a book, the children have been writing paragraphs to define and explain concepts they are learning. They choose the three most important pieces of information, arrange them into sentences, and combine the sentences to make a paragraph. Here are several of their paragraphs:

Moon
The moon is a ball of rock. It goes around the earth. It has no air or atmosphere.

Asteroids
Asteroids are chunks of rock and metal. They orbit around the sun. Many asteroids are in the asteroid belt between Mars and Jupiter.

The Inner Planets
The inner planets are Mercury, Venus, Earth, and Mars. They are closest to the sun. All four are made of rock.

The children write the paragraphs on chart paper using interactive writing, and Mrs. McNeal supervises their work, making corrections and teaching spelling, capitalization, and punctuation skills as needed. It's important that the paragraphs are written conventionally because they're posted in the classroom for children to read and reread.

The first graders participate in other unit-related activities at eight centers that Mrs. McNeal has set up in her classroom. They participate in all of the centers, with certain ones assigned each day. They go to some centers only once a week and others, such as the research center, more often. Here are the centers:

◆ **Art center** Students use paint to create a map of the solar system with a parent volunteer's assistance at this center. They dip nine round sponges of varying sizes (one for the sun and eight for the planets) into paint and stamp them on a wide sheet of construction paper. After the paint dries, the students label the planets, add moons, rings, and the asteroid belt using marking pens.

◆ *Listening center* Each week, the children listen to a different book from the text set of books about the solar system and draw pictures and write words to complete a chart about the book. This week, they're listening to Frank Asch's *The Sun Is My Favorite Star* (2000).

◆ *Writing center* The students make a pattern book based on Pat Hutchins's *Rosie's Walk* (1968), a story the first graders know well. Mrs. McNeal writes one line on each page of the book, omitting the last word or phrase. She compiles the pages and binds the book together so that all children have to do is supply the underlined word or phrase and add an illustration to complete the page. Here is Jacky's completed book:

> *My star and I traveled through <u>space</u>*
> *Across the <u>clouds</u>*
> *Around the <u>moon</u>*
> *Over the <u>stars</u>*
> *Past the <u>space shuttle</u>*
> *Under the <u>meteors</u>*
> *Through the <u>milky way</u>*
> *And I got back in time for my <u>birthday</u>.*

The underlined words are the ones that Jacky chose for her book. After she finished her book, she put it in her personal box of books to read and reread at home and during the first 10 minutes of the school day.

◆ *Word wall center* Children use a pointer to reread the words on the solar system word wall. Then they participate in other activities, including writing the words on dry-erase boards, spelling them with magnetic letters, and matching word cards to pictures.

◆ *Research center* Children write and illustrate books about the solar system at the research center. Every other day, Mrs. McNeal focuses on one of the planets and records information about it on a large data chart hanging on the wall next to the center. The completed data chart is shown on the next page. Then children each write a paragraph-long report about the planet that contains three facts. They refer to the chart as they write their reports, and through this activity, they are practicing what they've been learning about writing paragraphs with three facts. Alex's report about Jupiter is shown in the box on page 466. He has incorporated three facts from the data chart, and most of the words are spelled correctly because he could check the spellings on the data chart.

◆ *Computer center* Children use the Internet to check the NASA website for photos of the planets taken by Voyager and other spacecraft, and the National Geographic site for a virtual tour of the solar system. Mrs. McNeal has bookmarked these two sites, and children navigate the World Wide Web with the assistance of a Tech Liaison from the local high school.

◆ *Library center* Children read books from the solar system text set at this center. They are especially interested in reading and rereading the leveled books and in poring over the photos in the informational books.

Data Chart on the Planets

Planet	Where is it?	How big is it?	Does it have moons or rings?	Is it hot or cold?	What does it look like?	Is there life?	Other facts
Mercury	first, closest to the sun	second smallest	no	roasting hot or freezing cold	dry, airless, rocky, lots of craters	no	about the size of our moon
Venus	second	about the size of earth	no	hotter than an oven	thick, yellow clouds and tall mountains	no	air is poisonous, easiest planet to see in the sky
Earth	third	a middle-sized planet	1 moon	just right for life	made of rock and mostly covered with oceans	yes	we live here
Mars	fourth	half the size of earth	2 tiny moons	colder than earth	red dirt desert and pink sky	no	nickname is the Red Planet because of rusty iron in the soil
Jupiter	fifth, outside the asteroid belt	biggest planet, the "king"	16 moons 2 rings	cold	giant ball of gas, has a great red spot, covered with clouds	no	all the other planets could fit inside it
Saturn	sixth	second biggest planet	17 moons thousands of rings	very cold	giant ball of gas, covered with clouds	no	most beautiful planet
Uranus	seventh	third biggest planet	15 moons 10 rings	freezing cold	giant ball of gas, bluish-green color	no	lies on its side, spins differently
Neptune	eighth	fourth biggest planet	8 moons 4 rings	freezing cold	giant ball of gas, also bluish-green color, has a great dark spot	no	takes a rocket 8 years to go from Neptune to the sun

🔹 *Poetry center* Children reread poems about the sun, moon, and planets written on chart paper that they have practiced reading as a class. They also take the poems written on sentence strips out of pocket charts and rearrange the lines to create new versions. This is a popular center because one child gets to pretend to be Mrs. McNeal and use a pointer to direct the other children in the group as they read the poems.

Mrs. McNeal has a magnetized dry-erase board that she uses to direct children to centers, and they check off the centers they complete on a chart hanging near the board so that Mrs. McNeal can keep track of their work. At the end of each week, children are expected to have completed six of the eight centers, including the art, writing, and research centers.

As they approach the end of the unit, Mrs. McNeal brings the class together to talk about their final project to extend their learning and demonstrate all they have learned. They talk about several possibilities, but they decide to invite their parents to come to the classroom on Friday afternoon to listen to oral presentations about the planets and to see their work. They divide into groups of two or three, and each group chooses one planet to report on. They make posters with drawings of the planet and three facts about it. They check the information on the data chart and practice what

Alex's Report

2 rings

16 moons

Jupiter is a giant ball of gas. It is outside the asroid belt. Did you no all the other planets could fit inside it?

they will say. They also ask Mrs. McNeal to take the parents on a tour of the class-room, showing them their books, charts, centers, and other activities. Many parents, grandparents, and friends come to the after-school presentation, and they're im-pressed with all that their children have learned, especially the new information that the NASA spacecraft have discovered.

*T*eachers often search for the one best way to develop units or design language arts instruction, but there isn't one best way. Instead, teachers pick and choose from thou-sands of books, activities, and assignments as they plan literature focus units, litera-ture circles, reading and writing workshop, and thematic units. In this text, you've read about these components of language arts instruction:

- Creating a community of learners
- The reading and writing processes
- Language arts procedures, concepts, strategies, and skills
- Word walls and vocabulary activities
- Journals and other ways to use writing as a learning tool
- Three purposes for listening

- Grand conversations and other talk and drama activities
- Language arts centers
- Reading and writing stories and learning about the structure of stories
- Reading and writing information and learning about expository text structures
- Reading and writing poetry and learning about poetic forms and stylistic devices
- Spelling, handwriting, and grammar

Teachers pick and choose among these components as they plan for instruction. Choosing to have students write in reading logs or create a story quilt is not necessarily better than having them write sequels or collect sentences from a book to examine sentence structure. Teachers begin with frameworks for the three instructional approaches and then select literature, activities, and assignments based on their instructional goals and beliefs about how children learn.

As teachers gain experience developing units, they often go beyond the "What shall I do with this book?" or "What shall I teach in this unit?" questions to think about the choices they make as they plan instruction and teach (McGee & Tompkins, 1995). Teachers need to think about why students should choose many of the books they read and why skill and strategy instruction should be taught in context. Through this reflection, teachers realize how theories about how children learn, along with their instructional goals, provide the foundation for language arts instruction.

As you continue reading, think about how you will organize for language arts instruction and how you will design literature focus units, literature circles, reading and writing workshop, and thematic units. Consider these key points:

- ◆ How do teachers design, teach, and assess literature focus units?
- ▶ How do teachers organize, monitor, and assess literature circles?
- ◆ How do teachers set up, manage, and assess reading and writing workshop?
- ◀ How do teachers develop, teach, and assess thematic units?

LITERATURE FOCUS UNITS

Teachers plan literature focus units featuring popular and award-winning stories for children and adolescents. Some literature focus units feature a single book, either a picture book or a chapter book, whereas others feature a text set of books for a genre unit or an author study unit. During these units, students move through the five stages of the reading process as they read and respond to stories, learn reading and writing strategies and skills, and engage in language arts activities.

How to Develop a Literature Focus Unit

Teachers develop a literature focus unit through an eight-step series of activities, beginning with choosing the literature for the unit, continuing to identify and schedule activities, and ending with deciding how to assess students' learning. Whether or not teachers are using trade books, they develop a unit using the steps outlined in the LA Essentials box on page 468 and described more fully in the following sections. Teachers need to make the plans themselves because they're the ones who best know their students, the standards their students are expected to meet, the reading materials they have available, the time available for the unit, the skills and strategies their students need to learn, and the language arts activities they want to use.

Literature focus units featuring a picture book are usually completed in 1 week, and units featuring a chapter book are completed in 2, 3, or 4 weeks. Genre and author units may last 2, 3, or 4 weeks. Rarely, if ever, do literature focus units continue for more than a month. When teachers drag a unit out for 6 weeks, 2 months, or longer, they risk killing students' interest in the particular book or, worse yet, their love of literature.

STEPS IN DEVELOPING A LITERATURE FOCUS UNIT

1. Book Selection
Select the book to be featured in the literature focus unit, obtain a class set of books, and collect a text set of related books.

2. Instructional Focus
Identify the focus for the unit and the standards to address during the unit.

3. Strategies and Skills
Choose the language arts strategies and skills related to the standards to teach during the unit.

4. Reading Process Activities
Plan activities representing all five stages of the reading process.

5. Grouping Patterns
Coordinate whole-class, small-group, and individual grouping patterns with the activities.

6. Technology Resources
Locate technology resources related to the featured book.

7. Assessment
Plan how students' work will be assessed, and make an assignment checklist or other grading sheet.

8. Schedule
Create a time schedule and lesson plans.

Step 1: Select the Featured Book. Teachers begin by selecting the featured book for the literature focus unit. The book may be a story—either a picture book or a chapter book—or an informational book. The reading materials should be high-quality literature and should often include multicultural selections. Sometimes teachers select several related books representing the same genre for a genre study or books written by the same author for an author study. Teachers collect multiple copies of the book or books for the unit. In some school districts, class sets of selected books are available for teachers; however, in other school districts, teachers have to request that administrators purchase multiple copies of books or buy them themselves, often through book clubs.

Once the book (or books) is selected, teachers collect related books for the text set, including other versions of the same story, other books written by the same author, books with the same theme or representing the same genre, or related informational books or books of poetry. Teachers collect one or more copies of each book for the text set, which they place on a special shelf or in a crate in the library center. At the beginning of the unit, teachers introduce the books in the text set and encourage students to read them during independent reading time.

Step 2: Identify the Instructional Focus. Teachers identify the instructional focus for the unit by matching the book's strengths with the language arts standards they'll teach. Some standards, such as interpreting words with multiple meanings, can be taught using almost any book, but others, such as comparing and contrasting tales from different cultures, are book-specific. Teachers also identify standards that focus on listening, talking, writing, and other language arts to teach as students participate in the unit. For example, when teachers plan to read the featured book aloud, they identify listening comprehension standards to address, and when students will write sequels to the story, teachers identify standards dealing with the writing process and writing mechanics to teach. Teachers identify what they want students to know and be able to do at the end of the unit, and then these standards become the focus of both instruction and assessment.

Step 3: Specify Language Arts Strategies and Skills to Teach. Teachers review the standards they've selected and decide which strategies and skills to teach using the featured book. Sometimes the standard specifies the strategies and skills, but at other times, teachers analyze the standard to determine which ones their students need to learn. In addition, teachers consider students' observed needs. Sometimes they plan minilessons to teach strategies and skills directly, but at other times, they plan to model how to use the strategies and skills as they read aloud or to ask students to share how they use the strategies and skills during grand conversations.

Step 4: Plan Reading Process Activities. After determining the instructional focus, including the strategies and skills they plan to teach, teachers decide which activities to include in the unit. The activities they choose need to fit into the five stages of the reading process. Questions teachers can ask themselves at each stage of the reading process are listed in Figure 14–1. Teachers also make sure that students have opportunities to engage in listening, talking, reading, writing, viewing, and visually representing activities during the literature focus unit. Of course, not all six language arts fit into every unit, but for most units they do.

Step 5: Coordinate Grouping Patterns With Activities. Teachers think about how to incorporate whole-class, small-group, buddy, and individual activities into their unit plans. It's important that students have opportunities to read and write

---

FIGURE 14–1

Questions to Use in Developing Literature Focus Units

Prereading
- What background knowledge do students need before reading?
- What key concepts and vocabulary should I teach before reading?
- How will I introduce the story and stimulate students' interest for reading?
- How will I assess students' learning?

Reading
- How will students read this story?
- What reading strategies and skills will I model or ask students to use?
- How can I make the story more accessible for less capable readers and English learners?

Responding
- Will students write in reading logs? How often?
- Will students participate in grand conversations? How often?
- What scenes from the book will students want or need to dramatize?

Exploring
- What words might be added to the word wall?
- What vocabulary activities might be used?
- Will students reread the story?
- What skill and strategy minilessons might be taught?
- How can I focus students' attention on words and sentences in the book?
- How will books from the text set be used?
- What information can I share about the author, illustrator, or genre?

Applying
- What projects might students choose to pursue?
- How will books from the text set be used?
- How will students share projects?

---

independently as well as to work with small groups and to come together as a class. Small groups are especially effective for English learners because they feel more comfortable in these settings, and classmates help to clarify confusions and support their learning (Brock & Raphael, 2005).

Step 6: Locate Technology Resources. Teachers locate technology resources to use in the unit, including Internet sites with author information and information on related topics, CD-ROM and video versions of stories for students to view and compare to the book version, and audiotapes of stories to use at listening centers. Teachers also plan how they will use computers for writing and researching projects and digital cameras for photographic essays related to the unit.

Step 7: Plan for Assessment. Teachers plan for two types of assessment—assessment of students' learning and monitoring of students' work during the unit. Teachers provide opportunities for students to pursue authentic assessment projects that are based on standards and that show the relationship between instruction and assessment rather than paper-and-pencil tests. Students usually choose the projects they'll create to demonstrate their learning, and they often get involved in the assessment process when they self-assess their work and what they've learned.

Teachers often use unit folders to monitor students' work. Students keep all work, reading logs, reading materials, and related materials in the folder, which makes the unit easier for both students and teachers to manage. Teachers also plan ways to monitor students' work at centers during a literature focus unit. The Weaving Assessment Into Practice feature on page 472 shows a centers assessment checklist prepared in booklet form for a first-grade unit on *The Mitten* (Brett, 1989). Students color in the mitten on each page as they complete work at the center.

Teachers also plan ways to document students' learning and to assign grades. One form of record keeping is an assignment checklist. This sheet is developed with students and distributed at the beginning of the literature focus unit. Students keep track of their work during the unit and sometimes negotiate to change the sheet as the unit evolves. They keep the lists in unit folders, and they mark off each item as it is completed. At the end of the unit, students turn in their completed assignment checklist and other completed work.

An assignment checklist for an upper-grade literature focus unit on *The Giver* (Lowry, 2006b), a story about a "perfect" community that isn't, is presented in the Weaving Assessment Into Practice feature below. Although this list doesn't

Weaving Assessment Into Practice

AN UPPER-GRADE ASSIGNMENT CHECKLIST FOR *THE GIVER*

Name _____

Student's Check		Points
_____	1. Read The Giver. (20)	_____
_____	2. Write at least ten entries in your reading log. Use a double-entry format with quotes and your connections. (20)	_____
_____	3. Participate in small-group grand conversations. (5)	_____
_____	4. Create a storyboard. Chapter # _____ (5)	_____
_____	5. Make an open-mind portrait of Jonas with four mind pages. (5)	_____
_____	6. Write an essay about the theme of the book. (10)	_____
_____	7. Choose and analyze ten words from the word wall according to prefix, root word, and suffix. (5)	_____
_____	8. Read one book from the text set. Write a brief summary in your reading log and compare what you learned about societies with The Giver. (5)	_____

Title _____

Author _____

| _____ | 9. Make a square for the class story quilt. (5) | _____ |
| _____ | 10. Create a project and share it with the class. (20) | _____ |

Project _____

Date shared _____

Total _____

A CENTERS ASSESSMENT BOOKLET FOR A UNIT ON *THE MITTEN*

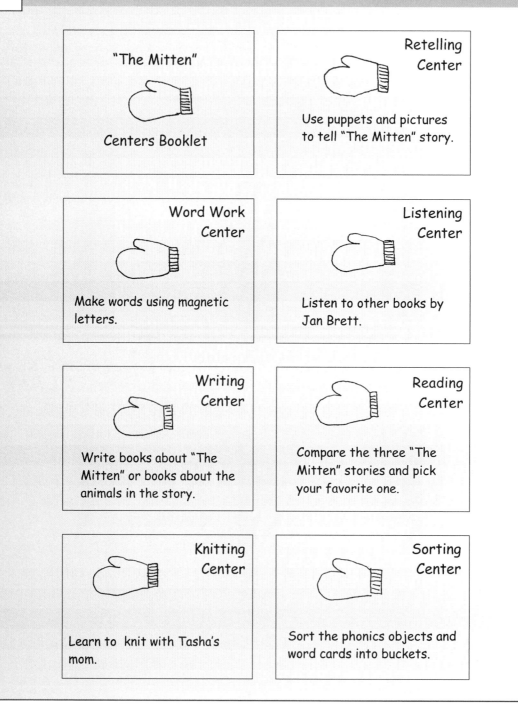

"The Mitten"

Centers Booklet

Retelling Center

Use puppets and pictures to tell "The Mitten" story.

Word Work Center

Make words using magnetic letters.

Listening Center

Listen to other books by Jan Brett.

Writing Center

Write books about "The Mitten" or books about the animals in the story.

Reading Center

Compare the three "The Mitten" stories and pick your favorite one.

Knitting Center

Learn to knit with Tasha's mom.

Sorting Center

Sort the phonics objects and word cards into buckets.

include every activity students are involved in, it does list the activities and other assignments that the teacher holds students accountable for. Students complete the checklist on the left side of the sheet and add titles of books and other requested information. The teacher awards points (up to the number listed in parentheses) on the lines on the right side of the sheet, and totals the number of points on the bottom of the page. Then the total score can be translated into a letter grade or other type of grade.

Step 8: Create a Time Schedule. Teachers create a time schedule that allows students sufficient time to move through the five stages of the reading process and to complete the activities planned for the focus unit. Literature focus units require large blocks of time each day, at least 2 hours, in which students read, listen, talk, and write about the featured book.

A Primary-Grade Literature Focus Unit on *The Mitten*

Jan Brett's *The Mitten* (1989), a cumulative picture-book story about a series of animals that climb into a mitten that a little boy has dropped in the snow on a cold winter day, is the featured selection in literature focus units taught in many primary-grade classrooms. A planning cluster for a literature focus unit on *The Mitten* is shown in Figure 14–2. Teachers use the big book version of *The Mitten* to introduce the unit and to examine Brett's innovative use of borders. Children retell the story with the teacher's collection of stuffed animals and puppets representing the animals in the story—a mole, a rabbit, a hedgehog, an owl, a badger, a fox, a bear, and a mouse. They read the story several times—in small groups with the teacher, with partners, and independently. The teacher also reads aloud several other versions of the story, such as *The Woodcutter's Mitten* (Koopmans, 1990) and *The Mitten* (Tresselt, 1989), and children make a chart to compare the versions. The teacher presents minilessons on phonemic awareness and phonics skills, creates a word wall, and involves the children in word-study activities. They participate in sequencing and writing activities and learn about knitting from a parent volunteer. The teacher also sets out a text set of other books by Jan Brett and reads some of the books aloud. As their application project, children divide into small groups to research one of the animals mentioned in the story. Fifth graders work with the primary-grade students as they research the animals and share what they learn on large posters.

An Upper-Grade Literature Focus Unit on *The Giver*

Upper-grade students spend 3 or 4 weeks reading, responding to, exploring, and applying their understanding of Lois Lowry's Newbery Medal book, *The Giver* (2006b). Lowry creates a "perfect" community in which the people are secure but regulated. Jonas, the main character, is chosen to be a leader in the community, but he rebels against the society and escapes. To introduce this book, teachers might connect the book to the United States Constitution and the Bill of Rights, or discuss the problems in U.S. society today and ask students to create a perfect society. Or, students might think about how their lives would be different in a world without colors, like Jonas's.

Students can read the story together as a class, in small groups with the teacher or in literature study groups, with buddies, or independently. Students come together to

FIGURE 14–2

A Planning Cluster for a Primary-Grade Unit on *The Mitten*

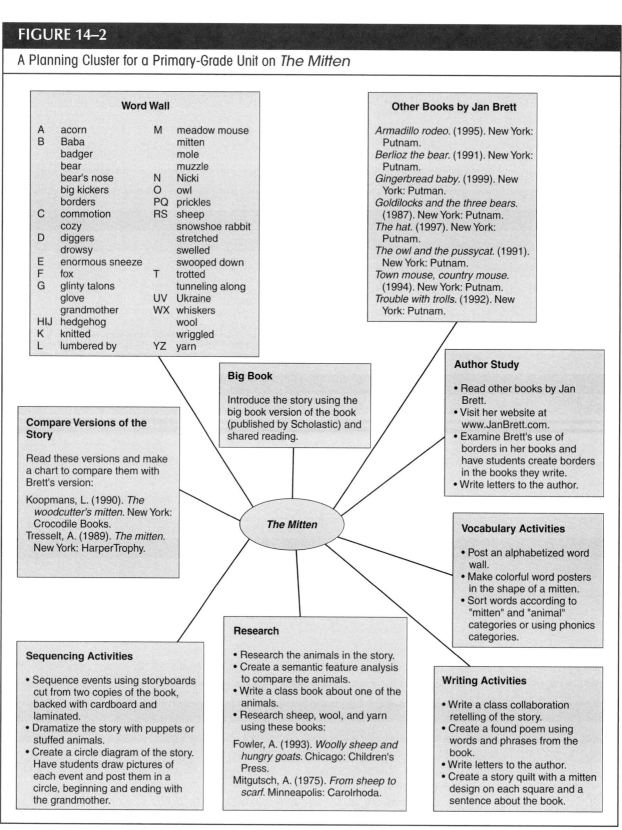

Word Wall

A	acorn	M	meadow mouse
B	Baba		mitten
	badger		mole
	bear		muzzle
	bear's nose	N	Nicki
	big kickers	O	owl
	borders	PQ	prickles
C	commotion	RS	sheep
	cozy		snowshoe rabbit
D	diggers		stretched
	drowsy		swelled
E	enormous sneeze		swooped down
F	fox	T	trotted
G	glinty talons		tunneling along
	glove	UV	Ukraine
	grandmother	WX	whiskers
HIJ	hedgehog		wool
K	knitted		wriggled
L	lumbered by	YZ	yarn

Other Books by Jan Brett

Armadillo rodeo. (1995). New York: Putnam.
Berlioz the bear. (1991). New York: Putnam.
Gingerbread baby. (1999). New York: Putman.
Goldilocks and the three bears. (1987). New York: Putnam.
The hat. (1997). New York: Putnam.
The owl and the pussycat. (1991). New York: Putnam.
Town mouse, country mouse. (1994). New York: Putnam.
Trouble with trolls. (1992). New York: Putnam.

Big Book

Introduce the story using the big book version of the book (published by Scholastic) and shared reading.

Author Study

• Read other books by Jan Brett.
• Visit her website at www.JanBrett.com.
• Examine Brett's use of borders in her books and have students create borders in the books they write.
• Write letters to the author.

Compare Versions of the Story

Read these versions and make a chart to compare them with Brett's version:

Koopmans, L. (1990). *The woodcutter's mitten.* New York: Crocodile Books.
Tresselt, A. (1989). *The mitten.* New York: HarperTrophy.

The Mitten

Vocabulary Activities

• Post an alphabetized word wall.
• Make colorful word posters in the shape of a mitten.
• Sort words according to "mitten" and "animal" categories or using phonics categories.

Sequencing Activities

• Sequence events using storyboards cut from two copies of the book, backed with cardboard and laminated.
• Dramatize the story with puppets or stuffed animals.
• Create a circle diagram of the story. Have students draw pictures of each event and post them in a circle, beginning and ending with the grandmother.

Research

• Research the animals in the story.
• Create a semantic feature analysis to compare the animals.
• Write a class book about one of the animals.
• Research sheep, wool, and yarn using these books:

Fowler, A. (1993). *Woolly sheep and hungry goats.* Chicago: Children's Press.
Mitgutsch, A. (1975). *From sheep to scarf.* Minneapolis: Carolrhoda.

Writing Activities

• Write a class collaboration retelling of the story.
• Create a found poem using words and phrases from the book.
• Write letters to the author.
• Create a story quilt with a mitten design on each square and a sentence about the book.

discuss the story in grand conversations and deal with the complex issues presented in the book in both small groups and whole-class discussions. They also write in reading logs. Teachers identify skills and strategies to model during reading and to teach in minilessons. Students write important words from the story on the word wall and engage in a variety of vocabulary activities. They also learn about the author and examine the story structure in the book. After reading, they can do a choral reading, create a story quilt, compare U.S. society with the society described in the book, and create other projects. Figure 14–3 shows a planning cluster for *The Giver.*

LITERATURE CIRCLES

Students divide into small groups, and they read and respond to a self-selected book together during a literature circle (Daniels, 2001; Evans, 2001; Frank, Dixon, & Brandts, 2001). Students read independently, and then they come together to participate in grand conversations to discuss the book. They also write in reading logs and sometimes create projects related to the book. For students to be successful in literature circles, a community of learners is essential. Students need to develop responsibility, learn how to work in a small group with classmates, and participate in group activities.

How to Organize for Literature Circles

Teachers move through a series of steps as they prepare for literature circles. Even though students assume leadership roles and make a number of decisions as they participate in literature circles, the success depends on the teacher's planning and the classroom community that has been created. The LA Essentials box on page 477 outlines the steps in organizing literature circles.

Step 1: Choose Books. Teachers choose five, six, or seven books and then collect six copies of each one. To introduce the books, teachers give a book talk about each one, and students sign up for the book they want to read. One way to do this is to set each book on the chalk tray and have students sign their names on the chalkboard above the book they want to read. Or, teachers can set the books on a table and place a sign-up sheet beside each one. Students take time to preview the books, and then they select the book they want to read. Once in a while, students don't get to read their first-choice book, but they can always read it later during another literature circle or during reading workshop.

Traditionally, students read stories during literature circles, but teachers have found that students also enjoy reading informational books (Heller, 2006/2007; Stein & Beed, 2004). Students read and discuss nonfiction much like they do stories, talking about what they liked about the book as well as the big ideas and what they learned. In fact, teachers report that literature circles are an effective way to increase students' interest in informational books.

Step 2: Identify Strategies and Skills. Teachers identify the reading and literary response standards to address as students participate in literature circles, and then they decide which strategies and skills to emphasize. Sometimes the standard specifies the strategies and skills, but at other times, teachers analyze the standard to determine which ones their students need to learn. Teachers plan to emphasize

FIGURE 14–3

A Planning Cluster for an Upper-Grade Unit on *The Giver*

Introducing the Book

- Read the book when studying ancient civilizations and focus on the traits of a civilization.
- Discuss the problems in U.S. society, and ask students to create a perfect society.
- Create a world with no colors.
- Share objects from a book box, including an apple, a bicycle, a sled, the number 19, a stuffed bear or other "comfort object," and a kaleidoscope of colors.

Story Structure Activities

- Create a set of storyboards, one for each chapter, with a good title for the chapter, a picture, and a summarizing paragraph.
- Create a plot diagram to graph the highs and lows of the book.
- Make an open-mind portrait with several mind pages to track Jonas's thinking through the book.
- Compare Jonas's character to Kira's in Lowry's *Gathering Blue* (2000a) or that of another familiar character.
- Draw a setting map of the story.
- Analyze the theme of the book and create a story quilt to represent it.

Vocabulary Activities

- Post an alphabetized word wall in the classroom, and have students make individual word walls.
- Draw word clusters.
- Sort words according to "Jonas," "Giver," and "Community" categories.
- Teach minilessons on dividing long words into syllables or identifying root words and affixes (e.g., *obediently, distrustful, apprehensive*).
- Teach minilessons on etymology (e.g., English, Latin, and Greek words).
- Collect powerful sentences and write them on sentence strips.

Comparing Societies

Students read a book about U.S. democratic society and compare it with the perfect society in *The Giver*.

Cowman, P. (1995). *Strike! The bitter struggle of American workers from colonial times to the present.* New York: Millbrook.
Fleming, R. (1995). *Rescuing a neighborhood: The Bedford-Stuyvesant Volunteer Ambulance Corps.* New York: Walker.
Haskins, J. (1993). *The march on Washington.* New York: HarperCollins.
Hoose, P. (1993). *It's our world, too! Stories of young people who are making a difference.* New York: Joy Street.
Meltzer, M. (1990). *Crime in America.* New York: Morrow.

The Giver

Author Information

- Collect information about Lois Lowry, including "Newbery Acceptance" by Lois Lowry, published in the July/August 1994 issue of *Horn Book* (pp. 414–422).
- Read other books in the series, including *Gathering Blue* (2006a) and *The Messenger* (2006c).
- Read Lowry's autobiography, *Looking Back: A Book of Memories* (2000).
- Write letters to the author.

Grand Conversations

- Have students share their ideas about the chapters they have read.
- Have students choose an appropriate title for the chapter.
- Have students share favorite sentences from the chapter.
- Have students make predictions about the next chapter.

Writing Projects

- Write found poems, "I Am" poems, or other poems.
- Write an essay comparing Jonas's society with ours.
- Write a reaction to this quote: "The greatest freedom is the freedom of choice."
- Write a simulated letter from one character to another in the story.
- Write a prequel or a sequel to the story.

Reading Log

- Keep a simulated journal, written from Jonas's viewpoint, after reading each chapter.
- Write a double-entry journal with quotes from the story in one column and personal connections or predictions in the other column.

Word Wall

A	anguished assignment	PQ	permission precision punishment
B	bicycle		
CD	ceremony community	R	Receiver regret released ritual
EF	Elders elsewhere		
GH	Gabe guilt	S	sameness stirrings successor
I	ironic		
JK	Jonas	T	transgression transmit tunic
L	luminate		
M	memories		
N	Nurturer	UV	
O	obediently obsolete	WX	
		YZ	yearning

STEPS IN ORGANIZING LITERATURE CIRCLES

1. Books
Choose six or seven titles and collect five or six copies of each book for students to read.

2. Strategies and Skills
Identify the standards to address and the language arts strategies and skills related to the standards to teach.

3. Groups
Organize the circles by giving book talks and having students sign up for the book they want to read.

4. Roles
Decide on roles for group members and clearly explain the responsibilities of each role.

5. Schedule
Set the schedule for literature circles and have students in each small group decide how they will schedule reading, discussion, and other work times.

6. Grand Conversations
Conduct grand conversations to monitor students' reading, and support students as they respond to and deepen their understanding of the book.

7. Reading Logs
Set guidelines for how often students will write in reading logs and the types of entries they will make.

8. Assessment
Plan ways to monitor students as they read and respond to the book in small groups.

particular strategies and skills as they determine which roles students will assume or plan questions for grand conversations and reading log entries. They also think about how they can model the use of strategies and skills as they interact with the students in the literature circles.

Step 3: Organize the Circles or Groups. The books in the text set often vary in length and difficulty, but students are not placed in groups according to their reading levels. Students choose the books they want to read and, as they preview the books, they consider how good a fit the book is, but that's not their only consideration: They often choose to read the book they find most interesting or the one their best friend has chosen. Students can usually manage whatever book they choose because of support and assistance from their group and through plain and simple determination. Once in a while, teachers counsel students to choose another book or provide an additional copy of the book to practice at home or to read with a tutor at school.

Step 4: Decide on Roles for Group Members. Teachers decide how to structure the literature circles and what roles students will assume. Sometimes students in a group choose their own group leader, or a natural leader emerges when they first get together; however, at other times, teachers identify the group leader. In addition to the leadership role, each group member assumes a role, and students also select these during the first meeting of the group. When teachers have students assume roles, they must clearly outline the responsibilities of each group member. Teachers often spend a great deal of time at the beginning of the school year teaching students how to fulfill the responsibilities of each role.

Students assume roles to facilitate the group's understanding of the book they're reading: One student becomes the Passage Master, and other group members assume the roles of Word Wizard, Connector, Summarizer, Artist, and Investigator. When students are reading informational books, some roles remain the same, but teachers and students create other roles that focus on the unique characteristics of nonfiction. Stien and Beed's (2004) students added a Timeline Traveler, who creates a timeline of historical events, and a Fantastic Fact Finder, who shares interesting facts; and when students read biographies, an additional role was Vital Statistics Collector, who shares personal information about the person being profiled.

Some teachers continue to have students use the same roles for each literature circle during the school year, but others find that after students learn to use each of the roles they can assume them flexibly as they read and think about the book. One way to do this is by "tabbing" (Stien & Beed, 2004): Teachers pass out packs of small self-stick notes, and students use them to make notes applying what they've learned about the different roles as they read. On some notes, students ask a question, choose an interesting passage to read aloud, note an interesting word to look up in the dictionary, or jot a personal, world, or text connection, for example.

Step 5: Set the Schedule. Teachers set a time schedule for the literature circle, and then each small group of students decides how to use the time to read the book and participate in grand conversations. During group meetings, teachers often participate in grand conversations and add their ideas to the discussion. They also monitor that students are completing their reading assignments and fulfilling the responsibilities of their roles. While the teacher meets with one group, the other groups read independently or participate in other activities.

Step 6: Conduct Grand Conversations. Students alternate reading and discussing the book in grand conversations. At the beginning of the literature circle, students decide how often to meet for grand conversations and how much of the book to read before each discussion. Sometimes teachers participate in the conversations and sometimes they don't. When the teachers are participants, they participate as fellow readers who share joys and difficulties, insights and speculations. They also help students develop literary insights by providing information, asking insightful questions, and guiding students to make comments.

Step 7: Write in Reading Logs. Students often write in reading logs as part of literature circles. Teachers make decisions about the types of entries they want students to make as they read. Sometimes students write entries in their logs after each chapter, and at other times, they write once a week. Students may write their reactions to the chapters they have read or write about issues that arose during the grand conversation. They may also write predictions, collect vocabulary words, and record powerful sentences from the book in their journals. Depending on the complexity of the book and the issues the teacher wants students to think about, the teacher may ask students to respond to a question after reading a particular chapter.

Step 8: Plan for Assessment. The assessment focuses on students' comprehension of the book they've read and their participation in the literature circle. The standards that teachers select guide the assessment. When teachers choose a standard that focuses on analyzing the theme of the story, for example, they check students' reading logs and listen to their comments in grand conversations. Teachers also plan how they will assess students' participation in the literature circle. Most teachers observe students as they move around the classroom and participate in grand conversations. Many teachers also use an assignment sheet to assess students' work. A fifth-grade grading sheet is shown in the Weaving Assessment Into Practice feature on page 480.

READING AND WRITING WORKSHOP

Nancie Atwell (2007) introduced reading workshop as an alternative to traditional reading instruction. In reading workshop, students read books that they choose themselves and respond to them through writing in reading logs and conferencing with teachers and classmates. This approach represents a change in what we believe about how children learn and how literature is used in the classroom. Atwell developed reading workshop with her middle school students, but it has been adapted and used successfully at every grade level, first through eighth. There are several versions of reading workshop, but they usually contain these components: reading, sharing, minilessons, and reading aloud to students (Serafini, 2001).

Writing workshop is similar to reading workshop, except that the focus is on writing. Students write on topics that they choose themselves, and they assume ownership of their writing and learning (Atwell, 1998; Calkins, 1994; Fletcher & Portalupi, 2001). At the same time, the teacher's role changes from that of being a provider of knowledge to that of serving as a facilitator and guide. The classroom becomes a community of writers who write and share their writing. There is a spirit of pride and acceptance in the classroom.

A FIFTH-GRADE GRADING SHEET FOR LITERATURE CIRCLES

ASSESSMENT CHECK

Name _____   **Book** _____

Circle Members

1. _____   3. _____   5. _____

2. _____   4. _____   6. _____

Write a schedule of your activities. What was your role?

M	T	W	T	F

M	T	W	T	F

M	T	W	T	F

Reflect on your work in this literature circle. Score yourself, and then write about your work on the back of this sheet.

1. Read the book.   A B C D

2. Complete your group role.   A B C D

3. Participate in grand conversations.   A B C D

4. Write in your reading log.   A B C D

5. Make a group project.   A B C D

6. Share your project.   A B C D

Writing workshop is a 60- to 90-minute period scheduled each day. During this time, students are involved in three components: writing, sharing, and minilessons. Sometimes a fourth activity, reading aloud to students, is added to writing workshop when it's not used in conjunction with reading workshop.

Establishing a Workshop Environment

Teachers begin to establish the workshop environment in their classroom from the first day of the school year by providing students with choices, time to read and write, and opportunities for response (Overmeyer, 2005). Through their interactions with students, the respect they show to students, and the way they model reading and writing, teachers establish the classroom as a community of learners.

Teachers develop a schedule for reading and writing workshop with time allocated for each component, or they alternate between the two types of workshops. They allot as much time as possible in their schedules for students to read and write. After developing the schedule, teachers post it in the classroom, talk about the activities, and discuss their expectations with students. Teachers teach the workshop procedures and continue to model them as students become comfortable with the routines (Kaufman, 2001). As students share what they're reading and writing at the end of workshop sessions, their enthusiasm grows and the workshop approaches are successful.

Students keep two folders—one for reading workshop and one for writing workshop. In the reading workshop folder, students keep a list of books they've read, notes from minilessons, reading logs, and other materials. In the writing workshop folder, they keep all rough drafts and other compositions. They also keep a list of all compositions, topics for future pieces, and notes from minilessons. They also keep language arts notebooks in which they jot down images, impressions, dialogue, and experiences that they can build on for writing projects (Calkins, 1991).

How to Set Up a Reading Workshop

Teachers move through a series of steps as they set up their classroom, prepare students to work independently in the classroom, and provide instruction. These steps are summarized in the LA Essentials box on page 482.

Step 1: Collect Books for Reading Workshop. Students read all sorts of books during reading workshop, including stories, informational books, and books of poetry. Most of their reading materials are selected from the classroom library, but students also bring books from home and borrow others from the public library, the school library, and classmates. Students read many award-winning books, but they also read series of popular books and technical books related to their hobbies and special interests. These books are not necessarily the same ones that teachers use for literature focus units, but students often choose to reread books they read earlier in the school year or during the previous year in literature focus units and literature circles. Teachers need to have literally hundreds of books in their class libraries, including books written at a range of reading levels, in order to meet the needs of English learners, advanced readers, and struggling readers.

Teachers introduce students to the books in the classroom library so that they can more effectively choose books to read during reading workshop. The best way

STEPS IN SETTING UP A READING WORKSHOP

1. Books
Collect a wide variety of books at varying reading levels for students to read, including stories, informational books, poems, and other resources, and place them on a special shelf in the classroom library.

2. Workshop Procedures
Teach reading workshop procedures so that students know how to choose and respond to books, participate in conferences, and share books they've read. Reading workshop operates much more smoothly when students are familiar with the procedures.

3. Minilessons
Teach minilessons on topics drawn from standards as well as other strategies and skills that students are using but confusing.

4. Read-Aloud Books
Choose read-aloud books to introduce students to new genres, authors, literary elements, or series stories that they might want to continue reading on their own.

5. Schedule
Design a reading workshop schedule that incorporates reading, sharing, minilessons, and reading aloud to students.

6. Conferences
Plan a schedule for conferences so that you can talk with students individually or in small groups about the books they're reading, and monitor their comprehension.

7. Assessment
Monitor students' work and assess their reading with state-of-the-class charts, observations, and conferences.

to preview books is using a very brief book talk to interest students in the book. In book talks, teachers tell students a little about the book, show the cover, and perhaps read the first paragraph or two (Prill, 1994/1995). Teachers also give book talks to introduce text sets of books, and students give book talks as they share books they have read with the class during the sharing part of reading workshop.

Step 2: Teach Reading Workshop Procedures. Students need to learn how to choose books, write responses to books they are reading, share books they have finished reading, and conference with the teacher, as well as other procedures related to reading workshop. Some of these procedures need to be taught before students begin reading workshop, and others can be introduced and reviewed as minilessons during reading workshop.

Step 3: Teach Minilessons. Minilessons are an important part of reading workshop because the workshop approach is more than reading practice. Instruction is important, and minilessons are the teaching step. Teachers present minilessons on reading workshop procedures and on reading concepts, strategies, and skills. They identify topics for minilessons based on the standards they are addressing and students' observed needs. Teachers use examples from books students are reading, and students are often asked to reflect on their own reading processes.

Step 4: Choose Books to Read Aloud to Students. When teachers include the reading-aloud component with reading workshop, they carefully choose the books they will read. These books may be more difficult than those students can read independently, or they may be chosen to introduce students to a genre, an author, or a literary element. Sometimes teachers read aloud the first book in a series and then invite students to continue reading the sequels themselves. Teachers choose books to read aloud for a variety of specific instructional purposes.

Step 5: Design a Schedule for Reading Workshop. Teachers examine their daily schedule, consider the other language arts activities in which their students are involved, decide how much time is available for reading workshop, and allocate time to each of the reading workshop components. Some teachers make reading and writing workshop their entire language arts program. They begin by reading aloud a book, chapter by chapter, to the class and talking about the book in a grand conversation for the first 30 minutes of reading workshop. During this time, teachers focus on modeling reading strategies and talking about elements of story structure. For the next 45 to 50 minutes, students read self-selected books independently. The teacher conferences with small groups of students as they read and presents minilessons to small groups of students as needed. Then students spend the next 15 to 20 minutes writing about their reading in reading logs. Sharing is held during the last 15 minutes, and students do book talks about books they have finished reading.

Other teachers coordinate reading workshop with literature focus units. For example, they decide to allocate one hour to reading workshop at the beginning of their language arts block. Students begin with 30 minutes of independent reading and then use the next 10 minutes to share books they have finished reading with the class. The last 20 minutes are used for a minilesson. Then students move into a literature focus unit for the next 90 minutes. In some classrooms, teachers alternate reading and writing workshop, either by month or by grading period.

Step 6: Plan for Conferencing. During reading workshop, students are reading independently, and teachers must find ways to monitor their progress. Many teachers begin each reading period by moving around the classroom to check that students have chosen books and are reading purposefully and then use the rest of the reading period for individual and small-group conferences. Teachers create conference schedules and meet with students on a regular basis, usually once a week, to talk about their reading and reading skills and strategies, listen to them read excerpts aloud, and make plans for the next book. Teachers take notes during these conferences in folders they keep for each student.

Step 7: Plan for Assessment. Teachers use a classroom chart to monitor students' work on a daily basis. At the beginning of reading workshop, students or the teacher records on a class chart what book students are reading and the activity in which they are currently involved. Atwell (1998) calls this chart "the state of the class." Teachers can review students' progress and note which students need to meet with the teacher or receive additional attention. When students fill in the chart themselves, they develop responsibility for their actions and a stronger desire to accomplish tasks they set for themselves.

To monitor primary-grade students, teachers often use a pocket chart and have children place a card in their pocket, indicating whether they are reading or responding during reading workshop or at which stage of the writing process they are working during writing workshop.

Teachers take time during reading workshop to observe students as they interact and work together in small groups. Researchers who have observed in reading and writing workshop classrooms report that some students, even as young as first graders, are excluded from group activities because of gender, ethnicity, or socioeconomic status (Henkin, 1995; Lensmire, 1992). The socialization patterns in classrooms seem to reflect society's patterns. Henkin recommends that teachers be alert to the possibility that boys might share books only with other boys or that some students won't find anyone willing to be their editing partner. If teachers see instances of discrimination in their classrooms, they should confront them directly and work to foster a classroom environment where students treat each other equitably.

How to Set Up a Writing Workshop

As teachers set up a writing workshop classroom, they collect writing supplies and materials for making books for the writing center. They set out different kinds of paper—some lined and some unlined—and various writing instruments, including pencils and red and blue pens. Bookmaking supplies include cardboard, contact paper, cloth, and wallpaper for book covers; stencils; stamps; art supplies; and a saddleback stapler and other equipment for binding books. Teachers also set up a bank of computers with word-processing programs and printers or arrange for students to have access to the school's computer lab. Teachers encourage students to use the classroom library, and many times, students' writing grows out of favorite books they've read.

Teachers also think about the classroom arrangement. Students sit at desks or tables arranged in small groups as they write. The teacher circulates around the classroom, conferencing briefly with students, and the classroom atmosphere is free enough that students converse quietly with classmates and move around the classroom to collect materials at the writing center, assist classmates, or share ideas. There is space for students to meet for writing groups, and often a sign-up sheet for writing groups is posted in the classroom. A table is available for the teacher to meet with individual students or small groups for conferences, writing groups, proofreading, and minilessons.

In addition to collecting supplies and arranging the classroom, teachers need to prepare students for writing workshop and make plans for the instruction. The steps in setting up a writing workshop are summarized in the LA Essentials box on page 486.

Step 1: Teach the Stages of the Writing Process. Teachers often begin writing workshop by teaching or reviewing the five stages of the writing process, setting guidelines for writing workshop, and taking students through one writing activity together.

Step 2: Teach Writing Workshop Procedures. Teachers need to explain how students will meet in groups to revise their writing, how to sign up for a conference with the teacher, how to proofread, how to use the publishing center, and other procedures used in writing workshop (Ray & Laminack, 2001). A set of guidelines for writing workshop that one seventh-grade class developed is presented in Figure 14-4.

Step 3: Identify Topics for Minilessons. As with reading workshop, teachers teach minilessons during writing workshop related to the standards they've identified. Teachers present minilessons on procedures related to writing workshop and writing concepts, skills, and strategies that students can apply in their own writing. Other topics for minilessons come from teachers' observations of students as they write and the questions students ask.

Teachers also share information about authors and how they write during minilessons. For students to think of themselves as writers, they need to know what writers do. Each year, there are more autobiographies written by authors. For example, Tomie dePaola has written a popular series of autobiographical picture-book stories for young children, including *Things Will NEVER Be the Same* (2003), and Lois Lowry has written *Looking Back: A Book of Memories* (2000). Each chapter focuses on a memory prompted by a photo; this is a format students can imitate when they write autobiographies. A number of well-known authors and illustrators are profiled in the Meet the Author series published by Richard C. Owen, including *Can You Imagine*, by Patricia McKissack (1997), *If You Give an Author a Pencil*, by Laura Numeroff (2003), *From Paper Airplanes to Outer Space*, by Seymour Simon (2000), and *Firetalking*, by Patricia Polacco (1994). Students like these picture-book autobiographies because they provide interesting information, and the authors come to life through the color photographs on each page. They can be read aloud to primary students, and older students can read them independently. Video productions about authors and illustrators are also available. For example, in the 27-minute video *Eric Carle: Picture Writer* (1993), Eric Carle demonstrates how he uses paint and collage to create the illustrations for his popular picture books.

Step 4: Design a Writing Workshop Schedule. An important instructional decision that teachers make is how to organize their daily schedule and what portion of the language arts block to allocate to reading and writing workshop. Some teachers

STEPS IN SETTING UP A WRITING WORKSHOP

1. Writing Process
Teach the stages of the writing process so that students understand how to develop and refine a composition.

2. Workshop Procedures
Teach writing workshop procedures so that students know how to meet in revising groups, sign up for conferences, and publish their writing, for example. For students to be successful, it's essential that they know the procedures they will be expected to use.

3. Minilessons
Identify topics for minilessons to teach during writing workshop while anticipating that other topics will arise from strategies and skills that students are using but confusing.

4. Schedule
Design a writing workshop schedule that includes writing, sharing, and teaching minilessons. Consistency is important so that students know what is expected of them and can develop a routine.

5. Conferences
Plan how you will conference in small groups and individually with students so that you can monitor their work, provide feedback about their writing, and assess their progress.

6. Sharing
Include opportunities for students to share their published writing with classmates.

7. Assessment
Plan to monitor and assess students' work using state-of-the-class reports, conferences, writing-process checklists, and rubrics.

make reading and writing workshop the focus of their language arts program. During the writing workshop portion, students move through the writing process as they write on self-selected topics for 45 or 50 minutes. The teacher meets with small groups of students or with individual students as they draft, revise, and edit their compositions during this writing time. Next, teachers use a 15- to 30-minute block of time for minilessons during which they present minilessons on writing workshop procedures and writing concepts, skills, and strategies to the whole class, small groups of students, or individual students as needed. Sharing is held during the last 15 minutes, and students read their finished compositions aloud to classmates, often sitting in the author's chair.

Other teachers coordinate writing workshop with literature focus units. For example, they may allocate the last hour of their language arts block for reading and writing workshop, and alternate reading workshop and writing workshop by month or by grading period. Another way some teachers allocate time for writing workshop is during the last week of a literature focus unit, when students are developing a writing project. For example, in the literature focus unit on *The Mitten* discussed earlier

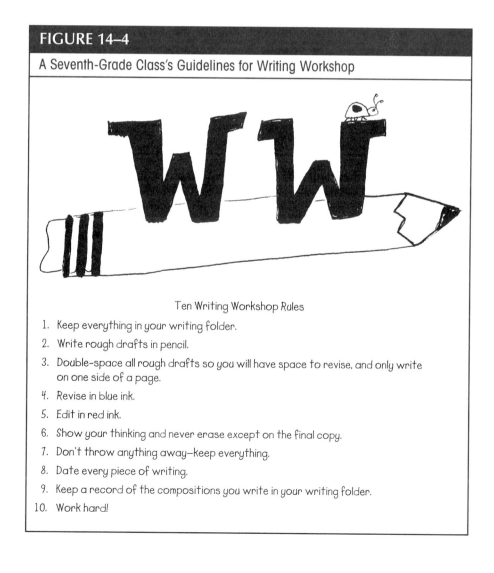

FIGURE 14–4

A Seventh-Grade Class's Guidelines for Writing Workshop

Ten Writing Workshop Rules

1. Keep everything in your writing folder.
2. Write rough drafts in pencil.
3. Double-space all rough drafts so you will have space to revise, and only write on one side of a page.
4. Revise in blue ink.
5. Edit in red ink.
6. Show your thinking and never erase except on the final copy.
7. Don't throw anything away—keep everything.
8. Date every piece of writing.
9. Keep a record of the compositions you write in your writing folder.
10. Work hard!

in this chapter, primary-grade students use a writing workshop approach as they research one of the animals mentioned in the story and create posters to share what they learn.

Step 5: Plan for Conferencing. Teachers conference with students as they write (Calkins, Hartman, & White, 2005). Many teachers prefer moving around the classroom to meet with students rather than having the students come to a table to meet with them because too often, a line forms as students wait to meet with the teacher, and students lose precious writing time. Some teachers move around the classroom in a regular pattern, meeting with one-fifth of the students each day. In this way, they can talk with every student during the week.

Other teachers spend the first 15 to 20 minutes of writing workshop stopping briefly to check on 10 or more students each day. Many use a zigzag pattern to get to all parts of the classroom each day. These teachers often kneel down beside each student, sit on the edge of the student's seat, or carry their own stool to each student's desk. During the 1- or 2-minute conferences, teachers ask students what they are writing, listen to students read a paragraph or two, and then ask what they plan to do next. Then these teachers use the remaining time during writing workshop to conference more formally with students who are revising and editing their compositions. Students often sign up for these conferences. Teachers make comments to find strengths, ask questions, and discover possibilities during these revising conferences. Some teachers like to read the pieces themselves, whereas others like to listen to students read their papers aloud. As they interact with students, teachers model the kinds of responses that students are learning to give to each other.

As students meet to share their writing during revising and editing, they continue to develop their sense of community. They share their rough drafts with classmates in writing groups composed of four or five students. In some classrooms, teachers join in the writing groups whenever they can, but students normally run the groups themselves. They take turns reading their rough drafts to one another and listen as their classmates offer compliments and suggestions for revision. In other classrooms, students work with one partner to edit their writing, and they often use red pens.

After proofreading their drafts with a classmate and then meeting with the teacher for a final editing, students make the final copy of their writing. Students often want to put their writing on the computer so that their final copy will appear professional. Many times, students compile their final copy to make a book during writing workshop, but sometimes they attach their writing to artwork, make a poster, write a letter that is mailed, or perform a script as a skit or puppet show. Not every piece is published, however. Sometimes students decide not to continue with a piece of writing; they file the piece in their writing folders and start something new.

Step 6: Include Sharing. For the last 10 to 15 minutes of writing workshop, students gather together as a class to share their new publications and make other, related announcements. Younger students often sit in a circle or gather together on a rug for sharing time. If an author's chair is available, each student sits in the special chair to read his or her composition. After reading, classmates clap and offer

Weaving Assessment Into Practice

AN EXCERPT FROM A FIFTH-GRADE STATE-OF-THE-CLASS CHART

Names	Dates 10/18	10/19	10/20	10/21	10/22	10/25	10/26	10/27
Antonio	4 5	5	5	6	7	8	8	8 9
Bella	2	2	2 3	2	2	4	5	6
Charles	8 9 1	3 1	1	2	2 3	4	5	6 7
Dina	6	6	6	7 8	8	9 1	1	2 3
Dustin	7 8	8	8	8	8	8	9 1	1
Eddie	2 3	2	2 4	5 6	8	9 1	1 2	2 3
Elizabeth	7	6	7	8	8	8	9	1 2
Elsa	2	3	4 5	5 6	6 7	8	8	9 1

Code:

1 = Prewrite   4 = Writing Group   7 = Conference
2 = Draft   5 = Revise   8 = Make Final Copy
3 = Conference   6 = Edit   9 = Publish

compliments. They may also make other comments and suggestions, but the focus is on celebrating completed writing projects, not on revising the composition to make it better. Classmates help celebrate after the child shares by clapping, and perhaps the best praise is having a classmate ask to read the newly published book.

Step 7: Plan for Assessment. Teachers monitor students' work in several ways. They monitor students' progress from day to day with a state-of-the-class report; an excerpt from a fifth-grade writing workshop chart is shown in the Weaving Assessment Into Practice feature above. Teachers can also use the chart to award weekly effort grades, to have students indicate their need to conference with the teacher, or to have students announce that they are ready to share their writing. Teachers also develop checklists with which students keep track of their work and monitor their application of strategies and skills that are being taught. In addition, teachers use rubrics to assess the quality of students' published compositions.

THEMATIC UNITS

Thematic units are interdisciplinary units that integrate reading and writing with social studies, science, and other curricular areas (Kucer, Silva, & Delgado-Larocco, 1995). Students take part in planning the thematic units and identifying some of the questions they want to explore and activities that interest them

(Lindquist & Selwyn, 2000). Students are involved in authentic and meaningful learning activities, not simply reading chapters in content-area textbooks in order to answer the questions at the end of the chapter. Textbooks might be used as a resource, but only as one of many available resources. Students explore topics that interest them and research answers to questions they have posed and are genuinely interested in answering. They share their learning at the end of the unit and are assessed on what they have learned as well as on the processes they used in learning and working in the classroom.

How to Develop a Thematic Unit

To begin planning a thematic unit, teachers choose the general topic and then identify three or four big ideas that they want to develop through the unit. The goal of a thematic unit is not to teach a collection of facts, but to help students grapple with several big understandings (Tunnell & Ammon, 1993). Next, teachers identify the resources that they have available for the unit and develop their teaching plan. Ten steps in developing a thematic unit are summarized in the LA Essentials box on the next page.

Step 1: Collect a Text Set. Teachers collect stories, poems, informational books, magazines, newspaper articles, and reference books for the text set related to the unit. The text set is placed in the special area for unit materials in the classroom library. Teachers plan to read some books aloud to students, students will read some independently, and they will read others together as shared or guided reading. These materials can also be used for minilessons, to teach students about strategies and skills. Other books can be used as models or patterns for writing projects. Teachers also copy some poems on charts to share with students or arrange a bulletin-board display of the poems.

Step 2: Set Up a Listening Center. Teachers select recordings to accompany stories or informational books or create their own tapes so that absent students can catch up on a book being read aloud day by day. Also, the recordings can be used to provide additional reading experiences for students who listen to a recording when they read or reread a story or informational book.

Step 3: Coordinate Content-Area Textbook Readings. Sometimes content-area textbooks are used as the entire instructional program in social studies or science, but that's not a good idea (Robb, 2003). Textbooks typically only survey topics; other instructional materials are needed to provide depth and understanding. Students need to read, write, and discuss topics. It's most effective to use the reading process and then extend students' learning with projects. Developing thematic units and using content-area textbooks as one resource are a much better idea. Tierney and Pearson (1992) recommend that teachers shift from teaching *from* textbooks to teaching *with* textbooks and incorporate other types of reading materials and activities into thematic units.

Step 4: Locate Technology Resources. Teachers plan the videotapes, CD-ROMs, charts, time lines, maps, models, posters, and other displays to be used in connection with the unit. Children view videos and explore Internet sites to provide background knowledge about the unit, and other materials are used in teaching the big ideas.

STEPS IN DEVELOPING A THEMATIC UNIT

1. Text Set
Collect a text set of books to use in the unit. Set the books out on a special shelf in the classroom library.

2. Listening Center
Set up a listening center and collect recordings of various books in the text set.

3. Textbooks
Coordinate content-area textbook reading with other activities in the unit.

4. Technology Resources
Locate Internet and other technology resources and plan ways to integrate them into the unit.

5. Word Walls
Identify potential words for the word wall and activities to teach those words.

6. Learning Logs
Plan how students will use learning logs as a tool for learning.

7. Strategies and Skills
Identify language arts strategies and skills to teach.

8. Talk and Visually Representing Activities
Plan ways to involve students in talk activities, such as instructional conversations and oral presentations, and in visually representing activities, such as graphic organizers and quilts.

9. Projects
Brainstorm possible projects students can create to apply their learning, but usually allow students some choice in which projects they develop.

10. Assessment
Plan ways to monitor and assess students' learning with assignment checklists, rubrics, and other assessment tools.

Materials can be viewed or displayed in the classroom, and students can make other materials during the thematic unit.

Step 5: Identify Potential Words for the Word Wall. Teachers preview books in the text set and identify potential words for the word wall. This list is useful in planning vocabulary activities, but teachers don't use their word lists simply for the classroom word wall. Students and the teacher develop the classroom word wall together as they read and discuss the big ideas and other information related to the unit.

Step 6: Consider How Students Will Use Learning Logs. Teachers plan for students to keep learning logs in which they take notes, write questions, make observations, clarify their thinking, and write reactions to what they're learning during thematic units. They also write quickwrites and make clusters to explore what they're learning.

Step 7: Identify Strategies and Skills. Teachers identify the language arts standards they will address and plan minilessons to teach strategies and skills, such as expository text structures, how to locate information, report writing, and interviewing techniques. Minilessons are taught so that students can apply what they are learning in unit activities.

Step 8: Plan Talk and Visually Representing Activities. Students use talk and visually representing to learn during the thematic unit and to demonstrate their learning. These are possible activities:

- Give oral reports.
- Interview someone with special expertise related to the unit.
- Participate in a debate related to the unit.
- Create charts and diagrams to display information.
- Role-play a historical event.
- Assume the role of a historical figure.
- Participate in a readers theatre presentation of a story or poem.
- Tell or retell a story, biography, or event.
- Use a puppet show to tell a story, biography, or event.
- Make a quilt with information or vocabulary related to the unit.
- Write and perform a skit or play.

Step 9: Brainstorm Possible Projects. Teachers think about possible projects students may choose to develop to apply and personalize their learning during thematic units. This advance planning makes it possible for teachers to collect needed supplies and to have suggestions ready to offer to students who need assistance in choosing a project. Students work on projects independently or in small groups and then share them with the class at the end of the unit. Projects involve one or more of the six language arts. Here are some suggestions:

- Read a biography related to the unit.
- Create a poster to illustrate a big idea.

Weaving Assessment Into Practice

AN ASSIGNMENT CHECKLIST FOR A MIDDLE-GRADE THEMATIC UNIT ON FLIGHT

Name _____ Date _____

	Excellent	Good	Fair	Poor
1. Make a K-W-L chart on flight.	____	____	____	____
2. Read five books on flight and write a note card on each one.	____	____	____	____
3. Write 10 pages in your learning log.	____	____	____	____
4. Make a word wall on flight with 50 words.	____	____	____	____
5. Make a cluster about birds.	____	____	____	____
6. Make a time line about flight.	____	____	____	____
7. Write a compare-contrast essay on birds and airplanes.	____	____	____	____

_____ Prewriting
_____ Drafting
_____ Revising
_____ Editing
_____ Publishing

8. Make a report poster on flight. Choose four ways to share information.   ____   ____   ____   ____

_____ report   _____ diagram   _____ photo
_____ poem   _____ picture   _____ quote
_____ story   _____ Internet   _____ other

- Write and mail a letter to get information related to the unit.
- Write a story related to the unit.
- Perform a readers theatre production, puppet show, or other dramatization.
- Write a poem, song, or rap related to the unit.
- Write an "All About . . ." book or a report about one of the big ideas.
- Create a commercial or advertisement related to the unit.
- Create a tabletop display or diorama about the unit.

Step 10: Plan for Assessment. Teachers consider how they will monitor and assess students' learning as they make plans for activities and assignments. In this way, teachers can explain to students at the beginning of the thematic unit how they will be assessed and can check that their assessment will emphasize students' learning of the big ideas. An assignment checklist for a unit about flight for middle-grade students is shown in the Weaving Assessment Into Practice feature on this page.

FIGURE 14–5

Guidelines for Using Content-Area Textbooks

Comprehension Aids
Teach students how to use the comprehension aids in content-area textbooks, including chapter overviews; headings that outline the chapter; helpful graphics, such as maps, charts, tables, graphs, diagrams, photos, and drawings; technical words defined in the text; end-of-chapter summaries; and review questions.

Questions
Divide the reading of a chapter into sections. Before reading each section, have students turn the section heading into a question and read to find the answer to the question. As they read, have students take notes about the section, and then after reading, answer the question they created from the section heading.

Expository Text Structures
Teach students about expository text structures and assist them in identifying the patterns used in the reading assignment, especially cause and effect or problem and solution, before reading.

Vocabulary
Introduce only the key terms as part of a presentation or discussion before students read the textbook assignment. Present other vocabulary during reading, if needed, and after reading, develop a word wall with all important words.

Big Ideas
Have students focus on the big ideas instead of trying to remember all the facts or other information.

Content-Area Reading Techniques
Use content-area reading techniques, such as PReP, exclusion brainstorming, and anticipation guides, to help students identify and remember big ideas after reading.

Headings
Encourage students to use headings and subheadings to select and organize relevant information. The headings can be used to create a graphic organizer.

Listen-Read-Discuss Format
Use a listen-read-discuss format. First, the teacher presents the big ideas orally, and then the students read and discuss the chapter. Or, have students read the chapter as a review activity rather than as the introductory activity.

Using Content-Area Textbooks

Content-area textbooks are often difficult for students to read—more difficult, in fact, than many informational books. One reason textbooks are difficult is that they mention many topics briefly without developing any of them. A second reason is that content-area textbooks are read differently than stories. Teachers need to show students how to approach content-area textbooks and teach them how to use specific expository-text reading strategies and procedures to make comprehension easier. Figure 14–5 presents guidelines for using content-area textbooks.

Teachers can make content-area textbooks more readable and show students ways to remember what they've read (Robb, 2003). Some activities are used before reading and others after reading: the before-reading activities help students activate prior knowledge, set purposes for reading, or build background knowledge, and the after-reading activities help them identify and remember big ideas and details. Other activities are used when students want to locate specific information. Here are some activities to make content-area textbooks more readable:

◆ *Preview.* Teachers introduce the reading assignment by asking students to note main headings in the chapter and then skim or rapidly read the chapter to get a general idea about the topics covered.

◆ *Prereading Plan (PReP).* Teachers introduce a big idea discussed in the reading assignment and ask students to brainstorm words and ideas related to the idea before reading (Langer, 1981).

◆ *Anticipation Guides*. Teachers present a set of statements on the topic to be read. Students agree or disagree with each statement and then read the assignment to see if they were right (Head & Readence, 1992).

◆ *Exclusion Brainstorming.* Teachers distribute a list of words, most of which are related to the key concepts to be presented in the reading assignment. Teachers ask students to circle the words that are related to a key concept and then read the assignment to see if they circled the right words (Johns, Van Leirsburg, & Davis, 1994).

◆ *Graphic Organizers.* Teachers distribute a cluster, map, or other graphic organizer with the big ideas marked. Students complete the graphic organizer by adding details after reading each section.

◆ *Note Taking.* Students develop an outline by writing the headings and then take notes after reading each section.

◆ *Scanning.* Students reread quickly to locate specific information.

Students in the upper grades also need to learn how to use the SQ3R study strategy, a five-step technique in which students survey, question, read, recite, and review as they read a content-area reading assignment. This study strategy was devised in the 1930s and has been researched and thoroughly documented as a very effective technique when used properly (Anderson & Armbruster, 1984; Caverly & Orlando, 1991). Teachers introduce the SQ3R study strategy and provide opportunities for students to practice each step. At first, students can work together as a class as they use the technique with a text the teacher is reading aloud. Then they can work with partners and in small groups before using the strategy independently. Teachers need to emphasize that if students simply begin reading the first page of the assignment without doing the first two steps, they won't be able to remember as much of what they read. Also, when students are in a hurry and skip some of the steps, the technique will not be as successful.

A Middle-Grade Thematic Unit on Flight

Middle-grade students connect science and language arts in a thematic unit on flight. To begin the unit, students and the teacher create a K-W-L chart and students write facts about how birds and airplanes fly, space flight, and famous aviators. They also identify questions they will investigate during the unit. The teacher sets out a text set of stories, poems, and informational books about flight for the students to read. Some of the books are on tape or CD, which students can listen to at the listening center. Students list important words about flight on a word wall and participate in a variety of vocabulary activities. Students research flight-related questions using books and Internet resources and through interviews with a pilot, flight attendant, astronaut or other knowledgeable person. Students present oral reports or prepare multigenre papers to share what they learn. A planning cluster for a thematic unit on flight is presented in Figure 14–6.

FIGURE 14–6

A Planning Cluster for a Middle-Grade Thematic Unit on Flight

Books

Bellville, C. W. (1993). *Flying in a hot air balloon.* Minneapolis: Carolrhoda.

Bernhard, E. (1994). *Eagles: Lions of the sky.* New York: Holiday House.

Borden, L. (1998). *Good-bye, Charles Lindbergh: Based on a true story.* New York: McElderry.

Busby, P. (2003). *First to fly: How Wilbur and Orville Wright invented the airplane.* New York: Crown.

Johnston, S. A. (1995). *Raptor rescue: An eagle flies free.* New York: Dutton.

Kalman, B. (1998). *How birds fly.* New York: Crabtree.

Lopez, D. (1995). *Flight.* New York: Time-Life.

Maynard, C. (1995). *Airplane.* London: Dorling Kindersley.

Peters, L. W. (1994). *This way home.* New York: Holt.

Ryan, P. M. (1999). *Amelia and Eleanor go for a ride: Based on a true story.* New York: Scholastic.

Weiss, H. (1995). *Strange and wonderful aircraft.* Boston: Houghton Mifflin.

Yolen, J. (2003). *My brothers' flying machine: Wilbur, Orville, and me.* Boston: Little, Brown.

Word Wall

AB	airflow	H	helicopters
	airfoil	I	instruments
	airplane	JK	jet
	airport		jet stream
	altitude	L	landing
	Amelia Earhart		lift
	astronauts	MNO	migration
	aviation	PQ	passengers
	aviator		pilot
C	Charles Lindbergh		pitch
	Chuck Yeager		propeller
	controls	RS	roll
D	drag		rudder
E	engine	TUV	takeoff
F	FAA		thrust
	flapping wings		tilt
	flight attendant	WX	weight
	flightless		wing
	flyways		Wright brothers
	fuselage	YZ	yaw
G	glide		

Charts and Diagrams

- Make a time line of the history of flight.
- Draw diagrams of birds' wings or airplanes.
- Make a Venn diagram comparing birds and airplanes.
- Make a data chart of information about animals that fly, including birds, bats, insects, and fish.

Multigenre Projects

- Prepare a multigenre project about flight.
- Prepare a multigenre biography of an aviator, such as Chuck Yeager, Charles Lindbergh, or Amelia Earhart.

Vocabulary Activities

- Post words on an alphabetized word wall hanging in the classroom.
- Use words on the word wall for a minilesson on dividing words into syllables.
- Make word clusters and hang them on airplane and bird mobiles.

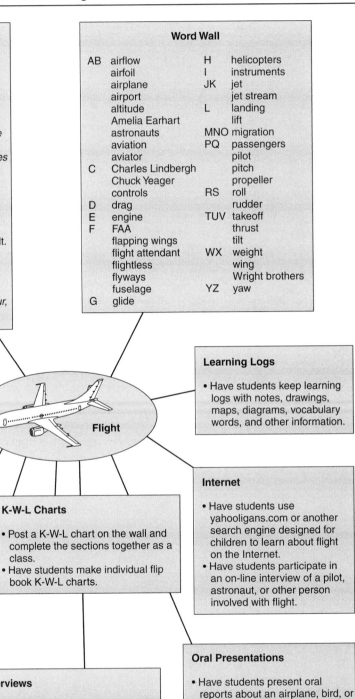

Flight

Learning Logs

- Have students keep learning logs with notes, drawings, maps, diagrams, vocabulary words, and other information.

Internet

- Have students use yahooligans.com or another search engine designed for children to learn about flight on the Internet.
- Have students participate in an on-line interview of a pilot, astronaut, or other person involved with flight.

K-W-L Charts

- Post a K-W-L chart on the wall and complete the sections together as a class.
- Have students make individual flip book K-W-L charts.

Interviews

- Interview a pilot, flight attendant, astronaut, zookeeper, ornithologist, or someone else knowledgeable about flight.
- Participate in an on-line interview of a pilot or astronaut.

Oral Presentations

- Have students present oral reports about an airplane, bird, or aviator.
- Have students do an oral presentation of a poem from Fleischman, P. (1985). *I am Phoenix: Poems for two voices.* New York: HarperCollins.

Review

Designing language arts instruction that reflects the theory and research about language and how children learn is an important responsibility. Teachers follow a series of steps to develop literature focus units, literature circles, reading and writing workshop, and thematic units. Here are 10 key concepts presented in this chapter:

- Teachers develop literature focus units featuring award-winning and other high-quality books that students could not read independently.
- Teachers develop activities using all five stages of the reading process for literature focus units.
- Teachers organize for literature circles so that students can read and respond to self-selected books in small groups.
- Teachers create a community of learners so that students can work successfully in small groups.
- Teachers organize reading and writing workshop with plenty of time for reading and writing, and they present minilessons on procedures, strategies, and skills.
- Teachers provide opportunities for students to read and write independently during reading and writing workshop.
- Teachers can adapt and combine the patterns of practice to fit the needs of their students and their curriculum.
- Teachers focus on several big ideas as they develop thematic units.
- Content-area textbooks can be used as one resource in thematic units, but they should never be the only books that students read.
- Teachers design assignment checklists that students complete to document their learning during thematic units.

Professional References

Anderson, T. H., & Armbruster, B. B. (1984). Studying. In P. D. Pearson, R. Barr, M. L. Kamil, & P. Mosenthal (Eds.), *Handbook of reading research* (pp. 657–679). New York: Longman.

Atwell, N. (1998). *In the middle: New understandings about writing, reading, and learning.* Portsmouth, NH: Heinemann.

Atwell, N. (2007). *The reading zone.* New York: Scholastic.

Brock, C. H., & Raphael, T. E. (2005). *Windows to language, literacy, and culture: Insights from an English-language learner.* Newark, DE: International Reading Association.

Calkins, L. M. (1991). *Living between the lines.* Portsmouth, NH: Heinemann.

Calkins, L. M. (1994). *The art of teaching writing* (2nd ed.). Portsmouth, NH: Heinemann.

Calkins, L., Hartman, A., & White, Z. R. (2005). *One-to-one: The art of conferencing with young writers.* Portsmouth, NH: Heinemann.

Carle, E. (1993). *Eric Carle: Picture writer* (videotape). New York: Philomel.

Caverly, D. C., & Orlando, V. P. (1991). Textbook study strategies. In D. C. Caverly & V. P. Orlando (Eds.), *Teaching reading and study strategies at the college level* (pp. 86–165). Newark, DE: International Reading Association.

Daniels, H. (2001). *Literature circles: Voice and choice in book clubs and reading groups.* York, ME: Stenhouse.

Evans, K. S. (2001). *Literature discussion groups in the intermediate grades: Dilemmas and possibilities.* Newark, DE: International Reading Association.

Fletcher, R., & Portalupi, J. (2001). *Writing workshop: The essential guide.* Portsmouth, NH: Heinemann.

Frank, C. R., Dixon, C. N., & Brandts, L. R. (2001). Bears, trolls, and pagemasters: Learning about learners in book clubs. *The Reading Teacher, 54,* 448–462.

Head, M. H., & Readence, J. E. (1992). Anticipation guides: Meaning through prediction. In E. K. Dishner, T. W. Bean, J. E. Readence, & D. W. Moore (Eds.), *Reading in the content areas* (2nd ed., pp. 229–234). Dubuque, IA: Kendall/Hunt.

Heller, M. F. (2006/2007). Telling stories and talking facts: First graders' engagements in a nonfiction book club. *The Reading Teacher, 60,* 358–369.

Henkin, R. (1995). Insiders and outsiders in first-grade writing workshops: Gender and equity issues. *Language Arts, 72,* 429–434.

Johns, J. L., Van Leirsburg, P., & Davis, S. J. (1994). *Improving reading: A handbook of strategies.* Dubuque, IA: Kendall/Hunt.

Kaufman, D. (2001). Organizing and managing the language arts workshop: A matter of motion. *Language Arts, 79,* 114–123.

Kucer, S. B., Silva, C., & Delgado-Larocco, E. L. (1995). *Curricular conversations: Themes in multilingual and monolingual classrooms.* York, ME: Stenhouse.

Langer, J. A. (1981). From theory to practice: A prereading plan. *Journal of Reading, 25,* 152–157.

Lensmire, T. (1992). *When children write.* New York: Teachers College Press.

Lindquist, T., & Selwyn, D. (2000). *Social studies at the center: Integrating kids, content, and literacy.* Portsmouth, NH: Heinemann.

McGee, L. M., & Tompkins, G. E. (1995). Literature-based reading instruction: What's guiding the instruction? *Language Arts, 72,* 405–414.

Overmeyer, M. (2005). *When writing workshop isn't working: Answers to ten tough questions, grades 2–5.* York, ME: Stenhouse.

Prill, P. (1994/1995). Helping children use the classroom library. *The Reading Teacher, 48,* 363–364.

Ray, K. W., & Laminack, L. L. (2001). *The writing workshop: Working through the hard parts (and they're all hard parts).* Urbana, IL: National Council of Teachers of English.

Robb, L. (2003). *Teaching reading in social studies, science, and math.* New York: Scholastic.

Serafini, F. (2001). *Creating space for readers.* Portsmouth, NH: Heinemann.

Stien, D., & Beed, P. L. (2004). Bridging the gap between fiction and nonfiction in the literature circle setting. *The Reading Teacher, 57,* 510–518.

Tierney, R. J., & Pearson, P. D. (1992). Learning to learn from text: A framework for improving classroom practice. In E. K. Dishner, T. W. Bean, J. E. Readence, & D. W. Moore (Eds.), *Reading in the content areas: Improving classroom instruction* (2nd ed., pp. 85–99). Dubuque, IA: Kendall/Hunt.

Tunnell, M. O., & Ammon, R. (Eds.). (1993). *The story of ourselves: Teaching history through children's literature.* Portsmouth, NH: Heinemann.

Children's Book References

Asch, F. (2000). *The sun is my favorite star.* New York: Scholastic.

Brett, J. (1989). *The mitten.* New York: Putnam.

dePaola, T. (2003). *Things will NEVER be the same.* New York: Putnam.

Gibbons, G. (1997). *The moon book.* New York: Holiday House.

Hutchins, P. (1968). *Rosie's walk.* New York: Macmillan.

Koopmans, L. (1990). *The woodcutter's mitten.* New York: Crocodile Books.

Lowry, L. (2000). *Looking back: A book of memories.* New York: Delacorte.

Lowry, L. (2006a). *Gathering blue.* New York: Delacorte.

Lowry, L. (2006b). *The giver.* New York: Delacorte.

Lowry, L. (2006c). *The messenger.* New York: Delacorte.

McKissack, P. (1997). *Can you imagine.* Katonah, NY: Richard C. Owen.

Numeroff, L. (2003). *If you give an author a pencil.* Katonah, NY: Richard C. Owen.

Polacco, P. (1994). *Firetalking.* Katonah, NY: Richard C. Owen.

Simon, S. (2000). *From paper airplanes to outer space.* Katonah, NY: Richard C. Owen.

Tresselt, A. (1989). *The mitten.* New York: HarperTrophy.

NAME INDEX

SUBJECT INDEX